1 YEAR UPGRADE
BUYER PROTECTION PLAN

CONFIGURING WINDOWS 2000

WITHOUT

Active Directory

Carol Bailey

Dr. Thomas W. Shinder Technical Editor

KEY	SERIAL NUMBER
001	MKE783FV2P
002	BH8UZ237VB
003	DNVN5T5QL9
004	JDKJR4PP9D
005	ZLA99G2FLW
006	234UFVKLMA
007	94JGV3MDK2
008	FKA3234KP3
009	J3AWV4MLSD
010	NK3VL8SE4N

PUBLISHED BY
Syngress Publishing, Inc.
800 Hingham Street
Rockland, MA 02370

Configuring Windows 2000 Without Active Directory

Printed in the United States of America

1 2 3 4 5 6 7 8 9 0

ISBN: 1-928994-54-7

Technical Editor: Dr. Thomas W. Shinder
Co-Publisher: Richard Kristof
Acquisitions Editor: Catherine B. Nolan
Developmental Editor: Jonathan Babcock
Freelance Editorial Manager: Maribeth Corona-Evans

Cover Designer: Michael Kavish
Page Layout and Art by: Shannon Tozier
Copyedit by Syngress Editorial Team
Indexer: Julie Kawabata

Distributed by Publishers Group West in the United States and Jaguar Book Group in Canada.

Acknowledgments

We would like to acknowledge the following people for their kindness and support in making this book possible.

Richard Kristof and Duncan Anderson of Global Knowledge, for their generous access to the IT industry's best courses, instructors, and training facilities.

Ralph Troupe, Rhonda St. John, and the team at Callisma for their invaluable insight into the challenges of designing, deploying and supporting world-class enterprise networks.

Karen Cross, Lance Tilford, Meaghan Cunningham, Kim Wylie, Harry Kirchner, Kevin Votel, Kent Anderson, and Frida Yara of Publishers Group West for sharing their incredible marketing experience and expertise.

Mary Ging, Caroline Hird, Simon Beale, Caroline Wheeler, Victoria Fuller, Jonathan Bunkell, and Klaus Beran of Harcourt International for making certain that our vision remains worldwide in scope.

Anneke Baeten and Annabel Dent of Harcourt Australia for all their help.

David Buckland, Wendi Wong, Daniel Loh, Marie Chieng, Lucy Chong, Leslie Lim, Audrey Gan, and Joseph Chan of Transquest Publishers for the enthusiasm with which they receive our books.

Kwon Sung June at Acorn Publishing for his support.

Ethan Atkin at Cranbury International for his help in expanding the Syngress program.

Author

Carol Bailey (MCSE+Internet) is a Senior Technical Consultant working for Metascybe Systems Ltd in London. Metascybe is a Microsoft Certified Partner that develops its own PC communications software as well as offers project work and consultancy. In addition to supporting these products and services for an internationally diverse customer base, Carol co-administers the company's in-house IT resources.

With over 10 years in the industry, Carol has accumulated a wealth of knowledge and experience with Microsoft operating systems. She first qualified as an MCP with NT3.51 in 1995 and will remain qualified as MCSE as a result of passing the Windows 2000 exams last year. Her other qualifications include a BA (Hons) in English and an MSc in Information Systems.

Well known for her Windows 2000 expertise, Carol has a number of publications on this subject, which include co-authoring the following books in the best-selling certification series from Syngress\Osborne McGraw-Hill: *MCSE Windows 2000 Network Administration Study Guide* (Exam 70-216). ISBN: 0-07-212383-4; *MCSE Designing a Windows 2000 Network Infrastructure Study Guide* (Exam 70-221). ISBN: 0-07-212494-6; and *MCSE Windows 2000 Accelerated Boxed Set* (Exam 70-240). ISBN: 0-07-212383-4.

Technical Editor

Thomas Shinder, M.D. (MCSE, MCP+I, MCT) is a technology trainer and consultant in the Dallas–Ft. Worth metroplex. He has consulted with major firms, including Xerox, Lucent Technologies, and FINA Oil, assisting in the development and implementation of IP-based communications strategies. Tom is a Windows 2000 editor for Brainbuzz.com and a Windows 2000 columnist for Swynk.com.

Tom attended medical school at the University of Illinois in Chicago and trained in neurology at the Oregon Health Sciences Center in Portland, Oregon. His fascination with interneuronal communication ultimately melded with his interest in internetworking and led him to focus on systems engineering. Tom and his wife, Debra Littlejohn Shinder, design elegant and cost-efficient solutions for small- and medium–sized businesses based on Windows NT/2000 platforms. Tom has authored several Syngress books, including *Configuring ISA Server 2000: Building Firewalls for Windows 2000* (ISBN: 1-928994-29-6), *Configuring Windows 2000 Server Security* (ISBN: 1-928994-02-4), *Managing Windows 2000 Network Services* (ISBN: 1-928994-06-7), and *Troubleshooting Windows 2000 TCP/IP* (ISBN: 1-928994-11-3).

Contents

Why Use Windows 2000 without Active Directory?

There is more to Windows 2000 than just Active Directory features—as this book shows. But there's no doubt that Windows 2000 was written with Active Directory in mind, which is reflected in the standard documentation that accompanies the software. Chapter 1 will begin to answer these questions.

TIP

You can always check the current version of Windows (build and Service Pack if applied) by running **WinVer.exe**, which displays the About Windows dialog box.

Chapter 3 Laptops   129

**Switching between
Working Environments**

There are a number of
features that help users
switch seamlessly between
their different working
environments. These
include:

- Power management
  and preservation
- Offline folders and
  synchronizing data
- Dialup access

Chapter 4 File and Print Services   185

NOTE

The general advice when planning disk space for indexing is to allow at least 30 percent and preferably 40 percent of the total amount of disk space you index (known as the *corpus*). It would also be prudent to host the index catalogs on a different disk from the operating system.

Understand the specific technical features and options available with Windows 2000 Terminal Services, including:

- Fast connections over low bandwidths
- Remote administration
- Tighter security
- Shadowing (remote control)
- Seamless integration between PC and server

Justifications for running DNS include:

- Having UNIX computers
- Running Internet services
- Running Active Directory
- Preparing for Active Directory
- Looking to integrate UNIX and Microsoft communication

Chapter 7 Internet Services   423

NOTE

Internet Explorer 3.0, Netscape Navigator 2.0, and later versions of both browsers support the use of host header names. Older browsers do not. Additionally, you cannot use host headers with SSL because the host header will be encrypted—this is an important point for Web servers using SSL for additional security.

Chapter 8 Secure Communication   491

Secure communication can be broken down into the following five components:

- Nonrepudiation
- Antireplay
- Integrity
- Confidentiality
- Authentication

**Setting the Tunneling
Value, Necessary for
L2TP/IPSec Support**

VpnStrategy Value	Description
1	PPTP only (the default)
2	Try PPTP and then L2TP/IPSec
3	L2TP/IPSec only
4	Try L2TP/IPSec and the PPTP (Windows 2000 default)

Chapter 10 Internet Connectivity   625

Q: I'm interested in publishing a VPN server behind the ISA Server. I understand IPSec can't be translated, but is there a good reason why I can't run a PPTP server on my internal network configured as a SecureNAT client?

A: There is a good reason why this won't work—the SecureNAT element works only with TCP and UDP ports. PPTP uses the GRE protocol (number 47) in addition to TCP port 1723, and there's no way to translate this when it comes into the ISA server from an external client. You can create VPN connections from the internal network, and you can run a VPN server on the ISA server itself or on a DMZ, but you cannot publish a VPN server as a SecureNAT client.

Taskpad views are HTLM pages that can contain a number of items:

- MMC Favorites
- Wizards
- Scripts
- Programs
- URLs

Foreword

There is a tremendous variety and volume of literature available these days on how to install and configure Windows 2000, so you may ask "How is this book different?" As the title indicates, this book concentrates on configuring Windows 2000 *Without* Active Directory. It's about making the most of those Windows 2000 features and services that can be used independently of Active Directory—whether that's in an existing NT4 domain environment, Novell's NDS, UNIX, or even a standalone workgroup.

I was motivated to write this book because the existing books on Windows 2000 invariably explain the new features only in the context of Active Directory, with the result that many people just do not realize what is possible without Active Directory. This approach ignores the reality that many companies don't want or need the services Active Directory offers and would prefer to keep their legacy services intact. Of course it's easy enough to get a Windows 2000 computer up and running so it's functional without Active Directory, but it's entirely a different thing to fully use and exploit Windows 2000's new features to your advantage. And yet, these exciting new features are there, and are yours for the taking.

This book is not anti-Active Directory. I won't tell you why you should or shouldn't use Active Directory. I won't tell you which alternative directory service to use, or advocate everybody should be running P2P. Rather, this book is an acknowledgement that many corporations are currently running Windows 2000 without Active Directory for many reasons. Some of those reasons may boil down to timing and budget constraints, or perhaps a lack of suitably trained staff. It can take many months of designing, planning and testing before a migration deployment can even begin. Still recovering from Y2K upgrades, and with an economic downturn with fewer staff and restricted budgets, IT Managers need to make the most of the resources they already have with minimal risk of disruption to existing services—and Active Directory migration does not neatly fit into this category.

Other reasons for not migrating to Active Directory include a lack of confidence in Microsoft's first version of an enterprise directory service, simply because it lacks maturity. It hasn't yet stood the rigors and test of time that make IT Managers feel comfortable enough to pull the plug on existing and working systems in a production environment. An Active Directory upgrade or migration is not in the same league as any other Microsoft upgrade to date, and getting it wrong or running into problems has far-reaching consequences across the whole enterprise network. In comparison, this book shows you how to take relatively small, isolated steps with Windows 2000 systems without having to restructure existing infrastructures. This allows you to gradually introduce Windows 2000 at your own pace, allowing more staff to gain valuable experience in the new operating system to help ease the learning curve. In fact, introducing Windows 2000 this way into your network offers a good stepping-stone as part of a company's gradual migration process to Active Directory, rather than aiming for the "Big Bang" approach of implementing Active Directory first. This book is just as much about strategic decisions as it is technical implementation details. As such, it is equally applicable for both IT Implementers and IT Managers.

The first chapter examines in some detail why many companies have not migrated to Active Directory, with some of the technical, political and strategic decision markers you may also want to take onboard. If you are an IT implementer rather than a decision maker, you may still find this information useful so you have a better understanding of how some of the problems you may face will be more than just technical. It has long been said that politics make up the 8th layer of the OSI 7 layer model, and this is becoming increasingly true in today's networks where the IT infrastructure *is* the business and profit of the corporation.

Just as it's important to know about the features and services you can implement outside Active Directory, you should also be aware of which features and services cannot work without Active Directory. Too often Windows 2000 literature concentrates on the benefits of Active Directory, but without clearly identifying which of those benefits are dependent upon an Active Directory environment. The first chapter includes a section on these features and looks at both their advantages and disadvantages. This puts you in a better position of being able to make an informed decision on whether they justify implementing Active Directory, or whether they will change any migration plans or timescales. The more objective information you have, the more empowered you become to make the right decision for your particular circumstances, rather than having to make decisions based on literature with a marketing bias.

Subsequent chapters deal with technical implementation details of how to configure specific Active Directory independent features and services. However, there's still strategic information available: for example designing, deploying, or upgrading issues that you may want to consider as part of longer-term plans, or configuration options which take into account political issues in addition to just technical problems.

Unfortunately, this book cannot cover every single Windows 2000 feature that can be used without Active Directory (or I would still be writing it!), but it does aim to cover the main areas that I think have most impact for the majority of company networks. This includes features that are particularly relevant to workstations, laptops and servers (for example, exactly how the security and reliability features work, which have already earned high praise in the industry), and specific services such as IIS5 and the highly acclaimed Terminal Services. Many of the improvements in Windows 2000 were on the networking side simply because they were necessary to accommodate Active Directory. This book shows you how you can cash in on those networking service improvements even though you're not running Active Directory—which include DDNS, DHCP, WINS, NLB, and complimenting services such as Certificate Services, IPSec, RAS and IAS, ICS/NAT, and even an introductory look at ISA Server.

Chapter 1 also contains a section outlining subsequent chapter contents in more detail which provides more information on the breath and scope of the book, and the Windows 2000 features that will be covered. You may also find this section useful if you want to dip into chapters out of sequence. Each chapter was written to stand alone as much as possible, but occasionally it was necessary to refer to material in previous chapters to prevent duplication. When this has been the case, the reference is clearly stated.

A walkthrough accompanies each chapter, and these aim to provide useful, practical, hands-on exercises that should be possible even on production computers. This book aims to bring Windows 2000 features out from the test network, and into the production environment. Written by somebody working in the industry full time, it is aimed at real-world networks, real-world computing practices, and real-world relevance, today.

Note: This book was completed shortly after Windows 2000 Service Pack 2 was released. As such it includes information appropriate to companies working with Windows 2000 at this time—including information and references to hotfixes, Microsoft Knowledge Base articles, downloadable white papers, online resources, Service Pack 1, Service Pack 2, and the Windows 2000 Resource Kit utilities and documentation.

—*Carol Bailey*

Chapter 1

Why Not Active Directory?

Solutions in this chapter:

- **Why Use Windows 2000 without Active Directory?**

- **The Purpose of This Book**

- **Active Directory Integration**

☑ **Walkthrough: Managing User Accounts and Securing the Local Windows 2000 Administrator Account**

☑ **Summary**

☑ **Solutions Fast Track**

☑ **Frequently Asked Questions**

Introduction

Welcome to *Configuring Windows 2000 WITHOUT Active Directory*, which quite simply aims to demonstrate how you can make the most of Windows 2000 outside an Active Directory environment. Microsoft spent considerable time and money, and bet its future business, to update its already successful platforms of Windows NT 4.0 and Windows 98 to be today's version of Windows 2000. Although it's true that Windows 2000 was written around and for Active Directory (Microsoft's first offering of an enterprise directory service), it also offers many new and improved features that you can take advantage of immediately, with little or minimal risk to your existing network infrastructure, because they are independent from Active Directory.

If you are running a Windows NT 4.0 style domain, a Novell NDS or equivalent alternative directory service, a workgroup (peer-to-peer) network, or even have a standalone computer, you can still benefit greatly from Microsoft's new technologies if you have computers running Windows 2000. You may already have Windows 2000 computers on your network—laptops, desktops, and servers—but not realize their full potential simply because you are unsure about which of the new features will work independently from Active Directory or because you do not know how to configure and use them in your own network environment. This book is for you—to show you what features can be used outside Active Directory and how to get the best out of them in a production environment today.

Why Use Windows 2000 without Active Directory?

We're actually asking two different questions here: Why use Windows 2000 at all, and why use Windows 2000 without Active Directory? There is more to Windows 2000 than just Active Directory features—as this book shows. But there's no doubt that Windows 2000 was written with Active Directory in mind, which is reflected in the standard documentation that accompanies the software. Both questions deserve a separate look.

Why Use Windows 2000?

Before we begin answering this first question, we might take it back one more step and ask ourselves why use a Microsoft operating system computer at all?

Despite the accolades of alternative platforms, it has to be recognized that no computer system (hardware or software) is 100 percent perfect. You may have personal preferences based on experience and knowledge—and therefore you have to decide which operating system best fits your requirements.

The Acceptance of Windows into the Corporate Workplace

In this context of no computer system is perfect, many corporations decided on Microsoft operating systems because they offer an easy-to-use interface. This factor alone substantially reduces costs for both end-user training and network administration. It also makes recruiting staff easier simply because there's a better choice and greater availability of people in the marketplace with varying degrees of experience with and competence in this operating system.

Additionally, Windows comes from an established company, is widely available, is widely supported by the industry, and offers solutions within the budgeting requirements of most companies and even individuals with home networks. True, there are cheaper alternatives—but the overall cost of a computer is more than the cost of its initial hardware and operating system. These days we are more aware of Total Cost of Ownership (TCO), which takes into account factors such as ease of installation, ease of use and maintenance, choice of hardware, choice of drivers and packages, and availability of training material, qualified staff, and vendor support, among other considerations.

It is also true that there are alternative platforms that can boast a history of offering better security and reliability, but at the cost of lack of flexibility, less support for third-party drivers and applications, more extensive training requirements, and higher recruiting costs. Taking the whole equation into account, it's no wonder that many corporations today include Microsoft operating systems on both workstations and servers.

The Acceptance of Microsoft in the Corporate Workplace

This book isn't about the question of whether to use Microsoft systemst, but instead a realization that Microsoft systems do exist in the workplace and will continue to do so for the foreseeable future. In fact, I would guess that the majority of people reading this book will not even have a choice of which operating system to use. For every IT manager with the power to make this decision, the majority inherit the choices of their predecessors and know it is unrealistic to replace a working system with an alternative (unless there are exceptional circumstances). And for every IT manager with the authority to make that choice, there are many more people working in the IT industry who simply do not have that decision to make. Their job is to implement and support the current and past choices of other people. Corporate networks are built on historical decisions and politics rather than purely technical choice.

The Emergence of Windows 2000

Microsoft spent more than three years on improving Windows NT 4.0 and Windows 9x before finally releasing its next version, which it decided to call Windows 2000. And for all the current marketing about Windows XP, and Windows.NET, these too will be built on today's standard Windows 2000 technologies.

As somebody who is involved with both producing software solutions and supporting them, I'm aware that the best products are a result of evolution. They build on previous technical knowledge and experience while incorporating feedback from the trenches. By "best" I include good design (both visually and structurally), reliability, and a feature set that is both useful and relevant to the end user (rather than simply bloatware). The maturity of the product and company is important simply because it is against the odds that a completely new product will meet these needs if it has no such foundation. More often than not, perspiration wins over inspiration.

Although heralded as a new operating system, Windows 2000 is evidently more the result of a reinvention rather than a new invention—which offers a confidence factor appreciated by those not willing to learn by fire. When redesigning Windows NT 4.0 for Windows 2000, Microsoft had the luxury of learning from past mistakes and improving on successful features. This learning wasn't just from its own products but also from other peoples' products that had earned market share and stood the test of time.

I think there's plenty of evidence that when designing the Windows 2000 feature set, Microsoft responded to requests for ease of use together with business-oriented features and improved reliability. Its aim was to take advantage of today's expanding new technologies and meet the requirements of enterprise and Internet-related businesses. Today more people are beginning to realize that Windows 2000 can deliver on its marketing promises for features and reliability.

Windows 2000 Track Record

Over a year from its release and two service packs later, Windows 2000 is no longer bleeding-edge technology. Many companies have been successfully running Windows 2000 in various guises (with and without Active Directory) for some time with proven successful results. It's steadily gaining an almost begrudging respect from the previously cynical IT users who were all too familiar with regular blue screens and lockups and the need for third-party applications to supplement limitations in the operating system's feature set. Now that the MCSE Windows NT 4.0 exams are officially retired by Microsoft, more IT staff by necessity (to retain their MCP or MCSE titles) are learning Windows 2000 and its new features.

TIP

For more information on current Microsoft certifications, see "Microsoft Technical Certifications" on the Microsoft site (www.microsoft.com/trainingandservices/default.asp?PageID=mcp&PageCall=certifications&SubSite=cert).

Windows 2000 Today

Windows 2000 is the current Microsoft operating system today, which is reflected in the computing resources available from Microsoft and elsewhere. Your trusted Windows NT 4.0 and Windows 9x are already branded *down-level*, which is synonymous with *legacy* to clearly indicate that they are not considered current. These operating systems now have a ticking shelf life—Microsoft has announced that it won't be supporting them beyond June 2003, and the decision to not roll out any more service packs for Windows NT 4.0 is perhaps indicative that Microsoft is gearing down its support for the older platforms.

New computers arrive with Windows 2000 preinstalled, and the mass of new literature is aimed at the current, not down-level, systems. More IT professionals are becoming certified in the new Windows 2000 exams, and Windows 2000 is usually assumed in their daily digestion of mailing lists, magazines, and newsgroups. If you have had no exposure to Windows 2000 yet, you must be in the minority. Like it or not, it is Microsoft's current operating system, and the future will build on it.

Why Not Use Active Directory?

Despite its title, this book is certainly not anti–Active Directory. In fact, because I know Active Directory is built on the tried and test distributed technology of Exchange 5.5, which has proved successful for some time, I probably had more faith in Microsoft's first release of a distributed directory service than many. As a network administrator, I'm well aware of the benefits a hierarchical directory can offer with scalable and central administration, and the ability to delegate and fine-tune control at lower levels. And, finally, there's the recognition that applications don't always run only over reliable and fast networks!

I'm also aware, though, that many companies are running Microsoft operating systems in a non–Active Directory environment for any of the following reasons:

- The company doesn't have the resources to migrate to Active Directory in the short or even medium term.

- The company has experienced delays in the migration design, testing, and rollout phrase.

- The company has decided not to trust Microsoft's as yet relatively new technology—particularly if a working Windows NT 4.0 domain structure is already in place with an alternative directory services infrastructure and the company cannot afford disruption to the everyday running of IT services.

- The company has decided that the overheads of both upgrading and maintaining Active Directory are not cost-effective when set against its network requirements.

These might not be popular decisions with Microsoft's marketing strategy, but they strike a welcomed chord of common sense to those of us actually working in the field. In fact, Microsoft itself endorses the need for carefully planning the design and thoroughly testing and training before deploying Active Directory. The bottom line is that it's not good business practice to rush something that will have far-reaching consequences across the whole of your enterprise network. It's very difficult to redress an Active Directory design flaw once it's got to the deployment stage, and Active Directory consultants with experience now behind them acknowledge that a design mistake is very costly in terms of money, time, and lost productivity—and it certainly doesn't help the confidence factor. In many cases, a design mistake has meant undoing everything and starting from scratch.

With no current *grafting* and *pruning* facilities (where domain trees can be merged, split, and renamed) and a lack of current management tools (for example, simple drag-and-drop features), many companies just aren't prepared to risk an Active Directory migration until the product offers the improved versatility and flexibility that are required for an existing enterprise network. In fact, it speaks volumes about the lack of built-in tools to handle existing networks when you realize that Microsoft itself resorted to a third-party domain migration tool to help migrate its Windows NT 4.0 domains (**Fast Lane Technologies DM/ Consolidator**). Its own utility, **Active Directory Migration Tool** (ADMT), just isn't suitable for all but the simplest and smallest of Windows NT 4.0 domain migrations. For a start, it can't handle in-place upgrades—it works only when the Active Directory domain you're migrating to is in Native mode, and many corporate network administrators will need and want to remain in Mixed mode for a safety period.

But it's not just domain restructuring and moving users you need to consider—you also need to factor in an extensive and thorough inventory of hardware/memory/BIOS versions and software packages to identify required upgrades. There's also the tedious and time-consuming logistical nightmare of moving a considerable amount of data for servers that are migrated or consolidated. All this takes time.

Added to all this, you have IT managers and administrators who remember the teething problems and rather painful learning curves that accompanied Novell's NDS when it was first available. I think we're a little wiser and more cautious these days, learning from experience that it takes time for such a product to be robust enough, and flexible enough, to meet the requirements of a true production environment.

Designing and Deploying Active Directory: More Than a Technical Challenge

Many people have questioned why Active Directory hasn't been as widely adopted as supposed—quoting the technology involved isn't particularly difficult. But designing and deploying Active Directory is much more than technological challenges or meeting the resource needs of upgrades, training, recruiting, and testing. Networking services today are inextricably woven into the very heart of a corporation's management policy, which means that restructuring the network not only introduces a high risk, but involves management just as much as (if not more than) the actual IT implementers. Changes on an enterprise scale necessitate political choices and decisions that must meet the requirements of disparate managerial sections.

It's all very well for Active Directory migration documentation to talk glibly about "involving all parties for a consensus design," but in reality achieving that can be near impossible simply because of internal politics. Some companies have resorted to creating multiple forests simply because a consensus was not a workable solution. Each forest can then be configured to trust each other forest—but then you lose the power of a single enterprise directory and end up with little more than your original Windows NT 4.0 multimaster domain configuration. It's not a scalable solution, and it is not future-proofed. For example, installing a product that modified the schema (for example, Exchange 2000) would not be able to extend further than the current forest. With no grafting and pruning facilities, the only alternative would be to start over.

From a business perspective, Active Directory adoption is also a difficult project to quantify and qualify. Many companies quote the lack of a compelling business reason as one of the main reasons why they haven't yet migrated to Active Directory. Although they can perceive long-term benefits, these have to be offset against the immediate costs and risks associated with restructuring and redesigning an existing working network infrastructure from the top down.

In fact, you can see the cost justification in delaying because the longer a company doesn't migrate to Active Directory, the more the product will mature as bugs will be discovered and fixed, customer feedback will be integrated into new releases, and a greater choice of third-party products becomes available. Additionally, there will be a wider choice of staff in the marketplace with Windows 2000 experience and qualifications.

You can easily appreciate how an IT manager reading through some of the bugs listed as fixed in the two Windows 2000 service packs will rejoice in the company's inertia and be grateful it wasn't his or her network that was vulnerable to particular critical problems. With the Microsoft marketing machinery now revving up for Windows XP and Windows.NET Servers, it makes it an even easier excuse to put off the migration process and wait for these to be released and fixed—and you're back where you started!

With these political issues in mind, the question of "How soon should we migrate to Active Directory?" often turns into "How late can we migrate to Active Directory?"

There's even the additional technical (and political) consideration of whether to use Microsoft's directory service at all because it doesn't offer cross-platform support. This issue is crucial to many corporations that rarely run just Windows but usually have a mixture of other platforms. Such corporations will want to carefully consider whether a cross-platform directory service would offer a better alternative to Active Directory before committing themselves to a restricted solution. The concept of being sucked into a Microsoft monopoly at the moment is a very sensitive issue, and it is just as much a political issue as a technical one.

Designing & Planning...

Substantiating Return on Investment (ROI)

Some Active Directory adoptions have occurred after identifying two specific business justifications. The first has been when the company has identified a product its business requires that will run only on Active Directory (the most obvious current example is Exchange 2000). The second has been for new networks where upgrading hardware, modifying existing services and procedures, and restructuring considerations have not been an issue.

In addition, many of the companies that migrated to Active Directory so that they could run Exchange 2000 were previously running Exchange 5.5. This meant the IT staff could leverage their Exchange 5.5 knowledge to more quickly understand and apply the similar concepts and building blocks in Active Directory. This no doubt helps to alleviate the retraining and staffing issues that many corporations flag as being one of the problems with an Active Directory migration.

The Purpose of This Book

Most Windows 2000 books (and Microsoft references) either cover very basic material on Windows 2000 (for example, how to drive the new interface) or expect you to migrate fully over to Active Directory. Any Windows NT 4.0 domain or workgroup seems to exist only with a view of upgrading/migrating later—and all the new features are just around this corner. Very few (if any) concentrate on how to get the best out of Windows 2000 before or without running Active Directory—for example, features that are completely unaware of Active Directory or some that can be run with some limitations. In fact, when the media talks about Windows 2000 Server, this product seems to be synonymous with Active Directory, as if Windows 2000 Server cannot work without Active Directory and people cannot differentiate between the two.

This viewpoint also makes it difficult to pinpoint features that run independently from Active Directory so that even if your network has migrated to Active Directory, those who are non-Enterprise administrators can be aware of how to get the best out of their departmental servers.

As somebody who works full time in the IT industry, I see the need for this information every day, without it being met elsewhere. To date, the only Windows 2000 information I've seen falls into the following categories:

- Plenty of literature from Microsoft (for example, Resource Kits, TechNet, MS Press) that assumes people either have migrated or are migrating whole-heartedly over to Windows 2000 and Active Directory.

- Study guides aimed at those wishing to upgrade their MCP and MCSE (and equivalent) to the new Windows 2000 track, where all the new features exist only in an Active Directory environment.

- *From the Field* references from the few that have actually migrated over to Windows 2000 and Active Directory and can pass on relevant, practical information to those about to walk in the same footsteps.

- Specialized books on certain Windows 2000 topics, such as Web hosting, DNS, Exchange 2000, security, and more.

As previously mentioned, the purpose of this book is to cover some of the main features in Windows 2000 that you can use immediately and independently from Active Directory. This approach is much more than simply making a Windows 2000 computer function in your existing environment—we're looking at using and exploiting to the full new features that might not be immediately obvious and that can all be configured independently from Active Directory.

This approach also provides a way of allowing you to adopt Windows 2000 slowly, at your own pace. Many companies seem to be adopting a mixed deployment where Windows 2000 computers coexist with down-level systems as desktops and servers are gradually replaced with upgrades in line with natural refresh cycles. In many cases such in-place upgrades are seen as seamless because the new version offers the same functionality as the previous, so the risk is minimal.

This is very different from Microsoft's pro-Active Directory stance and its assumption that everybody will be running Active Directory networks sooner rather than later. I can't help thinking that it is a more sensible approach to take, and one that even Microsoft will benefit from in the long term.

By explaining how to configure and use Windows 2000 services that do not rely on Active Directory, I'm hoping that this book will redress the power and control people feel they have lost as a consequence of Microsoft's pro-Active Directory stance. And for those companies that *are* planning to move to Active Directory, it offers an interim compromise and stepping stone as you move from your stable Windows NT 4.0 networks to Windows 2000 Active Directory.

Who Should Read This Book

This book is for two different, and yet complementary, types of IT people: IT managers and IT implementers. The distinction between the two is blurred these days, and I recognize that many job functions will involve both roles.

IT Managers

I wanted to provide information for what I saw as a rather badly represented target audience: IT managers. I've seen books and whitepapers and I've attended seminars that are supposedly aimed at the "IT Decision Maker," which I've taken to mean IT managers. But they rarely seem to successfully address the requirements of the IT managers I come across every day in my work.

In my experience, IT managers are the people who have a high level of IT knowledge and can appreciate what is technically possible, together with knowing how to amalgamate this with business acumen within the restrictions of their company resources. They are the ones who make the important decisions to translate theory into practice, within the context of company policies. They have to battle with resource deficiencies and company politics. They risk their job, reputation, and blood pressure on making such decisions.

This book aims to provide useful information on what is *technically* possible (and how) while still taking into account real-life issues such as minimal risk, minimal cost, and identifying isolated steps that offer easily obtainable goals and short-term practical results. Once armed with this information, you will be in a stronger position to decide how and when to translate these new features into project plans and schedule realistic time frames and resources to put them into action.

The book contains special information sidebars for IT managers where the topic identifies a **Designing & Planning** consideration to help highlight important information you may want to consider.

IT Implementers

Second, this book is also aimed at the IT implementer, who is usually a network administrator looking to configure and install Windows 2000 in an existing environment, but without having to also take on Active Directory. All too often, standard Windows 2000 literature discusses new features only in the context of Active Directory so that you may not be aware of what features and services you can use (and how) independently from Active Directory. Therefore, you're being asked to learn Active Directory, the new features, *and* the new interface all at once—which usually relegates it to a testing environment or your home study network. This book aims to provide the information you need to start using Windows 2000 productively in your current working environment.

Armed with this information and a clear view of what is possible with Windows 2000 when running it outside an Active Directory domain (and what isn't possible without Active Directory) you will then be better equipped to dive into the standard Microsoft documentation and build on this knowledge. This then may or may not include Active Directory features—but the choice will then be yours, rather than having it decided for you.

By knowing what is possible without Active Directory and how to implement it, you should gain a level of knowledge and a perspective that is difficult to obtain from the standard Microsoft documentation. Throughout the book we will have special information sidebars for IT implementers where the topic identifies a relevant **Configuring & Implementing** consideration to help provide additional technical information.

Microsoft Certified Professionals and System Engineers

Although not specifically aimed at MCPs and MCSEs, this book may also be of benefit to MCP/MCSE candidates looking to supplement their Windows 2000 exam knowledge and extend it into the realities of the workplace.

It may also help NT professionals transition their skills to Windows 2000 because new features can be learned within the context of a Windows NT 4.0 domain, instead of trying to take these on board at the same time as learning Active Directory. There's nothing so reassuring as starting from familiar ground rather than feeling as if you're starting everything from scratch again. Interestingly, Microsoft's fairly recent addition of exam 70-244, "Supporting and Maintaining a Microsoft Windows NT Server 4.0 Network" (available since April 2001), shows its acknowledgment that Windows NT 4.0 domains are still prevalent in the workplace and as such need to be supported by competent professionals.

While the other Windows 2000 exams assume an Active Directory context, in reality MCP/MCSE professionals will find it the exception and not the norm that they will be given Active Directory Enterprise permissions—so they must know which features they can configure and use independently from Active

Directory in a typical departmental setting. Note, however, that this book is *not* written as a MCSE study guide for a specific Microsoft exam; there are plenty of good alternatives for these already.

What This Book Will Cover

This book will cover a wide range of topics that encompass a diversity of the new features and services that Windows 2000 offers. This will include everything from features particularly relevant for workstations, laptops, and servers, to specific services such as IIS and Certificate Services, Terminal Services, and Remote Access to networking services such as Domain Name System (DNS) and Dynamic Host Configuration Protocol (DHCP), Internet Protocol Security (IPSec), and Network Address Translation (NAT). All these and more will be explained outside the context of Active Directory—clearly outlining what is possible and what isn't, and also what is possible with certain limitations.

Additionally, each chapter contains a walkthrough that includes step-by-step information on how you might implement some of the features covered in the chapter. These are practical exercises that reinforce some of the chapter contents and that should be useful on most production environments to help provide some hands-on experience.

Chapter 2: Workstations

Many people have Windows 2000 now as their standard desktop operating system, but they might not realize how to make the most of the new features it offers. In fact, I've often seen people treat Windows 2000 as if it were Windows NT 4.0 with the interface annoyingly changed, totally unaware of the new features and benefits "under the hood," just there for the taking! The new interface isn't to everybody's liking, but it is highly configurable—if you know where to look.

Windows 2000 is often chosen for stability and reliability reasons, and it has certainly earned its reputation for better stability and reliability than previous operating systems. Are you aware, though, of how that is accomplished and how you can configure and fine-tune this? For example, Windows File Protection helps to address the "DLL hell" we got used to seeing with incompatible versions of files, but it comes at the cost of disk space. Knowing how this works and how you can configure it gives the choice back to you, rather than relying on the operating system to make choices for you. When disk space on the operating system partition is tight (often an issue if upgrading), knowing how to configure the DLL cache can make the difference between being able to upgrade to Windows 2000 without repartitioning your disk and not being able to install it.

Active Directory Group Policies have had a lot of coverage as being one of the biggest reasons to migrate to Active Directory so that you can centrally control and secure users' and computers' environments. They offer far more extensive configuration options than System Policies ever did—and they do so without *tattooing* the registry. But did you realize that you can use them outside Active Directory, even within a Windows NT 4.0 domain? Local Group Policies are one of Windows 2000 best-kept secrets! Using them together with security templates, you can centrally configure and deploy your security and administrative templates on Windows 2000 computers—for example, you can lockdown desktops for users and enforce tight security configurations.

Chapter 3: Laptops

It's not difficult to see why the laptop market was the first to embrace Windows 2000. It offered the Plug and Play (PnP) features and Device Manager loved in Windows 9*x*, but with the secure logon and NTFS security that was needed for a mobile existence. Added onto that, EFS, the Encrypting File System in Windows 2000, offered increased protection, which was a new security feature that was easy to use immediately without Active Directory. But you do know how to best use EFS and what restrictions and limitations it has? Do you want to disable it to ensure that you don't end up with inaccessible files, but you are not sure how to do that without Active Directory?

Those are some of the best-known features and reasons for running Windows 2000 on laptops, but it also offers some great new features for integrating a mobile environment with the corporate network—including automatic hardware profiles and a Synchronization Manager. Files and content can be cached when the laptop is online, which can then be used when the laptop is disconnected and synchronized when next online. This can greatly improve productivity, reduce bandwidth, and help eliminate the problems of lost modifications when multiple versions are used.

Other new features applicable for the laptops include the new Power Management options and general Windows 2000 maintenance and troubleshooting utilities that are particularly relevant for laptop users—such as the Task Scheduler and advanced boot options for when the laptop is urgently needed but many miles away from the IT Help Desk!

Chapter 4: File and Print Services

The workhorses of the network that fulfill various file and print services have a lot to gain from Windows 2000. Storing and retrieving data can be made easier with features such as Distributed File System (Dfs) to help you reorganize shares without actually moving any data, an Indexing service that lets users search for files and content across the network, and disk quotas to help you control and plan disk storage and capacity.

Disk management has become easier with the new dynamic disk storage providing on-the-fly changes without rebooting. Remote disk management is now possible, and the Remote Storage service can provide instant increased disk storage by dynamically migrating less often used data to tape. The built-in backup utility has an improved interface with an inbuilt graphical scheduler, and you can now leave Performance Monitor running as a service to help keep an eye on the general health of your servers (for example, emailing the administrator when critical factors such as low disk space and memory are identified).

There's plenty of printing improvements too, including support for the new Internet Printing Protocol (IPP), which allows intranet and Internet users to install and manage their printers through a browser.

Chapter 5: Terminal Services

I think Windows 2000 Terminal Services earns its spot as my favorite feature in the Windows 2000 feature set. Now part of the base operating system rather than a separate product, Terminal Services is installed as a service just like any other operating system service. Best of all, it comes in two flavors: Administrator Mode and Application Mode.

Administrator Mode requires no additional licensing considerations with the only drawback being the maximum simultaneous connections being restricted to two. It allows administrators to remotely log onto a Windows 2000 server (running this service) and remotely administer it as if they were sitting in front of it. It's ideal for low-bandwidth connections because all the programming execution stays on the server—only screen and mouse/keyboard data is transmitted. And it's secure because you can use 128-bit encryption, and it's firewall friendly in that it doesn't use remote procedural calls (RPC) that most firewalls block. It's difficult to see why you wouldn't install this on all Windows 2000 servers.

Application Mode is how most people currently think of a terminal server—servicing applications to users in a true multiuser environment. It's an easier environment to control and maintain because everything is held centrally in one place. Conversely, there may be times when you want to integrate that environment with the user's local operating system, so you need to know whether this is possible and how. Terminal Services means that any Windows 32-bit user can have a Windows 2000 operating system environment—without having to change his or her hardware. This could be a permanent arrangement in an attempt to centralize all applications and administration or a stepping-stone as you slowly migrate users' desktops to Windows 2000.

There are some great new features and improvements in Windows 2000 Terminal Services that previously were possible only with the Citrix add-on, Metaframe—for example, improved throughput, mapping of local printers and drives, copying files between the two systems, and, of course, shadowing (which Microsoft calls Remote Control), which lets an administrator see and take over a user's session. Particularly for remote sites, the last feature can be a godsend for IT Help Desks and dramatically reduce user problems and increase the turnaround of logged calls.

I found that additional features supplied with Service Pack 1 (interestingly no longer included with Service Pack 2 but downloadable from the Microsoft site), and from the Windows 2000 Server Resource Kit were indispensable for production use of Terminal Services, and so I've included these in this chapter.

The only fly in the ointment with Windows 2000 Terminal Services is the new requirement for running Terminal Services Licensing. You must run these when running Windows 2000 in Application Mode. They require consideration before installation, and for this you have to know exactly how they work and what configuration options you have. Once you have identified Terminal Services as a possible resource for your company, learn about Terminal Services licensing requirements before you make any deployment plans!

Chapter 6: Networking Services—DNS, DHCP, WINS, and NLB

At the heart of any network lie the networking services that make it possible for computers to communicate with each other. With the acceptance that not all networks have high bandwidths and must often integrate with other networks (including the Internet) and non-Windows computers, Windows 2000 networking services such as DNS, DHCP, and WINS have had a vital overhaul. Microsoft has had to do this because Active Directory has been its focus of Windows 2000, and Active Directory relies on a reliable networking infrastructure. Quite simply, if there are TCP/IP problems there will be Active Directory problems. Although you might not be ready to move to Active Directory, there is no reason why you can't benefit from those networking services improvements.

Although DNS, DHCP, and WINS are independent services, they work so closely together to produce the same goal of computer-to-computer communication that it is difficult to talk about one in isolation from the others. Each involves central management, configuration control, and security. The Network Load Balancing (NLB) built into Windows 2000 Advanced Server (and Datacenter Server) also offers high availability and load balancing of networking services. With a view to distributed networking, scalability, and reliability, Network Load Balancing complements the Windows 2000 networking services very well.

Chapter 7: Internet Services— IIS5 and Certificate Services

There are some great improvements to IIS, which no doubt help to account for some of the Windows NT 4.0 server upgrades to Windows 2000 outside Active Directory. There are improvements in reliability, administration, security, and performance—all good news for standalone public Web servers. Many of these are hidden, behind-the-scenes changes, so it pays to know exactly what they are and how they function.

There are also improvements for the intranet environment with **WebDAV** (Web Distributed Authoring and Versioning), as Microsoft continues to blur the distinction between Web servers and file servers, making the browser a universal desktop interface.

Certificate Services is a separate service to IIS, but it's easy to see how the two complement each other—particularly outside Active Directory. Certificate Services complements IIS by offering server and user certificates for a highly secure form of authentication and encryption. IIS5 complements Certificate Services by offering its Web-based certificate forms for requesting and receiving certificates. These certificates can be for both user authentication (for example, used with Web authentication) and also computer authentication (for example, used with IPSec).

When installing and configuring Certificate Services outside Active Directory, you have the choice only of installing it in Standalone mode, not in Enterprise mode, which requires Active Directory. Most Windows 2000 documentation that covers Certificate Services assumes an Enterprise installation, and so it can be frustratingly difficult to try to use Certificate Services and associated utilities outside Active Directory. This chapter is the exception, where it assumes and concentrates on a Standalone installation.

Chapter 8: Secure Communication—IPSec

This chapter builds on the previous chapter because it covers using computer certificates that are requested and granted with Certificate Services and IIS5. Computer certificates are an alternative authentication method to Kerberos when using IPSec, and although Kerberos is the default authentication (except with L2TP/IPSec) you cannot use Windows 2000 Kerberos outside Active Directory. Computer certificates make IPSec possible and secure when used outside Active Directory.

In addition to explaining the authentication methods, this chapter explains how the built-in IPSec policies work and how you must modify them when outside Active Directory. It also explains the various components and utilities that support IPSec. Additionally, it covers how to build your own custom policies so that you are firmly in control of what traffic you accept and block and how to track and monitor it.

This chapter is very much a need-to-know and hands-on, practical look at implementing IPSec rather than offering a theoretical exploration of how cryptography-based security works. I've found this level of detail very difficult to find elsewhere, particularly when implementing IPSec outside Active Directory. And yet to me, this is what network administrators should focus on as a starting point in implementing IPSec.

Chapter 9: Remote Access— RAS, VPN, IAS, and CMAK

The improved VPN support is well known in Windows 2000, and it's usually L2TP/IPSec that grabs the limelight for this. I think the new remote access policies are the greatest improvement for securing and fine-tune configuring a server for remote access connections. These apply for dialup, for PPTP and L2TP/IPSec VPN connections, and when using IAS (Internet Authentication Service). Somehow remote access policies have earned the reputation of not being applicable outside Active Directory, and this is just not true. What is true is that they must be configured slightly differently when used on a Windows 2000 member server within a Windows NT 4.0 domain, so it's vital to understand exactly how they work.

Although L2TP/IPSec can offer greater security, it will not be the best choice for everybody because it has greater overhead in terms of server resources and administrative overhead (server and remote computer both need computer certificates, for example). Not all platforms support IPSec either. When L2TP/IPSec is not an appropriate choice, you need to know how to configure PPTP with the tightest security.

When L2TP/IPSec can be used, this chapter explains how this can be configured outside Active Directory, exactly what security is being used, and how you can monitor it. You may be surprised by some of the defaults Microsoft selects for you, and you may want to change them.

CMAK is the Connection Manager Administration Kit, which allows administrators to deploy central connection details bundled into a dialer. This means remote users have to run only your supplied executable to easily connect to your remote access services. You can use either a static phone book to supply the actual connection details or a dynamic phone book that the user checks each time he or she connects and automatically downloads any changes. Not only can this look very professional—for example, by customizing the dialer with company logos and a personalized message with Help Desk details—but it can also dramatically reduce Help Desk calls from remote users trying to set up and/or amend the required connection details. For example, although Windows 2000 Professional can automatically prompt for an underlying ISP connection to be made before a VPN connection, down-level clients do not. Many users simply do not understand or forget that they should first connect to their ISP and then make an additional connection to the VPN server. The custom dialer can be configured to do this automatically for the user.

Chapter 10: Internet Connectivity— ICS, NAT, and ISA Server

All three of these Microsoft solutions—Internet Connection Sharing, Network Address Translation on RRAS, and the Internet Security and Acceleration Server—offer different solutions for connecting multiple workstations on a local area network to the Internet, by means of one computer that is connected to both the internal and external network.

Obviously, they differ in complexity and functionality, and it's important to know their differences as well as similarities so that you can better judge which of these solutions (if any) is suitable for your network's Internet connectivity. ICS as the poor relation often gets bad press because of its simplicity, but when you look at its actual abilities, it's surprisingly adept at meeting many connectivity needs. NAT, it is true, does offer much better monitoring facilities and more flexibility in configuration—for example, it is able to take advantage of multiple public addresses and reserve certain addresses for specific services. Neither, however, can accommodate controlling access by users—and to do this you'll need something more like ISA Server, which is the Windows 2000 upgrade to Microsoft Proxy Server 2.

ISA Server has a lot more to offer than just controlling user access—highly configurable caching, bandwidth control, and firewalling features are only some of its impressive feature set. As an additional product (not built into the operating system like ICS and NAT), it's important to appreciate exactly how this product works with its limitations and restrictions as well as its features. For example, although it was written to integrate with Active Directory, unlike Exchange 2000 it can be used both inside and outside Active Directory. Some of the features you might want to use may be available only when it's integrated with Active Directory, and it's important to realize this if you are currently running a Windows NT 4.0 domain. This is particularly important if you're planning to upgrade Proxy Sever 2 while Microsoft is offering an attractive upgrade deal. If you are not installing ISA Server into Active Directory you may lose some of the functionality you had (such as arrays). It's very important to realize all the implications of upgrading, and I've found that Microsoft documentation generally assumes that an ISA Server that is required for caching will be installed in Active Directory, and that only the firewall features will be installed on computers outside Active Directory. While this chapter cannot cover each ISA feature and how to configure it, it will outline the new features and cover upgrading issues and how to configure/install it outside Active Directory.

Appendix A: The Windows 2000 Microsoft Management Console

Common to most Windows 2000 graphical configuration utilities is the Microsoft Management Console (MMC). In my experience, most people find this intuitively easy to use at its basic level, and so throughout the book I've made the assumption that step-by-step instructions are not required on how to navigate around the MMC when using the built-in Administrative tools.

Some people, though, may not be as comfortable with creating custom MMCs, and these can make an administrator's life much easier—for example, having one MMC configuring/monitoring one service that is running on multiple servers. Or conversely, monitoring multiple services from the same computer that are logically linked—for example, DNS and DHCP, or the Security event log with IPSec policies so that you can easily monitor which policies are being used.

I don't understand why administrators don't use custom MMCs like this more often and logically group together tools that they frequently use. It's so much easier to call up a single MMC with everything you need rather than having to load lots of different MMCs and then on each having to navigate to the correct level. It's incredibly quick and easy to create custom MMCs, so I can only conclude that most administrators are not aware or forget that this is possible. This technique also works well with remote administration and the powerful RunAs command that lets you call up an application with an administrator's privileges while still logged on with a standard user account.

Other people may not be aware of the true flexibility and power of the MMC—for example, creating and using Taskpads as simpler GUI utilities that can be easily distributed for delegated administration or integrated into applications. ISA Server, for example, makes good use of MMC Taskpads, as Chapter 10 shows. With its Web-based support, I suspect using MMC Taskpads is another area that Microsoft and vendors will continue to develop, in line with the PC-to-Web integration concept that is prevalent throughout Microsoft's new features and platforms. This appendix serves as a good introduction to creating your own Taskpads without any programming knowledge so that you too can leverage the simplified user interface.

What This Book Won't Cover

Because this book is aimed at explaining and highlighting what is possible without Active Directory, it won't cover the basics of Active Directory architecture, how to migrate to Active Directory, or how to configure features within Active Directory. It will not concentrate on Windows 2000 features that rely on Active Directory, although these may be pointed out where applicable. For example, we may cover features that can be used outside Active Directory but in a limited form or that will be enhanced or changed once running in an Active Directory environment. These can then be flagged as considerations for a future migration—for example, influencing your Active Directory design or timescales. Or you may need to add to the Active Directory deployment additional reconfiguration to ensure that the new features can be used.

One example of this is making full use of dynamic name registration with Windows 2000 DNS and DHCP, which is possible even if you're running down-level clients in a Windows NT 4.0 domain. Without Active Directory you won't be able to benefit from two features that rely on running in Active Directory. These require configuring your DNS zones to be Active Directory integrated, which can be done only when running DNS on a Windows 2000 domain controller in an Active Directory domain. Once this is applicable, however, you can then reconfigure the zone type and capitalize on the two new features, which are better fault tolerance and secure updates. Whether these new features are important enough for you to change your plans or priorities to migrate to Active Directory is up to you to decide. This book makes no assumptions that benefits are "must haves" because everything comes at a price.

Just as you should be aware of which Windows 2000 features you can implement outside Active Directory, so you should be aware of which Windows 2000 main features depend on an Active Directory infrastructure. When you are not running Active Directory, you will not be able to use the following:

- Exchange 2000 and other Active Directory dependent applications
- Intellimirror features
- Enterprise-related Group Policy Objects (GPOs)
- Quick resource searches across the enterprise network, with the ability to extend the schema
- Universal groups, group nesting, and changes in group membership
- Task delegation (the Windows NT 4.0 domain administrator remains the lowest level of administrative authority)
- Kerberos rather than NTLM authentication
- Automatic transitive trusts
- Multimaster replication
- Enterprise Encrypting File System (EFS) recovery agents
- Enterprise Certificate Authorities (CAs)
- Quality of Service (QoS)

Exchange 2000 and Other Active Directory Dependent Applications

Exchange 2000 was the first product on the market that *required* Active Directory—it will not run on a Windows 2000 member server in a Windows NT

4.0 domain, for example. One of the reasons for this is that it must communicate with a Windows 2000 Global Catalog, and the Exchange directory is now merged with the Active Directory rather than being separate as it was with Exchange 5.5 and Windows NT 4.0. This explains the emergence of the new group type in Active Directory, called **Distribution** and shown in Figure 1.1. Unlike standard group assignments that we know in NT that are used for assigning permissions, it is instead used for identifying email distribution groups.

Figure 1.1 Distribution Groups in Active Directory—Designed with Exchange 2000 in Mind

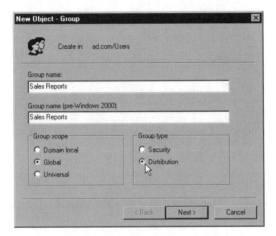

For companies wanting to take advantage of some of the benefits Exchange 2000 offers, it has been a decisive turning point to adopt Active Directory. Exchange 2000 now boasts an impressive list of new features such as Instant Messaging, Conferencing, Web Storage, and XML—in addition to Active Directory integration where the two user directories (for network accounts and mail accounts) have been amalgamated for a single, central point of configuration.

Figure 1.2 shows an Active Directory user account properties updated with Exchange options that in Windows NT 4.0 had to be accessed with a separate Exchange Administrator program.

We may soon see other Active Directory–enabled products that similarly rely on Active Directory, and if they offer options and features not to be found elsewhere, you may also decide that is good enough reason to go with Active Directory. Other products may offer a restricted feature set unless it is installed in an Active Directory domain—Microsoft's ISA Server is a good example of this. You should take the time first, though, to understand what the new Active Directory dependent features are and whether you really need them.

Figure 1.2 Active Directory User Properties after Exchange 2000 Installation

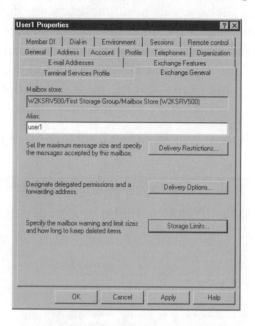

Designing & Planning...

Additional Considerations for Active Directory Dependent Applications

Make sure you know exactly what the new features offer from an Active Directory dependent product and whether they require additional supporting services. For example, Exchange 5.5 included Web hosting only as an optional service if Outlook Web Access was required. In Exchange 2000, Web hosting is now tightly integrated with the product.

A thorough understanding of how the product actually works will allow you to more accurately access whether it is justified when set against the costs of implementing Active Directory in-house. If you decide your business can benefit from these features, but you don't want the burden of Active Directory migration, look to see whether the product can be offered externally as an outsourced service (for example, from ASPs). This could give you the best of both worlds with access to the new features but without having to restructure your network.

Continued

You may find it useful to refer to Chapter 2, "Making the Decision to Deploy," from the Exchange 2000 Server Resource Kit (also available from the Microsoft site at (www.microsoft.com/TechNet/exchange/guide/plan/p_02_tt1.asp) and refer to a list of Exchange 2000 featrues from www.microsoft.com/exchange/evaluation/features/default.asp.

Intellimirror Features

Admittedly, the Intellimirror features of centrally controlling users and computers are one of the biggest advantages in favor of Active Directory because they offer an easy-to-control facility not found with Windows NT 4.0 domains. For example, you can redirect key user folders, such as My Documents or My Pictures, to ensure that users save personal work to a central server. Central servers are easier to protect against lost data because they are usually protected with Uninterruptible Power Supply (UPS) systems, hardware RAID, carefully and controlled backup routines, and they allow access to the data from any workstation.

Independently from Active Directory, you can still use home directories and mapped drives so that user data can be saved centrally, and roaming profiles are still supported so that users can log on to any desktop and retrieve their own familiar desktop profile.

Active Directory allows Microsoft Installer (MSI) applications to be automatically installed to users or computers, which is a great way to manage software deployment outside SMS. Many companies already have in place a successful mechanism for application deployment, and they have no need to change their tried and tested rollout methods. Many of these include the ability to push the installations/upgrades at a planned schedule—for example, at a quiet time overnight when the network load is light and the disruption to users is minimal. At the moment, automatic installations with GPOs lack this built-in facility and installations are either applied when the PC is booted up or when the user logs on (slowing down the bootup/logging on process considerably and reducing bandwidth when it is most needed).

Remote Installation Service (RIS) is a new feature that is very prominent in Microsoft literature. It allows a computer with suitable hardware to install Windows 2000 just by turning it on. It sounds wonderful, and yet there's a considerable amount of behind-the-scenes work before this is possible. For example, this includes the workstations being restricted to using a limited set of PCI network adapters or using PCs which are PXE compliant. Because of these restrictions, they immediately rule out installing to laptops, which would have been one of the most obvious contenders to benefit from RIS. Additionally, there's the need to configure a source server (which must have multiple disks). You also have to set up the relevant permissions for joining computers to the domain, finding and entering each computer's GUID if you require greater security, and only being able to install Professional (not Server). Another restriction that's applicable to existing networks is that you can only install to the workstation's C drive, which means that you cannot install onto dual-booting machines. In my experience, RIS has more disadvantages in practice than theory—unless you are building a new network from scratch with RIS in mind. The majority of these advantages could easily be met with an old-fashioned scripted installation either from a server (if the client already has network support) or with the help of a floppy disk that holds an *unattend* file, if the client computer can boot from a CD that contains the Windows 2000 distribution files. An example of the RIS Configuration Settings Window is shown in Figure 1.3.

Figure 1.3 One of the Many RIS Configuration Settings

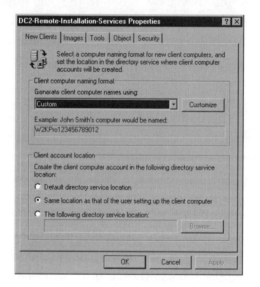

Configuring & Implementing...

RIS Supported Adapters

There are a limited number of PCI cards supported with the RIS boot disk if your desktop isn't PXE compliant. Note that you cannot manually add support for additional adapters although Microsoft might extend the range at a later date. The adapters supported include the following:

- 3Com 3C900B-Combo
- 3Com 3C900B-FL
- 3Com 3C900B-TPC
- 3Com 3C900B-TPO
- 3Com 3C900-Combo
- 3Com 3C900-TPO
- 3Com 3C905B-Combo
- 3Com 3C905B-FX
- 3Com 3C905B-TX
- 3Com 3C905C-TX
- 3Com 3C905-T4
- 3Com 3C905-TX
- AMD PCnet Adapters
- Compaq NetFlex 100
- Compaq NetFlex 110
- Compaq NetFlex 3
- DEC DE450
- DEC DE500
- HP DeskDirect 10/100 TX
- Intel Pro 10+
- Intel Pro 100+
- Intel Pro 100B
- SMC 8432
- SMC 9332
- SMC 9432

Continued

> In case this list has changed since this book went to print, you can always check the full current range after installing RIS and then running the RBGG utility (which produces the floppy disk for RIS clients) from \\<server_share>\RemoteInstall\Admin\i386 Once loaded, select the **Adapter List** button.

Enterprise Related Group Policy Objects

Group Policy Objects (GPOs) are a big thing in Active Directory—and they can really be seen as part of the Intellimirror set that aims to centrally control users and computers. Similar in concept to the Windows NT 4.0 system policy, they provide a mechanism for network administrators to control behavior and settings—for example, they remove the capability to change their network settings.

GPOs are seen as vastly superior to Windows NT 4.0 system policies for two reasons. First, they don't *tattoo* the registry of the client computer, which means that once applied the settings remain in effect for the next person. Second, they offer a greater range of options for both computers and users—and at different levels. For example, an enterprise administrator can set an option that cannot be changed by lower-level administrators with the No Override option. By default, options are inherited as they go down the levels (site, domain, and OU), but an administrator with appropriate privileges can decide to block this inheritance—if the No Override option hasn't been set, as shown in Figure 1.4.

Figure 1.4 Active Directory Group Policy Settings—With and Without Override

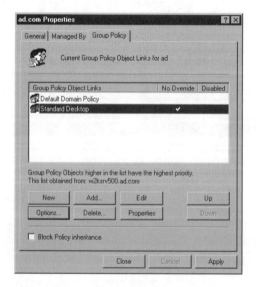

While GPOs offer great advantages in central administration, they can also be a minefield for troubleshooting if the end result isn't what was expected or desired. They require competence and experience to both design and configure them effectively across the different levels of authority we didn't have with Windows NT 4.0 networks—local, site, domain, and OU and any nested OUs. I suspect in reality what will happen is that administrators will "fire-fight" to get the result they want without regard to company policy with a complete mishmash of contradictory and superfluous options. At the moment I don't think Microsoft offers practical tools to help with this new area of Active Directory—and practicalities will mean that Microsoft will either have to supply this in a later version or a third-party vendor will step in.

Outside an Active Directory network, you can still make use of local GPOs that allow options such as computer startup scripts, hiding certain options, and enforcing strong passwords. Beware, however, that in an Active Directory environment such local GPOs could be overwritten by site, domain, or OU GPOs. Chapter 2 will cover local GPOs in more detail.

NOTE

For more information on GPOs, see Chapter 4, "How Group Policy Works," and Chapter 5, "Developing a Group Policy Implementation Strategy," in the Microsoft *Change and Configuration Management Deployment Guide*.

There are also some white papers that can be downloaded from the Microsoft site such as "Introduction to Windows 2000 Group Policy" at www.microsoft.com/windows2000/techinfo/howitworks/management/grouppolicyintro.asp, and "Windows 2000 Group Policy" at www.microsoft.com/windows2000/techinfo/howitworks/management/grouppolwp.asp.

Quick Resource Searches across the Enterprise Network, with the Ability to Extend the Schema

This is what Active Directory is all about: having a scalable directory service across your enterprise network that allows for details about computers, users, and services to be easily available for administrators, users, and computers alike. These details are distributed and replicated across both local area networks and wide area networks. Quite simply, NT networks were not designed with this sort of scalability in mind, although various workarounds and improvements have evolved to help meet this requirement.

The Active Directory schema—which details the way such objects are defined and searched—allows for more extensive properties to be attached to each object than the Windows NT 4.0 Security Accounts Manager (SAM) allowed. For example, a user can search for a printer that has a high color resolution or one that is physically close to him or her—rather than relying on an administrator's manual share description to include these facts. Figure 1.5 shows the administrator's interface to the schema using the Active Directory MMC.

Figure 1.5 The Active Directory Schema MMC

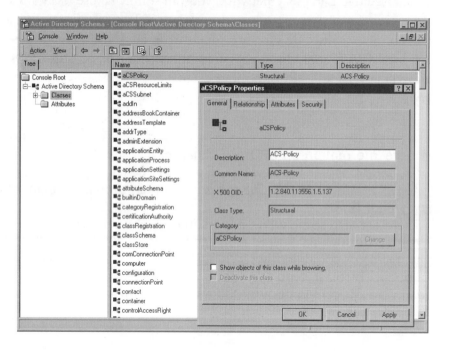

Additionally, Active Directory allows you to extend the schema, which means if there is an additional attribute you would like included—for example, you would like to be able to add a new field to each user's account so you can specify their qualifications—you can do this with Active Directory, but you cannot do so with NT domain accounts. It's probably more likely that this feature will be used by applications offering directory-related services. When such products add their own extensions to the Active Directory schema, this allows them to leverage the benefits of having a directory presence such as checking user permissions and being *site aware* (that is, they know the boundaries of well-connected networks and function appropriately).

All this sounds attractive, but beware! In practice, extending the schema should be done only as a last resort and only after much testing. You should be aware of the consequences of extending the schema, which includes additional replication traffic right across the Active Directory network—and take into account latency so that you know when the change is consistent throughout the network. Also, be aware that currently a schema change once made cannot be deleted, only
disabled. It's not for nothing that Microsoft didn't include the Active Directory Schema MMC as a standard Administrative Tool, made the schema read-only by default, and created an Enterprise Schema group to restrict and discourage such capability!

NOTE

For more information on the Active Directory Schema, see Chapter 4, "Active Directory Schema," from the Windows 2000 Server Resource Kit.

Limitations regarding Active Directory's schema have been a key reason for distrust among administrators. It lacks flexibility to roll back to a known state, delete modifications, or tidily uninstall applications that have modified the schema during installation. Installing Exchange 2000, for example, makes over a thousand modifications to Active Directory. Administrators want the ability to clean and tidy the directory schema for efficiency and to prevent problems with developers attempting to access or modify disabled schema details.

Fortunately, Microsoft has listened to such concerns and will be adding a **Schema Delete** functionality into Active Directory—but it won't go into Windows 2000. Instead, you'll have to wait until the next version, Windows .Net Server, is released (first available release of this feature will be in Beta 3).

Another useful schema improvement in Windows .Net Server will be **Cross-Forest Trust**, which will allow schemas across forests to communicate with each other—this is currently not possible in Windows 2000 Active Directory. Although Microsoft originally envisaged that customers would have only a single forest, for many reasons this has not proved a popular assumption in real-world environments.

NOTE

For more details on Windows .Net Server (the next version of Windows 2000 Server and code-named Whistler), refer to "Looking Forward to Windows .NET Server" on the Microsoft site: www.microsoft.com/WINDOWS2000/future/whistler.asp.

Universal Groups, Group Nesting, and Changes in Group Membership

Groups for handling multiple users confusingly change rules under an Active Directory domain—and, even more confusingly, they change again when the Active Directory is switched to native mode (running on Windows 2000 domain controllers and no Windows NT 4.0 BDCs).

The same basic concept of defining global groups for grouping users, then adding global groups to local groups still applies. But there are no longer local groups on Windows 2000 domain controllers; instead, you have domain local groups. Also new is Universal groups, which break all the Windows NT 4.0 rules by allowing their membership to be global, local, and users—offering an easier way to give users access to resources throughout the Active Directory domain without regard to their domain membership. Universal groups, however, must be replicated across the whole network; therefore, they should never contain users, but rather stable groups that are unlikely to change. In a fire-fighting situation, though, it must be very tempting to add users to universal groups without regard to the impact on the replication traffic.

In short, the changes to groups offer a greater flexibility to meet the needs of an enterprise network. Make sure these changes are fully understood with company policies drawn up before implementing them! Table 1.1 summarizes the Windows 2000 groups and membership rules.

Table 1.1 Windows 2000 Groups and Membership in Active Directory

Name of Windows 2000 Group	Membership in Mixed Mode	Membership in Native Mode
Universal Groups	(Not supported)	User accounts and global groups from any domain and other universal groups
Global Group	User accounts from the same domain	Users and global groups from same domain
Domain Local Group	User accounts and global groups from any domain	User accounts, universal groups, global groups from any domain, and domain local groups from the same domain

Task Delegation

When you are running an Active Directory network, the domain still remains the security boundary (for example, password policies apply only to the domain), but the administrator can now delegate tasks such as resetting passwords, unlocking an account, and joining computers to the domain. This is made easier with the Delegation of Control wizard within the Active Directory MMC, which is shown in Figure 1.6.

Figure 1.6 Delegation of Control Wizard in Active Directory

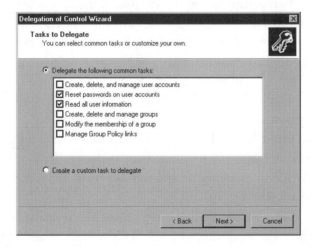

NOTE

For more details, see the "Microsoft Step-by-Step Guide to Using the Delegation of Control Wizard": www.microsoft.com/windows2000/ techinfo/planning/activedirectory/delegsteps.asp.

Not being able to delegate administrative control is one of the things I most lament about Windows NT 4.0 domains because it resulted in too many users having administrative control (which made no distinction between the critical and noncritical admin tasks), or simple administrative tasks were left for too long because they are given to a small team of users that already had too much to do.

Delegating control is not without its own pitfalls however, and as part of your Active Directory design you must decide in advance on company policies for who can delegate control and to whom, what tasks, and how to monitor them.

Kerberos Rather Than NTLM Authentication

Kerberos offers both a more secure password authentication (for example, it offers mutual authentication) and a quicker one over NTLM (it uses delegation). You can also control Kerberos settings (such as the maximum lifetime of a user ticket) to fine-tune your requirements. Whether these are good enough reasons to implement Active Directory will depend on your security needs.

Note that Kerberos will be used on an Active Directory network only when both client and authenticating server is running Windows 2000—Kerberos will not be used if both client and server are not running Windows 2000, irrespective of whether your domain is Active Directory. For example, a Windows 2000 Professional that must authenticate with a SQL database that is running on a Windows NT 4.0 server will use NTLM. NTLM is also used on standalone Windows 2000 servers and for all Windows 2000 computers in a workgroup.

Another exception is if you set up a trust relationship between domains in two forests. At the forest level (the root) trusts to other Active Directory forest will use Kerberos. But when the external trust is domain to domain (for example, required for efficiency in a deeply nested domain structure), the trust will use NTLM rather than Kerberos.

So is NTLM such a bad authentication protocol? Actually, NTLM authentication supports three different methods of challenge/response authentication with varying levels of security to suit your environment and client technology. The weakest form of security is LAN Manager (or LM), which is used in workgroups to provide downward compatibility for Windows for Workgroups, Windows 95, and Windows 98 for file sharing. The next level is NTLM v1, and it is used when you have a Windows NT 4.0 domain with a domain controller running SP3+. The highest level is NTLM v2, which is used on Windows 2000 clients in a Windows NT 4.0 domain if all domain controllers are running SP4+. By default, all three authentication mechanisms are enabled, but you can strengthen your authentication policy by disabling the weaker levels you don't need. For example, if you run Windows 2000 Professional and/or Windows 2000 Server in a Windows NT 4.0 domain and all the domain controllers are running SP4+, you can set the Windows 2000 computers to use NTLM v2 only with a local group policy. Chapter 2 covers such security group policies.

NOTE

There are plenty of additional resources with technical information on how Kerberos works and the differences between it and NTLM. Try, for example, the following:

- Whitepaper called "Windows 2000 Kerberos Authentication" from the Windows 2000 Server Technical Notes or the Microsoft site: www.microsoft.com/windows2000/techinfo/howitworks/security/kerberos.asp
- Knowledge-Based article Q217098, "Basic Overview of Kerberos User Authentication Protocol in Windows 2000": http://support.microsoft.com/support/kb/articles/Q217/0/98.ASP
- Microsoft's "Step-by-Step Guide to Kerberos 5 (krb5 1.0) Interoperability": www.microsoft.com/windows2000/techinfo/planning/security/kerbsteps.asp.

Automatic Transitive Trusts

Unlike Windows NT 4.0, trusts between domains (if within the same forest) are transitive—there is no need to explicitly define a trusting/trusted relationship between two domains. So, for example, if you have two domains—one called COMPANY1.COM and one called CHILD.COMPANY1.COM (with the latter being a child domain of the former)—then both domains would automatically trust each other. Similarly if you had COMPANY1.COM and COMPANY2.COM, which crucially both belonged to the same forest, they would still automatically trust each other. And if you had other child domains such that they were six levels deep, they would all still trust each other.

Configuring and maintaining trust relationships between Windows NT 4.0 domains was very cumbersome; hence the domain models were used and adapted to suit most environments. In truth, I suspect there are more multiple-trust domains (often more affectionately known as the absolute chaos model) than there should be, simply as a result of fire-fighting permission problems. But with the greater complexity came greater control—it was often easier to restrict security when using a single trust. If your Web server belonged to a trusting domain and was breached so that its local SAM was exposed, your domain accounts were still safe and so were other servers outside the Web domain.

You have no such control over domain trusts within an Active Directory forest. Although you can create a shortcut trust (one that has a direct trust relationship to speed the authentication) and you can create external trusts, you cannot revoke a trust within an Active Directory forest for additional security or control. The only way to do this would be by having multiple forests and explicitly defining one-way trust relationships between the two (or more) domains. Multiple forests, however, also mean multiple computer and administrative overheads, multiple directories, and multiple schemas.

Multimaster Domain Controllers

Windows NT 4.0 domains had a single PDC (Primary Domain Controller) with multiple BDCs (Backup Domain Controllers), which resulted in only one computer having read/write access to the domain accounts and the others having read-only access. This meant that if the PDC was offline, while the BDCs could still authenticate clients, new accounts couldn't be created or passwords couldn't be changed—and hence a BDC would have to be promoted to PDC status.

Active Directory Domain Controllers all have read/write access to the accounts, which means that any domain controller can be used for writing to the directory. This offers better fault tolerance than the Windows NT 4.0 structure. The downside of this is that each domain controller should have a higher degree of security than BDCs might have had—with permissions and rights, and physically secured. Because they now offer write access, to all the accounts throughout your enterprise you *must* ensure that BDCs upgraded to Windows 2000 domain controllers are secure. This is a point often overlooked, and it is particularly important for remote branch sites, for example, that don't have a local administrator.

Despite the initial promise of all domain controllers in Active Directory being equal, which makes for greater fault tolerance and true distributed computing, this turned out to be less than true for all domain controller functions. In fact, there's more server maintenance required with Active Directory because now you have more to worry about than just a local security database. Active Directory requires specific services that domain controllers in your forest and domain must assume for the smooth running of the enterprise network. They are often referred to as FSMO roles: **Flexible Single Master Operations**. These are as follows:

- Domain Naming Master (one per forest)
- Relative Identifier Master (one per domain)
- Infrastructure Master (one per domain)
- Primary Domain Controller Emulator Master (one per domain)
- Schema (one per forest)

For an Active Directory network to function correctly, all these need to be available as critical services. The more domains you have in your forest, the higher the overhead of maintaining these services (the actual number of services will be <number of domains x 3> + 2; for example, in a forest of only 5 domains, you'll have 17 critical services to maintain). Added to that, there are also the servers that hold the Global Catalog service, and you're encouraged to have at least one domain controller with this role per site.

For better fault tolerance and load balancing, it is advised that you split these roles between domain controllers, and even geographically if possible. Figure 1.7 shows the dialog box from a domain controller where you configure and maintain three of the roles that can be transferred. Domain controllers that hold these roles should be rigorously backed up and physically secured. Although the roles can be transferred between working domain controllers (hence they are referred to as *flexible* and originally as *floating*), it is more difficult to resume the service when one of these domain controllers unexpectedly fails. You can seize the role with another domain controller—which is why Active Directory designs with fault tolerance in mind ensuring that a spare domain controller is available, specifically for standby reasons. Some of the roles cannot be transferred back once seized; your only option is to reinstall the operating system.

While it is nice to have any domain controller able to modify accounts and groups, clearly the reliance on these FSMO roles brings with it a heavier burden of maintenance, possibly the need for more servers, and more potential points of failure in the network. Added to that, when the domain is switched to Native mode, users will not be able to log in unless they can contact a domain controller that has the Global Catalog service, so this too requires redundancy.

Figure 1.7 Configuring and Maintaining Three of the Five FSMOs Roles

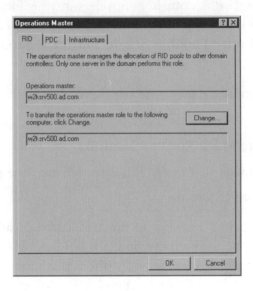

The simplistic PDC/BDC multiple domain arrangement has its limitations—but it was never this complicated! You may even argue that its simplicity and limitations were actually one of its strengths. What you gain in Active Directory with the multimaster domain controllers, you certainly lose in terms of additional overheads when it comes to the overall picture of maintaining Active Directory domain controllers.

Enterprise Encrypting File System (EFS) Recovery Agents

EFS offers a higher degree of security for protecting confidential data stored on disk (that is, it is not protected when being transmitted across the network). Only the person who encrypted the file and by default the administrator can decrypt an encrypted file. The administrator can act as a recovery agent to ensure that a file is always accessible if needed (for example, the employee leaves the company). EFS will be covered in Chapter 3.

When you're running an Active Directory network the network Enterprise administrator is designated the default recovery agent—and you can add more recovery agents for this task. When you're not running Active Directory by default the local machine's administrator can act as a recovery agent, so your EFS protection is only as secure as your local administrator account.

It's always good practice to secure your local administrator account, irrespective of whether you're planning to us EFS. Use the simple method of renaming your local administrator account, and create a bogus account with the same name and no rights. For your true administrator account, make sure you choose a complex and difficult-to-guess long password—and use it only when you have to. For everyday work, make sure you use a standard local User account, a local Power User account, or a user domain account—and if needed, supplement this with the new **Run as** Windows 2000 command (Shift+Right-Click program, or type **runas** on the command line) to run a command or program in a different context.

Enterprise Certificate Authorities

Windows 2000 Certificate Authorities (CAs) that can issue user and computer certificates may be either Standalone or Enterprise CAs. Standalone CAs have no interaction with Active Directory, whereas Enterprise CAs fully integrate with Active Directory. There are advantages and disadvantages to both modes of running, but if you do not have an Active Directory network, clearly the choice is made for you.

The main disadvantage of not being able to run an Enterprise CA is that you can't automatically issue certificates with the use of predefined certificate templates—for example, for use with IPsec. You can still use computer certificates, however, by manually requesting them (through a browser) and manually (or programmatically) granting the certificates. Whether this is a viable option will depend on how many computers require certificates together with time delays, administrative overheads, and/or development resources. An exception to this is the use of smart cards for a more secure logon that will work only with computer certificates issued from an Enterprise CA.

> **NOTE**
>
> For more information on using smart card logon, refer to the Knowledge Base article Q257480, "Certificate Enrollment Using Smart Cards": http://support.microsoft.com/support/kb/articles/Q257/4/80.ASP.

Taking the automation out of granting certificates does afford a greater degree of security and control that some network administrators would welcome rather than deplore. An Enterprise CA must be constantly available on the network because it works in tandem with Active Directory, whereas Standalone CAs have the flexibility of working even when detached from the network (because everything is stored locally), which again provides greater security and control. Standalone CAs will be covered in greater detail in Chapter 7.

Quality of Service

The technologies and concepts of having Quality of Service (QoS) have been around for many years, first introduced by necessity with the slow X25 networks, then Frame Relay, then ATM. It is difficult and complex to implement QoS outside a single WAN environment because it must be supported end-to-end (that is, every component in the often heterogeneous network from computer, to switch/hub/bridge, to router must similarly support the same QoS communication). It is even more difficult to implement in an Ethernet environment where the original goal of this medium was to transmit as much traffic from each client as fast as possible, and it is typically used with bursty traffic. This is clearly at odds with QoS, which has to predict and manage traffic.

The need for Quality of Service in a LAN environment became recognized first with the advent of bandwidth-hungry applications such as streaming video and audio, which are also sensitive to latency and jitter. Nowadays the management of traffic is just as relevant for any service that is bandwidth hungry, time sensitive, or mission critical—spilling over to e-commerce services and enterprise resource planning applications, for example. Modern networks (and those of the future where the Internet will become the universal backbone) need to encompass business requirements, not just technical issues. The answer isn't always to over-provision—to provide more and more bandwidth—but to manage sensibly and coordinate the increasing amount of traffic we expect our networks to handle.

Quality of Service isn't so much a single service, or even a single technology; rather, it encompasses various technologies and concepts with the same aim of managing traffic (for example, prioritizing). The more you realize what's involved, the more you appreciate the limitations and restrictions of converting what seems a simple concept into practice.

You can configure Microsoft's implementation of QoS with Windows 2000, but it does rely on Active Directory. This is because it uses ACS (Admission Control Service) on each subnet, which acts as the network's central nervous system with which to govern and control the QoS requests from each requesting computer before the communication traverses the network. In this way, an inappropriate QoS request can be stopped quickly, rather than getting to the destination (for example, a conferencing server) and then being rejected.

The ACS does this policing in two ways; first, it acts as the Subnet Bandwidth Manager (SBM) to confirm that the overall subnet bandwidth can currently accommodate each client's request for a certain amount of bandwidth. But before it even gets that far, it checks for identity and permissions (for example, at the user, group, OU, or enterprise level) to make sure that the requested level of service should be permitted. Unlike the subnet's current bandwidth status (which is dynamic), this is determined beforehand by a network administrator—for example, that John Smith in Marketing can use the video conferencing service.

Although the actual permission policy is held locally on the ACS (in the Local Policy Module or LPM), the identity lookup procedure uses an LDAP call to Active Directory. There is no mechanism within the Windows 2000 QoS to perform this user lookup to a Windows NT 4.0 domain or a local group on a member server. The only scope for maneuvering outside Active Directory is the LDAP API, which can be used by a third-party vendor to reference an alternative LDAP directory to Active Directory (for example, Novell's NDS).

Although great in theory, implementing QoS in an existing LAN environment is fraught with complexities and problems. One of its biggest problems is that it must be supported end-to-end—and this isn't easy to achieve retroactively. Let's look at some of the QoS components:

- **Operating System Level** Each node on the network (for example, the original client computer) must have QoS components built in to the operating system (which Windows 2000 does) in order to request and honor QoS and communicate with the ACS. This is implemented as a Policy Element (PE), which in Windows 2000 is supplied as MSIDPE.DLL.

- **Application Level** The client and server need to run an application that is QoS aware—that is, one that can ask for and receive QoS commands. Some Microsoft applications have this built in to them, including NetMeeting and Windows Media Player. Microsoft offers a QoS API or Traffic Control API for developers.

- **Network Adapter** The network card in the computer needs to be able to send out a QoS request in its Ethernet frame that requires that 802.1p is supported to denote the relative priority. 3Com, Intel, and Compaq are examples of vendors supplying NICs that support 802.1p.

- **Hubs, Bridges, and Switches** These must also support 802.1 to honor and keep the QoS requested. Cisco, 3Com, ExtremeNetworks, and Intel are examples of vendors supplying these devices that are QoS compliant.

- **Routers** These work at the network level, ignoring Ethernet frames. There must be a way of mapping the same QoS information at this level if it is to cross subnets. This is done by using the DiffServ Codepoint (DSCP) in the IP header (this supercedes the IP Precedence field), which provides a method of marking and maintaining a packet's relative priority.

These are only some of the components that must be taken into consideration before you can hope to implement Windows 2000 QoS across your network. You need a very good foundation of networking knowledge to coordinate all these and be ready to do battle with the plethora of acronyms that abound around QoS. Unfortunately, because QoS is a technically complex subject, the documentation that describes its implementation and configuration is not the easiest to understand either because it's invariably written by QoS specialists for other QoS specialists that make few concessions and many assumptions for those not on the same level of experience/knowledge.

It should also be noted that Microsoft's implementation of QoS has its critics who contest that it cannot scale well and is therefore suitable only for small networks and/or limited implementation. ACS as the nervous system becomes a bottleneck when tasked with many requests from many computers, with each device initially signaling whether it can support the requested service. The signaling protocol in this case is RSVP (the Resource Reservation Protocol), which carries with it a lot of personalized information (such as user name, application name, the requested service, the projected impact on the network, and what parts of the network will be affected), and this in itself can demand a lot of network overhead. It is well suited, though, to small LANs, and if you are planning to migrate to Active Directory and want to use Microsoft's QoS, you may want to take this information about RSVP and ACS into account when designing your sites. This type of QoS implementation is referred to as **Integrated Services** (or more commonly, **Intserv**), which uses a *per-flow management* on a one-to-one basis, which has high overheads but can be managed and controlled very precisely.

As soon as Windows 2000 QoS crosses a router it then uses **Differentiation Services** (**DiffServ**), which mark the packet with a differentiated priority class so that it has a relative priority over other packets. At this point there's no checking back with the ACS or with the next device (router) in the path—it simply forwards the packet according to the priority class, and when each router is configured similarly this works very well. The simplicity of this arrangement means has it fewer overheads and is much simpler (although less precise), which, in turn, allows for multiple sessions to be processed at once (aggregation-flow management), which makes for better scalability.

Diffserv has been heralded as the way forward for implementing wide-scale QoS implementations across large networks, and particularly across networks owned by different companies. The barriers to achieving this lie just as much in business technicalities as in technological issues—and until these can be resolved it is unlikely that QoS will be a reality over the Internet, even if it were supported on all network components.

Microsoft would argue that its implementation of a mixed Intserv and Diffserv offers the best of both worlds, and it remains to be seen whether the per-subnet ACS and RSVP traffic presents a bottleneck that prevents true scalability. I can see that the time will come when QoS will become a necessity and not a luxury across your enterprise network, but I don't think the technologies or industry vendors can easily deliver it today.

TIP

The best analogy I've seen for explaining the differences between Intserv and Diffserv uses another form of transportation: airplanes. Intserv is like each person having his or her own personalized jet to travel to the destination—lots of expensive overhead but offering a very personalized service. Diffserv is like having a standard chartered airplane that sections multiple passengers into First Class, Business Class, and Economy—everybody travels in the same vehicle, but each class has different levels of comfort, allowing more people to travel at once with some degree of personalization.

Active Directory Integration

Even if your Windows 2000 computers are operating in a Windows NT 4.0 domain or a workgroup, there may be occasions when you will still need to integrate with Active Directory. The first (and perhaps most likely) is that in the middle of migrating your company network to Active Directory, there will be a time when your network must encompass both types of domain structures. Or your company may have deliberately decided on a hybrid network where just a portion of the network runs an Active Directory structure. Another possibility is if you have external links—for example, the need to share resources with partners who have an Active Directory network, or perhaps your company has merged with or acquired another company that has an Active Directory network.

It's important to realize how external trusts work with Active Directory. As a Windows NT 4.0 network administrator, you will probably find this less confusing than an Active Directory network administrator. As far as your Windows NT 4.0 domain is concerned, setting up a trust to an Active Directory domain is no different from setting up a trust with another Windows NT 4.0 domain. You still use User Manager for Domains, and you specify one-way trusts with the NetBIOS naming format of the domain with which you want to communicate (this equates to the down-level domain name in Active Directory). If you want both domains to trust each other, this still means you have to configure two different trusts (Trusted and Trusting)—as does the Active Directory administrator with the Active Directory Domains and Trusts MMC, as shown in Figure 1.8, where external trusts exist between the Windows NT 4.0 domain called COMPANY and the Active Directory domain called ad.com.

Figure 1.8 Configuring External Trusts between Windows NT 4.0 Domains and Active Directory

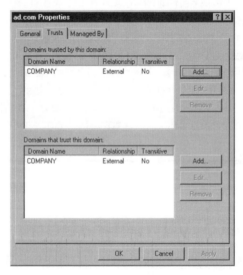

One of the nice configuration features with the Active Directory configuration is that, unlike Windows NT 4.0 Trust Relationship configuration, you can verify that a trust is currently working. To do this, select the listed trust and click the **Edit** button. You'll see details of the trust configuration and also a **Verify** button, which when selected will check the current status of the configured trust, as shown in Figure 1.9.

Although Active Directory domains have automatic transitive trusts, this does not mean that your single external trust to an Active Directory domain gives you access to the whole Active Directory forest. As you can see from the information in Figure 1.8, the trust in this case is not transitive. External trusts do not extend beyond the domain with which they are created—just as Windows NT 4.0 domain trusts work. Therefore, if you need access to more than one Active Directory domain, you will need to configure additional trusts with each Active Directory domain.

Figure 1.9 Verifying an Active Directory Trust Current Status

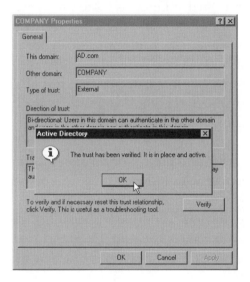

Migrating Networks

Obviously, large existing networks with multimaster Windows NT 4.0 domains cannot be turned into a pristine Active Directory network overnight. Depending on the restructuring and domain consolidation that is needed, the actual migration process can take many months. The standard advice is to start at the top (the root) and move down the network structure, looking to migrate user domains first and then resource domains.

If you are the administrator of a Windows NT 4.0 domain and your company is in the middle of migrating to Active Directory, you will obviously still need to run your Windows NT 4.0 domain for some time and ensure that you can access resources in the new Active Directory when required, and vice versa. To do this, you will need to ensure that you have configured an external trust with one or more Active Directory domains. If your company is running a model single-domain Active Directory structure, this will be much easier than a multiple-domain structure.

During this migration period you can prepare your domain for Active Directory by upgrading any hardware, and you can upgrade computers to run Windows 2000. Use this book to learn which features and services you can use on your Windows 2000 computers while your domain is still running Windows NT 4.0.

Fractional Networks

It's entirely possible for an Active Directory forest to appear on your company's network in the middle of its logical hierarchy, and which was never designed with enterprise goals in mind. This happens naturally, for example, when the IT department start testing and piloting Active Directory as a dry run that will later be scrapped. It may or may not integrate with the rest of the network—for example, if you're testing migration tools you usually need to configure trusts with the existing domains.

It's just as possible that an Active Directory forest is created for nontesting purposes, perhaps as a result of a project or division identifying a specific requirement that could not be met within the existing network structure. For example, a division may need to run conferencing services with Exchange 2000, or a new project with the budget for new hardware has identified substantial cost savings in terms of startup and maintenance using the Intellimirror set. Or the company wants to be able to use multiple ISA servers configured as an array for distributed and fault-tolerant caching.

Although we haven't heard much about such isolated Active Directory forests occurring within corporations, I can see how they could easily happen, particularly if new Microsoft products require Active Directory. After all, it's not difficult to set up a small Active Directory domain—the minimal requirement is one reasonably specified Windows 2000 Server running DNS. I'm sure it's not how Microsoft envisioned Active Directory being implemented, with or without external trusts to other Windows NT 4.0 domains on the network. But it's certainly possible.

Without pruning and grafting facilities to merge two or more forests, these fractional networks could be fraught with long-term consequences. When you are asked to create a trust to and from an Active Directory forest that was designed and created to consist of only a fraction of your network, make yourself and others aware of the limitations and restrictions this will have for future network growth. It is entirely possible, though, that this kind of arrangement could suit your current requirements and provide a way of utilizing Active Directory features in the short term without having to wait for large-scale migration.

Dangers of Fractional Networks Running Active Directory

The scalability of fractional networks will probably be restricted because they are unlikely to be suitable for extending to the rest of the network. The first domain in an Active Directory becomes the root domain, which should be created at the top of the logical hierarchy with everything cascading from that. If it's not, this can present problems with the domain namespace and replication issues. For example, if a division created an Active Directory forest so it could run Exchange 2000 Server and called its Active Directory domain EX2K.com, this is hardly a suitable namespace for the whole of the company (the root domain cannot be renamed), and yet any child domains would have to inherit this name as the parent domain. It is possible to have multiple trees within one Active Directory forest, but the EX2K.com domain would still remain the root domain simply because it was created first.

It would be worse if more than one Active Directory forest were created in this way because then you get into the situation of having multiple forests in the same company. You can link these with external trusts, but you lose the benefits of having a common schema and directory. For example, if you wanted to apply a GPO throughout the whole network, you would have to create and configure it multiple times on each forest and assign it on each forest, rather than having to do this only once. Directory searches would extend only as far as the current forest, and it wouldn't be possible for a user in one forest to know whether a negative search was a result of the resource not existing or not existing in the current forest. A user would have to know in advance exactly where a resource was in another forest to be able to use it because he or she would not be able to leverage the directory to find it. And similarly, services in one forest would be unaware of services in another forest, which means your ability to leverage fault tolerance and scaling is restricted.

External Networks

Your existing network infrastructure may have to accommodate and integrate with a new network as a result of a merger or acquisition. Long term, no doubt the aim will be to consolidate and merge the resources into one logical network if possible, in order to minimize maintenance costs and maximize resources. But when resources are required from both networks, it is likely that trusts will be needed in much the same way as they would be needed in the migration networks.

Partner relationships are a little different because usually the aim is not so much allowing cross-network sharing as restricting access to only the resources required. In these circumstances, the transitive nature of Windows NT 4.0 trusts can be very useful in limiting the trust boundaries. With the transitive nature of automatic trusts within an Active Directory forest, this is not possible, and instead NTFS permissions must be more tightly monitored. Because external trusts do not extend beyond the domain, this could be another reason to create smaller domains in an Active Directory forest if you have such partner relationships and take a tip from Windows NT 4.0 domain style structures.

If you have a small company that consists of a workgroup rather than a Windows NT 4.0 domain, you may still be able to integrate with other networks running Active Directory. Because you have no Windows NT 4.0 domain controller, you cannot configure a domain trust. However, if you can physically connect to a network running Active Directory (through a router), you will be able to map drives to shares in an Active Directory network if you can be authenticated This can be with either an Active Directory user account or a local account on a specific computer. If the username and password configured for you on the Active Directory domain are different from the credentials you're using in your workgroup, you should use the Connect As option when creating the external mapping. If the credentials are the same, you should be connected immediately.

NOTE

Workgroups utilize Peer-to-Peer (P2P) architecture, which may be suitable for the following situations:

- Smaller companies that decide they don't require the overheads of a centralized directory structure
- Branch offices without a network administrator
- Home networks that are cropping up as a result of home computing and working at home

In all of these circumstances, Windows 2000 is a good choice for its feature set, reliability, and security, but it's rare to find documentation that acknowledges Windows 2000 computers being used in a PnP environment. This book encompasses the configuration of Windows 2000 on standalone computers, on workgrouped computers (rather confusingly, Microsoft terms Windows 2000 servers in a workgroup as standalone), and Windows NT 4.0 domains.

Walkthrough: Managing User Accounts and Securing the Local Administrator Account

Managing local accounts on a Windows 2000 computer is one of the first basic administrative tasks you should know how to do. Irrespective of whether you're going to use Windows NT 4.0 domain accounts or local accounts on your Windows 2000 computers, it's important to secure the local administrator account and enable the Guest account only if really needed.

Chances are, when you installed Windows 2000, you provided a password that was easy to type and remember for the local administrator. Now that it's up and running, you should secure the local administrator account and confirm that the Guest account is disabled (although it is by default). If you are going to log in locally to the computer, you should also create an account for you to safely use on a day-to-day basis—one that doesn't have full administrator rights. This walkthrough will take you through the following steps:

- Adding a new user
- Changing the administrator's password
- Confirming that the Guest account is disabled

NOTE

This walkthrough will not tell you what passwords to use; this is up to you. A secure password is usually one that is at least seven characters that include alphanumeric characters (numbers and letters) and characters like !@#$%^&*.

1. Make sure that you are logged in with the local Administrator account, and then click on **Start | Settings | Control Panel** and load **Users and Passwords**.

2. When first loaded and no other local accounts have been added, the Users and Passwords looks like Figure 1.10 with only the local Administrator account and the Guest account listed as **Users for this computer**.

Figure 1.10 Users and Passwords

3. You'll notice the **Users must enter a user name and password to use this computer** near the top of the dialog box. This should be checked so that a user must log on before being able to use the computer. If you uncheck this, you'll be prompted to specify an account that will be used automatically each time Windows is loaded. Unchecking this would not be a secure solution, so we will leave this checked. The first thing we will do is create a new user so that you can log in without having to use the Administrator account. Click on the **Add** button, which starts the Add New User wizard. Where prompted, type in a User name and optionally the Full Name and Description, similar to Figure 1.11.

Figure 1.11 Adding the New User

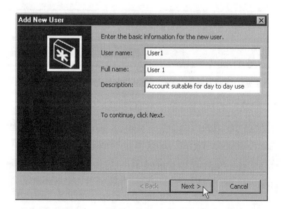

4. Click on **Next**, and you'll be prompted to supply a password, and then type it again to confirm. Select a password that you can easily remember, but that is still secure (see the previous Note before the steps in this walkthrough for tips on what is considered a secure password).

5. Click **Next**, and the following dialog asks what level of access you want to grant (see Figure 1.12). Keep the default of **Standard user**, which equates to a Power User. This is the most powerful local group after the local Administrators group.

Figure 1.12 Specifying the User Access (Group Membership)

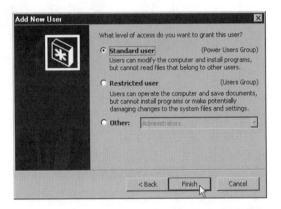

6. Click on **Finish**, and you should then be looking at the Users and Passwords with your new user added to the list of **Users for this computer**, similar to Figure 1.13.

7. You'll notice that when your new user account is selected, you can use the **Remove** button to delete the account, the **Properties** button to change any of the options we have just supplied, and the **Set Password** to change the password. We need to change the password of the Administrator account, but you'll notice that this cannot be similarly changed with the **Set Password** button. If you highlight the Administrator account, the **Set Password** button becomes unavailable and you're told to use **Ctrl+Alt+Del** and **Change Password** instead. You could change the Administrator password this way, but there's another method that we'll use because it also allows us to verify that the Guest Account is disabled. Click on the **Advanced** tab and then the **Advanced** button under the Advanced User Management section. This loads up the Local Users and Groups MMC, as shown in Figure 1.14.

Figure 1.13 New User Successfully Added

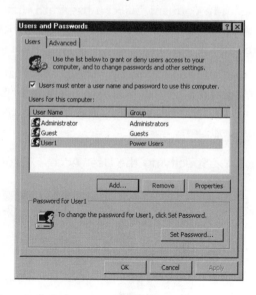

Figure 1.14 Local Users and Groups MMC

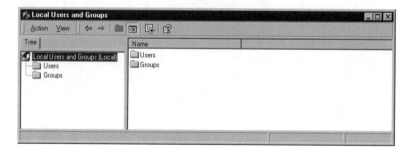

8. Click on **Groups**, and you'll see the six local built-in groups you can
    use on a Windows 2000 computer. One of the nice things about
    Windows 2000 MMCs for administration is that the built-in options
    have long and useful descriptions to accurately describe what they are
    and their purpose. It's worth reviewing these. For example, you'll see that
    the Power Users group we selected for our new user account has the
    following description:

    ```
    Power Users possess most administrative powers with some
    restrictions.  Thus, Power Users can run legacy applications
    in addition to certified applications.
    ```

If the built-in groups are not sufficient, you can create your own group by right-clicking on Groups, and then selecting **New Group**.

9. Click on **Users**, and you'll see our three user accounts again, similar to Figure 1.15. Only this time you'll notice that the Guest account has a red cross over it, which denotes that this account is disabled.

Figure 1.15 Local Users and Groups—Displaying the User Accounts

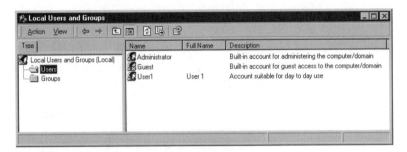

10. To confirm that this account is disabled or to enable it, double-click it to display its Properties; you'll see the following dialog box (Figure 1.16) with more options than we had previously. Unless you have a good reason to use the local Guest account, do not change these options, and click on **OK**.

Figure 1.16 Guest Properties, Confirming the Account Is Disabled

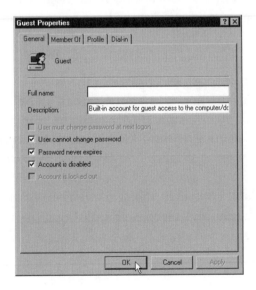

11. We still need to change the Administrator account password, which we can do from here. You can quickly rename accounts and reset their passwords by right-clicking the relevant account and selecting **Set Password** or **Rename** as required. For greater security, some people rename the local Administrator account to a less obvious name and then create a regular account with no privileges and name that "Administrator." In this walkthrough we'll just change the password. Right-click on the **Administrator** account, select **Set Password**, and you'll be prompted to type in and confirm the new password, as shown in Figure 1.17. Remember to select a password that is secure; refer to the Note at the beginning of the walkthrough steps for tips on what constitutes a secure password.

Figure 1.17 Changing the Administrator's Password

12. If you have previously changed your password through Ctrl-Alt-Del and Change Password, you'll notice that here you don't have to specify the old password first. Click **OK**, and if both fields match, you'll see an information box indicating **The password has been changed**. Click **OK**, and you'll be back in the Local Users and Groups MMC, which we can now close, and click **OK** to close the **Users and Passwords**.

13. In future, if you want to just use the Local Users and Groups MMC, rather than getting to it from **Control Panel | Users and Passwords**, you could use Computer Management from **Start | Programs | Administrative Tools | Computer Management**. However, a much quicker way is to right-click **My Computer** on the desktop and select **Manage**. You'll see a number of different administrative options related to the local computer, and at the bottom of the **System Tools** section is **Local Users and Groups**. Expand this, and you'll see the same **Users** and **Groups** as before, as shown in Figure 1.18.

Figure 1.18 Local Users and Groups within Computer Management

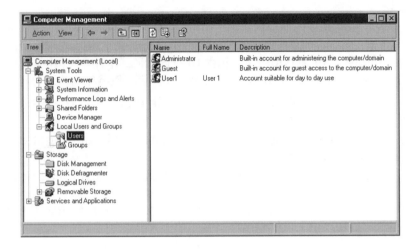

NOTE

The Local Users and Group is an MMC in its own right, which means you could also create a custom MMC to load just this if you preferred. See the Appendix for how to create custom MMCs if you're unsure how to do this.

14. Finally, we need to log off and log in with the new account we've created. Press **Ctrl+Alt+Del** and select the **Log Off** button. Confirm that you want to log off. You'll be presented with the **Log On to Windows** prompt where you need to change the **User name** from **Administrator** to the name of your new account (our example was User1), supply the password you provided, and click **OK**. A successfully logged-on new account will display the **Getting Started with Windows 2000**, which you can close with **Exit**. Try to change the Administrator account password again; you should see an **Access is denied** message, which confirms that your account does not have full Administrator rights and as such presents less of a security risk when you're using it (for example, if you inadvertently run a dangerous macro or Trojan horse that requires administrative privileges to harm your PC).

NOTE

If you need to run tasks and utilities that require Administrative rights, use the powerful new *Run as* facility so that you can specify the Administrator account for just that particular task without having to log off from your current session. You can use RunAs in one of three ways:

1. Shift and right-click on the file that loads the program, and then select **Run as**.
2. Create a shortcut on the desktop, shift and right-click it, and then select **Run as**.
3. Use the **Runas** command on the command line or in scripts. See the Appendix and Table A.1 for a list of the Administrator MMCs, with the following Note on how to use them with the **Runas** command.

Summary

This chapter has outlined how and why so many companies use Microsoft operating systems and will continue to do so. Windows 2000 is the current Microsoft operating system, which offers both reliable and business-oriented features that can take advantage of today's technologies. Although new versions of Microsoft's operating systems (Windows XP and Windows.NET) are already around the corner, they are considered minor upgrades to Windows 2000 in comparison to the upgrade jump from down-level operating systems (such as Windows NT 4.0 and Windows 9x) to Windows 2000.

There may be many reasons why a company is not currently adopting or migrating to an Active Directory network—and yet there are few resources available that explain how to make the best of Microsoft's current operating system outside an Active Directory environment. This book hopes to address this need for both IT managers and IT implementers while also offering some supplemental material for the MCPs and MCSE candidates looking to transition their Windows NT 4.0 knowledge and experience.

This book will cover a diversity of options that Windows 2000 can offer you immediately, independently from Active Directory. This covers features that are particularly relevant to workstations, laptops and file and print servers, and key services such as Terminal Services, RAS and VPNs, IIS and Certificate Services, and also networking services such as DNS, DHCP, WINS, IPSec, and NAT. It's just as important to identify what's possible only when you are running Active Directory so that you're aware of any restrictions in configuring Windows 2000 without Active Directory. When you know more about each feature (both advantages and disadvantages) you can make the informed decision about whether your network requires these and plan accordingly.

Despite your network not running Active Directory, there may be occasions when you need to configure external trusts with an Active Directory domain so that network resources from each network can be used. This can be as part of the initial testing and piloting of Active Directory, as part of the migration deployment, or as a result of a partner company or a merger or acquisition. It can even be as a result of a subsection of your company's network that has decided to run a small Active Directory network to take advantage of features that can be run only in an Active Directory domain.

Solutions Fast Track

Why Use Windows 2000 without Active Directory

☑ Microsoft Windows offers a good business solution as an operating system because of its easy-to-use interface, its acceptance as a mature product in the market place, its widespread acceptance and adoption by other vendors, and availability of staff to support it.

☑ Windows 2000 builds on past experience and incorporates customer feedback for more business-oriented solutions that meet today's enterprise networks.

☑ Windows 2000 is gaining acceptance in the workplace with claims of better reliability and stability confirmed by customers. Not everybody has or is migrating to Active Directory for a variety of reasons that include business, technical, and political reasons.

The Purpose of This Book

☑ Most Windows 2000 literature seems to assume an Active Directory context—whereas in reality this does not reflect the current marketplace, which is assuming a gradual, mixed deployment of Windows 2000 computers into the existing network infrastructure. This makes it very difficult for IT managers and IT implementers to know which Windows 2000 features can be used independently from Active Directory and how to configure them.

☑ This book is just as relevant for IT managers as it is for IT implementers, so that they are aware of what is possible to implement independently from Active Directory (and how and whether it has restrictions outside Active Directory) and which features cannot be implemented without Active Directory.

☑ This book will cover a variety of Windows 2000 features and services that can be implemented independently from Active Directory—from workstations, laptops, and servers, to specific services like IIS5 and Terminal Services, to networking services like DNS, DHCP, NLB, IPSec, and NAT.

☑ There are a number of features in Windows 2000 that will work only in an Active Directory environment. These include, for example, Exchange 2000 and other Active Directory dependent applications, Intellimirror features, Kerberos authentication, automatic transitive trusts, Enterprise CAs, and Quality of Service. It's important to familiarize yourself with what these features are and how they work (advantages *and* disadvantages) and whether alternatives can be found.

Active Directory Integration

☑ Just because your current networking environment is not running on or migrating to Active Directory doesn't mean that you can afford to ignore it. There may be occasions when your network integrates with an Active Directory network, which can work to everybody's advantage.

☑ Examples of a Windows NT 4.0 domain integrating with Active Directory are in either the planning or testing stages of Active Directory migration or during the actual migration.

☑ Other examples of Active Directory integration include external links to partner companies, where they need to access resources on your network (or vice versa), or company mergers or acquisitions, where the new network is running Active Directory.

☑ It's also possible that only a fraction of your company network is running Active Directory without enterprise ambitions, but simply to use specific Active Directory dependent features. This can have both advantages and disadvantages—for example, with external trusts with your Windows NT 4.0 domain you may be able to use Active Directory dependent applications, but this arrangement is unlikely to scale well.

Frequently Asked Questions

The following Frequently Asked Questions, answered by the author of this book, are designed to both measure your understanding of the concepts presented in this chapter and to assist you with real-life implementation of these concepts. To have your questions about this chapter answered by the author, browse to **www.syngress.com/solutions** and click on the **"Ask the Author"** form.

Q: Will we be able to continue using our Windows NT 4.0 domain structure indefinitely?

A: In theory, yes, although in practice I suspect this will not be practical as time goes on. First, Microsoft has already retired many Windows NT 4.0 exams to encourage certified engineers to be qualified in the Windows 2000 track, which will mean that there will come a time when it will be easier to recruit IT staff with qualifications in Windows 2000 than qualifications in Windows NT 4.0. Second, Microsoft's own resources are clearly aimed at supporting and developing its current and new operating systems, so it's obvious that the company is aiming for little (if any) response to problems and development requests on Windows NT 4.0. Networks might not change as quickly as Microsoft would like, but there's no stopping technology, and there's no doubt that Windows NT 4.0 cannot take advantage of many of today's business and technological requirements. Support from Microsoft for down-level clients will officially stop by the end of 2003, and it's likely that other vendors in the industry will follow this lead.

Q: I recognize the need for an enterprise directory service but have IBM AS/400s, Nortel PBXs, and Solaris and Linux boxes on our network in addition to Windows machines. I'm concerned that Active Directory is restricted to just Windows. Are there alternative directories that can embrace all these platforms?

A: Siemens and Worldtalk are just two examples of cross-platform directories you may want to consider.

Q: I've heard a lot of conflicting information about the Kerberos authentication protocol used with Active Directory. Rather than wading through long white papers, is there a succinct way I can have key questions answered?

A: There's an excellent Knowledge Base article Q266080 called "Answers to Frequently Asked Kerberos Questions" that is a great place to start. It covers standard questions dealing with information on RFCs, interoperability, Microsoft extensions, time synchronization, and more.

Q: I'm aware that there's a deluge of information about Active Directory available that makes it very difficult to know where to start. Do you have a personal recommendation for a starting point?

A: One of my personal favorites is David Iseminger's book, *Active Directory Services for Microsoft Windows 2000 Technical Reference* (MS Press, ISBN 0735606242).Despite the dry title and initial appearance I found this book an enjoyable read, and I thought it brought together both technical and managerial issues nicely. Ironically in this pro-Active Directory book there's one of the few admissions that using Windows 2000 outside Active Directory is both possible and positive: *You don't have to wait until your Active Directory services infrastructure is in place before you upgrade desktops (to Windows 2000 Professional) or member servers (to Windows 2000 Server, Windows 2000 Advanced Server, or Windows 2000 Datacenter Server). Although certain Windows 2000 features won't be available until Active Directory services are available, gating the rollout of desktops and servers based on Active Directory isn't necessary.*

Q: I'm rather confused about how stable Windows 2000 is and what level of service pack it should be running. What's your advice?

A: At the time of writing, Service Pack 2 has just been released and Microsoft doesn't advise that you install it unless you have specifically identified a problem that it resolves. There have been a number of hot fixes specifically for security issues, so for servers and particularly those that have an Internet presence (those running DNS, IIS5, NAT, and ISA Server) this is more relevant. It's less important for workstations and internal servers that have no identified problems. I think it's too early yet to tell how stable Service Pack 2 is or to advocate that everybody should upgrade to it immediately—although I appreciate that it's easier to support a single, common platform. In comparison, Service Pack 1 has been out for some time, and I would encourage anybody running Windows 2000 in its release version to upgrade to Service Pack 1. It introduced few known problems, and it comes with many additional features/services (particularly for Terminal Services) that make it worthwhile.

Q: Should we look to upgrade workstations or servers to Windows 2000 first?

A: This is an interesting question. Technically, you should look to upgrade servers first because overall this offers a quicker ROI because each server benefits multiple clients immediately. Additionally, the services that run on a server are more powerful than those that typically run on workstations. As an extreme example, Windows 2000 Terminal Services on an upgraded NT4 server would provide a greater asset than a more reliable workstation. However, it seems that many companies are more comfortable with a longer-term, cautious approach and have upgraded many more workstations than servers. Maybe part of the caution is not realizing what services and features can be configured outside Active Directory or not being able to distinguish Windows 2000 Server from Active Directory as a result of the standard documentation. Or perhaps the upgrades reflect natural computer refresh cycles and servers that have a higher specification from the outset have longer refresh cycles. I think it's interesting that companies went their own way and ignored official advice—and I think there's no right or wrong way. If you are comfortable with your current upgrade policy and have substantiated that it's the right course for you, I'm not going to disagree!

Q: I've read that computers installed with Windows 2000 should be clean installations, so why have the upgrade option from Windows NT 4.0 and Windows 98?

A: Technically, you should always do a clean installation rather than an upgrade if this is feasible. This is for a number of reasons, including a safer installation (less likely to hang) and not inheriting any bad or lax configuration issues from the previous version (for example, bloated profiles and registries). An upgrade means you shouldn't have to reinstall and reconfigure existing settings, which can save you consideration time. When default operating system settings have changed with Windows 2000, the original will be kept if upgrading—this may or may not be something you want. Any changed default values in Windows 2000 will be flagged in the book as upgrading considerations.

One of the other arguments for doing a clean install is that an upgraded system doesn't have the same high security inherently built into the system (registry and system files), but this can be retroactively fixed by applying a Basic security template (covered in Chapter 2). Disk configurations are another area of consideration when thinking about an upgrade or clean installation—for example, you can create new fault tolerance configuration only when disks have been converted to dynamic, whereas an upgraded Windows NT 4.0 server carries over disk fault tolerance with basic disks (more details on this in Chapter 4).

Q: Where can we get hold of Microsoft's Active Directory Migration Tool?

A: This is downloadable with documentation from http://microsoft.com/windows2000/downloads/tools/admt/default.asp.

Q: Is there a way we can migrate existing down-level system policies to Active Directory Group Policies?

A: Although similar in concept, GPOs in Windows 2000 employ very different technologies to the old style System Policies; for this reason it's usually recommended that you build the GPOs from scratch. If you really have to migrate existing System Policies, there's a Windows 2000 Resource Kit tool called **Gpolmig.exe** that was designed with this aim. It's recommended that you thoroughly test the results afterward to ensure that your settings were successfully migrated. Chapter 2 contains information on using local Group Policies, which is a good starting point for understanding the new technology; it also contains references so that you can read up on Active Directory GPOs.

Q: What third-party migration tools are available?

A: There are now a number of migration utilities available, and I encourage you to do your own reading on what is currently available and other people's reviews on testing and using them. Each has its own advantages and disadvantages, and what's best for your network could depend on factors such as whether you need to restructure and when (before or after migrating to

Active Directory), whether you need to migrate users from non-Windows NT 4.0 domains and include Exchange migrations, the speed of conversion, the need to migrate online data, and the amount of cleanup and tracking you require.

There's no single tool that you can load, press a button, and a little while later you're presented with an Active Directory forest. Rather, you have to wade through a suite of tools and use those you require. Four main players in this market are Aelita Controlled Migration Suite, BindView bv-Admin, FastLane DM/Suite, and NetIQ DMA. You can get more information on each of these products from their Web sites (www.aelita.com, www.bind-view.com, www.fastlane.com, and www.netiq.com). As a bonus, most of these sites include downloadable white papers on Active Directory migration and troubleshooting. There's plenty of information from Microsoft on migrating, but one resource you will want to include is its *Domain Migration Cookbook* available from www.microsoft.com/windows2000/techinfo/planning/ activedirectory/cookbook.asp.

Q: What third-party tools are currently available for Active Directory to help make up for the lack of ongoing maintenance tools supplied with Active Directory?

A: Again, it pays to shop around to find out what's available and check magazine reviews of these products, but the third-party companies that ship migration tools usually have maintenance tools as well, so these are a good starting point. For example, NetIQ supplies **OnePoint Directory and Resource Administrator** to help with administration, and **AppManager for Active Directory** to help troubleshoot and maintain the network. Additional companies in this market are NetPro with its **DirectoryAnalyzer**, NetVision with the **DirectoryAlert for AD**, and **Full Armor** with a utility specifically aimed at administrating and troubleshooting GPOs. But don't forget to also check the utilities that are supplied with the Windows 2000 Resource Kit.

Q: I've heard Windows XP will have many of the features that are already included in Windows 2000 and as such can be considered more of an upgrade than a new version jump. Is there somewhere I can check the differences and new features between the operating systems?

A: I found Microsoft's Windows XP Professional Comparison Guide (www.microsoft.com/windowsxp/pro/guide/featurecomp.asp) to be very useful for this. It lists Windows XP features in comparison to Windows 2000, Windows NT 4.0, and Windows 9x/Me. Obviously, it's a list of new features specifically to promote Windows XP and doesn't, for example, list all the new features in Windows 2000. Nonetheless, it provides a useful guide for improved and new features that will be available in Windows XP. I'm just waiting for an equivalent document for Windows .NET Server so we can see the new features and improvements that will be in the next version of Windows 2000.

Chapter 2

Workstations

Solutions in this chapter:

- **Using Local Group Policy**
- **Security Configuration Using Templates**
- **Improvements in System Reliability**
- **Improvements in Usability**

☑ **Walkthrough: Configuring Local Group Policy**

☑ **Summary**

☑ **Solutions Fast Track**

☑ **Frequently Asked Questions**

Introduction

This chapter introduces you to the power and flexibility of Windows 2000 Professional in a typical desktop environment and the improvements this operating system has over previous versions. These features are applicable to corporate desktops, home computers, and even laptops running Windows 2000 Professional—although the next chapter covers laptop-specific features in more detail.

If you are running Windows 2000 Professional in an NT4 domain, a Novell or Unix network, or even in a workgroup, and want to know how to get the best of the new features of Windows 2000, this chapter is for you. In fact, this chapter also has relevance even if your Windows 2000 Professional is running in an Active Directory domain and you want to understand what configuration options you have independent of Active Directory.

Some of the topics covered in this chapter are particularly difficult to find elsewhere outside the context of Active Directory, because standard Windows 2000 Professional literature assumes that you are configuring the desktop within an Active Directory environment. For example, you will find references that state "Group Policy depends on Active Directory" which is somewhat misleading because it implies Group Policy cannot be used outside Active Directory at all. Certainly some settings can be used only with Active Directory—for example, RIS settings (RIS can be used only with Active Directory), automatic software deployment, and folder redirection.

Whereas a single, central setting that can apply throughout your network at many different levels is ultimately more powerful than settings residing on each machine, it's still possible to achieve many similar configurations at a local level. You can set startup/shutdown and logon/logoff scripts for example. You can enforce passwords' complexity and how often they are changed. You can lock-down the desktop and prevent users from seeing or setting certain options such as network settings and sharing printers or folders. You can set Internet Explorer configuration, disable registry changes and the command prompt, configure the Start menu and task bar, allow users to have elevated privileges for when they are installing applications, and so on.

Unlike standard literature on Windows 2000 Professional, this chapter assumes you are not running in an Active Directory environment or that your Active Directory configurations do not affect (override) local settings covered here. However, you should be aware that if and when your network does migrate to Active Directory, local settings can be overridden by central settings.

Using Local Group Policy

Group Policy is big news with Windows 2000. It's one of the most complex new features you need to grasp when looking to deploy Active Directory. It offers a way of centrally controlling settings at a computer and user level throughout an enterprise at many different levels. For example, you could specify that your company virus checker load at computer startup on every machine in your enterprise without exception (and install or repair it automatically, if necessary). You could also specify that a specific department load up an internal company database when users in your marketing team log on. You could set very restrictive permissions for temporary employees whenever they log on, irrespective of which computer they use.

In a nutshell, group policies are the next generation of system policies that were used in NT4 domains to control workstations centrally. They are vastly more extensive (for example, over 450 settings that affect registry-based configurations and over 100 security-based options alone) and superior in design because they no longer permanently affect the registry, can be reapplied at regular intervals (not just logon or startup), can be applied at different levels (local, site, domain, organizational unit), and can be filtered. *Filtering* means that you can determine which groups or users will be affected by the settings and which users can read and/or modify them (that is, not just administrators).

Many administrators coming to Active Directory from NT4 find group policy one of the hardest new features/concepts to grasp: I know I did. The practical application of using the standard tools provided by Microsoft doesn't help either—it's very easy to set options and lose them in the myriad of levels. You've also got to contend with Inheritance and No Override issues—whether an option set at a higher level propagates down into the next level—and which users will be affected by the settings and which users will be able to modify them. On top of all that, you have to know how to troubleshoot group policies—when an option isn't set as you expect, where do you start to look? Is it a group policy inconsistency, a group membership issue, or a network latency issue? You must also take into account efficiency of processing because multiple and complex group policies can slow up startup times considerably—particularly if processing over a remote link. And unlike system policies, group policies continue to generate network traffic as any changes are reapplied at regular intervals (by default every 90 minutes on desktops) and replicate to other domain controllers.

I think configuring, deploying, and maintaining group policy in Active Directory is very powerful. However, the problems faced by Information

Technology (IT) managers and implementers are, first, one of training—administrators must be proficient in understanding this new technology, what its capabilities are, and the nuts and bolts of how it works. Second, IT managers must plan and design effective and efficient group policies—and be sure these can be tested, documented, enforced, and monitored. Group policies that spring up ad hoc are a nightmare waiting to happen.

By concentrating initially on local group policies—settings that affect only one Windows 2000 computer—managers and implementers can start to feel their way with this new configuration feature. If you can plan and configure group policy on the simplest level, it is then easier to scale up and plan on an enterprise level. For environments that never migrate to Active Directory, managers and implementers can still make the most of this technology by exploiting the local configuration options to their fullest potential—which is what this particular topic is all about.

NOTE

For more information on designing Group Policy within an Active Directory environment, see Chapter 5 "Developing a Group Policy Implementation Strategy" from Microsoft's *Windows 2000 Server Deployment Planning Guide* which is available online at www.microsoft.com/TechNet/prodtechnol/windows2000serv/reskit/deploy/ccmdepl/ccmch05.asp.

WARNING

Do not confuse policies with *user preferences*, and *profiles*. Policies are set and enforced by administrators. User preferences are desktop settings that users can set (if allowed), for example, their choice of screensaver, folder options, and so on. Profiles contain user-specific configurations such as desktop shortcuts, program settings unique to the user, and so on. Policies have a higher precedence than the other two and, as such, are more powerful.

Group Policy Objects

The actual configuration settings are stored in what is termed a *Group Policy Object*, which is frequently abbreviated to just *GPO*. Physically these reside in subfolders off **%systemroot%System32\GroupPolicy**, and logically they are split between computer settings and user settings.

Computer settings are options that always apply to the local computer, irrespective of who (if anybody) is logged on to the computer (for example, computer startup/shutdown scripts). User settings are options that apply for the duration of a user's session on the computer (for example, logon/logoff scripts).

Group Policy settings can be configured with a status of **Not Configured**, **Enabled**, **Disabled**, or **Not Granted**, together with a setting appropriate for the actual option itself (for example, the minimum number of letters for passwords, the logon text message you want displayed, the name of programs that are allowed to be run, and so forth).

Unlike Active Directory GPOs, local GPOs cannot be filtered—that is, you cannot configure a local Group Policy and set it such that it affects only a certain group of people and not others. However, what you can do is set NT File System (NTFS) permissions on the **Group Policy** folder itself (**%systemroot%System32\GroupPolicy**). For a GPO to be applied to a user, that user must have read access to the settings. So you can remove the effect of the local GPO by removing read access to those users or groups.

For example, if your Windows 2000 Professional is shared between full-time employees and students on work experience, and you want to tightly lockdown the desktop when any of the students logs on—you would ensure that all users who weren't students were members of a group and then deny that group access to the **Group Policy** folder (see Figure 2.1).

NOTE

The **%systemroot%System32\GroupPolicy** directory and subdirectories by default give *Full Control* to Administrators and the operating system, and *Read* to Users. If you decide to control local GPOs with access control lists (ACLs), you may need to reset these if you later move to Active Directory GPOs.

Figure 2.1 Setting Permissions on the Group Policy Folder

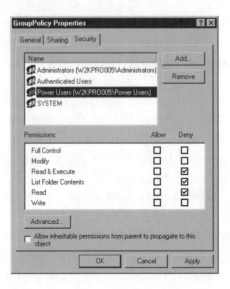

Whenever anybody but members of that group logged in, the restrictive lockdown GPO would be applied. Note that if administrators do not want the restrictive GPO to apply to them, they will need to deny themselves read access to the GPO itself after configuration. If they later need to read or change the local GPO, they will first have to take ownership of the directory and all subdirectories, and then give themselves Full Control.

Locating Local Group Policy

Local Group Policy configuration is rather strangely hidden away on a Windows 2000 computer—probably to encourage you to use Active Directory Group Policies instead! A subsection of it that covers security options is easily accessible from the desktop under **Local Security Policy**. However, to access all the local Group Policy options, you have to work a little harder by either running **gpedit.msc** or by adding the Group Policy snap-in to a new or existing Microsoft Management Console (MMC). To configure local Group Policy, you must belong to the local Administrator's group.

> **NOTE**
>
> MMC is commonly used these days, and with its default Explorer-like interface, it is intuitive enough for even novices to use without problems. For this reason, this book assumes that people are comfortable using the MMC interface for configuring Windows 2000. However, Appendix A, The Windows 2000 Microsoft Management Console (MMC), provides more information on the standard configuration utility of Windows 2000 for those who want to know a little more about it and how to realize its full potential by utilizing its highly customizable interface.

Local Security Policy

Local Security Policy can be found under **Control Panel | Administrative Tools**. This provides access to the following:

- Account Policies (password and account lockout policies)
- Local Policies (auditing, user rights, and security options policies)
- Public Key Policies
- IP Security Policies on Local Machine (Internet Protocol Security (IPSec) Administration)

If you expand all the available folders on the left, you will see any subfolders and finally the actual group policies that you can set. Figure 2.2 shows all local security settings expanded with the options for the Password Policy displayed on the right with the name of the option, the Local Setting, and the Effective Setting. When using local GPOs only, the last two columns will usually be the same, but in an Active Directory environment they could be different if site, domain, or OU GPOs were overriding your local GPO.

Complete Local Group Policy Settings

To set and configure the full set of local Group Policy settings—both the Computer Configuration settings and the User Configuration settings—you must either run **gpedit.msc** (for example, from the command line, or **Start | Run**) or add the Group Policy snap-in into a new or existing MMC. You should then see an MMC similar to Figure 2.3.

Figure 2.2 Local Security Settings Displaying the Password Policy

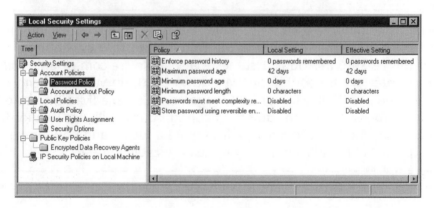

Figure 2.3 Local Group Policy Settings

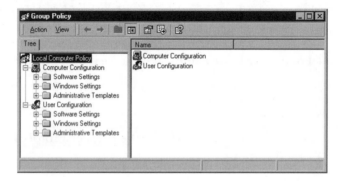

As you see when you expand all the folders, the options available are many and varied. You will also notice that buried under **Computer Configuration | Windows Settings** are the security settings we looked at earlier with access to Account Policies, Local Policies, Public Key Policies, and IP Security Policies on Local Machine.

The same set of folder options is common to all Windows 2000 GPOs. However, Active Directory GPOs have some additional options within these folders. Because some options are not applicable to Local Group Policies they will have no options to configure, which can look a little odd at first—such as Software Settings (used within Active Directory to assign or publish software for automatic maintenance).

Configuring Local Group Policy

To set most Group Policy options you either double-click the option, or right-click the option, select the appropriate option (for example, **Security** or **Properties**), and configure the required setting.

So, for example, to set the local Security Policy such that a minimum of seven characters is required for the password, you would double-click **Minimum password length** under **Account Policies | Password Policy** and then specify **7** characters, as in Figure 2.4.

Figure 2.4 Setting the Local Password Policy to Require a Minimum of 7 Characters

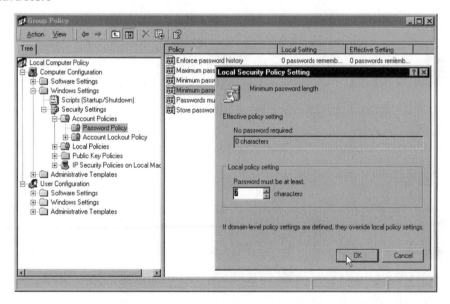

Most GPO options are self-explanatory. Unfortunately, if you need further clarification, the GPO settings are not covered in the Help, and the context-sensitive help for these dialog box options is very minimal. A better bet, when provided, is the additional Explain tab, which displays a fairly extensive explanation.

Figure 2.5 shows an example of one of the Explain tabs. However, the official reference for all GPO settings (the effects of enabling, disabling, and not configuring each policy, and the interaction between them) is Microsoft's *The Group Policy Reference*, available in the Windows 2000 Server Resource Kit. You will also find plenty of additional third party resources for configuring GPOs (complete books!) because it is such a powerful and complex configuration set—but most will be based on Active Directory GPOs.

Figure 2.5 Example of an Explain Tab for a Group Policy Setting

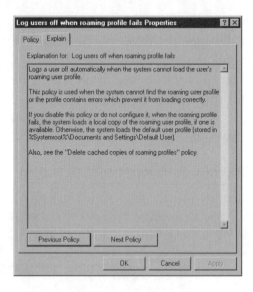

Also within the Resource Kit you'll find the utility **Gpresult.exe**, which when run, displays information about both domain and local Group Policy settings for the computer and currently logged-on user.

Configuring & Implementing...

Internet Explorer Exceptions

Exceptions abound for Internet Explorer (IE) when it comes to configuration and GPOs. First, if your organization has used the Internet Explorer Administration Kit (IEAK) to configure Internet Explorer, you shouldn't use the kit on computers running Windows 2000 if you are going to use Local GPOs.

Instead, GPOs are the preferred method of configuring Internet Explorer on Windows 2000. (Internet Explorer options are located under **Administrative Templates | Windows Components** for both the Computer Configuration and the User Configuration.) Second, rather bizarrely, the gpresult Resource Kit utility doesn't display Group Policy options for Internet Explorer.

Useful Group Policy Objects

It is beyond the scope of this section to list each and every local group policy setting. Your best bet is to load Local Group Policy on a Windows 2000 computer and browse through the various options available to see which could be used effectively in your environment. Many of the options covered later in this book have associated GPO settings which are explained within their own section.

However, this section outlines some of the more commonly used GPO settings to give you some idea of the types of options that are possible. These include the following:

- Computer startup/shutdown and user logon/logoff scripts

- Password options such as how often they should be changed and complexity of chosen passwords

- User rights such as the ability to access the computer over the network, shut down the system, and so forth

- Security options such as displaying the last username in the logon box, and logon message text

- Deleting cached copies of roaming profiles and clearing the pagefile on shutdown

- IE settings such as Proxy Server settings, IE Favorites, and disabling user configuration

- Preventing installations from floppy disks, CDs, and DVDs (removable media)

- Removing options such as **Run** and **Network and Dial-up Connections** from the Start menu

- Logoff and shutdown options, such as adding Log Off to the Start menu and disabling the **Shut Down** command

- Desktop options such as removing My Documents and My Network Places, disabling Active Desktop, and only allowing bitmapped wallpaper

- Disabling Control Panel altogether or selecting which Control Panel applets and/or options you will allow (for example, disabling Add/Remove Programs)

- Configuring the company screen saver and enforcing password protection on it

- Restricting network and dial-up configuration

- Disabling the command prompt, disabling the registry editor, and running only specified Windows applications

Many of these are easy to find and self-explanatory to configure. However, those that deserve a little more information are covered in greater detail below.

Computer Startup/Shutdown and User Logon/Logoff Scripts

Logon scripts (which are files that automatically process one or more commands as soon as the user logs on) have become the essence of controlling user settings. Logoff and startup/shutdown scripts are a very welcome addition missing from previous versions of Windows, and I can see these being used extensively in every environment—whether it's for additional security, controlling network mappings, updating settings, removing temporary files, and so on.

Computer startup and shutdown scripts can be configured under **Computer Configuration | Windows Settings**, where you can specify script names, and any accompanying script parameters required that will be run automatically when the computer boots into Windows 2000, or restarts or shuts down. By default each specified script waits to complete before the next specified script is run.

The default setting is for these scripts to run hidden, but they can be configured to appear within a command window with another setting called **Run startup scripts visible** and **Run shutdown scripts visible**, which are both found under **Computer Configuration | Administrative Templates | System | Logon**.

User Logon/Logoff scripts can be configured under **User Configuration | Windows Settings | Script (Logon/Logoff)**, which allows you to specify script names that contain any commands you want to execute as the user logs on and off (for example, drive letter mappings or importing software settings). These run before any logon script specified as part of the user's account properties (specified under the **Profile** tab).

Unlike computer startup scripts, however, multiple user logon scripts run synchronously (simultaneously) rather than waiting for each to complete. Therefore, if you are running commands that are time or process dependent, you are advised to run just one logon script with wait statements if necessary.

Additionally, if your logon scripts take a long time to process, it is possible they may not complete before the user is able to use the computer. If it is imperative that all logon scripts complete before the user can do anything in a session, you can set another option called **Run logon scripts synchronously**, which can be set under **Administrative Templates | System | Logon** under both **Computer Configuration** and **User Configuration** (Computer Configuration takes precedence). Setting this option is at the risk of delaying the logon process.

By default, all scripts should complete within 10 minutes. Any scripts that haven't completed are terminated with an error logged to the System Event Log. This safety setting ensures a computer doesn't lock up if a command is unable to complete—due to, for example, missing files, a bad network connection, and so on. If you need to modify this timeout, there's yet another setting—called **Maximum wait time for Group Policy**, which is located under **Computer Configuration | Administrative Templates | System | Logon**.

WARNING

Do not fall into the trap of specifying multiple logon scripts with conflicting commands because it is unpredictable which setting is used. This makes for a very frustrating and time-consuming troubleshooting exercise! For example if a user had multiple scripts assigned at logon, with the first script mapping LPT1: to an Epson printer and the second script mapping LPT1: to an IBM printer, you could not guarantee which printer would be used when the user logged on and then printed to the LPT1: port.

By default all logon/logoff scripts also run hidden but, similarly to startup/shutdown scripts, they can be configured to appear with a command window with the **Run logon scripts visible** setting under **User Configuration | Administrative Templates | System | Logon/Logoff**.

Password Options

Password options are part of the Local Security Settings GPO we covered earlier but, with security being such an important issue, this section covers some of the password options you can set in a local GPO.

Your Windows 2000 computer's greatest threat to security is unauthorized access to a powerful account such as one that is a member of the Administrator's group, or the local Administrator account itself. If an unauthorized user logs into your Windows 2000 computer with the local Administrator account, most security measures are next to useless.

For example, the administrator can install viruses and Trojan horses, delete or modify crucial data files, take ownership of all files and reassign permissions, and decrypt any EFS files. Having a suitable and enforceable password policy helps to thwart many of these attacks.

You will find the Password Policy under **Computer Configuration | Windows Settings | Security Settings**. Because none of these settings has the Explain tab, I think it's worthwhile to list additional information on each of them. These settings are:

- Enforce password history
- Maximum password age
- Minimum password age
- Minimum password length
- Passwords must meet complexity requirements
- Store password using reversible encryption for all users in the domain

Enforce Password History

The **Enforce password history** option allows enhanced security by ensuring that old passwords are not continually reused when users are prompted to change their passwords. By default, it is not set (0) but can be set up to 24.

Maximum Password Age

Maximum password age determines how often users will be prompted to change their password on this machine. Specify the number of days that a password is allowed to be used. A value of 0 will effectively disable this option (the same password can be used indefinitely), or you can specify up to 999 days.

The default value on a local GPO is 42 days and for greater security should be used together with the **Enforce password history** option.

Minimum Password Age

I'm always getting **Minimum password age** confused with **Maximum password age**, but this setting determines how many days a new password must be used before a user allowed to change it. A value of 0 means that a new password can be changed immediately. The maximum setting is 999 days. Note that the setting here must be less than the **Maximum password age**. This option is used to make sure the password history option is effective—otherwise users could repeatedly cycle through passwords until they can reuse a certain one (that is, their favorite).

Minimum Password Length

The **Minimum password length** option at least is intuitive—specify the minimum number of characters you want used in passwords. Note that it is not set by default (0 characters), and it is usually recommended that a password should be at least seven characters long. However, before setting this, you may find the next option, **Passwords must meet complexity requirements**, more appropriate to enforce a more secure password setting that, for example, will help to combat *dictionary attacks*.

Passwords can be up to 14 characters outside an Active Directory domain, and up to 104 characters when in an Active Directory network.

Passwords Must Meet Complexity Requirements

When **Passwords must meet complexity requirements** is enabled, new and modified passwords must fulfill the following criteria:

- Must not contain all or part of the user's account name
- Must be a minimum of six characters long
- Must contain characters from three of the following four categories:
    1. English uppercase characters (A..Z)
    2. English lowercase characters (a..z)
    3. Base 10 digits (0..9)
    4. Nonalphanumeric characters (for example, !,$#,%)

These complexity criteria are configured within the Windows default password filter: **passfilt.dll**. You cannot modify these configurations, but you can create your own custom password filters with the Microsoft Platform Software Development Kit.

> **NOTE**
>
> Strong password enforcement is also available with NT4, but few people know about it because is not automatically included, nor does it have a graphical user interface (GUI). However, this same function has been available since NT4 Service Pack 2 (SP2) (although I recommend using it from the latest Service Pack available).
>
> If you are running NT4 domains, it is particularly recommended that you use this on both primary domain controllers (PDCs) and backup domain controllers (BDCs), and on any NT4 servers that run services connected to the Internet, such as Internet Information Server (IIS) and Exchange Server.
>
> The Knowledge Base article "How to Enable Strong Password Functionality in Windows NT" [Q161990] provides instructions on how to do this. The process involves copying over the .dll, modifying the registry, and rebooting the computer. Thankfully, the automatic inclusion of this option in Windows 2000 makes it much easier to configure!

Store Password Using Reversible Encryption for All Users in the Domain

Store password using reversible encryption for all users in the domain is hardly an intuitive label, is it? Despite sounding as if it has no relevance for a local GPO, it applies to both the local GPO and Active Directory GPOs. What you must know before considering enabling this is that setting this option is functionally the same as storing passwords in clear-text within the account database, rather than storing them in encrypted format. Obviously this is a very undesirable security risk and should only be enabled if a specific application requires it and you have determined that the need to run this application is greater than the security risks to password integrity.

One example of when you have to use this setting is if your remote access users have to use the less secure authentication protocol Challenge Handshake Authentication Protocol (CHAP) (for example, non-Windows users) when authenticating with a Remove Access Server (RAS). If your Windows 2000 server will be hosting RAS services for users that must authenticate with CHAP, you must enable this option in the Local Group Policy of your RAS server.

Note that there are further GPO options linked with password policies, such as those found under the Account Lockout Policy (for lockout thresholds, duration, and automatic reset) and auditing logon successes and failures as part of the Audit Policy.

Internet Explorer Settings

Although a few Internet Explorer settings exist for the Computer Configuration under **Administrative Templates | Internet Explorer**, most are within the **User Configuration** section of **Local Group Policy**. You have settings under **Internet Explorer Maintenance** (under **Windows Settings**), which is where you specify your Proxy Server settings, and **Favorites and Links**, together with security settings and IE associated programs (for example, HTML editor, e-mail program, and so forth).

You also have a whole host of settings under **Administrative Templates | Windows Components | Internet Explorer**, which fully allow you to control and configure just about every aspect of Internet Explorer, such as disabling the Internet Connection Wizard, not allowing well-known controls such as Shockwave Flash and Microsoft Media Player, setting subscription limits to restrict downloading content for offline viewing, disabling the **Save this program to disk** option, and disabling individual configuration pages.

Disabling Installation from Removable Media

Disabling installation from removable media prevents users from installing software from floppy disks, CDs, and DVDs—effectively forcing them to install only from network distribution points that house company approved software. It won't however, stop users from attaching to any unofficial shares to install software—and if this is a possibility, look to other measures to control this (such as restricting Internet access, restricting who can create shares, and regularly reviewing shares on your network).

This useful GPO option is called **Disable media source for any install** and can be found under **User Configuration | Administrative Templates | Windows Components | Windows Installer**.

Controlling Access to Control Panel and Components

You can fine-tune the behavior of any component within the Control Panel, stored under **User Configuration | Administrative Templates**. However, three of the main GPO options for controlling Control Panel and its various components are the following:

- Disabling Control Panel
- Hiding specified Control applets
- Showing only specified Control Panel applets

Disabling Control Panel

The most restrictive of the options is **Disable Control Panel** under **User Configuration | Administrative Templates | Start Menu & Taskbar**. Enabling it prevents control.exe, which is the program that actually loads Control Panel, from running. This prevents users from running Control Panel or any of its associated components (for example, Hdwwiz.cpl for the Add/Remove New Hardware Wizard), even if they were to specify the program from a command line.

It also removes Control Panel from the Start menu and from Windows Explorer. And if a user tries to select a Control Panel item from the Properties item on a context menu, he or she will see a message explaining that a policy prevents this.

Hiding/Showing Specified Control Applets

The less restrictive options **Hiding/Showing specified control applets** are found under **User Configuration | Administrative Templates | Control Panel** and only hide or show your choice of specified Control Panel applets from the user by removing them from the Control Panel window and the Start menu. Experienced users will still be able to access these applets by running them from the command line—such as Appwiz.cpl for the Add/Remove Program and Netcpl.cpl for Network and Dial-up Connectivity.

> **NOTE**
>
> All Control Panel programs are stored in the **%systemroot%\system32** directory with a .cpl extension. If you are unsure of the actual name of the program, search this directory for the .cpl extension—most names are fairly easy to recognize. You can find the complete list in the Knowledge Base article "How to Hide Selected Control Panel Tools in Windows 2000" [Q261241].

Screen Saver Options

Screen savers are very simple to set and configure, and more important than protecting your monitor, they are instrumental in protecting unattended logged in workstations. However, you may want to enforce a corporate screen saver and ensure that it is activated after a specific period of inactivity and protected with a password.

Many performance problems and reliability issues are often tracked to users installing their own choice of screen savers. GPOs allow you to control this easily with settings under **User Configuration | Administrative Templates | Control Panel | Display**, where you can set the name of the screen saver to be used (which prevents users from changing it under **Control Panel | Display**), specify that it be password protected (which disables the **Password protected** check box on the **Screen Saver** tab in **Display** in **Control Panel**), and for good measure you may decide to disable the Screen Saver tab altogether from Display in Control Panel by setting the **Hide Screen Saver tab** option.

Disabling the Command Prompt, Disabling the Registry Editor, Running Only Specified Windows Applications

Most of the GPO options **Disable the command prompt**, **Disable the registry editing tools**, and **Run only specified Windows applications** are self explanatory but valuable enough to point out where they are, along with any additional information that should be considered when enabling them.

Disable the command prompt is located under **User Configuration | Administrative Templates | System** and prevents a user from running **Cmd.exe** (Windows 2000's interactive command prompt). However, it also prevents the computer from running script files that use the command interpreter (those that end in .cmd and .bat). If you use this policy, ensure that none of your startup/shutdown or logon/logoff scripts use .cmd or .bat files. Look to use alternatives such as cscript files.

You can disable both registry editors (regedt32.exe and regedit.exe) with the GPO setting **Disable registry editing tools**, which is located under **User Configuration | Administrative Templates | System**.

You can restrict which programs can be run with two options: **Run only allowed Windows applications** and **Don't run specified Windows applications** under **User Configuration | Administrative Templates | System**. By specifying permitted programs or restricting selecting programs, users will not be able to run then from Windows Explorer. They will, however, be able to run them from the command prompt *if* they have access to the command prompt.

Deploying Local Group Policy Objects

Unfortunately, local Group Policy by definition is local to each Windows 2000 computer and as such there is no Microsoft central configuration tool to help you define a standard LGPO you want to deploy onto each machine. You can't, as you might think, simply copy a configured computer's GPO folder onto another computer.

If you are using disk imaging, there's no reason why new computers installed with Windows 2000 cannot start with the same local Group Policies. Beware that an administrator with full access to the appropriate Group Policy folder can make modifications.

However, you can export and import the security policy within the local GPO together with additional security settings such as registry settings, service configurations, and ACLs. This is done using Microsoft's Security Configuration and Analysis, which is covered next.

Security Configuration Using Templates

This section discusses one of Microsoft's simplest and yet most powerful configuration utilities for Windows 2000 computers that aren't part of an Active Directory domain: Security Configuration Manager. Although this section is in the workstation chapter, it applies equally to servers since it concentrates on the security configuration of a Windows 2000 computer. However, it ties in nicely with local Group Security Policies in the previous section and offers a solution to the central deployment and maintenance of standard security options on multiple computers.

Microsoft's Security Configuration Management uses templates and a security database to store, compare, analyze, import, and export various security configurations on a Windows 2000 computer. It allows the following:

- You can import whichever of Microsoft's built-in security templates most closely fits your requirements and either apply it to your Windows 2000 computer without modification, or make minor changes first.

- You can import your own previously defined security template and either apply it to your Windows 2000 computer without modification, or make minor changes first.

- You can analyze the current security settings on a computer and export them into a template of your own choice.

- You can analyze current computer settings against a template to see where differences arise and then choose whether to resolve these differences (and how).

You can do all this both with an easy to use MMC snap-in, and with a command-line utility. More on both of these later.

For example, if your Windows 2000 computers had been in use for some time on your network, you could check how secure they were with regards to user rights, password policies, account policies, services, registry options, group membership, file permissions, and shares—and compare them against the standard Microsoft template that most closely resembles your requirements.

Or, if you had a customized security template that you wanted to apply to all Windows 2000 Professional desktops, and another to apply to Windows 2000 member servers, you could periodically import them (for example, within a startup script) to ensure the security options on these computers were kept constant.

Moreover, multiple templates can be used on one computer such that the end result is a layer of multiple options in which the last applied option takes precedence. This allows you to have a smaller overall number of modular configurations to be used throughout your organization to minimize redundancy, rather than having to use and maintain a large number of templates with only small changes that can be used only once on a computer. For example, you may have a base template for all your Windows 2000 computers, and then apply more or less restrictive templates on top of that depending on each computer's role.

Security Templates

The Microsoft built-in security templates are located under **%systemroot%Security\Templates**. Basically, these break down into templates designed for Windows 2000 workstations, servers, and domain controllers (obviously, Windows 2000 domain controllers apply only to Active Directory domains). The standard categories are the following:

- Default

- Secure

- Highly Secure

- Compatible

- Out of the Box (Setup Security)

For example, you'll have three possible Default Security templates—one for workstations, one for servers, and another for domain controllers. The different levels denote increasing levels of security, as it is generally assumed that a server will require higher security than a workstation. However, if you are running in a highly secure environment you may want to use the server template on your workstation—check the security differences closely rather than blindly adhering to Microsoft's label.

You'll easily be able to see which is which by the name of the template—if it ends in **wk** it denotes being suitable for a workstation. The ending **sv** is for server, **ws** is for workstation *or* server, and **dc** is for domain controller. All templates have an INF extension and are text files that you can read and edit—although it is not advisable to modify them with a text editor.

So, for example the default security template for a Windows 2000 Professional workstation is **defaultwk.inf**, and the secure template for a Windows 2000 workstation or server is **securews.inf**.

Don't worry too much about the names for now because you'll normally work with these templates within an easy to use MMC snap-in that handily displays their descriptions—although if you have to check the file quickly, these descriptions are also listed on the very last line of the .INF file itself under the **<name>ProfileDescription = parameter**.

NOTE

These templates are designed to be applied in layers—so for example, you would usually apply a default template to every Windows 2000 computer you wanted to secure. Then for computers requiring a secure template, you would then add the secure template in addition to the default template.

Default Security Template

The Default security template contains default settings for account and local policies, plus typical values for event log maintenance and basic permissions for system services. It also includes default access permissions for system files, directories, and registry keys. It doesn't include modifications to user rights, so that if you or applications have modified these they will be retained. which makes it a suitable template to apply to an upgraded Windows 2000 computer or one that has had applications installed on it.

There are different versions for workstation, server, and domain controller that are worth noting. The workstation version has default startup settings for system-related services, whereas the server version also adds server-related services onto this list (for example Simple Mail Transfer Protocol (SMTP) and License Logging). In comparison, the domain controller version omits any service-related settings so it would be appropriate on any machine where you have fine-tuned service startup to suit your requirements.

Secure Security Template

There are only two versions of the Secure security template: one for domain controllers and a combined one for workstations and servers. These offer a medium level of security that encompasses stricter settings for password and lockout policies, no guest access to the Event Log, and the enabling of some key auditing options. The auditing options include unsuccessful login events and privilege use, together with successful/unsuccessful account management and policy changes. With the addition of this auditing, there's sensibly also provision for a larger Security Event Log. Note that this template, despite its name, contains no settings for files, folders, and registry keys since these are presumed secured by the underlying default template.

Highly Secure Template

There are two versions of the Highly secure template, and neither of them is applicable outside an Active Directory domain since they require the highest security features within a native-mode Active Directory environment. They set the requirement of having digital signatures on both client- and server-side communications, along with signing and encrypting all network data. Computers running these security options are not able to communicate with any down-level client.

Compatible Template

The Compatible template offers a lower level of security than the Default template in the interests of application and service compatibility and may be more applicable if your Windows 2000 installation is an upgrade rather than a clean installation, or if it is running applications that are not fully Windows 2000 compatible.

Similar to the Default template, this template removes Authenticated Users from the Power Users group but compromises on security by lowering the permissions on folders, files, and registry keys typically accessed by applications.

Out of the Box Templates

The Out of the Box template has the description "Setup Security" to indicate that it is often used as the first base of your own modifications. It offers Microsoft's default shipping security settings that you would get on a clean installation of Windows 2000 for your workstation or server, with additional security settings if running on a domain controller. It allows you to reset back to a known default state.

NOTE

There is another template available from Microsoft aimed at stand-alone Web servers, called hisecweb.inf, which is available to download at: http://download.microsoft.com/download/win2000srv/SCM/1.0/NT5/ EN-US/hisecweb.exe.

Viewing and Modifying Templates

The easiest way to view and modify templates is by using the Security Templates snap-in. When it is loaded you will see all the templates available on your computer. Figure 2.6 shows the list of templates available to a clean installation of Windows 2000 Professional, with the templates' long descriptions to summarize their contents and purpose.

Viewing Template Settings

To view each template's settings, double-click the template and you will see the categories in Figure 2.7.

Figure 2.6 List of All Default Security Templates with Corresponding Descriptions

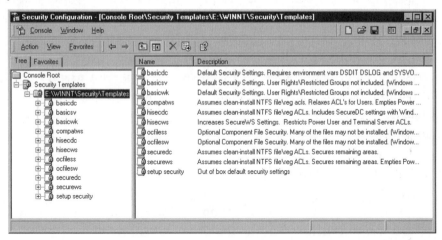

Figure 2.7 Security Template Categories

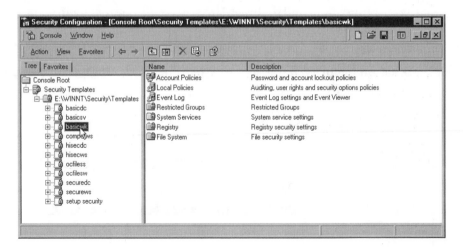

If you browse through the categories, you will see the types of options that can be set—for example, the same security options we saw in the Local Security for password policies and account locks, user rights, security options, and so on. I think two of the most useful options are checking for shared directories and NTFS permissions (under File System) and the Restricted Groups. The Restricted Groups category isn't overly intuitive with the default templates, so if you are unsure about these check the following section.

Restricted Groups

Restricted groups are for controlling membership of certain groups that are security conscious—usually because they have greater privileges in the way of user rights and file/folder permissions. Typical examples of restricted groups to configure are the built-in local Administrator's group and the Power Users group. However, the same principle applies to your own groups—for example, an SQL Administrator's group that is used to grant its members full access to your company database.

In an ideal world, each local group on your Windows 2000 computer would contain only the members it should have and no more. However, in the real world it's very easy for groups to acquire new members for troubleshooting purposes, intended for a temporary solution only and yet they remain forgotten. This option allows you to monitor certain groups and define the correct membership. Members that are not included in the template are removed.

Using this security option is a double-edged sword. It's great for housekeeping and tidying up group membership that might compromise security, but ensure that your template is updated regularly or you'll remove legitimate users who will no longer be able to work!

Figure 2.8 shows an example of a modified Restricted Group setting in the Default Workstation Security Template, in which the local administrator is the only permitted member of the Administrator's group.

Figure 2.8 Example of a Restricted Group Added to the Security Template

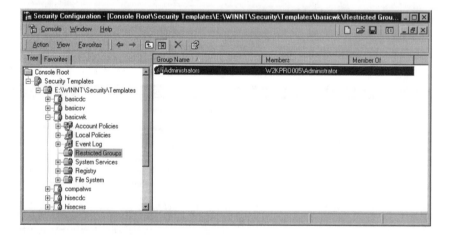

Modifying Template Settings

You can either modify the supplied templates or, more prudently, modify a copy to preserve the original. To use a copy you can either copy or rename within Explorer and then open your own template in the Security Templates snap-in, or perhaps more simply you can load a supplied template and choose **Save As** from the context-sensitive menu, as shown in Figure 2.9. Notice that this context-sensitive menu also allows you to set your own description for easier identification.

Figure 2.9 Copying an Existing Template to Preserve the Original

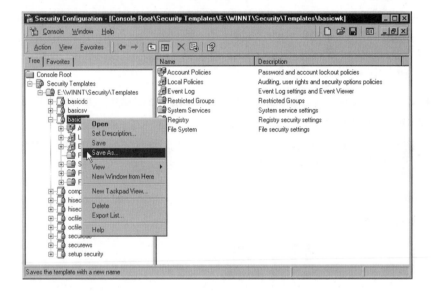

Applying Templates

Applying templates is done either with another MMC snap-in called **Security Configuration and Analysis**, or with a command line utility called **Secedit**. Both are discussed in the following sections.

NOTE

A further option exists for importing the template's security options into your local Group Policy. When editing your local Group Policy, right-click **Security Settings** and select **Import Policy**, which will allow you to select a security template.

However, keeping these configuration options as templates provides more flexibility because you can automatically import them periodically within scripts—as we shall see later.

Security Configuration and Analysis

When loaded for the first time, the **Security Configuration and Analysis**
MMC snap-in prompts you to open a new security database. You can load this
snap-in into its own MMC or add it to the same MMC you used for the templates. You are then prompted to import a security template to act as a starting
block. Choose the template that closest matches your requirements.

Now that you've loaded a security template, the power of this snap-in
becomes evident with the new Actions that are available from the **Security
Configuration and Analysis** root. As the text explains in the right pane, you
can either configure your computer or analyze your computer security settings
by comparing them against your chosen template. These options are shown in
Figure 2.10. After analyzing your computer, the Export Template option also
becomes available.

Figure 2.10 Options Available After Opening a Security Database—Include
Analyze and Configure

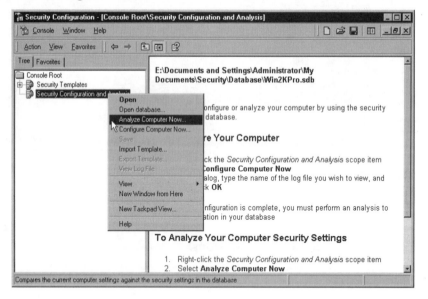

Configure Computer Now

Selecting **Configure Computer Now** first prompts you for the log path location, then you will see a dialog box similar to Figure 2.11, showing the progress
of configuring your security settings to match those in your chosen imported
template. Don't forget you can add layers of templates to one computer—use the

Import Template command if you want to do this before selecting **Configure Computer Now**.

Figure 2.11 Progress Display When Configuring Your Computer with Your Chosen Security Templates

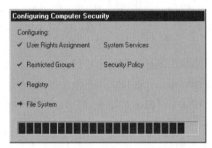

To see what changes took place and any errors that occurred during the configuration process, right-click **Security Configuration and Analysis** and select **View Log File**. This loads the text file in the right pane of the MMC. To return to the normal view, right-click **Security Configuration and Analysis** again and deselect the **View Log File** option. A sample log file is displayed in Figure 2.12.

Figure 2.12 Example of a Security Log File

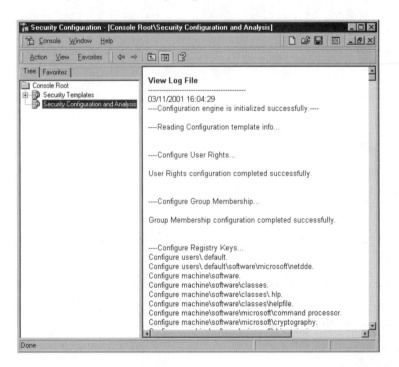

Analyze Computer Now

Selecting **Analyze Computer Now** also prompts you for the log path location, then you will see a dialog box similar to Figure 2.11, only this time it shows the progress of analyzing your current security settings against those in your imported templates. When it is finished, you can view your effective security settings by browsing through the template settings in each of the expanded Security Configuration and Analysis options.

This time you will see a column for the Database Setting and a column for the Computer Setting. When the policy has not been defined in the security template, it will appear as **Not defined** under the Database Setting. Where the policy options have been defined and are identical you'll see a green tick next to the policy. Where the two differ, you'll see a red cross against the policy, with the two settings displayed. For example, Figure 2.13 shows that the local policy has a text message of "Please contact the Help Desk if you cannot log on to this workstation," which does not exist in the template.

Figure 2.13 Results After Analyzing the Security Database against the Computer's Settings

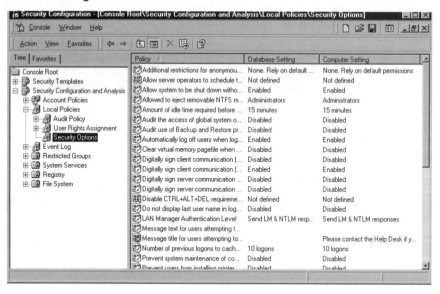

If you then decide you want to add the current computer setting into the security database so that future tests don't flag the discrepancy, double-click the policy and define the new policy in the security database.

After you have analyzed your computer you can view the resulting log, similar to the process described in the previous section. But perhaps more exciting is the now new option to export your current security settings to a new template that can then be imported to another computer in the same way as we previously ran the **Configure Computer Now** process.

Deploying Security Templates Automatically with Secedit

Although the security snap-ins make easy work of configuring, importing, and exporting security settings on a single computer, Security Configuration has a sister command line utility that is more useful for importing security options to multiple Windows 2000 computers: **Secedit.exe**. This can be run in conjunction with startup scripts, logon scripts, or automatically called periodically with the Task Scheduler.

Run **Secedit** without any parameters from the command line and you will see help information automatically displayed that provides a description and information on how to use the command for analyzing, configuring, refreshing security settings, exporting security settings, and validating a template.

For deploying security templates automatically, use the **secedit /configure** option and ensure that the template you want to use is available to the computer. This can be in a central location (for example, a mapped network drive) if you use the /CFG parameter, which allows just one template to be used for multiple computers.

Another useful option when configuring security is to use just certain areas of a template rather than apply the whole template (which is the default). The areas you can choose include the Local Security Policy (for example account policies, password settings, audit policies, and so forth), restricted group settings, user rights, registry options, file storage (permissions and shares), and service configuration.

Secedit /Configure Options

The complete syntax of the **Secedit /configure** command is the following:

```
Secedit /configure DB<filename> [/CFG<filename>] [/overwrite]
[/areas<area1 area2 ..>] [/log<logpath> [/verbose] [/quiet]
```

For example, to configure all the Windows 2000 Professional computers in the Accounts department with a centrally stored security database called

ACCOUNTS.SDB in \\W2KSRV05\Security using a template called
ACCOUNTS.INF in \\W2KSRV05\Security\Templates, the script for these
computers may contain the following:

```
Secedit /configure DB\\W2KSRV05\Security\accounts.sdb
 /CFG\\W2KSRV05\Security\Templates\accounts.inf /overwrite
 /quiet
```

Table 2.1 further explains these available options.

Table 2.1 Options Used with Secedit /Configure

Option	Explanation
/DB<*filename*>	This must be specified and provides the path to the security database that will be used.
/CFG<*filename*>	This specifies the path to the security template to be used.
/overwrite	Valid only when using the /CFG switch; when specified this results in overwriting rather than appending the composite template results.
/areas <*area1 area2 ..*>	When the whole of the template isn't required, use this switch to specify which of the following areas should be configured: SECURITYPOLICY, GROUP_MGMT, USER_RIGHTS, REGKEYS, FILESTORE, SERVICES. Each specified area should be separated by a space.
/log<*logpath*>	When specified sets a non-default path for the log file.
/verbose	When specified produces detailed progress information.
/quiet	Suppresses both screen and log output.

Improvements in System Reliability

Reliability was certainly one of the goals of Windows 2000, aiming for a higher
uptime and better user experience with fewer reboots, fewer DrWatson errors,
and fewer lockups. This section looks at some of the new features that undoubtedly have helped to build Windows 2000's reputation for offering a more robust
operating system.

For IT implementers, these native and often behind the scenes functions prevent time being wasted by attempting to troubleshoot sporadic stability issues. For IT managers, these improvements in reliability mean users can spend more time working and less time waiting for data to be restored from backup, rebooting, and putting in Help Desk calls about system reliability issues. These reasons alone make a good argument for using Windows 2000 on the desktop. The features covered in this section are the following:

- Device Driver Signing
- Windows File Protection (WFP) and System File Checker (SFC)
- Service Pack Application

Device Driver Signing

Badly written hardware drivers are one of the main causes of stability problems and you are most likely to discover this after installing a new device and rebooting, only to be faced with the infamous Blue Screen of Death (BSOD). The road to restoring completely from backup at that point is an unhappy, but all too familiar, one. Thankfully, this has been addressed in Windows 2000 with the help of signed drivers and with the Recovery Console (the Recovery Console will be covered in Chapter 3).

All drivers on the Windows 2000 HCL are digitally signed by Microsoft to indicate that they pass their various stress and reliability tests. This offers more protection than we had under NT4, in which you had no idea whether the driver had been thoroughly tested at all (let alone by Microsoft) but your computer would happily let you install it without a murmur. Of course, there are drivers available for Windows 2000 that aren't signed and are perfectly reliable (or rather, as reliable as software can be!), but installing a signed driver puts the odds in your favor and helps with the confidence factor.

TIP

Microsoft's Hardware Compatibility List can be found online at www.microsoft.com/hcl/default.asp and Windows Update at http://corporate.windowsupdate.microsoft.com.

Whereas we may build Windows 2000 computers strictly adhering to the HCL (all drivers on the HCL are signed), it is often very difficult afterwards to maintain the same level of restriction as more devices are required and installed, often ad hoc. The Driver Signing options available in Windows 2000 at least allow us to be aware of this potential and either warn before installing an unsigned driver, or even prevent installation of unsigned drivers.

Most device drivers are installed when new hardware is added to the computer and either Plug and Play (PnP) automatically starts the Add New Hardware Wizard, or the user manually selects the **Add/Remove Hardware applet** from **Control Panel**. However, you can also update an already installed driver.

By default, users and even Power Users can't install device drivers. You would normally need administrative rights (controlled with the Group Policy **Load and unload device drivers** under **Security Settings | Account Policies | User Rights**).

Driver Signing Options

Driver signing options are found with the Driver Signing button on the System Properties, Hardware tab. The various options are:

- **Ignore** Install all files, regardless of file signature.

- **Warn** Display a message before installing an unsigned file (this is the default).

- **Block** Prevent installation of unsigned files.

And there's a final option that only administrators can set, called **Apply setting as system default**, which means that a local administrator's choice will be set per machine and not just in his or her profile. A user can then set a more restrictive option for himself, but not a less restrictive option.

Additionally, a Group Policy option called **Code signing for device drivers** is the equivalent to this administrator's setting. This policy is under **User Configuration | Administrative Templates | System**.

Driver Signing Verification

You can verify that a driver device is digitally signed (and view its version number) by checking the Properties of the device under **Device Manager** (load this from **Control Panel | System | Hardware** tab **| Device Manager** button). When you display the properties of a device, go to the **Driver** tab to see displayed the vendor and the digital signature (if it has one). Microsoft's digitally

signed drivers appear as **Microsoft Windows 2000 Publisher**, as you can see in
Figure 2.14.

Figure 2.14 Example of a Microsoft Signed Device Driver

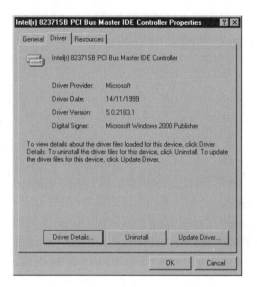

Windows File Protection and System File Checker

Windows File Protection and System File Checker directly attempt to address the
problem of DLL Hell (DLL being dynamic link library) experienced by so many
previous Windows users, in which different application installations would each
install their own version of a system file, overwriting the previous version
without choice. Whereas the newly installed application might work fine, previously installed applications that also made use of these system files but weren't
written or tested with the same version of these files could have problems. The
result could be the infamous DrWatson message, a complete lock up, or even a
system reboot.

Windows File Protection (WFP) in Windows 2000 protects key system files
at all times, and should one of them be deleted or replaced with an alternative
version, WFP automatically reinstalls the original. It uses file signatures, a file catalog, and a Dllcache folder working in conjunction with another Windows 2000
feature called the System File Checker (SFC). Together these features protect the
integrity of critical files that are integral to the computer's reliability.

Even though WFP works automatically on every copy of Windows 2000, it is in your interest to understand how it works, what configuration options there are (to decide if they are relevant to your setup), and what limitations it has.

How Windows File Protection and System File Checker Work

Windows File Protection works because Microsoft digitally signs all the system files that ship with Windows 2000. This allows them to be checked by the operating system for integrity. Immediately after installation of the operating system, a copy is made for backup purposes with a corresponding catalog maintained of all essential files and version numbers. This may easily explain loss of hard disk availability—by default the Dllcache folder is 50MB on Professional and unlimited on Server (this can be modified with the Group Policy **Limit Windows File Protection cache size**).

The backup directory is a hidden protected system folder called **Dllcache**, which is stored under **%systemroot%\system32** by default. Despite its name, it holds more than DLLs and includes most of the system files (DLLs, driver files, font files, .INF files, ActiveX controls, and executable files). In all, there are about 3000 files that are protected, and therefore duplicated, on your system. These mainly come from your **%systemroot%** directory, the **%systemroot%\system** directory, and the **%systemroot%\system32** directory.

When WFP detects that a protected file or folder has been deleted, it automatically replaces it with the copy in the Dllcache. When a protected file is replaced with another version that isn't digitally signed by Microsoft, WPF looks to replace it with the backup version. However, it first verifies the integrity of the backup version to make sure this hasn't also been replaced (for example, by the installation program), and if necessary it will look to replace it automatically with the original from your installation source.

If you installed from a network installation share and it's still available, or if you installed from CD and the CD is still in your CD-ROM drive, this will happen behind the scenes. If retrieval from the installation origin fails (for example, the CD is back on the shelf), then the user is prompted to supply the distribution media. Unfortunately, there's no browse option at this point so you can't use an alternative location. If you must cancel the request, an error message appears and a WFP error is written to the System Log with information on the missing file being cancelled by the user and a warning that it is required for system stability.

NOTE

If you want to change the saved source path for the Windows 2000 distribution media, there are several places in the registry where this is stored. These include:

HKEY_LOCAL_MACHINE\SOFTWARE\Microsoft\Windows\
    CurrentVersion\Setup\Installation Sources
HKEY_LOCAL_MACHINE\SOFTWARE\Microsoft\Windows\
    CurrentVersion\Setup\SourcePath
HKEY_LOCAL_MACHINE\SOFTWARE\Microsoft\WindowsNT\
    CurrentVersion\SourcePath

The System File Checker tool (**sfc.exe**) can be run independently by an administrator to scan all protected files to verify versions and replace them immediately or at the next bootup.

Figure 2.15 displays a typical Windows File Protection information message in the System Log, which shows that an unauthorized version of the file cmd.exe was replaced, and WFP was consequently activated automatically and restored the original version. When this happened, the user was unaware that anything was wrong because it all happened "behind the scenes."

Figure 2.15 Windows File Protection in Action

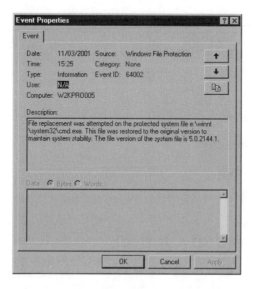

Running System File Checker on the Command Line

The available command line options you can use with the **sfc.exe** command are listed in Table 2.2.

Table 2.2 System File Checker Command Line Switches

Command Line Switch	Description
/Scannow	Immediately scans all protected system files.
/Scanonce	Will scan all protected system files on next bootup, but not on subsequent boots.
/Scanboot	Will scan all protected system files every time the computer boots.
/Cancel	Cancels any outstanding SFC commands.
/Quiet	Replaces protected files without prompting the user.
/Enable	Prompts user to confirm replacement of protected system files.
/Purgecache	Immediately deletes all existing files in the Dllcache folder, and rescans all protected files.
/Cachesize=x	Reconfigures the size of the Dllcache folder. Value must be set in MB—for example, /Cachesize=10 sets the size of the Dllcache folder to 10MB.
/Help or /?	Displays Help for all options and descriptions.

So, for example, if you suspected your Dllcache folder had become corrupt, you could use any one of the following commands to repair it (though the last two would require a reboot first):

- **SFC /Scannow**

- **SFC /Purgecache**

- **SFC /Scanonce**

- **SFC /Scanboot**

WFP Configuration Options

WFP is one Windows 2000 feature that doesn't need to be installed or configured before it works, but there are some configuration options that may better suit your working environment.

- Limit the WFP cache size
- Modify the WFP cache location
- Configure frequency of file scans

Limit the WFP Cache Size

You can limit the WFP cache size both with the SFC command using the **/CACHESIZE=** switch and with a Group Policy called **Limit Windows File Protection cache size** under **Computer Configuration | Administrative Templates | System | Windows File Protection**.

The folder size is specified in Megabytes with 1 being the minimum and 4294967295 the maximum (the latter meaning that it's unlimited). If you either disable this policy setting or don't set a maximum size, the WFP folder defaults back to being 50MB for Professional and unlimited for Server. The new setting takes effect after a reboot, and if you have already exceeded your maximum size you should also run SFC with the **/PURGECACHE** option before the reboot.

Configuring & Implementing...

Setting WFP Limitations on Setup

If disk space is short and you want to set a minimal cache right away when you install Windows 2000, you can do so if you're performing an unattended install. You need to have the following in your script file:

```
[SystemFileProtection]

SFCQuota=0
```

This makes the cache as small as possible to help preserve disk space. When a backup file is required, the user is prompted for the Windows 2000 distribution files so they can be retrieved.

For more information on performing unattended installations see the following: Chapter 3: "Deploying Windows 2000 with Unattended Installations" in Microsoft's Desktop Solutions Deployment Guide available with TechNet and also available online at the following URL: www.microsoft.com/TechNet/prodtechnol/office/deploy/chapt3.asp.

Modify the WFP Cache Location

You can modify the WFP cache location with the Group Policy **Specify Windows File Protection cache location** under **Computer Configuration | Administrative Templates | System | Windows File Protection**.

Hard disk space is less of an issue these days, but you may want to use an unlimited cache and not have the room to accommodate that on your system partition. Use this option to specify an alternative full path to where you want to store protected files (for example, on an alternative disk), but it mustn't be a network location.

Configure Frequency of File Scans

System File Checker by default automatically scans files for WFP only during setup. You can configure the **Set Windows File Protection scanning** Group Policy under **Computer Configuration | Administrative Templates | System | Windows File Protection** to change how often and when SFC runs. This has no effect on background protection WFP offers or allowing you to run sfc.exe manually. The options you can enable are:

- **Do not scan during startup** The default setting. Scanning normally only occurs immediately after Windows 2000 is installed.

- **Scan during startup** Scanning will occur each time you load Windows 2000 for additional protection at the cost of a delayed startup response.

- **Scan once** Scanning occurs the next time the system is restarted.

WFP Limitations

So what's the catch? With any added protection you are going to experience some disadvantages. Many of the disadvantages have already been noted, such as redundant data taking up a large chunk of your hard disk, delayed response time, and the inability to specify an alternative distribution source (good enough reason to install from an available network distribution share!).

One of the limitations to watch out for is the buffer limit for detecting changes to protected files. If a user deletes a large number of system files at once, WFP may not be able to keep up and may discard some changes. You may still be able to recover all files, however, by either initiating the **SFC /Scannow** command, or with the **Windows File Protection scanning** policy set to scan on every startup, you could simply instruct the user to reboot.

Service Pack Application

Service Packs are the product of continued development work by Microsoft in that they contain application bug fixes, security fixes, updated drivers, and sometimes system administration tools and additional utilities or components that were not available when the base version of the product was released. The general advice is to apply the latest Service Pack after confirming reliability within your own environment. For most of us, Service Packs fix more problems than they create.

However, one of the problems with previous versions of Windows and Service Packs was remembering to reapply the Service Pack after installing anything from the base distribution CD. There was no prompt or warning and often this task was forgotten if it was possible to postpone it until later. Only when reliability became an issue with odd error messages and stability problems did we think to reapply the Service Pack. I know, I've done it too when I've been in a hurry or the Service Pack CD wasn't readily at hand! I'm sure many of us are guilty of contributing to reliability problems simply due to this lack of methodical reapplication of Service Packs. But then, Microsoft made it too easy for us to do this.

Windows 2000 is different. If you install a new component after the installation of a Service Pack, by default you'll be asked to supply the Service Pack at the time of installation in addition to the distribution CD. It won't let you install the new component without access to the Service Pack—which is bad news for a busy administrator who has temporarily misplaced that elusive CD, but good news for reliability. Microsoft's thinking is: better no new component at all than risking an unstable one.

TIP

You can always check the current version of Windows (build and Service Pack if applied) by running **WinVer.exe**, which displays the About Windows dialog box.

Slip-Streaming Service Packs

If you have already installed Windows 2000 and now want to install a Service Pack, you simply run **update.exe** from the Service Pack CD or equivalent media. However, if you are installing Windows 2000 from scratch, there is no longer any need to install the base version first and then install the Service Pack on top. Instead you can *slip-stream* (integrate) the Service Pack into the installation so that only the newer files are installed.

To apply a Windows 2000 Service Pack to an existing distribution point, use the **-s:<folder>** switch with the **update.exe** program, which overwrites the existing distribution files with the later service pack files. So, for example if you would normally install Windows 2000 Professional from a network share using the command: **\\Server05\Distribution\Win2KPro\i386\winnt.exe**, then type: **update -s:\\Server05\Distribution\Win2Kpro** to slipstream the Service Pack into this directory for new installations.

Limitations of Service Packs

The integration of Service Packs with the operating system is certainly a good move toward making easier an administrator's job of providing a reliable platform. However, there are still a couple of limitations and problems that administrators must address.

The first is how to update currently installed systems with a new Service Pack. It's great that new installations can automatically include the latest Service Pack by slipstreaming, but that doesn't help those systems that were installed before the Service Pack was available. Of course you can install the Service Pack independently, but you still need both a mechanism for identifying these computers and a deployment method.

The second issue is how to deploy hot fixes. Hot fixes are patches from Microsoft that address known problems but are not available in the current Service Pack. Occasionally they will fix a functionality issue, but more likely they will be security patches for recently exposed security issues.

Most workstations will not require hot fixes to be installed. It is more likely you will need to install these on vulnerable servers such as those that offer Internet services, for instance, computers running IIS, ISA, NAT, RAS, and so on. The standard advice from Microsoft is to monitor their security bulletins and apply hot fixes as and when they are applicable to your particular setup. However, it can become a full-time job to monitor the reported problems and fixes that appear every day, obtain the hot fixes, test them offline, and then install them on multiple computers. How much time and effort you decide to devote to this will be a rather unpalatable resourcing issue in which you have to balance idealism with reality.

What can help is augmenting your deployment with a third party Service Pack Management tool that can centrally keep track of which computers have what installed. With it you can centrally and automatically update computers with the latest Service Pack and latest hot fixes. It won't do anything you couldn't do manually, but it can save a great amount of time and effort in anything but the smallest of networks, and will help you formulate and keep to a company deployment policy.

Improvements in Usability

I'm aware that ease of use is both relative and subjective. But Microsoft has made significant changes to both the look and feel of the desktop interface (presented within Windows Explorer) and features that are aimed at making users more productive more quickly.

This section doesn't list all of the new features, nor will it be a "How to Use Windows 2000" tour. However, it will list some of the new features I think make Windows 2000 a better choice over previous versions of Windows. These include the following:

- Desktop changes
- Hardware support
- Wizards and Help

Designing & Planning...

More Information

For more information on how ease of use contributes to greater productivity, you may find the following white paper useful: "General User Productivity Improvements": www.microsoft.com /WINDOWS2000/ guide/professional/solutions/productivity.asp.

Desktop Changes

People who are used to previous versions of Windows can find the desktop changes annoying—simply because they're not what we're used to. Most people's first experience of Windows 2000 was frustrating, bewildering, and exasperating as they tried to find where the familiar tools and options were hidden, with a yearning for the old, familiar Windows. Certainly it takes longer to relearn than if you're coming fresh to Windows 2000. Much the same was also true when Windows 95 first shipped, yet after a while people did find it much easier to use than previous versions, and the cry for a similar interface with the NT kernel spawned the advent of NT4.

And yet after a relatively short time of working with Windows 2000, I now find it difficult to drive the legacy desktops. The familiar Microsoft Management Console (MMC) has lived up to its aim of providing a reassuringly common shell that loads and runs all native Windows 2000 configuration options. I have to admit that many default desktop settings both annoyed and frustrated me at first, but I do acknowledge that default settings are suitable for everyday users, if not administrators.

The new desktop often tries to make intelligent choices for users who have little computing knowledge. For the most part these choices are acceptable—especially for corporate America, which is Microsoft's main market. It's a pity Windows 2000 doesn't offer two desktop options—one for everyday users and another for administrators. However, as it is it's left to administrators to tweak any desktop changes that best suit their users and configure their own desktop to best suit their own needs.

Of course you can use Group Policy to help customize your Windows 2000 desktop—for example, removing certain menus and disabling dangerous configuration options. You can also create useful shortcuts on the desktop and remove unwanted desktop clutter just as you could with NT4 and Windows 9x. However, this section looks at some aspects of the new desktop configuration. Some of the most commonly changed desktop features include the following:

- Personalized menus
- Start menu settings
- Display options
- Folder options

Personalized Menus

Personalized menus explain the missing menu items you're expecting to see. When you use the Start menu to access programs, by default you won't see all the menu items available to you—they are kept hidden initially. To access them, either wait a few seconds or click the chevrons (down arrows) at the bottom of the menu items. Figure 2.16 shows personalized menus in use.

Figure 2.16 Example of Personalized Menus in Which Menu Options Are Cropped

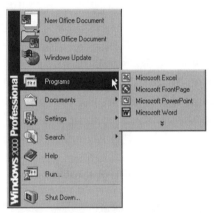

The reasoning behind personalized menus is to keep the desktop clean so frequently used programs are easier and faster to access. If, like me, you dislike this option, deselect the **Use Personalized Menus** check box from **Start | Settings | Taskbar & Startup Menu | General** tab.

Start Menu Settings

Now that you have found the **Taskbar and Startup Menu**, you'll find really useful options on the next tab, **Advanced**. This contains options for the following, most of which are self-explanatory:

- Display Administrative Tools
- Display Favorites
- Display Logoff
- Expand Control Panel
- Expand Network and Dial-Up Connections

- Expand Printers
- Scroll the Programs menu

Expanding Options

Perhaps expanding options requires a little explanation, as the term *expand* isn't overly intuitive and personally I find this one of the most useful and little-known desktop configuration options. The Help tells you that selecting an expand option displays the contents of your chosen option in a menu instead of a window.

Still not clear? I think this is best explained by examples. Although expanding My Documents may be useful for everyday users, let's take as an example the administrator's most often visited desktop item: the Control Panel.

Normally you would load an applet within Control Panel by clicking **Start | Settings | Control Panel**, which loads a window from which you can choose the applet you require. Figure 2.17 shows the default setting for the Control Panel with large icons—although many people switch to the **Details** option in the **View menu**.

Figure 2.17 Default Display for Control Panel

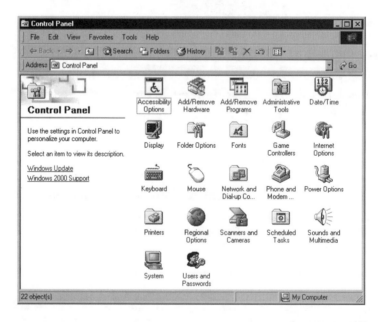

Select **Expand Control Panel** in the **Taskbar and Start menu**, and now your Control Panel applets and folders are accessible right off the Start menu, as shown in Figure 2.18.

Figure 2.18 Expanded Display for Control Panel

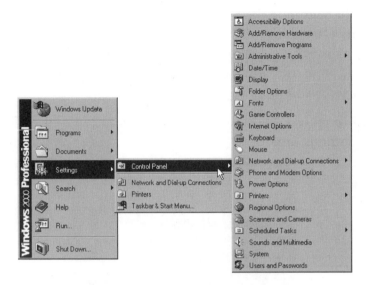

Display Options

Display options are fairly self-explanatory. They can be accessed quickly by right-clicking your desktop and choosing **Properties**. You will then see six tabs that allow you to choose display configuration options, including appearance, screen savers, choice of desktop icons, resolution, and colors. Perhaps two options worthy of note simply because they are new and fairly well hidden, are the following:

- Automatic powering down of the monitor
- Advanced settings

Monitor Power Options

The **Power** button is located on the **Screen Saver** tab and provides a selection of Power schemes in which you can control when and if your monitor and hard disks will automatically power down after a period of inactivity. For a standard Desktop configuration this is set at 20 minutes for the monitor (and never for hard disks). The rest of the options available here are more applicable to laptop users who wish to make the best use of battery conservation; these will be covered in the following chapter.

Advanced Settings

The **Advanced** button on the **Settings** tab takes you straight into the monitor device properties, as shown in Figure 2.19. From here you can select options such as small fonts, whether the computer should be rebooted after making display changes, device properties of the display adapter and monitor, refresh frequency, and hardware acceleration.

Figure 2.19 Monitor Properties from Advanced Button under Display Properties | Settings Tab

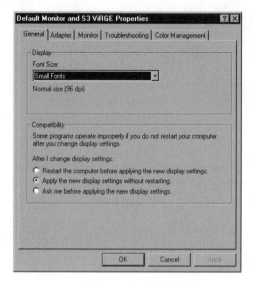

Folder Options

I have to admit, as an administrator I cannot work with the default folder options, and one of the very first things I do on a new Windows 2000 computer is change these! Remember that the default shipping options are suitable for everyday users, not administrators who need to see hidden and system files with easily displayed file properties. I would guess I use Windows Explorer more than any other Windows utility, and if that sounds similar to how you work, it is important that its options be set to suit your requirements. Choose **Folder Options** from **Control Panel**, or select it from the **Tools** menu within Explorer. The most important tab here (for me, anyway) is the **View** tab, as shown in Figure 2.20.

Figure 2.20 Default Settings for Folders Options, View Tab

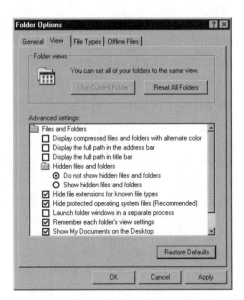

You can see that this allows you to fine-tune how files and folders are displayed. I usually end up doing the following:

- Setting **Show hidden files and folders**

- Unchecking **Hide file extensions for known file types**

- Unchecking **Hide protected operating system files (Recommended)**

I also find the option **Display compressed files and folders with alternate color** very useful.

Use Windows Explorer's **View** menu to change to the **Details** display (if not already selected). Then you can use the **Like Current Folder** button, seen in Figure 2.20, to apply the same settings to all folders—there's nothing more annoying than turning on hidden files only to find your choice applied to just one folder!

Hardware Support

It's well known that Windows 2000 now supports the much needed Plug and Play (PnP) capability we first saw with Windows 95, and it comes with enhanced reliability. Thankfully, this makes the job of adding new hardware much easier for both novice users and seasoned administrators alike since the process is now often as simple as Windows detecting the correct device and automatically installing the correct driver for it. Together with support for digital signatures to verify that the driver has been tested by Microsoft (as covered in the System Reliability section) hardware support has become much easier.

Other enhancements include support for Universal Serial Bus (USB) devices, Firewire, and Infrared, which means that Windows 2000 supports today's more advanced technologies to provide a variety of hardware solutions.

> **NOTE**
>
> The easy to use PnP capabilities of Windows 2000 make it an immediate choice for traveling businesspeople who know little about configuring computing devices, have no time or patience to configure computer devices and hardware, and understandably enough simply want to use their laptop without worrying about such issues.

Wizards and Help

Windows 2000 is aimed to achieve maximum productivity from both users and administrators, and two significant changes in this version of the operating system are the widespread use of wizards and a comprehensive online Help system.

Today's computer users are becoming more computer literate and often have a good idea of how to maintain and configure their own computers. It's more unusual these days for end users to contact the IT Department for help with simple operations and minor configuration changes. And the Help Desk Manager can afford to have less highly trained personnel to offer first level support because of the easy to use configuration tools and user-friendly interfaces that offer sensible defaults in times of doubt.

Wizards

Windows 2000 abounds with wizards that guide you through setting up and configuring software and hardware. For the most part, they are intuitive to use, provide adequate information with sensible defaults, and summarize your options and choices at the end before you commit yourself to making those choices.

Most wizards have alternative, manual methods to do the same job, which better suits the more advanced administrator. Some of the most commonly used wizards in Windows include the Add New Hardware Wizard, the Configure your Server Wizard, the Internet Connection Wizard (for Internet Explorer connection options), and the Network Connection Wizard.

Despite personally finding some of these wizards annoying when I would prefer an easy to find single property page for the configuration options I know I want, I have to admit that the only time I've had a homeworker successfully create a VPN (virtual private network) connection on the first attempt has been with the Windows 2000 Network Connection Wizard. That is certainly an improvement on methodically talking through each configuration option and setting in Windows 9*x* and Windows NT4! So there's no doubt these wizards do help with ease of use and a quick productivity level.

Another useful wizard is the Hardware Troubleshooter, which is a kind of hybrid of wizard and online Help. Each device has a status display to indicate whether Windows 2000 thinks it is working properly—although any device problems would also be flagged in the Event System Log and in Device Manager. Figure 2.21 shows the report on a network card that Windows 2000 detects to be working normally.

Figure 2.21 Example of Device Status

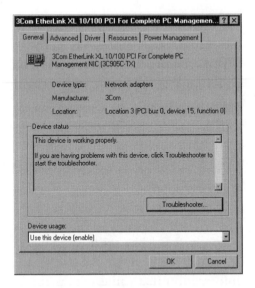

If your device isn't detected as healthy, or if you don't believe the status is correct, you can click the Troubleshooter button to launch the Hardware Troubleshooter, as shown in Figure 2.22.

Figure 2.22 Hardware Troubleshooter Being Used to Help Diagnose and Remedy Problems with the Network Adapter

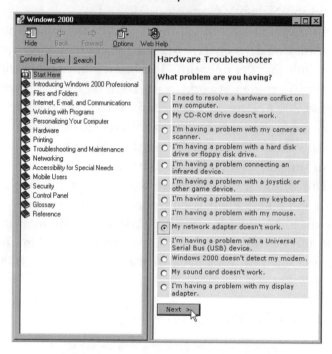

Select the relevant problem (for example, "My network adapter doesn't work.") and click **Next**. You'll be presented with more choices and/or more information to help diagnose the problem and suggest things to check. Effectively it's a graphical user flow chart of troubleshooting questions with relevant suggestions and information. Thankfully, they include a pass option: "I want to skip this step and try something else." You'll notice that the left pane includes traditional Help-style information that you can browse through by topic, or use the Search and Index facilities.

Help

One of the steepest learning curves I had with Windows 2000 was remembering that the online Help was actually very helpful! I had gotten used to the rather sparse and out of date information that came with previous versions of the operating system and quite simply got out of the habit of using it. Instead I would turn immediately to other resources, such as TechNet, the Resource Kits, and Microsoft's site. However, being able to use these external resources isn't always within the capabilities or experience of end users.

Now the online Help in Windows 2000 lives up to its name. It's been completely revamped with easy to find and easy to digest information on just the options and features you're interested in. It offers different levels of information too—for example, the more verbose theoretical explanation, and step-by-step "How To:" instructions that can launch the relevant program or utility for you so you can see and work with both side-by-side. For those with access to Microsoft's Web site it also offers links where relevant, and the end of each topic has a Related Topics link.

I think the new-style Help and mass of useful information it contains are a vast improvement in Windows 2000. My only complaint would be that it often suffers from the same limitations and restrictions of all hypertext documentation in that it's often easy to get lost and sometimes annoying to discover the information you want is scattered across multiple pages and sections in the attempt to provide small chunks of modular information at a time. Easily accessible help also comes in the form of context-sensitive Help within dialog boxes and tooltips.

Context-Sensitive Help

A quick explanation is available for each and every dialog box option (both ones you can change and display only boxes). Make full use of these when viewing and changing options you are not sure about. To use the context-sensitive Help, either use the **question mark** in the upper-right corner of the dialog box and then click the option, or right-click the option and then select **What's This?**.

Tooltip Sensitive Help

If you leave your cursor over a menu item that has a tooltip, you will see displayed a short and concise explanation of the item the cursor is currently hovering over (the item doesn't need to be selected). The idea is that if you're slow to actually select an option, you must be hesitant for a reason—is it the right option you need? The tooltip aims to provide enough information to determine whether you've about to select the right item.

For example, recently loaded Documents appear on the desktop under **Start | Documents**, which makes it easy to reload a document you have edited recently. But what if you had two different versions of the file (for example a local one and a centrally stored version) and weren't sure which version you had edited last. When you load the document from Start, Documents, which version are you loading?

It's impossible to tell from the name alone. But the tooltip for each document will display the location of the file. In the example in Figure 2.23, we can quickly see that our document was last edited on a network share and not, for example, locally under My Documents (or similar).

Figure 2.23 Tooltip Displaying the Location of a Recently Edited Document

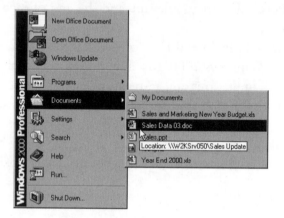

Other tooltips describe the function of the program—for example, if you have forgotten which Control Panel applet to use to specify environment variables, pass the mouse over the Control Panel applets you think are good contenders, and the tooltip for System will display "Provides system information and changes environment settings," which saves you from loading different applets and checking all the property pages until you find the one you want. You may also find tooltips particularly useful for those small tray icons—for example, the time display tooltip tells you today's date, a network adapter's tooltip tells you its transfer rate, and the battery icon tooltip on laptops immediately indicates how much power you have left.

Walkthrough: Configuring Local Group Policy

This example will take you through the steps of configuring Windows 2000 Professional such that it has the following settings:

- Automatic lockout of an account after four attempts
- Auditing turned on for failed logon attempts
- Last username not displayed in logon box
- Welcome Screen not displayed
- Access to Windows Update disabled
- A default screen saver set

1. To load Local Group Policy: Select **Start | Run** and type in **gpedit.msc,** which should load Group Policy in a MMC snap-in with Local Computer Policy showing at the root.

2. To set the account lockout settings: Expand **Computer Configuration** and then move through **Windows Settings | Security Settings | Account Lockout Policy**. In the right-hand results pane you should now see three possible policies, as shown in Figure 2.24.

Figure 2.24 Locating Account Lockout Policy in the Local Group Policy

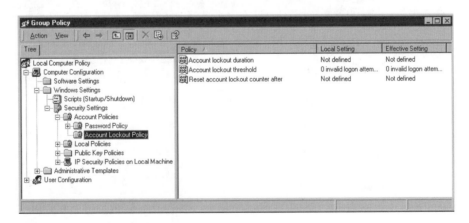

3. Double-click **Account lockout threshold** in the right pane, and set the number to be **4**. Click **OK** to save this setting. You will notice that it's

suggested you also change the other two options (Account lockout duration and Reset account lockout counter after), as shown in Figure 2.25. Because you don't want to have to unlock accounts manually (unless it's an emergency), click **OK** to accept the suggested changes. Note that if you want to use these options but with different values from the default of 30 minutes, you would have to select Cancel and then select both separately to set the values you want to use.

Figure 2.25 Suggested Settings After Setting Account Lockout Threshold

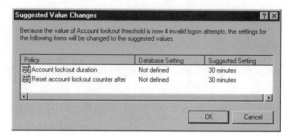

4. To turn on Auditing for failed login attempts: Expand **Local Policies | Audit Policy**. In the right pane, double-click **Audit account logon events**. Select the **Failure** setting, as shown in Figure 2.26.

Figure 2.26 Setting Group Policy Auditing On for Failed Logon Attempts

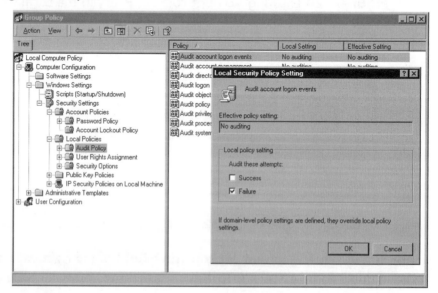

5. To disable displaying the last username on logon: Expand **Security Options** and in the right pane search for the policy called **Do not display last username in logon screen**, as shown in Figure 2.27. Double-click the policy to set it to **Enabled**.

Figure 2.27 Security Option to Not Show the Last Username in the Logon Screen

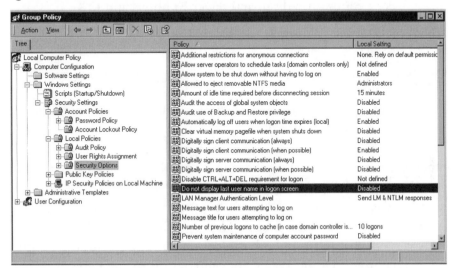

6. To disable the Welcome screen: Expand **Computer Configuration | Administrative Templates | System** and locate the policy **Don't display welcome screen at logon**. Double-click this to edit it, and select **Enabled** and **OK**. You will notice that the **Explain** tab for this policy tells you that users can still access the "Getting Started with Windows 2000" welcome screen by selecting it from the Start menu, or by typing **Welcome** in the Run dialog box.

7. To set a default screen saver: Expand **User Configuration | Administrative Templates | Control Panel | Display** and find the policy called **Screen saver executable name**. Double-click the policy to edit it, and set it to **Enabled** and type in **logon.scr**. You will notice the **Explain** tab on this policy provides more information—for example explaining that default screen savers reside in **%systemroot%System32** and have a .scr extension (which must be specified). You must specify the full path if your screen saver isn't in this default directory. You might now also want to set the screen saver to be password protected, which

you can do by selecting the **Next Policy** button and specifying **Enabled** and clicking **OK**, or if you don't want to password protect the screen saver simply click **OK**.

8. To disable Windows Update: Expand **User Configuration | Administrative Templates | Start Menu & Taskbar** and locate the policy called **Disable and remove links Windows Update**. Double-click on this to edit it, and select **Enabled** and **OK**.

The Group Policy settings you have changed will take effect immediately.

Summary

This chapter has looked at some of the important changes and options available on every Windows 2000 computer—whether Professional, Server, or Advanced Server. But many of these are particularly applicable to the desktop PC that is either not networked, in a workgroup, in an NT domain, or in a Novell environment. You don't have to run Windows 2000 Professional in an Active Directory environment before you can benefit from many new features and options.

In particular, we covered Local Group Policy, which allows you to configure many options that relate to both the computer settings and user settings. Whereas most literature on Group Policy concentrates on Active Directory GPOs, this chapter explained the full potential of configuring local GPOs and how these can be exported and imported between computers.

Security templates offer another way to control all these settings and, additionally, security settings such as registry keys, NTFS and share permissions, group membership, service configuration, and so on. You can use the templates supplied by Microsoft or define your own template and then compare it against the computer's settings. You can use the Security Configuration and Analysis snap-in to define your own template, compare a template's settings against the computer's settings, and configure the computer with template settings. More powerfully, you can use the **secedit** command to push these settings (which can be held centrally) onto multiple computers.

In the year since it was released, Windows 2000 has earned the respect for stability that Windows NT never had. This has been helped by device driver signing to help installers identify which drivers have been tested and approved by Microsoft, Windows File Protection to prevent an unreliable mixture of system files, and the integration of Service Packs into the operating system. These features help to provide a more stable system, but it's important to know how they work so you can make modifications if necessary to suit your requirements, and to understand any limitations.

Finally, this chapter covered some of the usability improvements in Windows 2000 that help to increase user productivity and efficiency, and reduce help desk calls. However, the new desktop changes were aimed at end users and not administrators so you may have to modify these to ensure you can also do your job easily and efficiently. Some of the new features and options are less obvious and may require user training to help users make the most of their desktop environment.

Solutions Fast Track

Using Local Group Policy

- ☑ Group Policy offers comprehensive settings that can affect the computer and user—such as computer startup/shutdown scripts, user logon/logoff scripts, password options, user rights and auditing, Internet Explorer configuration, desktop lock down features, and so on.

- ☑ Whereas Active Directory is needed to control and deploy Group Policy Objects (GPOs) centrally at a more sophisticated level, local GPOs can be used to good effect outside Active Directory.

- ☑ Although Active Directory GPOs are more powerful, they are also more complex—requiring more planning, more training, more testing. They are also more difficult to troubleshoot.

- ☑ Local GPOs cannot be filtered like Active Directory GPOs, but you can control whether their settings are effective or not by using NTFS permissions on the Group Policy directory **%systemroot%\System32\GroupPolicy**.

- ☑ **Local Security Policy** is available under **Administrative Tools**, which is a subset of **Local Group Policy**. For the complete local GPO settings you must either load **gpedit.msc** from the command line, or load the **Group Policy** snap-in into a custom MMC. Consider complementing these with the **Group Policy Reference** and **Gpresult** tool from the Resource Kit.

Security Configuration Using Templates

☑ Security Configuration Management uses templates and a security database to store, compare, analyze, import, and export various security configurations on a Windows 2000 computer.

☑ You can use either one or more Microsoft preconfigured templates, modify these, or specify your own to configure all the GPO settings, plus service configuration, registry options, group membership, file, and share permissions.

☑ You can use the command line tool, **Secedit** (which can be run from within startup and logon scripts, for example), to deploy and enforce GPO settings and security configurations—even if the settings (templates and security database) are stored centrally on a file server.

Improvements in System Reliability

☑ Device driver signing helps to eliminate problems that accompany badly written drivers. You can configure the computer to differentiate between drivers that have been tested and signed by Microsoft, and those that haven't. You can choose to warn the user before installing unsigned drivers, block unsigned drivers, or install them without warning.

☑ Windows File Protection (WFP), together with System File Checker (SFC), helps to eliminate DLL Hell by monitoring key operating and system files. Only new files that are digitally signed by Microsoft are allowed to overwrite the originally installed versions. An attempt to replace the original file by an unsigned version results in the original file being replaced by a copy in the Dllcache folder.

☑ There are several WFP settings you may want to bear in mind, such as changing the size of the cache folder and its location.

☑ Service Packs are now integrated into the operating system such that after installation stability will not rely on the administrator remembering to reapply the Service Pack after system changes. You can also slip-stream a Service Pack into an installation so that you don't have to install the base version and then apply the Service Pack separately.

Improvements in Usability

- ☑ Desktop changes in Windows 2000 may confuse those used to the desktop in previous versions. The default desktop configurations are aimed at the end user and not experienced administrators, so you may need to make some changes so you can work effectively and quickly.

- ☑ Some new options are hidden away and not obvious, such as expanded menu options and folder options.

- ☑ The number of Plug and Play (PnP) devices available makes configuring hardware devices much easier, with the list of available devices now extended to USB, Infrared, Firewire, and so on.

- ☑ Online Help and information are much improved with wizards, context-sensitive help and topic help, troubleshooters, and tooltips.

Frequently Asked Questions

The following Frequently Asked Questions, answered by the author of this book, are designed to both measure your understanding of the concepts presented in this chapter and to assist you with real-life implementation of these concepts. To have your questions about this chapter answered by the author, browse to **www.syngress.com/solutions** and click on the **"Ask the Author"** form.

Q: I've heard of No Override options for Group Policy. How can I set this for our local Group Policy so that when we upgrade to Active Directory, our local settings won't be lost?

A: The simple answer is, you can't. The No Override and Block Inheritance GPO options are only for Active Directory GPOs. For greater security, local Group Policy can always be superceded by Active Directory GPOs, such as those linked at the site, domain, or OU level. However, when you upgrade to Active Directory, you could export your local settings before setting up any Active Directory GPOs and then import them into an Active Directory GPO.

Q: I don't get the same security template names as yours—mine has a dedicadc.inf and no hisecuredc.inf. How come?

A: You're running a version of Windows 2000 that was upgraded from a beta version (where they used slightly different names for these templates). I am unsure exactly what (if any) security options changed between beta versions and the release version, but from experience I strongly advise you to start over and do a clean installation of Windows 2000 rather than risk running a version that has upgraded a now unsupported Beta configuration.

Q: I'm looking to upgrade my Windows 98 to Windows 2000 Professional. I frequently use a USB scanner. How can I check whether the scanner is supported by Windows 2000 before upgrading?

A: First point of call is Microsoft's Hardware Compatibility List (www.microsoft.com/hcl/default.asp). If it's not listed, try also Windows Update on http://corporate.windowsupdate.microsoft.com. Finally, try the manufacturer's Web site or contact them directly.

Q: Before installing a new device, I always like to update the Emergency Repair Disk first, but the usual RDISK command doesn't work. What's the equivalent in Windows 2000?

A: There is no command line equivalent in Windows 2000. Instead you create an Emergency Repair Disk using **Start | Programs | Accessories | System Tools | Backup**. Make sure your floppy disk is inserted, and click **Emergency Repair Disk** on the **Welcome** tab.

Q: How can I find out what drivers are loaded on a Windows 2000 computer?

A: If you have access to the Resource Kit, this contains a useful little command line utility called **Drivers**. When run it lists all the drivers currently running from the **%systemroot%\System32\Drivers** folder—which you can port to a file. Another alternative is to use Boot Logging, which lists in the file **%systemroot%\ntbtlog.txt** all the drivers Windows 2000 loads (or attempts to load) on bootup with their name and status (either **Loaded driver** or **Did not load driver**). You enable Boot Logging by pressing **F8** on startup when you see "For troubleshooting and advanced startup options for Windows 2000, press F8" and then selecting **Enable Boot Logging** from the **Windows 2000 Advanced Options Menu**.

Q: Where can I find some really simple explanations of how to drive the Windows 2000 desktop, such as setting up shortcuts, setting screen savers, customizing the toolbar, using the new Search utility, and so on?

A: You may find the following useful:

- *Step-by-Step Guide to Usability Improvements in Windows 2000 Professional*: www.microsoft.com/windows2000/techinfo/planning/client/ prousability.asp

- *MS Windows 2000 Professional Getting Started*: Chapter 4, "Windows Basics": www.microsoft.com/TechNet/win2000/win2kpro/manuals/ progs/pgsch04.asp

- "Personalizing Your Computer" from Windows 2000 Professional Help.

Chapter 3

Laptops

Solutions in this chapter:

- **Integrating Mobile Computing with the Corporate Network**

- **Securing Data Outside the Company Environment**

- **Mobile Maintenance and Troubleshooting**

☑ **Walkthrough: Using Offline Files**

☑ **Summary**

☑ **Solutions Fast Track**

☑ **Frequently Asked Questions**

Introduction

The need for computing resources to travel with us has become the norm rather than the exception. No longer the realm of traveling salesmen, laptops have become a necessity for the growing number of people who don't work in a single environment but rather have a virtual working environment that they take with them as they travel from site to site, or from the office to home. A laptop has to cater to a wide variety of people and tasks, essentially allowing mobile users to work effectively wherever they are.

When you think about it, that's a tough order. We still expect the same functionality, reliability, and security from laptops that we have from a corporate desktop—only squeezed into a smaller and lighter package that can function independent of any other device (including an external power source). Not only that, we also frequently require added flexibility and functionality that desktop computers don't need—such as additional hardware for backing up, printing, and scanning.

We also need laptops to be able to cope easily with the transition from being a stand-alone unit that's acting independently, to being connected with the corporate network, so it can benefit from company resources such as central servers and printers, and be able to share and synchronize data with coworkers. But most importantly, in order to be able to work effectively, we need to spend minimal time and effort on using and maintaining these computers. Laptops should be a tool to help you do your job, not become another job in itself.

There are some great innovations and features in Windows 2000 specifically aimed at mobile users, which no doubt explains why the laptop market was the first to enthusiastically embrace Windows 2000. In the past, many people used Windows 95 and Windows 98 on laptops for their ease of use (in particular, Plug and Play technology) but lamented the lack of security and stability that NT could provide. Windows 2000 resolves the Plug and Play issues and adds support for other new technologies such as hot pluggable devices that require minimal installation and configuration. It has an operating system that offers higher stability and better security than NT and adds additional features, which make using and supporting laptops a more trouble-free experience for everybody.

This chapter looks at some of the features that have helped to make Windows 2000 so popular on laptop computers. Of course, because these features are built into the base operating system, many of them can also be applied to standard workstations and servers running Windows 2000. For example, sometimes the distinction can become blurred between the computing needs of a corporate desktop computer, a laptop, and a home PC. Because Windows 2000 builds its features into the operating system, you can capitalize on this flexibility by applying and using the features that best suit your particular requirements on each computer.

This chapter concentrates on features that a mobile user will use and require from his or her computer—such as how to integrate different working environments (stand-alone and networked), how best to secure data, and what simple maintenance and troubleshooting utilities are available to keep the laptop up and running.

Integrating Mobile Computing with the Corporate Network

One of the major design challenges for mobile computing is in creating an automatic and consistent working environment. In reality, a corporate environment and a stand-alone environment are about as different as you can get, but that shouldn't be the concern of the laptop user. Business users don't care—and shouldn't have to care—how technology works "under the hood." They just want it to work with as little effort and expertise from themselves as possible so that they can get on with their job.

Fortunately, when you're using laptops with docking stations, Windows 2000 automatically creates two hardware profiles such that appropriate device drivers are automatically loaded when the computer it turned on according to whether it is *docked* or *undocked*. However, if the laptop is not being used with a docking station, or is not fully Plug and Play (PnP) compliant (that is, Windows 2000 cannot detect whether it's docked or not), you'll have to create a new hardware profile manually; using **Hardware Profiles** and **Device Manager** via the **Hardware** tab under **System Properties** to create two different hardware profiles that load up the devices in different environments.

When the laptop boots, the user has a choice of which hardware profile to choose, and/or to default to one after a timeout period. Figure 3.1 shows an example of using three manually created hardware profiles for a user's different working environments.

Thanks to PnP support in Windows 2000, a laptop that is used with a docking station may dynamically switch hardware profiles without having to be powered down. However, a manually created hardware profile requires a laptop to be restarted so that the user can select the hardware profile required (or a default is selected after a timeout).

Figure 3.1 Creating Hardware Profiles for Laptops without Docking Stations

Also thanks to Plug and Play, a number of devices and peripherals can easily be added to laptops (sometimes without powering down) without expert assistance from support personnel, so that users can add additional monitors for presentations, for example, or scanners for home use.

Whenever possible, software should be installed when the laptop is in the office environment, and tested for both network use and non-network use. If the laptop is for somebody who is fairly technically competent and who may need to install, uninstall, and configure software and PnP hardware when away from the corporate network, it is generally advisable to grant membership in the Power Users group on the laptop rather than give the user an Administrator account.

Power Users membership provides the user with the ability to install, uninstall, and configure software and PnP hardware if a device fails or if software needs to be installed away from the corporate network. An Administrator account should be granted only if the user needs to configure and install legacy (non-PnP) devices. If possible, to help ensure the stability of your laptops, grant only user membership, which restricts users from installing, uninstalling, or configuring software and devices.

Designing & Planning…

Strategies for Supporting Laptops

Network administrators usually have less control over the configuration of laptops, because users often require a dynamic system that can accommodate new devices and different configurations. Therefore, it's a good idea to think about the level of administrative control a laptop user should have and to weigh users' requests for control against the need to support standard and stable systems. You can use local Group Policy (covered in the previous chapter) on laptops to good effect by selectively enabling or disabling the elements you don't want users to configure or change. When configuring local Group Policy, don't forget to configure security-conscious settings for things like account lockouts, enforcing passwords, and so on.

Other tips for supporting laptop users includes ensuring that they have a regular and adequate backup routine—it's very easy to forget what you don't see! Also, consider documenting each laptop's configuration before handing over control to a user. One of the easiest ways to document Windows 2000 setup information is by exporting the System Information for each hardware profile. To do this, load the **Computer Management** MMC (Microsoft Management Console) and navigate to **System Tools | System Information**. Right-click and choose either the **Save As Text File** option or the **Save As System Information File** option.

Switching between Working Environments

There are a number of features that help users switch seamlessly between their different working environments. These include:

- Power management and preservation
- Offline folders and synchronizing data
- Dial–up access

Power Management and Preservation

Even if mobile users didn't have to install software or devices, chances are they would still need to consider their laptop's battery management. When a user is working at a desktop computer with a constant external power source, getting power to the computer is not a concern. In comparison, a laptop user who wants to use the computer when not attached to an external power supply has to contend with managing and maximizing battery consumption.

When needed, balancing the requirement for performance against necessary power conservation is always a tricky equation. Windows 2000 is particularly geared toward handling this type of situation with support for Advanced Configuration and Power Interface (ACPI) and Advanced Power Management (APM) technology. If either of these is being used, a laptop running Windows 2000 is able to manage its power system more efficiently in response to applications, device drivers, and user configuration options. And even if neither ACPI nor APM is supported, a user can still configure limited power management options for disks and monitors using the **Power Schemes** under **Control Panel**.

A laptop using power management may be able to take advantage of two additional power modes called Hibernate and Standby. Hibernate mode can be used to save the current system state (applications and network connections) to disk, and then power down. On a restart, although (by default) the user is prompted to enter his or her username and password, the existing state is reloaded so that the user is up and running again easily. This option is appropriate if the user will not need the computer resources for an extended period of time.

Standby mode is where the monitor, hard disk, and other hardware devices are put into a low power state, but without actually saving the information or powering completely down. Note that because the existing state is not saved to disk, the laptop is vulnerable to data loss if the computer suffers a power shortage.

Figure 3.2 shows an example of a laptop that supports both Hibernate and Standby modes, so that when the user asks to shut down, he or she has the usual choices of logging off, shutting down, or restarting, but also of putting the laptop into Standby or Hibernate.

WARNING

Some environments require that laptops be turned off for security reasons—for example on airlines, in hospitals, and at military sites. Although a laptop may look as if it is turned off when in Hibernate or Standby mode, that is *not* the same as being turned off, and you will not be able to guarantee that the computer will not reactivate.

Figure 3.2 Shutdown Options with Standby or Hibernate

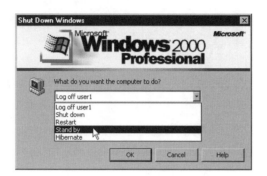

Configuring and Installing ACPI/APM

ACPI is the newer "OnNow" design initiative for power management, giving the operating system complete control of the power being used by devices. APM is the older implementation, in which the Basic Input/Output System (BIOS), rather than the operating system, is responsible for controlling power management and monitoring battery status. APM has several limitations over the newer ACPI, including devices being turned off at inappropriate times, unknown suspend states, inconsistent configuration interfaces, being restricted to detecting activity for devices that reside on the motherboard, and not supporting multiprocessor systems.

BIOS versions are everything when it comes to supporting ACPI and APM. When Windows 2000 is first installed, it checks the BIOS to see what it can support and then installs the appropriate Hardware Abstraction Level (HAL).

If ACPI is supported and compliant with Windows 2000, you can make the most of power management features in Windows 2000. To confirm that support for ACPI has been installed and detected, check for the presence of **Microsoft ACPI-Compliant System** under the list of **System devices** in **Device Manager**. Figure 3.3 shows an example of a laptop with ACPI support.

If the BIOS supports ACPI but Windows 2000 didn't install support for it, the version might not be supported, in which case it needs to be upgraded before you can use ACPI with Windows 2000 (contact the BIOS manufacturer for an upgrade). However, after flashing a new BIOS version onto your computer, you'll have to reinstall Windows 2000—so it's better to confirm the version before installation! You can confirm BIOS ACPI compatibility with Windows 2000 with the Microsoft Windows Hardware Compatibility List (HCL) or with the BIOS manufacturer.

Figure 3.3 Device Manager Showing ACPI Devices

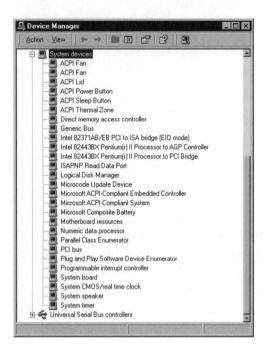

Windows 2000 also checks for APM BIOS compatibility at the time of installation. APM must be enabled in the BIOS before setup is run. You can use the Windows 2000 Support Tool, **Apmstat.exe**, to check APM BIOS compatibility. To confirm APM support has been installed, check for the presence of **NT Apm/Legacy Support** in **Device Manager** after enabling **View | Show hidden devices**.

You should then be able to use the power management features in Windows 2000, though without the same degree of reliability and control as you would have if using ACPI (for example, to bring the computer out of a suspended mode requires activity from the keyboard or mouse, so it wouldn't detect an incoming network connection or the automatic firing up of maintenance tasks such as backup).

Configuring Power Options

Irrespective of whether you have ACPI or APM support, you should enable and configure **Power Options** under the **Control Panel**. This includes the following:

- Choosing/Configuring a power scheme

- Enabling Hibernate mode and the battery status indicator

- Configuring the power button setting

- Setting a battery alarm

In comparison with a standard desktop or server computer, a laptop has two different settings for each power scheme, which are divided into **Plugged in** and **When running on batteries**. Although the default power scheme, even on laptops, is **Home/Office Desk**, more appropriate power schemes are **Portable/ Laptop**, **Presentation**, and **Max Battery**. You can select one of these predefined schemes or create your own. The exact settings for each depend on what your computer can support—for example, you do not see settings for Hibernate if your laptop is not configured to support hibernation. Figure 3.4 shows the settings on a laptop configured for the **Max Battery** scheme, which is designed to prolong battery consumption at the expense of computing efficiency and performance.

Figure 3.4 Power Schemes Configured for Max Battery

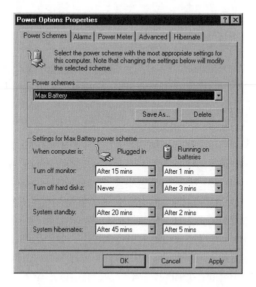

Hibernate mode is disabled by default and must be enabled through the **Hibernate** tab under **Power Options** (if the **Hibernate** tab is not displayed, this feature is not supported on the computer's hardware). Because hibernation requires the current state of the system to be written to disk, it uses as much free disk space as you have RAM. Fortunately, when you set this option, the amount of free disk available and the disk space required are displayed in the dialog box, as shown in Figure 3.5 (here, on a laptop with 128 MB RAM).

Figure 3.5 Setting Hibernate Support on a Laptop

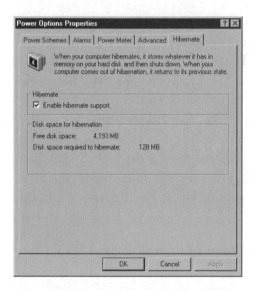

When the laptop is using Standby, by default it prompts the user to log back in when restarting from Standby. However, you can change this by clearing the **Prompt for password when computer goes off standby** on the **Advanced** tab under **Power Option Properties**, as shown in Figure 3.6.

Note that the **Power buttons** option in Figure 3.6 allows you to select **Power Off**, **Standby**, or **Hibernate** for when you close the lid, press the Power button, or press the Sleep button, so that the laptop can automatically go into one of these modes. However, the Power Off option is not the same as using the **Shutdown** command, which gracefully shuts down the laptop by flushing cached data to disk and prompting you to save any open documents—in comparison, the Power Off option is literally the same as pulling the power, without saving any data or closing gracefully, and so is not recommended. However, on a non-ACPI or –APM enabled laptop, Power Off may be the only option available, and you must remember to use the **Shutdown** command.

Battery monitoring and management are only available on ACPI- or APM-enabled laptops when your computer is using a Smart Battery subsystem interface or a Control Method Battery (CMBatt) interface. By enabling the **Always show icon on the taskbar** option on the **Advanced** tab under **Power Options**, users can easily monitor the current battery level. When they leave the cursor over the power meter on the taskbar, a tooltip displays the amount of battery power remaining. They can also double-click the power meter to see more information, for example, whether a second battery pack is being used. Figure 3.7 shows information from the power meter icon, which tells the user that 71 percent of the batter power remains, and the second battery is not inserted.

Figure 3.6 Advanced Power Options

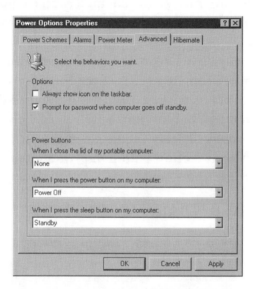

Figure 3.7 Power Meter Information from the Taskbar

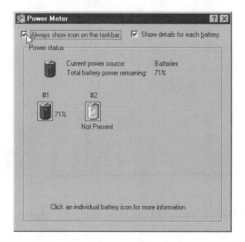

> **NOTE**
>
> Single-click the power meter icon in the taskbar, and you can easily toggle between the different power schemes.

Additionally, you can set alarms for low battery and critical battery levels that you define. When these are reached, the computer can trigger a visual or audible alarm, execute a program, or change the power state (to Standby, Hibernate, or Shutdown).

For example, you may define a low battery alarm to display a message but not change the power mode when 10 percent of the battery power remains. Your critical battery alarm could be triggered when 3 percent of the battery power remains, displaying a message but this time automatically changing the power mode to Standby to conserve energy. Figure 3.8 shows an example of alarm settings, in which each **Alarm Action** button displays another dialog box where you can define the settings you want.

Figure 3.8 Configuring Low Battery Alarm Actions

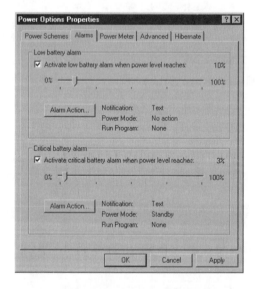

Offline Files and Synchronizing Data

Combining the concepts and strengths of Internet Explorer's Offline Favorites and Briefcase from previous incarnations, **Offline Files** and **Synchronization**

Manager in Windows 2000 offer a great way to manage data when the computer is no longer connected to a resource—whether it's a network server or a Web site.

Offline Files simply caches data on the local drive so it can be accessed when offline. When the computer is reconnected, Offline Files and Folders synchronizes the files stored on the local drive with the files on the network. If there are any version conflicts, you'll be prompted for which one to keep.

When the computer is offline, files and folders appear in the same directory as they did online, which makes them easy to find. Such offline resources are visually indicated with roundtrip arrows in their bottom-left corner. Figure 3.9 shows an example of making the **May Data** folder available offline, so that data in this folder, together with the **Forecasts Year End 2001** folder, will be available even when the computer isn't connected to the network.

Figure 3.9 Making Files and Folders Available Offline

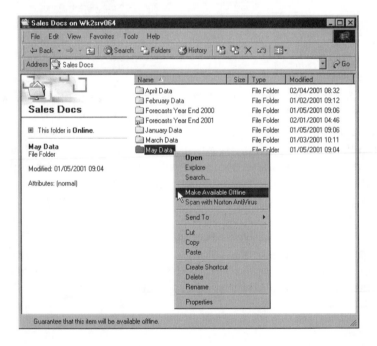

As you can see from Figure 3.9, making a file or folder available offline with Windows 2000 Professional is as simple as right-clicking it when connected to the resource, and selecting **Make Available Offline**. The first time you do this, you'll see the Offline Wizard prompting you for settings that include whether you want notice reminders on the task bar about the online/offline status, and whether to create a shortcut on the desktop (see Figure 3.10). You'll also be prompted for when to synchronize data (whenever logging on/off, or manually,) and to enter network credentials (username and password) if these are required for the network resource.

Figure 3.10 The Offline Files Wizard

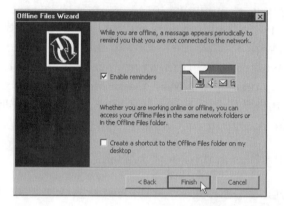

NOTE

Whereas users can select which drives, folders, and files they want to use offline, network administrators can also set *caching permissions* on Windows 2000 network shares. As we shall see in the following chapter, the share's **Caching Settings** can be set to prevent a user from making any data within the share available for offline use (for example, on sensitive data), or automatic caching options could be set so that users didn't have to set anything on their laptops. The default network share Caching Settings on a Windows 2000 shared resource are to allow caching and to allow users to set their own caching choices.

If you right-click a drive, folder, or file and the **Make Available Offline** option is not available, the network share caching permissions have been set centrally by the network administrator.

In a similar way, you can make Web content available offline with Internet Explorer by adding the current page to your Favorites list, and selecting the **Make Available Offline** option, as shown in Figure 3.11.

When setting up Web content for offline use, clicking on the **Customize** button loads the Offline Favorite Wizard. which prompts you to set the level you want to make available, as shown in Figure 3.12. For example, if you need only the information on one page, you don't need to download further levels, and you can conserve disk space and make your synchronization quicker.

Figure 3.11 Making Web Content Available Offline with Favorites

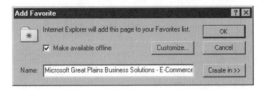

Figure 3.12 Configuring the Amount of Web Data to Make Available Offline

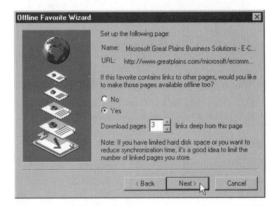

When synchronizing Web content, you can define a schedule to do this automatically, for example, at a time when the site is less likely to be busy, and when your computer is otherwise idle. You'll be prompted to enter log-on credentials, if required, on the Web site—just as you were prompted for network credentials on network resources. But for both types of Offline resources, you can use the **Synchronization** utility under **Accessories** (or from Windows Explorer's **Tools** menu) to update manually any type of data that's marked for synchronization, as well as configure it to synchronize automatically.

Configuring Synchronization

Load **Synchronization** and you'll see a list of the items you've marked to make available offline. By default, they will all be included, but you can deselect items when you manually synchronize, as shown in Figure 3.13, in which one of the Web offline items has been deselected.

Figure 3.13 Selecting Items to Synchronize

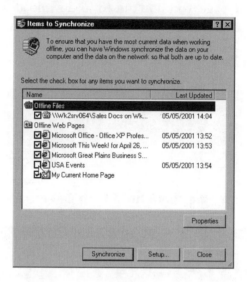

Click the **Synchronize** button, and the computer attempts to synchronize with the items selected. If this requires a dialup connection to succeed, you'll automatically be prompted to do this.

When **Offline Files** is selected (as in Figure 3.13), the **Properties** button shows the files currently stored in the offline cache. You see the name and type of file, its synchronization status, whether it is currently available, its access permissions, whether the source is currently available (online or offline), its location (share or URL), the size of the file, and when it was last modified. The **Properties** button, when an individual item is selected, shows you that item's synchronization status, such as when it was last synchronized, its download size, and any synchronization errors. You are also able to configure its schedule and download settings.

The **Setup** button is used to configure synchronization for each connection type (for example, your local area network [LAN] connection, your Internet Service Provider [ISP] dialup connection, and your company virtual private network [VPN] server), with tabs for **Logon/Logoff**, **On Idle**, and **Scheduled**. Figure 3.14 shows how only the company network resources should be synchronized when using the VPN connection—it wouldn't make sense for Web content to be updated with this connection.

As you can see in Figure 3.14, the **Logon/Logoff** tab allows you select which items you want synchronized automatically whenever you log on or log off, and you can choose to be prompted to do this rather than making it automatic. For example, if you were about to take the laptop off the company network, it would make sense to synchronize before logging off. If you had been working offline and were about to reconnect to the company network, it would make sense to synchronize on logon.

Figure 3.14 Setting Synchronization Settings for Each Connection

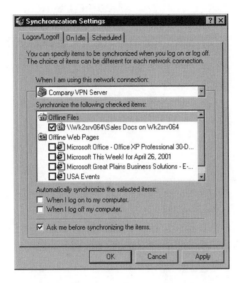

The **On Idle** tab allows you to set synchronization to occur when the computer is idle. Again, you can configure which items to synchronize depending on the connection being used. The **Advanced** button has settings for defining idle time, if using that option (the default is 15 minutes), whether and how often to repeat synchronization automatically at regular intervals when the computer is idle (the default is every hour), and finally, whether to prevent synchronization when running on battery power.

The **Schedule** tab allows you to change and define automatic synchronization, using the Scheduled Synchronization Wizard. This steps you through setting a schedule for each connection (with a starting time and date), along with how often the synchronization should occur (daily, weekdays, or after a defined number of days). Once you have defined your basic schedule, you can then refine options to be more sympathetic to a laptop with settings specifically aimed at using an internal power supply. Figure 3.15 shows these options, available on the **Settings** tab.

When synchronizing files, the status display includes a **Details** button, which when selected, expands the status to show each item being synchronized and its progress, as shown in Figure 3.16. If a particular item is taking too long to synchronize and you want to cancel it, highlight it and click the **Skip** button. Clicking the **Stop** button stops all current synchronization. When no changes are detected (as shown on two items in Figure 3.16), no synchronization of data occurs, which prevents needless data transfers.

Figure 3.15 Defining Settings for a Scheduled Synchronization

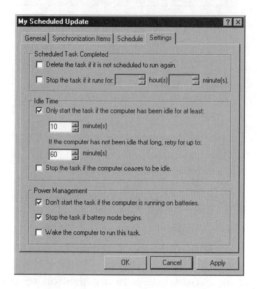

Figure 3.16 Synchronizing Data

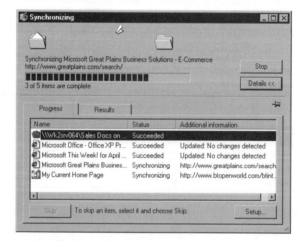

Configuring the Offline Files Folder

We've seen how the Offline Properties show an administrator the details of the Offline Files folder. You can actually delete individual files directly from this hidden folder, but you'll be prompted to confirm this with the special **Confirm File Delete** dialog box, shown in Figure 3.17.

Figure 3.17 The Confirm File Delete Prompt

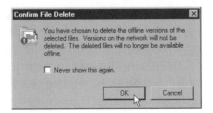

Access to the hidden Offline Files folder is available through the **Synchronization** tool, but you'll notice it doesn't let you configure its size or location. Another method of deleting offline files that does let you configure its size, is through Windows Explorer's **Tools** menu, under **Folder Options**, on the **Offline Files** tab. This dialog box (shown in Figure 3.18) allows you to configure Offline Files settings and set the size of the Cache folder.

Figure 3.18 Offline Folder Settings

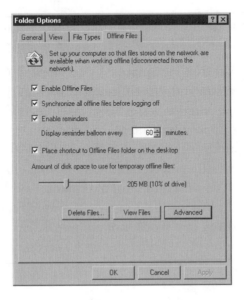

The **Delete Files** button actually takes you to a view of each folder rather than each file, letting you conveniently delete all the offline files stored in individual folders. Many unnecessarily stored offline files are temporary files, and this option gives you the choice of just deleting all the temporary files, or deleting all the files in the folder.

NOTE

The Offline Files folder is shared among all the users on the computer. This doesn't present a security risk when the Offline Files folder resides on an NT File System (NTFS) volume, since files stored there retain their NTFS permissions. If a user is no longer working on that computer, you could delete any files he or she used, in order to make more space available for the computer's other users. However, because the Offline Cache works on the First In, First Out (FIFO) principle, these files would be discarded eventually anyway.

If you're confident you don't want to keep any cached files (including any modified offline files), and want to start with a completely clean Offline Files cache, you can do this by reinitializing the Offline Files cache. To do this, press **Ctrl+Shift** while clicking the **Delete Files** button. You'll be asked to confirm and then reboot the PC.

Configuring Offline Files with Local Group Policy

There are a number of configuration options you can use with Local Group Policy, under **Administrative Templates | Network | Offline Files** for both **Computer Configuration** and **User Configuration**. When both are used and conflict, the Computer Configuration settings take precedence. Figure 3.19 displays the ones available under Computer Configuration.

Note that these options may apply to a Windows 2000 server if you are controlling Offline Files centrally (covered in the following chapter).

As well as *enable* and *disable* types of options, most Local Group Policy options for Offline Files are ones that can be configured through the dialog boxes we have already seen. However, one worth noting here is the **Files not cached** option. By default, Windows 2000 does not cache certain files, those with the following extensions:

- .slm (Microsoft Source Library Management)

- .mdb (Microsoft Access database)

- .ldb (Microsoft Access security)

- .mdw (Microsoft Access Workgroup)

- .pst (Microsoft Outlook personal folder)

- .db? (Generic database)

Figure 3.19 The Offline Files Group Policy Options

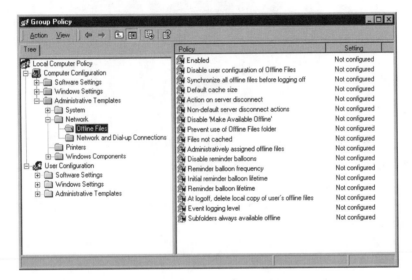

You can use the **Files not cached** option to define your own file extensions that identify files you do not want to be cached. However, configuring this policy will overwrite the default filters, so if you want to keep the default filters and add your own, you need to define all the default filters as well as your own in this policy. Each extension should be defined in the policy, separated by a semi-colon. Figure 3.20 shows an example of using all the default Microsoft Access filters, plus .tmp and .bak files.

Another Group Policy option worth noting is the **Event logging detail**. By default, only corrupted offline files are logged to the Event Log, but this group policy allows you to record other events, such as when the server goes offline and back online, and when a client is offline.

Figure 3.20 Using the Files Not Cached Local Group Policy

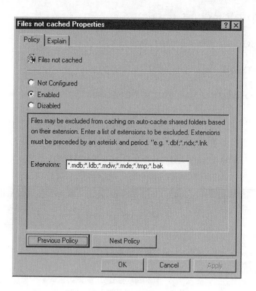

Changing the Offline Files Folder Location

You might have noticed one missing configuration option: how to change the location of the Offline Files folder. Most laptop users use a single partition, and so they have no need to do this. But if you've partitioned your laptop disk, and an alternative partition to the one that holds your operating system has much more free disk space, it would make sense to move the Offline Files cache to where more disk space is available.

By default, the Offline Files cache location is **%systemroot%\csc** (the *csc* stands for Client Side Caching). You can change the location (but not the name or the size) with the **Cachemov.exe** utility from the Windows 2000 Resource Kit.

When you first run this utility, it checks to make sure you have more than one available partition, and that you have local administrative rights. You'll be prompted to select an alternative location, and it would be prudent to choose one that's both formatted with the Windows NT file system (NTFS) and has plenty of disk space. The utility displays its progress as it disables offline files, copies the files and security settings, re-enables offline files, and deletes the old cache. Figure 3.21 shows the **Offline Files Cache Mover** utility.

Since the only input required is the alternative drive location, this utility also works unattended using the command **cachemov –unattend <drive>:** (for example: **cachemov –unattend D:**). Only when used in unattend mode will it write its success or failure to the Application log—but note that it doesn't record to which drive the cache was moved.

Figure 3.21 The Offline Files Cache Mover Utility

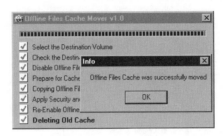

Dialup Access

The new **Network Connection Wizard** in Windows 2000 makes it easy for mobile users to connect to the Internet and use a dial-up connection as their means of keeping in touch with coworkers, sharing and retrieving data over the company network, sending and receiving e-mail, and having Web and newsgroup access.

Thanks once again to PnP, most modems are auto-detected and now very easy to install and use. The Network Connection Wizard guides a user through setting up dial-up access if this is not already configured. This should be sufficient for users to get the standard Web access through their local ISP.

If users want to use their dial-up connections for other services, such as connecting to your company remote access server (RAS) or VPN server, or accepting limited incoming connections, they can simply use **Add Network Connection** under **Start | Settings | Network and Dial-up Connection**, which will guide them through configuring the network type they need. Figure 3.22 shows the initial choices the Network Connection Wizard presents.

Of particular relevance is the ease of creating a VPN connection. Thanks to VPN support now being built into the operating system and this Network Connection Wizard, it's very easy for users to configure a VPN connection for themselves with minimal assistance from support staff.

For example, a VPN connection prompts for the underlying ISP connection to be used, as shown in Figure 3.23. Previously, making a VPN connection was a two-step manual process that required the user to connect to the ISP first and then connect the VPN connection.

Figure 3.22 The Network Connection Wizard

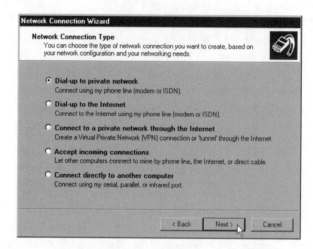

Figure 3.23 Automating the Underlying Connection for VPN Access

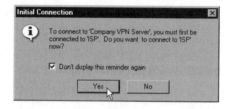

NOTE

Chapter 9 covers how to set up and configure Windows 2000 remote access servers and connection configurations for both dial-up and VPN.

Once connected, the user will be authenticated onto the company network, and if allowed remote access permission, will be able to use company network resources just as if he or she were connected in the office—only with a slower transfer rate. Users could combine periodic remote connections with synchronizing their Offline Files.

Securing Data Outside the Company Environment

Securing data on portable computers that leave the company network is certainly more difficult than securing it within your company infrastructure, where you can physically protect the computer, and monitor company boundaries with routers and firewalls. Laptops, by virtue of being portable and expensive, are very easy and attractive prey to thieves.

Unfortunately, they are also incredibly susceptible to being simply forgotten and left behind on public transport, in hotels, and in meeting rooms. Whereas the cost of downtime and replacing the computer is regrettable but expendable, it's much harder to put a cost on confidential information falling into the wrong hands. Typically many laptops carry such confidential information, whether by traveling salesmen with customer information and company sales figures, or managers with confidential company business information, or technical staff with prototypes and source code.

Securing data, especially on laptops, has been a big problem of late. With physical access to the hard drive (for example, by putting it into another computer or booting from floppy or CD to install a new copy of the operating system), you can use a new local administrator account to take ownership of any files on the disk, and thus gain access to original NTFS-protected files. For this reason, Jaz drives are even more susceptible, and unfortunately, as far as security is concerned, they are more portable and vulnerable than laptops.

There have been various third-party utilities available on the market to encrypt data, but they usually require the user to remember to encrypt the data manually and supply a password to decrypt the data. These utilities not only have a higher overhead in terms of monetary and support costs, but are often invasive and not seamlessly integrated with a user's working environment.

Thankfully, the Encrypting File System (EFS) in Windows 2000 addresses these problems. Provided that the drive has been formatted with Windows 2000 NTFS, you can use the new **Encrypt** attribute to protect data such that only the original user and a recovery agent (typically the local administrator outside an Active Directory environment) can access it.

If another version of the operating system were loaded onto the computer, or if the disk were loaded into another computer, the new administrator would not be able to access a file that was encrypted with the original operating system. He would be able to see the file and its encrypted attribute, but not view its contents, move it, copy it, rename it, or change the encrypt attribute—he would see an Access Denied message.

He would, however, still be able to delete the file. Encrypting grants no protection against deletion. NTFS permissions protect the file such that *other users* cannot delete it—but in the case of a new operating system version being installed, this would not protect the file from deletion by a new administrator, who could simply take ownership of the file, grant himself Full Control and delete it. But he wouldn't be able to read its contents first.

EFS works with a public/private key mechanism that safeguards the integrity of data and allows for seamless and quick encryption and decryption. When a computer has no trusted certificate authority (CA), users are automatically granted a self-signed certificate (self-signed by the operating system) when they first encrypt a file. Because EFS doesn't let you encrypt a file without at least one EFS recovery agent, it also creates an EFS recovery certificate. Only the original user and the recovery agent (the person who holds the recovery certificate—by default the local administrator outside Active Directory) is able to decrypt the encrypted data.

Chapter 7 discusses in more detail the installation and configuring of Certificate Services for user/computer certificates, when they're used with Web authentication and encryption, and the Internet Protocol Security (IPSec) protocol. However, you can use EFS automatically without having to configure anything additional, which means you can take advantage of this high security feature with minimal administrative overhead.

Configuring & Implementing…

Protection against Inaccessible Files

The Encrypting File System (EFS) is another good reason you shouldn't let a user log in with the local administrator account on a laptop. Only the local administrator has access to the EFS recovery certificate. If that certificate were to be deleted without a backup, it's possible to have inaccessible files on the computer if the user encrypted files and then their account was removed.

Whenever possible, folders rather than files should be configured for encryption—so that files within the directory will automatically be

Continued

encrypted. Because encryption is native to the operating system, programs run by the same user should not have a problem with encrypted files.

For additional security, you should look to encrypt a user's My Documents folder, along with all contents, any temporary directories, and any printer spool files. System files cannot be encrypted (to protect the system from becoming inoperable), and any folder that contains a system file is not able to be encrypted. In the normal course of events, you would usually keep system files away from user files, so this shouldn't be a problem. What might be more of a problem, however, is juggling between compressing and encrypting folders. You cannot do both to the same folder.

Encrypting Folders and Files

It's incredibly simple to encrypt a file or folder. Simply right-click it and select **Properties**, then click the **Advanced** button and you'll see the following options for compressing or encrypting (Figure 3.24).

Figure 3.24 Setting Encryption on a Folder

Note that the dialog box in Figure 3.24 warns you you'll be asked whether to apply the Encrypt attribute to all subfolders and files—which is usually advisable. You can change this encryption attribute in exactly the same way, by deselecting the check in the **Encrypt contents to secure data** check box.

Additionally, you can use the **Cipher** command line utility to set the Encrypt and Decrypt attribute on multiple files and folders. Used by itself without parameters, it will display the encryption state of the current directory and any files it contains. Use **Cipher /?** to see a full list of available command-line switches.

Limitations and Considerations When Using EFS

We've already covered a few caveats for using EFS, one of the most important being that you are unable to both compress and encrypt a file or folder. Other restrictions and considerations that should be noted include the following:

- Only files and folders on Windows 2000 NTFS volumes can be encrypted. If users copy their EFS files to another disk, they must be formatted with NTFSv5 to keep the Encrypt attribute.

- Decryption is possible only for the original user and a recovery agent. Remember that a user will have a different security identifier (SID) when logging on locally than when logging on to an NT4 domain—and as such, encrypted files may be inaccessible.

- EFS files copied across the network transfer as clear text, unless additional mechanisms such as IPSec or Point-to-Point Tunneling Protocol (PPTP) are used to protect them.

- Shared files should not be encrypted because only the original user (and administrator) will be able to read them.

- Drag-and-drop should not be used with encrypted files—cut and paste instead to ensure the Encrypt attribute is not lost.

Disabling EFS

Most of the time, the benefits of EFS far outweigh any disadvantages. However, it is possible for files to become permanently inaccessible with EFS (if there are problems with the recovery agent), or you may find the need to share files is more important than the security EFS offers, or that users inappropriately encrypt files.

You can disable EFS in one of two ways. In an Active Directory environment, you configure an empty EFS policy and assign this to the computers on which you want to disable EFS. On PCs outside Active Directory, you can effectively do the same thing, but you'll have to configure this individually at each PC.

Because encrypting a file requires the presence of at least one EFS recovery agent, if you remove that recovery agent (the local administrator's EFS recovery certificate), users will no longer be able to encrypt files. When they try to, they'll see an error message similar to Figure 3.25 and have to cancel the request to encrypt the file.

Figure 3.25 Error When EFS Is Disabled

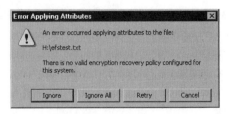

Rather than just deleting the local administrator's recovery certificate, however, it would be prudent, to export it before deleting it, just in case there are any encrypted files on the computer. You can then import the certificate to decrypt them. You do all this by loading the Local Group Policy editor (**gpedit.msc**) and navigating to **Computer Configuration | Windows Settings | Security Settings | Public Key Policies | Encrypted Data Recovery Agents**; there you should see the local administrator's recovery certificate (identified by the Intended Purposes displaying **File Recovery**). You can export the recovery certificate from there and import it again later if needed. When you have safely exported it, you can delete it by right-clicking it and selecting **Delete**. To export the recovery certificate, follow these steps:

1. Right-click the **Administrator's File Recovery Certificate** and select **All Tasks | Export**, which starts the Certificate Export Wizard.

2. In the wizard, select **No, do not export the private key**, **Base–64 encoded X509 (.cer)**, and specify a filename such **as A:laptop001 admin EFS recovery certificate**.

To import the recovery certificate, follow these steps:

1. Right-click **Encrypted Data Recovery Agents** and select **New | Encrypted Recovery Agent**, which starts the Add Recovery Agent Wizard.

2. In the wizard, select the **Browse Folders** button, and navigate to your stored exported EFS recovery certificate (with the .cer extension). This will appear under Users as **USER_UNKNOWN**. When you click **Next** and **Finish**, you'll also see "The certificate cannot be validated;" these errors are normal outside Active Directory.

Remote Access Security

We've already seen how easy it is for a user to create a dial-up connection to your company RAS or VPN server. When a user is connecting point-to-point to a RAS server, the security concerns about encrypting data are fewer. However, when connecting over an unsecure medium with an unknown route (such as the Internet), it is imperative that company data be secured as it travels from laptop to company network, using the Internet as its carrier.

PPTP provides adequate security protection for most companies, and more importantly, it can be used out of the box with Windows 2000. On a laptop running Windows 2000, there's nothing additional to install and little to configure on the VPN connection, except to specify that you want a VPN connection and supply the server's Internet Protocol (IP) address or Domain Name System (DNS) name.

Windows 2000 also supports Layer 2 Tunneling Protocol (L2TP)/IPSec for VPN connections, which offers a more secure tunneling protocol for when security is paramount. This cannot be used straight of the box however, for it requires a computer certificate on both the Windows 2000 client and the Windows 2000 VPN server. Chapter 9 covers this in detail.

Another option for securing data over a remote link may be to use a Terminal Services client connection, which offers built-in encryption of up to 128-bit—even when your version of Windows 2000 doesn't support 128-bit encryption. Particularly when speed and low bandwidth are an issue, Terminal Services could offer you a means of transferring data remotely from laptop to corporate network that is both secure and more efficient.

Chapter 5 covers installing, configuring, and using Terminal Services, which has many new options for Windows 2000 and may, therefore, provide you with an alternative means of protecting company data when it needs to be accessed by a mobile user.

Mobile Maintenance and Troubleshooting

Hopefully, many of the new technologies and features will mean that users have fewer problems with their laptops. As any network administrator who's had to support mobile users knows, supporting this type of user is much more difficult than supporting standard desktop users, for many reasons.

One reason is simply because laptops support a wider variety of hardware, and therefore are more likely to differ from a standard, corporate build. Support staff will be asked to diagnose exotic hardware with which they've had little (if any) experience, and if the user and nonfunctioning computer are not physically present, it can often be a daunting and fruitless process.

How much control you give your mobile users over corporate laptops will be a matter of judgment and balancing different requirements. Some companies tightly lock down what users can do and see on a laptop (you can make good use of local Group Policy here) and will insist that any installations, upgrades, and problems are resolved on site at the company.

For other companies this will not be necessary, or even possible, if users are to be efficient and productive. These days many users are more computer savvy and are both willing and able to carry out some simple maintenance and trouble-shooting on their laptops should the need arise.

There are a number of utilities that a mobile user can use to help keep himself up and running as efficiently as possible. Any Windows 2000 computer and user can use the three utilities described in this section, but I think they are particularly suited to laptop users:

- Safe Mode and the Recovery Console
- Task Scheduler
- Task Manager

Safe Mode and the Recovery Console

To my mind, there's nothing worse than going to an important meeting, or having a tight deadline to meet, for which everything is on your computer—which won't boot up. My heart goes out to anybody in this situation. It's bad enough when desktop computers won't start, or servers failover and/or need rebuilding. But when you're on the road, away from the corporate network and company resources, the world is a lonely and desperate place when your single laptop is effectively dead metal.

In these circumstances, knowing about and having access to a few advanced boot options can make all the difference to your laptop, and to your sanity. In these circumstances, reinstalling Windows 2000 from scratch or restoring a full backup or a disk image is not a viable option—you need to get the computer up and functioning as quickly and as easily as possible, even if that means not every service or device is working.

Despite reservations about whether some of your mobile users will be competent enough or happy about using these advanced boot commands, consider including these in their overall user training, and/or talking them through the use of them when needed. They could literally make the difference between the user being productive that day, or not.

The **Last Known Good Configuration** and **Safe Mode** options on the **Advanced Options** menu on a Windows 2000 computer are automatically available by pressing **F8** during the boot process. If the laptop has just had a new device, service, or even application installed, or perhaps had a configuration change, and afterwards refuses to boot, it's well worth trying the **Last Known Good Configuration**. It's easy enough to try, requires the least knowledge and skill of the commands we'll cover here, and it can't do much harm—at worst, the computer will boot, without the last lot of configuration changes, but at least it will be functional.

When trying **Safe Mode**, it's logical to first try **Safe Mode with Networking**, which tries to load using just key services to get the operating system, the network card, and basic networking services up and running. However, if it's a laptop that isn't booting, how important is networking? You cannot modify which devices and services start when you try Safe Mode and Safe Mode with Networking. However, the exact list of what will be tried is in the registry (if you've had the foresight to check it before running into problems) under the following registry keys:

> HKEY_LOCAL_MACHINE\SYSTEM\CurrentControlSet\
> Control\Safeboot\Minimal
>
> HKEY_LOCAL_MACHINE\SYSTEM\CurrentControlSet\
> Control\Safeboot\Network

These generally translate into the devices and servers listed in Table 3.1.

Table 3.1 Devices and Services Included with Safe Mode Boot Options

Devices and Services	Safe Mode	Safe Mode with Networking
Locally attached media devices such as CD-ROM /Jaz drives and hard disks	X	X
Input devices such as keyboard and mouse	X	X
Basic display driver (VGA)	X	X

Continued

Table 3.1 Continued

Devices and Services	Safe Mode	Safe Mode with Networking
Mass-storage devices (IDE/SCSI controllers)	X	X
Event Log	X	X
Logical Disk Manager	X	X
Plug and Play	X	X
Remote Procedure Call (RPC)	X	X
Network Cards (including PCMCIA)		X
Computer browser service		X
DHCP client driver service		X
DNS resolver cache service		X
Messenger service		X
Netlogon service		X
Server service		X
TCP/IP NetBIOS helper service		X
Workstation service		X

If the computer boots up using one of the Safe Mode options, look in the Event Log for a service or device that isn't listed in Table 3.1 in the mode used, and look to disable, stop, or reconfigure it temporarily to regain stability on a normal bootup.

Finally, if these don't work and you suspect the monitor display settings or Explorer.exe is corrupt, you could try **Enable VGA Mode** and **Safe Mode with Command Prompt**, in the **Advanced Options** menu.

However, if these bootup options don't get the computer up and running, another troubleshooting avenue could be using an emergency repair disk (ERD)—if the user has access to the Windows 2000 source files (including Service Packs). Unfortunately, this isn't often the case with mobile users. Whenever disk space permits, copy the source files onto the hard disk, or onto a removable disk (taking the risk that a removable device will be accessible).

When access to the source files is viable, make sure the user regularly creates ERDs with the **Backup** utility under **Accessories | System Tools**, and also has to hand the three floppy disks required to boot into Windows 2000 setup (use the **makeboot** utility in the **Bootdisk** folder on the Windows 2000 CD).

Then the user will be able to boot from the floppy disks and select to repair a damaged installation. At this point they can either supply the ERD, or even better, let the setup program find the latest repair settings on the hard disk so that the registry and system files can be returned to a known state.

However, having access to all the source files is not an option for many laptop users until they're back in the office. If this is the case, the **Recovery Console** could be the final resort. Fortunately, it's a very powerful resort.

It's true that this requires the local administrator's password and rather more skilled usage, but this is still something you could talk a user through, step-by-step, in an emergency. The Recovery Console is very powerful, operating independent of the operating system, and allows you to do any of the following:

- Use, copy, rename, or replace operating system files and folders

- Enable/disable services or devices from starting on the next reboot

- Repair the file system boot sector or the Master Boot Record (MBR)

- Create and format partitions on drives

Configuring & Implementing…

Local Group Policy Settings for Recovery Console

While installing the Recovery Console, you may also want to consider changing two local Group Policy settings under **Computer Configuration | Windows Settings | Security Settings | Local Policies | Security Options**, which are:

- Recovery Console: Allow automatic administrative logon
- Recovery Console: Allow floppy copy and access to all drives and all folders

The first isn't generally recommended for security reasons, because it would allow nonauthorized users access to low-level devices and services. However, the Recovery Console allows only three logon attempts and then reboots—which you may want to bear in mind for remote troubleshooting situations and stressed users!

Continued

The second option is more useful. It allows you to use the **SET** command within the Recovery Console to set **= TRUE** the following four options:

- **AllowWildCards** (for example: dir *.exe)
- **AllowAllPaths** (can traverse mounted volumes)
- **AllowRemovableMedia** (can copy from computer to floppy disk or Jaz drive)
- **NoCopyPrompt** (doesn't prompt if a file is about to be overwritten)

Although they are less secure, you may find the **AllowWildCards** and **AllowRemovableMedia** options very useful. For example, a user could more easily find a certain driver you request without being sure of the exact name/spelling and could e-mail you the file to check for corruption. However, I really don't recommend setting the last option for novice users!

However, the Recovery Console is not installed by default and normally requires the Windows 2000 Professional CD and either a bootable CD-ROM drive or the four Windows boot disks. I don't think that's reasonable to expect on most laptops, so I would recommend that it be installed on the hard disk in advance of any problems. It's true this requires about 7MB of precious disk space, but that could be a small price to pay for a recovered laptop in an emergency.

To install the Recovery Console onto the laptop (or any other Windows 2000 computer), run **winnt32/cmdcons** from the i386 on the Windows 2000 CD. This will add another entry onto the boot options called **Windows 2000 Recovery Console**, which makes it much easier for a user to access quickly. If you want to install this as part of your unattended setups, use the **winnt32.exe/cmdcons/unattend** command under the **[RunOnce]** section of the answer file, or within the **Cmdlines.txt** file.

Using the Recovery Console

After loading the Recovery Console, you'll see a display that informs you the computer is running the Windows Boot Console Command Interpreter with a dire warning that's enough to worry even desperate users: *This is a limited function command prompt intended only as a system recovery utility for advanced users. Using this utility incorrectly can cause serious system-wide problems that may require you to reinstall Windows NT to correct them.*

You're further informed that typing **exit** will unload the recovery console and reboot the computer, and you're prompted to enter the number of the operating system you want to log on to (most likely going to be 1:\WINNT on a laptop), and by default you'll be prompted for the local administrator password to access the Recovery Console.

Type **HELP** to get a list of the (limited) commands available when working within the Recovery Console. These commands are listed in Table 3.2. However, in the majority of troubleshooting cases, you'll probably use only a limited number of these, with the most popular being those having to do with renaming and copying files, listing available services, and disabling services. You may also want to run Checkdisk (**CHKDISK**) with the **/P /R** switches, which forces an exhaustive check of the drive with corrections if any problems are found.

Table 3.2 Available Recovery Console Commands

ATTRIB	DIR	FORMAT	RD
CD	DISABLE	HELP	REN
CHDIR	DISKPART	LISTSVC	RENAME
CHKDSK	ENABLE	LOGON	RMDIR
CLS	EXIT	MAP	TYPE
COPY	EXPAND	MD	SYSTEMROOT
DEL	FIXBOOT	MKDIR	
DELETE	FIXMRB	MORE	

When using the Recovery Console, you have access only to the following folders:

- The root
- %systemroot% and subfolders of the operating system you're currently logged onto
- Cmdcons
- Removable media drives such as CD-ROM drives

For a full description of each command and examples of how to use them, reference the Knowledge Base article "Description of the Windows 2000 Recovery Console" [Q229716], which is available online at http://support .microsoft.com/support/kb/articles/q229/7/16.asp.

NOTE

When copying, deleting, or renaming system files, you will probably need to use the **ATTRIB** command to set or reset an attribute using + or – **R** for *Read-only*, **S** for *System*, and **H** for *Hidden*. Most nontechnical users will not be familiar or comfortable with using a command to set file attributes before being able to manipulate files, so don't take this exercise for granted but talk them through it slowly.

Task Scheduler

The useful graphical user interface (GUI) utility **Task Scheduler** lives under **Accessories | System Tools** and is new to Windows 2000. Previously, with NT4, you had to use the rather complicated **AT** command to schedule certain programs and tasks to run automatically. It wasn't really suited to users who frequently power down their machines and who are more comfortable with a graphical utility and wizards to step them through configuration.

The new Task Scheduler addresses these issues by allowing both users and administrators to set up scheduled tasks to run either while the computer is idle, or while it is being used. Tasks are configured and performed using standard Windows 2000 security permissions, so you can set permissions on each task to protect it from being changed by users.

For example, you can specify that a task runs with an Administrative account when it is required by the program that is being run. In this way, an administrator can configure administrative maintenance tasks to run automatically and periodically, and the user cannot change that. This could include periodically clearing out all temporary files with Disk Cleanup (**Cleanmgr.exe**).

NOTE

Scheduled Tasks run according to the computer's date and time—so ensure that these are set correctly on the computer before configuring any scheduled tasks.

Being able to set administrative tasks (such as batch files) to run automatically is a great boon for laptops that are configured to restrict user access, and when the laptops may not be brought back onto the company premises for some time.

In addition, this utility is power management friendly because the default setting is to not run scheduled tasks when running on battery power (although you can change this). For ACPI-enabled laptops, you can also select to have the computer wake to run the task, as shown in Figure 3.26.

Figure 3.26 Scheduled Tasks Are Power Management Friendly

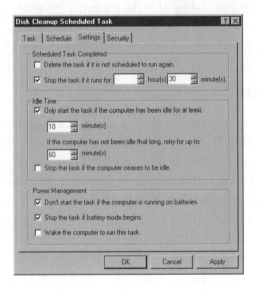

Configuring Scheduled Tasks

It's simple enough to use Scheduled Tasks now that it comes with a graphical front end. Either use **Add Scheduled Task**, which you'll find displayed within the Scheduled Tasks utility (much like **Add Printer** in the Printers folder, or **Make New Connection** under Network and Dialup Connections), and use the wizard to step you through creating a task, or right-click within the Scheduled Tasks and select **New | Scheduled Task** to go straight into modifying the Task, Schedule, Settings, and Security tabs. Or you can drag an application or file directly from Explorer into the Scheduled Tasks utility.

You'll be prompted to supply a user account and credentials to run the application if it's not running under a System account. Note that the account has to be locally accessible to your machine. For example, you couldn't specify the local Administrator account on a different machine and then copy the task onto that machine. Instead, you would have to configure the scheduled task remotely.

Although you can copy configured tasks from one computer to another, the original account information is not saved. When the new user pastes the .JOB task into her Scheduled Tasks, the account information will be changed to her own, and she will have to supply her own password for the task to succeed. You cannot modify this directly in the file either, because the .JOB is not in human-readable format. Each time you modify the task's properties, you'll be prompted to supply the account's password.

You can keep an eye on scheduled tasks with the **View Log** command in the **Advanced** menu. This is a text file called **SchedLgU.txt**, which lives in the system root (by default \WINNT), that simply lists when the Task Scheduler Service started and finished and which tasks were run, and records a result. For example, a normal result would be: **Result: The task completed with an exit code of (0)**, whereas failures are more verbose about why the task failed, with suggested methods to remedy the problem.

NOTE

For scheduled tasks to complete unaided, they must be able to run auto-mated, either configured to do this within the program's configuration, or by supplying command-line switches. Many workstation-based appli-cations are designed to be interactive only, and so can only be loaded waiting for input rather than load, execute, and exit.

Setting Security Permissions for Scheduled Tasks

Each task has its own Security tab where you can add users and set NTFS per-missions on the task. These permissions are in addition to any permissions actu-ally on the files the tasks will be running—and are more relevant when multiple users use the same computer.

This is the case when you configure tasks with an Administrator's account and you don't want users to change the task (for example, to delete it). Table 3.3 shows how the NTFS permissions relate to the actual scheduled tasks.

Table 3.3 Schedule Task Permissions

Permission	Explanation
Full Control	User can view, run, change, delete the task, and change the owner.
Modify	User can view, run, change, and delete the task.
Read & Execute	User can view and run the task.
Read	User can view the task.
Write	User can view, run, change, and delete the task.

Task Manager

Most users are happy with the concept and use of Task Manager—if only to end a hung application! However, Task Manager can offer much more functionality in terms of basic information about the PC and troubleshooting in real time. It's certainly not as sophisticated as using the Performance utility (covered in Chapter 4), and doesn't allow you to save any historical data, but it does provide a wealth of information to help the user with basic troubleshooting for his or her PC, or relaying that information back to the Help Desk.

Most users are happy to call up Task Manager with **Ctrl+Alt+Delete** or **Ctrl+Shift+Esc** (or by right-clicking the task bar), view the tasks running, and use the **End Task** button for the culprit application that is "Not Responding." A few users look at the Performance tab, which provides a snapshot and some historical data of how memory and CPU usage are performing. It won't tell you which application is hogging resources, but it will give you a good indication of the overall state of the computer. Figure 3.27 shows an example of memory counters in use while running a few typical desktop applications, some of which are performing background tasks.

Table 3.4 lists the various memory counters with an explanation of what memory each is recording.

Table 3.4 Task Manager's Performance Memory Counters

Memory Counter	Explanation
Physical Memory Total	This is the total amount of RAM installed on the computer.
Physical Memory Available	This is the amount of RAM available for CPU processes.

Continued

Table 3.4 Continued

Memory Counter	Explanation
Physical Memory System Cache	This is the amount of RAM being used by the file cache. (What does the File Cache do? Is the memory dynamically allocated?)
Commit Charge Total	This shows the size of virtual memory (page size) in use, which matches the number shown in MEM Usage.
Commit Charge Limit	This is the size of the paging limit.
Commit Charge Peak	This shows the highest amount of virtual memory used since Task Manager began tracking usage.
Kernel Memory Total	This shows the amount of paged and nonpaged memory used by the operating system's kernel.
Kernel Memory Paged	This shows the amount of virtual memory set aside for the kernel.
Kernel Memory Nonpaged	This is the amount of RAM dedicated to the operating system's kernel.

Figure 3.27 Using Windows Task Manager Performance View

When Task Manager is minimized to the taskbar tray, you can easily view how stressed the computer is by the rising and falling bar in the icon. Leave your mouse over the icon and a tooltip reports the current CPU usage.

Task Manager becomes more powerful as a troubleshooting tool when you use the **Processes** tab, which lists all the currently running processes, along with other information about them. At first sight, this doesn't seem to offer much more useful information than you've got on the performance, except for breaking down the information into individual processes. However, use **View | Select Columns** to add additional information, and you instantly have a more powerful troubleshooting tool. Figure 3.28 shows the available columns you can select.

Figure 3.28 Task Manager's Available Processes Columns

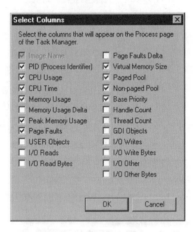

When you look at the information you've now got on available processes, you'll see a much more serious in-depth analysis. For example, the VM Size column (for virtual memory size) helps to identify any application that is leaking memory—as the specially created *LeakyApp* (from the Windows 2000 Resource Kit) is doing in Figure 3.29. Note also how this can identify the processes' priority, and you can change this, as well as end the process and end the process tree by right-clicking the actual process.

Figure 3.29 Using Task Manager's Processes Information

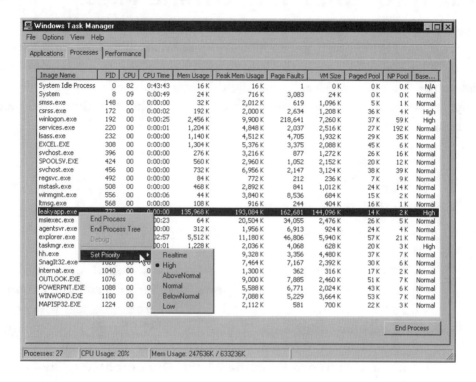

Walkthrough: Using Offline Files

This exercise requires two computers, the laptop (or workstation) running Windows 2000 Professional and another computer that offers files within a shared folder. You don't necessarily have to use dialup access to see how Offline Files work—we can just as easily simulate this on a local area network. The other computer doesn't have to be running Windows 2000. The steps this walkthrough covers include the following:

- Configuring Offline Files

- Working Offline

- Synchronizing data when back online

- Resolving conflicts with Offline Files

1. On the computer you're going to use as your server (this can be a Windows 2000 Professional, Windows 2000 Server, a computer running NT, and so on), create a shared folder with permissions that your laptop can access. Our example uses a directory called **Shared Docs** with the same share name. Create a few text files in there. Our example has five text documents named **Document1.txt**, **Document2.txt**, and so on.

2. From the laptop PC, map a drive to this shared folder using Explorer. You should then be able to see all the text documents you created. Right-click one or more documents, and select **Make Available Offline**. Each time you do this, you'll quickly see a synchronization dialog box as the remote document is cached. When a file has been marked for Offline use, you'll see the blue round trip arrows on the bottom left of the document icon, as shown in Figure 3.30, in which all but the last document have been marked for Offline use.

3. If you right-click these marked files, you'll see they still have the **Make Available Offline** option, but this time it's ticked to show the option is already selected. Select this option again if you want to toggle off the Offline marker.

4. At this point we're going to simulate a dropped connection—pretend we've disconnected from the VPN connection, or have powered down and are working at home. To do this, change the IP address on your laptop to one that is outside your local subnet. For example, click **Start | Settings | Network and Dial-up Connections**, edit the Properties

of your local area network adapter, and edit the TCP/IP Properties. Make a note of the settings before changing them to a static address that is outside your standard subnet range. My laptop uses DHCP, but by using **ipconfig** on the command line I can see it's currently in the 10.2.0.0/16 network so I'm going to change this to the static address of 192.2.0.2/16 with no default gateway.

Figure 3.30 Marking Files for Offline Use

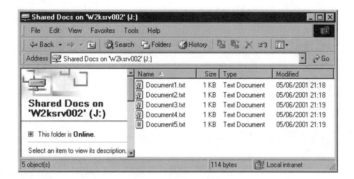

5. Because a Windows 2000 computer IP address changes dynamically, there's no need to reboot the laptop. Immediately, you should see a new icon in the system tray—a blue computer. If you leave your mouse over this, you'll see it displays **Offline Files – Computer(s) offline**.

6. Back in Explorer, you'll see that the drive has a red cross underneath it to denote it's no longer connected—but any files you marked as Offline are still visible, as shown in Figure 3.31. Any files you didn't mark are no longer visible. You might also notice that the status on the left has changed from **This folder is Online** to **This folder is Offline**.

7. Load one of the documents and edit it so it has easily recognizably changed contents. My original contents of Document2.txt said "This is document 2," which I'll change to "This is document 2 after it has been edited offline." Save and exit the file.

8. Restore your TCP/IP properties to how they were. We're now back online. If you wait a few moments, the blue computer icon on the system tray will display an information symbol over it. Leave your mouse over it and the tooltip tells you **Offline Files – Computer(s) available for reconnection**.

Figure 3.31 Offline Files on an Offline Drive

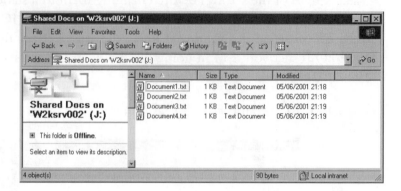

9. Click the **Offline Files** icon and it displays the Offline Files Status, similar to Figure 3.32.

Figure 3.32 Offline Files Status

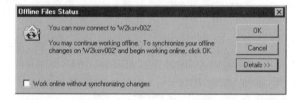

10. You'll see that you can connect to your original share or continue to work offline. Click the **Details** button and you'll see how many files have been modified that need synchronizing. Click **OK** to reconnect. You'll again see the Synchronization dialog box as the modified file is updated on the original shared drive. At this point, the Offline Files icon on the system tray disappears, because you're now working online with all files synchronized.

11. To confirm that the edited file did synchronize successfully, load it from the other computer and confirm that it contains your edited text.

12. What would have happened if somebody else had edited the same file as you, while you were offline? Go offline with your laptop again by changing the IP address again. Edit one of the files marked as Offline on both the laptop *and* the original computer on which is it stored. Make the edits such that you recognize which computer was used—for example, include the word LAPTOP or SERVER as appropriate. Save

both files and restore your laptop's IP address. This time when you try to synchronize you'll see a display similar to the one in Figure 3.33, in which you're prompted to resolve the conflict by keeping one of the versions—or both of the versions, but the laptop version will have a new name that includes the username and version number. You can use the **View** buttons to see the contents of each version so you can be sure which version you're keeping.

Figure 3.33 Resolving Offline File Conflicts

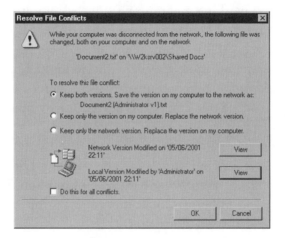

13. Decide how to resolve the conflict. When the files have finished synchronizing, load the file on the original computer and confirm that the version there is the one you selected to keep.

WARNING

Do not keep a document open while attempting to synchronize—close it first. If you try to synchronize a file while it is still open, you may see a warning message that prompts you to close all open documents first. However, the **OK** button on this warning dialog is to confirm that the documents are closed—not to confirm that you want them closed. Clicking **OK** will synchronize your files even if they are open, which may result in some corruption.

Summary

There are so many improvements in Windows 2000 that specifically address the needs of mobile users that it's no wonder this market was the first to eagerly embrace Windows 2000 as soon as it was released. It combines all the security features of NT4 with the flexibility of devices that Windows 98 was known for—and then considerably adds onto these with its own improvements.

Hardware profiles and caching files are two ways in which Windows 2000 makes integration between the corporate network and offline easier for the user by offering similar working environments in the two different states. Power management with Advanced Power Management (APM) or Advanced Configuration and Power Interface (ACPI) means that mobile users are now able to match their computing requirements more closely with the limited battery supply that a laptop offers, either with preconfigured power schemes and settings, with power management–friendly applications and devices, or by manually intervening so they can quickly adapt to immediate circumstances.

There are a number of options and settings in the Power Options as well as in selecting a power scheme, which include enabling Hibernation, configuring the Power button, and monitoring battery consumption. The two laptop power states of Standby and Hibernate offer users choices for preserving power without actually powering down the computer.

Offline files and the Synchronization utility are a great improvement on NT4's Briefcase utility. They allow a user to cache files locally when online so that the files will remain accessible when the user is offline. Synchronization updates the latest versions when next connected to the network. When the file server folders and files required by mobile users reside on a Windows 2000 server, the network administrator can configure the server so that files are automatically cached and the user has nothing to configure—or they can prevent caching, which may be prohibited in the interests of security.

However, the default setting is to allow the user to decide whether he or she wants to cache the files, and this provides the most flexibility for mobile users as they can precisely configure the Offline File settings themselves. You can even configure different files to synchronize, depending on which connection you are using, all with power management–friendly settings.

Connecting with dial-up access is now much easier for a user to configure by using the Network Connection Wizard, which guides a user through the different types of network connection configurations. These include dialup to an Internet service provider (ISP) or remote access server (RAS), or a virtual private network

(VPN) connection where the underlying ISP connection is automatically dialed first. You can secure data traveling over a VPN connection easily with the Point-to-Point Tunneling Protocol (PPTP), which is now built into the operating system rather than being an additional component; if you use computer certificates, you can take advantage of the stronger security offered by the Layer 2 Tunneling Protocol /Internet Protocol Security protocol (L2TP/IPSec).

The Encrypting File System (EFS) secures data on laptops to make them inaccessible to anybody other than the original user and a designated recovery agent (who is, by default, the local administrator outside Active Directory). EFS works seamlessly from the point of view of the user, who is unaware that the data he or she accesses is being encrypted/decrypted. It's good practice to enable EFS on folders rather than individual files so that new files created in the same folder will be automatically encrypted—don't forget to encrypt the Temp folder! EFS has some limitations, however; for example, you cannot both encrypt and compress a file. You can disable EFS by removing the recovery agent.

Windows 2000 includes more troubleshooting boot options such as **Safe Mode** and **Last Known Good Configuration**, which are particularly suitable for a mobile user needing to try to get a laptop up and functional again quickly. When these don't work, the Recovery Console offers a powerful, low-level utility that bypasses the Windows 2000 operating system to disable devices and services that might be responsible for the computer no longer booting up.

For mobile users who would not be able to carry around the original source media, installing the Recovery Console on their laptops in advance will mean it's accessible from the boot menu. There are two Recovery Console policy options that you may want to use on laptops, which allow an automatic logon and less restrictive access to drives and folders (for example, allowing the wildcard to be used when searching for files, and copying files to a floppy disk).

The Task Scheduler allows scripts and programs to be run automatically under a different security context for the currently logged-on user. This flexibility has advantages for both users and administrators, and the graphical interface and wizard make defining and configuring the tasks easy. You can also use standard NTFS security to control who can view, change, and run each task. Tasks are power management–friendly and can be configured sympathetically when limited power resources are available.

The Task Manager offers a surprisingly powerful troubleshooting tool for users so they can monitor CPU and memory usage in real time and also track the resources for each running process. It also allows them to end a *hung* application, and to identify those applications that are taking up a disproportionate amount of resources, which may identify problems with individual applications, or identify inadequate resources on the laptop.

Solutions Fast Track

Integrating Mobile Computing with the Corporate Network

☑ Hardware profiles allow for a laptop user to alternate easily between different computer configurations, depending on whether they are connected to the corporate network or not. When used with docking stations, Plug and Play ensures that the correct hardware profile will be selected automatically.

☑ Consider in advance the support strategy your company has with laptops—they often require a fine balance of tight administrative control (for minimal maintenance), and more lenient administrative control (because the user needs more control and flexibility over his or her own computer, which may not see the company IT department on a regular basis).

☑ The new power management facilities in Windows make good use of ACPI and APM with defined power schemes, battery management, and two new power states called Standby and Hibernate.

☑ Offline Files and Offline Web Content, used together with the new Synchronization utility, make it easier for mobile users to work offline seamlessly, by caching networked resources to disk.

Securing Data Outside the Company Environment

☑ Encrypting File System (EFS) is new in Windows 2000 and is a much welcomed addition to help secure data on vulnerable computing resources like laptops and removable drives.

☑ Only the original user and a designated recovery agent (typically the local administrator) can view, move, change, or delete a file with the Encrypt attribute.

☑ No additional configuration is needed for EFS to work—you can use it immediately without Active Directory or a certificate authority (CA).

☑ There are some limitations and restrictions when using EFS. For example, you cannot both encrypt and compress a file. Also, it's possible for the Encrypt attribute to be lost if the file is copied to a disk that isn't formatted with Windows 2000 NTFS.

☑ You can disable EFS if you prefer, simply by deleting the administrator's recovery certificate. However, it would be prudent to export (back up) the certificate before deleting it from the computer, in case there are any encrypted files already on the computer.

☑ Remote access over a dial-up connection is now easier for the user to configure, and offers more powerful security features such as L2TP/IPSec for VPN access, and 128-bit encryption for Terminal Services.

Mobile Maintenance and Troubleshooting

☑ For a nonbooting laptop, a user has recourse to Last Known Good Configuration and the Safe Mode options, which require minimal technical knowledge.

☑ The Recovery Console can be used when the simpler methods fail, and offers a very powerful mechanism to correct basic problems that might be preventing Windows 2000 from starting.

☑ The Recovery Console offers a basic set of commands, which, although they have limitations in use and scope, can be extended slightly with options in Local Group Policy.

☑ The Task Scheduler offers a new graphical interface for users and administrators to schedule tasks and programs to run at a specified time, under their own security context.

☑ Task Scheduler is also laptop-friendly and can take into account battery management and automatic wakeup.

☑ You can set security permissions on the tasks themselves to prevent users from seeing or changing them on their computers.

☑ Task Manager offers non-administrators some basic and useful information about what's happening on their computer, in addition to being able to close down errant programs that are "Not Responding."

☑ Specifically, Task Manager is good at identifying memory requirements and distinguishing between the different types of memory (for example real and virtual), and separating each process' resources to identify rogue applications.

Frequently Asked Questions

The following Frequently Asked Questions, answered by the author of this book, are designed to both measure your understanding of the concepts presented in this chapter and to assist you with real-life implementation of these concepts. To have your questions about this chapter answered by the author, browse to **www.syngress.com/solutions** and click on the **"Ask the Author"** form.

Q: I love the concept of Infrared devices, which are now supported by default in Windows 2000. There's virtually nothing for the user to configure, no extra cables to remember or break, and no time lost trying to untangle and plug the cables in to all the right holes. But does Infrared really work or should I hang onto those cables?

A: I can quite easily see why Infrared devices appeal to both laptop users and IT support staff. Yes, they certainly work, but the rate of data transfer—and therefore efficiency—is not the same as old-fashioned cabled transfer. If you need to copy across only a couple of small files, for example, it's ideal. But if you're planning to transfer your meaty PowerPoint presentation from your laptop to a standard workstation just before the meeting starts, you need to start hunting for those cables! I'm sure the technology will improve, but at the moment there are efficiency issues.

Q: We use laptops for presentations and multiboot between Windows 2000 Professional and Server, depending on the product being demonstrated. I've noticed that the Standby option isn't available on some of the laptops when booted in Server, but is on others—and it's always available when booted in Professional. Why is this?

A: Check to see whether the laptops missing the Standby option are using APM rather than ACPI. APM is not supported on Windows 2000 Server—only on Professional. If using Standby and having better reliability with power management is important to you, look to see if you can upgrade the BIOS to support ACPI, which is supported on Windows 2000 Server. Or try to use the laptops with ACPI for those that can boot into Server.

Q: I've got a user who complains that synchronizing her PowerPoint presentations to an NT4 file server takes much longer than if she synchronizes the same files to a Windows 2000 file server. Other users haven't mentioned any issues when synchronizing their files to the NT4 server. What's going on?

A: What this user is seeing is actually the difference between how the two operating systems read and write large files. Windows 2000 is trying to use Large File support when sending the files, whereas NT4 only has Large File support for reading files—so there's a disparity. You won't notice this on small files (PowerPoint presentations aren't usually the most streamlined files!). If this disparity is causing you a problem, you can add a new DWORD value called **SizReqBuf** and set it to (decimal) **65535** under the following registry key on the NT4 server: HKEY_LOCAL_MACHINE\SYSTEM\CurrentControlSet\Services\lanmanserver\parameters.

Note that adding this value will require a server reboot before it takes effect, and will take up slightly more memory on the server. It may be preferable simply to reorganize users and file servers so that users with Windows 2000 Professional store large files on Windows 2000 file servers and not NT4 file servers. This performance issue of slow writes is covered in the Microsoft article "Slow File Write from Windows 2000 to Windows NT 4.0 Server" [Q279282], which is available online at http://support.microsoft.com/support/kb/articles/Q279/2/82/asp.

Q: I appreciate that the Network Connection Wizard makes it easier for users to create new dial-up connections, but I would really rather RAS and VPN connections be automated for my less technically savvy users who just don't have the time or patience to follow written instructions on what they need to do. I don't fancy configuring each laptop for them individually, and besides which, they're rarely in the office. Can I define connections for them on my workstation and somehow deploy it centrally so users don't have to configure anything?

A: Fortunately you can—with the Connection Manager Administration Kit (CMAK). With this you define the connection details, package up the necessary files, and let users install the setup file—for example, when they're in the office and can connect to a shared folder, or you can send the file by e-mail, or they can transfer it from your FTP site. CMAK is covered in detail in Chapter 9.

Q: Why is there what looks like a stationery pin visible when my data is synchronizing?

A: This is because making a folder or file available offline is called *pinning* by Microsoft—and hence the picture of the pin!

Q: Can I use the Offline Files technique for desktop users, for example, as a guarantee in case their remote link goes down?

A: Yes you can—and this is one of the good things about features being built into the operating system, because you can choose how and when to use them. Although Offline Files are most suited for mobile users, there's no reason you couldn't use the same feature in this way. However, if your server is running Windows 2000, you would do better configuring this on the server rather than individually on each remote desktop. Configuring file servers for Offline Folders is covered in the next chapter.

Q: What sort of servers can I use with Offline Files? Do I have to use a Windows 2000 or NT4 server?

A: You can use Offline Files with any server that supports Server Message Block (SMB) file sharing, which includes: Windows 2000 (but not Windows 2000 Terminal Services), NT4, Windows Me, Win9x, and Unix servers running Samba. Note that Novell servers cannot be cached because they do not support SMB.

Q: If I'm using the Windows 2000 Backup on a laptop which has another user's encrypted files on it, will the backup program be able to backup those files and if so, will it keep the Encrypted attribute?

A: Yes, the backup program will be able to backup files irrespectively of the encryption attribute. If you restore it to a partition which has been formatted with NTFS by Windows 2000, the encryption attribute will be kept. However, if you restore it to a partition which is formatted with FAT or FAT32, the encryption attribute will be lost. It will also be lost if you restore it to a partition which has been formatted with NTFS by NT4.

Q: Is there a way to check quickly what files have been encrypted on a laptop?

A: You can use the **EFSInfo** command from the Windows 2000 Resource Kit, which displays encryption information on files and folders. You can use it to display this information for a specific file or folder, for the current directory (the default, if no switches are specified), or for the current directory and all subdirectories. For example, to check the whole of the C drive and output the information to file called **esfinfo.txt** so you can check it later, type **esfinfo /s:c:\ >esfinfo.txt**. Use **esftinfo /?** for a list of all command line options, or refer to the **Tools Help** documentation in the Resource Kit.

Q: One of the dangers of prompting a user to delete old files is the risk that they get impatient while it scans the disk and they get into the habit of clicking Cancel. Can I fully automate the Disk Cleanup utility so it requires no input from the user?

A: Yes, you can. This is actually a very deceptively powerful utility that runs well as a scheduled task. The Knowledge Base article "Automating Disk Cleanup Tool in Windows 2000" [Q253597], which is available online at http://support.microsoft.com/support/kb/articles/Q253/5/97.ASP, describes how to do this. Because Disk Cleanup supports lots of different choices (for example, deleting temporary setup files, old chkdsk files, and temporary offline files; compressing unused files; emptying the Recycle Bin; and so forth—you first need to run **cleanmgr.exe** with the **/stageset<number>** switch to define the particular cleanup configuration you want. This is then stored in the registry so that you can then run **cleanmgr.exe** with the **/stagerun<number>** switch, which defines which configuration you want to use. So for example, you could define a quick cleanup of temporary files every day, but a more thorough cleanup every week.

Q: I'm used to using the **AT** command to set up routine batch commands. Can I still use this with Windows 2000?

A: Yes, the **AT** command is still supported and in fact works together with the Task Scheduler. Two advantages the Task Scheduler has over the **AT** command is being able to run under different security contexts, and having its own reporting log. However, you can continue to build and use **AT** commands to work in Windows 2000—and you'll find they automatically appear under the Scheduled Tasks window. You can either manually reconfigure them, or use the Task Scheduler to reconfigure them—but once you've used the Task Scheduler you cannot then go back and edit them manually as an **AT** command.

Q: My Task Manager doesn't have tabs, the status bar, or menu bars. Where have they gone?!

A: This happens when Task Manager is running in what's called "Tiny Footprint" so it takes up less screen space. Double-click the border at the top of the window to return it to the normal view. Double-click in the empty space around any of the borders and it's back into Tiny Footprint display— which is very confusing the first time you do it accidentally!

Q: What's this **csrss.exe** process I can see in Task Manager, that's running at High Priority, and why can't I end it?

A: There are a number of Windows processes that are critical to the system and as such cannot be ended from Task Manager. This is one of them, with the cryptic name standing for *client/server run-time subsystem*, which is the user mode portion of the Win32 subsystem. It's used for console windows, for creating and deleting threads, and is involved in providing the 16-bit subsystem. Other critical Windows processes you can't end include:

- **Lsass.exe** The local security authentication server, responsible for authenticating users

- **Mstask.exe** The Task Scheduling service we just looked at

- **Smss.exe** The Session manager subsystem, responsible for starting the user session

- **Spoolsv.exe** Used for printing

- **Svchost.exe** Used with other processes running from DLLs

- **Services.exe** Responsible for controlling all the Windows services

- **Taskmgr.exe** Used to run Task Manager itself

- **Winlogon.exe** Responsible for managing user logon and logoff

- **Wingmt.exe** Used for client-side management

For more information on these, refer to the Knowledge Base article "Default Processes in Windows 2000" [Q263201], which is available online at http://support.microsoft.com/support/kb/articles/Q263/2/01.ASP.

Chapter 4

File and Print Services

Solutions in this chapter:

- Sharing Data: Storing and Retrieving
- Sharing Printers: Installing and Managing
- Managing Servers

☑ Walkthrough: Setting an Audit Policy

☑ Summary

☑ Solutions Fast Track

☑ Frequently Asked Questions

Introduction

For all the exciting new technology services that are being sent our way, such as those supporting e-commerce and mobile business (m-business), the old workhorse file and print servers remain the cornerstone of each company's network services. The need to easily and safely share, retrieve, and store data among users is precisely why networks came into being in the first place. These basic demands on a company network haven't changed, although our requirements for the amount of data we need to share, retrieve, and store have grown enormously over the years. Fortunately, new technologies are able to offer new solutions that make this job easier and more efficient.

Upgrading existing file and print servers to Windows 2000 offers an immediate and relatively isolated way of being able to realize some of the latest technology improvements without impacting the rest of your network infrastructure. Not only will you gain the immediate performance and reliability inherent to Windows 2000 while supporting a wide range of modern hardware, but you can also capitalize on specific Windows 2000 services and features that are typically used in a file and print environment.

By upgrading or installing Windows 2000 servers as member servers in your existing NT4 domain (or even in workgroups), you will benefit from a fast return on investment. Its server role means that many clients will benefit with minimal (if any) disruption. Not all features will be fully available for connecting legacy clients, but you can upgrade these clients to Windows 2000 gradually at your own pace and prioritize those clients that require the new client features or see if an upgrade or patch offers the same functionality without changing the operating system.

Some file and print features will not be fully available to the server outside an Active Directory environment, but that's no reason not to take immediate advantage of those that are available. You can later decide whether these features are important enough for you to include in the equation when deciding whether to migrate to Active Directory or not.

We've already looked at the new Windows client operating systems in desktop and laptop environments, and later chapters cover specific server services such as Terminal Services, Internet Information Services (IIS), and networking services. This chapter looks at some of the Windows 2000 server feature set, which typically benefits file and print servers most, but bear in mind that many of these features can also apply to other computers running Windows 2000 that aren't dedicated file and print servers.

This chapter covers data storage and retrieval, including using the Distributed File System (Dfs) to reorganize the way users access their data and how the indexing service has been integrated into Windows 2000 operating system for faster and more efficient searching. We also cover improvements and changes in printing (for example, the new Internet printing protocol). Finally, we look at how you can more easily manage and monitor these servers in terms of data storage, security, and maintaining crucial uptime and availability.

Sharing Data: Storing and Retrieving

This section looks at how data is stored on file servers and how users can easily access the information they need when they have the appropriate permissions to do so. Many of the basic concepts of making network data available to users are the same for a Windows 2000 computer as they were for NT4. You still organize data into folders, and you share the folders so that users can find them, attach to the share, and access the data they contain.

There's really very few good reasons why a member server offering file and print services should be running a file system other than the New Technology File System (NTFS), which (among other things), provides greater folder and file permission protection in addition to your share-level permission. Users rarely need to log on locally to a file and print server, so a standard practice with share permissions on these servers is to use **Full Control** Share Permission for **Everybody** and then control the actual folder or files with NTFS permissions. Users can access these shared folders when they browse the network, map a drive to the share, or have drive mappings automatically configured for them (for example, within application configurations or login scripts).

Shares continue to be configured with Windows Explorer via the Sharing tab on the folder's Properties. The only difference from configuring NT shared folders is the **Caching Settings** for offline use. Chapter 3 discussed the use of Offline Files and covered Windows 2000 features for laptop users, since this feature will most likely benefit mobile users. We saw how a user could make network files and folders available for offline use by caching them to disk.

However, on a Windows 2000 server, it's possible for the administrator to configure the folder on the server such that shared data (documents and programs) is automatically cached for users. This would be more appropriate if you were sharing a folder that desktop users didn't access, because there's little point in these computers automatically caching data and needlessly eating up disk space and bandwidth.

The default caching setting for a folder that has been shared on a Windows 2000 computer allows caching and lets the user configure the caching setting. However, as you can see in Figure 4.1, you can change this default on the server by selecting the Caching button on the folder's Sharing tab, which then allows you to modify the Caching Settings.

Figure 4.1 Configuring a Shared Folder's Caching Settings

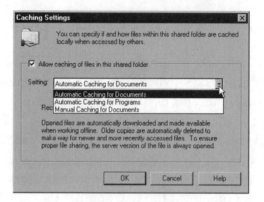

On an NT4 server, you monitor shares (which shares are available, opened files, and which users are connected) with Server Manager. On a Windows 2000 server, this has been moved to the Shared Folders as one of the System Tools within Computer Management.

You can access Computer Management through **Administrative Tools** or by right-clicking **My Computer** on the desktop and then clicking **Manage**. Figure 4.2 shows an example of the Shared Folders on a server that includes the built-in default shares (all hidden by the use of the **$** character at the end of the share name) and the shares that have been configured for users so that they can easily find and retrieve their data.

Note that **Shared Folders** is an MMC snap-in in its own right, so you could use a custom MMC that included only the Shared Folders if you preferred this less cluttered interface. When you add the Shared Folders snap-in, you'll be asked whether you want it for the local computer or a remote computer.

In this way you could have a single MMC with all the shared folders for your servers, which you monitor from one utility. Although Shared Folders by default lists **Shares**, **Sessions**, and **Open Files**, you can individually choose which of these to include in the snap-in. Figure 4.3 shows an example of a custom snap-in monitoring shares from four different servers.

Figure 4.2 Monitoring and Managing Your Server's Shared Folders

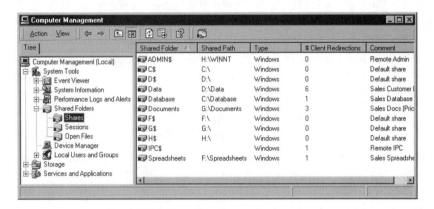

Figure 4.3 Monitoring and Managing Shared Folders from Multiple Servers

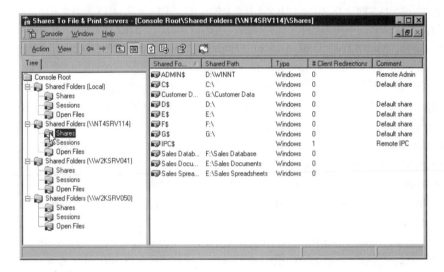

Another benefit of logically pooling your servers this way is the ability to send a single message to each of the servers. To do this, right-click a server and select **All Tasks | Send Console Message**. You'll be able to type your message in the top box, and beneath that will be a list of the recipients to whom the message will be sent.

By default, all servers in your MMC will be selected, but you can use the Add or Remove buttons to include or exclude other computers before hitting the Send button. Providing that the Messenger Service is running on the remote server, your message will appear on the server's console display with the originating server name as well as the date and time that the message was sent.

Chances are, your company network's shares won't look as tidy as the example in Figure 4.3! Typically, network shares increase exponentially over a period of time, which makes it more difficult for users to find the data they need.

For example, when browsing the network, users need to have a good idea of which server actually stores the share—so they need good memories, or finding the data they want will be a lengthy and rather hit-or-miss affair. This process is made more complicated when a server's disk capacity can no longer hold all the data that is needed, so some of the data is moved to a different server. That's not so difficult for a user if, for example, that user's SALES server holds the majority of his data and a SALES2 server is added for data that's required less often. But what's more likely to happen is that another server with additional capacity will be used instead, so that the user must remember that some of his sales data is actually held on a server that might be called PRODUCTION.

Worse still for users, share names often don't conform to a company standard, which makes it even more difficult for browsing users if they have to deal with different naming formats—for example, server names and shares that are a mixture of department, function, and geography (not to mention arbitrarily chosen names) and all of which might be out of date.

For example, how is a new employee in the Dallas office to know that his marketing data is actually stored on a server called HOUSTON with a share name of Advertising? This scheme might have once made sense, at least before this server was physically moved and departments were merged. Of course, it would make more sense for this server and share to be renamed to something more intuitive for the users actually using them now.

But as any network administrator knows, changing server names and share names can spell disaster because it's difficult to accurately track down all the instances that use the old names. Login scripts are easy enough when they're all centrally stored, but local configurations are more difficult to track down, and discovering which applications have stored these names (and where) is even more difficult and time consuming. From a technical and logistical point of view, it's easier and safer to leave badly named servers and shares and take the responsibility of users not always finding the networked data they require. However, it's hardly ideal.

Some built-in Windows 2000 services and features can help with this dilemma at very little cost and risk. For example, Dfs allows you to reorganize your company shares from the user perspective but without actually renaming any servers or any shares. On top of that, it can also offer high availability of data if multiple servers host the same data, because you can configure *replica sets* into one share such that the user will automatically be directed to an alternative source if the first source is unavailable.

It's true that not *all* Dfs features and functions can be realized outside Active Directory, but even it just used for the reorganization of existing shares, this solution is well worth considering in your existing NT4 environment. Additionally, the use of *mounted volumes*, now possible with the latest version of NTFS, gets around the problem of splitting logically grouped data across drives and machines while also minimizing the number of mapped drives users require. Finally, via the built-in *Indexing Service* on your Windows 2000 file and print servers, users will be able to more easily and quickly find the data they need.

Distributed File System (DFs)

The concept behind Dfs is very simple: It offers a share of shares. You create a new share (called your *Dfs root*) that will be your new starting point for users to locate data—so make sure that it has a generic but intuitive name for users to find easily. Under this new share, you create new shares with new names that actually point to existing shares anywhere on your network. In this way, you're logically renaming shares and their hierarchical positions.

For example, let's say that a user in the Sales department requires data on the network, which is held in the following shares:

> **\\SALES1\Documents**
>
> **\\SALES1\Projections**
>
> **\\SALES2\Spreadsheets**
>
> **\\JUPITER\Sales_Additional**
>
> **\\WESTST\Memos**

The user has the first four of these shares mapped to different drives as part of her login script, and the last one is mapped ad hoc when needed. This means that the user will have five more drives to contend with when opening, saving, and searching for documents. Not all the shares or servers have intuitive names to help the user remember which one she needs. Wouldn't this be easier for her if she had a single mapped drive called SALES, under which she had five subfolders, all with appropriate names to help identify what they contained? Each subfolder displays the new name and logically links to the old mapping (but the user won't see the original share name). So the user's new, single mapped drive in Explorer will look something like Figure 4.4.

Figure 4.4 New Single Share for All Mapped Drives Using Dfs

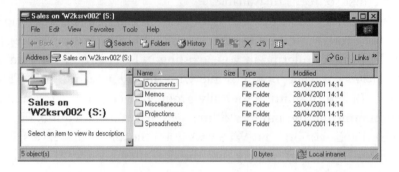

You can only have one Dfs root on each server. In our example, we called our Dfs root **Sales**. Part of your Dfs design plan must include how many Dfs roots you want to use. As in our example, you could have a Dfs root for a division, a department, or even a region. Alternatively, you could decide to have one single root share for the whole of your company—for example, call it *Network Data* and create many more logical shares underneath it.

Each logical share that you add to the Dfs root is called a *Dfs link*. An additional feature of Dfs makes these links fault tolerant by specifying multiple sources for the same link so that, should the first become unavailable (server down or network down), the user is automatically directed to the alternative source. Such an alternative source is called a *Dfs replica* because it holds a replica of the data.

Outside Active Directory, you can't have multiple sources (effectively, copies) for each Dfs root. This means that if the server hosting a Dfs root is not available, users will not be able to locate resources using that Dfs's links. However, in this circumstance, users will still be able to reach the resources through their original, full path. If and when you migrate to Active Directory, you can use fault-tolerant Dfs roots that safeguard against this single point of failure.

Also available when hosting Dfs in Active Directory is the automatic File Replication Service (FRS) that domain controllers use to replicate the data between the Dfs replicas. However, relying on FRS when the data is volatile has its dangers because the FRS uses a loose consistency; there could be as much as 15 minutes' latency between changes on one Dfs replica propagated to another Dfs replica within the same subnet.

This latency increases when the replicas are in different subnets, resulting in out-of-date information being returned to a user. Worse, if a connectivity issue rather than a server issue prevented the user from accessing the data behind the Dfs link, different users could be making different changes to the same data at the same time. When this happens and both replicas are back online, some changes will be lost. (The last changes take priority.)

In addition to this disadvantage of risking data loss with Dfs replicas when automatically replicating data, data that constantly changes will cause a great deal of network traffic, which might not be acceptable during working hours over slow links.

While there are undoubtedly some advantages to using automatically repli-cating data (which is only possible to configure in Dfs when in an Active Directory domain), Dfs replicas work best with nonvolatile (preferably read-only) data. When using Dfs in Active Directory, you can also set the replication to be manual rather than automatic—but don't forget, you can do exactly the same thing *outside* Dfs by running a copy routine from your designated *master* source to the alternative sources.

Designing & Planning...

Using Dfs for Central Distribution Points

A good example of a read-only folder is one that holds installation sets for application packages. For example, if licensing is permitted, you could hold all the setup files to install your most commonly used appli-cations so that they are always available on the network for people who are authorized to install them. Such distribution sets, called *central dis-tribution points,* or *CDPs,* tend to take up a lot of disk space, so these may be scattered throughout your network on different servers and even on more than one server. You could host a Dfs root called *Distribution* and gather all the application setup directories under it, making replicas of any servers that host the same files, for additional fault tolerance.

Another advantage of replicas within Active Directory is that that they are *site aware*—that is, a client automatically chooses the replica link that is physically closest. In comparison, outside Active Directory, a client always tries the first listed replica and goes on to try the next listed replica only if the first wasn't available.

How can a client know his share or folder is a Dfs share or link rather than a normal share or normal folder, and which physical location is actually being used? A Dfs share or folder on a Windows 2000 client has a Dfs tab available on the folder's Properties, which shows the real physical mapping, displaying which paths are available and which of those paths are active.

Additionally, a Check Status button allows availability to be verified, as shown in Figure 4.5, where the Miscellaneous Dfs link has a replica using both the Jupiter and Saturn servers. The first server is unavailable, so the alternative is automatically chosen for the user.

Figure 4.5 Additional Dfs Tab Displaying Actual Location and Availability

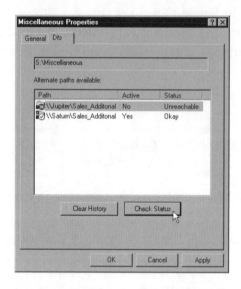

Having such an automatic backup location makes server maintenance easier because you can temporarily a server bring offline (for example, to upgrade software, make system changes that require a reboot, or add and remove hardware), and users automatically use the replica link without needing to change their drive mappings. If you use Dfs and do a little advance planning, off-hours maintenance work could become a thing of the past!

Configuring Dfs

Dfs is automatically installed on a Windows 2000 server but in a nonconfigured state. Load it from **Administrative Tools**; from within the Dfs MMC, right-click your server and select **New Dfs Root**. This launches the New Dfs Root Wizard, which guides you through this process.

Configuring & Implementing…

Using Dfs for IIS Directories

When configuring the directories your IIS servers will use, remember the power behind Dfs. You can use Dfs shares to logically bring together disparate servers and shares under one logical share so that they all have a unified namespace. So, for example, your company Internet Web site could point towards one share that contains subfolders, which actually house content from different departmental servers. Should the content be moved from one server to another, the IIS administrator doesn't need to change the IIS configuration or check for HTML embedded links to change, because these changes should be tracked centrally on Dfs.

Additionally, you can add automatic fault tolerance for the Web site by configuring each link for alternative locations so that data will still be returned, even if the primary file server fails.

You will first be prompted to select the type of Dfs root you want, **Domain** or **Standalone**. Outside Active Directory, standalone is your only choice, so select it. You're prompted to name your server and then either choose an existing local share as your Dfs root or specify a new one with its path and share name. Remember, this share name is the starting point for Dfs clients, so choose it with care. Remember too that you are choosing a name for your users and not yourself; a name like *DfsRoot* will mean nothing to them! The next dialog box allows you to put in your own comment or description to help you more easily identify this share. (Users can't see this comment.)

Now that you've got your Dfs root, you can add Dfs links to it by simply right-clicking the root and selecting **Dfs link**. This step prompts you for the link name (the new name that the user will see) and the actual share it maps to. Figure 4.6 shows a new link for the Marketing_Folders Dfs root, called Brochures.

When you've got a Dfs link, you can add a Dfs replica to it by right-clicking the link and selecting **New Replica**. You'll be prompted to select an alternative location to use. You'll notice the Replication Policy settings (**Manual replication** and **Automatic replication**) that are available only in an Active Directory domain—but don't forget, you could use your own manual replication outside Dfs, if required.

Figure 4.6 Adding a Dfs Link

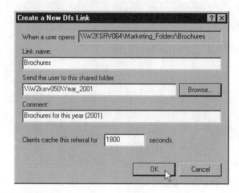

Figure 4.7 shows an example of setting a Dfs replica for our Brochures folder. Notice that it has an entirely different underlying directory structure, here going to an NT4 server. The important thing to remember is that your alternative location must contain the same data!

Figure 4.7 Defining a New Dfs Replica

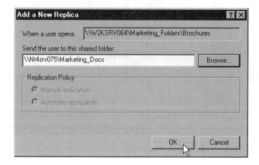

> **NOTE**
>
> Dfs should be used for the convenience of users rather than when you are configuring applications (the IIS service being an exception here). For example, in configuring a backup schedule, it might be easier to use the Dfs share name, but doing so will unnecessarily increase network traffic and doesn't offer a reliable path, because Dfs shares are by nature logical placeholders. What happens when an administrator later changes the Dfs link to a different server or adds a replica? With such a configuration, you won't be sure exactly which server or what data is being accessed.

Once you've defined a replica, you can take it offline rather than delete it, if you want to temporarily make it unavailable for users. Simply right-click it and select **Take Replica Offline/Online**, which toggles the availability of the link when the client asks for locations.

Caching Values

You can set caching values on the Dfs root and the Dfs links, which work in much the same way as time-to-live (TTL) values work on Domain Name System (DNS) referrals. With *caching referrals*, clients remember the Dfs link rather than having to go back to the Dfs root server each time, so performance is increased and network traffic reduced.

The default caching interval on a Dfs root is 300 seconds (5 minutes) and 1800 seconds (half an hour) for each link. You can change the caching referral value on the Dfs root and Dfs link properties; you can also change Dfs links when defining them. You might remember seeing these values when looking at the properties of the Dfs root and links. Figure 4.6 shows the caching interval for a Dfs link.

As with setting TTL values on DNS entries, a longer referral time means less network traffic but at the risk of the link being out of date. When your network is stable, use longer referral periods. When your network is more volatile—for example, prior to server consolidation or before data migration—configure the referral values to be shorter. Note that you can have different referral values for each Dfs link to reflect its volatility, so when you know a server share will be moved, change only its Dfs link to have a shorter referral period so that the increase in referral traffic will only be for that Dfs link rather than all the links.

NOTE

Remember that Clear History button on the Dfs tab we saw in Figure 4.5? This clears the referral cache so that the client checks up-to-date information directly with the Dfs root server.

Volume Mount Points

Improvements in NTFS v5 in Windows 2000 means that you can now mount a new drive and assign it a path on an existing drive. This means fewer drives for a user to navigate and allows you to more logically group file locations in a hierarchical manner on the same server.

Remember our previous example shown in Figure 4.4, in which the Sales department had two different shares, called Documents and Projections, on the same server? If the data within these shares logically belongs together but resides on two different drives on that server, they have to be mapped to two different drives. Wouldn't it be nicer if the user had just one mapping that contained the two folders?

A *mounted volume* or drive allows you to do this by using an empty directory to point to the new partition (for example, within the Documents folder or on the same level as the Documents folder). So, instead of the user having a share called Documents mapped to their M drive, and another share called Projections mapped to their N drive, he could have just one drive mapping under M that includes:

\Documents

\Documents\Projections

This allows you to include a nested hierarchical structure to your user's shares, which you can't do with Dfs outside Active Directory. Dfs would be able to rename the share and hide the actual location, but it wouldn't be able to put a share within another share.

By mounting new drives in this way, you're effectively increasing the logical disk space as far as your users are concerned, even though physically you've added another drive.

Another good use of mounted volumes is deliberately using different drives to distinguish between volatile and nonvolatile data so that they can be treated differently for fault tolerance. For example, you could have a static customer database that you mirror to ensure high availability. You may then put dynamic data, such as day-to-day customer information, on another partition, which is not mirrored for performance reasons (or you may put this on a striped set for faster access).

From a user's point of view, these two lots of data are logically grouped together, yet are stored on different drives. It would make more sense for them if all their customer information appeared on the same drive, which you can do with a mount volume. Mount the drive that will contain the volatile data in an empty folder on the mirrored drive. The fault-tolerance mirroring would mirror the empty folder as a placeholder to mount the dynamic customer data, without actually mirroring the dynamic data to which it points.

NOTE

You'll often see the new drive mounting feature referred to as *mount volumes* rather than *mount drives*, *mount disks*, or *mount partitions*. Volumes rather than disks usually refer to Windows 2000 dynamic disks (which we'll cover later). However, you don't need to use dynamic disks to mount a new drive. Although the empty folder into which you mount the drive must be NTFS v5, the new drive can be formatted as NTFS, FAT, or FAT32.

Configuring Mounted Drives

Mounted drives, although they use NTFS v5, are configured with Disk Management, which uses the Computer Management MMC. Although a mounted drive requires an empty folder on another local NTFS drive, this folder doesn't have to be created in advance. After creating your new partition, you will be prompted to assign it a drive letter or path. Select the option **Mount this volume at an empty folder that supports drive paths**, and select the **Browse** button.

At this point, you'll see a list of all local drives that can support your mounted drive (NTFS v5). You can expand a drive and navigate to the folder you want to use, or you can select the drive and then click **New Folder** to create it. Don't worry about whether an existing folder is empty or not; the OK button won't be available until you select an empty folder. When the empty folder is selected, you'll be prompted to format it and assign a label, just as you would any other new drive.

If your new drive or partition already has a drive letter, you can still mount it onto another drive. Right-click the drive, select **Change Drive Letter and Path**, then select **Add**.

Figure 4.8 shows an example of creating a mounted drive. The D drive on the server that contains the customer information is full, so an additional drive has been added to the server. A user maps to this drive as his F drive, with other mapped drives using G, H, and I going to different shares on different servers. If your new drive were configured without using a mounted drive, users would have to access its data on a separate drive letter, either using J or unmapping their existing drives so that this additional drive becomes G and then remap their old drives to new letters. Any network administrator smells disaster here! But by mounting the new drive under your server's D drive, users simply see a new directory under their existing F drive.

Figure 4.8 Mounting a New Drive to Logically Extend an Existing Drive

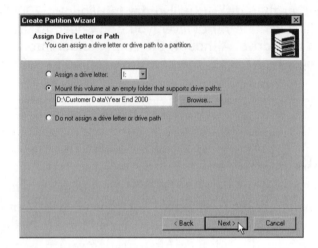

Indexing Service

The indexing service was originally shipped as part of IIS as the Content Indexing Server so that, when users were connected to your Web server, they could search through indexed Web documents to find and retrieve the information they requested. Like many additional services that were previously bolted onto NT4 and have stood the rigors of time, the Indexing Service has been improved and woven into both Windows 2000 Professional and Windows 2000 Server.

Thanks to new features and enhancements, the Indexing Service now extends its comprehensive indexing and fast searching capabilities not only to HTML files but to text, Internet mail and news, and any Microsoft Office documents (version 95 and later) such as Excel spreadsheets and Word and PowerPoint documents. Additionally, you can index any file that has a document index filter available for it. These index filters are provided by the vendor or can be customized using the Software Development Kit. You can choose to index all files, even if they have no known filters.

The new use of **Native Property Sets** in NTFS v5 means you can now search for a file by name and by all content and all properties (such as size, data modified, number of characters, or author's name). Additionally, for Microsoft Office documents, you can also search on any of the Summary information properties (for example, key words and company).

By default, each Windows 2000 computer is configured to automatically index local drives, but the Indexing Service isn't set to start automatically. When you use the Search facility available when you right-click **Start** on the desktop, you can expand the **Search Options** to display additional search options for **Date**, **Type**, **Size**, and **Advanced Options** with a link to Indexing Service. Until the Indexing Service is enabled, you cannot choose these advanced search options.

Selecting the Indexing Service link displays the dialog box in Figure 4.9, which allows you to start indexing when your computer is idle so that it can build a local catalog of your local files. If you click the **Advanced** button, you'll see your computer's index catalogs (System and, if IIS is installed, Web), which, when the service is running, will show details of the index such as its size and total number of documents.

Figure 4.9 Indexing Service Settings Access through the Desktop Search Facility

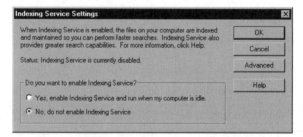

NOTE

Any drive that has **Allow Indexing Service to index this disk for fast file searching** as its property (under the **General** tab) will be included in the Indexing search and retrieval.

You can also access the computer's Indexing Service through **Computer Management** and then navigate to **Services and Applications | Indexing Service**, or you could load Indexing Service in its own MMC.

An index catalog details which drives and directories are to be used in searching and retrieving files as well as which directories are explicitly configured to be exempt from the index (in the case of the default system catalog, this list will be **Application Data**, **Temporary Internet Files**, and **Local Settings**, all under the **Default User**). Figure 4.10 shows an example of the automatically selected directories that are indexed in the System catalog for a server that has four drives.

Figure 4.10 Default System Index Catalog

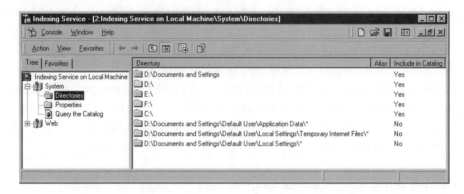

As an alternative to using the Search command from the Desktop, you could use the **Query the Catalog** option, which displays the default query form shown in Figure 4.11.

Figure 4.11 Default Index Query Form

After the Indexing Service is running (right-click **Indexing Service on Local Machine** and select **Start** if it's not already running) and has completed its index (which can take some time), you can submit your searches through this Query form as an additional form of searching for locally stored documents.

Because you can add remote directories to your System catalog, you could index directories from other file servers, which would provide you with a central location to search for all remotely stored data. But wouldn't it be useful if *users* had access to such a central index to help them track down the documents they need? For example, if a user wanted a document he knew he edited in the last week and that he could identify by author and keywords, but he didn't know on which server it was stored, a central catalog that quickly searches through multiple file servers could save him a lot of time and frustration.

To build a central catalog for remote users, you'll have to define a custom catalog with the directories you want to index, specifying the full (network) path so that users will be able to open the file references directly from their desktops.

You can quickly test the functionality of a remote catalog by logging in to another Windows 2000 computer with an account that has administrative privileges and loading an Indexing MMC that is focused on your file server. Then run the **Query the Catalog** option and check that remote documents can be loaded from the search retrieval lists. Figure 4.12 is running on a remote Windows 2000 computer that hosts two custom catalogs: Marketing and Sales. It's using Query the Catalog against the Sales catalog, testing a search for documents that contain details on installation services.

NOTE

The important thing is for you as a network administrator to build a catalog that includes the directories users need. All the developers need is access to the catalog.wci, and they can build their applications around it. The MSDN site has extensive information on building applications using the Indexing Service: http://msdn.microsoft.com/library/default.asp?URL=/library/psdk/indexsrv/indexingservicestartpage_6td1.htm.

This site covers how to use index catalogs with scripting (APIs, VB scripting, Jscript), programming applications (Visual Basic, Visual C++, Visual J++), and Web applications. It also provides a number of samples, including using the OLE DB Provider for Indexing Service API, OLE DB Helper API, Microsoft ActiveX Data Objects (ADO) API, Admin Helper API, and Query Helper API.

Figure 4.12 Remotely Querying a Custom Catalog

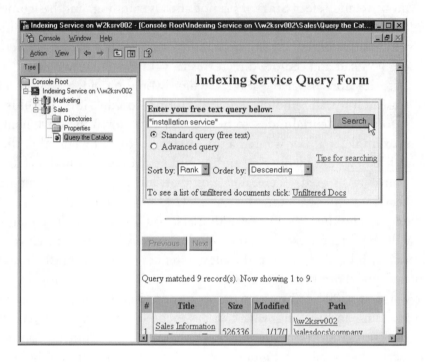

When a document is selected from the list, it should successfully load the document within Internet Explorer, ready for viewing, editing, or printing.

To offer this service for users, you'll need to either use your intranet to offer an equivalent Index query form (with a standard HTM and IDQ file) so that users can access their index catalogs through their browsers, or you can build your own customized server application, which then interacts with your servers' index catalogs.

Configuring Index Catalogs

Although you can add directories to your existing catalogs (System and Web), for remote users you'll need to specify and define a new catalog. Bear in mind that similarly related documents should be grouped together in a catalog to restrict the scope of the search. When users search on a specific catalog, only documents contained within that catalog's index are searched (although a customized search could search through multiple catalogs consecutively).

For example, you could create a catalog for each department (for example, Sales, Marketing, and HR) and under each catalog add only the servers and directories that host documents for that department. Alternatively, for larger organizations, you could create a catalog by country, division, or geographical area to help users seamlessly search through multiple servers to (hopefully) find the documents they need. Figure 4.13 shows an example of a server running three different index catalogs for the Sales, Marketing, and HR departments.

Figure 4.13 Customized Index Catalogs for Different Departments

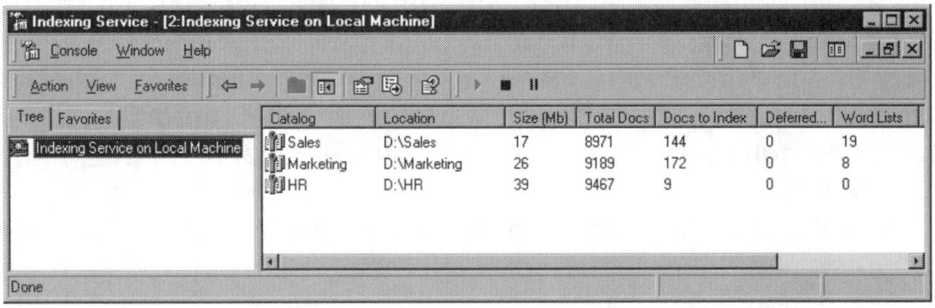

Catalog	Location	Size (Mb)	Total Docs	Docs to Index	Deferred...	Word Lists
Sales	D:\Sales	17	8971	144	0	19
Marketing	D:\Marketing	26	9189	172	0	8
HR	D:\HR	39	9467	9	0	0

To create a new catalog on your server, right-click **Indexing Service on Local Machine** and select **New | Catalog**. Specify the local directory where you want to create the index, and make sure that it has plenty of free disk space. Then you'll need to add into this catalog the directories you want to include (and exclude) in that particular catalog. To do this, right-click the catalog and select **New | Directory**. Make sure that you specify the directory as a network path that your users will be able to use.

Specify the path and directory with authentication needed to access all the files in the directory, and then choose **Yes** or **No** to specify whether this directory should be included or excluded from the catalog index. Figure 4.14 shows an example of adding a new directory to an index.

Figure 4.14 Adding a New Directory to an Index

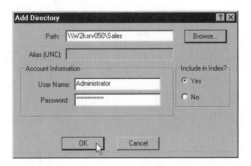

> **NOTE**
>
> When configuring the index catalog, use the full path rather than the UNC share because a UNC share could return the names of files to users who have no access rights to read those files. When you use the full path, NTFS permissions are respected in the index retrieval, which means that a user will not see a document returned in her search if she doesn't have access permission to it. So, for example, if documents you want to index on the W2KSRV001 server are contained in a share called DOCS, but the full path to this share is D:\Marketing\Shared\Docs, you need to specify the full path of \\W2KSRV001\ Marketing\Shared\Docs, and not \\W2KSRV001\DOCS.
>
> Novell and UNIX permissions are not respected in the search retrieval. Encrypted files are not indexed. If a file that is already added to the catalog is changed to encrypted, it is automatically removed from the index.

Performance Tuning Indexing Service

For the majority of the time, the Indexing Service works just fine without any reconfiguration. However, you can easily change how much memory and processing should be dedicated to this service by right-clicking **Indexing Service** when it's stopped, then choosing **All Tasks | Tune Performance**. You'll see the dialog box shown in Figure 4.15.

Figure 4.15 Tuning Indexing Service Performance

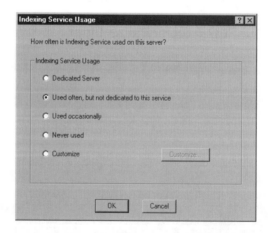

Obviously, you can increase performance by running the Indexing Service on a server with plenty of resources (particularly RAM) and ensuring fast and reliable access to those disks that are indexed. (Using striped disks helps in this task in a predominantly read environment.) You might consider running multiple catalog indexes on multiple servers to distribute the load. Make sure that you use servers with plenty of available disk space to generate the indexes, because when you start to add directories, they can get quite expansive!

NOTE

The general advice when planning disk space for indexing is to allow at least 30 percent and preferably 40 percent of the total amount of disk space you index (known as the *corpus*). It would also be prudent to host the index catalogs on a different disk from the operating system.

However, one other configuration you might want to change is the default time when the Indexing Service merges its temporary indexes into one master index. This process is both disk and processor intensive and can take a long time, depending on the number of temporary indexes that must be merged. By default, this merge occurs at midnight, which might clash with automatic backups and virus-checking routines. You can change this time by editing the following registry key and specifying the number of minutes after midnight when this process should occur: HKEY_LOCAL_MACHINE\SYSTEM\CurrentControlSet\Control\ContentIndex\MasterMergeTime.

Sharing Printers: Installing and Managing

Although a print server can be any computer that manages one or more printers, most people think of a print server as a member server that hosts one or more central printers for multiple users. Often, print servers are also used as file servers; thus *file* and *print* often go together. Despite the call for paperless offices, there's no doubt that people still need to print for various reasons and with various processing demands.

However, the printer is connected to the print server (for example, through a local or network port), it's still the printing software that makes the printer visible to networked users and that services their print requests. Windows 2000 makes network printing easy for users. Once you set it up, users can browse for the printer they want to use and select it.

As a network administrator, you have a few NT4 tricks up your sleeve that helps to manage shared printers, such as printing pools (load balancing print requests with multiple printers) and printing priority (so that long batch reports can take lower precedence than a few short pages that urgently need to be printed). All these have been carried forward into Windows 2000.

With a greater range of newer technologies supported and with Plug and Play support and wizards, installing printers is easier with Windows 2000, which now requires little in terms of configuring the appropriate driver, printer language, and port. Many printers can now be installed on the fly without having to reboot the server; this in itself is one of the biggest advantages of using Windows 2000 on your busy print server. It doesn't sound like a big deal to have to reboot in order to install a new printer, but when your file and print server is almost constantly in use by a large number of users, this feature becomes very important!

Table 4.1 lists the types of printers you can attach to a Windows 2000 computer as well as their associated installation procedures. When the printer is installed, configured, and shared, a number of network clients can use it, as shown in Table 4.2.

Table 4.1 Installing Various Types of Windows 2000 Printers

Printer Type	Installation
Universal Serial Bus (USB) and Firewire (IEE 1394) printers	These are detected instantly because they are designed to support *hot plugging*, which means that these types of devices can be added and removed while the computer is running.
LPT printers (parallel ports)	If these are added when the server is powered down, they will be found on a restart, and Windows 2000 will automatically start the Found New Hardware Wizard. However, you can also initiate this wizard by selecting hardware detection from the Add/Remove Hardware Wizard or by selecting **Add Printer | Local Printer** and then selecting **Automatically detect my printer**. However, unless you can find a parallel printer that supports hot swapping, parallel printers usually require the server to be rebooted before they are available to users.

Continued

Table 4.1 Continued

Printer Type	Installation
Infrared (IR) enabled printers	You must have an infrared transceiver installed (use the Add Hardware Wizard to do this) so that the IR port appears under the list of printer ports. As long as the IR-enabled printer is within one meter, it should be automatically detected and installed without the need to reboot.
Non-Plug and Play printers	When printers have to be connected through a serial port or with a network interface card, they are usually non-Plug and Play and are not detected or automatically installed. You must manually install these with the Add Printers wizard, and the server will require a reboot.

Table 4.2 Clients Supported on a Windows 2000 Printer Server

Printing Client	Comments
Windows 2000	No additional drivers need to be installed.
Windows NT4 and Win9x	Either install drivers for these platforms on the server itself (using the Additional Drivers button under the Sharing tab and selecting the platforms to support), or clients can locally install the printer driver.
Windows 3.x and MS-DOS	These drivers cannot be installed on the print server and must be installed locally on each client.
NetWare clients	These require the File and Print Services for NetWare installed on the print server, with the IPX/SPX transport protocol installed on both server and clients.
Macintosh clients	These require the Print Services for Macintosh installed on the print server, with the AppleTalk Transport Protocol installed on both server and clients.
UNIX clients	These require Print Services for UNIX installed on the print server, with the clients running their LPR program, which connects to the server's LPD service.

NOTE

One of the advantages of upgrading a print server to Windows 2000 is that you can install *all* 32-bit printer drivers so that users don't have to install drivers locally. When a few Windows 2000 computers creep onto your network, remember that each requires locally installed printer drivers for each printer it uses—with the additional support costs this requirement incurs. Be ahead of the game and have these drivers installed centrally first!

There are a number of other enhancements to printing in Windows 2000, some of which we'll discuss next:

- Standard TCP/IP port monitor
- IP printing
- Better monitoring
- User options

Standard TCP/IP Port Monitor

The Windows 2000 TCP/IP port monitor replaces the NT4 LPRMON protocol for TCP/IP printers connected directly to the network through a network adapter. The addition of this standard port greatly simplifies installing TCP/IP printers by automatically detecting the network settings needed to print. It's also much faster (supposedly 50 percent faster) than standard LPR printing because it uses only single spooling.

IP Printing

IP printing extends printing capability to the browser if the client supports the Internet Printing Protocol (IPP) version 1.0 (which effectively means Windows 2000 computers and Windows 9x computers). Clients can browse for printers both locally and over the Internet if they know the print server's name (or IP address) and print directly to an IPP printer with a URL format. The Windows 2000 print server must be running IIS.

Windows 2000 computers have IPP support built in, but Win9x clients need to run **wpnpins.exe** from the **\Clients\Win9xipp.cli** directory on the

Windows 2000 Server CD in order to support the IPP features described in this section. There is no support for IPP on NT4 computers.

WARNING

Before using IIS with Windows 2000, please read the following: "Unchecked Buffer in ISAPI Extension Could Enable Compromise of IIS 5.0 Server," available from www.microsoft.com/technet/security/bulletin/ms01-023.asp. This is a serious security hole in IIS and is now fixed with Service Pack 2. You can also download the following patch: www.microsoft.com/Downloads/Release.asp?ReleaseID=29321.

Within an intranet environment, IIP uses RPC communication for faster processing, but when used over the Internet, it use only HTTP over port 80, so there's no need to reconfigure your existing firewalls.

For example, on your company network, you could manage all your printers from Windows 2000 Professional through your browser by calling up http://<server_name>/printers, which displays the shared printers on that server. In a similar way, a user with IPP support on her computer could connect to her printer that way rather than using the Add Printer Wizard (or equivalent). Figure 4.16 shows an example of printers displayed on a local Windows 2000 print server using IPP through the browser to IIS on the server. Note that the Location field, shown in Figure 4.16, isn't displayed outside an Active Directory environment.

Figure 4.16 Viewing Available Printers with IPP

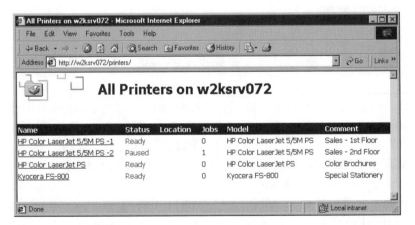

Only shared printers, rather than all the printers on the server, are displayed from the Web server. Any shared printers the user doesn't have permission to use (specified on the printer **Properties | Security** tab) display as "Access Denied" under the Status column rather than the Ready or Paused status shown in Figure 4.16. As such, these printer pages use Active Server Pages (ASP), which are automatically created on the fly when a user accesses the Web server.

With the appropriate printer permissions, you can then manage the displayed printers. For example, after connecting to the paused printer, you could choose the **Resume** option under the **Printer Actions**. Figure 4.17 shows this printer after Resume was selected and the display was updated to show details of the current document being printed.

Figure 4.17 Viewing and Managing Printers with IPP

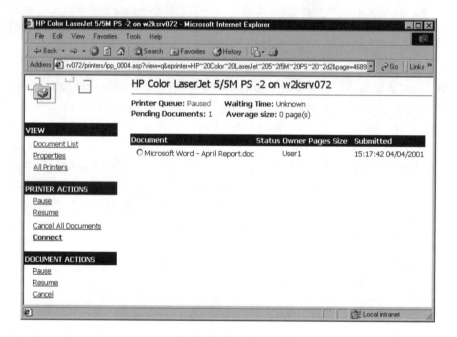

You'll see the same display when you type the URL on Internet Explorer's Address bar (v4.0 or higher). For example, the first HP Color LaserJet printer in Figure 4.17 has a share name of HPCOLORL, so the user would type **http://w2ksrv072/hpcolorl** and see the same hypertext display.

Users have an easy point-and-click printer installation by selecting the printer they want to install and then clicking **Connect**. They'll see a prompt to add a printer connection for their selected printer, as shown in Figure 4.18, where this time, the connection is over the Internet.

Figure 4.18 Installing a Printer with IPP

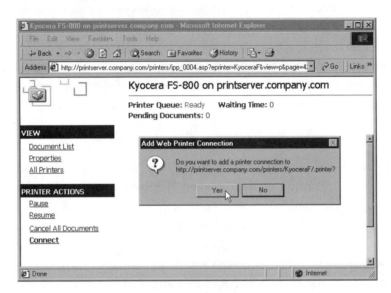

Once the user confirms that he wants to install the printer, IIS locates the correct printer drivers and packages them on the fly into a cabinet (.cab) file to download to the client computer. (This .cab file does not remain on the client computer after installation.) The user will see a progress bar to indicate the driver download and by default will be prompted to supply a network password (logon information that checks that the user has permission to use the printer). When the installation is complete, the user is informed with a link that takes him to his Printers folder.

> **WARNING**
>
> I had problems getting a connection to a virtual printer site using an alias for the server. I was hosting the printers on the company Web server, which has the standard name of www.company.com. Because I wanted to use printserver.company.com for printing so users would more easily remember the name, I created an alias called *printserver* in my company.com domain. IPP wouldn't work with my alias! It would work only with the proper host name of www. So I ended up changing them around—making this server's proper host name *printserver* and its alias *www*—which resolved the problem. Why IPP doesn't seem to like aliases, I don't know. This was true for both intranet and Internet use.

The extension of the Web server into a printing server to manage and install printers with IPP becomes quite exciting when used over the Internet, because home users can print directly to a company print server with an Internet connection, and public Web applications can be built that use the printer URL to directly send prints to your printers. As you can see, IPP offers significant new features for users and network administrators on both the local intranet and over the Internet.

Printing Permissions Over the Internet

By default, the virtual printing directory on your IIS server (%systemroot%\ web\printers) is configured for **Integrated Windows authentication**, which means that it authenticates users against your NT4 domain SAM if your Windows 2000 print server is a member server in an NT4 domain, or against local accounts if your Windows 2000 print server is a standalone server.

Alternative authentication methods you could use are *Anonymous authentication*, which lets anybody use it (which could be dangerous!), or *Basic authentication*, which is less secure than Integrated Windows authentication (because the password is sent in clear text) but is supported by all client browsers. Only Internet Explorer users can use Integrated Windows authentication, and you might have problems with it and proxy servers or firewalls.

If you will be offering printing over the Internet, you'll need to consider how and what authentication to use. You might find it useful to read Chapter 7, which explains the various types of ITS authentication and how to configure them.

For example, you might decide to use certificates for greater security if Integrated Windows authentication cannot be used. However, as far as security goes with IPP printing, you should treat your printer's virtual directory the same as any other Web directory, in addition to setting the appropriate permissions on the printer itself.

Better Monitoring

Long overdue, a **Print Queue** object has been added to **Performance** so that you can monitor critical counters on your print servers for individual printers as well as monitoring all printers. Printing demands tend to be very sporadic, so being able to constantly monitor this service helps enormously when you are trying to ascertain just how much your print server is used and stressed by the various printing demands placed on it. The new counters are these:

- Add Network Printer Calls

- Bytes Printed/sec

- Enumerate Network Printer Calls

- Job Errors

- Jobs

- Jobs Spooling

- Max Jobs Spooling

- Max References

- Not Ready Errors

- Out of Paper Errors

- References

- Total Jobs Printed

- Total Pages Printed

Figure 4.19 shows an example of adding the **Print Queue** object on a Windows 2000 print server.

Figure 4.19 The New Print Queue Object for Monitoring Print Servers

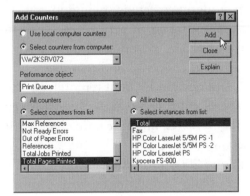

NOTE

As with any Performance counter, if you are unsure what it means, press the Explain button, which extends the current dialog box with a help explanation. More information on using the Performance utility is contained in the "Managing Servers" section of this chapter.

User Options

When a user selects the **Print** option (for example, within her word processing application), she can choose a number of advanced printing options that are supported on most printers and often overlooked. These include printing multiple pages on one page (**Pages per sheet**), printing multiple copies (**Number of copies**) even when not supported directly by the printer, and reversing the order of the prints (under **Options | Reverse print order**) for printers that print in reverse order.

It's worth looking over the printing options available to the user each time a print is requested, if only to familiarize yourself with what is possible and what a curious user can select just before calling the Help Desk!

Managing Servers

Plenty of new features in Windows 2000 help to make managing file and print servers easier than before. On the hardware side, this includes better disk management with new dynamic disks, a built-in disk defragmenter, and better support for remote media.

You can manage your data more easily with the help of the improved Backup program to more easily protect your data, with remote storage as an efficient method of extending your storage capacity, and with the long-awaited disk quotas that will safeguard users from unexpectedly filling up your valuable disk space.

Additionally, some improvements in performance monitoring can now run as a service. Auditing is also available, so you can monitor who is correctly (and incorrectly) trying to access your servers and resources.

Many of the MMC utilities can be used remotely as well as locally, as we've already seen. You can add all your servers into one MMC and monitor and manage them from a single MMC, or you can load an MMC ad hoc and simply focus it on a remote server.

If you're using Windows 2000 Professional, you'll need the Administration Pack to install the server utilities onto your desktop. This file is called ADMINPAK.MSI and can be found in the i386 folder of the Windows 2000 server CDs, although it would be better to install it from the equivalent directory on the Service Pack CD.

When installed, ADMINIPAK.MSI copies over all the administration utilities and puts them all under **Start | Programs | Administrative Tools**—all 27 of them! Because you might not need them all (in fact, outside Active Directory there's little point in having the three Active Directory utilities displayed), you should remove the ones you definitely don't need so you only have relevant links on your desktop. You can always reinstall them later.

You could also find that using a Terminal Services connection offers a better alternative to remote administration because it's less bandwidth hungry and easier to configure with firewalls, since it doesn't rely on NetBIOS. Instead, you'll need to configure the firewall for the RDP protocol. Using Terminal Services as a remote administration method is covered in Chapter 5.

Disk Management

One of the most significant changes in Windows is the support for two different storage types: dynamic and basic. *Basic disks* use normal partition tables that are supported by all versions of Windows, MS-DOS, and NT4 and can hold primary partitions, extended partitions, and logical drives. With NT4 you could configure these with volume sets, stripe sets, mirror sets, and stripe sets with parity; changes to the disk configuration meant rebooting the server, which is always problematic for network administrators who must ensure maximum uptime.

Dynamic disks are currently supported only with Windows 2000. You can configure disks initialized as dynamic without having to reboot the server, and you can move them from machine to machine because they are self-describing. This is possible by storing information about the disk on the last 1MB of the disk itself. The same types of disk configurations (mirrors, stripe sets, and so on) are possible with dynamic disks; you merely have to contend with slightly different terminology and remember the keyword *volume*. Table 4.3 lists the disk terminology for both basic and dynamic disks.

When you first install Windows 2000, all existing disks are installed as basic, but you can easily convert them to dynamic using the Disk Management MMC. Simply right-click the disk and select **Upgrade to Dynamic Disk**. It's that simple. However, be warned that changing the storage type will render the disk unusable to previous versions of the operating system.

You can change a disk back to basic, but doing so repartitions the disk and therefore destroys any data on it. This means that you shouldn't convert disks to dynamic format if there's any possibility they have to be read by another operating system—for example, if you've got a dual boot on your server with NT4 until you're confident Windows 2000 is offering a reliable service.

> **NOTE**
>
> New disks added after Windows 2000 installation can immediately be initialized as dynamic rather than initializing them as basic and then upgrading them.

You should be aware of a few more caveats to using dynamic disks before going for that Upgrade option:

- You cannot create new spanned, mirrored, or striped sets on basic disks in Windows 2000. They must be converted to dynamic first. However, these existing disk configurations from NT4 will be kept after the upgrade to Windows 2000.

- Although you can upgrade a basic disk to dynamic, a partition created on the disk when it was basic cannot be extended as it could be if the disk were upgraded to dynamic before creating the new volume.

- Disks configured as a set (for example, a mirror set or a stripe set) must all be the same storage type, which means that you cannot upgrade just one disk if it's part of a set; you must upgrade all or none.

- You cannot upgrade any removable disk, including disks in laptops, to dynamic.

- You must have 1MB free on the disk in order to convert the disk to dynamic.

- You cannot upgrade a basic disk to dynamic if the sector size of the disk is larger than 512 bytes.

In addition, you cannot install Windows 2000 on a dynamic disk that hasn't been upgraded from basic. This is because the Windows 2000 Setup program recognizes only dynamic disks that contain partition tables. When a new disk is found and immediately initialized as dynamic, it contains no partition table.

Table 4.3 Disk Terminology for Basic and Dynamic Disks

Basic Disk Terminology	Dynamic Disk Equivalent
Partition	Simple volume
Logical drive	Simple volume

Continued

Table 4.3 Continued

Basic Disk Terminology	Dynamic Disk Equivalent
Volume set	Spanned volume
Mirror set	Mirrored volume
Stripe set	Striped volume
Stripe set with parity	RAID-5 volume

NOTE

The storage type is independent from the file system used to format the disk. For example, a disk formatted with FAT32 could be converted to dynamic; it doesn't have to be formatted as NTFS. However, a disk must be formatted as NTFS if you want to extend a volume.

Even if you decide not to upgrade your disks to dynamic, you can still benefit from better disk management by being able to remotely configure disks by loading the Disk Management MMC and focusing it on a remote computer. To remotely manage another computer's Disk Management, the user must be a member of the Administrators or Server Operators group on the remote computer, and both computers must be in the same or in a trusted domain.

It would make sense to ensure your disks are operating at their optimum level by keeping them defragmented. There's no excuse not to do this now; Windows 2000 comes with a simple version of Diskeeper as a built-in Defragmentation utility, which is accessible on the Tools tab of a disk's Properties. You'll also find this utility as a snap-in under **Computer Management | Storage**. This utility allows data to be physically reorganized on the disk so that, where possible, it's stored contiguously for faster access time.

Because the operating system accesses and moves the data rather than the utility itself, the process is safer and can work even when the computer is being used. You can defragment FAT, FAT32, and NTFS volumes, but you can defragment only one volume at a time and only local volumes. Remember that defragmentation is more efficient and effective if there's plenty of free disk space.

NOTE

For regular and scheduled defragmentation, you need the full version of Diskeeper from Executive Software. This version doesn't ship with Windows 2000.

The new Windows 2000 Removable Storage Service manages removable storage media such as tapes and optical disks as well as robotic storage libraries. Such remote storage can now be grouped together and pooled for more effective and cost-efficient management, so different applications can use and share your remote storage. You can use Removable Storage to do the following:

- Track online and offline media
- Mount and dismount media
- Insert media to and eject media from a library
- View media and libraries
- Create media pools and set their properties
- Secure media and media pools
- Perform library inventories

Removable Storage is also part of the **Computer Management | Storage snap-in**, or you can load it as separate snap-in. It further divides into Media Pools, Physical Location, Work Queues, and Operator Requests.

Using the Disk Management Utility

You can access the local Disk Management through **Administrative Tools | Computer Management | Storage | Disk Management**, or you can load the Disk Management MMC snap-in separately. You'll see details of each volume (the file system, whether basic or dynamic, and so on) and details of each disk (its status, whether a primary or extended partition, free space, and the like). Because of the new dynamic storage type, better status information is available for these disks. Table 4.4 lists the possible disk status scenarios.

When you have problems accessing the disk but you've eliminated basic power, hardware, and cable problems and the **Reactivate Disk** command fails, you might have to resign yourself to the fact that a disk is bad and needs replacing. To replace it, use the **Remove Disk** command, power down the computer, and replace the disk. If possible, you should delete all volumes on this disk before removing it; but remember, deleting volumes irreversibly deletes any data, so you must be sure that the disk is bad before taking this step. If the disk is part of a mirror, break the mirror so that a good copy of the data remains.

Table 4.4 Disk Status Information in Disk Management

Status	Description
Online	The disk is accessible and has no known problems (normal disk status).
Online (errors)	Seen only on dynamic disks when I/O errors have been detected. If these errors are recoverable, the disk reverts to the Online status after you select the **Reactive Disk** command. If the errors are more serious, an underlying problem with the disk is indicated and you should attempt to resolve it (for example, replace the disk).
Offline	Seen only on dynamic disks when the disk is detected as not accessible, possibly because it is corrupted or intermittently unavailable. If the disk name appears as **Missing**, the disk can no longer be located or identified, perhaps as a result of being corrupted, powered down, or disconnected. Verify any basic hardware problems (such as power to the disk) and then try the **Reactivate Disk** command. A disk that is displayed with its correct name (rather than Missing) but with the Offline status may be recovered with the **Reactivate Disk** command.
Foreign	Seen only on dynamic disks that have been moved from one Windows 2000 computer to another. Before you can use it on your computer, you'll need to use the **Import Foreign Disks** command.
Unreadable	The disk is not accessible, possibly because of hardware failure, corruption, or I/O errors or because the disk is not yet fully initialized and read by Disk Manager. For example, the disk might still be spinning up when Disk Management is loaded. Try rescanning the disks. If this fails, reboot the computer.
Unrecognized	The disk cannot be used in Windows 2000. It could be a disk from a UNIX computer, for example.
No Media	Only applicable to removable disk types such as CD-ROM or removable drives. This will change to Online when an appropriate medium is inserted into the drive.

Data Management

In most people's minds, removable storage such as tape drives and zip drives are very closely linked with backing up data. You might already use a third-party backup program so you can recover data in the event of disaster (hardware problems, application corruption, and user error), which will continue to work just fine with Windows 2000—but don't forget to check that it will before upgrading to Windows 2000! This includes not just the hardware being used but also the backup facilities, such as support for some features, including EFS files and mount volumes, and support for removable storage.

Remote Storage

Additionally, Windows 2000 supports Remote Storage, which allows you to move unused files from your hard disks to tape when a predetermined disk capacity is reached. It does this in conjunction with removable storage and using *mount points*. Remember how you could mount a volume from another disk with a logical placeholder? You can use the same technique to have logical placeholders for files on your hard disks that physically reside on removable storage.

Files that haven't been accessed for some time are automatically moved (*truncated*) from the hard disk to tape, leaving behind a placement holder that points to where the physical file resides. From the users' (and applications') point of view, the file still remains on the hard disk with the full size reported. When users need the files, they are automatically brought back from the tape to the hard disk.

Configuring & Implementing...

Supported Media for Remote Storage

Unfortunately, Remote Storage works only with tape devices because, although removable storage detects other devices such as CD-RW, these devices themselves cannot be formatted by the operating system (they require third-party software). So Remote Storage recognizes these devices as read-only and therefore unsuitable for remote storage or backup.

After installing Remote Storage with Add/Remove Windows Components, run **Remote Storage** from Administrators Tools, which

Continued

launches the Remote Storage Setup Wizard. This series of steps automatically detects removable storage that is supported by Remote Storage, and the tapes you select to use are automatically created in a single media pool. Something else to be aware of is that Remote Storage supports only a single tape type that you specify on setup and that cannot be changed later.

This method provides you with a very cost-efficient way to combine disks and tapes to the best effect. The only disadvantage to the user is a slower access time when files are required from removable storage, but this is a small cost to pay and should happen infrequently because only the least used files are moved to remote storage.

It is important that backup programs honor the remote storage mount points; otherwise, your migrated data will be inaccessible when you restore from backup. In addition, if you want to back up all the data on both the computer's disks and tapes (local and remote), Windows 2000-compliant backup programs can be configured to back up the data directly on the remote storage rather than having to move it back onto the local disk before backing it up.

Note that the default setting for backing up remote storage data is to not back it up. Figure 4.20 shows the option that selects whether or not to back up remote storage using the Backup Wizard.

Figure 4.20 Backing Up Remote Storage

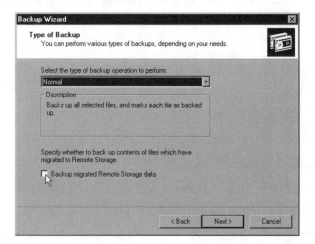

For non-Windows 2000-compliant backup programs, you can change a registry key so that the programs don't back up the remote files. To do this, set the following key to **1**:

HKEY_LOCAL_MACHINE\SYSTEM\CurrentControlSet\Services\RSFilter

Parameters\ SkipFilesForLegacyBackup

Remember to regularly verify the data on remote storage. Tape is particularly prone to wearing out when regularly accessed, so you risk lost data on bad tapes when automatically moving data from one source to another. This is why remote storage is not a substitute for archiving and backups; it offers more flexibility in how you store and manage your data but no protection for it. For additional protection, keep more than one copy of your remote storage, preferably offsite.

Windows 2000 Backup Utility

Windows 2000 comes with an improved backup program that is accessible from the Tools tab of a disk's Properties or by typing **NTBACKUP** from **Start | Run**. As you can see from Figure 4.21, the initial page of this utility offers a Backup and Restore Wizard to walk you through the steps required for these procedures. It also allows you to create an emergency repair disk (ERD).

Figure 4.21 The New Windows 2000 Backup Utility

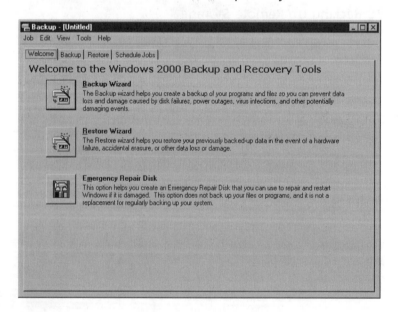

The following are important differences to note with the new Backup utility:

- You can now back up to a wider range of media, including files, instead of being restricted to tape.

- If you want to back up the registry, you must select the **System State data** option.

- The popular **RDISK** command is no longer available. You can create an ERD only through the Backup utility.

- You can now schedule backups graphically.

NOTE

With the new Windows backup utility, you can back up network drives (if you have the relevant permissions), but you can't remotely back up the system state on another computer. One way around this might be to configure each Windows 2000 computer to back up its own system state and then include those backups with your remote backups.

Disk Quotas

The other powerful tool in a network administrator's armory is the ability to set individual disk quotas for users on each partition or volume, which can be configured to warn users only or stop them from exceeding their limit. Quotas are not enabled by default and can be used only with NTFS formatted disks via the Quota tab on a disk's Properties. The benefits of using quotas include:

- Resource planning is improved because you can determine the maximum amount of disk space that user data can consume.

- Access to user data is more efficient if it is limited in size, which produces a faster user access time and faster backups requiring fewer overall disk resources.

- Storage is made more efficient by encouraging users to remove and back up old files that are not needed.

Designing & Planning...

Using Disk Quotas

The concept of using quotas sounds ideal to a network administrator who must constantly juggle disk resources. Quotas sound like a sure deal that can't go wrong. However, there are a few issues to bear in mind when you use quotas. First, you cannot set a serverwide or domainwide quota. Quotas do not span partitions or volumes, so on a file server with multiple disks, you must set quotas for each disk.

When planning how to organize your data, take this into consideration if you want to use quotas. For example, remember that mounted volumes, although they appear to logically extend a disk from a user's point of view, are actually a different physical disk that has its own disk quota. For example, if a user exceeded her disk quota and attempted to delete files but deleted them from a mounted volume, it wouldn't free up the disk space she was looking for.

Similarly, a user will have no concept of which disk is being used for each share, so if her Documents share resides on one disk and her Pictures share on another, deleting files from one directory wouldn't provide her with more space on the other disk's directory. This issue is even more prevalent when Dfs is used, because Dfs hides the actual physical location from the user. Using quotas with Dfs replicas can result in inconsistent quotas and could report inconsistent free disk space to users.

On the plus side, however, a user with a restricted quota will see only her quota as available space when she looks at the drive's Properties. If you want to use quotas, try to logically group together user directories on the same partition or volume.

Configuring Disk Quotas

Quotas work by charging users for each new file they create or modify using the NTFS owner attribute. Note that compressed files are expanded when they determine the overall quota limit, so compressing files will not effectively increase a user's quota. Disk quotas are set on the Properties of each disk, as shown in Figure 4.22.

The first thing you must do is set the **Enable quota management** option, which, when applied, will change the Status from **Disk quotas are disabled** and a red traffic light to **Disk quota system is active** and a green traffic light, as shown in Figure 4.22.

Figure 4.22 Setting Disk Quotas

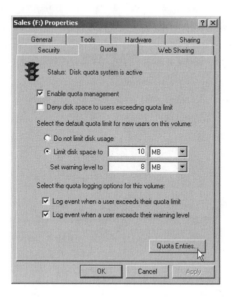

If all your users have the same quotas, you can configure everything from this dialog box, but if you want to further restrict some users, you'll have to use the Quota Entries button to specify settings for individual users. (You cannot specify quota entries for groups.) Note that disk quotas are never applied to administrators.

Notice how you can only monitor quotas or only warn users, or warn and deny disk space. You can also choose whether to log warnings and quota limits. These options appear under the System log as an NTFS event (for example, **Event ID: 37** with the description, **A user hit their quota limit on volume <x>:**).

By clicking the **Quota Entries** button, you'll see a dialog box similar to the one in Figure 4.23. Originally, this dialog box starts off with just one entry for the **BUILTIN\Administrators**, which has an unlimited disk quota, but you can still see the percentage of the disk quota (not the disk) used. Remember that most applications are installed by administrators, and these will count against the disk quota (another good reason that users shouldn't install shared applications).

To add a quota entry, click **Quota | New Quota Entry**, and you'll be prompted to select users from your domain or local computer. You can't select local groups, but you can select multiple users if you want to apply the same quota entries to them. When you click **OK**, the user will be temporarily identified as **<Multiple>**, and you can set individual quota settings, as shown in Figure 4.23. You'll see the default disk quota, which you can modify, or you can change the enforcement setting.

Figure 4.23 Adding a New Quota Entry

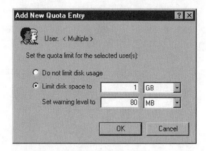

When you have set limits on individual users, you'll be able to see each user's quota and whether it's exceeded. Figure 4.24 shows an example of some quotas, with Users 1–6 having a more restrictive quota than the default on the disk (as shown under the **NT AUTHORITY\SYSTEM**). Users 7 and 8 have a smaller quota, with one showing the user has reached the warning level and the other one reaching the maximum.

Figure 4.24 Example Disk Quota Entries

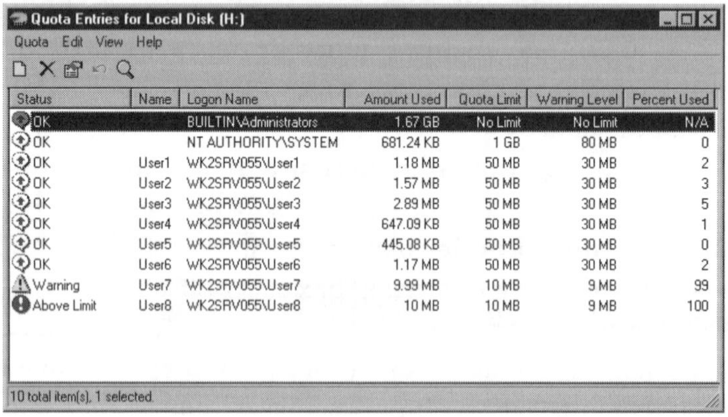

Status	Name	Logon Name	Amount Used	Quota Limit	Warning Level	Percent Used
OK		BUILTIN\Administrators	1.67 GB	No Limit	No Limit	N/A
OK		NT AUTHORITY\SYSTEM	681.24 KB	1 GB	80 MB	0
OK	User1	WK2SRV055\User1	1.18 MB	50 MB	30 MB	2
OK	User2	WK2SRV055\User2	1.57 MB	50 MB	30 MB	3
OK	User3	WK2SRV055\User3	2.89 MB	50 MB	30 MB	5
OK	User4	WK2SRV055\User4	647.09 KB	50 MB	30 MB	1
OK	User5	WK2SRV055\User5	445.08 KB	50 MB	30 MB	0
OK	User6	WK2SRV055\User6	1.17 MB	50 MB	30 MB	2
Warning	User7	WK2SRV055\User7	9.99 MB	10 MB	9 MB	99
Above Limit	User8	WK2SRV055\User8	10 MB	10 MB	9 MB	100

10 total item(s), 1 selected.

When you have a number of quota entries, it can take quite some time for them to be calculated and the logon name resolved from the security identifier, or SID. (Quotas work on individual SIDs rather than on account names.) By the same token, using quotas can decrease overall performance of your server because the additional checks and calculations must continuously be made whenever new files are created or ownership is transferred.

Designing & Planning...

Quotas and Deleted Files

Remember to factor in how deleted files are handled when you use quotas. For example, if you delete a user's directory directly on the server so that the user can save new files when his quota is reached, by default these files go into in the Recycle Bin and so are still actually on the server with the original SID. Although the user can't see his files any more, his quota percentage won't decrease unless you take ownership of the files first, delete them from a different computer, or remember to also delete them from the Recycle Bin.

Similarly, some companies use third-party utilities to retain deleted files on the server for a specified period so that they can be easily recovered if a user accidentally deletes vital files. Remember that if these users retain the file on the same volume with the same SID, the user's quota percentage used will not increase.

An interesting point arises when you try to delete a quota entry that belongs to a user who still has files on the monitored disk. You cannot delete a quota entry unless the ownership of that user's files is transferred to somebody else or the files are moved or deleted from the disk. Figure 4.25 shows the sort of dialog box you'll see if you try to delete a quota entry that includes current files.

NOTE

You can import and export quota entries between disks using the **Quota | Import and Quota | Export menu options**.

Monitoring

Part of your job of offering file and print services is to maintain them, which includes checking the overall health of the server in terms of hardware and

Figure 4.25 Deleting a Quota Entry for Current Files

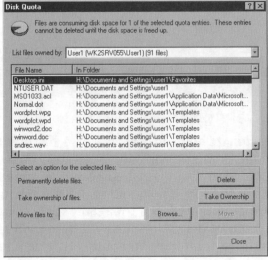

software performance and checking that only authorized users are using its resources. Two of the most valuable tools for handling these tasks are the Performance utility (formerly called *Performance Monitor* in NT4) and the Event Log.

The basic concepts behind these utilities haven't changed from NT4, but some of their functions and interfaces have improved features. This section takes a quick look at how these new features can be used to monitor the state and health of your servers. Of course, the same precepts can be extended to other computers running Windows 2000.

Performance monitoring at first glance looks very similar to performance monitoring with the System Monitor, which allows you view in real time various aspects of the computer, such as memory, processor usage, disk performance, and number of opened sessions.

Figure 4.26 shows an example of a System Monitor running as a chart and using the Add button to add different objects and counters to monitor. Notice how you can choose different computers here (providing that you have administrative rights to them) so that you can compare the same object across different servers. Use the Explain button to get help on what each counter means.

You can switch between Chart view and the Histogram and Report views (see Figure 4.27) by using the buttons on the toolbar. Report View is often the easiest to use rather than having to sort through the various fluctuations and colors of the other views.

Figure 4.26 Running the System Monitor Performance in Chart View

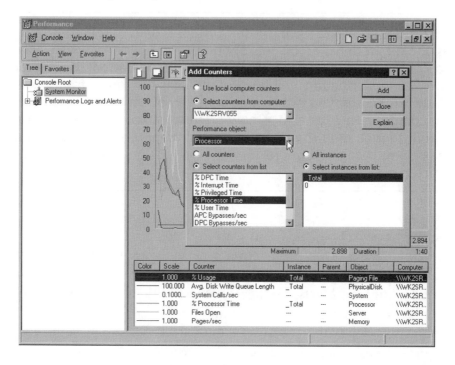

Figure 4.27 Using System Monitor Performance in Report View

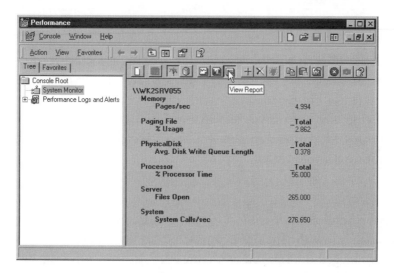

NOTE

Hidden away on the toolbar is the System Monitor Properties. You can't, as you might think, access this option by right-clicking System Monitor. If you're not familiar with the standard Properties button, use the tool tips over the buttons and you'll find Properties is the fourth from the end. Under Properties, you can change a wealth of configuration options, including the view, as well as how often to sample data; whether report and histogram data should be presented as current/average/minimum/maximum; changing options for the graph, colors, and fonts; and much more.

The Performance Logs and Alerts snap-in is useful when you're baselining your servers and comparing changes over time and usage trends or when you need to be alerted to critical conditions. This snap-in offers a choice of **Counter Logs**, **Trace Logs**, or **Alerts**. Configuring these options has changed from NT4. The new Performance utility is the least intuitive to use of the new MMCs, but it's worth persevering with it, because its tools are now more powerful and flexible. In particular, you can now configure logs to run as a continual service rather than having to leave the computer logged in and locked or monitor remotely from another computer.

Counter Logs

Counter logs are used to baseline servers and record performance over a period of time. You can view these logs in real time. Because they can be saved in a comma-separated or tab-separated format, you can easily export these logs into spreadsheets programs for analysis and manipulation. By running counter logs as a service, you can now define start and stop times to selectively and automatically log information when you want.

Alerts

Alerts notify an administrator when a certain condition is reached—for example, when disk space is low, the memory or processor is slowing considerably, or too many users are logged on. You can configure Alert to send a message to the administrator when such conditions are met, run a defined program (such as a batch file that pages an administrator), or start logging to find what is causing the alert.

Trace Logs

Trace logs are used by programmers and providers (for example, software vendors) to watch for certain activities by applications, services, or the operating system (such as page faults to track down a software bug) and record these when they happen rather than take recordings at certain intervals. A parsing tool is required to interpret the trace output, so this option is of little use to a standard administrator unless used in conjunction with developers.

Using Performance Data

How useful you find the information in the Performance logs depends on whether you have selected appropriate objects and counters and whether you can interpret the results efficiently. This often takes practice and experience, depending on your particular servers and what you want to monitor.

Of course, there are standard recommended thresholds to watch for any computer, such as the processor shouldn't show above 85 percent, pages per second shouldn't be above 20, processor queue length (per processor) shouldn't be above 2, and available memory bytes shouldn't be above 4MB.

However, you need to fine-tune these thresholds for your particular computer and add the counters that affect overall performance from the users' point of view. While a computer by definition always has one bottleneck, the idea is to make that bottleneck the user response rather than the computer's or network's response. When a computer is reacting as fast as a user requires, its performance is considered to be optimum. In reality, you must balance that ideal against finite resources and find the thresholds that offer an acceptable solution.

NOTE

You can often find more information and resolutions for events using the Event ID and searching through the Microsoft Knowledge Base, which is included with TechNet and available online at http://search.support .microsoft.com/kb.

Additionally, the Windows 2000 Server Resource Kit includes **Error and Event Messages Help**, which provides a detailed explanation and suggested course of action for most of the events you'll see in the Windows 2000 event logs. This feature is also available for free download from www.microsoft.com/windows2000/techinfo/reskit/ ErrorandEventMessages/default.asp.

In comparison to the freedom of selecting only the events you want with Performance logging, you have little control over what is logged in the System Event and Application Event logs. It's essential to keep an eye on these logs, which automatically generate error messages, warnings, and information about critical events so you can follow them up. Some applications do offer control over what sort of messages are logged, as we saw with the Quota entries. Figure 4.28 shows the System event logged for the user who reached his quota limit, which is shown as an NTFS information event, detailing the user, the workstation, the time, and the volume involved.

Figure 4.28 Example System Event for Quota Information

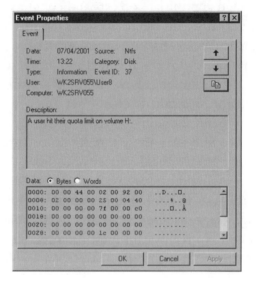

Auditing Events and the Security Log

You do have a high level of control over what events are logged in the Security log. Before anything can be logged to the Security log, you must enable **Auditing** under the local **Security Settings**, which we covered in Chapter 2, when looking at local Group Policies. You need to select what you want to audit from the nine different categories. To audit files and printers you'll need to enable object access and then use the **Security** tab on the resource (folder, file, printer), select the **Advanced** button, and use the **Auditing** tab to select which users or groups you want to audit for that particular resource. Figure 4.29 shows an example of setting auditing on a directory called Sales Projections, which is configured to track unauthorized access.

Figure 4.29 Example of Setting Auditing on a Directory

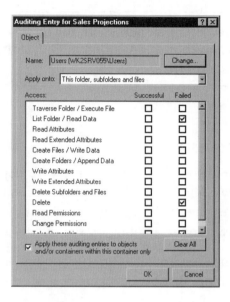

To audit printers, follow the same procedure, only this time the possible types to audit are appropriate only for printing, as shown in Figure 4.30, which shows an example of auditing a printer that uses special check-printing stationery. Because of its security implications, only a limited number of people should be using this printer.

Figure 4.30 Example of Setting Auditing on a Printer

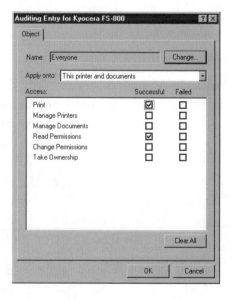

> **NOTE**
>
> You must be logged on as an administrator or as a member of the Administrators group to turn on auditing. Only administrators have access to the Security logs.

Auditing the Registry

A further type of auditing you might want to use with object auditing is on the registry. Ordinarily, only administrators should have access to critical areas of your server's registry, which ensures the integrity, confidentiality, and availability of services. But you might want to use auditing on the registry for two main reasons:

- To track which administrator is directly modifying the registry (usually required for settings that have no graphical interface), providing for accountability and a recorded event

- As a precaution to ensure that nonadministrators are not trying to access your server for malicious reasons (hacking)

Only keys and subkeys (not individual values) can be audited in the registry, using regedt32. Probably the most important areas of the registry to audit are the following:

- HKEY_LOCAL_MACHINE\System

- HKEY_LOCAL_MACHINE\Software

- HKEY_CLASSES_ROOT

If you are interested in auditing the registry for only the first reason shown (tracking changes administrators make), you need only select **Administrators** (local or domain) as your auditing choice. If, however, you're interested in ensuring the integrity of your server from nonauthorized access, you should choose **Everybody**.

To configure auditing on the registry, load **regedt32**, navigate to the key you want to audit, select the **Security** menu, go to **Permissions | Advanced | Auditing**, and set the options you want. Figure 4.31 shows an example of setting auditing for **Everybody** on all the keys under HKEY_LOCAL_MACHINE\ Software, which is where installed applications write their configuration information.

Figure 4.31 Setting Auditing on the Registry

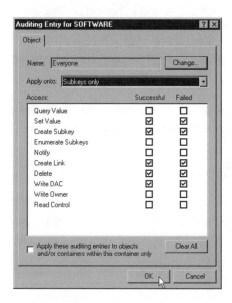

Auditing puts an additional stress on your server, so use it with caution if you don't want it to negatively affect performance. Additionally, the fewer audit checks you make, the less cluttered your Security log—and each audit event can create multiple security events, which makes it more difficult to identify the important information. The goal is to audit as little as possible while obtaining as much information as you need.

Auditing Administrative Actions

Although you might want to audit users most of the time, you might also consider auditing administrative actions, such as identifying which administrator changed the system time, who logged on locally and when, or who shut down the server—particularly when more than one administrator manages the server. These options come under auditing **Privilege use**, which tracks all your defined **User Rights Assignments**. Unfortunately, you can't selectively audit user rights; it's all or nothing (with the exception of **Audit access of global system objects** and **Audit use of Backup and Restore privilege**, which are set within the local Group Policy, under the **Security Options**).

You might also want to track who is logging on to the server and using your network resources (shares and printers). The **Audit Logon** is the one to use here; again, you can choose between success and failure or both. If you have many users, you would more likely want to audit who was failing to log on rather than who was successfully logging on. Exactly what you audit and how depends on what you want to achieve. Use auditing information for the following reasons:

- Individual accountability for changes on your central servers

- Recorded evidence for legal or administrative actions

- As a tool for planning and monitoring resources—for example, to confirm that security practices are being enforced

Configuring Counter and Alert Logs

When configuring counter logs, you can either start by modifying the built-in System Overview log or create a new counter from scratch. When you expand Performance Logs and Alerts and click Counter Logs, you'll see the built-in System Overview log, with a comment explaining "This sample log provides an overview of system performance."

If you look at the System Overview Properties by double-clicking it, you'll see a dialog box similar to the one in Figure 4.32, which displays on the General tab the log name and path, the counters used in the logging, and how often the logging is done (the interval and units). Use the Add and Remove buttons to modify the counters included in the log. The Log Files tab allows you to change log name and path, its naming format, the type of file, the comment, and whether to limit the log file. The Schedule tab allows you to control how and when the log starts and finishes.

For example, you can set the log to automatically start at a given time on a given day. You can specify when to stop the logging, which includes when the log file is full. By starting a new log file and/or running a specified command (for example, a batch file), you can also set what action to take when it stops.

To create your own counter log, right-click **Counter Log** and select **New Log Settings**, where you'll be prompted for a log name and can then define its properties. You can build up multiple logs on the same computer to, for example, group together specific activities or services you want logically kept together.

When the logs are running (either manually—for example, by right-clicking the log and selecting **Start**—or at their specified times), you'll see the log icon change from red to green. Figure 4.33 shows an example of several log files running on a server, all except the default System Overview log.

Figure 4.32 Configuring a Counter Log

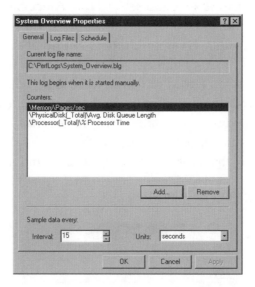

Figure 4.33 Running Counter Logs

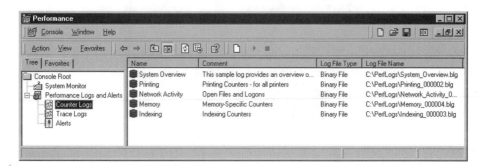

NOTE

The log type (specified under the **Log Files** tab in the log **Properties**) can be set to **Text File** (as a comma-separated or tab-separated variable) or **Binary** or **Binary Circular**. The text file format can be read by common applications such as Notepad, Excel, or Access and as such would be useful if you wanted to import the information and manipulate it. The binary files allow you to *play back* these logs later—for example, with the System Monitor, where you specify the log file under the **Source Properties**.

You configure Alerts in much the same way. Right-click **Alerts** under **Performance Logs and Alerts** and select **New Alert Settings** and the name of your alert log. You'll then be able to add counters you want to monitor and, for each one selected, set an **Over** or **Under** limit number you want to monitor. Note that the interval of sampling data is per log and not for each counter.

The Action tab should be used to define what to do when an alert action is recorded. You can simply log the entry in the Application event log, send a network message to a specified workstation name, start performance logging to capture more information, or run a specified program. Figure 4.34 shows an example of configuring an alert log that looks for known stress conditions every 10 minutes.

Figure 4.34 Configuring an Alert Log

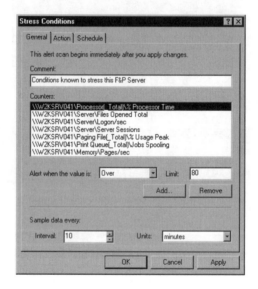

Configuring and Using the Event Logs

We've already discussed the logged information you'll see in the Event Log and how to configure auditing to enable the Security log. However, as a network administrator, you need to know about other options and configurations discussed in this section.

Each log has a Properties sheet, where you can configure options for its size, what to do when a log size is reached, set the low-speed connection by default, and so on. Right-click each log under Event Viewer and you'll see a dialog box similar to the one shown in Figure 4.35, which shows default values.

Figure 4.35 Viewing and Changing the Default Log Properties

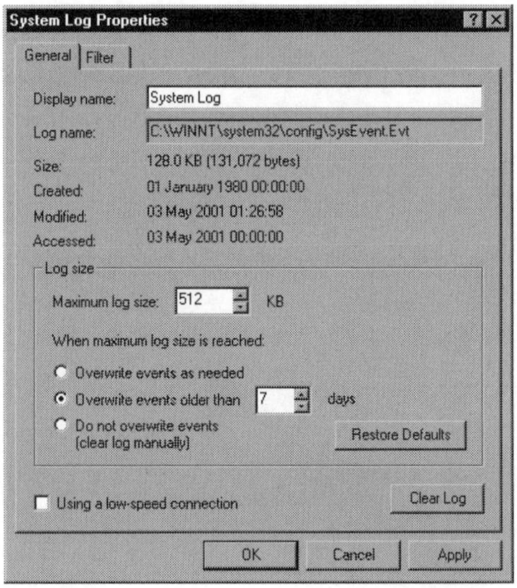

For a server, you'll probably want to increase the size of the log and decide whether to change what action to take when a log is full. This is particularly important for the Security log. If you're auditing, you can fill up an audit log pretty quickly, so ensure that you specify adequate disk space (something like 2MB to 4MB) and think about how to handle a full security log.

You might remember from Chapter 2 that one of the Local Group Policies under the Security Options was to automatically shut down the computer if the security log was full. This automatic shutoff prevents a user from overwriting evidence of unauthorized access attempts. Obviously, this is the more secure option, but it does rely on an administrator carefully monitoring the log and archiving events regularly to ensure that the server is available under normal conditions.

NOTE

You'll see from the System Log Properties the names and paths of the logs. On your server, these logs should be automatically protected from nonadministrators, but you might decide to secure them further by specifically granting or denying read access to specified users.

The Filter tab allows you to set criteria to help you more easily sift through the numerous logged events. The more specifically you can define the type of event you're interested in, the more precise your filter can be.

Figure 4.36 shows an example of using the Filter log to find when or if the Security log was cleared. If you're interested in a specific time period, you can define it by selecting **Events On** and fill in **From** and **To**. As you can see from the example, you'll see a neat little popup calendar to help you define the dates. This calendar easily identifies weekdays and today's date.

Figure 4.36 Configuring Filtering in Event Logs

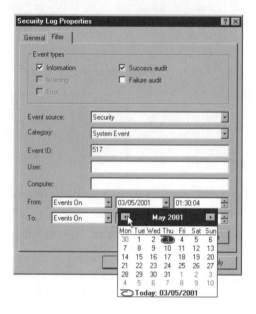

Once you've defined the filter, your results pane displays **Filtered view showing <number> of <number> event(s)** at the top to remind you that you're looking at a filtered display and not all the entries. Don't forget to turn off the filtering when you're finished!

Designing & Planning…

Analyzing the Logs

In reality, searching through all the Event logs is a pretty tedious and time-consuming process. It's difficult to get meaningful information from them in a usable form. What's worse, when you're responsible for multiple computers, you need to pool together the information from

Continued

them to find out, for example, how many failed network logons occur, how often network printers are used, how often servers are rebooted (immediately identifying downtime), and so on.

A number of tools help you use and manage the Event logs in the Windows 2000 Server Resource Kit. For example, **Seagate Software Crystal Reports 6.0** provides a utility to extract, view, and formulate the information from the logs into reports. You can export the information to a word processor, spreadsheet, or printer. The tool includes 12 pre-defined reports that you can use, or you can define your own.

Similarly, there's **CyberSafe Log Analyst (CLA)**, which isn't installed by default; you need to run the Setup program from the CD's \apps\log-analyst folder, which then creates **CLA** under your Administrative Tools. This utility allows you to select the logs you want to analyze from other computers, not just local logs. However, for remote logs, you must first select them with Event Viewer and save them as *.EVT logs or use an automatic event-dumping utility such as ELOGDMP.EXE (also from the Resource Kit). Then set the program to analyze them. You can then select the report you want to output the information you require, in the format that you want. You get a number of predefined templates (for example, Activity by User or Login Summary Report), which you can use as is or modify. You can also configure the report with your choice of title and company name; select the graph type, if any (bar chart , pie chart, 3D chart); and even add your company logo.

Crystal Reports 6.0 and CLA are both great utilities that fill a wide gap for administrators who need to monitor Windows 2000 computers. Not only do they help you sift through the information generated and present it in a clear and meaningful way, but more important, they allow you to pool together monitoring information throughout your network. It would make sense, for example, to group together similar computers to analyze, such as servers that require stricter security, like those that offer Internet services (IIS or VPN), servers that house sensitive data, or general workhorse file and print servers, and even monitor workstations.

Of course, if you have spare developers sitting around or the skills and time yourself, you could create a similar utility that is custom-built specifically for your requirements. Other tools related to Event logs include **Eventquery.pl** and **Logevent.exe**.

Walkthrough: Setting an Audit Policy

This exercise takes you through one of the most basic server maintain procedures: auditing your server. The concepts of server auditing have changed little from NT4, but the specifics of implementing an audit on a Windows 2000 server have changed. Obviously, you will need to decide on your own audit policy, judiciously selecting what you want to audit and how (the chapter contents includes more advice on this topic). The examples here should be enough to get you started. This example covers the following steps:

- Configuring auditing for network resources
- Configuring auditing for a file
- Configuring auditing on the registry

1. Setting a local audit policy is done through **Security Settings | Local Policies | Audit Policies** as part of the local group policy under the computer section (more information on this topic is covered in Chapter 2). You can take a shortcut to this section of the local group policy by clicking **Start | Programs | Administrative Tools | Local Security Policy**, which loads the Local Security Settings MMC, as shown in Figure 4.37.

Figure 4.37 Using Local Security Settings to Configure the Audit Policy

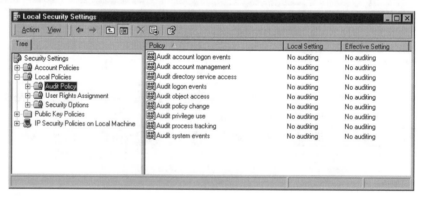

2. You'll notice that nothing is audited by default. As with NT4, you have to specifically set auditing. You'll also notice the columns **Local Setting** and **Effective Setting**. The reason for the two columns is mainly for

Active Directory environments in which you can set auditing policies at different levels—the domain level as well as an OU level. In an Active Directory environment, the local setting has least priority over the other levels, so any values you set here might well be overridden when and if this server is later joined to an Active Directory domain. Here is the place to check whether you have a conflict of settings and your local setting is being overridden by an Active Directory group policy object (GPO), in which case your auditing option might need to be set at a GPO on a different level GPO. However, for a Windows 2000 server in an NT4 domain or a workgroup, you fortunately don't need to worry about Active Directory GPO effective settings and any conflicts.

3. The first thing we want to audit is who is connecting to resources on this server. We set up this auditing with Audit logon events. For example, accessing a shared directory involves authenticating the user, irrespective of whether that authentication is local (the user has an account on the Windows 2000 server) or not (the user has an account on an NT4 or Novell server). Double-click **Audit logon events** and you'll see the dialog box shown in Figure 4.38.

Figure 4.38 The Audit Logon Events Dialog Box

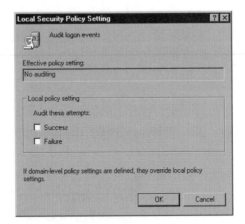

4. We have a choice here of defining an audit policy for users who successfully connect or for users who fail to connect (for example, use a bad password or the resource is denied), or both. Usually for network shares, you want to audit only failures rather than successes, so check the **Failure** box and click **OK**. Now anybody who tries to access any

resource on this server over the network and fails to authenticate will be logged in the Security log.

5. The process of auditing a specific file (or directory or printer) and the registry is a little different. First, we must enable auditing for object access, then separately configure the object that requires auditing. Double-click **Audit object access**, and this time click both **Success** and **Failure**. Then click **OK**.

6. At this point, your Local Security settings should look like those in Figure 4.39, with only **Audit logon events** and **Audit object access** configured. You can now close this MMC.

Figure 4.39 The Configured Audit Policy

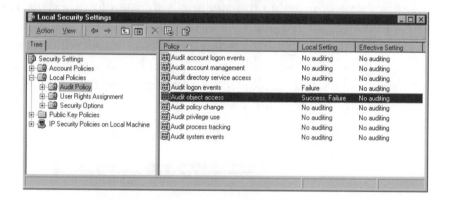

7. Load Explorer and create a folder on your server. Call the folder **Share**. Right-click the directory and configure the **Sharing** tab such that it's configured for **Share this folder**. For the purposes of this walkthrough, keep the defaults of **Everybody** having Full Control by clicking **OK** to close the folder properties.

8. Double-click your newly created folder called **Share** to open it. In the white space, right mouse-click, then choose **New | Text Document**. With the name of this document still highlighted, type **Test** and press **Enter**.

9. Right-click the file, choose **Properties**, then click the **Security** tab. You'll see the dialog box shown in Figure 4.40.

10. Click the **Advanced** button and then the **Auditing** tab. The Auditing Entries list is blank at this point. Click **Add** and double-click **Everybody**. This step loads the Auditing options we can set. We want to

audit who modifies this file, so click **Create Files/Write Data** under the **Successful** column. It should look like Figure 4.41.

Figure 4.40 Security Properties on a File

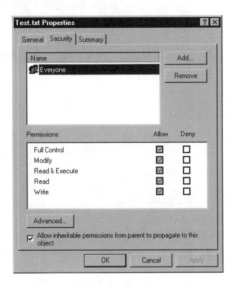

Figure 4.41 Setting the Write Audit Option

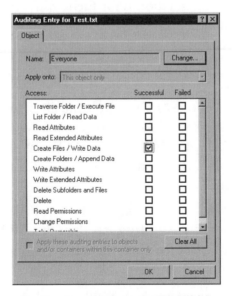

11. Click **OK**. Your Auditing Entries should now look like Figure 4.42.

Figure 4.42 Auditing Entry Added

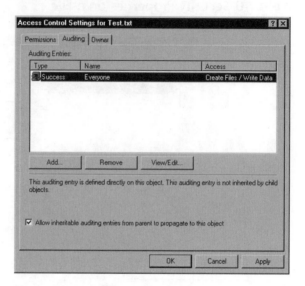

12. Use the **Add**, **Remove**, and **View/Edit** buttons if you want to refine auditing entries for this file. Click **OK**, then click **OK** again.

13. The final configuration is for the registry. Registry keys are also objects as far as auditing is concerned. Click **Start | Run** and type **regedit32** (*regedit* will not do here) and press **Enter**.

14. You would normally audit writing on specific main keys (identified in the chapter contents), but for simplicity in this exercise we'll audit a fairly innocent key so we can manually change one of the values and ensure that it's recorded in the registry. Navigate to the following key: **HKEY_LOCAL_MACHINE\SOFTWARE\Microsoft\ WindowsNT\CurrentVersion** and click the Security menu, then Permission.

15. Just as we did with setting auditing on a file, click the **Advanced** button, then the **Auditing** tab, then the **Add** button. This time we'll specifically select the local Administrator and then **Set Value** under the **Successful** column so it looks like Figure 4.43.

16. Click **OK**, then click **OK** again, and click **OK** once more.

Figure 4.43 Setting the Registry's Set Value Auditing Option

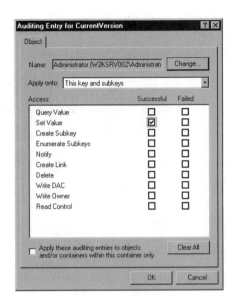

17. While the registry is still open, we can test this setting. Under
     CurrentVersion, you'll see a key for **RegisteredOwner**. Double-click it,
     and modify the string slightly (for example, add a space) and click **OK**.

18. Click **Start | Programs | Administrative Tools | Event Viewer** and
     click the **Security log**. You should see an entry with an Event ID 560,
     with the source Security and Category Object access. Viewing the
     Description, you should see more information, such as the exact key that
     was audited but not the actual value—remember, we set the audit on the
     key only as the lowest value you can audit in the registry. Figure 4.44
     shows an example of this type of audit. Scroll through your own
     Description to see additional details.

19. This will be followed by at least one Event ID 562, which is less useful.
     We'll come back to the Security log, but for now restore the registry
     string to its original state, remove the Auditing option, and close the
     registry.

20. We now need to test the network logon from another computer (which
     doesn't have to be Windows 2000). Make sure you log in to this work-
     station with a nonadministrative account.

Figure 4.44 Security Audit Event for the Registry

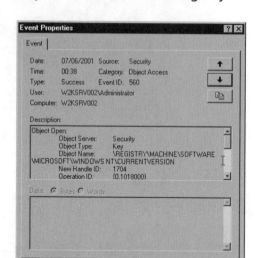

21. We need to test an unsuccessful logon to one of the server's resources, so with our nonadministrative account, we'll try to access a standard hidden administrative share on the server. This is a standard back-door way of gaining access to a Microsoft server's disk. Furthermore, we'll use the powerful **Net Use** command, which works from any Microsoft computer, often when Explorer won't. Load a command prompt and type **Net Use J: \\<server_name>\C$ /USER:ADMINISTRATOR** (changing the <server_name> to the name of your own server). You'll then be prompted for the server's administrative password. Make sure you type it in incorrectly. You'll see now the value of having a hard-to-guess administrator's password as well as renaming the account!

22. When you type in the password incorrectly, the Net command returns a "Logon failure" message about an unknown username or bad password. This message corresponds with a Logon/Logoff Failure with Event ID 529 in the server's Security log. Further more, this event lists the workstation and domain that issued the attempted logon, the username used, and the time. Note that it doesn't tell you which resource was tried. See Figure 4.45 for an example.

Figure 4.45 Failed Network Logon Audit Event

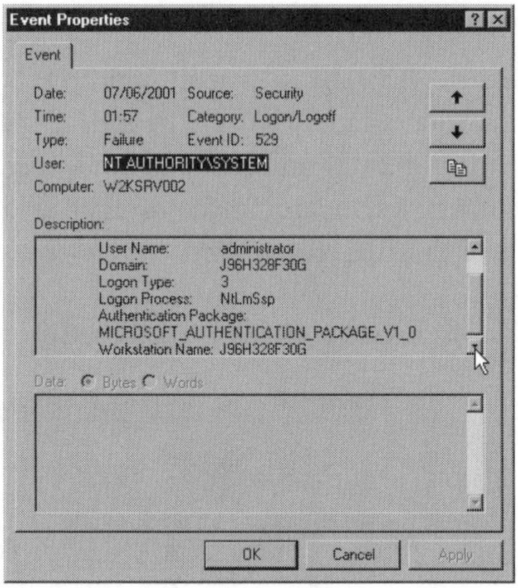

NOTE

When a user genuinely forgets his password, doesn't realize the Caps Lock is on, or tries to access something that he doesn't have permission to use, you will also see this audit event. However, repeated failed logon events like the one in our example should ring alarm bells for a number of reasons:

1. The username was Administrator, which is the most powerful account on the server and is the account a hacker would target first.

2. The computer is not logged into a domain. Notice that the domain name and the computer name are the same, which means they have logged on locally. This is unusual unless you're running in a workgroup environment. The Logon Type 3 confirms it was a network logon (local logons have Type 2).

3. The computer name is odd. It doesn't follow a standard naming format and certainly not the company's standard format.

4. The time stamp is long after office hours. Be sure to check that the clock is accurate on your servers! Unlike a standard user account, an administrator's account cannot be locked out after so many bad attempts, so a hacker has all night to guess alternative passwords, leaving a trail of these failed logon audit events.

23. It's time to check out the file auditing. Load Explorer, map a drive to the Share directory on the server, and load the text document. Add some text, save it, and exit.

24. In the Security Event log, you should now have two more entries, this time a Success audit with Category Object Access, Event ID 560 and Event ID 562. The first entry has all the relevant information, as Figure 4.46 shows, including the domain or user that accessed the file, the name of the file, and when it was accessed.

Figure 4.46 Successful File Audit Event

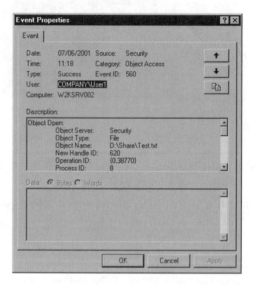

Summary

This chapter covered a lot of ground in examining how to run Windows 2000 Server for file and print services. Some of this information is equally applicable to workstations and other servers. However, the chapter concentrated on the main features and benefits of a typical file and print server environment.

When looking at how data was stored and retrieved, we covered Distributed File System (Dfs), which allows you to reorganize your existing network shares into a uniform namespace and provide fault tolerance by using replicas that point to multiple locations that host the same data. You can't use all the new features in Windows 2000 Dfs outside Active Directory—for example, the ability to host a domain Dfs root or have fault tolerance for your Dfs roots or automatic replication.

These features can be added when and if you migrate to Active Directory. However, despite Microsoft stating that standalone Dfs roots are there mainly for downward compatibility, there are some compelling reasons to utilize it to good effect in your NT4 environment.

We also looked at the Volume Mount Points feature. New in Windows 2000, this feature lets you mount a new or existing volume within an empty directory on another drive. Like Dfs, this feature provides a more logical and flexible view of data storage for users, which hides the complexities of the actual physical data storage from them.

The Indexing Service in Windows 2000 has been extended beyond offering a sophisticated and efficient search utility just for Web documents. It can now index documents of your choice across your network shares and disparate servers to help users quickly find the data they require from one single source.

Printing has been improved in a number of ways in Windows 2000, including the ability to support new technologies such as hot-pluggable USB and Firewire printers, in addition to supporting Plug and Play, which makes installing and configuring new printers much easier and quicker. The introduction of Internet Printing Protocol (IPP) to extend printing services to a Web server for both intranet and Internet setups offers exciting new possibilities and extends the flexibility and manageability of offering central printing services.

Finally, we looked at disk and data management, which included the new dynamic disk configurations that offer disk management without the need to reboot. We also covered the new Backup utility, defragmentation, removable storage, disk quotas, performance monitoring, auditing, and Event logs.

Solutions Fast Track

Sharing Data: Storing and Retrieving

- ☑ The process of configuring network shares for central data location hasn't changed much from NT4, except for the new Caching option, which you can configure so that mobile users automatically benefit from the new Offline Files feature.

- ☑ Distributed File System (Dfs) is a service that has many benefits in an NT4 domain, despite not having all the features available when it runs within Active Directory. Dfs allows you to reorganize existing shares into a single, simplified, and uniform namespace. It also offers better availability when you use replicas, whereby a single share can point to more than one location and the next location is automatically selected if the first becomes unavailable.

☑ Similarly to how Dfs makes locating shares easier for users by hiding from them the complexities of the physical locations, mount volumes can make data location more logical and easier to use. This is because a new or existing disk can be mounted into an empty directory on another disk, so the user simply sees a new directory in the existing location.

☑ The Indexing Service in Windows 2000 has been extended beyond the confines of indexing Web documents on an Internet server. It can now index any sort of file for both local resources and network resources. This flexibility provides users with a single, centralized search facility to locate and retrieve data from disparate servers. It supports fast retrieval with both simple and complex query languages.

Sharing Printers: Installing and Managing

☑ New hardware support such as USB, infrared, and Firewire might not require a server reboot when you are installing printers with these architectures.

☑ Plug and Play support makes installing and configuring printers both easier and quicker.

☑ A Windows 2000 print server can supply a wide range of client drivers, which clients automatically download when installing the printer, so there's no need to install and upgrade these locally.

☑ General improvements in printing include a new TCP/IP Port Monitor, Internet Printing Protocol (IPP), better performance monitoring, and new user options.

☑ IPP is a new and exciting extension to printing services that can be used in both an intranet environment and over the Internet. On an intranet, IPP uses RPC communication; on the Internet, it uses HTTP port 80 (so there's no need to reconfigure existing firewalls).

☑ Using IIP, you can monitor printers and documents and install a printer through a browser and Internet Explorer. IPP requires the print server to be running IIS on a Windows 2000 server or workstation.

Managing Servers

☑ Disk management has been improved with support for dynamic disk storage, bringing greater flexibility in configuring disks on the fly (no reboots) and remote configuration.

☑ Windows 2000 now supports Removable Storage to help more efficiently and effectively manage and pool remote storage such as tapes, optical disks, and robotic storage libraries. This can work in conjunction with Remote Storage and Backup.

☑ Remote Storage allows you to automatically migrate data you use less often to tape, making more space on disk for newer data. However, from the user's point of view, the data still exists on the disk and when accessed is automatically retrieved. The exception is the Backup program, which is Remote Storage aware and can be configured to back up the remote storage directly on tape.

☑ The Backup utility has changed in Windows 2000 and has an improved interface, including backup and restore wizards and scheduling.

☑ Disk quotas can be used to monitor, warn, and enforce disk space restriction on users. Disk quotas work per disk, per ownership (SID); as such, they must be used with caution in certain circumstances.

☑ Performance monitoring has been improved in Windows 2000 to include automatic logging that runs as a service.

☑ Event logs are now highly configurable and should be used to monitor the general health of your server. Auditing must be enabled before events are written to the Security log.

☑ Typical auditing information for file and print servers includes auditing success and failures on critical files, printers, privileged use, and the registry.

Frequently Asked Questions

The following Frequently Asked Questions, answered by the author of this book, are designed to both measure your understanding of the concepts presented in this chapter and to assist you with real-life implementation of these concepts. To have your questions about this chapter answered by the author, browse to **www.syngress.com/solutions** and click on the **"Ask the Author"** form.

Q: Is there a way to copy a share from one server to another, maintaining all the permissions?

A: First, copy the actual data across and create your new share. Then use the PERMCOPY.EXE utility from the Windows 2000 Resource Kit. It's very simple to use. For example, to copy the share OLD on the computer NT4SRV to a share called NEW on the computer W2KSRV, you would type **PERMCOPY \\NT4SRV OLD \\W2KSRV NEW**.

Q: Why don't my administrative shares from my NT4 server show up from my Windows 2000 server's Shared Folders—for example, my C$ and D$ shares?

A: This happens when a registry key has been added to the NT4 server, AutoShareServer, which is set to 0 under the following registry key: HKEY_LOCAL_MACHINE\System\CurrentControlSet\Services\ LanmanServer\Parameters. To reverse this, change the value from 0 to 1 with the registry editor, regedt32. You'll need to reboot the NT4 server for this change to take effect. There's an equivalent key for NT4 workstations, called AutoShareWks. However, network administrators might have configured this deliberately for security reasons.

Q: Wasn't Dfs available with NT4?

A: It was, but in a much simpler form. Dfs improvements in Windows 2000 now make this a compelling and integrated service to use. Now it's installed by default on servers and has a graphical configuration utility. Each link can have its own referral setting, status flags indicate the availability of replicas, and it can also be used with clustering. When you use it with Active Directory, you gain even more advantages, such as fault-tolerant Dfs roots, intelligent use of Dfs links according to site topology, and automatic replication of data if required. If you used Dfs with NT4, your settings are automatically kept and upgraded. If you didn't use Dfs before, now is a good time to start!

Q: What clients can be used with our standalone Dfs root as well as Windows 2000 computers?

A: NT4 clients with SP3 have Dfs client support, Windows 98 has Dfs client support out of the box, and Windows 95 has Dfs client support with an add-on (Active Directory Client Pack). Furthermore, 16-bit clients and NetWare clients cannot be Dfs clients. Note that with a standalone Dfs root, the client and server must be in the same domain. If you later move to Active Directory and use domain-hosted Dfs roots, you must use the Active Directory Client Pack for all down-level 32-bit clients (that is, NT4, Windows 98 and Windows 95).

Q: What's this "bulk ACL checking" that's in Windows 2000?

A: An Access Control List (ACL) records users' and groups' permissions on files and directories. NT4 stores an ACL for each directory and each file. In comparison, Windows 2000 stores only unique ACLs and indexes each occurrence of them. Chances are you'll have a lot of files and directories with the same ACL, so if all the directories and folders with the same permissions share just one ACL rather than duplicating the same ACL for each file and each directory, you'll be able to retrieve permissions much more quickly. For example, your Marketing group having read permission to 500 files would result in one ACL in Windows 2000 but 500 ACLs in NT4. You'll see the benefit of this system when you use the Indexing Service, which must check through a large number of files very quickly and honor the ACLs by returning only those files to which the user has access.

Q: I've heard that the Change Journal tracks all changes to files and directories. Can I use this to recover some important files I deleted by mistake?

A: The Change Journal is new in Windows 2000 and tracks all NTFS changes, such as whenever files and directories are added, deleted, or changed. The Change Journal tracks which object was changed and how (for example, write, move, delete, and so on). Unfortunately, this tool doesn't provide enough information to *undo* file system changes you've made, so you'll still need your trusty backup and restore system. However, it does produce an efficient journal of changes (hence the name) so that programs that need to track such changes (such as for backup, replication, and indexing) can consult the journal for an index of which files have changed, instead of having to check every file at runtime to determine whether it changed since the program was last run. When storing large amounts of data, having a Change Journal obviously offers a more efficient and faster method of accessing only the necessary (that is, changed) data.

Q: Is there a way of querying and saving the output of a server's disk configuration so that we have a historical record and can collate these records for all our new Windows 2000 servers?

A: Use the simple DmDiag tool from the Windows 2000 Server Resource Kit. This tool displays all the computer's system state and configuration with regard to disk storage, such as information on the computer name and OS version and any mount points, drive letters, or disk partitions. Running DmDiag on its own displays this information to the screen. Redirect the output using **DmDiag > filename.txt** so that you have a historical record.

Q: All the documentation says that you shouldn't upgrade a basic disk to dynamic if a down-level operating system needs to read it. Does this rule apply to clients accessing the disk over the network?

A: No, it doesn't apply to network access. The connecting client is blissfully unaware of the type of disk storage it is accessing, just as a Windows 95 client can happily access a NTFS drive, even though NTFS isn't supported natively on that client.

Q: Can we set quotas without having to go through the GUI?

A: Yes, you can, with the **DISKQUOTASETTINGS.PL** utility from the Windows 2000 Server Resource Kit. This tool lets you enable, disable, change, and display disk quota settings. The nice thing about this tool is that you can set quotas on multiple volumes simultaneously.

Q: Why can't I set an alert for the amount of free disk space? It seems such an obvious alert to set, and yet there's no counter for it.

A: You need the % Free Space counter from the Logical Disk object. Although physical disk counters are enabled by default in Windows 2000, logical disk counters are not. You need to type **diskperf–yv** at a command prompt, and then reboot the server. After that, you'll be able to monitor the Logical Disk % Free Space counter.

Q: We've got a departmental server that both serves as a file server and hosts an Access database, which runs very slowly. After we ran various performance tests, it seems that the processor is regularly peaking over 90 percent with a high queue length, but when the Access database isn't running the processor never runs above 50 percent and the queue length is never more than 1. What's the best thing to do here—add another processor or move this database onto another server?

A: You could add another processor and, to ensure that the database benefited the most from it, use the Processor Affinity with Task Manager to set a *hard affinity* of the database to the second processor. If it's a database that was written in-house, your developers might be able to set this programmatically. Keep an eye on RAM, too; running more than one processor requires more memory to support it, so you could find that you have to add another 64MB or so to achieve the same memory-level performance you had with only the single processor.

Q: What sorts of recommendations are there for configuring the page size?

A: In Windows 2000, you configure the computer's page file under **Control Panel | System | Performance**, then pressing the **Change** button. Ideally, your computer should rarely use the page file. It's an indication that physical memory was depleted and so used virtual memory by writing to disk. However, disk access and read/write are always slower than real memory, and some actions cannot be paged to disk. (Some system calls and network operations, for example, must use real memory.) However, configuring an adequate page file is essential to a file and print server, where memory is often the most stressed resource on the computer. It is recommended that your page file be at least 1.5 times the amount of RAM installed, but many people wouldn't dream of starting at less than double that amount. If you add more memory to the computer, don't forget to also increase the page size. You can further improve performance by setting a fixed page file size instead of a minimum and maximum; you'll get less fragmentation and a quicker response time when the additional space is required. Put the paging file on a different physical disk to the operating system and preferably over a stripe set (but not striped with parity, which takes more computing resources).

Q: I really need more help with understanding the performance counters than is provided with the Explain button. Where do you suggest I start?

A: The Windows 2000 Server Resource Kit includes a Performance Counters Reference that contains plenty of information on this tricky subject. It includes an overview of monitoring, how to detect bottlenecks, and describes each counter by feature and object, with suggestions for identifying specific types of bottlenecks, such as how to effectively monitor multiprocessor computers.

Q: I've heard that Windows 2000 supports I2O. Will using I2O mean better performance for my servers?

A: Support for Intelligent Input/Output architecture on multiprocessor servers allows you to achieve higher input/output by offloading certain I/O operations to a secondary processor. It is particularly suited to high-bandwidth applications such as client/server and video-based networking services. On a standard file and print server, the I/O operations are not likely to be the bottleneck; you're more likely to run into memory and disk access problems. But you might find that I2O will help with servers such as those running SQL or Exchange Server.

Chapter 5

Terminal Services

Solutions in this chapter:

- **Why Use Windows 2000 Terminal Services?**

- **Preinstallation Considerations**

- **Configuring and Managing Windows 2000 Terminal Services**

- **Configuring Clients to Use Terminal Services**

- ☑ **Walkthrough: Remotely Administering a Windows 2000 Server with Terminal Services**

- ☑ **Summary**

- ☑ **Solutions Fast Track**

- ☑ **Frequently Asked Questions**

Introduction

Thin-client environments have become fashionable of late, partly as a reaction to the problems of distributed computing, which include the administrative overhead of configuring and maintaining multiple and disparate systems. In the mainframe days, when one big computer held and processed all the applications and end users had no more than a dumb terminal with which to run their applications, support was much simpler. When an application needed to be installed, configured, or upgraded, it was done only once, and all users could simultaneously receive the changes. If a terminal broke, it was simply swapped out with a working one and the user could be just as productive immediately.

Nowadays it's a full-time job for a team of people to install, configure, and maintain end users' computers. Because data can be stored and configured locally, support overheads are greatly increased. A number of solutions, such as disk imaging, roaming profiles, home directories, and Systems Management Server (SMS) to remotely install and configure applications, aim to alleviate these problems. But such solutions come at the cost of purchasing them, training and testing, and deploying and maintaining them.

Certainly Active Directory is aimed precisely at addressing these problems of achieving a lower cost of ownership in terms of central control. It achieves this goal via a redesigned directory, employing technologies such as remote installation services, publishing and advertising applications, group policy settings at various levels of the network hierarchy, and redirecting folders to central servers.

However, many of these benefits (and more) can be achieved by employing thin-client solutions with terminal servers, where the applications are again stored and configured on a central computer. Indeed, you could argue that moving users over to thin clients on a Windows 2000 terminal server is more cost effective and easier to maintain than restructuring and migrating your existing domain architecture over to Active Directory.

True, a terminal server has high demands on its hardware—on the hard disk, memory, and processing capability. However, the cost of implementing sufficient Windows 2000 servers to efficiently run Active Directory services (including domain controllers running various services and Domain Name System [DNS] servers) could be higher than the money spent on implementing a farm of Terminal Servers.

For medium-sized to smaller companies for which the various costs (in terms of money, politics, time, and so on) of implementing Active Directory are considered too high, moving to Windows 2000 terminal servers as member servers in existing NT4 domains (or even in workgroups) could provide an attractive option. Alternatively, this solution could be used as a quick stepping-stone within these companies' migration plans.

Using Windows 2000 Terminal Services comes with one significant support advantage: being able to shadow a user so you can see and control that user's session. For companies with remote sites, or even for companies with a low ratio of support staff to users, this facility alone could bring a quick return on investment.

In short, Windows 2000 Terminal Services are one of the most exciting new features, if not *the* most exciting, to come out of the Windows 2000 feature set, which can be easily realized by network administrators in a very short time frame. Admittedly, Terminal Services won't solve every problem related to support and maintenance, but you might be surprised at just how many it does solve. Terminal Services in Windows 2000 has improved greatly from its predecessor, Terminal Services Edition (TSE). Read on to see what the product has to offer and how to configure it and your clients.

Why Use Windows 2000 Terminal Services?

The Introduction outlined the basic advantages of using a centralized computing model. Other chapters of this book cover Windows 2000 general features that, with the help of Terminal Services, can be immediately realized by a wide variety of clients without having to upgrade them to Windows 2000. Furthermore, because Terminal Services is now integrated with the base operating system, it is easier and simpler to support with standard Windows 2000 server utilities and features, whether the server is running Terminal Services or not. Additionally, there's only one common Service Pack to install for updates. This section details the specific technical features and options available with Windows 2000 Terminal Services, covering the following:

- Fast connections over low bandwidths
- Remote administration
- Tighter security
- Shadowing (remote control)
- Seamless integration between PC and server

Fast Connections over Low Bandwidths

With a terminal server client, the client to server traffic consists of keystrokes and mouse movements. The terminal server does all the data manipulation locally and passes back only the display update. In this way, network traffic is greatly reduced, and even a 28.8k modem connection can realistically use an application on a terminal server.

Designing & Planning…

Low-Bandwidth Connections

In the past, administrators and managers who had previous experience of unacceptable connection speeds on Terminal Server Edition (TSE) when using RDP often resorted to using Citrix Independent Computing Architecture (ICA) clients. This is because ICA is a faster and leaner protocol in comparison to RDP. However, I recommend you suspend your skepticism and try RDP5 before assuming the same performance speeds. Although the ICA protocol still remains quicker and can still accommodate a wider range of clients, I think the speed differences from RDP4 to RDP5 now make it a viable option.

Connection efficiency is a very dry subject to write about and can't do justice to the overwhelming priority it has in the real world. You must experience it to appreciate its importance. To witness a terminal service session perform as efficiently as if it were local is a very strange feeling when you know and understand the topology of the underlying network.

Users won't appreciate the faster connections because they always demand and assume every connection and application should behave as quickly and efficiently as if it were local. However, you'll definitely hear about it if the connection isn't good! Complaints about poor performance and unreliable connections are high on any network administrator's most dreaded reported problems, particularly when increasing available bandwidth is not an option.

Windows 2000 Terminal Services uses Microsoft Remote Desktop Protocol (RDP) for the client-to-server communication. RDP is based on the International Telecommunications Union (ITU) T120 protocol, which is an international standard multiple virtual channel conferencing protocol first used with Microsoft NetMeeting. RDP can only be used with the TCP/IP, however, rather than with NetBEUI and Internetwork Packet Exchange (IPX). This limitation is less a problem these days when TCP/IP is the default standard networking protocol. RDP can also be used with the Point-to-Point Protocol (PPP) for dialup Remote Access Server (RAS) connections, and it can be used with Point-to-Point Tunneling Protocol (PPTP) and Layer 2 Tunneling Protocol/IP Security (L2TP/IPSec) for virtual private network (VPN) connections.

The version of RDP that ships with Windows 2000 is version 5, which has a great many improvements over RDP4, which shipped with NT4 Terminal Server Edition. Not only is it more efficient in itself, but it can specifically accommodate low bandwidths by enabling data compression and caching bitmaps. These are set on a connection basis, as Figure 5.1 shows. Many of the new features in Windows 2000 are a result of RDP improvements in this later version.

Figure 5.1 Setting Data Compression and Bitmap Caching for Low-Bandwidth Connections

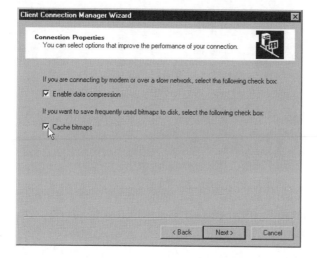

Remote Administration

Terminal Services in Windows 2000 now comes in two flavors that Microsoft calls *modes*. The traditional fat server that services thin clients is a mode called *Application mode*. New to this version is *Remote Administration mode*, which allows an administrator to remotely manage a Windows 2000 server using all the same technologies as thin clients but without the overhead on the server. Even better, you don't have to run a Terminal Services Licensing server (which we'll cover later) in order to handle this task.

You configure Terminal Services for one mode or another when you first install it. Thereafter you can change modes, but only through **Add/Remove Programs | Add/Remove Windows Components**. After you install Terminal Services, every time you run Add/Remove Windows Components, you'll be prompted for the mode Terminal Services should run in. If you want to change modes, this is the place to do it; otherwise, keep the default setting. Figure 5.2 shows the prompt you'll see for selecting one mode or the other.

Figure 5.2 Setting the Terminal Services Mode

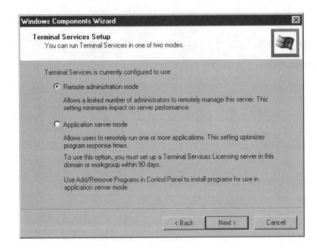

You can use this method for changing modes (for example, from Remote Administration to Application mode), but Microsoft advises you to decide in advance how you want to use Terminal Services, configure the appropriate mode you want, and keep to this setting to ensure that you don't run into application installation/configuration issues.

Remote Administration Using Terminal Services

Why use Terminal Services to remotely manage a server when you could use the standard Microsoft Management Console (MMC) utilities and simply connect to the remote computer? Even using Windows 2000 Professional is no setback when you can install the Remote Administration Pack (**adminPak.msi**) and configure all your server services from Windows 2000 Professional.

However, the main answer to this question lies in bandwidth: MMC-based utilities rely on a LAN-grade network and expect various remote procedure call (RPC) ports and services to be running (NetBIOS predominantly comes to mind here!). Therefore, remote administration with MMC utilities is not ideal when *remote* means over a wide area network (WAN) link or an Internet connection.

In comparison, using a Terminal Services connection requires little bandwidth. All the processing is handled on the server that is being configured, and only keyboard, mouse, and screen display data actually travels between the two computers. For firewalls, your only consideration is to configure them to allow the Windows 2000 Terminal Services protocol (RDP) on TCP port 3389.

The second reason is security. Not only is the data that travels between the two computers harder for an eavesdropper to interpret, but you can also encrypt it for additional security without having to set up IPSec and the administration, processing, and bandwidth requirements associated with it.

The third reason lies in platform compatibility. Because you can run a Terminal Services client on a variety of clients, including NT, Win9x, Windows for Workgroups, and even Windows CE and Windows Based Terminals (WBTs), you don't have to be running a Windows 2000 platform to perform administrative tasks on your Windows 2000 server. If you buy Citrix's MetaFrame add-on, you could extend this flexibility to include other clients such as UNIX workstations, Apple Macintoshes, and even DOS clients, if you still have any.

Using Remote Administration mode and a standard Windows 2000 Terminal Services client connection (which we'll cover later in this chapter), you can log on to the server as if you were physically sitting in front of it. Alternatively, you might prefer to use the Terminal Services Connection snap-in from Service Pack 1 (**\VALUEADD\TSAC\TSMMCSETUP.EXE**), which allows you to use the MMC snap-in called Terminal Services Connection. Figure 5.3 shows an example connection using this snap-in.

Note that you can add all your terminal servers in this one snap-in as additional connections. The Properties of each connection allow you to configure not only the connection name and terminal server name and address but also the screen resolution, an automatic logon, and a program to run automatically.

Terminal Services Remote Management Limitations

One of the limitations to using Terminal Services in Remote Administration mode, however, is that only two connections can be made at once. This restriction can be seen as a good safety precaution to ensure that multiple administrators don't try to change the same setting with different values. However, this restriction can be a problem in larger corporations where administrators connect to one server and from there connect to another server rather than initiating a new connection.

Figure 5.3 Using the Terminal Services Connection Snap-In

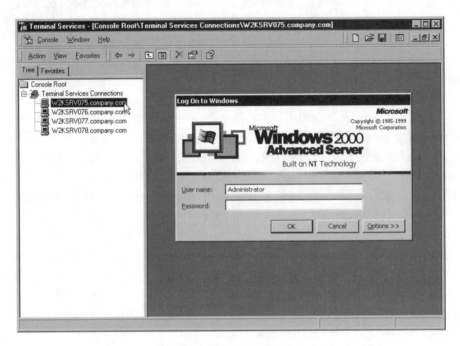

Another consideration is that the server running Terminal Services cannot cache other servers' folders or files for offline use (the client-side caching we saw in Chapter 3), although it can still have its own folders or files configured for offline use (the server-side caching we saw in Chapter 4). Any folders or files marked for client-side offline use on the server when Terminal Services is installed will have this feature disabled. This usually won't be a problem, since most servers are used to offer their local folders to users rather than connect to other shares. However, client-side offline caching can be used as a quick and inexpensive backup mechanism by synchronizing data between computers. Remember, this is no longer an option once Terminal Services is enabled.

Something else to consider is that although the visual display might look as though you're sitting in front of the server console, you're not, so you cannot see any popup messages sent to the console. Most popup messages have the same information written to the event logs, so checking the server event logs on a regular basis—specifically, after running an installation or a batch process—is more important when you are remotely administering a server using Terminal Services.

Recovering from Disconnected Sessions

If you use Terminal Services to perform server updates or start batched processing commands from a script and the network connection goes down due to, for example, a bad WAN link, by default the session will continue to run, although it will be disconnected. Whatever you were running will continue rather than be aborted, which leaves the server in an unstable state.

This setting is part of the user's account properties, under the **Sessions** tab, where the choices are **Disconnect from session** and **End session**. End session is the equivalent of using Task Manager to kill an open application, which is usually not a good idea when remotely administering a server! Note that if you didn't have a timeout on disconnected sessions (also set under the same Sessions tab), this is a very good reason why *two* remote administration connections are allowed: so that another administrator can connect and close the session when it's safe to do so.

NOTE

The user's setting can be overridden with the server's connection properties under the **Session** tab, which is configured via **Terminal Services Configuration | Connections**.

Microsoft recommends that all Windows 2000 servers have Terminal Services in Remote Administration mode enabled because its advantages are many and its disadvantages few. The impact on the server itself is minimal and offers administrators the ultimate "anywhere, anytime" administration and control. With Terminal Services in Remote Administration mode, you can do most things that you could do if you were physically sitting in front of the server and interactively logged on. You could even load up another Terminal Services connection and connect to another server.

However, if remote administration might include remotely rebooting the server (for example, installing a Service Pack or changing elements of the server's identity, such as name or domain), remember to never leave a floppy disk inserted in the drive. Better still, disable booting off the floppy disk and CD-ROM from within the BIOS.

Tighter Security

Many people think that running a terminal server is less secure than running a traditional client/server connection, because the user requires the Log On Locally permission, which you would never grant to users on domain controllers or critical member servers. However, for many reasons, a terminal server connection can be more secure than the traditional fat-client connection.

When you first choose to install Terminal Services and configure it for Application mode, you'll be asked what permissions to use: permissions compatible for Windows 2000 users or permissions compatible with Windows NT4. This choice is displayed in Figure 5.4.

Figure 5.4 Permissions Choice in Configuring Terminal Services for Application Mode

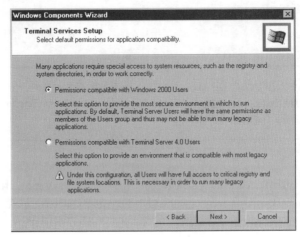

Whenever possible, choose the first (default) option, which offers a more secure environment. It makes terminal server users unable to install applications or access certain parts of the registry, even though they have the Log On Locally permission. Combined with standard NTFS permissions on the files or printers the server offers, this security measure offers immediate protection in that only administrators have access to and can configure crucial system settings.

Additionally, because your computing resources are concentrated on main boxes, you can more tightly control physical security. You can also make good use of Local Group Policy and security templates on Windows 2000 terminal servers (both these topics were covered in Chapter 2). For example, you can use auditing to ensure that only designated users successfully access the files and printers they should, and you can enforce strong passwords for local accounts.

Windows 2000 Terminal Services now also offers three different levels of encryption, making it very difficult, if not impossible, for an intruder to capture any useful network data. The three levels are low, medium (the default), and high.

Low-level encryption encrypts data sent from the client to the server only and is designed to protect password exchanges, using a 40-bit or 56-bit key. (Windows 2000 clients use the 56-bit key, and down-level clients use 40-bit.) *Medium-level encryption* encrypts data sent in both directions, again using a 56-bit or 40-bit key (depending on the client platform). *High-level encryption* encrypts in both directions using a 128-bit key if that capability is supported on the server. (You can easily check the cipher strength by looking at **Internet Explorer's Help | About** and use the High Encryption Pack—or install SP2—to upgrade it to 128 bit if required.) The encryption setting is a server setting and is configured as one of the connection properties with Terminal Services Configuration, as shown in Figure 5.5.

Figure 5.5 Setting the Encryption Level for a Windows 2000 Terminal Server Connection

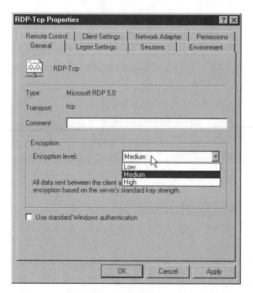

Note that if securing data across your network is important, this is a very easy way to implement that security. It has comparatively little of the overhead associated with IPSec processing and administration and is compatible with down-level clients. However, as with any application that uses 128-bit keys, the high-level encryption requires additional CPU resources on both client and server.

For multihomed servers, you can also specify which adapter should offer Terminal Services connections (and limit the number of connections if you want to safeguard server resources) by specifying the network adapter under the **RDP–TCP Properties | Network Adapter** tab. Although the default is **All network adapters configured with this protocol**, the drop–down box allows you to select a specific adapter on your server. The default is to use all adapters that have TCP/IP bound to them, but you could restrict the RDP protocol to just one adapter.

Configuring & Implementing...

Using Multiple Adapters for Different Settings

If you wanted to specify more than one adapter to use but not all the adapters, you would have to create a new RDP connection and specify the adapter to use as part of its configuration.

One situation in which you might want this type of installation is if you wanted to support different levels of encryption. If you wanted to use high-level encryption for the majority of your users but had some clients who couldn't use 128-bit encryption, you'd install two network adapters.

Configure one adapter for high-level encryption using one of the network adapters. Create a new RDP connection for the other adapter and configure it for medium-level encryption. Then configure your user connections for the various IP addresses or names such that users are matched according to the connection encryption level. This series of steps results in your terminal server using the highest level of encryption it can for all clients.

If you used only one adapter and one RDP connection, your choices would be to either run two different terminal servers or compromise on security by lowering the encryption strength to medium. Terminal Services clients using 56-bit encryption would not be able to connect to an RDP connection that was configured for 128-bit encryption. Unlike IPSec policies, you cannot negotiate down until a common security setting is found. However, 128-bit clients will be able to connect to an RDP connection that's configured for medium-level encryption.

Note that unlike many Windows 2000 services, you cannot use a different logical IP address. The RDP connection detail uses the adapter rather than the address.

If your user accounts will be local to the terminal server, the user portion of Local Group Policies will be available to all users, and you'll administer the user accounts under Local Users and Groups. Once Terminal Services has been installed, you'll find additional tabs on the account Properties that relate to Terminal Services. These tabs are **Environment**, **Sessions**, **Remote Control**, and **Terminal Services Profile**. Figure 5.6 shows a local user account on a standalone Windows 2000 server, showing the Terminal Services Profile tab, which is where you can grant or deny logon permission to the terminal server (on by default).

Figure 5.6 Windows 2000 User Account Properties with Additional Tabs for Terminal Services

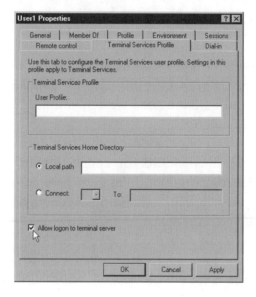

If, however, your terminal server will be configured as a member server in your NT4 domain and will use user accounts from your NT4 domain, the terminal server user accounts are subject to the same system policies and domain settings of your other users.

You can still use and configure the new Terminal Services properties using User Manager for Domains, which ships with Windows 2000 Server. To do this, you load **usrmgr.exe** from the server's **%systemroot%\system32** folder and choose the NT4 domain that holds your accounts. Figure 5.7 shows this Windows 2000 version of User Manager for Domains being loaded on a Windows 2000 member server that's configured with Terminal Services and validating users from an NT4 domain.

Figure 5.7 Using User Manager for Domains to Configure NT4 Accounts for Windows 2000 Terminal Services

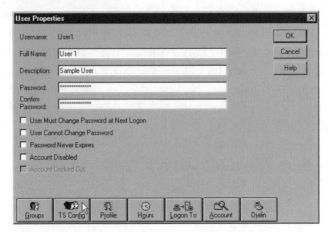

You can see the additional **TS Config** button at the bottom, which you wouldn't see on a standard NT4 User Manager for Domains. When you select this button, you can configure the same settings you have on a Windows 2000 account, as shown in Figure 5.8.

We'll cover the actual configuration options later, but another security option that can be set is to load an application on connection. In Figure 5.8, this option appears as the **Initial Program**. On a Windows 2000 account, it's specified under the **Environment** tab. When this setting is configured and the user connects to the terminal server, the specified application loads—and that's all the user has access to on the terminal server. When the user closes the application, the terminal server connection closes. This system offers very tight security because the user's connection can be used only for this one application.

Using the Application Security Tool

The Application Security Tool (**appsec.exe**) from the Resource Kit provides another way to secure the applications a Terminal Services user can run. It's designed so that users are allowed to run only listed applications, so it suits an environment in which only a limited set of user applications should be available. Note that this restriction is on the program executable name, which restricts use to both the command line as well as desktop shortcuts and menu items. Disabled applications apply only to users, never to administrators. Restrictions apply when the user next logs on.

Figure 5.8 Configuring Terminal Services Account Properties for an NT4 Account

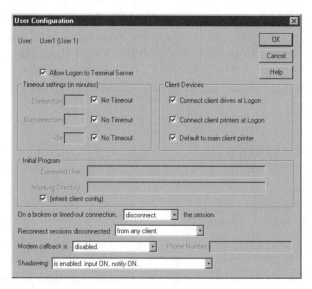

When you run this tool, you'll see a list of system files that are allowed by default, as shown in Figure 5.9. If you don't want a user to run any of these, highlight them and click the **Delete** button. Use the **Add** button to specify additional applications that users can use. If you are not sure which applications are run by users, use the Tracking mechanism provided with the **Add** button. When you are happy with your list, click **Enabled**. When **Disabled** is selected, users can run any application to which they have access and execute permission.

Figure 5.9 Running the Application Security Tool (AppSec)

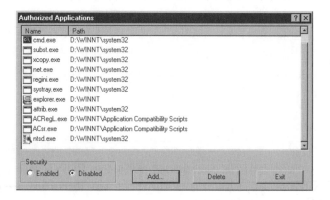

By default, 16-bit applications are disabled because the 16-bit subsystem (**ntvd.exe**) is not enabled. If you want to enable a 16-bit application, you must first add ntvd.exe to the allowed list and then specify the 16-bit application name.

Shadowing Users

The ability to *shadow* a user (to connect to the user's session, see what the user is seeing on his or her screen, and interact with that session) has previously been one of the biggest reasons to use the Citrix add-on called MetaFrame. This facility is now built into Windows 2000 Terminal Services. For remote sites and when the ratio of support staff to users is low, shadowing can dramatically improve the efficiency of end-user support. Administrators no longer have to either physically visit the PC that's experiencing trouble or talk through problems with the user on the telephone and ask for various files to be e-mailed in an attempt to find and diagnose a problem. Now support staff can simply connect to a terminal server's user connection and control the user's session.

Microsoft refers to this feature as *remote control* rather than shadowing, but this facility is so well-known as shadowing in Citrix circles that it will be a while before network administrators learn to call this old trick by its new name!

There are various settings you can configure for remote control. By default, remote control is enabled on every user account but requires the user's permission before the administrator can connect to the user's session. Another setting is to only view the user's session rather than interact with it. Figure 5.10 shows these options, which are configurable on each account, under the **Remote Control** tab.

When the administrator requests a remote control session with a connected user via the default settings, which requires a user's permission, the user will see on his or her screen the dialog box depicted in Figure 5.11.

The user's setting can be overridden with the **RDP-TCP Properties | Remote Control** tab, which is configured via **Terminal Services Configuration | Connections**.

Figure 5.10 Remote Control Options on a Terminal Server Account

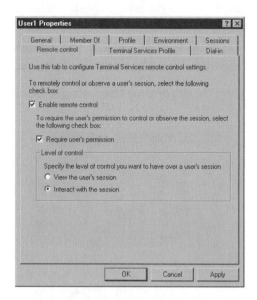

Figure 5.11 Remote Control Request

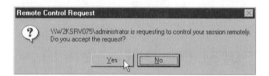

If the user clicks **Yes**, the session comes under the control of the administrator. If the user clicks **No**, the administrator is told that the remote control request has been rejected and the connection is refused. Note that the default user option is No, so a connection could be mistakenly refused by a user pressing **Enter** or **Return**.

Note also the political issues involved should the **Require user's permission** option not be set. The user would have no indication that an administrator was connecting to his or her session and either seeing what is on the user's screen and/or interacting with it without the user's consent. The administrator's convenience should be offset by a user's possible right of privacy and control over his or her own immediate working environment. The technical ability is there, but whether it should be used could be a matter of company politics and ethics.

In order for an administrator to initiate a remote control session, the administrator must use **Terminal Services Manager**, right-click the user's connection, and select **Remote Control**. By default the remote control session can be ended by pressing **Ctrl-*** (the * on the numeric keypad), but the hot key to be used for this task can be configured on the fly when the administrator attempts to initiate the remote control session. The administrator will see the dialog box shown in Figure 5.12, which allows him or her to accept the default setting (and gives a reminder of what that setting is) or select another hot key.

Figure 5.12 Configuring or Accepting the Remote Control Hot Key to End a Remote Control Session

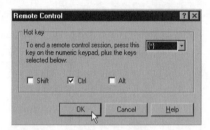

When the remote control session is ended, the user's Terminal Services connection will be disconnected from the administrator. From the administrator's point of view, the session is disconnected and ends. From the user's point of view, the user will once again be the only person connected to the session and so will have the same control over it as before the administrator connected with remote control.

Seamless Integration between PC and Server

At times, you might run a true thin-client environment with no local processing carried out on the client. However, in most environments, users run a mixture of local processing on their PCs and remote processing when they connect to the terminal server. This section looks at how the two types of connections are managed so that the user enjoys a seamless integration between the two environments. This integration includes the following features:

- Clipboard copy and paste
- Drive mappings
- Local printer support
- Profiles
- Home directories
- Scaling out
- Multilanguage support

Clipboard Copy and Paste

One of the new improvements with RDP5 is that the Windows 2000 terminal server's clipboard can now be used to copy text and graphics between the terminal server and the PC. So, for example, a user could open a large centrally stored document on the terminal server, copy sections from it, and paste these into a document that is stored and edited with the user's local version of Word.

Clipboard sharing is set on the server RDP connection rather than on a user basis. By default, clipboard sharing is enabled, but you can disable it in the **RDP-TCP Properties** with the **Terminal Services Configuration** utility, under the **Connections** folder, as shown in Figure 5.13. Note that setting this option would disable it, not enable it!

Figure 5.13 Disabling Clipboard Sharing

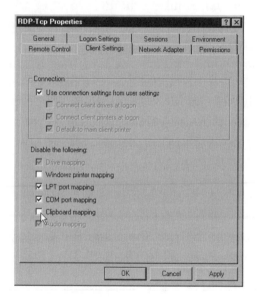

By default, you cannot use the clipboard to copy files and folders between the two systems. An attempt to do this will display the error message, "Cannot copy file: cannot read from the source file or disk." However, the **File Copy tool** (RdpClip) from the Windows 2000 Resource Kit remedies this problem. It requires you to make changes on the server as well as each Terminal Services client who wants to use this feature. Note that client versions vary, depending on whether the client is 32-bit or 16-bit. Rather than following the instructions in the Resource Kit for this tool, see instead the Knowledge Base article, "How to

Install File Copy in the Windows 2000 Resource Kit [Q244732]," which includes downloading a hotfix for missing files.

Drive Mappings

Drive Share is another useful Windows 2000 Resource Kit tool that allows you to map all local drives on the client computer into the terminal server session when the user connects, so that the user can access all his or her local drives within a Terminal Services session using a mapped drive.

For example, say that a user wants to access a floppy drive once she had connected to a terminal server so that she could save a file stored on the terminal server to a floppy drive. The floppy drive on that PC is designated as the A: drive. After you install Drive Share on both the server and client, the floppy drive would be mapped to the Z: drive within the terminal session, so the user could save the file as *X:filename.txt*. Similarly, the PC's local C drive would be mapped to the Y: drive within the terminal session, the CD-ROM on the D: drive mapped to X:, and so on.

To use Drive Share, you must copy the Resource Kit file **drmapsrv.exe** to the server's \System32 directory and then run **drmapsrv.reg** from the Resource Kit directory to modify the registry. On the client side, copy **drmapclt.dll** from the Resource Kit directory to the client's terminal server client installation directory (by default, **\Program Files\Terminal Server Client**), and then run **drmapclt.reg** from the Resource Kit on the client PC.

NOTE

If you want to use both Drive Share and File Copy, you must install them in that order. If you installed Drive Share after installing File Copy, you should reinstall File Copy.

Local Printer Support

When a user connects to a terminal server, any local printers in use on the local PC will be mapped to the terminal server's session by default, so the client can continue to use his or her own printers as well as any printers installed on the terminal server. This is a big improvement on the previous version of RPD. Note, however, that when the terminal session is disconnected, any pending prints to the mapped to local printer will be deleted.

This mapping of local printers is enabled by default on the user's account properties under the Environment tab, but it can be overridden on the terminal server with the **Client Settings** tab on the **RDP-TCP Properties** under **Terminal Services Configuration | Connections**.

> **NOTE**
>
> Automatic printer mapping is not supported for 16-bit clients and Windows Based Terminals (WBTs); these still must manually map printers using the Add Printer Wizard.

Profiles

Thanks to the automatic creation of two terminal server environment variables (**%SESSIONID%** and **%CLIENTNAME%**), Windows is able to determine whether or not the client is connected to a terminal server. This means that two different profiles can be used, one for when a client connects to terminal servers and another for when the client is not connecting to a terminal server.

Designing & Planning...

Using the Terminal Services Environment Variables

You can use these terminal server variables yourself to test whether a client is running a terminal server session or only a local Windows session. For example, you could create a single logon script that tests for the user's current environment and then loads certain applications, depending on the environment. Automatic loading of a virus checker is an obvious example. There would be no need for this feature on a Terminal Services login, where you can automatically scan for viruses on the server.

Profiles store user information such as application configuration, desktop icons, or color options. When the different environments offer different applications over different network connections, it could be particularly advantageous to apply two different profiles automatically.

When a user logs on to a terminal server, the server attempts to load a terminal server profile, if one is specified. If a terminal server profile isn't specified for that user, the server looks for a roaming profile, then the user's standard profile. Note that Terminal Services can also support roaming profiles, which could be useful if you have a terminal server farm and you want the user to have a common profile for all the servers. Make sure that you store the terminal server profile on a server other than the terminal servers so that it is always available. Also make sure that this server has plenty of disk space for the profiles, and enable read/write privileges to the shared directory for its users.

NOTE

When you use roaming profiles for terminal servers, it is important that each server should be configured similarly in terms of partitioning, directory structure, and application installations.

Home Directories

Just as a user can have a different profile for connecting to a terminal server, so the user can have a different home directory. Users typically use home directories to save personal files, which often include backup versions. Therefore, be prepared to allocate sufficient disk space for this eventuality, and consider enabling disk quotas so that a few users don't hog all the allocated disk space.

Whenever possible, it's a good idea to store volatile user and application data separately from the system files. *User data* refers to home directories, personal files, and profiles. *Application data* could refer to a shared database or spreadsheet. If you have only one server and one physical disk, you could partition your disk to keep the various types of data separate. (Better still, have separate disks.) If you have more than one terminal server, it is ideal to store any user and application data on a different server altogether. This setup will make the different types of data easier to protect, back up, and available to all terminal servers without the need for replication.

A good way to create user home directories is to create a server directory specifically for home directories and share it so that everybody has change permission access. Then specify each user's Terminal Services Home Directory to be

<SHARE>\%username% (for example, **\\SERVER1\HOMEDIRS\ %username%**) and map this drive to the same letter. Don't forget: If you're using Drive Share, the drives at the end of the alphabet will be used to map local devices, so you will be better off choosing a letter in the middle of the alphabet. Such a setting ensures that all users have the same drive mapping for their home directories (necessary for any application compatibility scripts), and Terminal Services will automatically create each user's home directory by creating a subdirectory under the share using the username, giving the user full control over it, while administrators can copy files into this directory but not read or delete files from it.

Multilanguage Support

With Windows 2000 support for multiple languages, you can now have a single version of Terminal Services that can service clients in any country, running a mixture of languages. Previously with Windows NT4 TSE, terminal servers were localized in individual languages, which meant buying a different version of Terminal Services for each language required, even if this support was required for just a few users.

The support for multiple languages on Windows 2000 Terminal Services makes for simplified administration as well as reduced costs—particularly in countries where multiple languages must be supported simultaneously. When installing Terminal Services for international use, you must install the languages you need to support on the terminal server. Should a user's profile specify a language that isn't installed, Terminal Services defaults to English.

NOTE

Terminal Services reports its local time to users (using the time zone on which it was installed) for all its applications. Therefore, if you have a user in a different time zone from your office, the time reported in that user's terminal session will not be the user's local time.

Preinstallation Considerations

Before diving into installing and deploying Windows 2000 Terminal Services, you must consider a number of issues. The process of deploying Terminal Services is a little more complex than deploying a standard file and print server—and getting it wrong could be costly in terms of money, time, and your reputation.

Some of the issues you need to think about even before the testing stage include the new Windows 2000 terminal server licensing issues, whether to upgrade existing terminal servers running Terminal Server Edition, how to include Terminal Services with an unattended installation, application suitability, hardware specifications for capacity and scalability planning, and identifying any limitations of Terminal Services that relate to your environment. Let's look at these issues in more depth.

Licensing

Licensing terminal server clients got a lot more complicated in Windows 2000. Running in Application mode, Terminal Services works in conjunction with a Terminal Services Licensing service, which must be activated (that is, given a computer certificate by Microsoft) and which hands out Terminal Services Client Access Licenses (TS CALs) for connecting clients. Licensing is no longer merely about monetary and paper issues; you must factor this new technology into your Terminal Services deployment.

You don't need to run a Terminal Services Licensing server if you want to use only the Remote Administration mode, but as soon as you change the Terminal Services configuration to Application mode, the terminal server will start to look for an activated Terminal Services Licensing server. When you're not in an Active Directory domain, this action will result in the terminal server broadcasting every 15 minutes until it finds such a licensing server. The Terminal Services Licensing server is needed to deliver TS CALs to the terminal server when clients connect.

You can install the Terminal Services Licensing on the server on which you're running Terminal Services, but it's usually preferable to run the licensing service on a standard file and print member server. When you're running Terminal Services within an Active Directory domain, you must install Terminal Services Licensing on a domain controller. So, if you're considering upgrading to Active Directory at a later date, you might want to take this factor into consideration now and install it on an NT4 domain controller that will be upgraded or on a member server that will be upgraded to a Windows 2000 domain controller.

The job of managing the terminal license servers will be much easier if you have Internet connectivity, because you need to enter information provided from the Microsoft Certificate Authority and License Clearinghouse. It is possible to do this without an Internet connection—say, via telephone or fax, but it's more difficult that way.

Once the license server is activated, you need to install client license packs (using an ID that identifies a number of TS CALs) so that the terminal server can deliver these to connecting clients. You still need to purchase the TS CALs through the standard channels (for example, Microsoft License Pak, Microsoft Open License, or with the Microsoft Select agreement) and then install them onto the licensing server so that connecting clients without a license can be allocated a license on a first-come, first-served basis. The good news is that you don't need to purchase or install TS CALs for the following clients:

- Windows 2000 computers (for example, Windows 2000 Professional)
- Non-Windows 2000 computers that are external to your company but that need to connect to your Terminal Services (for example, partner companies), which already have a Windows 2000 TS CAL installed

You must buy a Windows 2000 TS CAL for any other type of terminal service client—Windows NT4, Win9x, and Windows for Workgroups—in addition to the standard Windows 2000 Server CAL. Additionally, if you have some clients that will run the Citrix ICA client, you still need a Microsoft TS CAL for these devices, even if you plan to use only the ICA protocol.

The reason that you don't need to buy TS CALs if you have only Windows 2000 computers is that these machines have a built-in TS CAL, so they don't require additional licenses. However, you must still activate a license server. When you load the Terminal Services Licensing MMC, you'll see that it comes with unlimited Windows 2000 built-in licenses. These licenses are automatically issued to Windows 2000 clients as they connect, but you'll be able to see how many, and to which computers, with the **Terminal Services Licensing MMC** by checking the **Issued** count under the **Existing Windows 2000 License**, under which you'll see the names of the computers and when they were issued. Figure 5.14 shows a number of Windows 2000 TS CALs issued on a license server.

NOTE

In addition to the information in this section, you might find the following FAQ useful for more information on Terminal Services Licensing: Windows 2000 Terminal Services Licensing FAQ (www.microsoft.com/WINDOWS2000/server/howtobuy/pricing/tsfaq.asp).

Figure 5.14 Terminal Services Licensing Showing Details of Issued Built-In License Details

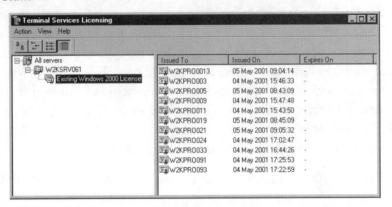

Installing Terminal Services Licensing

When you install Terminal Services Licensing as a separate Windows component (with **Add/Remove Programs**), you'll be prompted for the location of the license database (which defaults to **\System32\Lserver**). You'll see two role options, **enterprise** and **domain or workgroup**, as Figure 5.15 shows.

Figure 5.15 Installing the Terminal Services Licensing Service

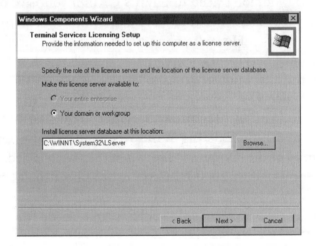

The Enterprise option, available only within an Active Directory domain, allows you to have one license server for each site that is registered within Active Directory. Outside Active Directory, in an NT4 domain and/or within a workgroup, you can only configure the Terminal Services Licensing service in a Domain/Workgroup role that works by mail-slot broadcasts.

In theory, this means that you need a license server for each subnet, but you can use a registry entry to preconfigure the NetBIOS name of a license server on a remote subnet, which allows you to consolidate license servers across your non-Active Directory network.

The registry value you need to add on the terminal server is of type REG_SZ and is called **DefaultLicenseServer**. Specify its string as the NetBIOS name of the license server. The new value should be added under the following registry path: HKEY_LOCAL_MACHINE\SYSTEM\CurrentControlSet\ Services\TermService\Parameters.

NOTE

After making this registry change, ensure that the terminal server can resolve the NetBIOS name correctly through WINS or add it into your local LMHOSTS file.

Configuring & Implementing…

Using the DefaultLicenseServer Setting

It's usual for TCP/IP settings to be able to specify more than one host (for example, you can specify alternative default gateways, primary and secondary WINS servers, and multiple DNS servers). However, you can specify only a single default (preferred) Terminal Services Licensing server with this registry setting. If the terminal server cannot connect to the server you define here, it resorts to broadcasting. Therefore, for maximum fault tolerance, you should consider specifying your DefaultLicenseServer as a server in a remote subnet, but ensure that you also have a license server on the same subnet. This setup reduces the broadcasts and, should the remote license server not be available, the terminal server will still be able to find a license server through broadcast.

The database size for storing the licenses is very low (for example, 5MB accommodates 6000 licenses), and the impact on the server's processing is almost negligible. In terms of memory, this service, whether idle or active, requires only about 10MB. However, even though it's tempting to use just one server for Terminal Services Licensing for the whole of your network, remember to factor in fault tolerance. Microsoft suggests that you should have at least one backup license server to ensure license server availability.

How Terminal Service Licensing Works

Once Terminal Services has been installed in Application mode, outside Active Directory it broadcasts for an activated Terminal Services Licensing server every 15 minutes. If more than one licensing server responds, one of these responses is chosen, and the terminal server continues to use that server as long as it is available. Windows 2000 Terminal Services communicates with its licensing server once every two hours to check that it is still available and, when the response is negative, it seeks another license server by broadcasting again.

When you first install Terminal Services and configure it for use in Application mode, you have a 90-day grace period in which to activate a license server and install TS CALs if they are required for your clients. You need to install TS CALs onto the license servers only for computers that aren't Windows 2000 computers. You can activate a license server with no client licenses. Connecting terminal clients that don't have built-in licenses (that is, non–Windows 2000 computers) are issued temporary licenses that expire after 90 days, and they will thereafter be refused access if no licenses are installed on the license server or servers.

NOTE

When you first install and configure Terminal Services for use in Application mode, you have a 90-day grace period in which to activate a license server. Use this grace period to your benefit so that you evaluate Terminal Services without having to commit to it until you've tested it in your environment.

When a client attempts to connect to a terminal server without a TS CAL, the terminal server contacts its Terminal Services Licensing server and asks for an available license. The license server checks to see whether it has an available (unallocated) license to give, and if it does, it passes this license to the terminal server and marks the license in its database as taken and therefore no longer available. The terminal server pushes the license to the client, where it's stored locally so that it can present it on subsequent connections, whether to the same or another terminal server. In this conversation, the client never talks directly to the terminal services licensing server. Terminal services licensing servers talk only to each other and terminal servers.

If the licensing server had no free licenses, it would try to contact other licensing servers for available licenses, and if those licenses were found, the licensing server would direct the terminal server to use this alternative license server. In this way, you can build up multiple license servers if required and not worry about on which license server you're installing the TS CALs. However, remember that license server discovery by default is done by broadcasting when it's not installed within an Active Directory domain. Therefore, to accommodate the cooperation between license servers, you need to run all the license servers in the same subnet.

If no free licenses are found, a temporary 90-day license can be issued to the client, and this is noted in both the license database on the terminal services license server (you'll see these under the **Temporary Licenses for Windows 2000 Terminal Services Client Access License**) and in the System Event Viewer so you are aware that a TS CAL is required.

Figure 5.16 shows two terminal services licensing servers, both activated, allowing all Windows 2000 computers to connect. However, the first server has a Client Licensing Pack installed (displayed as **Windows 2000 Terminal Services Client Access License**), which allows NT4 and Win9x clients to connect, whereas the second server has no Client Licensing Packs installed. Only temporary licenses will have an **Expires On** field defined.

When non-Windows 2000 clients connect without the Client Licensing Pack installed, this server issued clients with a temporary 90-day license (as shown under the **Temporary Licenses for Windows 2000 Terminal Services Client Access License**). Now that another license server is online with available TS CALs, clients that had a temporary TS license will be swapped to a full TS CAL from the other server.

Figure 5.16 Terminal Services Licensing, Both with and without Client License Packs Installed

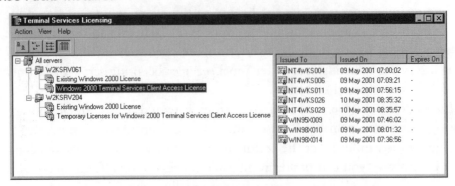

Activating a Terminal Services License Server

You can activate a Terminal Services Licensing server in one of four ways:

- Direct Internet Access
- Internet browser (World Wide Web)
- Telephone
- Fax

When you first load Terminal Services Licensing, it looks for all servers in the subnet running Windows 2000 Terminal Services Licensing using a broadcast and then displays them under **All Servers**. You activate a server by right-clicking it and selecting **Activate**, which then calls up the **Licensing Wizard**. You can choose the activation method you want to use.

The phrase *direct Internet access* sounds as if it should all happen automatically online, which it does except that it uses an e-mail to send you the activation code you need to complete the activation. Some administrators consider it easiest to use the Web access method, using either the browser on the same server that's using the Terminal Services Licensing or a browser from a workstation. From a security point of view, many network administrators don't allow Internet connectivity from member servers, so the Web access method from a workstation does offer a good solution.

To use the Web access method, run the Licensing Wizard from the license server and select the World Wide Web connection method, which then displays your Product ID and the URL you need to contact. Connect to this URL from your browser, and you'll see a page similar to Figure 5.17, in which you choose to activate the server. You'll be prompted to supply your credentials (company details) and product ID; a successful activation results in display of a page that shows your license server activation code. Print the page for future reference or take a screen-print and save it to disk. Type the activation code number in the Terminal Service Licensing Wizard to complete the server activation.

Figure 5.17 Connecting to Microsoft's Terminal Services Licensing Web Site

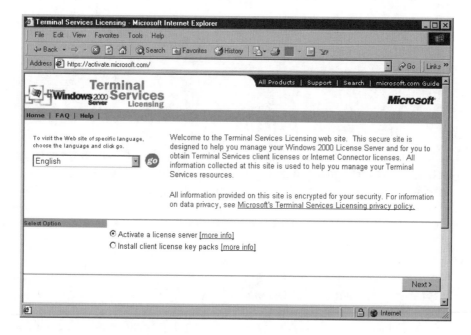

If you have bought client licenses, you can install them now or later. Remember, you need to install client licenses only for non-Windows 2000 computers, and these are per-seat rather than concurrent licenses.

An activated license server now displays its status as **Activated** within the Terminal Services Licensing MMC. Figure 5.18 shows an example of two activated license servers and one that is still **Not activated**.

Any Windows 2000 computers that connect to one of your Windows 2000 terminal servers will be automatically granted a TS CAL from one of your license server's unlimited pool of **Windows 2000 Terminal Services Client Access Licenses**. Non-Windows 2000 clients need to have license packs installed before they can be allocated a license, but if none is available, they will be allocated a license under the **Temporary Licenses for Windows 2000 Terminal Services Client Access License** pool, with their expiration dates set 90 days from issue. The date stamp is taken from the license server, not the client.

Figure 5.18 Activated and Unactivated Terminal Services Servers

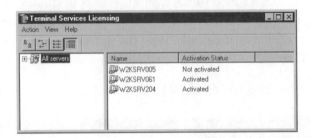

Designing & Planning…

License Reporting Tool

The Resource Kit contains a License Reporting Tool called **isreport.exe**, which can interrogate Windows 2000 Terminal Services Licensing databases and output the information into a tab-delimited text file, which you can then import into a spreadsheet or database for further analysis. Use the **/F** switch to specify the path and filename you want to use. Without this switch, the system defaults to **isreport.txt** in the current directory.

When you have multiple license servers, specify them with the command (after any switches). For example, to collect information into a file called **tssrv.txt** from terminal license servers TSLS1 and TSLS2, you would type: **lsreport /F tssrvt.txt TSLS1 TSLS2**. When no servers are specified, only the current license server will be used.

You can use **/T** to output only temporary licenses (for example, so you know how many you need to purchase) and specify your start and end dates for licenses using **/D start [end]**, where *end* defaults to today's date. For example, to collect information on temporary licenses issued in March 2001, you would type: **lsreport /T /D 03/01/2001 03/31/2001**. Note that this entry is for a server using the U.S. date format of *mm/dd/yyyy*.

Another Resource Kit tool is the License Server Viewer, **lsview.exe**, which executes license server discovery and then displays licenses by name, time they were discovered, and type (**domain** or **enterprise**). You can save this information to a log file. If you are not sure of the names of your servers running Terminal Services Licensing, you can use this information to broadcast in the local subnet. Remember, outside Active Directory, the system will not find license servers in remote subnets.

Upgrading from TSE

If you are already running a Windows NT Server 4 Terminal Server Edition, you are no doubt wondering whether to upgrade to Windows 2000 (and keep all your existing settings) or install a clean version and migrate users to Windows 2000.

The advantage of upgrading in-place is that it's a quicker process; there's no need to migrate users (if stored locally) and change their connection details or reinstall all the applications and reconfigure them. However, there are many advantages to installing a clean version; if at all possible, this is the better choice for security, reliability, and interoperability with other Windows 2000 Terminal Services.

When using multiple terminal services, you'll find them much easier to support and they will work together more smoothly if they have an identical configuration in terms of hardware, disk partitioning, operating system configuration, and (where licensing permits) applications. Hardware has recently changed considerably in terms of reliability, specification, and price. Chances are the hardware specification you're running on your current TSE is outdated, and you might not be able to (or want to) purchase the same hardware for new servers, so bear this factor in mind. Remember that skimping on the server specification is not a good idea for terminal servers unless their usage is very low.

In terms of operating system configuration, TSE and Windows 2000 running Terminal Services have some immediate differences, a fact that matters if you want multiple terminal servers to cooperate in terms of roaming profiles and application configuration. The directory structure differences include the following:

- The default operating system directory on TSE is **\WTSRV**; it is **\WINNT** on Windows 2000.

- Default profiles and user data on TSE are stored under **\WTSRV\PROFILES** and under **\Documents and Settings** on Windows 2000.

Other upgrading issues include the following:

- As with any Windows 2000 installation or upgrade, make sure that all hardware is supported, and remember that Windows 2000 itself requires more memory than NT4. Plenty of RAM should be at the top of your priority list for terminal servers. For this reason, run Terminal Services on a dedicated server, not one that's also a domain controller or running a server application such as DNS, SQL, or Exchange Server.

- TSE must be running Service Pack (SP) 4 or higher.

- An upgrade to Windows 2000 automatically installs Terminal Services configured for Application mode.

- If the version of Internet Explorer on the server is less than 5.01, the browser will automatically be upgraded, so you need to ensure that any installed applications work well with this version.

- Ensure all installed applications will work with Windows 2000 Terminal Services. Remember, it's not enough to check that they work with Windows 2000! Also be sure that you have any compatibility scripts required for your installed applications.

- If MetaFrame is installed, you must uninstall it (at the console) before the upgrade and reboot before upgrading to Windows 2000. If you want to use MetaFrame after the upgrade, you need to install a new version. If you leave the old version installed, it will not work after the upgrade.

- Domain trusts are unaffected by the upgrade.

- After the upgrade, the server can support both Windows 2000 Terminal Services clients and TSE clients. Many of the new features, such as PC/server integration with the clipboard and printers and improvements in performance and encryption, rely on the later client. However, remote control is a server enhancement, which therefore works with older clients.

NOTE

Ensure that users aren't logged in while upgrading, and use the **change logon/disable** command from a command prompt on the server to prevent users from logging on until the upgrade is complete. The **change logon /disable** command stops any new user sessions from being initiated over the network while still allowing local logons from the terminal server console. Any currently connected sessions, however, will not be disconnected by this command. This restriction is automatically lifted when the terminal server is restarted.

You can use **change logon /query** to find out the current logon status and **change logon /?** to get online help with the syntax and options for this command.

Unattended Installations

The various Terminal Services components (the Terminal Services service itself, the license server, and client distribution files) can be automatically included in a Windows 2000 Server unattended installation. The majority of the unattended installation settings are located under the **[Components]** section of the **unattend.txt** file and listed in Table 5.1. Additionally, to configure Terminal Services for Application mode (remember, Remote Administration is the default unless you're upgrading TSE), you need to change the **ApplicationServer** line under the **[TerminalServices]** section to 1.

Table 5.1 Terminal Services Related Lines for Unattended Installations

Line	Possible Values	Default Value	Explanation
TSEnable	ON or OFF	OFF	Installs Terminal Services.
TSKeyboardDrivers	ON or OFF	OFF	Copies all Windows 2000 keyboard drivers when Terminal Services is installed.
TSPrinterDrivers	ON or OFF	OFF	Copies all Windows 2000 printer drivers when Terminal Services is installed.
TSClients	ON or OFF	OFF	Installs Terminal Services client files (approximately 10MB) when Terminal Services is installed.
LicenseServer	0 or 1	0	Installs Terminal Services Licensing when set to 1.

Application Suitability

You must check that any applications you want to run on Windows 2000 Terminal Services in Application mode are compatible with both Windows 2000 and a terminal server environment. Usually, this means that user configurations are stored in the user portion of the registry, not as part of the computer configuration. Similarly, each user should have his or her own directories rather than a common directory to which all users have access.

With the increasing popularity of thin-client computing, most software vendors are aware of the need to support a terminal server environment. You should run into no problems with recent software releases when they are installed properly (in other words, either using the **change user/install** command or through Add/Remove Programs).

However, some applications need modification by means of a compatibility script that either runs as part of the installation or should be added to a user's login script before the user runs the application. Your Terminal Services server has a number of compatibility scripts automatically installed into the **%systemroot%\Application Compatibility Scripts** folder that your software vendor will advise you to use.

NOTE

The following Microsoft white paper has more up-to-date information on which application compatibility scripts are available with Windows 2000: www.microsoft.com/windows2000/techinfo/administration/terminal/ tsapcompat.asp. This white paper includes information on using SQL Server and VERITAS Disk Management in Remote Administration mode.

Additionally, compatibility scripts might be available for download from the Microsoft Windows Update site (http://corporate.windowsupdate .microsoft.com), which, for example, includes the following compatibility scripts:

- Lotus SmartSuite 9.5 (Ssuite95.cmd)

- Eudora 4.0 (Eudora4.cmd)

- Lotus Notes 4.x (Lnote4u.cmd)

- Power Builder 6.0 (PwrBldr6.cmd)

Microsoft Office 2000 is a good example of an application requiring additional installation procedures. When Office 2000 is installed on the same servers as Windows 2000 Terminal Services in Application mode, you'll see the dialog box in Figure 5.19.

Before Office 2000 can be installed, you need to obtain and copy to the server the Office 2000 Transform file (**termsrvr.mst**), which offers a specific Terminal Services installation. This includes settings more suitable for low-bandwidth usage, such as a more simplified splash screen and replacing the animated

Office assistant with a *still agent* to provide the same help information but in a more "terminal server-friendly" fashion.

Figure 5.19 Trying to Install the Standard Version of Office 2000 on Terminal Services

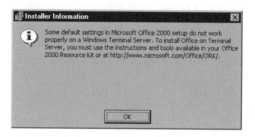

> **NOTE**
>
> For more information on installing Office 2000, refer to the following articles: "OFF2000: Installing Office 2000 on Windows 2000 Terminal Server [Q224313]" at http://support.microsoft.com/support/kb/articles/Q224/3/13.asp.

In the same way, you can make your own manual configuration changes within your server applications by reducing features and options that consume memory and bandwidth. There is a good reason that the following options are disabled by default:

- Client wallpaper (under **Terminal Services Configuration | Connections | RDP-TCP | Environment Properties**)
- Server's Active Desktop (under **Terminal Services Configuration | Server Settings**)

Finally, don't forget to thoroughly test your applications with a standard user connection (and don't forget to check 16-bit clients if you will be supporting these!). For applications that aren't strictly compatible with Windows 2000, you might have to use the less secure application compatibility setting of **Permissions Compatible with Terminal Server 4.0 Users** (refer back to Figure 5.4) as discussed under the **Tighter Security** section.

Capacity and Scaling

We've covered some of these issues in other sections, but it's worth reiterating them together in a single discussion. You could find that you need multiple terminal servers to support a growing number of users and/or applications, or you might decide to have multiple terminal servers to support different configurations (different security policies, for example) or to suit your network topology.

NOTE

Although it is tempting to keep all terminal servers physically together on the same subnet, when bandwidth is low you would do better to place the terminal servers nearest the resources they need, not closest to their clients. For example, terminal server users in a remote site who use an application that must query an SQL server will have a better response overall if their terminal servers were placed physically near the SQL server rather than physically near them. Remember that data from client to server is minimum, whereas data from the terminal server to other resources is just like any other LAN-grade connection.

Certainly if you're planning to use more than one terminal server, it makes sense for the servers to cooperate wherever possible. This includes having roaming Terminal Services profiles and storing them and volatile data (for example, home directories and application databases) on independent back-end servers. It would also be advisable to ensure these back-end servers had adequate storage capacity and a well-protected disk system (for instance, hardware RAID 5 with independent disk controllers) a UPS, and that they are bakced up regularly.

NOTE

You cannot use Cluster Service on the same Windows 2000 Server that's running Terminal Services. However, by deploying this back-end server topology, you can cluster the servers holding the volatile data, which is where you need the protection most.

We've already said that the ability to configure multiple terminal servers to work together is greatly increased if they have the same hardware and configuration. Remember that you can use the DNS round-robin for terminal server connections so that each client connection uses the same host name that is resolved to all the IP addresses of your terminal servers on your DNS server. This way, each address is handed out on a rotated sequence. However, a more elegant solution is to use Windows Network Load Balancing Service on a Windows 2000 Advanced Server, which can react to a downed server and connect a user to the least busy server. Network Load Balancing is covered in Chapter 6.

Configuring & Implementing...

Using Load Balancing with Session Disconnect

Take care with the **Session Disconnect** setting when you're using multiple terminal servers. A disconnected session (in comparison to a logged-out session) means that all the users' applications are kept running on the server, ready for the same user to reconnect. Logging off, in comparison, closes all applications and, on reconnecting, a user must start from scratch.

You should disable the Session Disconnect feature if you're using DNS round-robin to load balance between your terminal servers, because the user could easily be directed to a different terminal server on reconnection. In comparison, you might be able to use this feature with Windows Network Load Balancing, which can be configured to use **IP Affinity**. This means that the reconnecting client will be recognized by his or her IP address (assuming that the address hasn't changed or the client hasn't moved to another machine) and reconnected to the same server.

One of the burning issues related to terminal servers is the specification of the server. Thin clients come at the expense of fat servers, and I've never yet seen anybody in earnest run a terminal server that doesn't have four processors and less than 1GB of RAM. However, the exact server requirements depend on the number of clients server will be supporting simultaneously and the type of application the client will be using and how it will be used.

Specifications and scaling tests often categorize clients according to the type of work they perform as structured task workers, knowledge workers, and data entry workers, but you might find your users less easy to categorize. However, these categories serve as a good starting point and should be augmented with your own tests, always keeping an eye on acceptable thresholds values for memory, processor, network, and disk access.

Memory is invariably the single most important factor for a terminal server—and thankfully, memory is a much cheaper commodity these days. Start off with no less than 128MB RAM and try to allocate between 16MB and 20MB per session. The desktop alone requires about 13MB, and the rest depends on the applications being run. If running multiple terminal servers, try to group users on the same server that uses the same applications since executable code is shared across multiple instances.

It's easy to keep on eye on memory with the **Available Physical Memory** and **Page Inputs/sec** options with **Task Manager** on the **Performance** tab. Watch how these two elements decrease as another client connects. Find an average user and watch how much physical memory is used to get a good indication of a user's memory requirement. When the physical memory becomes less than twice the average user memory, it's time for more memory!

Another good indication that you need more memory is a dramatic increase in the page inputs/sec as physical memory runs out and the server resorts to virtual memory. The goal is to use as little virtual memory (page file) as possible rather than to simply increase the page file to make up for inadequate RAM. Not only is paging memory much slower, but many operations (including operating system and networking components) cannot be paged to disk.

NOTE

When allocating memory, try to eliminate any 16-bit applications on your terminal server. These require about 25 percent more memory than native 32-bit applications.

Refer to **Windows 2000 Terminal Services Capacity and Scaling** for more information and benchmark tests and results: www.microsoft.com/windows2000/techinfo/administration/terminal/tscaling.asp.

NOTE

When planning your hardware configuration, don't forget that Windows 2000 Server comes in two versions: **Server** can support a maximum of four processes and up to 4GB of RAM, whereas **Advanced Server** scales up to eight processors and 8GB of RAM.

The Resource Kit includes the following utilities to help with your own scalability tests:

- **RoboServer** (robosrv.exe)
- **RoboClient** (robocli.exe)
- **SmClient** (smclient.exe)
- **QueryIdle** (qidle.exe)

These utilities allow you to script a simulated client load and check on the server's performance. The two documents in the Resource Kit that describe these utilities in detail and how to use them are:

- Terminal Server Capacity Planning Tools Overview (tscpt.doc)
- Terminal Server Simulated Client (smclient.doc)

Limitations

Although Windows 2000 Terminal Services can do a great deal, it can't do everything. Some situations cannot be addressed with Terminal Services and its native Terminal Service client, and for these you need to find alternatives. These limitations include the following:

- Terminal Services is not suitable for applications that are graphics-intensive and require multimedia streaming capability (games and streaming media applications fall into this category).
- Terminal Services support only TCP/IP connections, not IPX or NetBEUI.
- Terminal Services cannot support Apple Macintosh, MS-DOS, or UNIX.

- Windows 2000 Cluster Service and Windows 2000 Terminal Services cannot be used on the same computer.

- All terminal server clients use the same IP address (of the server), so any application or device that relies on the IP address to identify a client will have problems. For example, firewalls and legacy hosts or applications might be able to use only the IP address rather than the host or workstation name. Whenever possible, change these to identify the client by workstation name, hostname, or logon name.

- Terminal Services cannot support more than 256 colors, and a client connection cannot use a higher screen resolution for the Terminal Services session than it is using locally. For example, if the client is configured to use 800 x 600, the Terminal Services connection could be configured to use 640 x 480 or 800 x 600, but it couldn't be configured to use 1280 x 1024, even if its monitor supported this setting.

- Terminal Services cannot be used with applications that require special hardware, such as barcode scanners or card swipes. The exception to this rule is if these pieces of hardware can be identified as a keyboard-type device, but devices attached by parallel or serial ports or an adapter card will not be recognized.

- Because multiple users share the same IP connection in a Terminal Services configuration, it is more vulnerable if a device or application were to subvert, lock, or monopolize that single connection.

Configuring and Managing Windows 2000 Terminal Services

There are two aspects of configuring Terminal Services: the server settings and client settings. Once a client is connected, you can manage the client sessions with the Terminal Services Manager. Server settings are few and are found with the **Terminal Services Configuration** using the **Server Settings**, as shown in Figure 5.20.

The **Terminal server mode** option you can see in Figure 5.20 exists for display purposes only. You can only change modes with Add/Remove programs. However, the Permission Compatibility, which is also set when Terminal Services is installed or configured, refers to the permissions we saw when configuring Terminal Services for Application mode. It allows you to change from one setting to another without having to reinstall. The **Delete temporary folders on exit**, **Use temporary folders per session**, and **Active Desktop being disabled** are all sensible defaults for Terminal Services.

Figure 5.20 Configuring the Terminal Services Server Settings

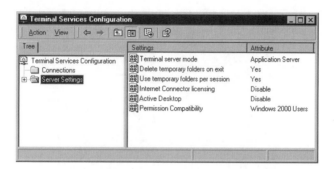

Internet Connector licensing can be changed only if you have an Internet Connector license installed, which is unlikely for most companies because it is aimed at application service providers (ASPs) and permits only anonymous access to nonemployees.

We've already covered some of the connection properties such as encryption level, remote control, drive, clipboard, and printer mapping. Some of these settings can be configured only at the server (for example, the encryption level and disabling the wallpaper). However, most can also be set on a client's user account (under the Environment, Sessions, Remote Control, and Terminal Services Profile tabs for Windows 2000 accounts and with the TS Config button on an NT4 account). The duplicated settings here, when set, override the client settings.

For example, you can set timeout values for disconnected, active, and idle terminal sessions, decide whether these should be disconnected or ended, and allow a reconnection from any client or (for Citrix ICA clients only) the original client. These options are shown for a Windows 2000 account in Figure 5.21.

The Connection settings in **Terminal Services Configuration** can override the client settings, although the default is to not override them. Figure 5.22 shows these same options on the server RDP connection. Note that on the server you are able to change only the **Allow reconnection** option if you have the Citrix MetaFrame add-on installed.

You can also override the starting program specified with the account or within **Client Connection Manager** (discussed in the next section). Setting the Starting Program as a server connection property makes sense if your terminal server offers a single application for all users connecting on that adapter, to save you having to specify this setting on individual client accounts and/or connection details.

Figure 5.21 Configuring a User's Account for Terminal Services Sessions

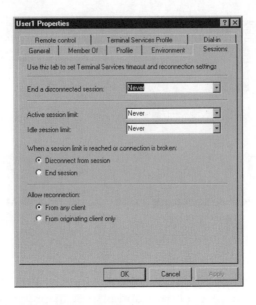

Figure 5.22 Configuring a Server Connection for Terminal Services Sessions

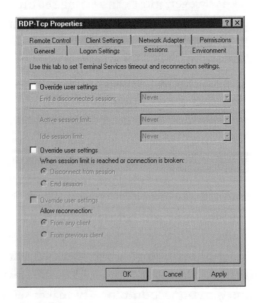

Being able to override client settings at the server connection explains one of the most often asked questions: "Why am I always prompted for a password when my full logon details are specified in my connection details?" This happens because the default settings under the connection's **Logon Settings** are to allow client-provided logon but always prompt for the password for greater security, as shown in Figure 5.23. If you want to allow automatic logon to include the password, deselect this option. You can also specify a default user account to be used automatically each time a client connects.

Figure 5.23 Allowing Automatic Logon with Terminal Services

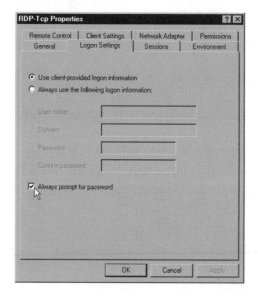

Another server connection property to note is the **Permissions** tab. By default, this property is configured for **User Access** and **Guest Access** to all users but additionally **Full Control** for administrators. The **Full Control** permission grants the administrators the permissions for remote control, sending a message, disconnecting a session, and so on. If you want nonadministrators to be able to have this administrative control just for terminal services, create a new group for them and grant that group **Full Control** on this tab.

An example is shown in Figure 5.24, where a new group called **TS Admins** has been added so that members of this group can support other terminal services users—for example, sending them a message and remotely controlling their sessions.

Figure 5.24 Granting Nonadministrators Permissions to Manage Connections

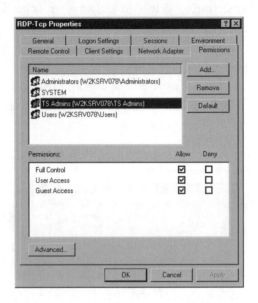

If you use the **Advanced** button and then choose the **View/Edit** button for the specified group, you'll see the individual permissions that can be granted to the terminal service connection. These are broken down into specific commands such as **Remote Control**, **Disconnect**, and **Message**, as shown in Figure 5.25. You can specify these individually if you want to fine-tune exactly which permissions a nonadministrator should have for managing terminal server connections (for example, being able to send a message to a connected user but not be able to disconnect their session). This then displays as **Special** rather than **Full Control** under the **Permission** column.

When clients are connected, you can use **Terminal Services Manager** to manage and view their sessions. However, Terminal Services Manager is itself designed to be used with a Terminal Services client rather than loaded directly from the console. When it is loaded locally, some options such as remote control are not available; and you'll get a warning message to this effect. Always run Terminal Services Manager from a client connection, even if it is loaded from the console itself.

As you can see from Figure 5.26, you can manage each session by right-clicking it under the **Users** tab and then choosing one of the available options. You can see that in our picture, there's only one disconnected session (user1), which would be possible to reset if you suspected that the user had accidentally disconnected rather than logged out, and there's no timeout set on his connection.

Figure 5.25 The Individual Permissions on a Terminal Server's Connection

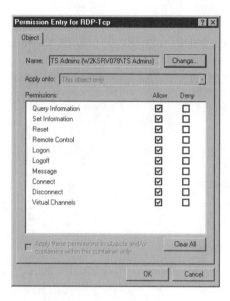

Figure 5.26 Using Terminal Services Manager to Manage Sessions

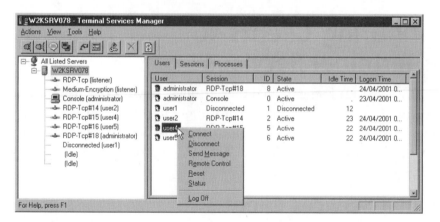

The **Status** option provides more information about this session—which adapter is being used, for example, and the number of incoming and outgoing bytes or frames as well as the compression ratio.

If you were to click the session from the left pane, you would see an **Information** tab on the right, which provides client information such as the username, workstation name, IP address, client directory, and other settings. Click the **Processes** tab instead and you'll see a list of processes (applications) that are

currently in use. Figure 5.27 shows an example of client information from a
Windows 2000 Professional client.

Figure 5.27 Client Information Displayed with Terminal Services Manager

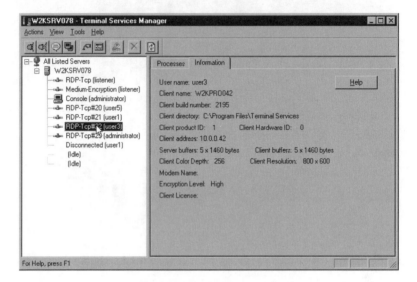

Configuring Clients to
Use Terminal Services

Although we've already mentioned the Terminal Services Connections snap-in
with regard to remote administration, it is more likely that users will use the
Terminal Services client or the Advanced Terminal Service client. The first is a
Windows program and the second an ActiveX control that is run within Internet
Explorer.

Terminal Services Client

This is the default client that ships with Windows 2000 Server versions. When
you choose to install Terminal Services, one of the options is to include the
Terminal Services Client Creator. This tool allows you run a program that
creates floppy disk set installations for 32-bit and 16-bit clients, as shown in
Figure 5.28.

Run this file, following the online instructions. Once installed, synchronize
the Windows CE device with the desktop to install the Terminal Server Client
onto the Windows CE device. As you can see from Figure 5.28, this process

requires only two disks for 32-bit clients (four disks for 16-bit clients). However, technology moves on and floppy disk installations are rather outmoded these days; indeed, many corporations actively disable the floppy disk drive for security reasons. A better bet is to use a network share to install the client files. To do this, navigate to **\System32\Clients\Tsclients\net** and share this directory with a name like *TSCLIENTS*. User connecting to this server will see two directories: one for Win16 and one for Win32. Within each of these is a setup program that installs the Windows Terminal Services client.

Figure 5.28 The Terminal Services Client Creator

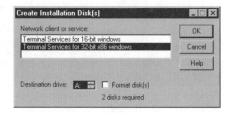

Configuring & Implementing…

Installing Windows CE Terminal Server Client

If you want to install the Windows CE Terminal Server Client (the full name being "Terminal Services Client for Windows CE Handheld PC Professional Edition v3.0-Based Devices") this is handled differently from the standard client install. For this, you need to install the file **hpcrdp.exe** onto the desktop PC, which can be found in the **\valueadd\ msft\mgmt\mstsc_hpc** folder on the Windows 2000 Server or Professional CDs. Alternatively you can download it from the Microsoft site: www.microsoft.com/windowsce/products/download/term-serv.asp.

In its default interactive setting, this client setup program prompts the user to agree to the licensing restrictions, ask the user to enter his or her name and organization, and prompts for an installation directory. As you can see from Figure 5.29, the default directory is **\Program Files\Terminal Services Client** on your installation partition.

The user is then asked whether the same Terminal Services settings should be used for all users on the computer or just the logged on user. After checking for necessary disk space (about 500KB), the system installs and creates the following two options under **Start | Programs | Terminal Services Client**:

- Client Connection Manager
- Terminal Services Client

Figure 5.29 Installing Terminal Services Client

Client Connection Manager is probably the most used utility to create connections to Terminal Services. Load it and click **File | New Connection** to load the **Client Connection Manager Wizard**, which steps you through creating a connection with prompts for the following:

- Connection name for easy recognition
- Actual server name or IP address of the terminal server (with a Browse facility)
- Automatic logon information, if required
- Screen resolution and whether to display the session in a window (the default) or full screen
- Enabling data compression and bitmap caching
- Program path and filename if the connection is to be used for only one application
- Icon and Program groups to be used

Once the connection is defined, the user can connect to the terminal server by double-clicking the icon created within the **Client Connection Manager** or right-clicking it from within **Client Connection Manager** and selecting **Connect**. As a third alternative, the user can select the connection name from **Start | Programs | Terminal Services Client**.

Right-clicking on the icon within the **Client Connection Manager** allows the user to create a shortcut on the desktop. Another option is Properties, where you can view and change any connection details with a three-tabbed dialog box. In this way you can build a collection of connections—to different servers or to the same servers but using different configurations (for example, each one starting a different program).

Figure 5.30 shows an example of connections suitable for an administrator that go to three different terminal servers. All three provide full desktop support, but connections are also configured for specific applications (the program path and filename prompted for in the wizard). When you specify a program to run as part of your connection details, your terminal server session opens using just that application. When you close the application, your terminal session ends. We saw previously how running a single application could be configured as part of the user account properties (the **Initial program** settings for an NT4 account or the **Starting program** under the **Environment** tab for a Windows 2000 account). By specifying the program on the client connection, you can configure multiple sessions for the same user that use different programs, as we have done here. So, for example, you could specify two user connections to the terminal server—one to use Word and another to use Excel. If you used the user account properties to specify the program, you would be able to specify only a single application for that user.

Figure 5.30 Example Client Connection Manager Sessions

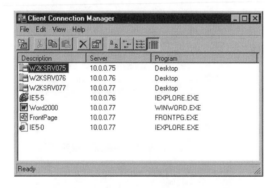

In our example, the administrator has used this feature and configured some terminal server connections to use different programs so that her connection runs only those applications. In particular, this configuration allows her to run different versions of the same application—in this case, Internet Explorer—which would be of more interest to developers and administrators than the typical end user, because different versions are useful for testing compatibility issues. The standard desktop connections in this example are using the default icon suggested by Client Connection Manager, while the program connections have been configured to use their own program icon to make them more easily recognizable. To change the default icon, use the Change Icon button to browse for the icon you want. You'll find the Change Icon button in the Client Connection Manager Wizard, or retrospectively, under the Program tab of the connection properties.

Using the File menu in the Client Connection Manager, you can export and import such connection details with a .CNS file. This then makes it possible to define users' connections centrally and distribute the .CNS files. You can export just one selected connection (with **File | Export**) or all connections (with **File | Export All**). If you export to an existing file, the original contents will be kept and the new connection or connections added to it.

One way to automatically distribute preconfigured Terminal Services connections is by including this file when the Terminal Services client is installed. You do so by copying it into the same directory as the setup program.

Terminal Services client is used more as a quick, ad hoc connection mechanism. As you can see from Figure 5.31, using this type of connection provides some but not all of the connection details we could specify with the Client Connection Manager. In particular, you can't launch a specific program and you can't provide logon details.

Figure 5.31 Using Terminal Services Client

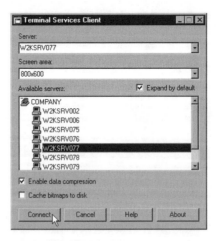

Note that as the number of Windows 2000 servers configured for Terminal Services increases within your domain, it's harder to find and select the server you require using this connection method. This point is particularly relevant if you plan to enable Terminal Services for Remote Administration mode on all your Windows 2000 servers in addition to the ones that will be in Application mode. You cannot separate the two different modes from this list, although doing so would be useful! Neither can you choose the order in which they are displayed; the order is alphabetical.

An interesting additional piece of information this program provides is confirmation of the key length used for encryption. The **About** button displays whether this client supports 56-bit or 128-bit encryption, as Figure 5.32 shows. This information is particularly important if you've configured your server connection for high encryption; such 56-bit clients would not be able to connect.

Figure 5.32 About Information from the Terminal Services Client Shows the Key Length Supported

Configuring & Implementing...

Upgrading to the "Full" Terminal Services Client from SP1

The **tsmisetup.exe** file, which ships with Service Pack 1 under the **\VAL-UEADD\TSAC** folder, offers a later version of the Terminal Services client within a Windows Installation File format (.msi). .Msi files are more applicable when you want to assign or publish software packages with Active Directory group policies. However, it's worth looking at this version, because it does contain a later version of the Terminal Services client.

When you install the **tsmisetup.exe** file, it creates a directory (by default, called **\Program Files\Terminal Services Client MSI**). Within that directory, you'll find the actual .msi file (called **Terminal Services Client.msi**). The readme file in this directory refers to this update of the Terminal Services Client the "Full Terminal Services Client."

Once installed, your Terminal Services client's About section displays a later Build Number (2221), and the cipher strength will have

Continued

automatically been upgraded from 56 bit to 128 bit. Note that this higher cipher strength affects only TS encryption levels, not the encryption levels in IE or IPSec. It is not the same as installing the High Encryption Pack.

Another difference is that this later version of the Terminal Services client allows you to run and configure the Terminal Services client from a command line (**mstsc.exe**), which you could incorporate into login scripts, startup folders, and so on. For example, to automatically connect to server W2KSRV077 using the connection IE, type: **mstsc "IE" –v: W2KSRV077**. For the full list of syntax commands, type **mstsc.exe /?** for the full list of syntax commands.

Terminal Services Advanced Client

Terminal Services Advanced Client (TSAC) has been available for some time as a free Microsoft download and was one of the best-kept secrets behind TSE. Now integrated into Windows 2000 Service Pack 1, you can install the browser-enabled version of the terminal server client from the \VALUEADD\TSAC directory. Run the file **tswebsetup.exe** on a server that is running IIS4 or IIS5, not the client computer or the terminal server computer (although you could run IIS on a terminal server if you were really short of file and print servers).

Running the **tswebsetup.exe** creates a virtual Web directory called TSWEB and within the file are a couple of sample Web pages, a cabinet file that downloads the TSAC ActiveX control, a Readme.htm, and a Word Deployment Guide.

TSAC works through automatic and central deployment from a Web site that delivers an ActiveX control and a connection page on which the user can type in details of the server to which he or she wants to connect. The initial connection to the Web server is standard HTTP over port 80, but once the ActiveX control has been installed, the subsequent connection from the client to the terminal server is RDP over port 3389, as if it was a standard Terminal Service client.

The beauty of using an ActiveX control for client deployment is that only one central version needs to be supplied and updated. Whenever Microsoft releases a new version of the control and it is copied onto the Web server, connecting clients are automatically updated with this new version. Previously, Citrix clients offered automatic client updates above Microsoft's RDP client. TSAC neatly combats this hurdle while also offering a browser application. Deployment couldn't be simpler from an administrator's point of view—simply send users a

URL that they click. This one-time 325KB download doesn't take too long to install, even over a WAN link.

The only limitation is that the client computer must be running IE4 or later. I would recommend IE5 or later for stable ActiveX control support. If you must use IE4, ensure that you have Internet Explorer 4 SP2 installed. In addition, the browser must be able to install a signed ActiveX control, as Figure 5.33 shows.

Figure 5.33 Prompt to Download and Install the TSAC ActiveX Control

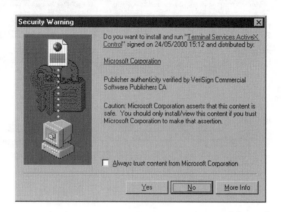

Some companies have a policy of never accepting ActiveX controls, even signed controls from reputable authorities such as Microsoft and VeriSign, and have configured their browsers accordingly. It also wouldn't be appropriate for roaming users (users who do not have a permanent desk or workstation but use any available workspace as needed) because, instead of storing these users' applications on a central file server so they are always available, this application needs to be installed locally (or wherever Internet Explorer is loaded). Some companies have a strict policy of deleting all downloaded Internet content every night in order to clean up disk space. This practice would remove this ActiveX control and requires it to be downloaded each day. Figure 5.34 shows TSAC correctly installed on a client workstation. Should you want to remove this ActiveX control, right-click it in your **Downloaded Program Files** file and select **Remove**.

Another security consideration is that ActiveX controls by definition shouldn't interact with any local resource, which goes against how the clipboard sharing and printer redirection as well as the Resource Kit tools Drive Share and File Copy work. This probably explains why the Resource Kit tools do not work with TSAC. You can disable the built-in Windows 2000 terminal server client features by adding the following keys to **HKLM\Software\Microsoft\ Terminal Server** with a **DWORD of 1**:

- DisableClipRedirection
- DisablePrinterRedirection

Figure 5.34 The Installed TSAC ActiveX Control

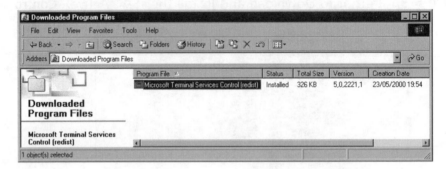

NOTE

The very fact that Microsoft calls its sample Web pages *samples* indicates that they were not specifically designed to be used out of the box. Rather, they are meant as a starting point for you to design your custom terminal server connection pages. For example, you need to modify the manyservers.htm sample in order to see multiple connections from different servers. The sample simply demonstrates that you can place the control on the same page any number of times.

The Microsoft Terminal Services ActiveX Client Control Deployment Guide (with the filename webclient.doc, installed into the TSWeb virtual directory on the IIS server) provides instructions on embedding the control within your own Web pages. It contains a section that explains how the sample pages work and how to modify them. For example, on **manyservers.htm**, you need to change each control's server value of **MyServer** to your own terminal server name. Alternatively, you could modify it so that it runs a specific program on the terminal server rather than providing a full desktop connection.

For most administrators and users, the Terminal Services Advance Client offers a neat way of providing a central deployment of the Terminal Services

Client without resorting to scripting and batch files. Certainly it makes a perfect complement to the Internet Connector License, but to control who can download it, you might want to set NTFS permissions on the TSAC Web site accordingly. If you want to audit who is downloading the control, the file you need to audit is **mstscax.cab**, which is the file that contains the ActiveX control.

Microsoft offers two sample Web pages that you can use out of the box, modify slightly for your own Web site, or replace with your own. The default page is simply **default.htm**, which redirects to connect.asp after prompting the user to type in basic connection details, as Figure 5.35 shows. For multiple servers, the **manyservers.htm** page shows four terminal server connections from the same server.

Figure 5.35 Using TSAC With the Default Connection Page for a Single Server

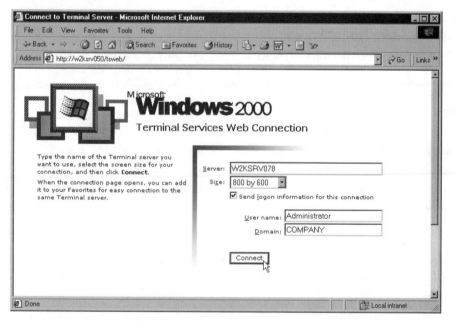

Automating Terminal Services Client Setup

The setup program that installs the Windows Terminal Services client can be partially or fully automated with the help of various switches and by supplying the connection file (***.cns**) with the files. This file allows you to send it to users in an e-mail or add it into their login scripts. Table 5.2 shows the various switches you can use with the setup program.

Table 5.2 Setup Switches for Automating Terminal Services Client Setup

Setup Command	Explanation
Setup /q	Installs the Terminal Services client, showing only the Exit dialog box. The user sees a blue background and software installation progress but cannot interact until finished and the Exit dialog box appears.
Setup /q1	Installs the Terminal Services client with no interaction required, but the user sees a blue background.
Setup /qt	Installs the Terminal Services client with no visual notification (the only indication will be the hard disk writes).
Setup /u /qnt	Uninstalls the Terminal Services client with no user interaction.

Other setup options you can use involve the **Conman** command that is supplied in the same directory as the client setup program. For example, you could include importing connections if you want to add connections into an existing .cns file. To do this, use **Conman –import:<path\filename.cns>**. For example:

```
Conman -import:\\W2KSRV077\Connections\sales.cns
```

You can also change the password on an existing connection with the command **Conman –p** using the format **conman –p: <connection name> <"password">**. Note that the password being set must always be enclosed in quotations. If the password is not specified or it contains a space or only quotations marks, the password is erased. The connection name need be enclosed in quotations only if it is longer than a single word. Table 5.3 gives some examples of changing the password on a connection.

Table 5.3 Automating Connection Password Changes

Example	Explanation
Conman –p IE "senate"	This changes the password on the connection called **IE** to **senate**.
Conman –p "Internet Explorer" "state government"	This changes the password on the connection called **Internet Explorer** to **state government**.
Conman –p "Internet Explorer"	This erases the password on the connection called **Internet Explorer**.
Conman –p "Internet Explorer" " "	This also erases the password on the connection called **Internet Explorer**.

Using TSAC as a Diagnostic Utility

You can modify the connect.asp page so that a client disconnection displays a disconnection code, which can help you narrow down and diagnose why connections are unexpectedly failing or disconnecting. To do this, make a backup of the connect.asp file in the **\Inetpub\wwwroot\TSWeb** directory. Then open the original connect.asp and find the following code:

```
sub MsTsc_OnDisconnected(disconnectCode)
    if not disconnectCode = 2 then
        msgbox ErrMsgText & MsTsc.Server<BR/>
    end if
        'redirect back to login page
        Window.Navigate("default.htm")
  end sub
```

And replace it with the following:

```
sub MsTsc_OnDisconnected(disconnectCode)
        msgbox ErrMsgText & MsTsc.Server & "disconnect code: " &
            disconnectCode
  end sub
```

Connect as usual from the client that's experiencing the disconnection problems (for example, call **\W2KSRV050/TSWEB** from within Internet Explorer and connect to your terminal server). When the session disconnects, a disconnect code will be displayed. You can match this code to one of the disconnection reasons outlined in Table 5.4.

Table 5.4 TSAC Disconnection Codes and Reasons

Disconnect Code	Disconnect Reason
1	Local disconnection (not an error)
2	Remote disconnection by user (not an error)
3	Remote disconnection by server (not an error)
260	DNS lookup failed
262	Out-of-memory condition
264	Connection timed out
516	WinSock socket connect failed

Continued

www.syngress.com

Table 5.4 Continued

Disconnect Code	Disconnect Reason
518	Out-of-memory condition
520	Host-not-found error (GetHostByName failed)
772	WinSock send call failed
774	Out-of-memory condition
776	Invalid IP address specified
1028	WinSock recv call failed
1030	Invalid security data
1032	Internal error (code 1032)
1286	Invalid encryption method
1288	DNS lookup failed
1540	GetHostByName call failed
1542	Invalid server security data
1544	Internal error (timer error)
1796	Timeout occurred
1798	Failed to unpack server certificate
2052	Bad IP address specified
2054	Internal security error
2308	Socket closed
2310	Internal security error
2566	Internal security error
2822	Encryption error
3078	Decryption error

NOTE

Remember that TSAC is an ActiveX control. As such, it can be scripted and used outside this environment—for example, within your own Web application or VB application. For more information on using TSAC, refer to the following Microsoft Developer Network (MSDN) article at: http://msdn.microsoft.com/library/techart/w2ktsac.htm.

Walkthrough: Remotely Administering a Windows 2000 Server with Terminal Services

There aren't too many reasons for every Windows 2000 Server not to run Terminal Services, at least in Remote Administration mode. This mode allows you to connect to each Windows 2000 server on your network from another computer, as though you were sitting in front of the Windows 2000 server. You can do this from any 16-bit or 32-bit Windows client (it doesn't have to be Windows 2000), with minimum bandwidth overhead so it's suitable for dialup connections. Furthermore, the connection can be secured with very strong encryption if both sides support 128-bit Terminal Services encryption. This even makes it suitable for connecting over the Internet if your firewall can be configured to permit RDP.

However, for the purposes of this walkthrough, we'll use Windows 2000 Professional as our connecting workstation and the Terminal Services MMC snap-in to remotely manage a Windows 2000 server. This snap-in requires access to the Windows 2000 Service Pack 1.

NOTE

The instructions for the walkthrough assume that you have access to Windows 2000 Service Pack 1; the files are not included in Windows 2000 Service Pack 2. However, if you do not have access to this Service Pack, you can download the Terminal Services Advanced client from the Microsoft site, currently available from: www.microsoft.com/windows2000/downloads/recommended/TSAC.

This walkthrough covers the following steps:

- Installing Terminal Services on a Windows 2000 server, configured for Remote Administration (this will require a reboot)

- Installing the Terminal Services MMC snap-in from the Windows 2000 Service Pack 1

- Connecting to the Windows 2000 server with the Terminal Services MMC snap-in

1. If Terminal Services is not already installed on your Windows 2000 server, you'll need to do this first. Make sure you're logged on with Administrative privileges and click **Start | Settings | Control Panel | Add/Remove Programs | Add/Remove Windows Components**. Scroll down the list and select **Terminal Services**. When you use Terminal Services for Remote Administration, you do not need to install Terminal Services Licensing. See Figure 5.36.

    Figure 5.36 Installing Terminal Services

    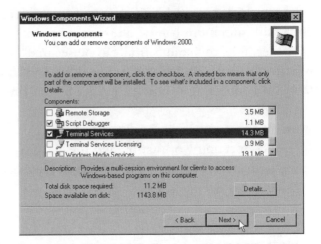

2. Click **Next** and the following dialog box asks you which mode you want to use with Terminal Services. Keep the default of **Remote Administration Mode** and click **Next**. After a little while, you'll see the Completing the Windows Components Wizard. Click **Finish** and **Close**. You'll be prompted to reboot. Unfortunately, although you have to reboot Windows 2000 far less often than NT4, making any changes to Windows 2000 Terminal Services from Add/Remove Programs invariably means that you have to reboot your server.

3. You now need to install the Terminal Services client on your Windows 2000 Professional (or another Windows 2000) server. Find the Windows 2000 Service Pack 1 and navigate to the **VALUEADD\TSAC** folder.

4. You'll find in this folder three .exe files and a Readme.htm. The file that you want to install the Terminal Services client snap-in is **tsmmcsetup.exe**. Double-click this file and you'll be prompted to confirm that you want to install the Terminal Services Connections

Snap-in. Click **Yes**. You'll be prompted to confirm the license agreement; read it and click **Yes** if you agree.

5. You'll be prompted to confirm or change the installation location, with the default being **\Program Files\Terminal Services MMC Snap-in**. When you are happy with the location, click **OK**. If the folder doesn't exist, you'll be prompted to create it. Click **Yes** to confirm.

6. At the end of the install, you are prompted to read the release notes. Click **Yes** or **No** to read them now. Then you should see confirmation that Terminal Services Connections MMC Snap-In Setup was completed successfully. Click **OK**.

7. Click **Start | Programs | Administrative Tools**. You should see a new option called **Terminal Services Connection MMC (tscmmc)**. Load this option and you should see the Terminal Services Connection snap-in load, as shown in Figure 5.37.

Figure 5.37 Loading The Terminal Services Connection MMC

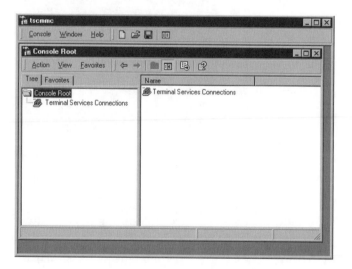

8. Right-click **Terminal Services Connections** and select **Add new connection**. You'll be prompted to fill in the server name or IP address, the name you want to give this connection, and optionally, any logon information.

9. You can use the **Browse** button to find the Windows 2000 server you just configured for Terminal Services, or simply type in the name or address. When you use Browse or tab to the next field, you'll see that the

Connection name is automatically filled with the same information. You can keep this name or change it as you like. This example used the Browse option to find the name of my server: **W2KSRV016**.

10. Click the **Log on automatically with this information** check box. Specify **Administrator** as the username, leave the password blank (for greater security, the password will be specified at connection time only), and fill in your domain name if your Windows 2000 server is joined to an NT4 domain. (Leave this blank if your server is in a workgroup.) Your connection details should look similar to Figure 5.38.

Figure 5.38 Specifying the Connection Details

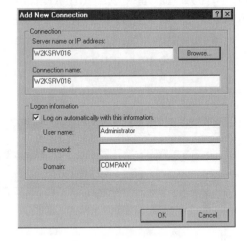

11. Note that you don't have to supply these logon details here. You could supply them each time you connect, but specifying them here will save you some typing later. Click **OK**.

12. You should now see your connection appear in the right pane. Right-click it, and select **Connect**. You should see your server's familiar **Log On to Windows** screen in the right pane, similar to Figure 5.39. (The figure has the Options button expanded so you can see it's already configured for the correct domain.)

13. If you see the logon screen but the resolution isn't correct—you can't see all the picture, for example (too small or too big)—you might need to change the screen resolution. Right-click the connection and select **Properties**. Under the **Screen Option** tab, you'll be able to change the desktop size, as shown in Figure 5.40. However, try keeping the default

of **Expand to fill MMC Result Pane** and click **OK**. This forced refresh might solve the problem.

Figure 5.39 Connecting to the Windows 2000 Server

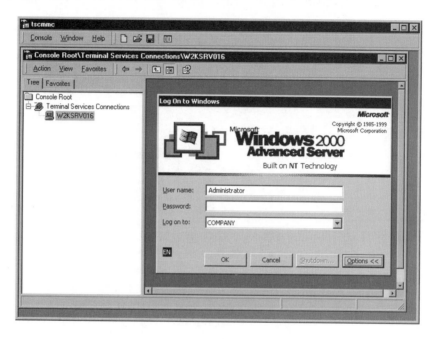

Figure 5.40 Changing the Screen Options

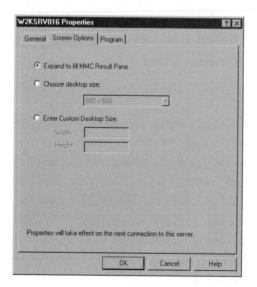

14. You should be able to log on and see the server's desktop displayed in the MMC. However, we'll tidy up this MMC by changing it from Author mode. Click **Console | Options** and change the Console mode to **User mode—full access**, as in Figure 5.41. Then click **OK**.

Figure 5.41 Changing the MMC Options to User Mode

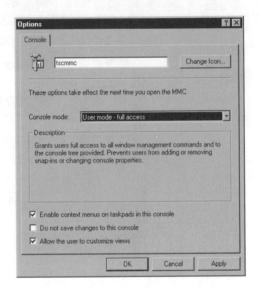

15. Exit the **MMC**, confirming that you want to save it when prompted. Call it back up again, and this time it should display more neatly, filling your screen. Connect to your server, log on, and you should be able to quickly navigate around the remote desktop. For example, run **Administrative Tools** or **Control Panel** applets, as shown in Figure 5.42.

16. Once you are connected, you might notice two things. First, the Start bar says **Windows 2000 Terminal** rather than **Windows 2000 Server** or **Windows 2000 Advanced Server**. That should help prevent you from getting confused about whether the session is local or remote. The second thing is that the **Windows Security** option under Settings calls up the standard **Windows Security** dialog box that you would normally see when you press **Ctrl+Alt+Del**. It's useful for checking logon details, locking the computer, logging off, accessing Task Manager, making password changes, and shutting down. If you press **Ctrl+Alt+Del** when using your Terminal Session, you'll get the **Windows Security** dialog box for your local Windows session, not the remote Windows terminal session. The equivalent key sequence to use is

actually **Ctrl+Alt+End,** but most people can't easily remember that! So Microsoft added to the Settings menu an item for this dialog box when in a Terminal Services session.

Figure 5.42 Using Terminal Services for Remote Administration

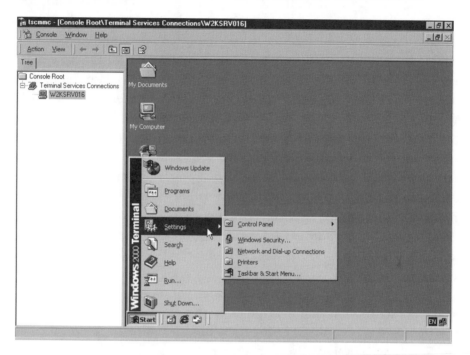

17. You can easily add servers into the same MMC by repeating the "Add new connection" procedure from Step 8 onward. That would provide a useful tool to connect to all your Windows 2000 servers from the same MMC. However, if you want multiple simultaneous connections, you have to create custom MMCs for each server.

Summary

This chapter outlined some of the main advantages of running a terminal services-type environment, specifically the advantages and features that now come built into the Windows 2000 operating system. These advantages can all add up to a much lower total cost of ownership because you can reuse legacy hardware while still getting the benefits of running a Windows 2000 environment. You can more tightly control and manage applications and users and improve security.

There are other advantages, including the ability to *shadow*, or remotely control (or view), a user's session such that remote support becomes a viable option. When users are running a mixture of local and remote processing, they can integrate the two environments by mapping the clipboard, drives, and printers. And last but by no means least, the RDP improvements mean the connection method between client and server is suitable for low bandwidths, which makes it a very attractive option for remote access users and remote administration.

However, before designing and installing your Terminal Services deployment, you should take into account a number of factors, including the new licensing service requirements, upgrades where applicable, unattended installations, and whether your applications are actually suitable or need modifying for Terminal Services. You'll also need to look at the whole area of capacity and scaling when usage will be anything other than very light and make the best use of multiple terminal servers working together for maximum uptime and minimum support.

We looked at configuring the terminal server itself, its terminal service connections, and Terminal Services-related options on user accounts. Both Windows 2000 local accounts and NT4 domain accounts can be configured for Windows 2000 Terminal Services, providing you use the User Manager for Domains included with Windows 2000 in order to configure the NT4 accounts. You should use the Terminal Services Manager within its own Terminal Services session in order to view and manage users and their connections. From this utility, you can send users a message, log users out, or remotely control their sessions.

Finally, we covered how to configure and distribute client-side connections, including the Terminal Service client, the Client Connection Manager, and the Advanced client (TSAC). The chapter's walkthrough stepped through using the Terminal Services Connection MMC for remote administration.

Running Terminal Services can open up a whole new way of offering and managing network services and users' desktops. Part of this methodology requires a new way of thinking, because we're so used to local users having local control, yet we have begun to realize that such personal freedom comes at the expense of high support overhead and less productivity. When deploying a thin-client solution, IT implementers and their managers inevitably face a learning curve, as the users often do. (Remember, not all users are familiar with the Windows 2000 desktop, let alone the requirement for new drive mappings.) This chapter covered enough ground to get you started and at least appreciate the underlying workings of a Windows 2000 Terminal Services solution.

Solutions Fast Track

Why Use Windows 2000 Terminal Services?

☑ Clients receive all the benefits of upgrading to Windows 2000 without actually being upgraded.

☑ The total cost of ownership is lower for support, installation, and maintenance.

☑ The Remote Desktop Protocol (RDP) connection is suitable for low bandwidths and can be configured to use different levels of encryption.

☑ You can use Remote Administration mode to remotely manage Windows 2000 servers with minimum overhead on the server and no need to run a Windows 2000 Terminal Services Licensing service or buy additional Terminal Services Client Access Licenses (TS CALs).

☑ Security can be tighter in a Windows 2000 Terminal Services environment.

☑ PC and server can integrate in terms of the clipboard, drives, and printers.

☑ Shadowing (remote control) is supported to help reduce support overhead, including configurable options such as allowing nonadministrators this right and specifying whether the user's permission should be obtained.

☑ Multilanguage support on a single server is now possible.

Preinstallation Considerations

☑ When running in Application mode, you must also run at least one Terminal Services Licensing Service, even if you have no need to buy TS CALs. All Windows 2000 computers have built-in TS CALs.

☑ License servers outside Active Directory can be set only to **Domain/ Workgroup**, which means that discovery is by broadcast. However, by editing the registry, you can use a license server on a different subnet than the terminal server.

☑ The Terminal Services Licensing helps you keep track of issued and available licenses. Temporary licenses can be issued for 90 days, giving you enough time to buy additional licenses.

☑ If you run Windows NT4 TSE, consider the advantages and disadvantages of upgrading in place or migrating users and applications onto a cleanly installed Windows 2000 server running Terminal Services.

☑ You can install Terminal Services and components in an unattended file.

☑ Check for application suitability by way of compatibility scripts and transforms. Consider manually modifying application configurations to make them more "terminal server friendly."

☑ Consider capacity and stress tests to help with server specification and how or whether multiple terminal servers should work together for load balancing and fault tolerance.

☑ Consider any limitations that make Terminal Services an unacceptable solution and whether this can be addressed with an alternative (such as installing Citrix MetaFrame).

Configuring and Managing Windows 2000 Terminal Services

☑ Use Terminal Services Configuration to set server and connection settings.

☑ The connection settings can override any client-configured connections.

☑ The connection configuration is where you set the encryption level and who is allowed to use remote control.

☑ Use Terminal Services Manager from within a Terminal Services client connection in order to view and manage client sessions. Here you can log off disconnected users, send messages, and initiate a remote control session.

Configuring Clients to Use Terminal Services

☑ Installing the Terminal Services Client Creator allows you to distribute the client software from floppy disks or by sharing the files over the network.

☑ Client installation results in installing the Client Connection Manager and the Terminal Services client. The Client Connection Manager lets you specify and save multiple connections, including a starting program and automatic logon; these connections can be exported or imported and automatically distributed with the installation. The Terminal Services client broadcasts for a list of terminal servers and allows a quick, ad hoc connection.

☑ You can upgrade the Terminal Services client to a later version from SP1, which is in MSI format and offers 128-bit encryption. You can now also run this version of the client from a command line.

☑ TSAC is also from SP1 and allows central and automatic deployment from a Web site that delivers an ActiveX control to a browser (Internet Explorer). The browser must be configured to accept signed controls for this to work. Note that some facilities either do not work with TSAC or could or should be disabled for greater security.

☑ You can fully automate the installation of the Windows 2000 Terminal Services client and change connection passwords with the **conman –p** command.

☑ You can use TSAC to help diagnose connectivity issues.

Frequently Asked Questions

The following Frequently Asked Questions, answered by the author of this book, are designed to both measure your understanding of the concepts presented in this chapter and to assist you with real-life implementation of these concepts. To have your questions about this chapter answered by the author, browse to **www.syngress.com/solutions** and click on the **"Ask the Author"** form.

Q: We're currently running WinFrame. Can we upgrade to Windows 2000 Terminal Services?

A: No, there's no direct upgrade path. If you want to keep all your terminal server settings, you'll have to first upgrade to Windows NT4 TSE and then Windows 2000. Consider in advance whether you need the Citrix MetaFrame add-on. Many of the features that caused people to buy MetaFrame are now in the latest version of RDP that comes with Terminal Services, so you might not need this additional upgrade.

Q: If Windows 2000 Terminal Services now supports shadowing, faster connections, automatic printer and drive mappings, automatic client deployment, single application connections, high-level encryption, a wider range of clients, and network load balancing, what's left for Citrix MetaFrame as an add-on other than support for non-Windows platforms and non-TCP/IP connections?

A: Admittedly, many of the features that sold Citrix MetaFrame to companies (such as faster connections and shadowing) are now included in Windows 2000 Terminal Services. For some companies, there will now be no need to include MetaFrame 1.8 for Windows 2000 on their Windows 2000 servers, unless they have to support a wide range of clients and platforms. However, MetaFrame 1.8 for Windows 2000 does have some new and improved features, including the capability of shadowing one-to-many and many-to-one (Windows 2000 Terminal Services can support only one-to-one shadowing). MetaFrame 1.8 offers *seamless windows*, in which the single application can be loaded in its own window and looks and behaves to the user just as though it were a local application. It can *publish* and *advertise* applications as being available rather than having to specify them directly in the connection details. Thirty-two-bit clients can participate in Citrix Program Neighborhoods so that all published applications can be used with a single sign-on. It has a more sophisticated mechanism for load balancing that can take into account factors such as processor use, pagefile use, and memory load. However, this includes only ICA clients, not RDP clients. One of the most potentially exciting new features is Application Launching and Embedding (ALE), which allows applications to be launched within a Web page. COM ports and audio mapping are also possible, as is video depth of up to 24-bit color. Finally, direct-dial ports are available without having to connect over a remote access server. Look for even more features and advantages at www.citrix.com. However, also remember to verify whether you actually need these additional features, because they come at a price in terms of finances, additional training, and administrative overhead.

Q: What happens if our server that was hosting Terminal Services Licensing dies?

A: You restore it from backup. (You *did* back it up, didn't you?!) It's really important to back up your Terminal Services License Service because it contains a Microsoft-issued computer certificate and holds your paid client licenses. When you back up the server (as you do regularly, of course), be sure to include the System State and license server directory, which, by default, is **%systemroot%\system32\Lserver**. When you restore, make sure that the Terminal Services Licensing Service is actually running. If you restore to the original server, you're back to where you started. If you have to restore to a new computer, any unissued licenses will be lost, and you must reinstall them using the telephone method, providing Microsoft with the information saved to the Event Log about the type and number of unissued lost licenses. You'll find the telephone number you need to call by changing your connection method to Telephone and selecting your country or region (under **View | Properties**), then clicking **Action | Install Licenses | Next**. The telephone number you need to call will be displayed in the next dialog box. What if you didn't back up your server at all? Call Microsoft and provide as much information as you can about your original license server.

Q: We've gone through a lot of our TS CALs much more quickly than expected. When I've checked the Terminal Services License Manager, it looks as though multiple licenses have gone to the same client. Is that normal?

A: No, it's not normal. Each device should have one TS CAL only, irrespective of how many Windows 2000 terminal servers it logs into. In truth, both Microsoft and customers are suffering a few "teething problems" with this first attempt at enforcing licensing for legitimate clients. Therefore, if you suspect that computers are taking multiple licenses, you need to look into it. For a start, if your devices that have multiple licenses are Windows Based Terminals (WBTs), which are usually displayed by their IP address or a universally unique identifier (UUID), check their firmware version with the manufacturer and upgrade if necessary. Some older versions of firmware fail to retain their licenses and so request new TS CALs on every restart. If, however, the device is displayed as a computer name, it's possibly a computer setup error as a result of cloning and a new computer name hasn't been correctly assigned. In this instance, the license count is correct but the names are invalid. Track these computers by IP address and manually set or change their computer IDs. Failing that, is it possible that some computers have been rebuilt? That would delete the original license so that the client needs to request a new one. Another potential cause of multiple client licenses is the Users group being denied Full Control to the following registry key and its subkeys: HKEY_LOCAL_MACHINE\Software\Microsoft\MSLicensing. It might also be worth checking the latest Knowledge Base articles for any other known problems. If you identify any genuinely misclaimed licenses, contact Microsoft Registration Authority and Clearinghouse by telephone so that you can reclaim your licenses.

Q: What's the TSInternetUser account?

A: This account is used only with the Internet Connector that services anonymous users. Just as IIS has an anonymous user account called IUSR_<computer_name>, so Terminal Services uses this account for anonymous access so that access permissions can be assigned appropriately.

Q: Can TSAC be used to securely administer servers over the Internet?

A: This is a very common question. The answer is yes, probably. However, just because your Terminal Services connection is within a browser and it supports 128-bit encryption, that doesn't mean it's using secure sockets (SSL over HTTPS), which is usually how information is secured with a browser. Using TSAC, the client-to-terminal server connection is still RDP, which can be encrypted with a 128-bit key. The browser simply presents a convenient way of deploying the client software and presenting the initial connection screen. So, data traveling between the client and the terminal server isn't the same as securing the data with SSL or a VPN connection. However, all these have a higher overhead than RDP in terms of bandwidth and processing. For example, not all the data is actually encrypted on an RDP connection, even with 128-bit encryption, which might surprise you. But the data that isn't encrypted usually wouldn't present a security risk. It includes packets such as the client computer name and client username when exchanging licensing information as well as packets used to acknowledge printing and printer announcements. Actual session data, print data, and mapped data (for example, copying and pasting data between the two computers) will be encrypted. So the real answer depends on your definition of *secure* and whether your firewall will let RDP traffic through.

Q: I'm having problems using Terminal Services from home, over the Internet. I've asked for our firewall to be configured for RDP traffic, but how can I check that my connection attempt is actually getting through to the Windows 2000 server?

A: Use the trusty network administrator's friend, Telnet. Simply connect to your server and specify **port 3389** instead of using the default Telnet port of 23. For example, at a command prompt, type **telnet <ip_address> 3389**. You should get a connection and see a blank screen with a flashing cursor. Get somebody on your company network to check the Terminal Services Manager, where your connection should appear as a blue icon with no additional information. Clicking it will display the message, "This session is not active. There is no information to display." However, this message proves that a TCP 3389 connection was successfully made from client to server. A failure to connect is likely to mean that TCP port 3389 is blocked at some point between you and the server. Note that it's possible to change the RDP port number, but doing so is not recommended. See the Knowledge Base article "How to Change Terminal Server's Listening Port [Q187623]" for steps on how to change the RDP port number.

Q: I've received complaints that using **Alt+Tab** to switch between applications within the terminal session doesn't work, and when users press **Ctrl+Alt+Del** to log off, they end up logging themselves out of their local computer.

A: And we thought everybody used a mouse these days! Unfortunately, *hot keys* aren't passed down from the terminal session to the local PC, so they work only for local PC sessions. For example, **Alt+Tab** switches between a terminal session and a local PC application; to the PC, the terminal session is just another program. This is a retraining issue, which is never simple or popular. If your users want to continue using these hot keys in their terminal services session, they can, but with new key sequences that are automatically mapped (and unfortunately can't be changed). The alternative key sequences are shown in Table 5.5. Note that these keys do not use the keys on the keypad.

Table 5.5 Alternative Key Sequences

Standard Windows Key Sequence	Terminal Services Key Sequence
Alt+Tab	Alt+PgUp
Alt+Shift+Tab	Alt+PgDn
Alt+Esc	Alt+Ins
Ctrl+Esc	Alt+Home
Alt+Spacebar	Alt+Del
Ctrl+Alt+Del	Ctrl+Alt+End

Chapter 6

Networking Services

Solutions in this chapter:

- **Name Resolution with DNS**

- **DHCP for Central Configuration and Control of Addresses**

- **Name Resolution with WINS**

- **High Availability with Network Load Balancing (NLB)**

- ☑ **Walkthrough: Configuring Standard Primary and Secondary DNS Zones**

- ☑ **Summary**

- ☑ **Solutions Fast Track**

- ☑ **Frequently Asked Questions**

Introduction

This chapter covers the behind-the-scenes networking services that today are essential to ensure computers can communicate with each other effectively and efficiently. Although the underlying mechanisms for doing this are of no interest or relevance for users or services, network communication underpins today's business infrastructures and as such deserves the highest priority in a company's IT department. After all, there's no point in having a highly specified server with expensive software, configured to perfection if nobody can connect to it and use its services.

For a variety of reasons, the TCP/IP protocol suite today has earned the place of being the standard networking protocol for almost every company and network. Once it was considered too complicated, too slow, and had too high an administrative burden to implement across an enterprise network. Now it has evolved to be more efficient in both functionality and design. And with central administrative services like DNS (Domain Name System) for name resolution, and DHCP (Dynamic Host Configuration Protocol) for automatically allocating addresses to computers, TCP/IP services now include central configuration that makes TCP/IP a viable protocol to implement, support, and work efficiently throughout today's large network environments.

There's no doubt that having an easy-to-use GUI interface to configure these services has helped promote TCP/IP's success just as much as Internet connectivity (which relies on TCP/IP) has helped its wide-scale adoption. Although some companies continued to use TCP/IP with command-line–based management and text files, many IT implementers and IT managers saw the benefits of using a GUI interface that made the administrative overheads easier, cheaper, and less prone to human error. Microsoft continues this trend with full support for these configuration services in Windows 2000 with regards to functionality and ease of configuration.

In fact, because TCP/IP is now the default protocol in Windows 2000, it has a very high prominence throughout the product suite. Microsoft can't afford customers not to have these TCP/IP services working efficiently because Active Directory is heavily dependent on TCP/IP—it can't function without it. To Microsoft, Windows 2000 and Active Directory go hand-in-hand—if one fails, they both fail. Because Active Directory depends on TCP/IP you can be sure a lot of attention went into ensuring that TCP/IP services were efficient and effective in use, configuration, and maintenance—good news to the IT implementer and IT manager alike.

You may already have basic TCP/IP services running on your UNIX servers, or you may have them (or some) running on Windows NT4 servers. It's even possible (but unlikely) that you are running no central configuration at all for TCP/IP. If you're responsible for implementing or managing network setups like these, you can take advantage of the improvements in these services that Windows 2000 offers. Even if you never plan to use Active Directory, you can still capitalize on Microsoft's improvements to these essential networking services. There's absolutely no reason why you can't run them on Windows 2000 Servers (as standalones or member servers) and benefit from the majority of the new features. The options and features that can be used only with Active Directory will be pointed out to help you better evaluate the priority of migrating (if at all).

For those of you definitely planning to migrate to Active Directory in the future, I would say it is *vital* you sort out your TCP/IP services before deploying Active Directory. In an Active Directory network, all clients *must* use TCP/IP, and you *must* use DNS throughout—these are no longer choices like they were with NT4. Once these are in place and running smoothly, you'll be in a much stronger position to move to Active Directory knowing that you're building on proven connectivity services. Then it will require very little work to make any configuration changes so you can take advantage of Active Directory-dependent options.

High availability and automatic fault tolerance with the ability to scale out (adding more servers to a collective unit) is also key throughout Microsoft's philosophy for Windows 2000. In addition to fault tolerant disks and clustered disks, Microsoft has now added the Network Load Balancing driver as standard on Advanced Server and Datacenter Server. This allows you to efficiently utilize multiple servers hosting vital network services to offer true network fault tolerance, network load balancing, and the ability to remove a server temporarily for maintenance with no disruption of service to users. Network Load Balancing is an ideal complement to some of the other services this book covers, including Terminal Services, IIS, VPN servers, and even ISA servers.

NOTE

This chapter assumes you are familiar with basic networking concepts such as what TCP/IP is and how it functions. For background information, a suggested starting point would be Chapter 1, "An Introduction to TCP/IP" from the Windows 2000 Server Resource Kit. More technical information can then be found in the following chapter in the same resource kit: Chapter 2, "Windows 2000 TCP/IP."

Name Resolution with DNS

Domain Name System is at the core of today's Internet successes because it allows nontechnology users to retrieve data and access resources easily, without any knowledge of where they are either physically (what server, what country, etc.) or logically (which of the many networks that make up the Internet). Users type in an easily recognizable name such as www.microsoft.com and their ISP is responsible for finding the corresponding IP address for them. Exactly the same methods have existed in UNIX-based companies where users need to access various servers easily without having to remember what IP address to use.

There was a time when these two DNS scenarios didn't meet, but today more and more companies are connecting to the Internet and integrating Internet resources inextricably with their business resources. Now the boundaries of DNS administration have blurred as the advantages of a truly distributed service are realized. IT managers have some important decisions to make, such as whether to host their own Internet DNS server with details of their Internet services, or to continue to use somebody's else's (for example, their Internet Service Provider's). Hosting your own DNS server means you have more control—for example changes can be made more quickly and it may be cheaper to use existing resources rather than pay for this service to be effectively outsourced. But the downside will be the responsibility of not just server maintenance and administration overheads, but also a greater security risk.

Added on to all this is the dependency of DNS within Windows 2000, since not only is TCP/IP the default protocol in Windows 2000, but Active Directory itself relies on having a DNS infrastructure. It's no wonder that DNS is a hot topic these days for anybody in IT!

It is outside the scope of this section to explain the concepts and workings of DNS. Rather it looks at whether you need to run a DNS service on your network, the advantages of running Windows 2000 DNS, and how to integrate Microsoft and UNIX platforms within a DNS environment.

Do You Need to Run DNS?

Rather than assuming you must have DNS on your network because everybody else seems to be doing it, it's worth reassessing the requirement for actually doing this. Personally I'm all for running only essential services and aiming for a clean and streamlined network that meets the needs of your business requirements. There's no point in using technology simply because it's there. The fewer services you have running, the less likely they are to conflict, and the fewer to cause problems. The fewer services you offer, the more IT staff can concentrate on the essential services, and the less training required. I always think it's better to do a few things well than many things that achieve (at best) only mediocrity.

If you are using or plan on migrating to Active Directory, you will have no choice over whether to run DNS, because you cannot run Active Directory without DNS. If a proportion of your computers run UNIX, no doubt this choice has already been made for you with an existing DNS service in place, which may or may not be used by Microsoft computers. Finally, if you want complete control over your own Internet servers' DNS entries, you will need to run DNS.

However, there's no doubt that hosting your own DNS service commands a high administrative overhead in terms of configuring, maintaining, trouble-shooting, and building in resilience. For example you should always have at least two DNS servers for each portion of your namespace to ensure that if one server went offline, this essential service could continue. If you intend to integrate your internal network DNS system with the Internet, you will also have additional security considerations.

Historically, DNS has not had a high prominence within Microsoft networks, although NT4 offered a DNS service for both client and server. This lack of prominence was simply because it wasn't needed in an all-Microsoft environment because NetBIOS and not TCP/IP was the common method of computer-to-computer communication. This was true even when a Microsoft computer ran only TCP/IP because Microsoft added a NetBIOS layer on top of TCP/IP (NetBT). Therefore, DNS on both the client and server side was added as an additional UNIX compatibility option.

If Windows computers needed to communicate with a UNIX computer, then they had to have some way of resolving host names to IP addresses. Typically, networks ran their DNS servers on UNIX and simply configured all computers to use these servers for host-name resolution. UNIX-based clients would use only DNS for name resolution, whereas Windows computers would use a mixture of NetBIOS and host-name resolution depending on whether they were connecting to a UNIX computer or another Windows computer. This dual method of name resolution continues with Windows 2000, as can be seen from the **DNS** tab and **WINS** tab under Advanced TCP/IP Settings as shown in Figures 6.1 and 6.2.

Figure 6.1 Advanced TCP/IP Settings for DNS

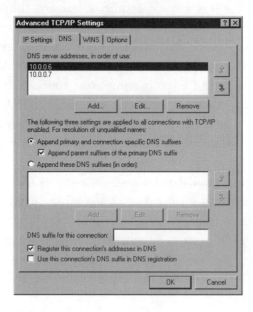

Figure 6.2 Advanced TCP/IP Settings for WINS

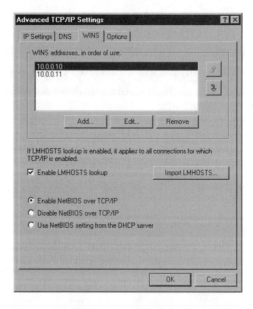

Few people ran the NT4 DNS service because although it offered a GUI interface for configuration, it didn't successfully compete with the stable UNIX-based systems that had been in place for years. However, it did have one major advantage for Microsoft environments, and that was its integration with Microsoft's NetBIOS name resolution methods. Microsoft's DNS service offered a WINS lookup if the name to be resolved wasn't found in the DNS database. In this way it offered a realistic method of tying together the two different types of name resolution.

By default, a Windows' host name and NetBIOS name were the same, and both means of resolution were tried when using TCP/IP to ensure maximum connectivity. Because WINS offered a dynamic service in that computers registered their names automatically on startup and released them on closedown, this allowed the NT4 DNS to offer dynamic NetBIOS name resolution by proxy. This meant that a UNIX client configured to use an NT4 DNS with a WINS lookup could resolve a name that hadn't been entered manually into the DNS database. Unfortunately, non–Windows clients still needed to be manually entered into the DNS database. So paradoxically it was UNIX clients that benefited the most from Microsoft's NT4 DNS service, rather than Microsoft clients.

Designing & Planning…

The Case for DNS Adoption

I can see good justification for gearing up for full-scale adoption of DNS throughout your networks *before* it becomes necessary. By its nature of being a truly distributed service, it's a complicated service to get running efficiently because each network is individual and has its own requirements. Therefore it makes sense to mitigate problems by early and gradual adoption before it becomes critical.

Knowing that you have more time allows you to plan carefully how you are going to implement this, taking into consideration training, upgrades, testing, monitoring and fall-back solutions. Just because you've identified that you don't need this service now doesn't mean you can afford to ignore it. There's no doubt that today's network reliance on TCP/IP will bring the need for DNS into your network sooner rather than later.

So, to recap, justifications for running DNS include:

- Having UNIX computers
- Running Internet services
- Running Active Directory
- Preparing for Active Directory
- Looking to integrate UNIX and Microsoft communication

You do *not* need DNS if the following do not apply and you are running an all Microsoft network – even if this includes Windows 2000 computers. Windows 2000 computers within an NT4 domain or workgroup continue to use NetBIOS for computer-to-computer communication even when running only TCP/IP—a much misunderstood fact that arose because of Microsoft's push towards Active Directory adoption and the marketing promotion of Windows 2000 into the UNIX arena.

Advantages of Microsoft's Windows 2000 DNS

Although NT administrators liked being able to use the standard Windows interface with the NT4 DNS service, and they liked the benefit of having a WINS lookup facility, it didn't eliminate the need to manually enter other records that couldn't be resolved by WINS lookup. Added to this, NT4 servers didn't have a good reputation for stability. When DNS is considered to be vital to the smooth running of your network, you naturally will look to put it on a stable platform, which often was reason enough to overlook NT4 Servers.

Windows 2000 DNS immediately overcomes these two hurdles by offering dynamic updates (where a client record can be added and removed automatically from the DNS database) and better stability through the improvements made to the operating system. It still offers the useful WINS lookup facility. Other features that now make it a very attractive choice of platform for your DNS service include the following:

- Support for SVR records
- Support for the underscore and Unicode
- Incremental Transfers
- Easy-to-use GUI administration

If you are interested in using any of these features, and you are currently using a UNIX-based DNS system, these features may also be available on this platform either in its existing state, or with a BIND upgrade. Table 6.1 contains a list of features that are supported on common DNS versions. However, you may decide that Windows 2000 DNS has other advantages (including the WINS lookup) and that the feature set offered by Windows 2000 DNS is reason enough to rethink your existing DNS services, and move to implement them on Windows 2000.

Table 6.1 Comparison of DNS Features on Different Platforms and Versions

	BIND 4.9.6	BIND 8.1.2	BIND 8.2.1	NT4	Windows 2000
Dynamic Updates	No	Yes	Yes	No	Yes
WINS Integration	No	No	No	Yes	Yes
Service Records	Yes	Yes	Yes	No	Yes
Unicode	No	No	Yes	No	Yes
Incremental Transfers	No	No	Yes	No	Yes

NOTE

Although technically dynamic updates are supported on BIND 8.1.2, the general advice is to use the later version of 8.2.1 for reliability.

Dynamic Updates

Dynamic update is one of the most useful features in Windows 2000 DNS. No longer dynamic by proxy with the help of a WINS server, now DNS can dynamically register and remove a client's host name into the DNS database.

This allows new computers to come onto your network and immediately ensures effective name resolution. And because it's automatic, the benefit isn't just one of timeliness, but of accuracy—the possible consequences of human error (especially when tasked with mundane jobs such as typing names to IP addresses) shouldn't be underestimated. It also means that DHCP can be fully utilized because it no longer matters that a computer frequently changes its IP address because this will be updated automatically in the DNS database.

NOTE

Dynamic updates are particularly effective when planning for network changes in terms of growth, reduction, and modifications. For example, a well thought out plan of disk imaging client computers together with Windows 2000 DHCP and DNS very quickly can bring online a large number of new computers with minimal network administration. Similarly, the decision to move from one network address range to another can be handled very easily without wide scale administrative changes. And mobile users who plug their laptops onto different networks throughout the enterprise can do so and have a timely and accurate name to IP address record in the DNS database.

All Windows 2000 computers can update their DNS server dynamically with their own host name. Down-level computers such as NT4 and Win9x can't, but they *can* do so through using Windows 2000 DHCP. Windows 2000 DHCP allows dynamic update by proxy so that when it successfully leased an IP address to a client, it can also dynamically update the DNS server with the details of name to IP address. And when the lease expires, it can remove the corresponding entry in the DNS database.

This combination of Windows 2000 DNS and DHCP makes a powerful choice for choosing to use Windows 2000 DNS. It can even be used to dynamically update UNIX clients that can't support this feature themselves.

Configuring Dynamic Updates

You might have spotted the relevant entry for using dynamic updates on a Windows 2000 computer in Figure 6.2. It's the **Register this connection's addresses in DNS** that is on by default. You can also choose whether you want to register a suffix with the host name (for example, company.com).

For down-level clients to dynamically register, they must be using a Windows 2000 DHCP server with the appropriate settings as shown in Figure 6.3.

Figure 6.3 DHCP Server Properties, DNS Settings for Down-Level Clients

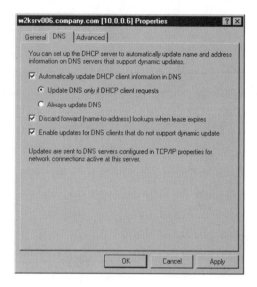

NOTE

If your Windows 2000 computers are using a DNS server that doesn't support Dynamic Update (for example, NT4 DNS) you should ensure these two options are not set. Trying to register a name when it's not supported will cause unnecessary errors and possibly problems on the DNS server being used.

The last important piece of information is configuring the DNS server to accept dynamic updates. Unlike the dynamic update setting on the client, a DNS server does not (for security reasons) allow dynamic updates by default. It must be enabled per zone, as shown in Figure 6.4 on the following page.

WINS Integration

On a Windows 2000 DNS server, this option to query a WINS server if it cannot resolve the host name itself is very useful when Microsoft computers are registering their NetBIOS names with a WINS server. In theory, if every Microsoft computer is using Windows 2000 DHCP that is updating DNS for them, this WINS lookup shouldn't be necessary. However, it is useful as a catch-all, and if you have some computers that are not yet leasing their addresses with a Windows 2000 DHCP.

Figure 6.4 DNS Zone Configured for Dynamic Updates

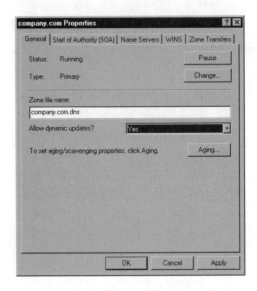

One important consideration to bear in mind when designing your DNS is how to configure this feature if you are mixing Windows and UNIX DNS servers. UNIX DNS servers have no concept of NetBIOS names and may well reject these records as corrupt. If this is the case you have two alternatives: don't replicate the WINS-related records, or create a WINS-only zone that is never used by any UNIX DNS servers. The latter may be a better choice anyway if you want to keep an eye on how often WINS lookups are occurring, rather than using standard DNS records.

WINS lookups and reverse lookups can also be configured with their own timeout values independently from other DNS records, and reverse WINS lookups can be configured to supply the DNS domain name as the NetBIOS scope.

Very few people use NetBIOS scopes and I've yet to come across a company that uses them on a production network. NetBIOS scopes provide a way of sub-sectioning your network, effectively creating virtual networks at the NetBIOS level. So for example, one computer belonging to a specified scope could communicate only with computers configured for the same scope. Scopes were seen as a low-level security option and/or a way to divide your network at the NetBIOS level. They have little place in today's networks where IP subnets, domains, and other security boundaries fulfill this role better.

Configuring WINS Forward and Reverse Lookup

The WINS forward lookup is configured as part of the Forward zone's Properties, under the **WINS** tab as shown in Figure 6.5. Enter the names of the WINS addresses and select the order of searching. The **Do not replicate this record** should be used when transferring this zone information to UNIX secondaries.

Figure 6.5 WINS Forward Lookups in DNS

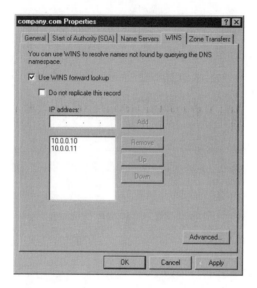

The WINS reverse lookup is configured as part of the Reverse Lookup Zone Properties with the **WINS-R** tab as shown in Figure 6.6.

On both of these dialog boxes the **Advanced** button allows you to specify the **Cache timeout** and **Lookup timeout** values in days, hours, minutes, and seconds as shown in Figure 6.7.

Service Records

So what's the big deal about Service Records, and what are they? Service Records (SRV) denote a certain type of DNS record that indicates a particular service such as a domain controller or a web server. If you have an all Microsoft network that isn't running Active Directory, it's unlikely you will need this particular feature. However, support for SRV records is the one requirement Active

Directory insists upon—it will not function without it because it is responsible for returning to the client a domain controller that can authenticate them onto the network.

Figure 6.6 WINS-R Reverse Lookup in DNS

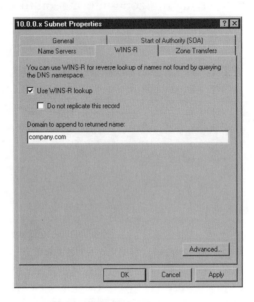

Figure 6.7 WINS Advanced Options

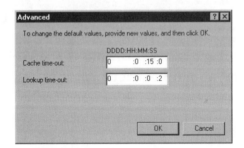

Previously this job of finding essential network services was done by NetBIOS names because Microsoft reserved the last character of the possible 16 for itself, to identify certain services. Therefore, when a TCP/IP NetBIOS client registers with its WINS server it can retrieve from the WINS database the names (and therefore IP addresses) of its domain, domain controllers, and master browsers. This method continues for Windows 2000 computers in workgroups and NT4 domains, which is why a robust WINS setup is still so important.

However, if you're planning on moving to Active Directory you will need to use a DNS server that supports SVR records.

Using Service Records

Fortunately for the network administrator, there's little need to manually configure Service Records with Windows 2000 DNS. When you configure a domain controller in your Active Directory, it will look for a DNS server that supports SRV records. If it can't find one, it will offer to install and configure Windows 2000 DNS and automatically add the required SRV records for you. However, if you're using a DNS server that supports SRV records but doesn't allow these to be added automatically, then you will have to add these records yourself, which is obviously time-consuming and error-prone.

Fortunately, manual addition is made easier by Windows 2000 DNS writing out the necessary records in text format to a file called **netlogon.dns** in your **%systemroot%system32\config** directory.

You won't see the Active Directory SRV records in your DNS Manager, but Figure 6.8 shows an example netlogon.dns file with all the SRV records required for a Windows 2000 domain controller called DC2 in the mycompany.com domain, using the address 172.16.0.2.

Figure 6.8 Example Netlogon.dns File Showing Active Directory SRV Records

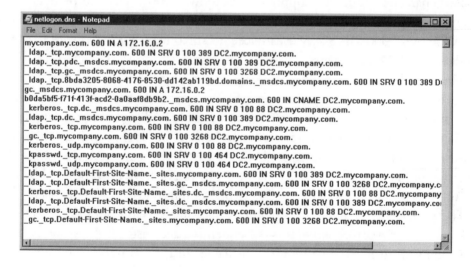

Unicode and the Underscore

Many DNS servers check for record integrity before loading, and anything found that does not conform with what they are expecting is marked as *bad* and either is not returned to clients, or can prevent the zone from loading. This is true for primary zones and secondary zones—in fact, a secondary DNS server may also reject bad records on transfer. This checking is also carried out when a client dynamically registers its name. Bad names should trigger an error or warning message on the DNS server. In order to know what is good and what is bad, obviously there must be set rules that define characters and formats that can be used.

Strict RFC 1123 defines acceptable host name specifications for DNS servers. This includes a–z, A–Z, 0–9, and the hyphen (sometimes called the *dash* or *en-dash* character). Anything else was considered *bad* and treated as such. This tight restriction causes problems with two definite scenarios—international countries that use extended characters sets and Microsoft computers.

Although English is generally considered the language of IT, it is perfectly understandable that users whose first language is not English will use local characters when naming their computers. Although it may be desirable to change these such that everybody is using only U.S. ASCII characters, it is often not practical. If it has been decided to link your network with a remote office in India using the same DNS system, you will need a way to accommodate non-standard characters. Unicode support in Windows 2000 is enabled by default, which provides the highest level of global interoperability. However, just because your Windows 2000 DNS server can accept Unicode, it doesn't ensure that non-Windows 2000 DNS servers do also. Before using Unicode characters, check to see whether it's also supported on other participating DNS servers.

Fortunately, having to support non-ASCII characters isn't a consideration for many of us. In comparison, however, support for the underscore is very applicable for Microsoft machines and this humble character offers some administrative nightmares when crossing the boundaries between NetBIOS name resolution and DNS name resolution. If you haven't come across this yet, or have been puzzled by the fury and exasperation this has caused network administrators, let me explain.

The underscore character is a perfectly acceptable—and often used—character within a NetBIOS name. It was frequently used instead of a space (which wasn't allowed) to make a name more readable. So for example, shares could be something like SALES_JAN, SALES_FEB, and so on, and machines named something like SQL_MAIN and SQL_BACKUP. The underscore causes no problems when used within a NetBIOS-only environment.

Configuring & Implementing...

What's in a Name?

Having the same name for both NetBIOS computer names and IP host names has helped to confuse many people about the differences between the two, and why the differences are important. In my company when we're testing connectivity issues, we make a point of having different names for each so we know easily whether NetBIOS or host name resolution has been made, without having to resort to a network analyzer. Don't use this technique yourself however, if you also have WINS lookup on your DNS!

Windows 2000 is the first version of Microsoft's operating system that no longer allows you to have different values for your host name and NetBIOS name.

An alternative is to use different names that aren't registered centrally—for example, choose a nonstandard name and ping it to make sure it's not resolved. Then add it into your LMHOSTS file and make sure it resolves. Do the same with a different name in the Hosts file. Don't forget to remove them after your testing!

However, by default Microsoft computers have the same host name as the NetBIOS name. If you configure a server to be called BIGSERVER_01 and install TCP/IP there, the default host name it will create for you automatically will be bigserver_01 (complete with the underscore). Although there's no technical reason to have the same name for both, it ensured maximum connectivity because name resolution would invariably fall back on the other method if the first failed. For example, if a NetBIOS application tried to resolve BIGSERVER_01 it would go through the standard NetBIOS resolution mechanisms first (NetBIOS cache, WINS server, broadcast, LMHOSTS file), and if that failed it would then revert to host name resolution (Hosts file, DNS).

NOTE

Although technically possible to reconfigure existing UNIX DNS servers, it may be politically expedient to try a different tack and consider instead creating a delegated zone for Microsoft computers. In the long run, this may be the most efficient and trouble-free solution rather than reconfigure existing UNIX servers, and/or instigating a computer renaming scheme. However, long term it would be a good idea to make sure all new computers are named without using the underscore.

The consequences of having the same name for both NetBIOS and host names can be seen when these computers that include an underscore in their names now need to participate in DNS. If your DNS server doesn't support the underscore character you are looking at either reconfiguring it to accept the underscore, upgrading it to accept the underscore, or reconfiguring all affected computers. A far easier approach is to use a DNS server that supports the underscore by default—which Windows 2000 does. However, it's still something to bear in mind if your Windows 2000 DNS will be communicating with non-Windows 2000 DNS servers (for example, Internet DNS servers).

WARNING

If you install Windows 2000 on a computer that has an underscore in its name, the setup program will automatically change the underscore to a hyphen without telling you. This is Microsoft's way of trying to encourage users to move over to standard DNS names and away from NetBIOS names! However, if you're sure your DNS servers can support the underscore (or maybe you're not using DNS) and you want to keep the original workstation name (perhaps it is included in scripts, for example), there's no reason why you cannot manually change the hyphen back to an underscore after the installation. When you do so, you'll see a rather cryptic warning message that the computer name may not work. This warning message relates to the use of the underscore with DNS servers that are strict RFC 1123.

Configuring Naming Formats

The option that governs which format is acceptable is under the server's **Properties | Advanced** tab as shown in Figure 6.9. You will also notice the **Fail on load if bad zone data** option under the Server option. The choices of name checking are:

- Strict RFC (ANSI)

- Non-RFC (ANSI)

- Multibyte (UTF8)

- All names

Figure 6.9 Configuring DNS Naming Formats

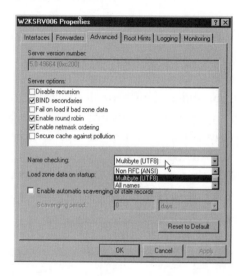

Strict RFC is a–z, A–Z, 0–9 and hyphen. **Non-RFC** is all these characters plus the underscore. **Multibyte** (UTF8) is for Unicode Transformation Format in 8 bit. If you are interested in learning more about UTF8, look up "Unicode character support" within the Windows 2000 Server Help.

All names effectively disables name checking because it configures the DNS server to allow all naming formats. This may be the easiest way to ensure that all workstations can successfully dynamically register their name—if you aren't integrating your DNS servers with other DNS servers that will reject these names. This option may be necessary, for example, if you used the special characters #, @, and $ for Windows 95 and Windows 98 computer names and cannot change them. With the default naming format setting on a Windows 2000 DNS, these characters will produce Event ID 5509 errors.

Incremental Transfers

Defined in RFC 1995 and often abbreviated to IXFR, incremental zone transfers allow for bandwidth conservation and faster transfers for sending and receiving zone information between DNS servers. There will always be some circumstances when a full zone transfer will be used (for example on startup, or when a large number of records have changed, or if the corresponding DNS server doesn't support IXFR). But when only a few changes have been made and a secondary DNS server requests an update, an incremental transfer will send just the changes rather than the complete zone (which is done in an AXFR). Incremental transfers are supported as standard on Windows 2000 DNS rather than a configurable option.

Easy to Use GUI Administration

Although you can configure and load your DNS entries from a text file, by far the easier way of configuring and maintaining Windows 2000 DNS is through the DNS MMC snap-in provided. This provides wizards for easy zone configuration, and easy to use dialog options. For example you can have a simple DNS forward and reverse lookup zone up and functioning within just a few minutes. There are context-sensitive dialog boxes for common administration procedures such as adding a new host, alias, mail server, and so on, so that only relevant information is prompted. These options can be seen in Figure 6.10.

Figure 6.10 Common DNS Administrative Options

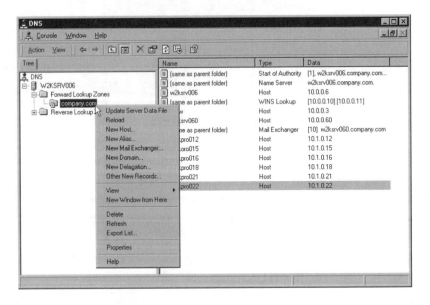

If the type of record you need to add isn't listed here, choose **Other New Records**, which provides you with a list of other record types with a helpful description displayed at the bottom of the dialog box. Once you have chosen the record type you are again prompted for only relevant information. Figure 6.11

shows the dialog you'll be presented with if you select to add an IPv6 host with the longer address field (note that Windows 2000 supports IPv6 hosts!).

Figure 6.11 Example of Configuring a Less Common Record Type—An IPv6 Host

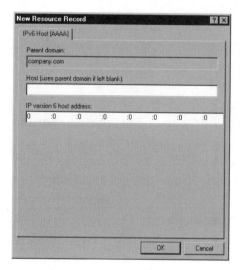

DNS also has its own Event Log so it's easier to identify and track any problems with this vital service.

Integrating Microsoft DNS and UNIX DNS

Some of the integration issues have already been covered, such as WINS lookups and name formats. However, this section looks at how you can mix and match and look to move a UNIX-based DNS structure onto a Windows 2000 DNS server. We will look at the following:

- Server Roles and Zones
- Transferring Zones
- Importing Zone Files

Server Roles and Zones

In UNIX DNS parlance a DNS Server holds one or more roles according to how it is configured and the number of zone files it stores. A zone is either Primary or Secondary. A Windows 2000 DNS zone can be either of these, with a third option called **Active Directory Integrated**. The last option is available only when you are running in a Windows 2000 Active Directory domain, and once enabled integrates the zone data into the Active Directory. This then makes for more efficient transfers, a multimaster update that offers a higher resilience, and allows you to configure secure updates whereby only the original owner can change its record details.

A Primary zone (referred as **Standard Primary** in Windows 2000) is the read/write copy of the database. When using dynamic updates, the DNS server hosting the Primary zone must be available or the update will fail. This is very important to remember when using dynamic updates outside Active Directory—because secondary zones are read-only, they cannot be used to update records.

A Secondary zone (referred to as **Standard Secondary** in Windows 2000) is a read-only copy of the primary zone. It obtains the copy through zone transfers—for example on startup, at designated intervals, or on a Notify command that changes have occurred. Having clients configured to use a Secondary DNS Server is useful for fault tolerance, load balancing client requests, and minimizing lookups over slow WAN links. For example, on a network with little change you might look to implement a secondary DNS server on a remote site and configure it to update every night. However, when using dynamic updates a client configured to use a secondary DNS server will be pointed to the Primary server in order to dynamically update its record. Only lookups will be serviced on the Secondary. If using dynamic updates in this situation, remember to prepare and monitor the additional bandwidth this will require.

The other type of DNS configuration we haven't discussed is Caching Only—using Forwarders and Forwarding DNS Servers, as shown in Figure 6.12. This involves configuring DNS servers not to use any zone—instead it is instructed to resolve names not from its own database, but by querying other DNS servers. It is useful for security reasons (it doesn't store any records), requires minimal administration overheads, and can help with reducing processing and bandwidth requirements if placed on remote sites. The longer they are up and running, the more records they hold in cache and the fewer queries it has to send out to other servers.

Configuring the Zone Type

When you create a new zone in Windows 2000 DNS, the New Zone Wizard will ask you which of the three zone types you want to use. The Active Directory Integrated option will not be available unless you are running DNS on a Windows 2000 Domain Controller. You will then be prompted for the relevant information. On both you will be asked whether it's for a forward or reverse lookup, the name of the zone (for example, company.com), and the name of the file that should store the records. If you're configuring a secondary zone you will also be prompted for the IP addresses of the primary (master) DNS servers that hold the zone information.

Figure 6.12 DNS Server Configured as a Caching-Only Server

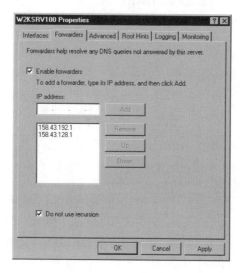

Once you have set the zone type, you can change it afterward, through the zone's **Properties** under the **General** tab using the **Change** button as shown in Figure 6.13.

Figure 6.13 DNS Zone Configuration—Set to Primary

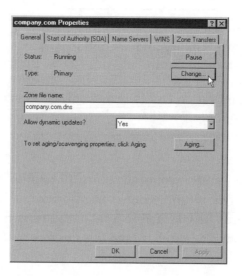

NOTE

If you are planning on migrating to Active Directory later make sure you install Windows 2000 DNS on servers that you have identified will be Windows 2000 domain controllers so that you can later change the zone type to be Active Directory integrated.

Transferring Zones

As we have seen, you can configure Windows 2000 DNS to be a Primary DNS server, or a Secondary. The zone transfer is always pulled by the Secondary from the Primary, never pushed from Primary to Secondary.

Despite the Secondary DNS servers initiating the zone transfer, you do have a high degree of control on the Primary. For example you can stop any zone transfers, or allow them to any server or to only specified servers. You can also specify *Notify*, which means that the Primary will contact Secondaries automatically when changes have been made so that the Secondaries can initiate a new zone transfer. This can be particularly useful in keeping the secondary DNS server up to date if you're using Dynamic Updates, but it has the potential to produce a lot of network traffic. If using DNS Notify, make sure your secondary DNS server supports incremental transfers.

NOTE

If using Notify, remember to disable this if/when you move to Active Directory and both Primary and Secondary DNS servers are running on Windows 2000 domain controller with Active Directory integrated zones. These DNS servers will exchange all Active Directory changes automatically every 15 minutes so Notify is not only not necessary, but will degrade performance.

By default, a zone transfer will occur every 15 minutes from a Windows 2000 Primary DNS server. This setting is determined by the Refresh Interval on the zone (**SOA** tab) and can be changed to a number that is then set to minutes, hours, or days. For example if you change this number to 1, it can then be set to every minute, every hour, or every day. This value is sent to the Secondary on each transfer so if you change it, it will come into effect only after the next transfer and not immediately.

Windows 2000 DNS servers configured as Secondaries must specify the IP addresses of any Primary servers. As a secondary it cannot specify how often zone transfers occur, but you can manually initiate them by right-clicking on the zone and selecting **Transfer from master**. A complete zone transfer also will occur when this zone is loaded.

Fast Transfers

By default, a Windows 2000 Primary DNS server will use Fast Transfers, which compresses the data to improve zone transfer performance. If you are using UNIX Secondaries, this might not be supported (for example, BIND versions earlier than 4.9.4). If this is the case, you should check the server's option **BIND secondaries**, which is found under the server **Properties | Advanced** tab. If fast transfer format is supported on your Secondary DNS server, this option should not be set. Note this is a server-only option, and cannot be set per zone.

Importing Zone Files

If you want to create a new zone on your DNS server, but want to use an existing zone file (for example, return to a consistent, known state), you can do this by copying the zone file into the **%systemroot%\System32\Config\DNS** folder and then specifying that this file should be used when creating the zone. Note that the file must be in the correct DNS format, and have a **.dns** extension.

In this way you can import DNS records from a UNIX DNS server instead of having to manually create them from scratch. Alternatively, if the UNIX DNS server is up and running you could simply transfer the records over by making your Windows 2000 DNS server a Secondary to the UNIX Primary. Once the records have transferred you can then change the zone on the Windows 2000 to be a Primary, and either decommission your UNIX DNS, or change it into a Secondary role to your server. If your UNIX DNS doesn't support dynamic updates, it would make sense to make your Windows 2000 DNS the Primary, and the UNIX DNS the Secondary.

Designing & Planning...

To Import or Not to Import?

Although it's highly tempting simply to import or transfer over existing DNS records from a working UNIX DNS server rather than creating them from scratch, beware you could also be importing over inaccurate and out-of-date information.

Many UNIX DNS servers have been operational for years with static records added manually over a period of time, probably on an ad-hoc basis, and probably by different administrators. You risk importing a lot of baggage in terms of unnecessary and out-of-date information. Your Windows 2000 DNS server cannot be justly blamed for returning wrong addresses to clients if that is what has been imported into the zone, but that won't stop other people from laying the blame at your server!

If you have to import static records (for example a large number of UNIX servers that have static addresses that cannot be changed to use Windows 2000 DHCP with reservations), importing may be your only recourse. However, with the "garbage in, garbage out" principle in mind, try to spring-clean the database before importing it, and then verify as soon as possible the imported information. Chances are, if you don't make this verification a priority at the outset, it will be forgotten.

Naming Formats for UNIX—Windows Zone Files

The naming format for a Windows 2000 zone file differs from the naming format on UNIX, so if you're planning on importing zone files from UNIX you not only have to copy them into the **%systemroot%\System32\DNS** folder, but remember to rename them. Table 6.2 compares naming formats and provides examples for a DNS name of company.com using the network address 10.10.5.0/24.

Table 6.2 Windows and UNIX Naming Formats

Zone Type	Forward lookup	Reverse lookup
UNIX Format	db.domain_name	Db.IP_network_forward_notation
UNIX Example	db.company.com	db.5.10.10
Windows 2000 Format	domain_name.dns	IP_network_reverse_notation.dns
Windows 2000 Example	company.com.dns	5.10.10.in-addr.arpa.dns

The other UNIX DNS file you can import is the Boot file, which you can move from your existing UNIX DNS server to your Windows 2000 DNS server. This will be called **named.boot** on UNIX; the equivalent is just simply **boot** in Windows 2000. If you want to use the boot file, you will also have to change the **Load zone data on startup** to be **From file** under the server's **Properties | Advanced** tab.

DHCP for Central Configuration and Control of Addresses

Dynamic Host Control Protocol provides a way for network administrators to centrally configure and control IP addresses and corresponding options for clients instead of having to configure them manually on individual computers. Because addresses are given to clients on a lease basis this allows more efficient pooling of addresses and provides an easy mechanism to change settings if required—for example, adding a secondary WINS server, moving users to a new domain name, and so on.

We have already seen how Windows 2000 DHCP can work with Windows 2000 DNS to offer dynamic updates for clients that aren't running Windows 2000. To me, this is one of the most compelling reasons to use Windows 2000 DHCP. However, Microsoft's latest version of DHCP also offers other incentives that you can utilize independently from DNS, in a workgroup, in an NT4 domain, in an Active Directory domain, or even just to service UNIX clients.

One of the reasons that network administrators haven't used DHCP to full effect in the past was because of its limitations when used in conjunction with DNS. Without dynamic updates in DNS, a network administrator has to create a static entry with a specific IP address. If that client were to use DHCP instead of having a fixed address, the network administrator couldn't guarantee that the client would receive the same IP address, which could then result in an incorrect DNS host record. The only alternatives were either to configure DHCP reserved addresses for each client (too high an administrative overhead to configure and maintain) or to use very long leases and hope for the best (which apart from being risky, immediately negated the benefits of address pooling and ensuring timely updates).

DNS dynamic updates now mean that network administrators can use DHCP to greatest effect on their network and automatically be assured of host record accuracy in DNS. In fact, because dynamic DNS greatly reduces the need to enter any static host records for clients, it frees administrators from this burdensome task considerably. For minimal network maintenance, you should aim for most computers using DHCP and dynamic registrations. Exceptions will be DHCP servers themselves, which must have a fixed address, although a Windows 2000 DHCP Server can natively update its own DNS record so there is no need to add static host records for these computers manually. Other exceptions will include non-Windows 2000 computers that cannot support DHCP (for example, some legacy UNIX computers and printers) and possibly key records that have to be added manually such as aliases, mail servers, and so on. For security reasons you may decide to add static records for all main servers such as DNS servers and domain controllers until you can enable Secure Updates, which is available on Active Directory networks.

When using static addresses, I strongly advise you to include these addresses in your DHCP scopes, and then mark them as excluded. This provides a more accurate centralized view of what addresses have been allocated, and therefore which addresses are still free. Otherwise it's very difficult to know which addresses are used if they have been configured statically—resorting to using Ping is *not* an acceptable solution!

For reduced future network administration, consider changing static addresses on servers that must keep the same address, to use DHCP with reservations. This has the advantage of being able to see centrally what addresses are being used, and efficiently control their settings without having to visit each machine. However, the disadvantage of using reservations is the administrative overhead of inputting them, maintaining them (for example remembering their record needs changing if their network adapter is replaced because reservations work on MAC address), and ensuring good connectivity between DHCP client and DHCP server.

Configuring & Implementing...

When Reservations Will Not Work

Because DHCP reservations work by checking the MAC address, this means reservations will not work if there is a router between the DHCP client and the DHCP Server. The reservation must be for a device on the same subnet on which the DHCP server resides.

Many corporations physically group together their key servers to better protect them and for easier administrative access. These servers are often put onto the first available subnet. If you followed such a pattern and wanted reservations for any of your key servers, this would work fine if the DHCP server was also on the same subnet. However, if you are providing multiple DHCP servers on different subnets (for example to spread the processing load, for bandwidth conservation, or because you cannot pass DHCP packets across subnets) you would need to add DHCP reservations on the DHCP server in the same subnet. Remember: If the DHCP client and DHCP Server are not on the same segment, reservations will not work.

A final consideration is protecting your DHCP configuration policy. Windows 2000 DHCP supports "Rogue DHCP Server Detection," which means that all Windows 2000 DHCP servers must be authorized. Within an Active Directory environment this ensures that only Enterprise administrators can bring online a Windows 2000 DHCP server. In an NT4 or workgroup environment, a Windows 2000 DHCP server still needs to be authorized by an appropriate administrator (e.g., local or domain). Hopefully this will help to reduce unauthorized users setting up DHCP servers.

The other side of protecting your DHCP policy is ensuring that users cannot change their DHCP setting to use a static address, which can quickly undo all your hard work! Look to restrict users from accessing these settings locally—for example, with system policies on Microsoft down-level client and a suitable group policy on Windows 2000 computers. For other clients, you will have to rely on user education alone, and bear it in mind when troubleshooting odd address-related problems.

This section will cover some of the other main advantages of using Windows 2000 DHCP under the following:

- TCP/IP Configuration Options
- Superscopes

TCP/IP Configuration Options

The minimum address configuration a TCP/IP client requires is IP address and IP address mask. Note that the mask is needed to determine the *true* host address when deciding whether another host is on the same subnet, or remote. All other options are considered optional.

Of course, the other TCP/IP address-related options seem far from optional to today's network administrator if they want to ensure effective communication with other computers. On all but single segment networks, a client should also have a default gateway defined. Other commonly required options include DNS servers and WINS servers. If any of these are not specified correctly, computer communication fails from the user's point of view.

The standard levels of applying these options (and more) with DHCP are at the server level (previously known as global options in NT4 DHCP), at the scope level, and on an individual reserved client. If there are conflicts, the scope-level options will take precedence over the server option, and if there are any conflicts with an individual client's option, the client option take precedence.

This multilevel approach allows you to fine-tune settings granularly, while still benefiting from global settings. Planning is all-important here to work out a sensible policy of which settings should be applied at which level—and to ensure administrators stick to it! To reduce duplicate configurations, try to identify early on which options will apply to everybody or to an acceptable majority (for example, the domain name, NetBIOS type). Then identify which scopes you want to use, and which options should be applied to them. You'll find some options will apply to all scopes, but you are unable to configure them at the server level—for example, the DNS integration options and whether to service DHCP or BOOTP clients. You'll find these listed as the scope's **Properties** rather than **Scope Options**. Finally, identify and configure settings exceptions for specific clients. If you have a consistent policy of where and how to set each option, it will pay dividends when reconfiguring or troubleshooting. Figure 6.14 shows a Windows 2000 DHCP server with typical options set at the scope level.

Figure 6.14 DHCP Scope Options with Typical Settings

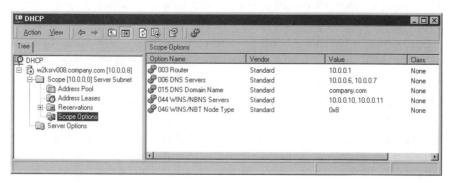

Vendor and User Class Options

To muddy the waters even more on the multiple levels of configuration, Windows 2000 now offers vendor and user class options. They are useful in further refining configuration and they may offer options not available on the standard levels. One good example of an additional setting you may want to use is releasing the IP address on shutdown, which is particularly relevant for mobile users plugging into different subnets.

Vendor classes are used so that a DHCP client can receive options based on vendor's identification and what class they want to use. Windows 2000 DHCP comes with three specific Microsoft vendor options and a default "other" (**DHCP standard**) for when no specific vendor setting is identified. The easiest way of explaining this is by example. You can have specific settings just for Windows 98 clients, and different options for Windows 2000-only clients. In addition to the preset Microsoft vendor classes, you could add others if supported by other vendors.

Although vendor classes cater for vendor options, user classes cater for a network administrator's logical grouping of computers. This allows the same logical group to be allocated the same settings, which are different from the standard server/scope options. An example of this would be to identify all laptops so they can release their IP address on shutdown, or computers on a remote site that should use a different default gateway and WINS server. Microsoft's DHCP server includes three built-in user classes: a default user class, a default BOOTP class, and one for Routing and Remote Access.

User classes allow a greater degree of control for the network administrator, but at the price of higher administration. For example a client cannot belong to multiple classes at once—one single user class is always a one size fits all. So, for example, if you defined two logical groupings and then found some computers needed the combination of the two, you would have to add a new user class and set the options all over again. If you decide to make good use of these logical user groupings, document them well and be sure to give them easily identifiable names.

The other downside of using vendor and user classes is the requirement to move away from a single, central configuration. This is because in addition to configuration on the DHCP server, each client that makes use of these class options must also be configured to ask for the class it requires using the **ipconfig /setclassid <adapter> <name of class>** command. Make sure you have good coordination of maintenance between the client configuration and the DHCP server.

Note that in the order of precedence, class options will override any options set at the server or scope level, but won't override any client settings.

NOTE

For more information on vendor and user classes, refer to the Microsoft Knowledge Base article "How to Create a New DHCP User or Vendor Class" [Q240247] which is available online at http://support.microsoft .com/support/kb/articles/Q240/2/47.ASP.

BOOTP and Multicast Scopes

Two new types of dynamic addresses that can be configured on a Windows 2000 DHCP Server are BOOTP addresses and multicast addresses. At the time of this writing, most companies will not commonly be using these—one because it addresses old technology requirements, and the other because it is addressing future technology requirements.

BOOTP was intended to configure diskless computers with an IP address and download an operating system to get it up and functional. The concepts behind BOOTP and DHCP are very similar, providing TCP/IP clients with a centrally configured and controlled startup environment. The packet structure for both types of clients is also very similar—both use the same service ports and both can be configured to use DHCP settings. It would make sense therefore, to offer both types of clients an IP address when requested.

MADCAP is used to support dynamic configuration of multicast addresses (those belonging to the Class D scope) for TCP/IP clients that already have a valid IP address but also require multicast addresses to participate in defined multicast groups. Multicasting provides a method of efficiently sending the same information once to a group of registered computers and is rumored to be a popular future direction for network services to ensure automatic and timely configuration with bandwidth conservation.

Two current examples of MADCAP applications are Microsoft's Phone Dialer and Exchange 2000's conferencing application. Microsoft provides seven MADCAP API functions in the Software Development Kit to help developers build their own MADCAP-enabled multicast applications.

BOOTP

Previously in NT4 DHCP, BOOTP clients were catered for only with reservations. Windows 2000 now offers dynamic addresses for BOOTP clients, which makes for more efficient allocation of addresses since unused ones can be reclaimed. However, it still cannot provide the client with the operating system files because this uses Trivial File Transfer Protocol (TFTP), which Windows 2000 doesn't support as a service. A Windows 2000 computer can only be a TFTP client, and not a TFTP server. Therefore, for Windows 2000 DHCP to fully support BOOTP clients, you have also have a third-party TFTP server that can provide the images the client needs to complete the BOOTUP process.

A Windows 2000 DHCP scope can be configured for DHCP clients only, BOOTP clients only, or either. If using either, bear in mind any scope settings will apply to both groups of clients. If these settings conflict, it may be preferable to put all BOOTP clients into their own scope. As an alternative, you could use the Default BOOTP User class, or for just a few BOOTP clients you could configure a BOOTP reservation and define the required client settings.

When using dynamic BOOTP scopes, you must define details for the TFTP server and boot image to be used. First of all, ensure that the **Show the BOOTP table folder** is enabled under the server **Properties | General tab**. This will display the BOOTP Table from where you can add the details of the boot image to be used.

MADCAP

Multicast Address Dynamic Client Allocation Protocol (MADCAP) adheres to RFC 2730. Its design is to provide requesting clients with an IP address and a least duration, nothing more. Multicast packets using this scope have a Default Time to Live setting of 32 seconds, which can be modified. The scope itself has an additional configuration option, its own Lifetime (how long the scope will be active). By default this is set to Infinite, but in the spirit of automatic configuration and clean up, it can be set to expire automatically on a given date.

To discover MADCAP servers on the network, clients multicast a discovery message to the address 239.255.255.254. Because this is a multicast discovery and not a broadcast discovery like DHCP, there is no need for DHCP forwarding on routers. However, you must make sure that routers will pass multicast packets or they will block the requesting clients' requests.

Automatic Private IP Addressing (APIPA)

This refers to the native ability of all Windows 2000 computers to self-configure an IP address if it is set to use DHCP (the default) and no DHCP server can be found. When this occurs, the computer chooses an address in the 169.254.x.x range with the subnet mask of 255.255.0.0, logs a warning in the System Event Log, and retries to contact a DHCP server in the background at regular intervals.

Where this option is most useful, I think, is when running a workgroup—for example, a home network or a small department. It allows all Windows 2000 computers in the same workgroup to obtain a valid IP address so that they can communicate with each other without the need for individually configuring them, or for using a DHCP Server. Where it is less useful though, is in a large network—and is one of my personal gripes with Windows 2000! When a computer boots up and can't find a DHCP server to provide one of our company allocated addresses, I want this to be easily recognizable to a user rather than the computer simply configuring itself for a 169.254.0.0/16 network that won't talk to anything else! To my mind, a valid but incorrect IP address that simply logs a warning event is worse than when a computer obviously has no IP address information and logs Red Errors in the Event Log! Most users when reporting network connectivity problems won't realize that their problem "I can't ping the server's address when everybody else can" is brought about because of something as fundamental as a faulty network adapter (the most likely reason).

Although Windows 98 also supported APIPA, Windows NT4 did not, so remembering the different effects of not contacting a DHCP server may be one of user education (remembering to check the IP address with IPCONFIG and what a 169.254.x.x address means). You may even consider disabling APIPA on key machines at either the computer level, or at the adapter level. This is something I certainly recommend for Windows 2000 servers that run RAS if that service is configured to use DHCP for client addresses.

Disabling APIPA on Windows 2000 Computers

Unfortunately this is one option that doesn't have a predefined group policy, although I think it should! Instead it requires adding the REG_DWORD type value **IPAutoconfigurationEnabled** and setting the value to 0.

This key must be added under: HKEY_LOCAL_MACHINE\SYSTEM\ CurrentControlSet\Services\Tcpip\Parameters.

APIPA will be disabled the next time the computer boots, and when it cannot contact a DHCP (and has no valid lease time from a previously leased address) it will not allocate any address information (all zeros or blank) and will log red Error messages in the System event log. Just as when using APIPA, it will try to find a DHCP server in background periodically so over a sustained period of time (the time it takes a user to realize they have a connectivity problem) it will have logged several of these Errors, which makes it much easier to immediately identify.

Superscopes

The easy setup and configuration of superscopes is another good reason to use Windows DHCP. Superscopes allow you to define multiple address ranges on just one adapter and offer a number of solutions for network administrators on more complex networks. These include the following:

- Support for more than one logical address range on a single physical segment, either because you have run out of available addresses, or because you want to logically separate computers. This arrangement is known as a *multinet*.

- DHCP server consolidation, providing DHCP addresses for clients in remote subnets.

- Address Migration.

Superscopes are simply a grouping of multiple DHCP scopes. You define your scopes first, then define your superscope and move the scopes into it (then known as child or member scopes).

Superscopes also provide some means of DHCP cooperation when using multiple DHCP servers. This is an important point because DHCP was not designed to be a distributed service like DNS. Each DHCP server knows nothing of the options and addresses offered by other DHCP servers on your network, which you are using for fault tolerance and bandwidth conversation. This easily can result in duplicated addresses being configured, conflicting options, or worse still, when a client has multiple valid addresses on different servers.

The last point about multiple addresses on different servers can arise if the server that offered the initial address doesn't respond in a timely fashion when a client attempts to renew. Instead, another DHCP server responds and because it has no scope defined for this client, sends back a negative acknowledgement that forces the client to ask for a new address from this server. At this point, both DHCP servers have addresses leased for the same client. When this happens too often, not only may a client be using an address that isn't optimal (i.e., not in its own subnet), but it's also a good way to quickly deplete addresses unnecessarily and give network administrators a hard job trying to resolve the situation.

Superscopes can be used such that all DHCP servers contain all the scopes you use throughout the network. On each server, mark each scope as excluded except the one(s) it is responsible for. This way not only will you be able to see a consistent view of all scopes and ranges that are being used on your network, it will also prevent multiple addresses being leased for the same client. With this setup, DHCP servers that receive a request to renew a lease that resides in an excluded scope range will be ignored and only answered by the DHCP server that originally leased it. If the originating DHCP server does not respond, the client will be forced to give up the address at the end of the lease and ask for a new address.

Multinets

A multinet is defined as a single physical segment network that has been logically divided by IP addressing. This situation might arise for two reasons. You might need more addresses than you have available on your subnet. Rather than resubnet your existing addressing infrastructure, you simply start a new network address. Create a new scope on your DHCP server for this new address range, and then create a superscope to move both scopes into. With this setup, clients requesting addresses will be located at an address from the first listed scope. When full, the DHCP server will then allocate addresses from the second scope.

In this scenario if clients from scopes needed to communicate with each other, you would have to ensure routing tables catered for this. One of the easiest ways to achieve this is to modify an existing router. If no router is being used, you could add a persistent route on each client to use its network card to forward both addresses.

Another reason for having a multinet is if you wanted to logically separate TCP/IP clients on the same segment—for example, to reduce network level (not MAC) broadcasts.

Server Consolidation

Superscopes allow you to concentrate your DHCP address leases onto fewer servers, and perhaps to move them to your tightly protected server subnet. Because of the inherent limitations of using multiple DHCP servers, the more you have, the more vulnerable you will be to conflicting configurations. Of course, there's also the additional server maintenance to bear in mind. Superscopes offer a good opportunity to consolidate DHCP servers onto as few servers as you think you require for fault tolerance and bandwidth conservation.

Providing your routers pass DHCP packets (RFC 2131 compliant) or you enable a DHCP Relay Agent (such as the one provided with Windows 2000 RRAS), one Windows 2000 DHCP Server can lease addresses to multiple remote subnets. When the DHCP server receives a request for an address, the server will automatically know from the router's subnet address (or relay agent) which scope the requesting client belongs to, and will allocate an appropriate address.

Figure 6.15 shows an example of a DHCP superscope for a number of remote subnets, displaying active clients on the 10.2.0.0/16 network. Although the computers are a mixture of Windows 2000 and down-level clients, the DHCP server is configured to update the DNS server for all clients. Accordingly, all the client icons show a pen to indicate that these addresses/names have been passed to a DNS server.

Figure 6.15 DHCP Superscope Servicing Clients on Multiple Subnets

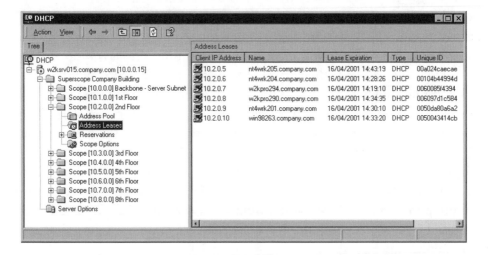

Migrating Users from One Scope to Another (Address Reallocation)

This rarely happens on a stable network that was designed with a policy that accommodated a flexible address allocation. However, poor decisions are inherited, circumstances change, and the IT industry often moves too quickly to keep up with the last lot of planning. Redesigning a network's address policy is not a happy choice to make, and must fill any network administrator with dread as the possible consequences of static addresses and hard-coded or saved addresses start to materialize. However, there may come a time when a radical change is the only sensible solution if your current IP address requirements cannot be met. For example, this may easily be the case if your company has merged with another and you need to integrate the two computing resources. Or your previous addressing scheme simply cannot cope with the recent expansion of new computers. Or perhaps after a security review a decision was made to move to using one of the private address ranges (private addresses should not be routed by Internet routers) in addition to a Proxy Server for Internet access.

Having a superscope on your DHCP server won't answer all your problems, but it can help in migrating users from one address to another by a single central configuration—providing they are DHCP users in the first place! The first thing you must do is plan in advance. Create a new scope for the new address range. If you don't already have a superscope defined for your DHCP server, create one and move the new scope(s) and the scopes to be retired into it. Make sure your routers have been changed so that communication between the two address ranges is possible. Then deactivate the scope that contains the address range you want to retire. New clients will receive an address from the new scope immediately. Old clients will have their renewal requests refused, which will force them to ask for a new address, which will move them onto the new scope. Do not delete the old scope until all active leases have disappeared or you will have clients running on their old addresses until the bitter end of their lease duration with no easy way of tracing them.

In theory, all clients should have moved automatically onto the new scope after half the number of days for which your old scope was configured. This is the minimum number of days you should allow for a gradual migration; it may obviously be more if a computer has not been turned on for a period of time (for example, a user on vacation or computer decommissioned).

Of course, you can always help speed this process if necessary by forcing a renewal on the client using the **ipconfig /renew** command or equivalent, which may be put into a computer startup script for Windows 2000 computers, or login script for down-level and legacy clients for either a specified period of time, or until it can be verified that the client is now using the new address.

When you are confident that all computers are now using the new address range, and after a suitable bedding down period, don't forget the housekeeping of deleting the old scope, removing the router entries, and removing any automatic script renewals!

Name Resolution with WINS

Windows 2000 has long been heralded as the kiss of death to NetBIOS—it wasn't going to be used any more with just native TCP/IP replacing all basic networking communication. For the first time, there's actually an option to disable NetBIOS on top of TCP/IP. Goodbye to NetBIOS broadcasts, network Neighborhood problems, and WINS servers? It may come as a shock to many people to learn just how inherently dependent Windows 2000 remains on NetBIOS. In fact, outside Active Directory, NetBIOS is used just as much as it was with NT4 and previous versions, so the need for a well-considered WINS design plan should deserve a high priority for any network administrator.

I've found many of today's network administrators fail to understand exactly how NetBIOS works and perhaps more importantly *why* it works the way it does. With the ascent of TCP/IP, the distinction between NetBIOS names and IP host names has become more blurred as the two move closer together in function, with their roles being to resolve a name to an IP address. Yet the two are very different, and it's important to know where these differences lie. I suspect it helps to understand and appreciate the use of NetBIOS and WINS if you understand Windows' networking pedigree.

To appreciate the history of NetBIOS, we could go beyond Windows NT, but we'll take that as our convenient starting point. Windows NT, when it first emerged, was aimed at multiple markets. This included the smaller NetBEUI networks that used to run LAN Manager, slightly larger networks that ran Novell, and almost as a "just in case" it offered a TCP/IP protocol so it could integrate with UNIX-based networks. In these early days, NetBEUI was the default networking protocol for NT.

Not only did offering three different protocols mean that Microsoft could target three different markets, but using the common method of NetBIOS communication with all three protocols meant that they could even offer all three at once on a single network card, while using just one communication interface for all Windows applications. That meant that an application had no knowledge of what underlying protocol was being used, which meant greater simplification for developers, which in turn offered customers a greater variety of software from which to choose, and customers could run them in a mixture of environments.

So, for example, users could connect to shared resources and authenticate using any one of the three protocols, providing that protocol was used by both client and server. This choice has never been there for UNIX servers, which natively run only TCP/IP and offer TCP/IP-dependent applications. Note that with the advent of Active Directory, this choice now no longer exists for Active Directory clients, which *must* run TCP/IP (although other protocols still remain supported).

NetBIOS is a broadcast-based protocol, which means it is suitable for single-segment networks with plenty of bandwidth. In its simplest form it is quick, lean, uncomplicated and has little to configure. However, it is clearly unsuited to today's networks where routers join multiple segments and bandwidth is often poor. TCP/IP on the other hand is a suitable protocol for more complex networks and Microsoft had to find a way to meet the requirements of both when customers wanted to use TCP/IP on Windows platforms. Their answer was Windows Internet Name Service (WINS), which functionally performed the same role of IP address to host name as DNS offered, but with IP addresses to NetBIOS names instead.

However, WINS also fulfills an additional service—providing a central store to identify essential network services. Just as the later DNS servers support the Service record (SVR) in order for clients to interrogate their DNS for a list of domain controllers, Microsoft uses an equivalent record demarcation by the use of the final letter in the NetBIOS name. NetBIOS names can be a maximum of 16 characters, but Microsoft computers such as those running NT4 will allow you to type only up to 15 characters when specifying a domain name, computer name, or username. This is because Microsoft reserved the last character for themselves so they could append a prefix that denoted a certain service. When you look at NetBIOS names (for example, locally on a client with **nbtstat –n**, or viewing the WINS database) you will see this final character being converted into a hexadecimal number. Locally with **nbtstat** this will be represented by the name, padded with spaces to make up 15, and then angled brackets containing the reserved service type. For example, **W2KPRO010   <00>** represents the workstation name. In the WINS database you will see this represented by square brackets in the format [xxh]—for example, **W2KPRO010   [00h]**.

Different types of services that can be used include those for the workstation, server, domain or workgroup, browser, replicator, RAS client, RAS server, network monitoring agent, and so on. Every Microsoft computer running NetBIOS on TCP/IP will by default register at least three different services (workstation, server, and messenger). For a server running additional programs, this is may be considerably more. Figure 6.16 shows an example of a server's list of NetBIOS names.

Figure 6.16 Example of a Standalone Server's TCP/IP NetBIOS Registered Names

NOTE

For a complete list of all the NetBIOS services and their corresponding numbers, refer to the Microsoft Knowledge Base article: "List of Names Registered with WINS Service" [Q119495], which is available online at http://support.microsoft.com/support/kb/articles/Q119/4/95.ASP.

Hopefully you can now appreciate how crucial a role NetBIOS plays in Windows' networking services. It has not died with Windows 2000, and even if you are running in an Active Directory there may be plenty of reasons why you will still need NetBIOS over TCP/IP for some time. As such, you cannot afford to have WINS servers either not returning their information, or worse, returning inaccurate information. Windows 2000 WINS features and options help to offer a reliable WINS solution with the following:

- Improved WINS Manager
- Data Integrity
- High Performance

Designing & Planning…

TCP/IP NetBIOS versus TCP/IP Direct Hosting

I had heard rumors that the primitive but powerful leftover from LAN Man days, the **Net** commands, would no longer work without NetBIOS. This flagged big alarm bells with me because not only are Net commands incredibly useful for quickly administering networking commands when the GUI utilities are too restrictive or you don't have the time to wade through them, but they're also the linchpin of many successful administration scripts.

Good examples of interactively using Net commands include **Net Use** for mapping a drive, **Net Send** for instant messages, **Net Config** to display a computer's configuration, **Net Helpmsg** for information on an error messages, **Net Session** and **Net Files** to see which computers are attached and which files are open. The most obvious use of Net commands in scripts is, of course, mapping drives in users' login scripts, but it can also be used with **Net Computer** to add multiple computers to NT4 domains, **Net Stop/Start** for controlling services, **Net Time** to synchronize server/workstation times, **Net Statistics** to find out some basic statistical information that is a good indication of a computer's health.

However, after some investigation I found that the Net commands will continue to work without NetBIOS, because of **Direct Hosting** that's supported on Windows 2000. Direct Hosting works only between two Windows 2000 computers (and later operating systems) and offers an alternative protocol to carry SMB (Server Message Block) traffic. Previous versions of Microsoft operating systems could only use NetBIOS to carry the application layer traffic of SMB, so to many (myself included), SMB became synonymous with NetBIOS.

Now Windows 2000 supports Direct Hosting as well as NetBIOS to carry SMB traffic, and a Windows 2000 computer can use both Direct Hosting *and* NetBT. If NetBIOS over TCP/IP is disabled, it will only use Direct Hosting. Microsoft's preferred method is Direct Hosting because it uses DNS rather than NetBIOS name resolution, which reduces the likelihood of broadcasts and the need to maintain two different mechanisms for name resolution (i.e., DNS and WINS).

But because Direct Hosting has to be supported by both communicating computers, a Windows 2000 computer won't know in advance whether the other computer also supports Direct Hosting. So it sends out its message using both, and the first one that is answered will be the

Continued

one that is used to complete the command. On a Windows 2000 computer, this could be either—it's literally down to timing. This can make for some puzzling network traces when SMB traffic is apparently used only intermittently with the NetBT protocol.

For those of you looking at network traces and filtering ports for firewalls and such, NetBT uses TCP and UDP ports 137 and 138; Direct Hosting uses TCP and UDP ports 445.

You can use **Net Config Redirector** and **Net Config** to find out whether NetBT and/or Direct Hosting are supported on a computer. NetBT will display as **NetBT_Tcpip** on individual adapters, and Direct Hosting will display as **NetbiosSmb (000000000000)**.

Unfortunately you can't disable Direct Hosting on a Windows 2000 computer (without also disabling File and Printer Sharing) so you know that all your SMB traffic will be over NetBT—you can only disable NetBT. But if you disable NetBT and use a networking command to a computer that doesn't support Direct Hosting, or where DNS name resolution fails, your networking command will fail. So the only reliable environment where only Direct Hosting can be used is in Active Directory (so workstations can find vital networking servers such as domain controllers) and where every computer on the network also supports Direct Hosting (that is, no down-level computers). I'm sure that time will come, but for many network administrators it won't be soon!

Even in this Active Directory environment with no down-level computers, I can still think of two other reasons to consider keeping NetBT on every Windows 2000 client: one for network administrators and one for users.

- For network administrators, **nbstat** offers a powerful tool, already mentioned in this book. I use it most when I have an IP address and need to know quickly which computer is using it and the name of the currently logged on user. I haven't yet found an equivalent command line utility to do this using Direct Hosting. This utility now comes with another switch, –RR (*ReleaseRefresh*), which is used to release the client's name in its registered WINS database and then renew it.

- For users, although it's one of my pet peeves, I have to admit many people would be lost without Network Neighborhood, which relies completely on NetBIOS. When I watch how users use their computers, I'm amazed at just how often they call up and use Network Neighborhood to do even the simplest of tasks when it would never occur to me to do the same

Continued

task in such an extracted and slow way! To remove Network Neighborhood would not be a popular move with most users and you would have to factor in additional user training to get them accustomed to using and searching with LDAP in Active Directory. This is why Direct Hosting only wouldn't be practical in a Windows 2000 workgroup, even with DNS— users wouldn't be able to see the network.

Improved WINS Manager

In truth, there aren't many configuration options available to the Windows 2000 WINS Manager through the MMC snap-in, and yet I find it very difficult to go back to using the equivalent under NT4. When first loaded you will see your server, with folder options for Active Registrations and Replication Partners.

Most of the interesting options are available when you right-click on your server, as shown in Figure 6.17. One of the more interesting options is the Export List, which allows you to output the current NetBIOS names to IP address mappings on your WINS server into a text or Unicode tab or comma delimited file. You can even choose to output the whole database, or just selected rows. This provides an easy way to sort and search through names when looking to do a little housekeeping—for example, identify names not adhering to your company naming policy. The other important option from this menu is, of course, the Properties where you can set the MMC refresh interval, the backup path and whether to backup on shutdown (recommended), record timeouts, database path, automatic database verification, and burst mode settings.

The Active Registrations folder you can see in Figure 6.17 is predominantly to find database entries by name or by address. This provides a great filter mechanism that was missing from NT4 WINS where you often had to scroll through a long list of entries. You can use wildcards if unsure of the exact address/name— for example, * on its own would return all entries. When searching by computer (Owner) you can also filter the results by record type, so for example, you could easily find the domain's master browser, or just a computer's current username. You can also define a static mapping through this menu, which might be used, for example, for a non-WINS client that cannot self-register or to reserve the name of a crucial server you need to take offline for some time (reserving the name will ensure no other computer *hijacks* the same name).

Figure 6.17 WINS Manager When First Loaded

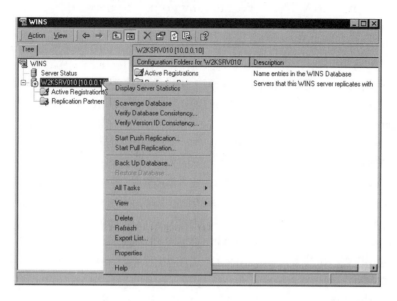

The Replication Partners folder allows you to configure how your WINS server should exchange its database information with other WINS servers. The standard advice is to configure both push and pull partners, although if you have a WINS server on a remote subnet with poor bandwidth it may be preferable to configure this as a pull partner to be initiated out of hours. To make life easier for you, you can even use automatic partner discovery, which uses multicasting with a push/pull configuration, and updates every two hours. Personally, for minimal administration I think the automatic partner discovery is a great idea with sensible defaults, although you must ensure any intervening routers support IGMP multicasting. Microsoft does not recommend using this option on large networks.

Data Integrity

WINS was not designed to be a truly distributed database. Just as NetBIOS was never originally designed to be used over multiple subnets but evolved with WINS to accommodate this need, neither was WINS really designed to work in harmony with multiple WINS servers but evolved with push/pull partnering to accommodate this requirement. Using multiple WINS servers is often at the heart of data integrity problems and the simplest advice to help combat this is don't do it. Or at least, minimize the number of WINS servers you run on your network to the lowest you think you can get away with, taking into account fault tolerance and slow links. Despite Windows 2000 now being able to be configured for

12 WINS servers, I think it is very telling that Microsoft themselves advise never running more than 20 WINS server on any complete network without contacting them for advice first.

Most network administrators underestimate how many WINS clients a single WINS server can service. You should always have at least two WINS servers so you have automatic fault tolerance, but bear in mind each server can service up to 10,000 clients. With the constant emphasis on timely responses and greater fault tolerance, it's perhaps no wonder that most networks run at least twice as many WINS servers as they need to do. Not only do the number of WINS servers increase your chances of data corruption and latency, but each server commands its own overheads in terms of maintenance.

You would be much better off running fewer WINS servers but for the ones you do run them on, ensure they are on highly specified computers. Always run them dedicated, and never on a domain controller or a mail server or any other service or application that competes for the computer's resources. In addition to a fast network card, consider using a dual-processor (increases performance by 25% on average). Because registrations, lookups, and the addition of replicated data accesses the physical database, this is going to be one of the server's components most highly stressed. Using a RAID array for a high performance disk subsystem will help, as will dedicated disk controllers.

These are the simple things you can do immediately to help protect your WINS data integrity, and they may be all you need to do. Other settings and options to help include the following:

- Backup Policy
- Controlling Replication Partners
- Replication Policy
- Removing Old Mappings
- Database Verification

NOTE

One other easy thing to check that will help ensure the integrity of your WINS databases is to ensure each WINS server has its Primary WINS setting configured for *its own IP address*.

Backup Policy

You can interactively backup your WINS database through the WINS Manager by right-clicking on the server and selecting **Back Up Database**. Once a backup has been done, you will also have Restore Database available from this context-sensitive menu.

A safer plan is to set the default backup directory under the server **Properties** (**Genera**l tab). This must be a local drive, but a good plan would be to put it onto a different physical drive. Once the backup directory path has been set the database will be backed up automatically once every three hours. As an added precaution you can also set the option to backup the database automatically on shutdown. Of course, you should always backup the whole server independently from the WINS settings.

Controlling Replication Partners

Just as you can set a Windows 2000 Primary DNS server to allow zone transfers with only known secondaries, you can configure WINS to replicate only with the servers you have configured as replication partners. This option is set on by default under the Replication Partners **Properties | General** tab. If this setting were not set, a user with appropriate permissions could select from the server's **Properties** either the **Start Push Replication** or **Start Pull Replication** and simply specify an IP address to use. Additionally, a push replication will prompt whether it should apply to just the selected server, or should propagate any changes to the selected server's replication partners.

The other option you have over controlling which replication partners you use is the **Block records for these owners** setting, which is under the **Advanced** tab of the **Replication Partners Properties**. This option was known as *Persona Non Grata* under NT4 and is suitable for removing WINS servers from your network because it prevents any further replication from that server that contains unwanted or out-of-date mappings.

Replication Policy

If you are defining replication partners manually rather than relying on automatic discovery, it's worth thinking about the trade-off between frequent replication with the increased chance of corruption, or fewer updates at the risk of greater latency. Most networks are actually fairly stable and would probably be fine replicating just once during a quiet period during the day, and once again after office hours. Remember, you can always initiate a replication if necessary, for example just after adding a new server onto the network that users need immediately.

A *Push* partner acts in the same way as Notify does in DNS. It informs its partner that it should ask to replicate. This can be configured for service startup, each time an address changes or on a frequency based on the number of changes.

A *Pull* partner is when the WINS server really does all the work, asking its partner for its database and resolving any differences. You can set a Pull to be initiated at service startup, at a certain start time and interval (in days, hours, and minutes), and how many times it should retry if unsuccessful.

Removing Old Mappings

When a WINS server confirms a client's registration, it also sets the Renewal Interval (equivalent to a TTL), which means the client must renew its name periodically in order to maintain its Active status in the database. Just as a DHCP client attempts to renew its lease after 50 percent has expired, so too does the WINS client. By asking the client to renew its mapping frequently, this ensures that Active entries are still valid.

The opposite of an active mapping is an *inactive* mapping, which should be triggered when a WINS client shuts down in an orderly fashion. When this happens the client sends a release message to its Primary WINS server so that the mapping can be marked as inactive. If the record remains inactive longer than the specified extinction interval (four days by default), the status will then change to *extinct*, and it is considered to be *tombstoned* (marked for deletion). It is important that the record is replicated as tombstoned rather than simply deleted outright because this could result in it reappearing as a result of other servers still having an active status for it.

The record remains tombstoned for a period called the *extinction timeout* (six days by default), after which the record is deleted as part of the automatic scavenging process. Note that you can also initiate scavenging from the WINS Manager by right-clicking on the server and selecting **Scavenge Database**.

The timeouts and interval settings are all configurable under the server **Properties | Intervals** tab. For the most part the defaults offer sensible settings to ensure that ghost mappings do not reappear; for this reason the dialog box also offers a button to restore the settings back to defaults. See Figure 6.18. One reason you may want to change these settings however, is to bring them into step with your DHCP lease settings.

Figure 6.18 WINS Server Properties | Interval Settings

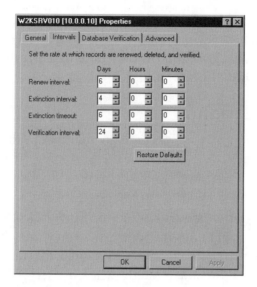

Manual Tombstoning

You can also choose to delete a mapping manually with the WINS Manager using the **Delete Owner** command from the Active Leases context sensitive menu. You will be offered the choice of deleting the record from your selected server, or marking it as tombstoned to be replicated to other servers. Unless you have a really, really good reason for not doing so, always choose the tombstone option if deleting a mapping and using multiple WINS servers. Always try to delete the mapping from the registering WINS server.

Database Verification

You can verify WINS database entries by performing a consistency check. When this is initiated on a WINS server, it compares its entries against entries on its replication partners' databases. When a local record is found to be identical to the owning replication partner's record, the WINS server has verified the record and accordingly updates the record's timestamp. When a local record is found to be older than the owning replication partner's record, it is replaced with the later version and its original is tombstoned.

You can initiate a database verification through the WINS Manager MMC, but you can also set this to occur automatically under the server **Properties | Database Verification** tab. Because the process is both processor and network intensive, it is better to perform this out of standard office hours.

High Performance

We have already covered how a single WINS server can service up to 10,000 clients and how a highly specified server will help with any bottlenecks. Two other features of the Windows 2000 WINS are **Burst Mode Handling** and **Persistent Connections**.

Burst Mode Handling

This allows a WINS server to support a high volume of simultaneous WINS registrations like you typically would find at the beginning of the working day. When the number of registration requests become so great that efficiency and accuracy is at stake, Windows 2000 WINS automatically switches into Burst Mode, whereby registration requests are immediately acknowledged without checking for duplicates and without adding the entry into the database. Instead, the acknowledgement that is sent has a very short TTL (time to live) so that the client can come back and renew properly when the server is less busy.

For the first 100 positive registration acknowledgements, the WINS server sets the TTL to five minutes. The next 100 positive registration acknowledgements come with a TTL of 10 minutes, and so on, incrementing the TTL by five minutes for each additional 100 requests. This continues until the TTL reaches 50 minutes (which is 1000 pending requests). At this point, the process starts over again with the WINS server sending out the next 100 TTLs with five minutes.

In this way, the WINS server has not turned away clients and has given them a temporary pass (which must be upgraded to a full pass) using varying timeout offsets. A Windows 2000 WINS server can process up to 25,000 registration requests using this method (after this threshold, requests are ignored).

Burst Mode settings are set under the server **Properties | Advanced** tab, as shown in Figure 6.19. The choices are for **Low**, **Medium**, **High**, and **Custom**. These represent the number of requests (registrations and renewals) that can be queued before **Burst Mode** is initiated. Low equates to 300, Medium to 500, High to 1000, and Custom can be between 50 and 5000.

Persistent Connections

Replication partners can now maintain persistent connections rather than tearing them down and setting them back up again with each replication. This option is set under Replication Partners properties, under both the **Push Replication** tab and the **Pull Replication** tab (both settings are on by default). Note this is not applicable for multicast partners. Figure 6.20 shows the Pull Replication settings for this.

Figure 6.19 Configuring WINS Burst Mode Settings

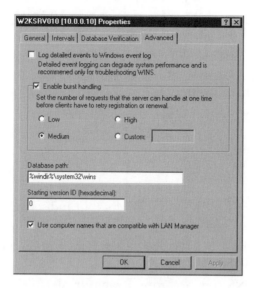

Figure 6.20 WINS Persistent Connection Settings for Pull Replication

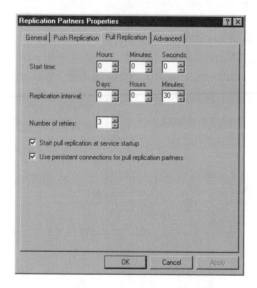

High Availability with Network Load Balancing (NLB)

The technique referred to as *round-robin* has long been used with DNS, and refers to two or more computers sharing the same name (alias) in the DNS database while having their own IP address. When a DNS client asks to resolve the name, the DNS server returns the first IP address. The next request will return the next IP address and so on, so the DNS server returns each address in a rotational fashion. This often explains why, when you ping a host name on the Internet, it can return a different IP address each time (if the ping request isn't blocked at routers!). It acts as a simple and unsophisticated fault tolerance and load balancing mechanism because the load is automatically (but indiscriminately) distributed between the computers that share the same name, and if one of the servers becomes unavailable the DNS server will send out a different address on the next request so the client will eventually connect.

Windows 2000 DNS supports round-robin by default (refer back to Figure 6.9), which can help out with fault tolerance and load balancing on your networking servers. However, DNS round-robin has its limitations and weaknesses. For example it has no idea when one of the servers go offline and it will continue to hand out an address that will not connect. Chances are, however, (particularly with services like Web traffic) that the client will retry the connection, and therefore will receive a different (and hopefully this time, available) address. You can supplement this technique with an additional monitoring service that checks on server availability (for example, pings the IP address) or service availability (for example, sends a simple application command that requests a response; therefore no response means the service is not functioning). When such monitoring devices detect a server or service has become unavailable they can send an alert to an administrator so that the problem can be rectified.

However, there is no inherent mechanism within DNS to detect a downed server because there is no continual conversation between a DNS server and its host entries to check whether they are online or not. The other problem with DNS round-robin is that it functions on name/address alone and cannot take into account the type of traffic (ports) using the host name. And you cannot proportion the amount of traffic between the computers with the same name—for example, giving out one IP address twice as often as the others because it has a faster network card.

Similarly DNS servers have no concept of *session state*—information that must be retained throughout the client's session. A single session can include multiple connections that may or may not be sequential, but in order to retain session state the client should be reconnected to the same server. The most common example to illustrate the need to retain session state is a Web browser shopping on an e-commerce site storing shopping cart items as it is browsing. However, perhaps a simpler and more obvious example for a network administrator is a Terminal Services client that disconnects its session rather than logging out in the hope of reconnecting later, and finds the same programs loaded as before.

WARNING

Windows 2000 DNS clients, unlike previous Windows DNS clients or UNIX workstations, have a local DNS cache that honors the TTL associated with the host record returned from the DNS server. This can give the impression that DNS round-robin isn't working because the client will continue to use the same IP address for subsequent connections rather than use the different addresses on the DNS server. You can view this cache on the client by typing **ipconfig /displaydns**, and empty the cache by typing **ipconfig /flushdns**.

The idea is that by caching host addresses, connections can be faster (because there's no delay waiting for the DNS server to respond) and network traffic is reduced. However, if you want to employ DNS round-robin for fault tolerance and load balancing, this may not work as expected with Windows 2000 clients because they don't request an address from the DNS server for each connection if the name is cached (and the TTL associated with the record hasn't expired). This is another reason why using Network Load Balancing is a better solution.

You can effectively disable the Windows 2000 DNS cache by modifying the registry, but this may not be practical for multiple clients, especially if they are not under your control.

If you want to effectively disable the DNS cache (set the TTL to 1 second) on a Windows 2000 client computer, you will need to set the value **MaxCacheEntryTtlLimit** to **1** under the following registry key: HKEY_LOCAL_MACHINE\SYSTEM\CurrentControlSet\Services\Dnscache\ Parameters.

Many of DNS round-robin shortcomings and limitations are addressed with Windows 2000 Network Load Balancing, which is supported on Advanced Server and Datacenter Server. Once this is configured on multiple servers, they all listen and respond to a shared IP address. Moreover they are aware of each other (by sending out *heartbeat* messages), which means they can react (converge) if one of the servers goes offline, is added back online, or if a server is added–in a similar way to how routers with routing protocols cooperate.

One of the best things about Network Load Balancing is that no special hardware is required (unlike Cluster service, which requires very specific hardware) and it operates completely independently from Active Directory. For once, there are few benefits of adding a Network Load Balancing server into Active Directory, except for being able to use Active Directory computer GPOs. Although two network adapters are not required when load balancing, the communication between the Network Load Balancing servers (the heartbeat messages) will be more efficient if each participating server has two network cards rather than the one.

NOTE

The exception to being able to use just one network adapter with NLB is if you're loading balancing PPTP traffic. This must use two adapters, each configured for a different subnet.

There are a few limitations of Microsoft's Windows 2000 Network Load Balancing service that won't often apply, but are worth noting from the outset:

- No support for Token Ring networks

- Not supported with layer three network switches (instead use a shared hub or layer two switch)

- All load balancing adapters configured as one unit (cluster) must be on the same subnet, with a maximum number being 32

- Each machine must be running TCP/IP and no other protocol

- Cannot be used on a server that is also configured for Cluster service (the Cluster service offers fault tolerance and load balancing of data with shares disks)

NOTE

Terminology can often get confusing here because Network Load Balancing and Cluster Service are both *clustering technologies* that deliver and ensure high availability with load balancing, fault tolerance, and recovery. Network Load Balancing offers this with a connectivity networking service, and Cluster Service does this with shared disks. Which one you use depends on whether you want high availability for connectivity, or for data.

However, they are often complimentary and can work together, but never on the same machine. For example you may have five or six Windows 2000 Advanced Servers all load balancing incoming Web traffic, and all Web servers use a shared backend database for storing and retrieving data. This database resides on a number of servers running Cluster service. In this way both the connectivity and the data is ensured high availability, but independently from each other.

Designing & Planning...

When the Maximum of 32 NLB Servers Is Too Few

We've already acknowledged throughout this book that Windows 2000 was designed for scalability. So what if you're hosting a big Web farm, and you can see that the maximum of 32 servers per Network Load Balancing cluster will not suffice? Fortunately, this is where DNS round-robin can come to the rescue. Because each Network Load Balanced cluster has a virtual IP address that all of the servers respond to, you can use DNS round-robin for multiple Network Load Balanced clusters on different subnets. This time, because the IP address doesn't resolve to just one machine, this technique is inherently more robust. Because you have the protection of numbers (multiple machines to one address) it's very unlikely that the whole of the Network Load Balanced cluster will become unavailable. This is the technique employed at Microsoft for their Web servers at Redmond.

Network Load Balancing is most often associated with and discussed in the context of Web services, but you can use exactly the same principles with other services for which you want to load balance and provide fault tolerance including Terminal Services, PPTP services, and even file and printing services (for example, providing fault tolerance for standalone Dfs roots discussed in Chapter 4). Remember, if you're load balancing servers that host data content, you must also have some mechanism in place to ensure data consistency across the servers—which is where a shared backend database (perhaps clustered for fault tolerance) can be very useful.

NOTE

L2TP and IPSec connections are not supported in a load-balancing environment. For this reason you can load balance VPN servers only if they are configured for PPTP ports. Special configuration is also required for load balancing PPTP, and where this is applicable will be noted in the following sections.

Network Load Balancing Components

Network Load Balancing uses a Windows 2000 networking driver that acts independently from the TCP/IP stack, and in fact sits between it and the network adapter driver(s). In this way it is able to filter packets before they reach the TCP/IP stack, which therefore offers an efficient service because the TCP/IP stack processes only relevant packets. Because this driver is present on every load-balanced server, there isn't the delay associated with sending all the packets to be examined by an independent load balancing host. And there's also no single point of failure as you would have with an independent load balancer. These external load balancers are often very expensive, and because they have this weakness of presenting a single point of failure, they then need to be supplemented with a standby for fault tolerance.

The load-balancing driver (**WLBS.sys**) works in conjunction with the Network Load Balancing control program (WLBS.exe), which is used to control the driver (start, stop, and query its status, for example). In this way, this networking service is very different from the other three networking services we have looked at in this chapter (and indeed from other services covered throughout this book). Although you might have expected to see or find a Network Load Balancing MMC as you would for any other Windows 2000 service, this is not the case with Network Load Balancing because it is actually implemented as a driver and not a service. Another driver implementation we have already looked at is EFS, which was covered in Chapter 3 when we looked at protecting data on laptops. You may remember that EFS similarly had no MMC to configure it, and it didn't appeared under the Services list, but instead was configured and monitored as an additional file/folder property, and with its own command line utility. Just as the EFS driver is installed automatically on Windows 2000, so the Network Load Balancing driver is installed automatically on both Windows 2000 Advanced Server and Datacenter Server, but by default is not enabled.

Before looking to enable and configure Network Load Balancing, we'll look at its individual components:

- Addresses and Priorities
- Port Rules
- The WLBS Command Line Utility

Addresses and Priorities

As previously noted, Network Load Balancing can work with one or two network cards in the server, but it must use TCP/IP, and the adapters that are configured for load balancing must be on the same segment.

As well as each card having a standard TCP/IP address, you must assign an additional address to identify the Network Load Balancing cluster, which has a virtual IP address (VIP). This is referred to as the **Primary** address within the Network Load Balancing cluster.

When you want client traffic to be load-balanced, it's this address you should specify (for example in your DNS database), and also use with the command utility WLBS.exe for monitoring and managing the cluster. However, each server in the cluster also has its real (or *dedicated*) IP address so you can communicate directly with each server if needed. For example you may decide to run an application on just one of the servers in the cluster (for licensing or disk space requirements), so for clients that need to access just that server within the cluster they use the dedicated IP address. Load balancing will never use the dedicated address, only the primary address.

If you're using two network adapters in your servers, the second adapter will be able to communicate with the other clustered servers or with backend databases or file servers. If possible put all these all their own subnet and their own hub/switch. Note you cannot use crossover cables between the servers for this intra-cluster traffic as you could if using Cluster Service with shared disks.

If you have already got TCP/IP working on your Windows 2000 server, you'll have already bound the dedicated IP address to a network card. But you'll need to add the Primary address (the VIP) as an additional address in the TCP/IP properties.

You specify the additional (VIP) address under **TCP/IP Properties | Advanced**, and then use the **Add** button under the **IP addresses** section. Make sure the dedicated address is bound first to the adapter. Figure 6.21 shows the server with the dedicated address of 10.0.0.78/16 adding the VIP address/mask of 10.0.0.50/16. Remember, all addresses in the same Networking Load Balanced cluster that are being used for load balancing must be on the same subnet.

Figure 6.21 Adding the NLB Primary Address (VIP) to TCP/IP Advanced Properties

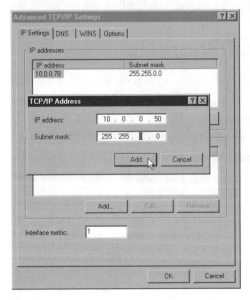

You will also need to enter both the VIP address and the dedicated address as part of the Network Load Balancing properties (which we'll cover later).

Finally, each cluster server must be assigned a **Priority** (**unique host ID**) in the range of 1–32. The host with the lowest number has the highest host priority, and is referred to as the **default host** because this is the server that traffic will go to if it's sent to the primary address but is not to be load balanced. Port rules (covered in the next section) decide whether traffic sent to the primary address is to be load balanced or not.

Using a numbering system to denote the Priority means that if the default host goes offline, a new default host can be elected automatically.

> **NOTE**
>
> When load balancing PPTP, the procedure for spwcifying the TCP/IP address is different. Because PPTP clients must use the same source and destination address, you cannot use a dedicated address on a Windows 2000 server that will be load balancing PPTP traffic. When your server will be load balancing PPTP traffic, remove the dedicated address from the TCP/IP properties and replace it with the VIP. You will also need to leave the dedicated address blank when configuring the Network Load Balancing properties.

Port Rules

Network Load Balancing uses port rules to decide what traffic will be accepted for load balancing, and how it will be load balanced.

The traffic that will be accepted for load balancing is identified by a port range, which can be split into TCP or UDP, or both. You can have one rule that encompasses all the traffic you need, or you can use multiple rules each defining different port ranges. Traffic that doesn't fall into one of the rules will be directed to the default host, as identified in the earlier section.

The default port range is both TCP and UDP, on all ports (0–65535). But, for example you could define that only http Web traffic should be load balanced by selecting Port TCP 80, and to do this you would specify TCP port range 80 to 80. To add https (SSL) traffic to also be load balanced, you would add another rule that included TCP port 443. If you wanted to use Network Load Balancing with Terminal Services you would define TCP ports 3389–3389 and so on.

How this traffic will be load balanced depends on whether you select **multiple hosts** or a **single host** (you can also select **Disabled**, which effectively acts as firewall filter block). Selecting multiple hosts is more usual when you want traffic for your selected ports to be sent to all the servers in the cluster. Single host might at first sound like a contradiction in terms when talking about load balancing, but it allows all traffic to go to the server with the highest handling priority. The handling priority allows for failover so that all traffic will go to a specific server unless it becomes offline. Then the cluster will elect the server with the next highest handling priority and send all traffic in this rule to this server instead, in the same way that the default host is dynamic and depends on current availability. When a server fails in this way, existing connections to that server will be terminated, and after a short delay the cluster will direct traffic to the newly elected server, which will prompt the client to log on again if authentication is required.

The final two elements in configuring port rules is the **Load Weight** and **Affinity** setting, for when you're using multiple hosts. By default these are set to **Equal** and **Single**, respectively.

Load Weight

When the Load Weight is set to Equal (the default), this means that all servers in the cluster will be sent an identical amount of load-balanced traffic. However, you could distribute the load unevenly among them by configuring on each what percentage of the load balancing traffic they should handle.

This is convenient when using servers with different specifications, or if the servers are not all running the same services. For example you may decide to have a low load weight on your default host if it has to cope with a fair bit of traffic that falls outside your port rules.

Designing & Planning…

Planning for Failure

Although the load-balancing feature is nice for distributing traffic, remember it's also there for fault tolerance. You should always look to provide sufficient server capacity within the Network Load Balancing cluster to absorb the additional capacity when one or more servers in the cluster fail. This is particularly relevant when you've configured a server in the cluster to have a low load weight. Remember, in theory this server could end up taking all the traffic if the other servers handling the same traffic fail. Although you may specify a load weighting of 1, if it is the only available server it will take 100 percent of the traffic.

Whether you're using Load weights or not, you may want to think of ways to limit or reduce the load to the remaining server/s and application/s if server failure happens. Otherwise, it won't be a lack of connectivity that brings down your critical services, but rather a server or application failure if it cannot handle the additional traffic.

Note that you don't have to meticulously divide all the servers into a percentage that equals 100, because servers can be dynamically added to or removed from the cluster. The actual percentage of load balancing will be determined at run time when the current cluster state is known, and reallocated dynamically as necessary. This is why this parameter is configured as a weighting and not a true percentage.

Affinity

When the Affinity setting is Single, this means that a client's session will remain with the same server once it has been chosen. So a client targeting a Web server that is part of a Network Load Balancing cluster will have one of the available Web servers allocated to it, depending on the current conditions and the port rules. But once it is connected to one of the Web servers, all subsequent traffic from the client will be directed automatically to the same server. This means that session continuity can be safeguarded—for example, if the Web server is tracking requests and navigation, or if fragmented packets are being transmitted.

NOTE

Single Affinity should always be used for PPTP traffic. You should also use single affinity with Terminal services clients if they are going to use the disconnect feature. For this to work correctly terminal services client must use the same IP address with either a reservation or a static address.

The Single Affinity setting is the safest configuration option, but it's the least efficient as far as load balancing is concerned because only the initial connection is load balanced. Consequently you would need to have many clients connecting with this configuration before you started to see the benefits of load balancing over multiple servers. Additionally, storing and retrieving connection information will require server resources.

If it's not necessary to keep track of which server is serving which client, and your inbound traffic will not be fragmented, you could choose to not use Affinity. For example if all session details that needed to be tracked were stored on a shared backend database or within the browser itself as cookies, and you knew that all incoming packets would not be fragmented, then using no Affinity would offer a much more efficient load balancing service and scale linearly.

A midway between the two Affinity options is the Class C option, and this is used primarily for when inbound packets originate from the same client but over multiple proxy servers. Organizations often group together proxy servers to distribute the processing and network load (Microsoft refers to this configuration as an array). Because each proxy server has its own IP address, packets from the same internal client can actually be sent from multiple external addresses (from different proxy servers). This setting looks to the first three octets of the source address, and if it finds a match with an existing connection will treat it as the same client. This is a good compromise at guessing whether a client's packet originated from the same destination even when it has a different IP address. When there is no match on the first three octets, the traffic is treated with no affinity.

The WLBS Command Line Utility

Although Network Load Balancing is installed as a network driver, it's administered with a command line utility called WLBS.EXE. This name is no doubt a throwback from its previous incarnation in Windows NT4 Enterprise Edition where it was called **Windows Load Balancing Service**. In fact, the two are interchangeable, which explains how you can mix and match both versions within the same Network Load Balancing cluster. You can then upgrade a load balanced NT4 server to Windows 2000 Advanced Server at your leisure (perform a *rolling upgrade* where you take the server out of the cluster, upgrade, and add it back into the cluster), and the upgrade will carry forward any WLBS configurations you had.

Using this program, administrators can remotely query and manage the cluster from any Windows 2000 or NT4 computer. Because it is a command line utility, it can also be used in scripts and with monitoring programs to help automate cluster control (for example, a monitoring program could e-mail an administrator when one of the servers goes offline).

With this utility you can start and stop individual servers within the cluster, or even the whole cluster. You can also enable and disable individual port rules (defined by their range), and block new traffic while permitting existing traffic for graceful removal of the server from the cluster (referred to as *draining*).

When run locally on the Network Load Balanced server, the same program has another couple of supported commands including displaying extensive current and past status information, and reloading the current configuration. Remote control can be password protected, or disabled for increased security.

Configuring Network Load Balancing

Because the Network Load Balancing driver is installed by default on Advanced Server (and Datacenter) you simply need to enable it and then configure the properties of the driver.

To do this, go into your network adapter's **Properties** (the adapter you want to use for Network Load Balancing), enable **Network Load Balancing**, and double-click it (or select and then click **Properties**). See Figure 6.22.

Figure 6.22 Enabling Network Load Balancing

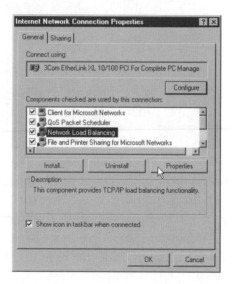

The Network Load Balancing properties consist of three tabs:

- Cluster Parameters
- Host Parameters
- Port Rules

Configuring Cluster Parameters

Here's where you specify the Primary address (otherwise known as the VIP), and the remote control configuration we covered in the earlier section. Strangely, on this first tab you'll also see a separate Help button for loading the WLBS.CHM help file on how to configure Network Load Balancing, which takes you through a checklist, best practices, how to, concepts, and troubleshooting. Figure 6.23 shows an example configuration of Network Load Balancing Cluster Parameters.

Figure 6.23 Configuring Network Load Balancing Cluster Parameters

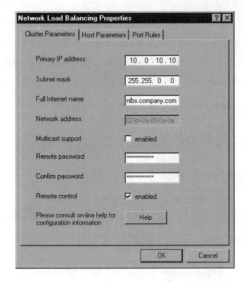

Although we've covered most of these options earlier, we haven't said anything that explains the Multicast support or the Network address. How traffic is delivered to all the servers in the clusters depends on whether they are listening on a shared *unicast MAC address* or a shared *multicast MAC address*.

If you are using only one adapter, then you have no choice; you can only use multicast. If you have two adapters you have a choice of unicast or multicast. Unicast is the default and not shown in Figure 6.23 as a selectable option because it's deselected automatically if you select **Multicast support** as an alternative. Personally, I think a radio button option would have made this clearer—that it's either configured for unicast or multicast.

Unicast hijacks the real MAC address of each adapter that has Network Load Balancing enabled, and replaces it with its own virtual MAC address (known as the cluster adapter). The cluster adapter always starts with **02bf** (as shown in

Figure 6.23) and then takes the rest of its address from the IP address assigned to the Primary host. In my example the 10.0.10.10 translates in hex to 0a000a0a. This now means that the Primary address (the VIP) resolves to this shared MAC address of 02bf0a000a0a, which all the clustered servers listen on.

> **NOTE**
>
> These unicast and multicast options are at the MAC layer—do not confuse this level multicast with IP multicasting at the networking level (which for example, we saw when looking at the multicasting scopes on the DHCP server and for auto-discovery for WINS replication partners).

However, you'll find that by default outbound packets from the cluster have a slightly altered MAC address and instead of **02bf** the **bf** is replaced with the Priority number (unique host ID), which is assigned to each of the servers. So in my example this server (which is the default host with a Priority of 1) will have a source address of 02010a000a0a. Changing the source address for each server is necessary for switch environments that expect unique source MAC addresses on each port.

Using the default of unicast support has two disadvantages. First, each server's real MAC address is not visible and cannot be used. Second, there is a performance hit when traffic is sent to a dedicated IP address because it must be processed by all servers and then discarded by all except the intended server.

A better method is multicast where the original MAC address of each server is retained, but the clustered servers all share a multicast address. This multicast address is **03bf** followed by the Primary server's IP address (in hex). Because each server retains its own unique MAC address, there is no requirement for a second adapter for traffic between the servers or backend servers. And there's none of the performance loss when using dedicated IP addresses. It's also possible to limit switch flooding (sending the same packets to all available ports) when using multicast by creating a VLN. However, you must ensure that a router in front of the cluster accepts the clustered multicast MAC address in response to a unicast ARP (Address Resolution Protocol). This potential problem may be overcome by adding a static ARP entry on the router for the VIP to multicast address. Use the **Cluster Parameters** tab to confirm the multicast address that will be used after enabling multicast support.

Where possible, use multicast instead of unicast, but make sure it is supported in your network infrastructure. All servers in the cluster must be configured similarly that is, either all unicast or all multicast. You cannot have a mixture within the same cluster.

NOTE

Cisco routers are a good example of when a static ARP entry is required when using a multicast (rather than unicast) MAC address with Network Load Balancing.

Configuring Host Parameters

Here is where you specify each server's Priority, its dedicated address/mask and whether you want the server to join the cluster immediately, or at a later time (for example, for minimal disruption to existing connections, you can configure it immediately but bring it online later with the WLBS utility). Figure 6.24 shows an example configuration of Network Load Balancing Host Parameters.

Figure 6.24 Configuring Network Load Balancing Host Parameters

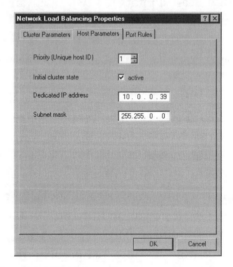

Configuring Port Rules

This is the most complicated dialog box to configure simply because it groups together a lot of configuration choices about how (and if) incoming traffic should be load balanced. Some options are mutually exclusive—for example, you can't configure the Handling priority unless you're load balancing on a single host (it doesn't apply to multiple hosts or if load balancing is disabled). We have discussed all the options in this dialog box under the Port Rules section earlier.

Figure 6.25 shows the default settings you'll see when you first display this tab where the default setting is a single port rule, which consists of all ports (range 0–65535), both TCP and UDP ports, and single affinity on multiple hosts with equal load weighting.

Figure 6.25 Default Configuration for Network Load Balancing Properties

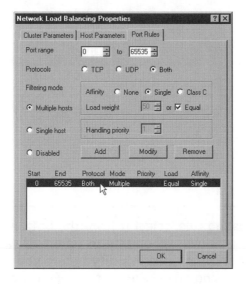

If you want to change these default settings, first select the rule in the bottom pane (highlighted in Figure 6.25, although it's not by default when this dialog box is first displayed), and then either select **Remove** or change the values and then select **Modify**. Although it looks as if you can select **Add**, you can't with this default rule, because it includes all possible port ranges. You must first either modify the default rule for fewer ports or delete it altogether and start from new.

As an example, Figure 6.26 shows three rules for a load balancing cluster server that hosts both Web services and Terminal Services. The first blocks any FTP requests (note that if a FTP rule were enabled it should include port 22, which is a good example of specifying a different start and end port range). The second load balances http traffic between all servers without using affinity but with a load weight of 20. The third is for Terminal Services (RDP only), which will direct all traffic to this server as long as it is online. With this configuration any other incoming traffic to be load balanced will go the default host.

Figure 6.26 Example Configuration of Network Load Balancing Port Rules

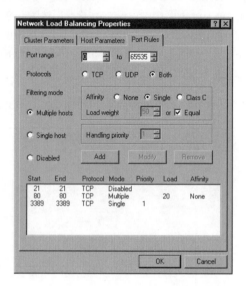

NOTE

To modify an existing rule, select it from the bottom pane and the con-figuration settings above will update to reflect its values. Change the values you want and then click **Modify** before you click **OK** (there's no warning before loosing any changes if you simply change values and click **OK** without clicking **Modify** first).

All servers in the same cluster must have matching port rules, or the server will not be initialized into the cluster and will log an error in the System Event Log. For example, all servers in this cluster must have exactly the same disabled port rule. The rule for terminal services must be the same except all servers must have a unique handling priority number to ensure failover. The rule for http traffic must be set to multiple hosts with no affinity, and each server can have the same or a different load weight.

Monitoring and Administering Network Load Balancing

You can use and load WLBS.exe locally or remotely. When used locally there is no need to specify the cluster address or assigned password. When used remotely (and remote control is enabled) you must specify the cluster Primary address (VIP) and the password. Note that a failure to supply the password will result in a bad *password error* rather than a prompt supply to it.

The full list of commands and syntax for this utility can be found by typing **wlbs /?** at the command line of any Windows 2000 Advanced Server (or Datacenter). If you want to run this utility from another Windows 2000 or NT4 computer, simply copy over the wlbs.exe file from the **%systemroot%\System32** folder.

At its simplest level you would use **wlbs <command>** locally on a clustered server. Remotely you would use **wlbs <command> <VIP> /passw <password>**. Examples of commands you can run both locally and remotely include **query**, **stop**, **start**, **drainstop**. So you might use the following to query the cluster with the VIP 10.0.10.10 with the remote control password of **abacus**:

```
Wlbs query 10.0.10.10 /PASSW abacus
```

You are more likely to drainstop a single server rather than the whole cluster, so for this you would need to specify the dedicated host name or address within the cluster; for example:

```
Wlbs drainstop 10.0.10.10:10.0.0.39 /PASSW abacus
```

You can similarly stop and start port rules and prevent any new traffic from using that port rule using the commands **disable**, **enable**, and **drain**, and then specifying the port range to identify the rule. For example, to prevent any new http traffic being load balanced on our server you would type:

```
Wlbs drain 80 10.0.10.10:10.0.0.39 /PASSW abacus
```

Two ways to record and identify historical cluster status is through the wlbs **display** command (which can only be run locally). This outputs a great deal of information including all the Network Load Balancing configuration stored in the registry (more than is configurable through the GUI), the last 10 System event messages, TCP/IP configuration, and the current status of the cluster. This information includes the time and date at the top. There's a lot of information here so I suggest you redirect it to a file so you can easily review and search through it—the time stamping makes it ideal as a historical record.

The second way to keep an eye on Network Load Balancing is with the System event log. Events sourced from WLBS will record events such as when servers went online or offline, convergence information (when all servers in the cluster know about each other and agree on each other's status), any remote control requests with the source IP address recorded (including rejected attempts from bad passwords), and any drainstop or equivalent commands.

Walkthrough: Configuring DNS Primary and Secondary Zones

This will take you through configuring a Windows 2000 Standard Primary DNS Server (root server) and a Standard Secondary DNS Server. These zones will have the following configurations:

- WINS lookups
- Dynamic Updates
- Secure Transfer with Notify

1. On your first Windows 2000 Server, install the DNS Networking Service if it is not already installed from **Control Panel | Add/Remove Programs | Add/Remove Windows Components | Networking Services**, and then select the **Details** button and make sure **Domain Name System (DNS)** is selected.

2. Load the DNS Manager from **Start | Programs | Administrative Tools | DNS**. This should load up with your server displayed in the left pane, and **Configure the DNS Server** message and explanation on the right.

3. Right-click your server in the left pane, and select **Configure the server**, which brings up the Configure DNS Server Wizard. Click **Next** and wait while it gathers setup information.

4. On the Root Server page, it will ask whether your server is the first DNS server on the network. Select the top option, **This is the first DNS server on this network** and click **Next**.

5. It will then ask whether you want to create a Forward Lookup Zone. Make sure the top option, **Yes, create a forward lookup zone** is selected and click **Next**.

6. On the Zone Type page, ensure the middle option, **Standard Primary** is selected and click **Next**.

7. On the Zone Name page, it will ask for a name of your zone. Type **company.com** or your choice of name and click **Next**.

8. The Zone File will ask for the name of the file that will hold the zone records. Accept the default suggested under **Create a new file with this file name** (e.g., company.com.dns) and click **Next**.

9. The Reverse Lookup Zone page will ask whether you want to create a reverse lookup zone. Accept the default **Yes, create a reverse lookup zone** and click **Next**.

10. On the Zone Type for your reverse lookup, select the middle option again—**Standard primary**—and click **Next**.

11. Type your network address—for example, if you are running in a 10.0.0.0/8 network, type **10** and click **Next**.

12. On the Zone File page for the reverse lookup zone, accept the default file name under **Create a new file with this file name** (e.g., 10-in-addr.arpa.dns) and click **Next**.

13. The last page of this wizard should present your choices so you can review them before clicking on **Finish**. They should look similar to Figure 6.27. If you agree with your settings, click **Finish**.

Figure 6.27 Final Page of the DNS Server Wizard to Review Choices

You should now have a Forward Lookup Zone and a Reverse Lookup Zone under your server, which when expanded should look similar to Figure 6.28.

Figure 6.28 Newly Created DNS Forward and Reverse Lookup Zones

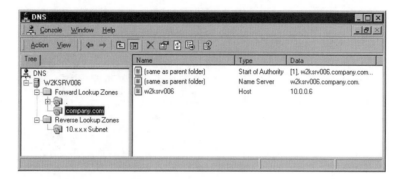

14. We could now add some static records into this zone, but instead we'll configure the zone properties. Right-click on the bottom forward lookup zone—in this example, **company.com**—and select **Properties**.

15. Change the **Allow dynamic Updates?** from **No** to **Yes**.

16. Under the **WINS** tab, click the **Use WINS forward lookup** and type in the address of your primary WINS server in the IP address field, and then click **Add**. Do the same for your secondary WINS server (if you have one). Because our secondary DNS server will also be a Windows 2000 DNS server that will recognize this type of record, we can leave unset **Do not replicate this record**.

17. On the Zone Transfer we'll specify that this server should transfer only to our known secondary DNS server. Type the address of your second DNS server and click on the **Add** button (see Figure 6.29).

18. We'll also specify the Notify option so that the secondary DNS will be notified of new records so it can ask for a transfer of this new information. Click on the **Notify** button and specify the IP address of your secondary DNS server and click **Add** so that it looks like Figure 6.30.

19. Click on **OK**, and **OK** again.

20. We'll go through the same configuration with our Reverse Lookup Zone. Right-click on it and select **Properties**. Set the dynamic updates under the **General** tab to be **Yes**.

21. Under the **WINS-R** tab, set the **Use WINS-R lookup** checkbox and type in your domain name (e.g., company.com) in the **Domain to append to returned name**.

Figure 6.29 Setting the Secure Zone Transfer Details

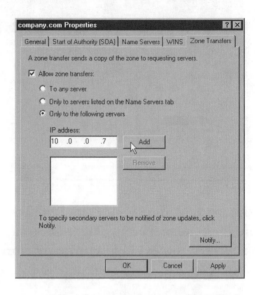

Figure 6.30 Setting the DNS Notify Settings

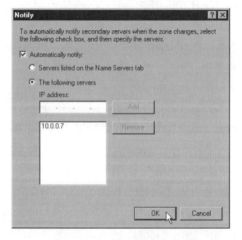

22. Under Zone Transfers, again type in the IP address of your second DNS server, and do the same for the Notify option. Click on **OK**, and **OK**.

23. We're now ready to configure our secondary DNS server. Install DNS on your second server if it isn't already installed.

24. We'll go through the Configure DNS Server Wizard again, configuring the same forward and reverse secondary zone. Click on **Next**, and **Next**

until you are asked what type of zone you want to create. This time, select the bottom choice of **Standard Secondary** and click **Next**.

25. On the **Name of the zone**, it must be named exactly the same as it was previously (e.g., company.com); click **Next**.

26. On the Master DNS Server page you'll be asked to specify the IP address of your first server. Type this in and click **Add** and then **Next**.

27. When asked whether you want to create a reverse lookup zone, select the top option to do so and click **Next**.

28. Select **Standard secondary** for your reverse lookup zone type and click **Next**.

29. Type in the same network address as you did on the first server (e.g., **10**) and click **Next**.

30. On the Master DNS Servers page, type the IP address of your first server, click **Add**, and then click **Next**.

31. You should now be looking at the Completing the Configure DNS Server Wizard with your choices. Click **Finish** if you don't want to go back and edit them.

32. Under the your second DNS server, you should now see the **company.com** Forward Lookup Zone, and the Reverse Lookup Zone for your subnet. Under each you should see the same host records as you saw previously on the first DNS server.

33. Now we'll prove that entries on the primary DNS server are updating automatically on the secondary by adding a new host record onto the primary DNS. To do this, go back to your Primary DNS server and right-click on the **company.com** Forward Lookup Zone.

34. Select **New Host**, and in the **New Host** dialog box, type **www** as if we were adding your company intranet Web server, and specify the IP address of **10.0.0.100**. Click the box **Create associated pointer (PTR) record** and click **Add Host**.

35. You should see a dialog message saying, **"The host record www .company.com was successfully created."** Click **OK** and then click **Done**. You should now be able to see the newly added host record, **www**, on your Primary DNS server.

36. Check that the reverse zone was correctly updated by navigating down the Reverse Lookup Zones until you see the name **10.0.0.100** with the Type **Pointer** and the Data showing www.company.com.

37. Check back on your secondary DNS server, on the same company.com and the same reverse lookup zone. You should now see the Web server record if you press **F5** to refresh.

38. If the entry hasn't automatically appeared, right-click on the **company.com** zone and select **Transfer from master**. If the data still doesn't transfer, check the DNS Event Log for any errors.

Note that you could add both servers to the same DNS MMC as shown in Figure 6.31 where the DNS MMC is running on the Primary DNS Server (W2KSRV006—the root server as shown by the *dot* zone above company.com), but I've also added my Secondary DNS Server (W2KSRV007). From this one MMC I quickly can check that both servers have the same information, and if not, I can issue a **Transfer from master** from the secondary zones. Add additional servers by right-clicking on the DNS root, and **Connect to computer** (then specifying the DNS server's name or IP address).

Figure 6.31 Multiple DNS Servers Displaying on the Same DNS MMC

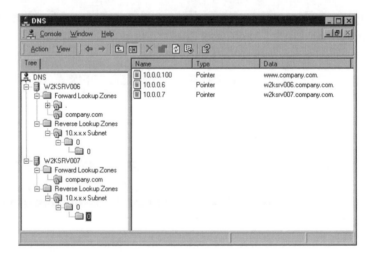

NOTE

Refer to the Appendix if you need more information about how to add servers to your DNS MMC, and about how to create customized MMCS.

Summary

This chapter looked at the essential networking services that provide name resolution and addresses to TCP/IP computers, and how Windows 2000 has improved these services. Without the smooth running of these services, many of today's companies would not be able to function. Working together, these networking services ensure communication between computers and provide a central point of administration that can automate and ease the administrative burden of configuring and maintaining hundreds of computers.

We first looked at DNS and questioned the requirement to run it on your network, and what Windows 2000 offered over other implementations. Some of these features included dynamic updates, support for newer record types and Unicode, incremental and secure zone transfers. You can fully integrate Windows 2000 DNS with other implementations of DNS, but take care when transferring records and data from your Windows 2000 DNS to a Secondary DNS server that might not support them.

Two new features that Windows 2000 DNS cannot use outside Active Directory include Active Directory integrated zones (which provide greater fault tolerance and improved efficiency of zone transfers), and secure dynamic updates (where only the original client can modify or remove a host record). Should you migrate to Active Directory later you can change your DNS configuration to support these features, but make sure you install the DNS service on servers that will be Windows 2000 domain controllers.

Windows 2000 DHCP working with Dynamic DNS together offers a centralized and automatic administration of addresses and names, even if your DHCP clients are down-level. This is because all Windows 2000 computers can dynamically register, modify, and unregister their host names with a DNS server that supports dynamic updates (like Windows 2000 DNS). This means that a Windows 2000 DHCP server can be configured to dynamically register host names in the DNS database for clients that cannot do this themselves.

Other advantages of using DHCP servers include having a centralized place to configure and monitor addresses and associated information such as router addresses, domain names, WINS servers, and so on. Consider putting all your allocated addresses into the DHCP databases even if they are marked as excluded or reserved. Reserved addresses act as functionally static addresses to ensure clients will receive the same address. You can also use reservations to configure individual configurations, but remember that the client must be on the same segment as the DHCP server.

We looked at the various TCP configurations you could set at the server, scope, class, and reservation level. Vendor and class options are new in Windows 2000 DHCP and provide greater flexibility in setting different options for a group of computers within your scope. We also looked at dynamic BOOTP and Multicast (both of which are new to Windows 2000 DHCP) and the uses and benefits of using Superscopes.

WINS was then covered—why it was such a crucial service for Microsoft computers and remains so even for computers that are running Windows 2000. This section covered the WINS database integrity and replication and how to configure these, and how burst mode and persistent connections can help with the efficiency of this service.

Finally we looked at network load balancing, which is installed automatically on Windows 2000 Advanced Server (and Datacenter Server) to provide clustering technologies for critical services. Highly configurable and versatile, it functions completely independently from Active Directory and requires no special hardware. Although it is most often discussed and associated with Web services, it is also suitable for providing the same load balancing and fault tolerance for other services covered in this book such as Terminal Services, file and print (including Dfs standalone hosts), PPTP, and ISA Server. In this way, network load balancing often overcomes fault tolerance and scaling restrictions and limitations that would otherwise require Active Directory.

Solutions Fast Track

Name Resolution with DNS

☑ DNS provides a distributed and hierarchical host name resolution to IP addresses. It is used increasingly in corporate networks and is an essential component of Internet communication.

☑ Just because Windows 2000 is more TCP/IP aware doesn't mean you have to run a DNS service on your network in order for Microsoft computers to communicate with one another. Valid reasons for running a DNS service include having UNIX computers, running Internet services, running or preparing for Active Directory, and integrating UNIX and Microsoft communications.

☑ Microsoft's DNS service that ships with Windows 2000 has many advantages and features that may not be found in other implementations. These include support for newer record formats (including Service records, which are essential for Active Directory), support for the underscore character and Unicode, easy-to-use GUI administration, incremental zone transfers, dynamic updates, and integration with WINS.

☑ All Windows 2000 clients can register their own host record with Windows 2000 DNS, and down-level clients can register by proxy if using a Windows 2000 DHCP server configured to allow this.

☑ Outside Active Directory, you can configure only Standard Primary and Standard Secondary zones, not Active Directory Integrated zones that support secure dynamic updates. This means that outside Active Directory only the Primary zone can support dynamic updates because the Secondary is a read-only copy to provide a quicker response (if the Primary is over a WAN link), fault tolerance, and load balancing. However, for greater security you can define which Secondary DNS servers can transfer zone information. And for greater efficiently in name resolution you can use Notify so that Secondary DNS servers are aware of new records that need to be transferred.

☑ Windows 2000 DNS can integrate fully with other versions of DNS, but be careful of transferring information they may not be able to understand (such as records for WINS, SRV, IPv6, ATMA, and Unicode). If transferring zone files between Windows and UNIX DNS servers, don't forget to modify the naming formats as appropriate.

DHCP for Central Configuration and Control of Addresses

☑ DHCP can greatly ease administrative overheads of configuring and troubleshooting IP addresses and associated information.

☑ Now that Windows 2000 DNS can support dynamic updates, DHCP clients can fully participate in DNS even if they are not Windows 2000 computers.

☑ DHCP offers central configuration and monitoring. Consider specifying all your TCP/IP client addressing information on DHCP; only the DHCP server itself requires a static address. Other computers that must have a stable address can be accommodated with reservations. Exceptions however are for clients that are not DHCP-enabled, and you cannot use reservations for clients that are not on the same subnet as the DHCP server.

☑ Windows 2000 DHCP also supports superscopes, dynamic BOOTP, MADCAP, Vendor, and User Class options for greater configuration and flexibility.

☑ You can set address configurations to a highly granular level—from server, to scopes, to class options, to individual reservations.

☑ Windows 2000 DHCP clients support APIPA, which means they will self-configure if they cannot find a DHCP server when set to do so, and periodically try to find a DHCP server. This accommodates single segment networks so that a DHCP server is not required for address allocation, and also accommodates a temporarily downed router if the DHCP server is remote. You may want to prevent this automatic behavior in certain circumstances (such as RAS servers).

☑ Superscopes provide addresses for multinets and multiple remote subnets, and offers benefits of fault tolerance, server consolidation, and server cooperation. They can also ease address reallocation.

Name Resolution with WINS

☑ NetBIOS name resolution remains a crucial part of networking communication for Microsoft computers and remains the default method of communication outside Active Directory.

☑ WINS is used not only to resolve names to IP address, but also for finding domain controllers in an NT4 domain and registering crucial networking services. The NetBIOS interface has offered a common programming interface for Microsoft applications for years so that software could be written without regard to the underlying protocol being used. Nowadays new applications also have a Winsock interface for IP and IPX clients, but many NetBIOS-only applications remain in circulation. Although you can disable NetBIOS over TCP/IP in Windows 2000, be careful that it is not needed!

☑ NetBIOS name resolution originally was not designed to be used over today's networks with remote subnets and limited bandwidth. WINS accommodates these conditions but you must carefully plan for integration between multiple WINS servers to ensure timely and accurate information with a suitable replication policy.

☑ WINS offers high performance with Burst Mode Handling to accommodate peak periods, and persistent connections between replication partners.

High Availability with Network Load Balancing

☑ This clustering technology ensures fault tolerance and load balancing at the network layer, which is more sophisticated than DNS round-robin, that has no automatic recovery or detection mechanism for downed servers. Although most often associated with Web services, Network Load Balancing can also be used with other services such as Terminal Services, file and print, and PPTP (although PPTP often requires special configuration).

☑ Network Load Balancing cannot be run on the same server as Microsoft's other clustering technology, Cluster service, which load balances and offers fault tolerance for critical data. However, the two services often complement each other. One other difference is that Network Load Balancing, unlike Cluster service, requires no special hardware (the only condition being it cannot be used with Token Ring adapters).

☑ Network Load Balancing is implemented as a network driver, rather than a service. It is automatically installed (but not enabled by default) on Windows 2000 Advanced Server and Datacenter Server (it cannot be used on Windows 2000 Server or Professional). It is configured at the driver level, and controlled and monitored with the WLBS.exe command line utility.

☑ Each Network Load Balancing server in the cluster is configured with addresses, priorities, and port rules. Port rules decide whether and how inbound traffic should be load balanced and includes options such as multiple/single host, load weight, and client affinity.

☑ The WLBS.exe utility can be loaded locally or remotely (if remote control is permitted), or called from monitoring programs or scripts. With it you can view and administer the current cluster status, servers within it, and even specific port rules. For example, you could prevent new traffic from going to one server while retaining existing connections for a graceful shutdown prior to removing it from the cluster (for example for maintenance).

☑ Both the System log and the WLBS local **display** command are good ways to keep historical information on NLB—for example, its current configuration and the status of the cluster, what commands were issued and from where, and so on.

Frequently Asked Questions

The following Frequently Asked Questions, answered by the author of this book, are designed to both measure your understanding of the concepts presented in this chapter and to assist you with real-life implementation of these concepts. To have your questions about this chapter answered by the author, browse to **www.syngress.com/solutions** and click on the **"Ask the Author"** form.

Q: We want to replace our UNIX DNS servers with Windows 2000 DNS to make the most of the new features it offers. We've imported the UNIX databases and it's all up and running fine. However, I'm concerned that we've inherited a lot of stale records that nobody is prepared to verify and I'm too anxious to simply delete them and hope for the best. I've noticed there's a scavenging option in the Windows 2000 DNS. If I enable this, will this be able to do the job for me and eventually help me to clear out unused records?

A: You can enable aging and scavenging on Windows 2000 DNS (it's not enabled by default), which is a good strategy when using dynamic host records that may leave behind out-of-date records. However, scavenging static host records is a little different. First, they must have the **Delete this record when it**

becomes stale option enabled on their properties after toggling on the **View | Advanced** option. Any static records with this setting will then be eligible for scavenging if they were created after scavenging was enabled on the DNS server. And this is the problem with your setup because scavenging is not enabled by default and only newly created host records will be scavenged once scavenging is enabled. You could start again from scratch, but enabling scavenging before importing the zone information. Perhaps more realistically you should bypass the friendly DNS Manager MMC and use the command line utility, **dnscmd.exe**. This is supplied in the Support Tools and is a very powerful command to do everything you can with the MMC and much more. See the online documentation for more information on how to use Dnscmd.exe. However, before enabling scavenging you may also want to read up on the aging and scavenging parameters you can define and the algorithms used to ensure you don't remove valid and needed records. There's a good section on this in the Windows 2000 Server Technical Notes "Windows 2000 DNS" whitepaper, currently available on the Microsoft site at www.microsoft.com/WINDOWS2000/howitworks/communications/ nameadrmgmt/w2kdns.asp.

Q: We are currently running NT4 DHCP servers. Rather than upgrade these to Windows 2000, can we simply move the existing DHCP database onto a cleanly installed Windows 2000 DHCP?

A: I would always recommend installing a clean version of Windows 2000 if possible, especially for a server that will be offering such an essential service as DHCP. However, I can appreciate the attractions of using an existing database that has defined all the server and scope options you need, plus any reservation details. There are two ways of doing this—the hard way or the easy way. Either way, back up your systems before trying this to ensure you can revert to a known state. Then reconcile all scopes on your NT4 DHCP server and stop the service.

The hard way to do this is to copy the DHCP database file from your existing NT4 server, **%systemroot%\system32\dhcp\dhcp.mdb**, and its DHCP settings under the registry (which are found under: **HKEY_LOCAL_MACHINE\SYSTEM\CurrentControlSet\Services\ DHCPServer\Configuration**. Then on your Windows 2000 Server, install the DHCP service, but make sure you don't load the DHCP Manager MMC. Stop the DHCP service on your Windows 2000 server and then delete everything in its **%systemroot%\system32\dhcp** folder (including any subdirectories). Copy your NT4's dhcp.mbd into the Windows 2000 server's **%systemroot%\system32\dhcp** folder, and then restore the registry key you saved from the NT4 server (same location). Start the DHCP service on the Windows 2000 server, load the DHCP Manager, and reconcile the scopes.

The easier way to move DHCP databases is with the little known utility called the **DHCP Import Export** tool (**DHCPExIm.exe**) from the Windows 2000 Resource Kit, Supplement 1. Not only is this easier because it does most of the hard work for you (no editing the registry), it also allows you to export/import specific scopes rather than the whole database. On the source server (your NT4 DHCP server), simply load the utility and choose which scopes you want to export, and save to a file. On the destination server (your Windows 2000 DHCP server) you then load the utility, open the previously saved file, and choose which scopes to import.

Q: We're looking to move to Active Directory later next year. In the meantime I want to get up and running a couple of Windows 2000 DHCP servers. Will this be a problem with "Rogue DHCP Detection" when we move to Active Directory?

A: Make sure you install your first DHCP Server on a member server within your NT4 domain, and not within a workgroup. Then you will have no problems.

Q: What are the DNS Users, DHCP Users, and WINS Users local groups created on our Windows 2000 Server after installing these services?

A: These automatically created local groups allow members to load and view these programs' MMC so they can view and check settings, but not to make any changes.

Q: We have a few BAD_ADDRESSES showing in our DHCP database. What do these mean?

A: Essentially they are indications that a duplicate address was tried and either the client or the server detected that an address it was configured to lease was already in use. The majority of Microsoft DHCP clients now check that the address they have been configured to use isn't already in use on the network. If the client detects that it is in use, it sends back a DHCPDecline message to the DHCP server so it can ask for another. The DHCP server marks any address that has responded with a DHCPDecline as a BAD_ADDRESS so it will not be offered to another client for the duration of its lease. If you cannot successfully track down the client that holds this address, your best bet (but not ideal) may to be exclude it so that it's not offered again when the lease expires. If you have legacy DHCP clients that cannot check for duplicate addresses themselves, you can enable the **Conflict Detection Attempts** setting under the server's **Advanced** properties so that the DHCP server itself checks for a duplicate address (the address is in use) before offering it to the client.

Q: What's the **Migrate On** option under the Windows 2000 WINS server Replication Partners? Is it anything to do with migrating to Active Directory and moving from NetBIOS names to IP host names?

A: No, it's nothing at all to do with migrating to Active Directory but everything to do with migrating to a WINS-enabled client. A non-WINS client normally would have a static mapping defined in WINS so other computers could find its IP address from its NetBIOS name. If that client were then migrated to be a WINS-enabled client, it would be able to register its own dynamic record. However, for security reasons, static mappings normally are not overwritten by dynamic name registration unless the Migrate On option is set.

Q: How can we work out the maximum convergence time for our WINS servers and what design is recommended?

A: Working out the convergence time is critical when planning for WINS servers deployment. You're effectively asking how long it would take for a change on one WINS server to be available on another WINS server. The answer is the sum of the replication periods from one server to the next over the path containing the longest replication period. It may help you to work this out and juggle figures by drawing out a logical diagram of your WINS servers. Draw a link between each connecting server, and specify by each link the replication interval being used. When you do this you will see why the simple hub and spoke topology is often the preferred method with all WINS servers configured as push/pull partners to a central server; this provides the shortest links from one server to another.

Q: Where can I tune Network Load Balancing performance—for example, how often heartbeat messages are sent, and when a server is deemed to be offline?

A: You'll find these under HKEY_LOCAL_MACHINE\SYSTEM\
CurrentControlSet\Services\WLBS\Parameters.

Q: Is there any way of monitoring the intra-cluster traffic—for example, the heartbeat traffic between Network Load Balancing servers?

A: There's no utility included specifically for this purpose, but you can use Network Monitor to capture the traffic and then decode it with the Windows 2000 Resource Kit load balancing parsers. These consist of two files, **wlbs_hb.dll** and **wlbs_rc.dll**, which must be copied to the **\Netmon\ Parsers** directory. You will then need to modify the existing files **mac.ini**, **tcpip.ini**, and **parser.ini** from the same directory so they include the new network traffice type.

Q: Is it a security risk to leave a failed network load balanced server in the cluster?

A: It may be, for example if you were using port rules to block traffic and the server is still accessible. You may find the Server Resource Kit tool, ClusterSentinel, useful; it works alongside monitoring service availability and the wlbs.exe utility. When it detects a server is unavailable it can remove the server from the cluster automatically, and similarly add it back into the cluster when it detects it's running normally again.

Q: When we initially tested our network load balancing cluster with three servers running IIS and talking to backend databases, we could tell that all three servers were load balancing requests. However, when we ran a load simulation program to see how this performance scaled up, only one of the network load balanced servers seemed to be working. Why is that?

A: Most load simulators are designed to test server performance rather than testing load balancing between servers. Chances are you ran the simulation from one computer, and had the cluster configured for either single affinity (the default) or Class C. With these settings all traffic with the same source address would be kept on one server in an attempt to conserve session state. To test load balancing with a simulation program you would either need to configure it to use different source addresses, or to change the cluster to use no affinity. If you're using backend servers, it's likely you would be able to store session state on these servers if you needed to retain this information, in which case you could use no affinity and benefit the most from Windows 2000 Network Load Balancing efficiency and performance.

Chapter 7

Internet Services

Solutions in this chapter:

- Installing IIS5

- Improvements in Reliability

- Improvements in Administration and Management

- Improvements in Security

- Improvements in Performance

- Document Collaboration with WebDAV

- Certificate Services

☑ Walkthrough: Configuring Multiple Web Sites on a Single Web Server

☑ Summary

☑ Solutions Fast Track

☑ Frequently Asked Questions

Introduction

Many of you reading this no doubt already run or have run IIS4 on Windows NT 4.0 and are wondering whether it's worthwhile running or upgrading to IIS5. What benefits and advantages does this later version of Microsoft's Internet Information System have, and how relevant are they to you if you're not running a Windows 2000 Active Directory environment?

Many people run their Web servers in a one-way trusted Windows NT 4.0 domain or even as a standalone server because they like the additional security benefits this approach automatically provides. Despite all the firewall procedures, proxying, Network Address Translation, intrusion detection, and hot fixes you can apply, it's comforting to know that should your Web server's security be breached there's still a boundary between this server and your users' accounts.

By contrast, a Web server that is part of Active Directory confers automatic transitive trusts with all other domains in the forest. These trusts cannot be revoked, and to control security access you have to rely on NTFS permissions, rights, and the integrity of your user accounts. Although not impossible to secure, it certainly radically changes the rules of security boundaries, which is not good news to IT managers and IT implementers alike.

For many organizations, running a Windows 2000 Server with IIS5 outside your standard network offers significant benefits in terms of reliability, performance, management, and security. A wide range of Internet servers stand to benefit from these improvements from modest Web servers with a few pages of static content to multiple high-processing servers delivering dynamic content with back-end database retrieval/storage.

With Windows 2000 Advanced Server you can also take advantage of scalability and fault-tolerant solutions with network load balancing and clustering services. And yet the same feature set can also be used to good effect within an intranet environment—particularly now that IIS5 has support for WebDAV, which allows users to access and modify documents stored on a Web server just as seamlessly as if the Web server were another internal file and print server. In addition to all these, of course, you'll also inherit the other benefits that come with Windows 2000, which are covered in other chapters.

This chapter will cover the improvements and new features to be found in IIS5 and its complementing service: Microsoft's Certificate Services. Much of the Windows 2000 documentation on the new Certificate Services concentrates on running an Enterprise Certificate Authority for granting certificates. Enterprise

CAs, though, are supported only in an Active Directory environment, so this section will concentrate on Standalone CAs only.

It is certainly true that running Certificate Services integrated within an Active Directory network makes it much easier to administer and deploy certificates. But you can still take advantages of Certificate Services outside Active Directory, and you may consider this to be a more secure solution anyway. The trick is knowing what you can do—and how to do it—when you are not running Active Directory.

This chapter cannot begin to do justice to the wide and complex subject of public/private key infrastructures or even hope to cover all the options and features that Certificate Services offers. But it will cover the basics of how to use Windows 2000 Certificate Services outside Active Directory so that you can use it with your Web server to offer a secure communication between client and server.

Installing IIS5

Internet Information Service is much easier to install with Windows 2000 because it's built into the base operating system. A clean installation of Windows 2000 Server and Advanced Server will automatically install IIS, although it's not automatically installed on Windows 2000 Professional. If you are upgrading to Windows 2000 and previously had IIS or Personal Web Server (PWS) installed, it will be automatically installed with the upgrade.

Many components make up IIS5, as you will see if you click the Details button when selecting to add it as an additional Windows component. For security reasons, the server version won't automatically install the FTP service or the NNTP service. Unlike earlier versions, however, it will automatically include FrontPage 2000 Server Extensions.

For developers, Windows 2000 Professional offers a cut-down version of IIS. This includes Personal Web Manager (PWM), which offers a simplified interface to the Web service, and the Internet Service Manager snap-in, which gives access to all IIS services. All components are selected by default.

When using the Internet Services Manager on Windows 2000 Professional, it's very easy to think it's exactly the same as that Internet Services Manager you get with the server version. In addition to Professional's allowing only a maximum of 10 simultaneous connections, there are also a few other subtle differences. These are as follows:

- It cannot create virtual Web or FTP servers.

- It cannot restrict access by IP address or domain name.

- It has no Operators.

- It doesn't offer HTML administration.

- It cannot log on to an ODBC database.

- It cannot use some of the new performance features (for example, compression and throttling).

NOTE

You cannot install IIS5 on any other operating system than Windows 2000, and conversely you cannot install a previous version of IIS on Windows 2000.

Designing & Planning…

Upgrading Considerations

One of your important choices will probably be whether to upgrade a working Windows NT 4.0 server with IIS4 or to upgrade it to Windows 2000, or migrate your IIS4 data to a clean installation of Windows 2000 with IIS5. While the general advice is to always do a clean install when you can (which also gives you an automatic standby if you keep your existing Windows NT 4.0/IIS4 available), you can take heart that Microsoft extensively tested this upgrade environment and declared it safe and reliable.

One important difference worth mentioning when mulling over the upgrade/install choice has to do with root directories. IIS5's installation (unlike previous versions) will not prompt you for your Web server's root directories (for example, \Inetpub\wwwroot and \Inetpub\ftproot). An interactive installation of IIS5 will *always* install these directories with their default names and on the same drive as your system directory (eg C:\WINNT). Many administrators like to put the Web server's root directories onto different partitions and use non-default names. This offers better security and means that you can use mirroring on just the system partition and/or place the Web content on striped drives.

Continued

If you are upgrading and have used nondefault names/locations for these root directories, obviously these will be carried over into Windows 2000 and IIS5. You can use alternative names/locations for these root directories when installing IIS5—if you use an unattended installation script. This doesn't mean you have to reinstall Windows 2000 from scratch, however because you can use Sysocmgr.exe to add/remove components after Windows 2000 has been installed. For more information on this, refer to the following Microsoft Knowledge Base articles:

- "How to Change the Default Installation Paths for FTP and the Web" [Q259671] (http://support.microsoft.com/support/kb/articles/q259/6/71.asp)

- "How to Add or Remove Windows 2000 Components with Sysocmgr.exe" [Q222444]: (http://support.microsoft.com/support/kb/articles/Q222/4/44.ASP)

Improvements in Reliability

There are many reasons why IIS5 could be said to be more reliable than its predecessor. Many are simply inherited from the more stable operating system that Windows 2000 provides. Others are a consequence of other new features. For example, a site that is more securely configured is also going to be more reliable. Similarly, being able to fine-tune and control performance such as bandwidth throttling will also have a positive effect on the server's overall reliability. Four features worth mentioning in their own right are these:

- Application protection
- IISreset command
- Easy backup and restore of IIS configuration
- FTP Restart

Application Protection

Web servers are very vulnerable to reliability issues simply from the applications they are asked to run. Should a Web application crash, you don't want it to crash all the other Web applications and/or the Web server itself as well.

IIS4 had two different modes for running applications: **In-Process** and **Out-of-Process**. The first allows all Web applications to run in the same memory space that the Web server is using which is certainly less secure but offers a faster processing and response return. Out-of-Process means each Web applications will run in its own, isolated memory space so that if one crashes, the other applications and the Web service itself are not affected. As you might have guessed, the greater security came at the cost of processing and response time, so choosing between the two was often difficult.

IIS5 offers a compromise between these two settings, called **Pooled Process**. This allows the Web services and other critical applications to run in their own memory space, with all Web applications pooled together using another, shared memory space. This means that if one of the Web applications crashes, it may affect other Web applications, but the Web server and system itself will remain unaffected. This helps to ensure the integrity of your Web server's system files, and it helps to protect against any unauthorized attempts to access files and services.

Setting Application Protection

This new setting is on as the default on new Web sites, and it can be set or changed under the Home Directory tab on the **Application Protection** option. As you can see from Figure 7.1, your choices are **Low (IIS Process)** for what was previously known as In-Process in IIS4, **Medium (Pooled)** for the new Pooled Process, and **High (Isolated)** for the Out-of-Process setting.

Figure 7.1 Application Protection Settings

IISreset

This is a simple but powerful command that is much overdue in IIS. It allows you to control all the IIS services as one logical service, without having to stop each one or reboot the server. You can run this from within the IIS Manager snap-in, locally from a command line, remotely from a command line, and, of course, you can incorporate it into scripts and even Windows Scheduler. This command can even take advantage of the improvements in the Windows 2000 Service Control Manager and automatically restart IIS if it should terminate unexpectedly, and it can be configured to reboot the server if a shutdown of the IIS services wasn't successful.

Because this command is so powerful, you'll be pleased to hear that it can also be enabled and disabled with the local administrator setting this locally on the Web server itself.

Restarting IIS from the Internet Information Services Snap-In

The **Restart IIS** command is available when you right-click on your Web server in the Internet Information Services MMC. Note that you can still stop, start, and pause individual IIS services. If IIS is already running, you will then have the choice of stopping IIS, restarting IIS, or rebooting the computer, as Figure 7.2 shows. When you click **OK** you'll then see a status box with an **End Now** button available in case the command cannot complete.

Figure 7.2 Restart Options from the Internet Information Services Snap-In

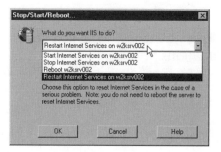

Restarting IIS Using the Command Line

Using the command line to issue an **iisreset** request has the following syntax:

```
Iisreset <computer_name> /<switch>
```

If you omit the computer name, the command will assume that it is for the local machine. And with no switch specified, the default is to restart the IIS services. So to stop or restart all IIS services on your Web server, you simply type **iisreset**. The complete list of switches is shown in Table 7.1.

Table 7.1 IISreset Switches and Explanations

IISreset Switch	Explanation
/RESTART	Stop and then restart all IIS services.
/START	Start all IIS services.
/STOP	Stop all IIS services.
/REBOOT	Reboot the computer.
/REBOOTONERROR	Reboot the computer if the command to stop/start/restart fails.
/NOFORCE	Do not force the IIS services to terminate if they do not stop gracefully.
/TIMEOUT:<secs>	Specify number of seconds to wait for IIS services to stop (can be used with the /REBOOTONERROR switch. If no value is specified defaults are 20 secs for restart, 60 secs for stop, and 0 secs for reboot.
/STATUS	Display status of each IIS service.
/ENABLE	Enable iisreset locally.
/DISABLE	Disable iisreset locally.

TIP

Need help with IISreset switches? Type **iisreset /?** to display the available switches and explanations.

Additional Control When Stopping IIS Services

Windows 2000 will automatically load **iisreset** when the IIS services stop unexpectedly. This is configured on the Recovery tab of the IIS Admin Service with all failures set to **Run a File**—which is **iisreset** (see Figure 7.3). You can change these settings if required—for example, you can run your own script or program instead.

Figure 7.3 The IIS Admin Service Recovery Options

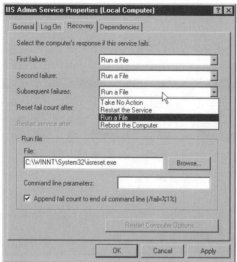

Backup/Restore Configuration

You know we should all create regular backups, particularly before making any changes. In reality, though, network administrators often make a number of changes in a single day so having to resort to restoring from backup will often lose a whole day's work and be a fairly lengthy process.

IIS5 comes with a very easy-to-use Backup/Restore Configuration that's available when you right-click on your Web server in the Internet Information Services MMC. This facility makes it very easy to create a backup before you make any changes and to restore a backup relatively quickly without having to take down the whole server and reboot. Obviously, it can't back up your Web content, but it will back up your Web server's configuration—for example, any changes you make within the Internet Information Services.

As you can see from Figure 7.4, this system is very simple to use. Click the Create backup button to name your particular backup configuration, and save it with the current date/time. To restore, select the backup you want to use and click Restore. When making incremental changes I find that it is useful to create a backup with a name that reflects the new changes I'm about to make as you can see in Figure 7.4. This allows you to easily retrace your steps to a known state. However, note that backups are listed alphabetically according to the name you give them; they do not appear in date/time order and you can't (as you might think) sort on the Date/Time column! If you want them listed in date order, consider prefixing each entry with the next letter of the alphabet—for example, "A-Base configuration," "B-Before bandwidth throttling," etc.

Figure 7.4 Backup and Restore Options

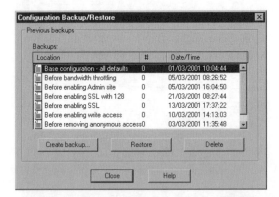

Backup Considerations

The majority of IIS configuration settings have been moved from the registry to the IIS metabase (metabase.bin), which greatly improves performance. This is what is being backed up here, not registry keys. It's important to remember that a registry backup is not sufficient to back up IIS5. However, there are still a few registry keys used in conjunction with IIS5, including the following:

- **HKEY_LOCAL_MACHINE \SOFTWARE\MICROSOFT\INETMGR** which holds information for Certificate Services, if installed.

- **HKEY_LOCAL_MACHINE \SYSTEM\CURRENT\CONTROLSET\SERVICES\INETINFO** which contains legacy information for Performance Monitor.

- **HKEY_LOCAL_MACHINE \SYSTEM\CURRENT\CONTROLSET\SERVICE\IIS ADMIN** which is used for backward compatibility with IIS4 so that you can configure an IIS4 server using the Windows 2000 Internet Information Services MMC snap-in.

You can create backups with both the Internet Information Services MMC and the browser-based version of Internet Services Manager (more on the browser-based version later).

Limitations of Backup/Restore Configuration

The two main limitations of this new feature are these:

- You cannot restore your backups using the browser-based version of Internet Information Services MMC (HTML Administrator interface).
- Backups are not portable—you cannot use them on other servers.

FTP Restart

Strictly speaking, this new feature combats unreliability on the client side, rather than adding reliability on the server. But reliability and performance from a user's perspective have such a close relationship that it's often difficult to distinguish between them cleanly. FTP Restart (as defined in RFC 959) allows a file transfer that has failed part way through to continue where it left off, rather than having to download the whole file again from the beginning. If you've ever had the experience of waiting for a large file to download, only to have it fail when it reaches the high 90 percent range, you'll appreciate a server that supports this feature!

Note that there are two benefits here. The first is obviously from the client's perspective because although the client may have to initiate the file transfer again (on some FTP clients it can be configured to start again automatically), it can begin transferring from where it left off rather than having to transfer the whole file, which saves considerable time. The second benefit is to the server because it doesn't have to retransmit redundant data, which obviously has an effect on the server's available resources and performance on other services (for example, Web sites).

Although the reason for the failed transfer may have nothing to do with the server (often the most likely reason is poor network conditions), the perception of file transfer reliability from the user's point of view will usually be thrown on to the FTP server.

Limitations of FTP Restart

Although FTP Restart is automatically available with IIS5, it's worth noting when it won't be used. These situations include the following:

- Uploading (PUT)

- Downloading a file greater than 4GB

- Downloading multiple files using wildcards (MPUT)

The last point is worth clarifying because often documentation simply states that FTP Restart doesn't work when using wildcards. It's more accurate to state that it will work only on a single file when it is interrupted midtransfer. This means that if a user is specifying a wildcard to download multiple files and the link goes down, FTP Restart will work with the actual file that was being transferred before the failure. But the server cannot restart a file transfer that was effectively never started. Therefore, the user must respecify any files that failed to download.

NOTE

The FTP client must also support the FTP Restart facility. Not all FTP clients do which includes Internet Explorer's FTP. There are a number of FTP clients that do support this, including Absolute FTP, BulletProof, Connexium, 3D-FTP 4.0, and FTP-Pro, to name just a few. There are a number of FTP clients available to download from http://alcom.tucows/com/win2k/ftp2k.html; look for the ones that mention *resume* in their list of features.

Improvements in Administration and Management

A number of improvements make IIS5 easier to administer and offer a service that was built to integrate with the operating system from the start. The first is simply using the common MMC snap-in, which is familiar to many IIS4 users. Not only does it offer familiarity, but it has greater flexibility than it did in previous versions because the MMC interface can be used to house additional Windows 2000 configuration utilities that are also used. These can include, disk management, users and groups, and local group policy, among others. You can now configure and manage the Web server under one configuration utility by adding the snap-ins required. Other areas of improved interface options for administering and managing include the following:

- Wizards and tools to guide you through setup and configuration
- Improved logging for Process Accounting
- Improved Remote Administration

Wizards and Tools

There are a number of wizards and tools in Windows 2000 to help guide you through common configuration requirements. They are particularly welcome with IIS where administration and management cover a number of different and complex areas. For example, security will be high on any administrator's list of priorities, and yet this covers a number of possible areas—from user accounts, security policies, to application security, NTFS permissions, and IIS authentication.

Security Settings Permission Wizard

The most basic (and useful) wizard to help out with configuring security in IIS is the **Security Settings Permission Wizard**, which is accessible when you right-click on a Web or FTP site or virtual directory and choose **All Tasks | Permission Wizard**. This wizard has two different modes of operation. It can configure your chosen site or virtual directory from scratch, based on two different templates. Or, more powerfully, it can be used to apply parent security settings to child sites or virtual directories.

To some extent, the latter can also be achieved by configuring the Master Properties on the server. This doesn't cover file and directory permissions, though. And if you want to host sites for both public access (Internet access) and private use (intranets) on the same server, only one Master Properties configuration can be used.

The two templates used are based on public and private access. In fact, there's very little difference between their settings except that the public sites uses only Anonymous authentication and the private site disables Anonymous and instead enables Basic, Digest, and Windows Integrated (security authentication is covered later). Both sites set the access permission to be Read and Script, giving NTFS permissions of Full Control to Administrators, and Read and Execute Scripts to all users.

As you can see from Figure 7.5, you can view the suggested settings and either accept or reject them. Once these have been accepted, you can then always modify these settings manually yourself.

Figure 7.5 Permissions Wizard Showing Settings for a Public Web Site

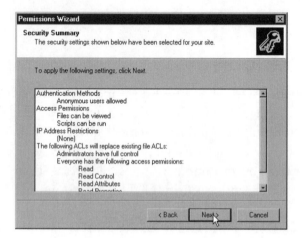

NOTE

Remember the limitations of wizards and especially this Security Permissions Wizard! It's very useful as a starting point, and it does offer sensible default values, but do not allow it to give you a false sense of security. Check that settings the wizard has changed are suitable. Don't just check that they still allow the site to be accessible for those who legitimately need to access it, but also look to see if you should further restrict the wizard's default settings. For example, the template for the intranet Web site includes Basic authentication, which doesn't encrypt the user's password (so it's clear text) as it is sent over the network. If all your users have Internet Explorer, you would be wise to disable this setting and only use Windows Integrated.

You may also find it useful to reference the Secure Internet Information Services 5 Checklist, which is available to download from the Microsoft site on: www.microsoft.com/technet/security/iis5chk.asp.

Windows 2000 Internet Server Security Configuration Tool

A more powerful security tool to automate security settings is the **Windows 2000 Internet Server Security Configuration Tool** (also known as "What If"). At the time of writing, this isn't incorporated into the product, although I'm guessing it may well be incorporated into future Service Packs. It is available without charge by downloading it from the following URL: www.microsoft.com/technet/security/tools.asp.

This utility is aimed at locking down a standalone Internet Web server, letting you select the security features and settings you want on your Web server. This is far more extensive than the simple Permissions Wizard, and clearly aimed at the server level and not at the application site level. It covers port access, services, script mappings, and removal of Web samples. Note that anything not selected will be disabled rather than left untouched, so the fewer features you choose, the more secure a setting you're automatically configuring.

WARNING

This is a very powerful and complex tool which makes it very easy to do substantial damage with ease! Use it and test it in a safe, non-production environment until you are sure the settings and changes are suitable. Remember that these settings are more extensive than the configuration options available with Internet Information Services so your IIS backups won't help you to restore back to a known state.

Undoing any settings with this tool depends on whether the configuration is set in your custom text file template or in the hisecweb.inf template. If set as one of your custom choices you can simply rerun the configuration tool again, and then change them and reapply. If set in the preconfigured hisecweb template, you'll have to load this and modify it with the Security Configuration Editor (covered in Chapter 2) and reapply. Alternatively, it may be easier (and safer) to simply restore your system from a full backup and then start again.

Your choices are saved to a custom template that you can then apply to either a local server or a remote server. Additionally, if you are running the tool to configure a local server, the utility will also apply a Windows 2000 standard security template called **hisecweb.inf**, which is designed for a standalone server (not a member server). Settings in this template don't allow remote logon, permit only Administrators to log on locally, set security options such as password policies, account lockouts, and auditing, secure the registry, and disable many unnecessary services (for example, the browser service).

Tip

The hisecweb.inf template can be used independently from this tool. As mentioned in Chapter 2, you can download it from the Microsoft site: http://download.microsoft.com/download/win2000srv/SCM/1.0/NT5/ EN-US/hisecweb.exe.

Certificate Wizard and Certificate Trust Lists Wizard

The two other new wizards built into Internet Information Services are the Certificate Wizard and the Certificate Trust Lists (CTL) Wizard. Certificates are required when using Secure Sockets Layer (SSL) on your IIS server to encrypt sensitive information and authenticate clients and you cannot employ SSL until your Web server has a valid certificate.

The Certificate Wizard is called automatically when you select the Server Certificate button under the Secure communication section of the site's Properties, Directory Security. It will automatically detect whether your IIS server already has a valid server certificate and even if it is about to expire. The wizard will step you through certificate managing. This example will include requesting a certificate, assigning a certificate to the server, and importing a certificate from a Key Manager setup. Figure 7.6 shows the last page of the wizard when requesting a Web server certificate.

The Certificate Trust Lists Wizard is available once your IIS server has one or more certificates and is called from the Edit button under the Secure communication section of the site's Properties, Directory Security. It allows administrators to configure which Certificate Authorities (CAs) should be used on each site. CTLs are mainly used when running multiple Web sites for different customers or departments that have different security requirements. For example, you use three different Certificate Authorities for issuing certificates, but each one is relevant to only one Web site you're hosting.

Figure 7.6 Completing the Web Server Certificate Server Wizard

Other wizards exist for creating new sites and virtual directories, prompting you for the information required. Simply right-click and select New from within the Internet Information Services MMC, as Figure 7.7 shows. Strangely absent from this wizard, in comparison to other Windows 2000 wizards, is the final summary page. You have to click Finish and manually check the properties of your newly created site or virtual directory—where, of course, you can also modify them.

Figure 7.7 Configuring a New Web Site That Calls Up the Web Site Creation Wizard

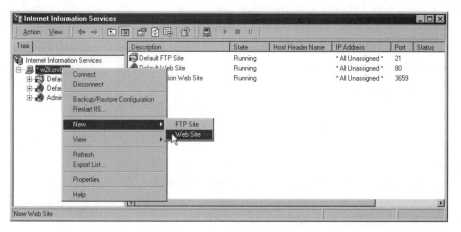

IIS Migration Wizard

Finally, another tool worth mentioning is the **IIS Migration Wizard** from the Windows 2000 Resource Kit. This is aimed at migrating Web servers from Netscape Enterprise Server 3.5 and Apache HTTP Server 1.3 to IIS5 by moving content and configuration settings. You'll still have to manually make some changes, such as modifying Unix style filenames. But it certainly offers a good jump start.

As a bonus, this utility can also be used with IIS servers—migrating IIS4 to ISS5, for example, if you want a clean installation of Windows 2000 but don't want to reconfigure your Web site from scratch. It can also be used to mirror an existing IIS5 site, which is useful for configuring standby servers and Web farms. For more information, see "Migrating a Web Server to IIS5.0" in the Internet Information Services Resource Guide.

Improved Logging for Process Accounting

IIS5 now lets administrators monitor and log how Web sites use processing resources on the server. This new feature is targeted at ISPs that may run a number of different Web sites for different customers and that want to know which sites are disproportionately taxing the server (and charge the customer accordingly). However, it's just as useful for Web administrators to identify a Web site's malfunctioning scripts and processes.

Process Accounting is enabled by selecting it as one of the extended W3C logging properties and then selecting from a number of events such as Total User Time, Total Kernel Time, Total Page Faults, and Total Processes (see Figure 7.8). It should be noted that this logging is on the site level only and cannot identify which of the site's applications or scripts are responsible for the collective logging. If the logging identified high readings, you would need to monitor and debug each site further for that level of information. Despite this limitation, Process Accounting remains a good indication of your server's general running state.

Note that if all Web sites are running high CPU usage, it's more likely a sign that your processor is underpowered and that you should add another processor, swap out the processor for another more powerful one, or look to move some Web sites to another server. Use Performance Monitor to baseline your server and then again during normal Web usage. If your processor is hitting above 80 percent, look to modify your hardware specification.

Process accounting is available only for Web sites (and not, for example, FTP sites) and can be used only with W3C Extended logging; it cannot be used when the site's Application Protection is set to Low (as discussed previously in the section on Reliability). A site that is using an unacceptably high level of CPU resources can also be *throttled*. For more information on this, see the section on Process Throttling under Performance, later in this chapter.

Figure 7.8 Setting Process Accounting Logging Options

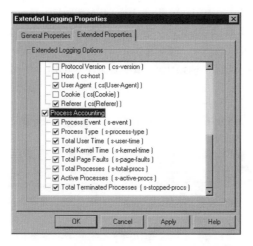

Improved Remote Administration

Remote in this context means not over a LAN-grade network. You can, of course, configure the Internet Information Services MMC to configure a non-local IIS server, but this will not be a viable solution over the Internet because the MMC is not firewall or proxy server friendly (or suitable for low bandwidths). Instead, you have a couple of solutions available to you when it comes to remotely administering your IIS5 server. The first is to make good use of the built-in Terminal Services, and the second is to use the browser-based Internet Services Manager (HTMLA).

Terminal Services comes with two licenses for remote administration so that you can remotely administer any Windows 2000 server with low bandwidth requirements as if you were logging on locally. It is suitable over the Internet if intervening firewalls and routers will allow through the RDP traffic (TCP port 3389), or it can be used with (dialup) PPP or with a VPN (PPTP or L2TP/IPSec).

If not using an additional encryption mechanism (such as the encryption inherent with VPNs), you may well want to set the Terminal Service Client's encryption level to high. Running Terminal Services in Remote Administration mode on the IIS server requires little processing overhead, which makes it a suitable remote administration utility even for IIS.

You must have installed on your local workstation (or server) a Terminal Services client, which can be either Windows based or browser based. Refer to Chapter 5 for more information on using Terminal Services in Windows 2000.

The browser-based Internet Services Manager (HTMLA) is the alternative IIS built-in solution for remote server administration (it is not available for IIS running on Professional). This has undergone a radical makeover from the IIS4 version, which was minimalist in functionality. This version in IIS5 purports to offer 98 percent of all administration functions within the Information Services MMC (see Figure 7.9).

Figure 7.9 Remote Administration of IIS5 Suitable for Internet Connections

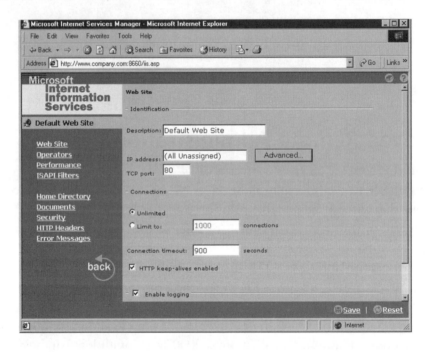

NOTE

By default, the administration site is denied access to all but localhost (127.0.0.1). To allow remote administration you must change this before you can remotely administer your Web site. You specify this under the **IP address and domain name restrictions** under the Administration Web Site's Directory Security tab.

It doesn't run the Certificate-based wizards (but it does have the Permissions Wizard), and it can show some options as configurable when they shouldn't be enabled. For example, you can configure SSL options without having a server certificate and set Digest authentication, which is applicable only to Active Directory domains. I have to admit that I'm not yet a fan of this remote administration tool, and I find it rather cumbersome to navigate and inelegant in design. But it certainly has improved from previous versions, and it could well make a very viable remote administration tool for IIS.

Remote administration can also be incorporated with the use of Web site operators that have limited administrative privileges on individual Web sites.

Web Site Operators

The use of Web site operators hasn't changed from IIS4 usage, but now that remote administration is more viable, I think it's worth revisiting. Web site operators are a group of designated users specified under the Web site's Operators tab who can modify properties only on sites on which they have been given permission. Through this mechanism, they have no access to IIS server-level settings, any Windows level settings, or the file system permissions. Web site operators can do the following:

- Set Web site access permissions
- Enable logging
- Change the default document settings
- Set content expiration
- Enable content ratings

Web site operators cannot do these tasks:

- Change the Web site's identification or port number
- Stop/start or pause the site
- Configure the anonymous username or password (or any other account)
- Throttle bandwidth
- Create virtual directories or change their locations
- Change the Application Protection setting

Designing & Planning…

Security Concerns Using Web Site Operators

There have been a number of security issues regarding Web site operator accounts because they offer a security account that is potentially easier to attack than the administrator's. Before using Web operators, be sure to read up on any potential vulnerabilities in this area, and if necessary install hot fixes to plug any potential risks.

Improvements in Security

We have already looked at a number of improvements in IIS5's armory with the new Permissions Wizard and Internet Server Security Configuration Tool. And as with previous versions of IIS, you can still grant or deny access to sites by IP addresses or domain names, and you can employ certificates for client/server authentication and encryption. This section looks at the authentication protocols available in IIS5 because these have changed and at first sight they can seem rather confusing. You need to strike that balance between enforcing strong authentication and ensuring accessibility to legitimate users.

Anonymous authentication remains as it was in IIS4. Using this type of authentication means that users do not have to identify themselves to be given logged-in access because they are using a special IIS anonymous account. By default, this account is called *IUSR_<computer_name>*, which is automatically generated for you. You can change the account name being used and its location.

For example, you may have one standard account on your domain that you use for all Windows anonymous access and that you prefer to use rather than multiple local accounts. You can also override the default IIS setting to automatically generate and manage this account's password. This is the main type of authentication used on the majority of sites so that users can access non-confidential data quickly and easily as a guest user, without being prompted for a username and a password.

The other types of authentication are used when either anonymous access is disabled, or access to files or directories being used within the site have restrictive NTFS permissions. Basic authentication is a fall-back authentication for when anonymous isn't appropriate, but when a stronger authentication protocol cannot be used. Basic is considered the most versatile of authentication protocols (most widely supported), but it is also the least secure because the password is sent across from client to server in unencrypted (clear-text) format.

Using clear-text passwords obviously makes the server vulnerable to *sniffing* with a network analyzer. When you know clients are able to use a more secure authentication protocol (for example, if all clients use Internet Explorer and do not go through proxy servers) this option should not be used. In an improvement from IIS4, you can now specify the location of the account if you don't want to use an account stored locally on the IIS server. This provides much greater flexibility. For example, you could use an account from your Windows NT 4.0 domain or even a Novell directory. New authentication protocols in IIS5 are these:

- Windows Integrated
- Digest
- Fortezza

The standard authentication protocols can be found under each Web site's Authentication Methods dialog box, as shown in Figure 7.10. This is accessed from the Directory Security tab, then the Edit button under Anonymous access and authentication control. Authentication control for FTP sites is found under the site's Security Accounts tab and note that your only choices for FTP are Anonymous and Basic.

Figure 7.10 Configuring Authentication Protocols

There may be occasions when these authentication methods are not adequate for your requirements. For example, this may include when you need to securely authenticate clients on browsers other than Internet Explorer and/or you need to encrypt data sent between client and server. When this is the case you're looking at using digital certificates, which will be covered in the section on Windows 2000 Certificate Services later in this chapter.

> **NOTE**
>
> Anonymous access is invariably selected by default. Bear in mind that a site that has this enabled will always try Anonymous access first, even if other authentication methods are specified and the user has a valid account.

Windows Integrated

For non-Active Directory networks, we can interpret this as "Windows NT Challenge/Response" (also known as NT LAN Manager, or simply NTLM). IIS5 documentation will often state that Windows Integrated is more secure than Windows NT Challenge/Response because it can use Kerberos.

Standard documentation, however, often fails to point out exactly when Kerberos will be used and when our old friend, NTLM, will be used. In a nutshell, if you're not authenticating within an Active Directory domain (that is, your Web server is either a member server or a Domain Controller within an Active Directory domain), you won't be using Kerberos. Even if you are authenticating within an Active Directory domain, Kerberos will be used only when the client is also running Windows 2000.

The two main limitations of using Windows Integrated authentication are that it is not browser independent (it works with only Microsoft Internet Explorer) and that it may not work across proxy servers. For these reasons, it is most commonly used in intranet environments, rather than for Internet services.

Digest

Defined in RFC 2069, this authentication protocol has the advantages of working across proxy servers and firewalls and offering better security than Basic because it encrypts the password. It can be used only with Active Directory user accounts, however. Therefore, IIS5 servers that are standalone, part of a Windows 2000 workgroup, or part of a Windows NT 4.0 domain will not be able to use this new authentication protocol. Its final restriction is that users must be running IE 5.0 or above. Clearly, it is not suitable for a general public Web site.

Fortezza

Support for this type of authentication has been provided primarily for U.S. government and military services; however, it's not actually provided within IIS5—you have to first install it as an add-on Cryptographic Service Provider (CSP). Support for Fortezza has been added to both Microsoft and Netscape client/server products including Internet Explorer, Microsoft Exchange Server, Microsoft Outlook, and Netscape Navigator.

Improvements in Performance

There have been a number of significant improvements to IIS5 so that it can deliver a faster service and run more Web sites. Some reports have claimed that IIS5 is four to five times faster than IIS4, but obviously each Web server's performance will have a number of different factors including hardware specification, bandwidth, scripting, and back-end processing (to name just a few!). The range of performance improvements means that you can realize some, and possibly many, performance gains on your IIS5 servers. None of these performance features is dependent on Active Directory.

NOTE

In the Performance section, it should also be noted that IIS5 benefits from other Windows 2000 related improvements such as clustering and load balancing. In particular, multiple processor support has been significantly improved in Windows 2000 so that servers can now scale up more reliably. Perhaps today's increased use in server-side scripting and SSL might explain why adding another processor has resulted in one of the most cost-effective performance benefits on an IIS5 server.

The following section takes a look at some of the key changes from an administrator's point of view. It is not intended as a programmer's reference but rather an overview of what these key features are, what are their advantages and any disadvantages or limitations, and how to configure them with the Internet Information Services utility. The new performance options are as follows:

- HTTP Compression
- ASP improvements

- Bandwidth throttling
- Process throttling
- Socket pooling

HTTP Compression

When the Web server can compress files before sending them over the network to the client, this can dramatically improve response times for a client in situations where bandwidth is low (for example, modem access). Both static and dynamic content can be compressed using the industry standard GZIP and Deflate algorithms. There are conditions and trade-offs for this setting that must be considered before enabling it on your IIS5 server.

First, because the client must decompress the files once they have arrived, this setting works only when the client can support HTTP Compression. All HTTP 1.1-compliant applications can support this compression which includes Internet Explorer 4 and above, and also Windows Explorer and My Computer in Windows 2000. Therefore, up-to-date Windows clients are more likely to benefit from this setting rather than legacy browsers.

Compression, like encryption, comes at a price. On the server end this means higher processing and the requirement for more disk space. If your Web server is already running at close to 80 percent processor usage or more, compression should not be enabled. Additionally, you should also have enough free disk space to comfortably store your files in both uncompressed and compressed formats. Although you can limit the disk space that is used to compress files, this will have a higher impact on the processor because it will result in data being compressed more than once.

You can choose to compress just static data, just dynamic data, or both. Static data stands to gain the most performance benefit because the files are compressed only once and then cached. Future requests for the same files mean that the cached files can be retrieved without recompression (unless they are no longer in the cache because disk space has been limited).

In comparison, dynamic content is compressed on demand because by its very nature it cannot be predetermined. This means that Web servers that hold a high percentage of static content stand to benefit the most from compression in terms of performance benefits. Conversely, Web servers that deliver mainly dynamic content to clients will see the least performance benefit and will have a higher demand on the processor.

Finally, one of the most important considerations about setting HTTP Compression when weighing the advantages and the disadvantages is that this is a server-wide setting. It cannot be set on individual Web sites, and as such it offers a rather inflexible, all-or-nothing choice per Web server.

Where you do have some flexibility is in defining how compression works (which algorithms are used, for example) and adding functionality (for example, encrypting compressed data). This is possible by defining custom filters with the Windows 2000 Software Development Kit.

Designing & Planning…

Compression Considerations

There are no hard-and-fast rules about when and whether to use this setting. It really is a case of weighing the advantages and disadvantages. Web servers that are accessed by dialup clients and that have a high percentage of static data will benefit the most—providing that the additional processing overhead doesn't throttle your server's CPU. With disk space and CPU prices being so cheap these days, there's an argument to enable this setting on all Web servers that have a reasonably powerful hardware specification. Be sure to monitor your server's CPU usage (use Windows 2000 Performance utility) to make sure this setting isn't negatively affecting your overall Web server performance. When the processing load reaches the 80 percent threshold, weigh the cost benefits of adding another processor before unsetting this option.

Configuring HTTP Compression

This option appears only in the WWW Service Master Properties, under the Service tab. Figure 7.11 shows the options that are available.

If you want to compress dynamic content, the **Compress application files** will affect files sent to the client when they have extensions of .dll, .asp, and .exe. If you choose only this type of compression, you don't need to specify any cache details because each file must be compressed on-demand before it is sent to the client. Setting this option on its own would be applicable if nearly all of your output was dynamic and/or if you didn't want to store compressed static files on the server. However, remember that less processing is required with compressing static files.

Figure 7.11 Configuring HTTP Compression and Options

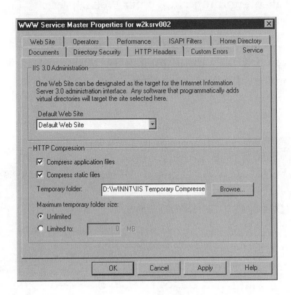

It is more likely that you would select the **Compress static files** option either by itself, or together with the **Compress application files** options. This setting affects files that have extensions of .htm, .html, and .txt. You must specify the Temporary folder where compressed files will be stored. By default this will be **%systemroot%\IIS Temporary Compressed Files,** but you can select an alternative location. The directory you choose must meet the following criteria:

- Local to the Web server
- Formatted as NTFS
- Not shared
- Not compressed

NOTE

You can modify the file extensions used to determine which files are compressed by editing the metabase entries: HcFileExtensions and HcScriptExtensions.

By default, the cache directory size is set to unlimited, but you can restrict this (in increments of 1 megabyte). When the restricted cache size is met, IIS will delete 256 files to make room for more files. Therefore, configuring a cache size that is too small will result in both a higher processing requirement and more read/write hard disk access.

Configuring & Implementing...

Testing Considerations

Remember that setting compression will have an effect only when files are requested by a compression-enabled client. This is true even when compressing static content because IIS compresses files only after they have been sent to the first compression-enabled client. Thereafter all additional requests for the same file can be met from the compression version. This allows IIS to intelligently compress and store only files that are requested without latency on startup.

These factors mean that when testing the performance results of setting compression, you should ensure that the client is compression enabled and that the files are requested more than once. To check that IE is configured to use compression, ensure that the **Use HTTP 1.1** option is selected under the **Advanced, Internet Options**.

ASP Improvements

Active Server Pages provide a server-side scripting environment so that you can create dynamic and interactive applications on your Web server. You can combine HTML pages, script commands, and Component Object Model (COM) components to create interactive Web pages or Web applications that are easy to deploy and modify.

A number of ASP features have been added in IIS5 that should help enhance performance and streamline server-side script. These include the following:

- New flow control methods
- Improved error handling
- Scriptless ASP

- Performance-enhanced objects

- Extensible Markup Language (XML) integration

- Windows script components

- New method of determining browser capabilities

- ASP self-tuning

- Server-side Include with SRC attribute

- Encoded ASP scripts

The IIS5 online documentation has more information on each of these new features within the Active Server Pages Guide under "What's New in ASP." The remainder of the guide contains extensive information on ASP including an introduction, how to develop Web applications with ASP, properties and methods, and samples.

Bandwidth Throttling

If your Web server has to share bandwidth between services (for example, www and email or even multiple Web sites) and it is important that a particular service doesn't hog all the available bandwidth, you can enable bandwidth throttling. IIS4 allowed you to set this on the server only, so that your bandwidth throttling applied to all www sites and FTP sites. IIS5 now lets you set this on a per-Web-site basis, which can override the server setting.

This setting is particularly useful if you need to regulate and control the amount of bandwidth each Web site will have to ensure that other services will have adequate bandwidth for themselves. However, this setting affects only static HTML files—not dynamic content such as ASP files. And it's important to realize that when socket pooling is enabled (the default), throttling the bandwidth on one site will result in throttling other sites if they share the same port number.

Configuring Bandwidth Throttling

To set this on a server level, **Enable Bandwidth Throttling** is under the server's **Properties, Internet Information Services** tab. Note that setting this option here also affects all FTP sites. To set this on a Web site level, this option is under the site's Performance tab, as shown in Figure 7.12. As you can see from the information provided in the dialog box, the Web site setting can override the server setting—even if the value on the server is less than the value on the site. The logic of being able to override a restricted option on the server with a less restrictive value on the site level is very unintuitive, so beware! You can use this reverse logic to good effect if you want to restrict your FTP sites. Set the bandwidth throttling at the server level, and then specify a higher bandwidth for each Web site.

Figure 7.12 Setting Bandwidth Throttling

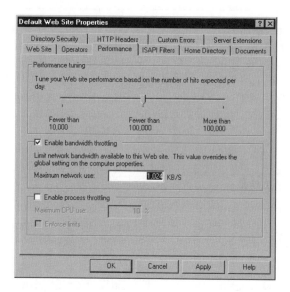

Process Throttling

Similar in concept to bandwidth throttling, process throttling allows you to control how much your server's CPU time is spent processing dynamic content produced by ASP scripts, Internet Server Application Programming Interface (ISAPI), and CGI applications. This can ensure that one Web site doesn't hog all CPU resources at the expense of other sites and other services.

It can apply only to sites that have been configured with Medium or High application protection (sites that don't share resources with IIS itself).

You can simply Log to the Application event log when the threshold is reached, or you can enforce the level. Enforcing has two automatic levels in addition to logging the event. When the processing usage reaches 150 percent of the threshold limit set, all the applicable applications will have their CPU priority set to Idle. Should the processing usage exceed 200 percent, all the applicable applications are stopped. This two-tiered enforcement allows IIS to intelligently detect malfunctioning scripts and limit the resulting damage by protecting other sites and services. In this way, this new option offers both better performance and reliability for the whole server.

Configuring process throttling is set under the **Performance** tab, as shown in Figure 7.12.

Socket Pooling

IIS4 allowed you to host multiple Web sites by three different methods. The first was to simply assign multiple logical IP addresses to the adapter and host each site on a different address. This was the simplest solution and the one most widely used for many companies. The second was to use host headers that relied on the browser correctly interpreting them and because not all browsers support host headers, this solution was used only with Intranet solutions where the browser version was known and controlled. The third was to use the same address but with a different port number. Because browsers default to using port 80 for Web sites, using a different port number meant users had to manually type it in with the URL, which wasn't an acceptable solution except for when making the site less available could be turned into a security advantage.

The disadvantage with the most common method of using different IP addresses was the additional resources it required from the server in terms of non-pageable memory. Each Web site had to create its own port—even though this was using port 80 on all addresses.

IIS5 now pools all ports with the same number together, which requires much less memory. The result is that you can run many more Web sites than you could before when you run them under a different logical address, all using the default port 80. Or, conversely, that the same number of sites will now free up more memory for other processes.

There are a few limitations to take into consideration. The first is that when configuring bandwidth and process throttling, those settings will affect all sites that are pooled and not necessarily just the Web site on which the setting is enabled. The second is that of application integrity, where it may be preferable for mission-critical applications to have their own dedicated socket pool. The third is that of network security because this setting means that IIS listens on all the server's addresses rather than being able to restrict addresses and adapters. When these factors are more important than the performance benefits you gain, you will need to disable socket pooling at the server level or for specific sites. Unfortunately, this is not possible through IIS's GUI utilities. Instead, you must modify the metabase using the ADSI scripting facility.

Document Collaboration with WebDAV

Although Web servers are now recognized as a great resource for providing a central place for users to access information, previous versions of IIS were geared toward offering read-only access for users. IIS5 implements Web Distributed Authoring and Versioning (better known as WebDAV), which conforms to RFC 2518 and is an extension of the HTTP 1.1 standard for exposing data over an HTTP connection.

At its simplest level, WebDAV allows users to modify and share documents on a Web server. IIS5 will automatically lock a file that is being modified while still allowing other users to read it. Obviously, this technology is more suited to intranet environments, but in theory there's no reason why the same technology cannot be applied to Web servers on the Internet.

WebDAV allows more than just modifying documents. However, it exposes the Web directory's file store just as if the user had logged on to the server locally. For example, a WebDAV-enabled directory allows users to modify, rename, delete, create, move, and search both files and directories (and their attributes where applicable). While this is very powerful, it's also very dangerous from a security point of view. Now HTTP offers more than just read and scripting access; you can no longer protect your Web server's content by blocking ports other than port 80.

WebDAV does not depend on Active Directory. Because securing access to a WebDAV-enabled Web server becomes more critical, it would be prudent to include in your security plans the highest authentication protocol that both server and clients can support. Ultimately, Kerberos can offer a higher level of security authentication for intranet sites and Digest for Internet Web server sites when using firewalls and proxies. Both of these protocols can be used only in an Active

Directory domain. Refer back to the section on Security for more information about authentication choices.

SECURITY ALERT!

WebDAV is a great new feature in IIS5 that extends the capabilities of a Web server to integrate a Web server's storage with traditional file server storage. It is particularly relevant for companies that are moving toward a browser-based desktop. However, it does pose a very serious new security consideration that not only must you be aware of, but so should other people who share responsibility for the integrity and security of your Web server. This includes your Web developers and network administrators (for example, those responsible for securing and monitoring firewalls and proxy servers). When your Web server is accessible from the Internet, this feature makes your server more vulnerable to attack (particularly Denial of Service attacks).

Be sure to read up on any security fixes and known problems to do with WebDAV if you choose to enable it—there have already been a number of problems reported. Also monitor carefully any changes to the IIS Write access on both existing sites and new ones and be extra vigilant about setting and monitoring NTFS permissions.

For security reasons, you may prefer to disable this feature altogether. It is possible to effectively disable WebDAV on the server (but not on individual sites on the server). To do this, stop the IIS services and from the **%SystemRoot%\System32\Inetsrv** folder type the following command: **CACLS httpext.dll /D Everyone** . Because WebDAV relies on the httpext.dll file, denying Everybody permission to use it effectively disables WebDAV (you cannot simply delete or rename it because of Windows File Protection). To reenable WebDAV, use Windows Explorer to modify this file's Security permission and simply remove Everybody and then restart IIS.

Using WebDAV

There is no WebDAV option to enable on each site. Instead, it is enabled on a site when you allow Write access. This potentially gives all connecting users seamless access to that site's filestore. To restrict what users can do and which users can do what, you use standard NTFS permissions on the site's files just as you would on a Windows 2000 file and print server. The only other protection you have is that IIS5 Write access won't let users modify any of the site's scripts (e.g., ASP scripts).

If you want users to be able to do this, set **Script source access** in addition to **Write** which will result in the script source being downloaded to the requesting HTTP 1.1 client.

Clients must be HTTP 1.1 compatible to take advantage of WebDAV, which includes not just IE4 and later versions, but also desktop applications such as the Microsoft Office 2000 suite. So, for example, a user can connect to a WebDAV directory by calling up the Add Network Place wizard and once connected can both manipulate the WebDAV filestore and modify the files with appropriate applications—subject to the NTFS permissions. Office 2000 applications can also directly connect to a WebDAV directory so that users can open, create, edit, and save documents in a WebDAV directory.

Figure 7.13 shows an example of using My Network Places to create a desktop link to a WebDAV virtual directory, and Figure 7.14 then shows the Web folder's contents just as if it were another remote directory.

Figure 7.13 Using My Network Places to Locate a WebDAV Site

Figure 7.14 A WebDAV Connected Site

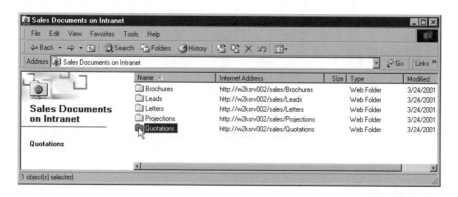

Certificate Services

Of all the services that have changed in Windows 2000 from Windows NT4, I think this one has probably undergone the most dramatic changes. Public Key Infrastructure (PKI) is heavily integrated with Windows 2000 networking. It is no longer a separated service relegated to public Internet Web servers, but instead it is seen as a viable authentication mechanism for domain users and external users alike.

The concept of using public/private certificates for authentication, confidentiality, and ensuring data integrity has not changed in Windows 2000, but it has been extended beyond using certificates for external Web and email services. It is now seen as a viable internal authentication method that can integrate with external companies as well as be used within the company network. Now, certificates can be used with Windows 2000 Encryption File Service (EFS), IP Security (IPSec), smart cards for logging in, and a whole list of other services.

The process of deploying these certificates has also been extended and improved so that certificates have become an integral part of the domain's network security. Unfortunately, much of the ease of deployment and some of the new features rely on Active Directory. It is very difficult, therefore, when reading up on the new features and options in Windows 2000 Certificate Service to decipher what is possible and what isn't when you are not running Active Directory. Most of the explanations and guides assume that you are running Active Directory, which leaves you perplexed about how to achieve the same things without Active Directory or uncertain about whether it's actually possible at all.

This section cannot do justice to explaining the background concepts and inner workings of public/private keys and PKI, or even cover every option and feature in Windows 2000 Certificate Services. But it will outline how to use Windows 2000 Certificate Services outside Active Directory, particularly with regard to using certificates on your Web server. As such, it will cover the following:

- Certificate authorities and roles
- Installing and configuring a standalone CA
- Server certificates
- How users request and manage certificates
- Configuring secure communication (SSL) on your Web server

Certificate Authorities and Roles

Public Key Infrastructure uses digital certificates issued and verified by trusted entities called Certificate Authorities (CAs). The Certificate Authority can be a body independent of your network such as VeriSign or Microsoft. Or you can host your own Certificate Authority to provide the most flexibility and control over how you issue and control certificates for your internal users, partners, and external customers.

Certificate Authorities adhere to a structured hierarchy of trust to offer the best flexibility and security in a distributed service. If you understand how the DNS hierarchy works, I think it helps to think of CAs as having a similar structure with trust and delegation running from the root (the top) down to the intervening servers and finally to the end hosts.

With Certificate Authorities, the top of the chain is the Root CA, which must be self-signed (there is no higher authority—much like a root DNS server). Below the Root CA you have subordinate CAs that obtain their certificate of trust from the Root CA and that can issue certificates to users and computers. The computer certificates can be for end services like IPSec, or they can be for a further subordinate CA. The final CA that issues users and computers with certificates is said to be the Issuing CA—although there's no reason why any CA shouldn't be an Issuing CA. The hierarchical structure used is entirely up to you. If you need to issue only a few certificates you can use your Root CA to do this.

Having a hierarchy of CAs means that you can distribute certificate services throughout your enterprise network, delegating control to different administrators and controlling network and server load. Despite each Windows 2000 CA being able to service up to 250,000 client certificates, the general advice is to treat your root CA like any root service, and not use it everyday to issue certificates. On all but the smallest of deployments, use the Root CA to issue certificates just for subordinate CAs.

Physically secure your Root CA, employ the highest security policies for it, don't run the service automatically, and back up the whole machine religiously. Most companies that have a distributed CA hierarchy would take the CA offline (physically remove the network card as well as powering off) to then be stored securely in a locked and protected environment. Then all that is needed is to renew the subordinate CA certificates or revoke subordinate CA certificates.

When you come to install Windows 2000 Certificate Services, you will be asked whether you are installing a Root CA or a subordinate CA. But more than that, you will also be asked whether you want to run an Enterprise CA or a

Standalone CA. This is the biggest difference from running Windows 2000 Certificate Services outside an Active Directory network—you will not be able to configure it as an Enterprise CA.

An Enterprise CA integrates with Active Directory for storage, security, management of certificates, and deployment. For example, with an Enterprise CA working with Group Policies, you can automatically deploy computer certificates when computers join the domain so that they can immediately use PKI services such as IPSec. You can predefine certificate templates for the services you want to use on your network so that when users request a certificate for a particular service they can simply choose from the list you have prepared. Certificate templates are not available with a Standalone CA. Users have to specifically request each detail when they request a certificate.

Another big difference is that because an Enterprise CA is tightly integrated into Active Directory, it can safely automatically grant certificates as soon as they are requested by users because Enterprise CAs have access to all the network security information about users and computers. In comparison, a Standalone CA by definition knows nothing about what options are allowed or whether the users' requests should be granted. Therefore, the Standalone CA administrator should manually check requests for certificates before granting them. This adds considerable administrative overhead in running Certificate Services outside Active Directory. The flip side is that you could argue that the lack of automation gives you a tighter control of what certificates are being requested and granted.

Note that you can also run a Standalone CA with Active Directory which provides additional benefits of centrally storing the certificate information but without the tie-in to the security account information.

To recap, without Active Directory you cannot use an Enterprise CA, but must configure Certificate Services to run as a Standalone CA. Standalone CAs cannot support the following:

- Certificate templates, which make it easier for users to request the certificate they require

- Automatic computer enrollment through Group Policies

- Automatic verification of certificates on demand

- Native smart card logon (although you can use third-party smart cards)

A Standalone CA can support the following:

- User certificates for Web access (SSL) and secure email (S/MIME)
- Computer certificates for IPSec

Installing and Configuring a Standalone CA

You install Certificate Services as you would any other Windows component with Add/Remove Programs and then Add/Remove Windows Components. Note these prerequisites before installing:

- You cannot rename the computer or move it into a different domain after installing Certificate Services (without invalidating the certificates it has issued).

- If you want to run both IIS and Certificate Services on the same server, make sure that IIS is installed first so that Certificate Services can add the virtual directories it needs. While it does this, IIS will have to be stopped during the installation.

- If you choose to install IIS and Certificate Services on a different machine, be aware that they communicate via DCOM, which is notoriously difficult (but not impossible) to configure through a firewall. When possible, try to make sure there is a good, uninterrupted network connection between your IIS server and the CA to which it will talk.

- Settings and information supplied when installing Certificate Services cannot be modified afterward, so supply them with care.

When installing, you will be asked a number of configuration options such as the role of your CA (Standalone vs Enterprise, and root or subordinate). If you select a Root CA, you will be asked to type in identifying information such as the name you want to give your CA and company details, the lifetime of the certificate (choose a long lifetime for the root CA and a shorter lifetime for subordinates), the key length (it is suggested you choose at least 1024), and where you want to store Certificate Services information. If all has gone well, you should then be able to load up the Certificate Authority MMC and see a display similar to the one shown in Figure 7.15.

If you are installing a subordinate CA, you will need to supply the root CA's name. If the root CA server is on the network it will attempt to find it and display the Parent CA name. You can request to send your certificate request online or save to a file. If you are unsure how to process an offline request and need to do so, refer to the section on Installing The Web Server's Certificate Offline with a Standalone CA later in this chapter.

Figure 7.15 Example of a Root Certificate Authority Called Company

Server Certificates

Before you can use certificates on your Web server, there are two server certificates that you must have. The first is for your Certificate Authority itself, and the second is for the Web server. You must have two different certificates for these two different functions—even if both reside on the same server.

If you install a subordinate CA, you will need to install a server certificate on your subordinate CA issued by the root CA. However, if you install your own root CA, the installation of your Root CA will automatically sign and issue this certificate for you. Figure 7.16 shows an example of a self-signed root CA certificate, which you view by right-clicking on your root server in the Certification Authority MMC, Properties, General tab and then selecting the View Certificate.

Once the CA is authorized by having its own certificate, it can now issue certificates to other computers and users. Now you can issue a certificate to your Web server so that it can authenticate user certificates. Without the Web server's certificate, the View Certificate and Edit buttons under the Secure communication section of the Directory Security tab will remain disabled.

One of the new IIS wizards is the **Web Server Certificate Wizard**, which helps to automate the requesting and deploying of Web server certificates. It's certainly an improvement on using IIS4's Key Manager. This wizard, though, is rather hampered when using a Standalone CA because you cannot request the certificate online, making it rather cumbersome to install. However, it's a one-off process, and once achieved it will get your Web site up and running with SSL.

Figure 7.16 Example of a Root CA Certificate

If you need help requesting a certificate offline, refer to the next section, which details how to install a Web server certificate offline. Installing a subordinate CA certificate can be done in much the same manner.

Installing the Web Server's Certificate Offline with a Standalone CA

The Web Server Certificate Wizard starts off so promising when you select the Server Certificate button under the Web site's Directory Security tab and choose the **Create a new certificate**. You can then select only the **Prepare the request now but send it later** option, which asks you for some identifying information and the length of the key requested. At the end, you save the request to a file with a .txt extension. This is known as a PKCS#10 certificate request file, which contains all the information needed to issue your certificate.

You then need to request your certificate outside IIS. Load the browser and type in **http://<computer_name>/certsrv**, which takes you to the Windows 2000 Certificate Services Web form, as seen in Figure 7.17. In this example, IIS and Certificate Services are running on the same machine, which means localhost can be used instead of the computer name.

When you select Request a certificate, the next screen asks you which type of certificate you're requesting. The default is **User certificate request** for a

Web Browser Certificate. Because you need to install a computer certificate and not a user certificate, this default is not appropriate, so you need to select **Advanced Request** and then the middle option, **Submit a certificate request using a base64 encoded PKCs #10 file**. This refers to your saved .txt file. Click on **Next** and use Internet Explorer to locate and load your text file, copy its contents, and paste it into the Web form's Saved Request entry, as shown in Figure 7.18.

Figure 7.17 The Windows 2000 Certificate Services Web Form

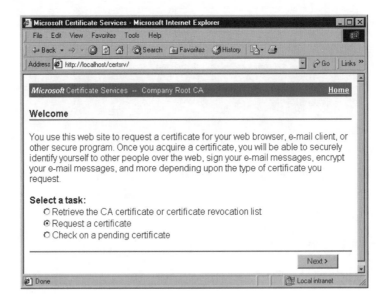

NOTE

When submitting the certificate request offline, you can use the **Browser for a file to insert** option shown in Figure 7.18 only if you change your IE security settings by adding this page to your list of trusted sites which also requires turning off the SSL requirement for all trusted sites. A browser is not supposed to access your hard disk which is a sensible choice. My advice would be to keep your browser security settings and copy/paste as described here.

Submit this and you will be told your certificate request is Pending. You should now see under your CA's Pending Requests folder an entry waiting to be granted, which you do by right-clicking on it and selecting **All Tasks | Issue**.

Figure 7.18 Submitting the Web Server's Certificate Request Offline

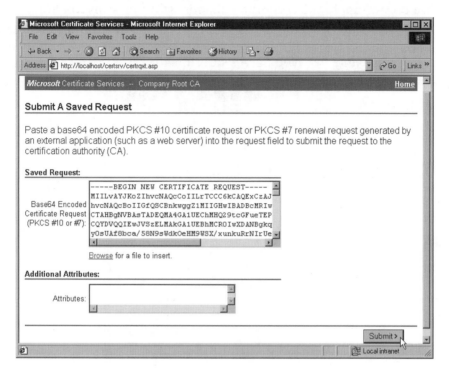

Go back into IIS and load up the Web Server Certificate Wizard again to install your Web server's now issued certificate. Once you have successfully installed it, the View Certificate and Edit button should then become available. You can check the validity of the certificate by selecting the View Certificate button. It will look similar to Figure 7.19 on the following page and this time you can see that the **Issued to** and **Issued by** are different, which confirms that this certificate is indeed different from the previously installed certificate on the same machine.

How Users Request and Manage Certificates

In order to use certificates on your Web server, a user has to be issued with a certificate from your Web server. A user has three different built-in resources for managing certificates (obviously you could extend these with your own programs). These include the Web forms we saw earlier, Internet Explorer's Internet Options, and the Windows 2000 Certificates MMC snap-in.

The browser-based Web forms are obviously suitable for all platforms and across the Internet. To request a user certificate for authentication on a Web site, the user will need to type in **http://<computer_name>/certsrv.** To request a certificate, the user should select the default User Web browser certificate. The user will need to supply the certificate's identification information because a Standalone CA cannot use templates to supply this information for the user.

Figure 7.19 Viewing the Web Server's Certificate

The Submit request should result in a Pending certificate on your CA server, which you must manually issue after checking that all the supplied details are satisfactory (you should deny the certificate if the details are not satisfactory). To retrieve the certificate, the user uses the same Web pages and this time selects to check on a pending certificate request. When the certificate has been issued, the user can install it for use.

The Internet Explorer configuration allows a user to view and manage certificates, but not request them. Under Internet Options, Content, Certificates button they will see a list of certificates installed on their PC, similar to Figure 7.20, which shows the top certificate as suitable for client authentication (for example, on a Web server). From here a user can view the certificate details, export it to a file, and import a certificate (for example, if issued from a CA that wasn't online).

A user running Windows 2000 Professional can also manage certificates directly from Users and Passwords, Advanced tab. From here the user can view, delete, and import/export certificates. For more advanced options and for servers running Windows 2000, you can also load the Certificates MMC snap-in (Figure 7.21) to manage certificates for the Current User, Services, and Computer. Despite this looking as though you can request a certificate from here (right-clicking on **Certificates—Current User | Personal | Certificates** and selecting **All Tasks | Request New Certificate**)—this option works only with Enterprise CAs. Similarly, because Certificate Services are so interwoven with Active Directory, the majority of options using these utilities will be applicable only if you are running Active Directory and using an Enterprise CA.

Figure 7.20 Internet Explorer 5 Showing the Computer's Installed Certificates

Figure 7.21 Windows 2000 Certificates MMC Snap-In which Has Limited Use Outside Active Directory

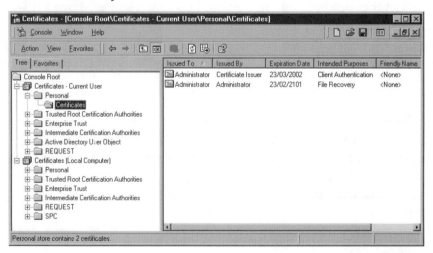

Designing & Planning...

Automating Certificate Requests

There is a CA option to automatically issue certificates without this need for an administrator to manually check and issue certificates, and without the resulting delay for the user. Set this option under the CA's Properties, Policy Module, Configure button and change the Default Action to be **Always issue the certificate**. Obviously, you would need to check credentials before issuing just any certificate, but there's no reason why this couldn't be scripted with your own customization. Similarly you could use your own methods for clients to request a certificate rather than relying on these built-in Windows Web forms.

You may find the following Microsoft links helpful for developing custom enrollments:

- **Certificate Enrollment Control:** http://msdn.microsoft .com/library/psdk/certsrv/xen_portal_6vtx.htm

- Certificate Services Web Enrollment: http://msdn.microsoft .com/library/psdk/certsrv/crtsv_using_3cj7.htm

Using Secure Communication (SSL) on the Web Server

Once your Web server has a certificate, you can configure the use of client certificates for authentication and encryption. This hasn't changed from IIS4, and your choices as shown in Figure 7.22 include using 128-bit encryption, accepting or requiring client certificates, enabling client certificate mapping, and enabling the certificate trust list.

WARNING

If you set the Require 128-bit encryption and clients connect with a valid certificate but with a browser that cannot support 128-bit encryption, they will not be able to connect. Note also that this option is available even if your IIS5 computer does not support 128-bit itself. Select this option with care!

Figure 7.22 Configuring the Web Server for Certificates

Client Certificate Mapping

Client certificate mapping allows you to map an issued certificate to a Windows user account. This is useful when you want to restrict access further than just the site access with NTFS on particular files and directories, for example. When you need more control with NTFS permissions, you must map certificates to user accounts because NTFS recognizes only accounts when restricting access, not certificates.

Client mappings can be either one-to-one (one certificate maps to a specific user account) or one-to-many (where multiple certificates map to just one Windows account). When defining many-to-one mappings, you will need to define rules so that the Web server can determine whether a supplied certificate should map to an account.

Although one-to-one mappings are the easiest to understand, many-to-one mappings are invariably more practical for a pubic Web site. Just as you wouldn't grant access to individual users but to a group, so it is easier to define a user account that a logical group of users can share.

For example, if you ran a Web site that needed to distinguish between non-subscribers and two different levels of subscribers, you could use anonymous access for non-subscribers and SSL for subscribers. Because you have two different levels of subscription, create two user accounts and then map each certificate you issue against the appropriate account. Should a user change subscription levels, you simply change the mapping from one account to the other. This makes it much easier to control than if each user had his or her own account.

Another benefit of using many-to-one mappings is that you don't have to use exported certificates, which is not the easiest procedure in the world!

Designing & Planning...

Mapping Considerations

Other considerations when deciding whether to use one-to-one or many-to-one mappings include security and flexibility. Usually these come at a cost to each other, and this is no exception.

One-to-one mapping is more secure than many-to-one because the user's certificate is actually checked (which is why it needs to be exported), whereas many-to-one mapping does not actually check the validity of the certificate. It simply looks out for matching fields.

The flip side to this is that should the user certificate expire and a new one be issued, the one-to-one mapping will need to be reconfigured for the new certificate whereas the many-to-one mapping will still work because it's not checking the validity of the certificate—just certain fields that will stay the same on different issues of the certificate.

Configuring One-to-One Account Mappings

This section will make the assumptions that you already have issued a certificate to a user and that you have created a user account you want to use for IIS.

One-to-one mappings require that the user's certificate be exported so that you can import it for the mapping. You can export the certificate from the client's PC using Internet Explorer's Internet Options, Contents, Certificates and then choosing the certificate to export and selecting the Export button. If the user is running Windows 2000 he or she can also export certificates by using the Certificates MMC. However, if you're configuring client mappings for a public Web service, neither of these is practical. Instead, you need to be able to do this from the server itself.

You export certificates on the Certificate Server by selecting the appropriate certificate under the Issued Certificates. The certificate will be easier to identify if you do this as soon as you issue the certificate from a Pending state. Double-click the certificate (or right-click and select Open), which will confirm to whom it was issued under the General tab. Click the Details tab, and then click the Copy to File button. This loads the Certificate Export Wizard. When asked which format you want, select **Base-64 encoded x.509 (.cer),** as shown in Figure 7.23, and then when you click Next, save the .CER file to a suitable location. It might be a good idea to create a directory especially for exported certificates.

Figure 7.23 Exporting a Certificate

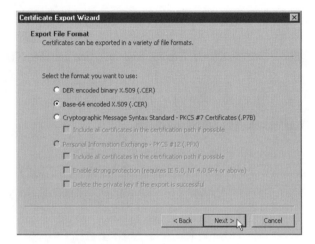

Once you have your exported certificate, you can go back into IIS's Secure Communication dialog box, **Enable client certificate mapping**, select **Edit**, and under the 1-to-1 tab, select the **Add** button. This will prompt you to locate your saved exported certificate. You will then be asked to select a name for the mapping (so you can easily identify it), together with the account name and its password. An example is shown in Figure 7.24.

Figure 7.24 Example of Configuring a One-to-One Certificate Mapping

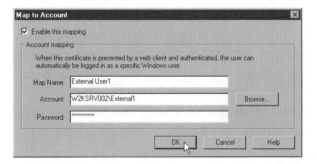

Once you OK this, the mapping should now show in the 1-to-1 dialog box, with the details of the Mapping Name and Windows Account on the left and certificate details displayed on the right for the selected mapping. Figure 7.25 shows an example of this. You simply repeat these steps for each certificate you want to map to each user account. Then you can restrict particular access with NTFS permissions by using your mapped account.

Figure 7.25 Example of How Your One-to-One Certificate Mapping Might Look

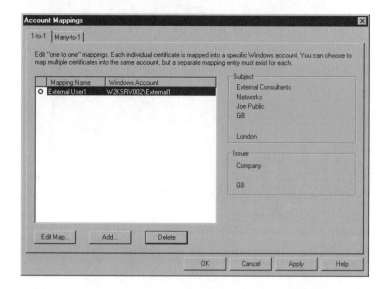

Configuring Many-to–One Account Mappings

This section will also make the assumption that you already have issued a certificate to a user and that you have created a user account to use for IIS.

Even though this many-to-one account mapping may look more complicated at first , it's much easier than one-to-one mapping. In the Many-to-1 dialog box, click **Add** where you will be asked for a Matching Rule name. This is for your reference only, and obviously it's more important to specify a distinguishing name if you plan on having many different rules for when you want to map certificates to accounts.

You will then have to define your rule, which simply means choosing a field and value in the certificate you want to use as identifying a particular certificate. You can use either the user's details (subject) or the CA details (issuer) and use various fields such as Organization, Department, Country/Region, State, or City.

As an example, we can see from our Joe Public's certificate that his Company is called External Consultants, his department is Networks, his city is London, and his country is Great Britain. We could use any of these (with wildcards for the values), or we could simply use the details of our CA and define the Issuer as **Company**, as shown in Figure 7.26.

Figure 7.26 Example of Configuring a Many-to-One Certificate Rule

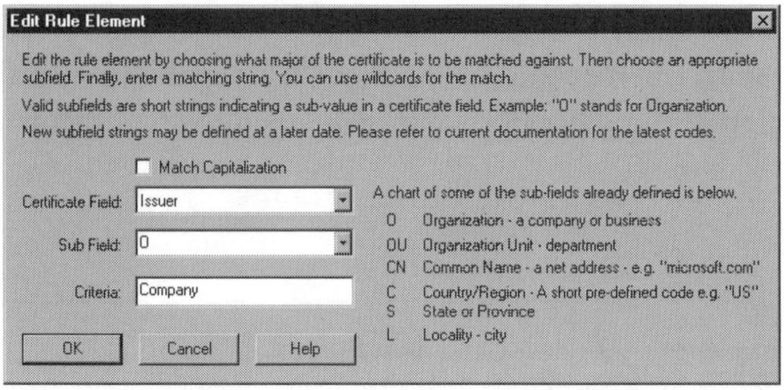

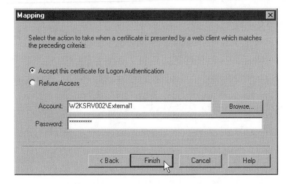

You can add multiple rules like this. For example, the next one saying the subject must be in London. When you have defined the rules you want, you must map them to an account similarly to the one discussed previously. Only this time, you also get the chance to refuse access, as seen in Figure 7.27.

Figure 7.27 Example of Configuring a Many-to-One Certificate Mapping

When you click on Finish (and confirm the password) you should then see an entry for your rule and Windows Account. To go back and edit or view these details, click the **Edit Rule** button, where a tabbed dialog box lets you go back over your choices.

Walkthrough: Configuring Multiple Web Sites on a Single Web Server

This walkthrough takes you through a common procedure for public Web servers—creating a new Web site using an additional IP address. IIS is well suited to hosting multiple sites, and there are a number of ways to achieve this including different IP address, different port address, and host header names. Using host headers is the most elegant solution if you are sure your browsers support this feature, so it is more appropriate for intranet Web servers. On a public Web site where the support for host headers cannot be assumed it is standard practice to use multiple IP addresses.

> **NOTE**
>
> Internet Explorer 3.0, Netscape Navigator 2.0, and later versions of both browsers support the use of host header names. Older browsers do not. Additionally, you cannot use host headers with SSL because the host header will be encrypted—this is an important point for Web servers using SSL for additional security.

Although you can follow this walkthrough with a Web server that's connected to the Internet, you can also use it on your intranet Web server because the concepts and procedures are identical. This walkthrough will use an internal Web server with just one adapter, but you can equally apply the same procedures to a public Web server with multiple adapters. The steps this walkthrough covers include the following:

- Adding a IP address to the Web server

- Creating a new Web site to use the second address

- Configuring the default Web site to use only the original address

- Testing the new Web site by address and name

1. The first thing we need to do is add a IP address to the Web server, which you do through the TCP/IP properties. On a Windows 2000 computer there are many ways to get to the TCP/IP properties; one way is to right-click **My Network Places** on the desktop, which takes you

straight into **Network and Dial-up Connections** where you should see your network adapter(s). Right-click the adapter you want to use, and select **Properties**. Double-click the **Internet Protocol (TCP/IP)** component, ensure that you have a static address defined similar to Figure 7.28, and then select the **Advanced** button.

Figure 7.28 TCP/IP Properties

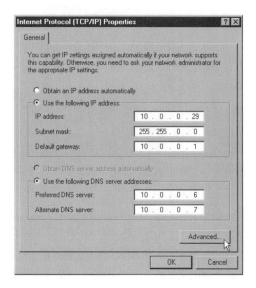

2. The **Advanced TCP/IP Settings** dialog box has tabs for **IP Settings**, **DNS**, **WINS**, and **Options**. Under the **IP Settings** tab you'll see your IP address and mask listed in the **IP addresses** section. Underneath this, click the **Add** button and type in the new IP address you want to use with your Web server. For this walkthrough, type in a free address on the same subnet as your original IP address. For example, this walkthrough will be using **10.0.0.30** with the subnet mask of **255.255.0.0**, which we are adding to our existing address of 10.0.0.29 with the same mask. Once you have typed in the second address and mask, click **Add** and you should now see both addresses listed in the **IP Settings** tab, similar to Figure 7.29.

3. Click **OK** to close this dialog box, **OK** to close the **Internet Protocol (TCP/IP) Properties** dialog, and **OK** to close the adapter properties, and close the **Network and Dial-up Connections**. From a command prompt, run **ipconfig** to ensure that both addresses have been successfully registered on the computer.

Figure 7.29 Additional IP Address Added

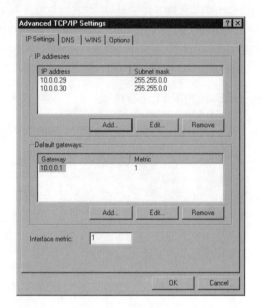

4. We now need to create the directory structure and files that will make up our new Web site. Usually your in-house Web developers will do this for you; or you can do this with an install program. For the purposes of this walkthrough, we'll manually create a new directory and copy some files into it. To do this, load **Explorer** and navigate to **\Inetpub\ wwwroot**. Select just a few files in this folder, then right-click and select **Copy**. Create a new folder in the **Inetpub** directory called **TestWeb** and paste your copied files into it (open the **TestWeb** folder and right-click **Paste**). It really doesn't matter which files you put in your new directory—they will be used only for display (as you will see later), rather than executed. Close Explorer.

5. Load up IIS by clicking **Start | Programs | Administrative Tools | Internet Services Manager** and click on your server's name in the left pane. You may not have all the IIS components installed (for example, FTP and SMTP), but you should see, as in Figure 7.30, that all Internet services are currently configured to use **All Unassigned** addresses, which means all IIS services are now currently listening on both of your IP addresses.

Figure 7.30 IIS Configured to Use All Unassigned IP Addresses

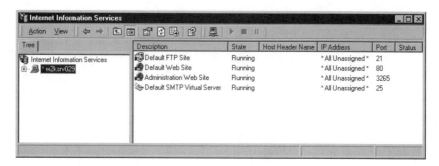

6. We want to add a new Web site, so right-click on your server in the left pane and select **New**, **Web site**. This loads the Web Site Creation Wizard. Click on **Next**.

7. On the **Web Site Description** page, type in an appropriate description (for example, **Test Web site for alternative IP address**), and click **Next**.

8. The **IP Address and Port Settings** page is where you specify your second IP address. For the **Enter the IP address to use for this Web site** use the drop-down list box to select the IP address you entered in Step 2, as shown in Figure 7.31.

Figure 7.31 Selecting the Alternative IP Address

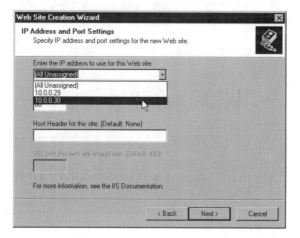

9. Click **Next**. On the Web Site Home Directory page, use the **Browse** button to specify the **TestWeb** folder, as shown in Figure 7.32.

Figure 7.32 Browsing for the New Web Site Directory

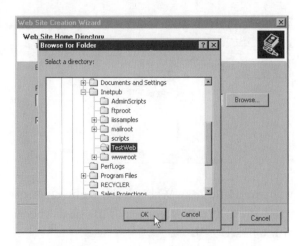

10. Keep selected **Allow anonymous access** to this Web site, and click on **Next**.

11. On the **Web Site Access Permissions** page, keep the defaults of **Read** and **Run scripts (such as ASP),** but we'll also add **Browse** as in Figure 7.33. Web sites don't often use Browse, but for the purpose of this walkthrough it allows us to easily identify this new site when testing.

Figure 7.33 Adding Browse Permission to the New Web Site

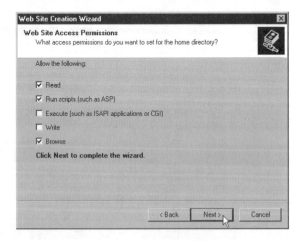

12. Click **Next** and **Finish**.

13. Back at the Internet Information Services MMC, you should now be able to see your new Web site listed, with your specific IP address displayed under the **IP Address** column, similar to Figure 7.34.

Figure 7.34 IIS Configured with New Web Site That Uses a Specific IP Address

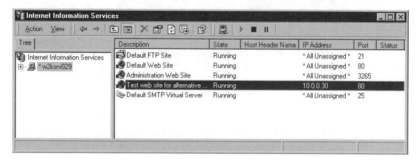

14. We must now change the Default Web Site so that it's no longer listening on both addresses, but just on the original IP address. To do this, right-click on **Default Web Site**, **Properties**. On the **Web Site** tab, change the **IP Address** from **(All Assigned)** to be the original IP address your Web server had, as shown in Figure 7.35.

Figure 7.35 Changing the Default Web Site's IP Address

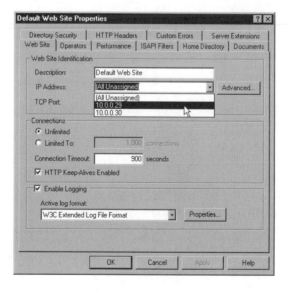

15. Click **OK**, and you should see the Default Web Site's IP Address update immediately in the Internet Information Services MMC, as shown in Figure 7.36. There's no need to stop/restart the service.

Figure 7.36 IIS Default Web Site Changed to Use a Specific Address

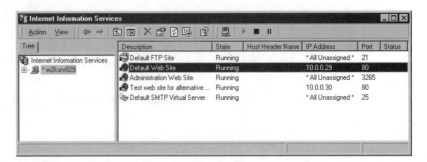

16. Note that you may similarly want to change which IP address is used on other IIS services. For example, your FTP service. When All Unassigned is used, the service will answer on all IP addresses that have been configured on your server.

17. We're now ready to test both Web sites. Assuming that your browser will accept local IP addresses in the address bar, load Internet Explorer on the Web server and type in your first IP address (**10.0.0.29** in our example). Note that if you are using a Proxy Server, you may have to first add your local network address to the Proxy Server Exceptions in Internet Explorer—you cannot use the server's NetBIOS name for this exercise. If you don't have your own Web site configured, this will display the default pages—localstart.asp when loaded locally, as shown in Figure 7.37.

18. Now load Internet Explorer, and type in the second IP address— 10.0.0.30 in our example. You should see a directory listing of the files you copied into this directory, similar to Figure 7.38. This proves that you're connecting to two different sites.

19. Because users connecting to a production server use Internet names rather than IP addresses, you would now need to add a new DNS host entry for your second site, giving it a new host name that resolves to your second IP address. This needs to be configured on the same DNS server that currently holds your Web server's www host entry which may be your own DNS server, or your ISP's DNS server. Because public Web sites use www as the host name, you will need to specify different

domain names for your two (or more) Web sites. If you decide to use a new domain name, ensure that it is registered for use on the Internet.

Figure 7.37 Connecting to the First IP Address

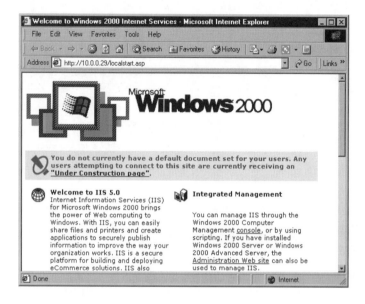

Figure 7.38 Connecting to the Second IP Address

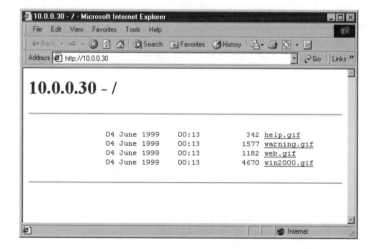

20. If you want to quickly test the two sites internally with DNS names, create entries in your local HOSTS file (found under **%Systemroot%\ System32\drivers\etc**) similar to Figure 7.39. Typing in the DNS names should then produce Internet Explorer displays similar to Figure 7.40.

Figure 7.39 Configuring the Hosts File to Test Both Web Sites with DNS Names

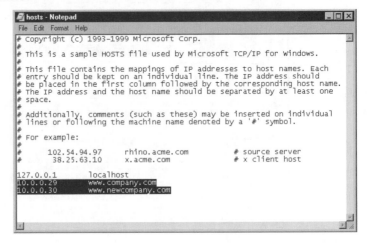

Figure 7.40 Using DNS Names to Connect to Both Web Sites

Summary

This chapter covered the new features in IIS5, which included improvements in reliability, administration and management, security, performance, and the new feature called WebDAV for document collaboration. Because Certificate Services is so closely integrated with IIS for SSL and client authentication, we also extensively covered setting up and configuring a standalone Certificate Authority so that you can control and issue certificates for your Web server and Web clients.

We saw how many of the new features are rather hidden, and while their default settings will provide overall better performance and reliability, some do come with limitations or configuration options that you should be aware of.

Security has always been a priority with Internet servers, and you can now use the new Security Settings Permission Wizard, the Security Configuration Tool, the Web server template, and the Certificate Wizard and Certificate Trust Lists Wizard to help make this job easier. As before, you can still permit/block on IP address/domain and use NTFS permissions on the files and directories. Some of the new authentication protocols (Kerberos when used with Windows Integrated and Digest) can be used only in an Active Directory environment.

The use of certificates with Web services offers a compelling choice for both strong authentication and encryption (SSL) for when Web servers are to be used over the Internet. There are some limitations to installing Windows 2000 Certificate Services outside an Active Directory (for example, no automatic computer enrollment or being able to request a certificate from within the Certificates snap-in), but this setup does offer considerable benefits and ultimately can be seen as more secure.

Although you can use a third-party Certificate Authority to provide the Web server certificate and client certificates, you will have more flexibility and control if you run your own CA. Many references on this subject assume you are running Active Directory and therefore provide poor advice and instruction on how to do this with a Standalone CA. As such, this chapter covered how to set up your own Standalone CA and how to issue a certificate for the Web server and clients. It also covered the steps required to map client certificates to Windows accounts.

Solutions Fast Track

Installing IIS5

☑ IIS5 is much easier to install than IIS4 because it's now integrated into the base operating system rather than requiring a separate installation.

☑ On both Windows 2000 Server and Professional you have the Internet Service Manager MMC snap-in to configure IIS services, and additionally Professional includes Personal Web Manager (PWM) for a simplified interface to the Web service.

☑ Although the Internet Service Manager looks the same on both Professional and Server, the version that installs on Professional doesn't include the more server-centric features such as the ability to create virtual sites, restricting access by IP address or domain, operators, HTLM administration, ODBC database logging, and some of the new performance features such as HTTP compression and throttling.

☑ Installing IIS5 no longer prompts you for root directories. There could be good reasons why you don't want to use the default paths. You can specify your non-default paths on an unattended installation, change them after the install, or choose to upgrade your existing IIS4 that already has the non-default paths.

Improvements in Reliability

☑ Application protection now allows you to configure a midway compromise between efficiency and reliability with the new Pooled Process application setting. This is identified as "Medium (Pooled)" under the site's Home Directory Application Protection.

☑ IISreset is a simple but powerful command that can control all the IIS services as one such that you can stop and start all IIS services without having to reboot the server. But you can also choose to reboot with this command if you prefer. You can issue this command locally from the Internet Information Service snap-in or from a command line. When using it from the command line you can use this on local and remote servers, enable/disable this service, and set additional options such as a timeout period to reboot.

☑ You can now back up and restore IIS settings to/from the metabase from within the Internet Information Service snap-in, which makes it very easy to return to a known, stable state.

☑ FTP restart allows an FTP client to resume an interrupted transfer so that the whole file doesn't need to retransfer. This helps reduce bandwidth and processing on the server and makes for more efficient transfers on the client side to help combat unreliable links.

Improvements in Administration and Management

☑ The Internet Service Manager can be combined with other snap-ins in the same MMC so that you have one central utility for configuring your Internet services (for example, disk management, local group policy, etc).

☑ Wizards and tools help guide you through setup and configuration. The Security Settings Permission Wizard can be used to set permissions based on two different templates (one designed for a secure intranet and another for a public Internet site), or it can be used to propagate permissions from the parent directory down onto the child directories to ensure a consistent policy.

☑ The Internet Server Security Configuration Tool can be downloaded free of charge to help you tightly secure a public Web server that is on a Windows 2000 standalone server. This uses a template for highly secured Web servers, together with the answers you supply about what services and ports should be allowed. Note that you can download and use the template independently if you prefer.

☑ The Certificate Wizard and Certificate Trust Lists Wizard help when you want to use certificates for authentication, and the IIS Migration Wizard from the Resource Kits helps you to migrate Web servers from Netscape Enterprise and Apache to IIS5.

☑ Other improvements include using Process Accounting logging and a redesigned remote administration Web interface.

Improvements in Security

☑ In addition to the Permissions Wizard and Security Configuration Tool, you can secure access by IP address/domain name, NTFS file permissions, certificates, and other authentication methods.

☑ NT Challenge/Response has been replaced with Windows Integrated, which includes both NTLM as before and Kerberos for when running in an Active Directory network.

☑ Digest is a new authentication protocol in IIS5 that, unlike Windows Integrated, will work across firewalls and proxy servers, but it is not available outside Active Directory.

☑ Support for Fortezza is now provided for U.S. government and military services.

Improvements in Performance

☑ HTTP compression helps to reduce bandwidth and therefore download times for clients that support this feature. You can choose to compress just static data, just dynamic data, or both. You can also choose where to cache the data on the Web server and the maximum size of the cache.

☑ A number of ASP improvements have been added to IIS5 to help enhance performance and streamline server-side scripting.

☑ Bandwidth and process throttling can ensure that a single service does not hog all the available resources so that other IIS services cannot run efficiently.

☑ IIS5 now pools all ports with the same number together (e.g., port 80), which requires less memory when running multiple sites.

Document Collaboration with WebDAV

☑ WebDAV (Web Distributed Authoring and Versioning) allows users to modify and share documents on a Web server.

☑ Microsoft Office 2000 applications and desktop applications are also WebDAV-aware so that they can use a WebDAV-enabled Web site just as it was another file server.

☑ While very flexible and extending the capabilities of a Web server to be another file server, WebDAV does expose your Web server to a higher security risk.

Certificate Services

☑ Certificate Services in Windows 2000 offers another authentication service (in addition to Kerberos and NTLM) that can be fully integrated with third-party companies. This includes certificates for EFS and IPSec as well as authenticating Web clients and offering a secure Web link with SSL.

☑ You can use a third-party Certificate Authority, or your own—or you can mix the two. When installing your own CA you can install a Standalone CA only if you are not running Active Directory. You can choose to install an Enterprise CA only in an Active Directory environment which then provides benefits of certificate templates, computer auto-enrollment, native smart card logon, and securely issuing certificates on demand.

☑ In a large organization that intends to use certificates extensively, you can employ a hierarchical setup with a root CA, subordinate CAs, and then issuing CAs.

☑ Before you can use certificates to authenticate Web clients, the Web server and client must have a trusted CA certificate in common, a Web server certificate, and client certificates. You can map a client's certificate to a single Windows account or map multiple certificates to a single account.

Frequently Asked Questions

The following Frequently Asked Questions, answered by the author of this book, are designed to both measure your understanding of the concepts presented in this chapter and to assist you with real-life implementation of these concepts. To have your questions about this chapter answered by the author, browse to **www.syngress.com/solutions** and click on the **"Ask the Author"** form.

Q: On our IIS4 servers, as a matter of security we used to delete the ISUR_<computer name> accounts and create our own that had less obvious names. They keep reappearing on our IIS5 server—what's going on?

A: Although you can still use alternative accounts for anonymous access, you can no longer delete the default accounts! Every time you load IIS it checks to see if the default accounts exist and if not, it creates them. Because each account has its own SID, this is most dangerous if a site is configured to use anonymous access and then the anonymous account is deleted. On the next IIS restart the account will be recreated in name only—its SID will be different, and the old site will look as if it should work, but it won't. If you don't want to use the default IIS accounts, your best bet is to disable them rather than regularly delete them and remember to always specify your alternative IIS account instead.

Q: On our Web server we have five different Web sites that we run for our customers. Each site requires its own access privileges, but we don't want the hassle of setting up accounts and asking the user to log in or issuing certificates. Any suggestions?

A: Sounds as if you need Anonymous Access, but with the ability to specify different access permissions on each site. That can be accomplished with multiple anonymous user accounts (in your case, five—one for each site). Then specify which account should be used with which site.

Q: We want to offer an FTP server so that customers can upload certain files to us, but we don't want them to be able to see what other customers have transferred to us. Do we need multiple FTP sites for this?

A: Not at all. Use Write but not Read for your user accounts, and make sure internal accounts (for example, the Administrator) have Read permission to see all uploaded files.

Q: What's Server-Gated Cryptography that I hear IIS5 can support?

A: This will not be available on your IIS5 server unless you install a special SGC certificate that has been issued by one of the CAs authorized to issue SGC certificates. Server-Gated Cryptography support is an extension to Secure Sockets Layer (SSL) which is provided for financial institutions that can use a strong 128-bit encryption. A SGC certificate must be issued to both the client and server, or the connection reverts to just SSL.

Q: Do Microsoft certificates adhere to an open standard, or are they proprietary?

A: Most digital certificates in use are now based on the X509 standard set by ITU-T and Microsoft uses X509 version 3, which allows interoperability with many other products and technologies that support public key cryptography.

Q: Is the default length of 512 bits suitable for our internal CA?

A: Probably not. Particularly if this is your root CA, it should be at least 1024 and perhaps even higher. Having a longer key length means you can afford to have a longer expiry time so you don't have to renew too often and risk the certificate being compromised. For a large company with a hierarchical CA infrastructure, Microsoft suggests a key length of 4096 and 20 years for a standalone root CA, 3072 and 10 years for intermediate CAs, 1024 key length and 2 years for Web servers, and 1 year for browser certificates. However, there are no hard and fast rules on this. It will depend on the level of security you want at the price of maintenance overhead and processing to produce the certificates. The only rule is abiding by the hierarchy—you cannot set a key length/lifetime that is higher than the level above. For example, you couldn't use a Web server certificate of 1024 bits valid for 5 years if your issuing CA had a bit length of 512 and was valid for 2 years.

Q: How much disk space does Certificate Services take up?

A: Allow about 1KB–20 KB per request. Therefore, up to 100 certificates requires between 200KB and 2GB, and up to 1,000 certificates requires between 2GB and 20 GB.

Chapter 8

Secure Communication

Solutions in this chapter:

- IPSec Planning—Working Out What You Want to Secure and How

- IP Security Utilities—For Configuring and Monitoring Secure Communication

- IPSec Built-In Policies—For Minimal Administrator Configuration

- IPSec Policy Components

- IP Security Protocols and Algorithms

- ☑ Walkthrough 8.1: Setting and Testing Custom IPSec Policies

- ☑ Walkthrough 8.2: Using IPSec to Protect a Web Server

- ☑ Summary

- ☑ Solutions Fast Track

- ☑ Frequently Asked Questions

Introduction

The need for secure communication over the Internet is always a hot topic because people need to encrypt sensitive information (for example credit card details) as it travels from computer to computer, and secure their computers from malicious attacks over the network. Accordingly, we use firewalls, application level security (like SSL for Web access, which was covered in Chapter 7), and accounts with strong password policies. Much less thought is given to traffic inside an internal network, however. Funny how we instinctively distrust people accessing our resources over the Internet and yet hold total trust for anybody who has access to the internal network. Firewalls and application layer security are rarely implemented within a company, unless the network infrastructure travels over WAN links. But many corporations have such good links between remote sites that they equate a LAN-grade network with LAN-grade low security and rarely think about the dangers of internal communication.

In fact, it's incredibly easy to get hold of a network analyzer and capture data as it travels over the network. You don't even have to be a comms expert these days to decode packets of hex data—the analyzers invariably do it for you (as we shall see in our walkthrough later). Such captured data can then be read, altered in transit, or replayed later. So all your attempts to physically secure machines, employ strong authentication with secure policies, and use EFS and NTFS permissions can count for very little if your data is exposed as it travels the network. Wouldn't it be great if you could protect it without having to buy additional software or hardware?

As you're probably aware, Windows 2000 ships with IP Security built into the TCP/IP stack. This allows machines that are running Windows 2000 to securely communicate with each other and authenticate/encrypt the data they transfer. Microsoft has not released IPSec client software for down-level clients such as Windows 98 and Windows NT, so this solution is only applicable for your Windows 2000 computers (and other IPSec-aware devices from other vendors). However, there's no reason why you can't employ IPSec selectively on your network and accordingly prioritize upgrades for computers identified as benefiting from IPSec. For example, this could be as simple as upgrading your Web servers and backend database servers to ensure customer information was kept secure. Or it could apply to a whole department—for example all users in the Accounts Department could be using Windows 2000 Professional with their main file and print server also being a Windows 2000 Server, but they still communicate with non-Windows 2000 computers for nonaccounts-related information.

One of the nice things about using IPSec is its flexibility. You can configure it to only allow secured communication (suitable for those Web and database servers) or you can configure it so that it responds with IPSec security when requested (suitable for those client workstations when connecting to the Accounts server) but won't initiate it (suitable for those client workstations when wanting to talk to NT4 servers such as your domain controllers, WINS servers, etc.). Or you can use *fall back to clear* which means that it will revert back to not requiring IPSec if the other side can't support it (useful if you are in the middle of upgrading your down-level clients to Windows 2000).

There's no doubt that IPSec is a great built-in security feature for Windows 2000. However, implementing it is fraught with complexities as you struggle with the plethora of acronyms and algorithms—to say nothing of coming to grips with the various utilities involved. Too often, discussions on implementing IPSec in Windows 2000 seem to concentrate on the theory side, and not enough on the practical side of implementing it. On top of all that, it is generally assumed you're running within an Active Directory network where Kerberos is used and computers have automatic certificate enrollment.

IPSec can be a very powerful and flexible security tool, so if you have computers running Windows 2000, why not make use of it? I have to admit that using IPSec outside Active Directory isn't exactly intuitive. Either Microsoft didn't want people to do this, or they didn't think people would want to do it. I also didn't find configuring the policies easy with the IP Security Policies snap-in because it's a mass of Russian dolls inside more Russian dolls. But it's worth persevering with, and it's not difficult to implement simple and effective IPSec policies.

This chapter will not provide an in-depth look at the theoretical side of IPSec, but it will guide you through the practicalities of implementing IPSec outside Active Directory for both simple and more complex scenarios. It's then up to you to decide how much of this you want to implement. Always remember security invariably comes at a cost in terms of maintenance (configuring and monitoring) and processing resources on the computers themselves.

IPSec Planning—Working Out What You Want to Secure and How

Despite our usual thinking about secure communication being synonymous with encryption, secure communication is more complex than this and can actually be broken down into the following five components:

- Nonrepudiation
- Anti-Replay
- Integrity
- Confidentiality
- Authentication

Nonrepudiation refers to not only verifying that the sender is who he claims to be, but also that he cannot later deny having sent the message (because only he could have sent it). *Anti-Replay* ensures that each IP packet is unique that protects data from being intercepted and later played back in an attempt to elicit the same response. *Integrity* refers to data being unmodified in transit—typically source or destination IP addresses to prevent spoofing, but can apply equally to the actual data itself. *Confidentiality* equates to encryption—ensuring the data cannot be read as it travels over the network. *Authentication* refers to each side proving they are who they say they are.

Secure communication can mean all or just some of these depending on your security requirements and priorities. If your priority is to prevent IP address spoofing (for example to ensure that all data destined for your server ends up on *your* server and not somebody else's) then you may have no need for encryption that inevitably adds a layer of complexity and additional processing. Similarly, just how strongly you protect your data will depend on what security algorithms are available to both sides and whether using them justifies the additional processing.

NOTE

There may be both political and legal reasons why you should not encrypt data, particularly if it is passing across international boundaries. Do not forget to check this!

Before diving into configuring IPSec, it's important to think ahead and plan first. Identify what data needs to be secured, in what way, how strongly, and on what machines it travels. If the data must pass through non–Windows 2000 computers that cannot support IPSec, think about upgrading these if possible, or consider alternative security measures. For example, not many people realize that you can use PPTP within a network just as effectively as over the Internet when using encryption with your VPN.

When both sides can support IPSec, check whether they can both support 128-bit encryption. Despite export laws being relaxed such that 128-bit versions are now available outside North America and Canada, not every computer is running or can run this version. One of the easiest ways to find out whether your Windows 2000 computer is 56-bit or 128-bit is to go to Internet Explorer's **Help | About**. If the Cipher Strength displays 56-bit, then the machine will not be able to support the stronger security mechanisms such as 3DES. The supplied built-in IP Security policies will negotiate down from the highest security to the lowest allowed, so 56-bit clients can communicate successfully with 128-bit servers.

However, if you want to use the stronger encryption and higher key lengths, upgrade your 56-bit clients to use 128-bit by installing the **High Encryption Pack** (available from the Microsoft site: www.microsoft.com/windows2000/downloads/recommended/encryption/default.asp). But beware that this will also affect EFS, NDIS connections, SSL, and Terminal Services. You cannot uninstall it (for security reasons), so test thoroughly on a nonproduction computer first!

NOTE

Installing Windows 2000 SP2 will also upgrade 56-bit Windows 2000 computers to 128-bit.

Work out whether you want an IPSec-enabled computer to *only* use secured communication (rejecting packets that are not IPSec), only respond with secured communication when requested, or use secured communication only when communicating with another IPSec-enabled computer.

If packet integrity is important to you, work out whether this should apply to IP addresses and ports in addition to the actual user data. Authenticating the IP header (addresses and ports) is more secure, but requires more processing.

Consider whether your secured communication should be on all traffic, to specified machines only (for example, certain IP addresses or a subnet), or only on certain ports. Note that some traffic cannot be secure—which includes broadcasts, multicasts, Kerberos, RSVP (the reservation protocol) and the IPSec protocol itself (ISAKMP). Work out whether you also want to secure ICMP traffic, which is—typically used with *ping*. Not securing ICMP makes it easier to troubleshoot connectivity issues, but because this is a control protocol (for example, redirecting packets) it will potentially leave your computers more vulnerable.

Designing & Planning...

Think Through the Consequences of Implementing Encryption

It's worth throwing in the reminder that if a no-good snooper cannot decode traffic as it traverses your network, neither can a well-intentioned network administrator who's trying to analyze network problems that involve corrupt and missing data. Unlike EFS recovery agents, there is no back door with IPSec except to disable it, which then leaves your network exposed. Often, resorting to a network analyzer to find out exactly where a packet is going awry is the final and definitive recourse for a network administrator—so beware that implementing IPSec could be removing this option from you. This is another good reason to selectively configure IPSec only where justified rather than implementing it throughout the company.

When thinking about authenticating each computer, it's time to throw a wrench into the works. IPSec can authenticate using Kerberos (the default, but not available to you if you're not running Active Directory), certificates, or a password stored in the registry. Before going any further, it's worth outlining the advantages/disadvantages of your two choices when running Windows 2000 with IPSec outside Active Directory.

Password Based

This is more commonly referred to as a *preshared key* in IPSec parlance. You simply type in the same string on both sides when configuring IPSec (Figure 8.1). This is undoubtedly the easiest way to configure IPSec, but it is also the least secure. This is because although the password is never sent across the network, it is stored as plain text (within the local security policy, which is stored within the registry). This means you must take additional steps to protect that setting from being read by unauthorized administrators.

For many people, using this method of authentication will not be adequate and certainly Microsoft itself does not suggest it is used except for testing or where interoperability requires it. But I think it's worth bearing in mind that if Active Directory and certificate authentication is not a viable option, using well secured passwords that are known to only a select few administrators has a lot to offer in the way of securing data. It's certainly very easy to configure and troubleshoot. Despite the dire warnings from official sources, don't reject it out of hand without considering the advantages!

Figure 8.1 Configuring IPSec to Use a Password (Preshared Key) for Authentication

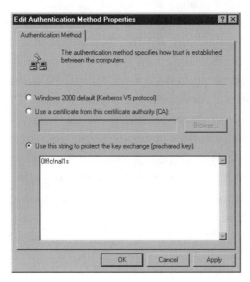

Certificate Based

Just as you can authenticate users on a Web server with digital certificates, you can authenticate computers with certificates when using IPSec. The only criteria are that both have a valid computer certificate (not user certificate unlike Web authentication or EFS) and that they both have a Certificate Authority (CA) in common. This CA can be either a third party (such as VeriSign, Microsoft, or a whole list of other well-known CAs), or your own CA.

> **NOTE**
>
> If you're planning on using IPSec with external customers, either business partners or customers over the Internet, they will probably feel more confident using a third-party Certificate Authority rather than your own internal CA.

Similar to Chapter 7's coverage of running your own CA for Web certificates, this chapter will assume you're running your own CA for IPSec certificates. However, the same principles will still apply if you use a third-party CA (except you'll part with more money, have less control, and have less to configure!).

The advantage of using certificates with IPSec is that it's inherently more secure, and offers interoperability with a wide range of other vendors. The disadvantage is it requires more complex configuration and overhead in terms of management. However, if you are already employing certificates for Web authentication, incorporating IPSec into this ready-made PKI infrastructure isn't such a big step. You can also extend it into your VPN solutions so remote clients use L2TP/IPSec to offer a more secure solution than PPTP.

If you later decide to migrate to Active Directory you can either keep your existing certificate authentication or easily move to Kerberos authentication while retaining the same IPSec policies that define what you want to secure and how. Always remember however, that Active Directory group policies will override local group policies, as discussed in Chapter 2.

It's important to note that when requesting a certificate from Microsoft Certificate Services, any valid computer certificate will suffice if it also has a corresponding CA certificate installed. Although the Advanced options list IPSec as a certificate type, this is effectively ignored by Windows 2000. You cannot currently limit whether a computer certificate will support IPSec or not.

Microsoft advises you to initially test IP Security with one of its certificates, but we'll cover installing the required computer certificates later in this chapter, using your own CA (Figure 8.2).

IP Security Utilities—For Configuring and Monitoring Secure Communication

There are a number of utilities you may need when configuring and monitoring IPSec. Thankfully, because you're not using Active Directory you don't also have Site, Domain, or OU Group Policies to worry about. All IP Security settings are configured locally in the local Computer Group Policy. Local Group Policy was covered in Chapter 2 to explain how this offers an extensive range of local configuration settings for both the user and computer. Although local Group Policy is (as its name suggests) *local*, it is possible to configure and control these settings centrally using security templates (also explained in Chapter 2). You can also export and import IP security policies between computers.

Figure 8.2 Configuring IPSec to Use a Certificate for Authentication

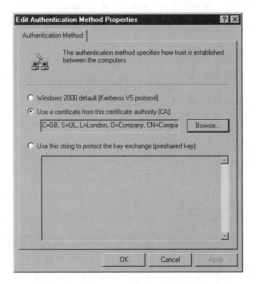

If you are using certificates for IPSec authentication, you will also need the Certificate Authority MMC snap-in we covered in Chapter 7 in order to issue certificates. Otherwise you'll predominately use the following:

- IP Security Policies on Local Machine
- IP Security Monitor
- IPSec Policy Agent Service
- TCP/IP Advanced Options
- Certificates Snap-in (to confirm valid computer certificates if using these for authentication)
- Security Log
- Netdiag Support Tool

Using IP Security Policies on Local Machines

We first saw the computer's Local Security Settings in Chapter 2 when looking at configuring and securing Windows 2000 computers. You can either access the IP Security Policies by loading up **Local Security Policy** under Administrative Tools, or use the Local Group Policy Editor (**gpedit.msc**) and navigate down the tree.

The **IP Security Policies on Local Machine** will be the utility you use most to configure what policies you want, how they are configured, and whether they should be in use. By default no IPSec policy is active on a Windows 2000 computer—a policy has to be specifically assigned. As shown in Figure 8.3, you will see three preconfigured built-in policies that we shall cover later.

Right-clicking on the **IP Security Policies | All Tasks** allows you create a new policy, manage filter lists and actions (covered later), check a policy's integrity, restore the default policies, and import/export policies. The last two options allow you to both backup and restore known, working policies. But perhaps more usefully, they also provide the means of quickly transferring IPSec policies between computers.

Figure 8.3 IPSec Policies Snap-In and Tasks

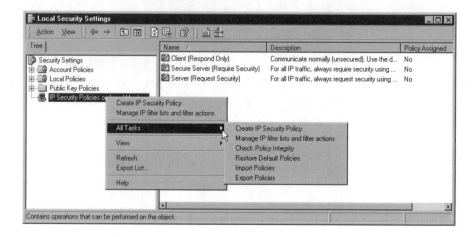

Using IP Security Monitor

This is a rather strange Windows 2000 utility, somewhat lacking in elegance and cohesion when compared with the standard utilities. There's some important information missing from here (which we'll cover later), but it does provide a basic graphical display of what's happening on your computer with regard to IPSec traffic.

You load this from the command prompt, or **Start | Run** and type **ipsecmon <computer_name>**. With no computer name specified, it will default to loading on the local computer. When you are monitoring a remote computer, this will be displayed on the title bar. (For example: **IP Security Monitor on W2KSRV005**. Otherwise a locally monitored computer will simply have **IP Security Monitor** on the title bar.)

Configuring & Implementing…

Command Line Alternative to the IPSec Policy Snap-In

For scripting enthusiasts, you can use the command line **ipsecpol.exe** tool from the Resource Kit which allows you to execute everything the IPSec Policy snap-in offers on both local and remote machines. Additionally, it has two modes of operation. The default is **Dynamic**, which means that any settings are not permanent but only last until the IPSec service (IPSec Policy Agent) is stopped or the machine is rebooted. The other mode is **Static**, which will preserve any changes made to the security policy. Type **ipsecpol.exe –h** for a complete list and description of how to use this scripting interface. Because there are no wizards to help guide you through adding new policies, you must be proficient in knowing exactly how policies work to use this tool.

Firstly it will tell you whether IPSec is currently enabled on the selected computer (bottom right hand corner). If it is and a computer is currently connected using one of your policies that results in transmitting data from the computer, this will be displayed in the active window with limited details such as the security protocols in use, the source and destination computer and so on. If it's using one of the built-in policies, the policy name will be displayed in readable form. However, any new policies you create will be displayed rather unhelpfully as a hex string identifier. We'll see later how to tie this back to the actual policy in use.

The example shown in Figure 8.4 is using a newly created policy called Certificate Policy (not that you'll know!) and you can tell it's currently sending out encrypted data because the Security column lists ESP which is short for **Encapsulating Security Payload**. You can also tell from this display that it has been encrypting data because of the byte count under the Confidential Bytes Sent/Received. At no time since the policy has been loaded has the computer sent any packets that haven't been secured (for example, with down-level clients). You can tell this because the number of Soft Associations (which refers to falling back to unsecured data) is set to zero.

Just why the Minimize button isn't on the title bar, I don't know! And the Options button, despite looking promising, only allows you to adjust the refresh rate from the default of 15 seconds.

Figure 8.4 Example Display When Running the IP Security Monitor

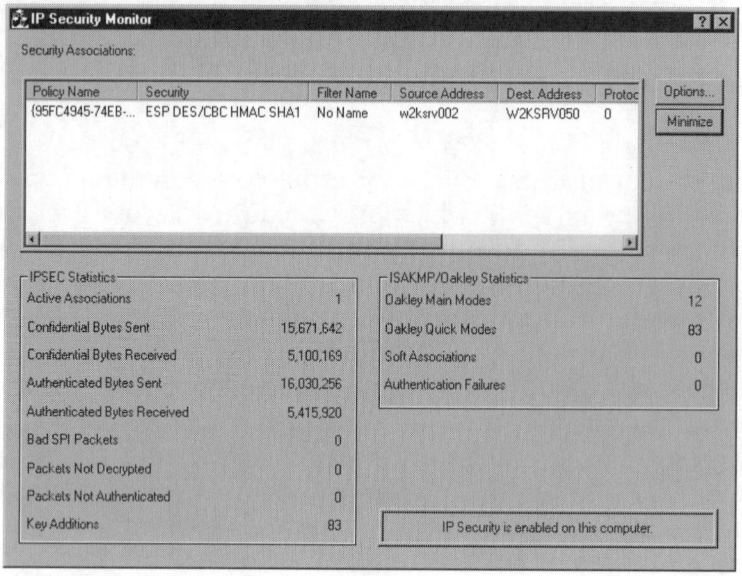

Using the IPSec Policy Agent Service

A Windows 2000 computer will automatically have installed and started the IPSec Policy Agent, which is responsible for retrieving the assigned IP Security Policy (if one is assigned) from the registry and passing the information within the policy to the IPSec driver.

The policy is retrieved at system boot up and checked at regular intervals for any changes (modifications). The default period is every three hours, but you can change this under the policy's **General** tab, as shown in Figure 8.5.

This setting is more relevant if you are running within an Active Directory and are centrally changing IP Security policies across the network or if you want to ensure that any locally changed policies cannot stay in place for a prolonged period of time. It is also relevant if you are centrally updating local group policies with security templates during the day (as covered in Chapter 2). However, in most instances I would have thought that retrieving policy information on a local computer every three hours was an unnecessary waste of processing, so consider increasing this default value on a stable network.

When modifying or changing IPSec values locally, it is recommended you use the **Check policy integrity** option we saw in Figure 8.3 to ensure that the new values have been committed to the registry. However, it's often safer to actually stop and restart the IPSec Policy Agent to ensure the "slate is clean." Although you can do this using the Services snap-in, it's much easier to call up a command prompt and type:

```
Net stop policyagent  #(to stop the service)
Net start policyagent #(to start the service)
```

Figure 8.5 Changing the Default Policy Retrieval Setting

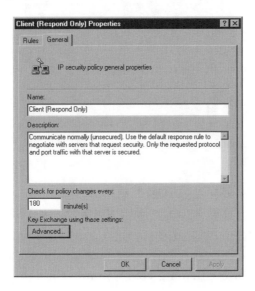

Using TCP/IP Advanced Options

This provides limited access to the IP Security Policies by selecting the **Advanced** button on your adapter's TCP/IP Properties, and then selecting the **Options** tab | **IP security** and then the **Properties** button.

As shown in Figure 8.6, you can see whether IPSec is currently enabled and toggle between using IPSec and not using it. The dropdown list box (**Use this IP security policy**) will display all the available policies with their description displayed directly below.

Figure 8.6 Changing IP Security Policies through TCP/IP Properties

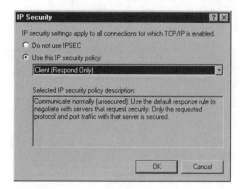

Using Certificates Snap-In

Obviously this is only used if you're using certificates for authentication. Although I said in Chapter 7 that using the Certificates MMC snap-in had limited use outside Active Directory (you can't use it to request a certificate, for example), it is useful for confirming your computer has the correct certificates for IP Security.

You have to load the Certificates snap-in into a new MMC or add it to an existing MMC if you haven't already done this. When adding the snap-in, you'll have the choice of selecting Certificates for the local machine, current user or services. It's important to remember that IP Security uses *computer* certificates, not user certificates, so be sure to choose the **Computer account** option. Remember that security is in effect even when nobody is logged on to the computer and that security is provided at the network layer which is why the certificate has to be a computer certificate rather than service or user.

When deploying IP Security with certificates there are two different folders of interest within the Certificates snap-in. The first is your CA certificate, which must be listed under the **Trusted Root Certification Authorities | Certificates**. The second is your computer's certificate which must be listed under **Personal | Certificates**. We'll step through requesting and using these certificates later.

Using the Security Log

To record IPSec related information in the Security Log, you must first enable Auditing through the **Security Settings | Local Policies | Audit Policy**. We covered local group policies in Chapter 2 if you need more information on how to do this, but essentially you can request auditing for things like account logon events and object access. For IPSec it's a good idea to request both Success and Failure audits so you're equally aware of when IPSec is failing as you are confirming that it's working, and with what security parameters.

When auditing is enabled and an IPSec policy is active, this will record various events such as whether a secure connection was established successfully and what security parameters were in place (for example, details on the certificate used for authentication, whether encrypting, and so on). Equally, when negotiations fail, the reason for this will be recorded. For example, you might see "IKE security association negotiation failed" with a Failure Reason such as "No response from peer."

To understand fully the recorded information in the audit logs, you need a good understanding of the IPSec security protocols, acronyms, and workings, which are covered in the final section of this chapter: **IP Security Protocols and Algorithms**.

The following output lists the full details from two example security events which together record a successful IPSec connection between two computers (10.0.0.2 and 10.0.0.30) using certificates for the computer authentication and using ESP to encrypt and authenticate the actual data:

```
IKE security association established.
 Mode:
Key Exchange Mode (Main Mode)


 Peer Identity:
Certificate based Identity.
Subject GB, UK, London, Company, w2ksrv002
Issuing Certificate Authority GB, UL, London, Company, Company Root CA
Root Certificate Authority GB, UL, London, Company, Company Root CA
Peer IP Address: 10.0.0.2


 Filter:
Source IP Address 10.0.0.30
```

```
Source IP Address Mask 255.255.255.255
Destination IP Address 10.0.0.2
Destination IP Address Mask 255.255.255.255
Protocol 0
Source Port 0
Destination Port 0


 Parameters:
ESP Algorithm DES CBC
HMAC Algorithm SHA
Lifetime (sec) 28800


Destination IP Address Mask 255.255.255.255
Protocol 0
Source Port 0
Destination Port 0


 Parameters:
ESP Algorithm DES CBC
HMAC Algorithm SHA
Lifetime (sec) 28800


IKE security association established.
 Mode:
Data Protection Mode (Quick Mode)


 Peer Identity:
Certificate based Identity.
Subject GB, UK, London, Company, w2ksrv002
Issuing Certificate Authority GB, UL, London, Company, Company Root CA
Root Certificate Authority GB, UL, London, Company, Company Root CA
Peer IP Address: 10.0.0.2


 Filter:
```

```
Source IP Address 10.0.0.30

Source IP Address Mask 255.255.255.255

Destination IP Address 10.0.0.2

Destination IP Address Mask 255.255.255.255

Protocol 0

Source Port 0

Destination Port 0


 Parameters:

ESP Algorithm DES CBC

HMAC Algorithm SHA

AH Algorithm None

Encapsulation Transport Mode

InboundSpi -1862285639

OutBoundSpi -1036219697

Lifetime (sec) 900

Lifetime (kb) 100000
```

Using the Netdiag Support Tool

Netdiag.exe is one of the Windows 2000 Support Tools. More information on its many uses can be found within the **Windows 2000 Support Tools | Tools Help**.

However, specifically for IPSec it can read and display all details of your current IPSec policy (this is where you can match your custom policy name to the long hex string displayed in IP Security Monitor!). Unlike IP Security Monitor, it can display a more accurate reading of your IPSec statistics.

Type **netdiag/test:ipsec/v** for full statistical details of your current IPSec policy, including the name of your custom policy. There's an awful lot of information here, so either scroll through it or redirect the output to a text file.

If you type **netdiag/test:ipsec/debug** you'll see configuration information on the policy in use. Beware that this will include your password in readable format, if using passwords rather than certificates. Figure 8.7 shows a small portion of this output that shows both the policy string, and the password (which in this case is KEY).

Figure 8.7 Example Output of Using Netdiag Showing the Custom Policy Name in Use and the Preshared Key

As you can see, Netdiag is very informative! Fortunately from a security point of view you can only run it locally, and nonadministrators will not be able to see this information. They will see information that displays "IPSec policy service is active, but test failed to get current policy information" with a later "Access is denied."

IPSec Built-In Policies—For Minimal Administrator Configuration

Windows 2000 IPSec comes with three built-in policies that you could decide to use as-is or modify one slightly. They're not ideal because they're not tailored to your particular requirements, but they do offer a good first base, and a quick jump start if you don't have the resources to configure your own policies.

They're certainly worth considering, if only to provide some examples of what you can configure IPSec to do, and how. Note that you cannot delete these, only modify them. However, if you are planning on modifying more than one or two options, it's probably better to create new policies and leave these as reference templates. The one thing you should change however, is the Kerberos authentication. The authentication should be configured for either preshared keys or certificate when used outside Active Directory.

It's a shame you cannot copy an existing built-in policy and rename it, as you can with the security templates. When you change something in one of the default policies, I suggest you document each step so you know how to reproduce it on other computers, and how to backtrack on yourself. It's very easy to lose options within the policies, and assuming you'll remember later what you changed is fatal if you have made multiple modifications! If you really get into a mess with your built-in policies such that you want to revert back to defaults, you can restore the built-in policies to their default values, restore from backup, or even remove TCP/IP and reinstall it. Note that restoring the default policies does not affect any custom policies, filters, or filter actions you have created.

> **NOTE**
>
> The standard advice about suspected corrupt or missing IPSec-related files is to uninstall TCP/IP and reinstall it. Because IPSec is inherently supported within the TCP/IP stack, this will reinstall all IPSec-related files and reinstate defaults. However, this step should not be necessary in the majority of cases because Windows File Protection (WFP) should automatically detect and recover these files if TCP/IP was installed when you first installed Windows 2000. Refer to Chapter 2 for more information on how Windows File Protection works and how to modify its behavior.

It's very simple to configure a computer to use a preconfigured IPSec policy. You can do this through your network card properties by calling up your **TCP/IP Properties | Advanced | Options | IP Security Properties** and then use the drop down list box: **Use this IP security policy**. Or you can use the **IP Security Policies on Local Machine**, right-click on the policy you want to use and select **Assign**. These built-in policies are:

- Client (Respond Only)
- Server (Request Security)
- Secure Server (Require Security)

Client (Respond Only)

This is suitable for workstations that must talk to both IPSec-enabled computers and non-IPSec-enabled computers. For example, a Windows 2000 Professional in an NT4 domain must communicate without IPSec to the NT4 domain controllers but may need to secure data transfers when accessing a Windows 2000 file and print server. This policy will never initiate IPSec but will respond with IPSec when requested by an IPSec-enabled computer.

> **NOTE**
>
> If two clients with this policy communicate together, the session would not be secured because neither side initiates security. As such this policy is

best suited to clients that only communicate with servers that are either non-IPSec-enabled or have one of the other built-in policies below set (or equivalent).

Server (Request Security)

This is suitable for a computer that responds to both IPSec-enabled clients and non-IPSec-enabled clients. For example, this might be a file and print server that has to accommodate some down-level clients but predominantly services Windows 2000 clients that have IPSec enabled.

If a connection is initiated with an IPSec-enabled client, and both sides agree on what is secure, the session will be secured. If a connection is initiated by a non-IPSec-enabled client, the connection will be accepted with what is called a *soft security association*, and the data will not be secured.

Secure Server (Require Security)

This is suitable for a server that can only allow secured communication. Any traffic not secured will be refused. Typically this would be used with file servers with highly sensitive data or security gateways at either end of an L2TP/IPSec tunnel.

SECURITY ALERT!

Use this policy with care! Remember this policy applies to all communications, which includes WINS servers, DHCP, DNS, domain controllers, etc. Unless these servers can honor the IPSec negotiation requested, these services will fail and clog up your Event Viewer with errors. Unless this server was running in a workgroup and not communicating with any other servers, it is unlikely this policy could be used without modification. However, you could easily change it such that certain computers or ports were exempt (e.g., those used for WINS/DNS, etc.).

However, despite its name it should not be considered secure enough for a server that is attached to the Internet that will communicate only with other IPSec-enabled computers. This is because it accepts incoming unsecured traffic (which exposes it to Denial of Service attacks) and doesn't protect the IP headers which means it is vulnerable to IP spoofing. For computers that communicate over an unsecured network like the Internet, you would be well advised to built a custom policy that blocked all but the ports you needed, only accepted communication with known computers, and rejected incoming traffic that wasn't secured.

IPSec Policy Components

The policies are said to be examples rather than designed to be used out of the box, but it's always advisable to check the examples provided rather than having a blank canvas! Whether you consider them to be good examples is a matter of opinion. Each IPSec policy consists of several security protocols that determine which encryption and algorithms are used and how to exchange keys. When you delve into the built-in policies, it becomes apparent they are made up of three main components:

- IP Filter rules
- IP Filter lists
- IP Filter actions

IP Filter Rules and Lists

A policy can have one or more rules, all of which can be active at once. For example, you could have one rule for LAN traffic and another for WAN traffic. Rules specify how and when communication is to be secured by providing the ability to trigger and control security based on the source, destination, and type of IP traffic. Each rule contains a list of IP filters and actions that take place when a match is made on the filter rule.

Each of the built-in policies contains the Default Response rule (which cannot be deleted, only modified or deactivated). This serves to respond to computers that request security when no other rule applies and therefore acts as a catch-all safety net. Additionally the server policies contain two built-in rules: **All ICMP Traffic** and **All IP Traffic**. As their names suggest, the first allows you to filter ICMP traffic so it can be subject to different rules (for example, allow it to pass unsecured) and the second filters all traffic. You can choose to use these rules as they stand, modify them (and their associated actions), or not use them in your policy.

Figure 8.8 shows the Secure Server (Require Security) policy with its default three rules listed under the IP Filter List, and all enabled. The only modification here is the Authentication on all three, which has been changed to use certificates rather than Kerberos (we'll cover how to do this later).

If you decide to create a new rule within a policy (using the Add button in Figure 8.8), it then becomes available for all new IPSec policies and can be configured outside the policy by right-clicking on **IP Security Policies on Local Machine | Manage IP filter lists and filter actions**.

Figure 8.8 Secure Server Policy Showing the Three Built-In Rules Enabled

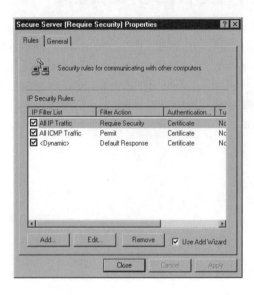

For example, within your Secure Server policy you might add a new rule that defines all DNS traffic from this machine because you want it to be exempt from security because your DNS server is not IPSec-enabled. Or conversely, on your Client (Respond Only) policy you want to ensure security on all traffic between your computer and your Windows 2000 DNS servers to enable host record integrity without using secure dynamic updates (which is only possible in Active Directory). Because you don't want to use the DNS servers' IP source addresses as the filter, but rather identify all DNS traffic from the computer, you decide to use the DNS port definition. Therefore you create a new rule that looks out for all packets with the remote TCP and UDP port 53, which then become available to this policy and all new policies. Figure 8.9 shows an example of how this newly defined rule within the Client (Respond Only) might look in addition to its Default Response rule.

NOTE

Editing a rule under one policy will change it wherever it is used in other policies. Similarly, if you edit the rule under the Manage IP Filter lists and filter actions, the modifications will be reflected in any existing policies that use the rule.

Figure 8.9 Client (Respond Only) Properties with a Custom Rule Added for DNS Traffic

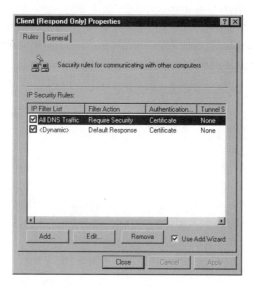

This new rule will then become available to all new policies (but not existing ones) and can also be modified under the **Manage IP Filter lists and filter actions**, as seen in Figure 8.10. Notice how you can add, edit, and remove these rules from this dialog box but you don't have access to the Default Response rule, which is only available within the policies themselves.

Figure 8.10 Built-In Default IPSec Filters, with a Custom Filter Added for DNS Traffic

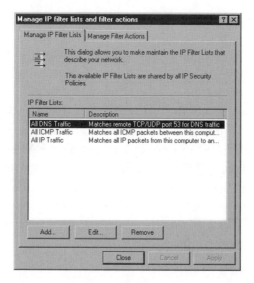

Recommendations for Defining Filter Lists

One of the essential components in making IPSec work is planning. It's a juggling act between aiming for the simplest policy possible, and ensuring it meets all requirements and exceptions. The following is a list of some recommendations that help to define efficient filter lists:

- If you need to cover a group of computers, try to do this with just one filter by using an IP subnet address or "Any IP Address" rather than individually specifying each computer's address.

- Try to logically group computers together whenever possible so that they can be included together in a filter.

- Try not to use overlapping and contradicting filters. An example of this might be one filter that identifies the subnet 10.10.0.0/16 and another that identifies destination computer 10.10.0.5/16. Another example might be a filter that identified all ports on a specific destination address, and another filter that identified a certain destination port on all addresses. It's important to remember that order in which IPSec filters are processed is not necessarily the same order as they are displayed in the configuration utility. All filters are simultaneously retrieved by the IPSec Policy Agent on computer startup and are sorted from most specific to least specific and then processed. It is unwise to assume that one filter will override another filter or the timing involved to do so. Therefore, it is simpler to strive toward filters that do not conflict.

IP Filter Actions

We've identified how to use rules within lists (for example, how to match traffic depending on the source or destination address, or protocol or port number). But we haven't yet said what action to take when a match is made. For example, how does the DNS filter know whether to secure this data or allow it to pass unsecured? This is where the Filter Action applies. You can see from Figure 8.8 on our modified Client (Respond Only) policy that the Filter Action is set to Require Security which means that all DNS traffic that goes out from the computer must be secured. The default Filter Actions available are:

- Permit
- Request Security (Optional)
- Require Security

If you look at the **Manage Filter Actions** tab under the **Manage IP filter lists and filter actions**, you'll see a description of each of these. Double-click on each filter action and choose the **General** tab so you can read the helpful, but long description that describes each action. As you might have guessed they range from most permissive (Permit) to most restrictive (Require Security), as can be seen from Table 8.1.

Table 8.1 IPSec Default Filter Actions

Filter Action	Description
Permit	Allows the identified traffic to be unsecured (not use IPSec).
Request Security (Optional)	Requests clients use IPSec if they are IPSec-enabled, but will fall back to using non secured communication if the client is not IPSec-enabled.
Require Security	Clients that are not IPSec-enabled will not be allowed to communicate. However, it doesn't guarantee that all communication will be secured because IPSec-enabled client may not request to use authentication or encryption.

NOTE

The Request Security option does not allow unsecured communication with clients that are IPSec-enabled. If the two IPSec-enabled computers cannot agree on a security negotiation, there is no fall back to using clear text. The ability to fall back to using clear text is only possible if the other computer does not respond at all to the IPSec challenge.

If these Filter Actions are not adequate, you can define a new filter action and you will be prompted whether you want to Permit, Block, or Negotiate security.

If you choose **Negotiate security**, you will also have to define whether this means not allowing communication with computers that aren't IPSec-enabled or falling back to unsecured communication. Then you must define whether you want the data to be encrypted and authenticated (High Security), or the whole packet authenticated (Medium Security), or define your own custom setting.

Recommendations for Defining Filter Actions

Similar considerations about simplicity should also apply when defining Filter Actions. Try to define actions that are general and consistent. Other recommendations include the following:

- If you want to prevent communication with rogue computers, ensure security is not negotiated for nonsensitive data or when communicating with non–IPSec-enabled computers. Instead, use blocking or fallback to clear policies.

- It is safe to set EFS confidentiality to none on sensitive data if a higher level application such as SSL and S/MIME will be securing the data.

- Consider specifying higher levels of security for remote gateways (such as VPN servers and routers on the Internet) that include authenticating the headers (AH), 3DES encryption, short key lifetimes (less than 50MB), and setting Perfect Forward Secrecy. If you know that authenticating computers can support these higher levels of security, remove any lower levels that can be negotiated down. An example of a custom filter with high security is shown in Figure 8.11.

Figure 8.11 Defining a Custom Filter Action with High Security for Remote Gateways

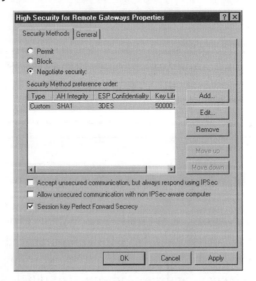

Other IP Rule Components—Authentication, Tunnel Setting, and Connection Type

Thankfully, these are less complicated! When editing your rule, these are the additional settings you can define. You should ensure that your computer Authentication is not set to Kerberos if you're not in an Active Directory domain. It's here that you specify whether to use either preshared keys or certificates.

The Tunnel Setting usually only applies if you want to protect data from one security gateway to another as it traverses a public network. So, for example, this would apply if you had two routers connecting over the Internet. IPSec then needs to be configured for Tunnel Mode rather than the default, Transport Mode. You do this by specifying the remote tunnel IP address.

The Connection Type refers to whether the traffic to be matched should be all traffic to/from the computer, or just LAN traffic, or just traffic that goes out over your dialup adapter(s). See Figure 8.12 where the connection type is set to **All network connections**. Specifying the connection type is a very easy way to differentiate IPSec behavior between traffic on your local network and traffic that goes over the Internet. However, remember that these settings are purely taken from the type of adapter used to send/receive data. IPSec cannot know whether data you send will remain on your local area network.

Figure 8.12 Setting the Connection Type for IPSec

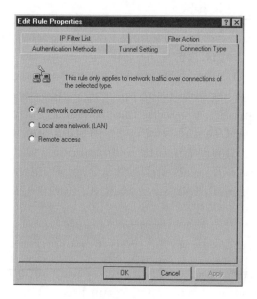

For example, all your Internet traffic may go via a proxy server, NAT server, or router rather than a dialup adapter. The job of securing data when it leaves these intermediary devices should fall on whoever is responsible for them, which is when it's vital to coordinate security policies with all network administrators. If you want to make sure that all data will be secured according to your policies, choose the **All network connections** option. Most intermediary devices will simply pass through the IPSec packets unchanged (providing the IPSec ports are not blocked).

> **NOTE**
>
> The exception here is that IPSec cannot be used with NAT (Network Address Translation) which involves changing the IP and/or TCP/UDP headers, which then invalidates the packet integrity. Make sure you do not send client IPSec packets to a NAT server. Consider using PPTP instead, which is NAT-friendly but has the disadvantage of only securing data between client and VPN server rather than offering end-to-end security.

Setting Computer Authentication Using Preshared Keys

You've probably worked out by now how to use preshared keys for authentication on a rule. Simply double-click the rule to edit it, select the **Authentication Methods** tab, and select either **Edit** or **Add**. If you specify more than one means of authentication, you can position the order in which they are tried.

As we saw in Figure 8.1, to specify the preshared key (password) you simply type it in after selecting **Use this string to protect the key exchange (preshared key)**. Any other Windows 2000 computer with the same password defined in their policy will be able to authenticate. Remember that authenticating computers with preshared keys means you must secure the local security policy.

Setting Authentication Using Certificates

Before you can authenticate using certificates, you need to have two computer certificates on each computer you want to run IPSec. The first is a Certificate

Authority certificate that is listed as trusted (either a root certificate or an inter-mediate certificate). The second is your actual computer certificate you're going to use for IPSec.

If you are using a third-party CA such as VeriSign or SecureNet, the first part could be incredibly easy. Under the **Authentication Method**, select **Use a certificate from this certificate authority (CA)** and use the **Browse** button to select your CA.

If you're not using a third-party CA but your own, you will need to ensure it is listed as a Trusted Root Certificate so you can select it from this list. If it's not on the list, you will need to request a CA certificate. You can use the Web enroll-ment pages we saw in Chapter 7, or you can script your own solution. This sec-tion will assume you're using the built-in Web certificate pages together with Windows 2000 Certification Authority snap-in. Following these steps should install your CA certificate:

1. Load your Web browser and connect to your Web server certificate enrollment page on **http://<server_name>certsrv**.

2. Choose the **Retrieve the CA certificate or certification revocation list** and select **Next**.

3. You should see your CA certificate listed, similar to the one in Figure 8.13 where my CA is called **Company Root CA**. Click **Install this CA certificate**.

4. The following page after selecting **Next** should tell you that "The CA certificate has been successfully installed."

NOTE

If your CA is offline, you will have to use the Web browser on the CA server itself and use the Download option and save to Base64 encoded format, and manually import the file using the Certificates snap-in.

To import the saved certificate, load a MMC snap-in using Certificates (Local Computer). Navigate to **Trusted Root Certification Authorities | Certificates** and right-click **All Tasks | Import** and follow the Certificate Import Wizard instructions to specify the file you saved on your CA server.

Figure 8.13 Installing Your CA Certificate

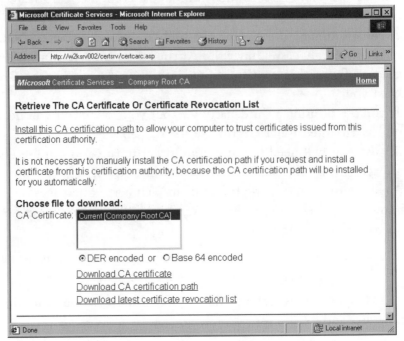

5. To confirm that your computer does now have your CA listed, it should appear under the **Certificates (Local Computer) | Trusted Root Certification Authorities | Certificates** along with the other third-party CAs. Figure 8.14 shows my CA added to this list which is called Company Root CA.

6. Now you should be able to select your CA from the list when using the **Browse** button under the **IPSec rule for the Authentication Method** tab and it should look something like Figure 8.2 when we previously discussed certificate authentication.

7. You now need a computer certificate. Back to the Certificate Enrollment page, this time select **Request a certificate** and then **Advanced request**.

8. Choose the **Submit a certificate request to this CA using a form** (assuming the CA is online; otherwise you'll have to choose the second option and save to a Base64 request file).

Figure 8.14 Confirmation of the CA Certificate Installation

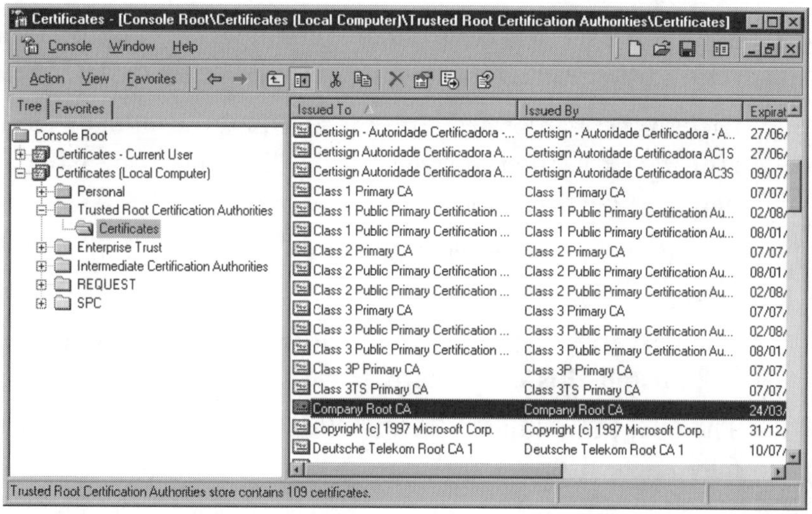

> **!** **WARNING**
>
> You may decide to remove certificates you don't want to use to ensure only your own CA is used on your computers. This is good security practice. However, there are six Trusted Root Certificates you mustn't delete because these are required by Windows 2000, even though some of the certificates have expired. They are:
> - Microsoft Timestamp Root
> - Microsoft Authenticode Root
> - Microsoft Root Authority
> - VeriSign Time Stamping CA
> - VeriSign Commercial Software Publishers CA
> - VeriSign Commercial Software Publishers CA

9. On the form, fill in identifying details under Name, Department, etc. The next important step is selecting the correct Intended Purpose. You don't, as you might think, select IPSec Certificate. Instead, select either **Client Authentication Certificate** or **Server Authentication Certificate**.

10. Make sure the **Create new key set** is selected and also select **Use local machine store**.

11. Click **Submit**, and you should be told that your certificate request has been received.

12. You should see this certificate request now listed under Pending in the Certification Authority. Right-click it and choose **All Tasks | Issue**.

13. Back in the Web browser, on the Certificate Pending page, select the **Home** link in the top right and this time select the **Check on a pending certificate**.

14. You should see your certificate listed. Make sure it is selected and click **Next**.

15. The next page should tell you that your certificate was issued. Select the link: **Install this certificate**.

16. The next page should tell you "Your new certificate has been successfully installed."

17. To confirm your computer certificate is successfully installed, load up the Certificates (Local Computer) snap-in and navigate to **Personal | Certificates**. You should see the certificate you just requested under here, and if you view its details it will tell you that it was issued by your CA, and its purpose is identification to a remote computer. Note this is different from the user certificates we created in Chapter 7 for Web authentication, where the details there display the certificate is intended to allow secure communication on the Internet. Your computer certificate should look similar to Figure 8.15.

With your CA selected as your choice of IPSec authentication, and a valid computer certificate, your computer is now ready to authenticate with another similarly configured computer.

NOTE

If you are using a third-party CA rather than your own, they will usually issue their own installation instructions that accompany their computer certificates.

Figure 8.15 Example of a Computer Certificate, Suitable for IPSec

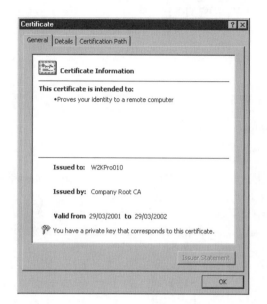

IP Security Protocols and Algorithms

So far, I've tried to steer away from the mass of acronyms, protocols and algorithms used with IPSec. There's no doubt that they confuse the uninitiated, which is a shame because you don't actually have to understand them to effectively use IP Security. But when setting up custom policies it helps to understand which options are appropriate, which you can do better if you understand what they are and how they work. However if in doubt, the defaults in the built-in policies offer a sensible starting place with the exception of changing the Authentication from Kerberos because this will only be used in an Active Directory domain.

It's a bit like owning a car—if the car is provided in working order, you don't have to fully understand all the components and how they fit together in order make minor modifications and take advantage of the vehicle's ability to get you from A to B. However, if you were to understand this level, you would be better able to appreciate what features suited your requirements, fine-tune the car, and be better able to troubleshoot any problems.

We've previously mentioned the two IPSec protocols in passing: **Authentication Headers** (AH) and **Encapsulating Security Payload** (ESP). Authentication Headers ensures the integrity of the whole IP packet (including source/destination address and ports) but cannot encrypt the data. Encapsulating Security Payload can encrypt the data being transferred and can ensure the integrity of this data (but not the headers).

Configuring & Implementing…

Testing IPSec

Hopefully, it goes without saying that you should fully test an IP Security policy with different clients, using different services and in every scenario you can identify, over a reasonable period of time. Even if you're not sure about the finer inner workings of certain settings, testing the actual output and looking at the results will provide a more thorough secure solution than if you relied on theoretical knowledge alone. Too often I've come across programmers who test by thinking through the logic of their code rather than actually testing it in production! Don't fall into this trap yourself. You don't have to be a security expert to use a network analyzer to check that data you want encrypted is encrypted, and that you're not preventing any important services from functioning or preventing legitimate access.

Remember also that routers and/or firewalls may have to be changed to accommodate IPSec traffic:

- **Protocol ID 50 and 51** For ESP and AH traffic
- **UDP port 5000** For IPSec negotiation traffic

Before two IPSec-enabled devices can use either AH or ESP, they have to agree on a set of security parameters to secure the communication. As such this section will cover:

- Data Authentication Algorithms
- Data Encryption Algorithms
- Key Exchange and Management
- Security Associations

> **NOTE**
>
> It's important to remember that *authentication* in the context of IP Security can refer to three different types of authentication, which can be very confusing if it isn't specified and the context isn't clear. The first is authentication of *computers*—each device proving it is trusted and who it claims to be. The other two types of authentication occur after the two devices have established a secure link and refer to the authentication of *data*—ensuring the data is unmodified in transit. This could be with AH (which can only authenticate), which ensures the integrity of the whole IP packet, or with ESP, which ensures the integrity of the data (but not the source/destination or port addresses).

Data Authentication Algorithms

The two Hash Message Authentication Codes (**HMAC**) available in IPSec to ensure data integrity are *MD5* and *SHA*:

> **MD5** (Message Digest 5) is based on RFC 1321 and makes four passes over data blocks using a different number constant for each message word on every pass. This produces a 128-bit key.

> **SHA** (Secure Hash Algorithm) was developed by the National Institute of Standards and Technology and described in FIPS PUB 180-1. Although similar in concept to MD5, it produces a 160-bit key and is considered a stronger authentication than MD5. This is why it appears higher in the built-in Default Response Rule.

Data Encryption Algorithms

Used with ESP, IPSec uses the US Data Encryption Standard (**DES**) algorithm, which was originally published in 1977 by the US National Bureau of Standards. DES works on 64-bit blocks of data with the algorithm converting 64 input bits from the original data into 64 encrypted output bits. However, while DES starts with 64-bit keys, only 56 bits are actually used in the encryption because the remaining 8 bits are used for parity.

A stronger version of DES is **3DES** (sometimes called *Triple DES*), so called because each block is processed three times which greatly increases the degree of complexity in the encryption. As we've noted previously, your computer must support 128-bit encryption in order to support 3DES and it is processor intensive.

DES can be combined with Cipher Block Chaining (CBC) to prevent identical messages from looking the same, even if the original data is resent identically. CBC is added automatically when using DES or 3DES in Windows 2000 IPSec—it is not a configurable option.

> **NOTE**
>
> If we look back at our example security policy displayed with the IP Security Monitor in Figure 8.4, we can see how the current policy is using ESP with Date Encryption Standard and Cipher Block Chaining and using the Hash Message Authentication Code of Secure Hash Algorithm 1. AH is not in use.
>
> If the policy had allowed security to be negotiated, other IPSec connections using the same policy may display different authentication and encryption algorithms.

Key Exchange and Management

A key is a secret code or number required to read, modify, or verify secured data and it is used in conjunction with algorithms to secure data. The Oakley protocol automatically handles key refresh and regeneration so that the same key isn't used for a long period of time or for a lot of data.

There are actually two different types of key exchanges used in IPSec: the Master Key and Session Key. The Master key is created when initially establishing the identity of both communicating computers – before any data is actually transferred. The Master Key is needed for the duration of the connection, and if the key's configured lifetime is less than the total connection time, a new Master Key will be generated. The default Master Key lifetime is set to 8 hours, although this can be modified in the policy under the **General** tab | **Advanced** button (Figure 8.16).

A Session Key is then required to safely transfer the actual data. Typically, to save time and processing the Session Key will not authenticate the computers again. Instead it borrows this information from the Master Key and only negotiates packet authentication and optionally encryption (if encryption is specified). However, if you want every packet transferred to independently authenticate each computer for higher security, enable the **Master Key Perfect Forward Secrecy** (sometimes abbreviated to PFS).

Figure 8.16 Modifying Key Exchange Settings

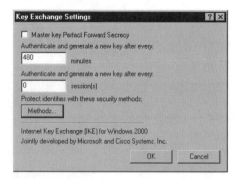

Since setting PFS has a performance overhead, you may decide on a midway solution and reauthenticate the computers after a certain number of Session Keys. Do this by specifying a number under the **Authenticate and generate a new key after every** option instead. Note that any value entered here will be overridden if the Master Key Perfect Forwarding Secrecy is set because that setting automatically reauthenticates with each Session Key.

Although reauthenticating undoubtedly adds an additional processing overhead, standard Windows 2000 IPSec literature warns of potential delays and an increase in network traffic caused by authenticating with domain controllers. When using authentication with certificates (instead of Kerberos, which is the default), authentication is local because these are stored locally, and such network resources are not required.

The **Diffie–Hellman** (DH) algorithm is used to secure key exchange so that both sides agree on a shared key without actually transmitting it over the network. Diffie-Hellman provides two groups to determine the length of the base prime numbers that are used during the key exchange. **Group 1** offers Low strength with 768 bits of key material, and **Group 2** offers Medium strength with 1024 bits. Obviously Group 2 offers a key that is more difficult to break but takes longer to generate. The choice of group cannot be switched during the negotiation and if the groups specified on the two computers don't match, negotiation will fail.

You can see these Diffie-Hellman groups specified as part of Windows 2000's **Internet Key Exchange** (IKE), as shown in Figure 8.17. You access these settings through the policy's **General** tab, **Advanced** button, and then **Methods** button. You can see how the most secure options are listed first with 3DES listed before DES, SHA before MD5, and the Diffie-Hellman Group 2 before Group 1. This ensures that security will be negotiated down only if necessary, so that if a connecting computer supports the highest algorithms, the stronger security will be used.

Figure 8.17 Key Exchange Algorithms Used for Negotiating the Highest Security

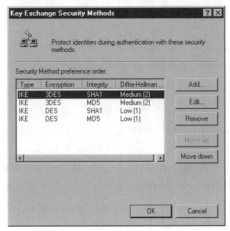

Configuring Session Key Settings

Session Key settings are configured as part of the Filter Action. This complicates things considerably because the active Session Key settings will depend on the filter that is being used, the filter's associated action, and, if the action includes negotiating security, the final setting will depend on which level was successfully negotiated.

Using the default built-in policies, the Session Key when using ESP (with DES or 3DES) will generate a new key every 100000 KB, and every 900 seconds. When just authenticating the packet (AH), the Session Key is also set to 100000 KB, but a new key will be generated every 300 seconds.

For example, the Require Security filter action has four levels of negotiation, all of which could have their own Session Key values. However, all of them require encryption (DES or 3DES) which means that they all have the same Session Key value of 100000 KB, and every 900 seconds. Figure 8.18 shows this (note the columns have been moved so these values can be seen all at once).

Figure 8.18 Default Session Key Values for the Require Security Filter Action

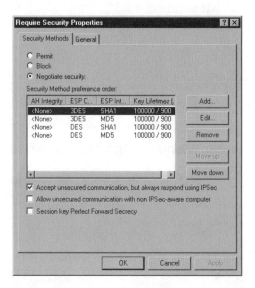

However, the Request Security filter action will negotiate down to using just Authentication (AH) if the client cannot support encryption (ESP). When AH is being used, the Session Key is also set to 100000 KB, but the lifetime value is set to 300 seconds. This is shown in Figure 8.19.

Figure 8.19 Default Session Key Values for the Request Security Filter Action

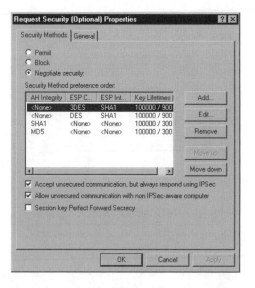

When you create a new filter action and use the default security method of either **High** (for ESP) or **Medium** (for AH), rather than the **Custom** option shown in Figure 8.20, this will result in a filter action that will not negotiate down and has no Session Key lifetime, which means that the same key will be reused for the duration of the connection. Figure 8.21 shows the result of choosing a new filter action choosing High Security that won't communicate with non-IPSec-enabled computers. You will see it doesn't use AH to protect the headers (IP addresses/ports) and it uses MD5 rather than the stronger SHA algorithm.

Figure 8.20 Choices when Manually Creating a New Filter Action

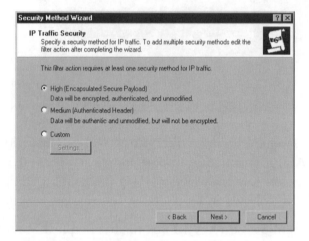

Figure 8.21 Resulting Key Options when Manually Creating a New Filter Action with High Security

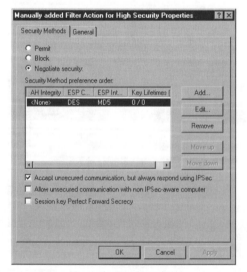

You must use the Custom option if you want to specify a new filter action that:

- Can negotiate different security options
- Will use the higher security algorithm
- Can protect the IP headers
- Prevents continual rekeying

Security Associations

Before two IPSec systems can exchange data, they need to agree on a set of security parameters that are allowed in their security policy, such as the authentication method between the two computers, the authentication algorithm, and the encryption algorithm. They also need to agree how they are going to handle key exchange for the algorithms chosen.

The set of security parameters negotiated in IPSec is collectively referred to as a **Security Association** (often abbreviated to just SA). The key exchange we looked at in the section above is handled by the key management protocol called **Oakley**.

Therefore, Security Associations in IPSec are negotiated and managed by a protocol security combination called Internet Security Association and Key Management Protocol/Oakley, which is usually abbreviated to **ISAKMP/ Oakley**. This is the name you'll sometimes see in the Event Log (Figure 8.22) when referring to IPSec policy settings. It's simply the full name that refers to Windows 2000 IP Security and its policies.

ISAKMP/Oakley consists of two different modes so that different types of Security Associations can be established, one for the initial exchange of information when two IPSec enabled computers communicate, and another for the actual data to be transferred. These are known as **Phase 1** and **Phase 2** to indicate the order in which they are initially made. Alternatively, they are also referred to as **Main Mode** and **Quick Mode** to reflect the usual efficiency of them. You may remember seeing Oakley Main Modes and Oakley Quick Modes statistics listed in the IP Security Monitor and the reference to these modes in the Security Log.

Phase 1 is activated by the source and destination addresses specified in the policy filter rules (note, not the port or protocol settings). It is used to authenticate each computer (for example, through certificates) so that a secure channel can be established between the two computers. The Master Key is agreed upon here.

Figure 8.22 Reference to the Full Security Protocol Combination, ISAKMP/Oakley

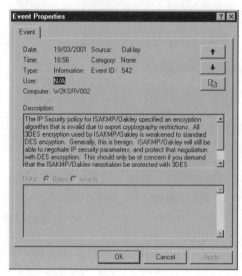

After the secure channel has been established, Phase 2 is used to both authenticate data and optionally encrypt the data sent over this established link. The first Session Key is agreed upon here. Phase 2 is quicker because, as we saw above, the Session Key typically borrows the same key information used in Phase 1 rather than negotiating this from scratch.

The two different types of SAs are referred to as the **IKE SA** and **IPSec SA**. You will not see details of the IKE SA in the IPSec monitor, but these can be displayed locally by using the netdiag support tool by specifying: **netdiag.exe /test:ipsec.v**, and in the Security Log if auditing is enabled.

Additionally, in Quick Mode the IPSec SA needs to allocate Security Parameter Index (**SPI**) numbers that will be used to differentiate packets. Because the IPSec SA is unidirectional, one is created for outbound traffic and another for inbound. If you look back at the Security Log example (under IP Security Utilities, Using the Security Log), these were listed right near the end of the second (Quick Mode) entry as **InboundSpi**, and **OutboundSpi**. On the IPSec monitor you will only see the outbound SA. After the inbound SA has been idle for five minutes, both IPSec SAs are terminated and the outbound SA will no longer display in the IP Security monitor. When data transfer recommences, two new SAs are created with new keys and new SPIs.

In case you noticed, the inbound and outbound SAs are catered for automatically in the policies with the **Mirrored** option when defining filters, as shown in

Figure 8.23. It would be unusual but not impossible to want to treat inbound traffic differently from outbound traffic. However, you can do this by deselecting the mirrored option—but use this with filters that permit or block rather than negotiate security.

Figure 8.23 IPSec Filters Are Automatically Mirrored

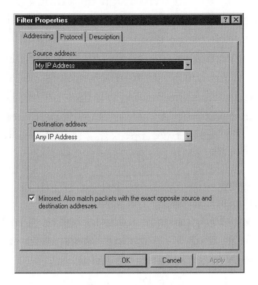

Walkthrough 8.1: Setting and Testing Custom IPSec Policies

In this walkthrough, we will not use certificates, but a preshared key (password). We'll create a test file and view the contents over the network, and then use two different IPSec policies, one with AH to sign the complete packet (protect both the headers and data from being modified) and another with ESP encryption added (to additionally encrypt the contents).

For this walkthrough, find two Windows 2000 computers that temporarily don't need to communicate with any other computer, and that are preferably physically near to one another (because you'll be working on both almost simultaneously). One of these must be Windows 2000 Server (because we'll use Network Monitor to capture network packets). If auditing is not already enabled, do this if you want to verify your computer's IPSec policy:

1. On the Windows 2000 Server, install Network Monitor if it hasn't already been installed. You do this with **Control Panel | Add/Remove Programs | Add/Remove Windows Components | Management and Monitoring Tools**, and with the **Details** button, select just the **Network Monitor Tool**.

2. Create a directory on your Windows 2000 Server and share it (for example, with the share name of IPSEC). Within this directory, create a text file called **ipsec.txt** and type in a single sentence, such as **This is my IPSec test document**.

3. On your Windows 2000 Professional computer, use Internet Explorer to map a drive to this share with the **Reconnect at logon** option set (you can disconnect it after the walkthrough). Make sure you can see the file you created (ipsect.txt). To make the network trace easier to read, we'll actually edit the file from a command prompt. So load a command prompt, and from there make sure you can load and edit the file. For example if you mapped the IPSEC drive to J, type **Edit J:ipsec.txt**.

4. Load Network Monitor on the server (**Start | Programs | Administrative Tools | Network Monitor**). If you're prompted to choose a network card, make sure you choose the MAC address that corresponds to your Local Area Network card that will be talking to the other IPSec computer. If you're not sure what address that is, from a command prompt type **nbtstat −A <your own IP address>** and the MAC address will be displayed at the bottom of the output.

5. You should now be looking at the Capture Windows (Session Stats) window (which is displayed on the window title) without any fields or windows being updated.

6. Before we start capturing data to and from this machine, we'll limit what we're capturing by filtering out traffic from any other computers. Click **Capture | Addresses**. Click the **Add** button to specify the address of your other IPSec computer. It should look something like Figure 8.24.

Figure 8.24 Adding an Entry into the Network Monitor Address Database

If you are not sure what address your other computer has, use the **nbtstat −A** command again (and if you know the name but not the IP address, ping the name to display the IP address first).

You can click the **Permanent Name** if you want to keep this name to MAC address mapping for the future. Click **OK**, and **Close**.

7. Back in the Capture Window, click **Capture | Filter** to specify the capture filter.

8. Double-click the **Address Pairs**, which takes you into the Address Expression box. Make sure the **Include** option is selected and the top (both ways) Direction, and under **Station 1** select the entry that corresponds to your local address, and under **Station 2** highlight your other computer (identifying it from the entry you've just added). It should look similar to Figure 8.25.

9. Click **OK**, and **OK** again to return back to the Capture Window.

10. Click **Capture | Start** and from your second machine and edit the file again from the command prompt. As soon as the contents are displayed, on your Windows 2000 Sever click **Capture | Stop and View**.

Figure 8.25 Configuring the Network Monitor Address Filter

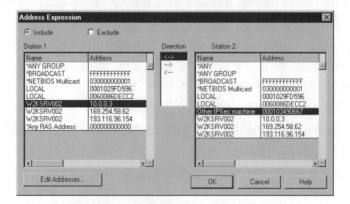

11.   You should see a number of frames displayed. From the bottom up, you are looking for one that has your other IPSec computer listed as the **Dst MAC Addr**, the **SMB** protocol type, and **Read** in the Description as shown in Figure 8.26.

Figure 8.26 Captured Packets from Network Monitor

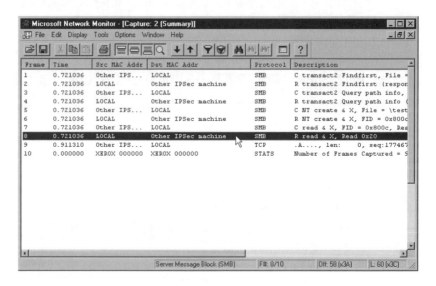

12.   Double-click on this entry to display the contents. If you scroll to the end of the bottom pane, you should see the contents of your test file displayed, similar to Figure 8.27. As you can see, it's not difficult to read data as it travels across the network!

Figure 8.27 Viewing the Contents of the Test Document with Network Monitor

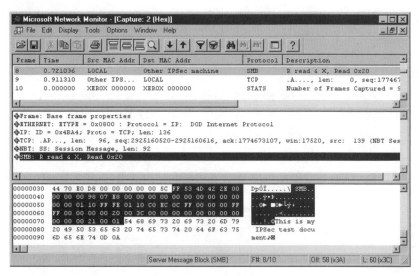

13. Now we'll create our two IPSec policies. For simplicity we'll create two exactly the same on each computer. On the first machine, load the **Local Security Settings**.

14. Right-click on **IP Security Polices on Local Machine**, and select **Create IP Security Policy**, which takes you into the IP Security Policy wizard. Click **Next** and name the policy (for example, **Testing with Password**). Click **Next** and on the next page, uncheck the **Activate the default response rule**. Click **Next** and select **Use this string to protect the key exchange (preshared key)** and type in **KEY**. Click **Next** and leave the Edit properties box checked and click **Finish**.

15. We now have a new policy with nothing defined. Make sure the **Add Wizard** box is checked at the bottom and click **Add** to add our new rule. That displays the Create IP Security Rule Wizard. Click **Next**, and on the next page, leave the **This rule does not specify a tunnel** and click **Next**. On the next page, leave the **All network connections** and click **Next**. Under the **Authentication Method** click the **Use this string to protect the key exchange (preshared key)** and type in **KEY**. Click **Next** and under the IP Filter List, select the **All IP Traffic** filter and click **Next**. Under the Filter Action we're going to add our own, so make sure **Use Add Wizard** box is selected and click **Add**.

16. This brings you to the IP Security Filter Action Wizard. Click **Next**. Name this filter **AH Only** and click **Next**. Make sure **Negotiate security** is selected and click **Next**. Make sure the **Do not communicate with computers that do not support IPSec** is selected and click **Next**. On the next page, we'll select **Medium** to only authenticate the packets (AH) rather than encrypt any data.

17. Click **OK | Next** and then **Finish**. You should now be able to select your new Filter Action. Select the **AH Only** filter and click **Next** and **OK**. You should now be back at the Rules dialog box such that it looks similar to Figure 8.28.

Figure 8.28 New Filter Action Added to All IP Traffic

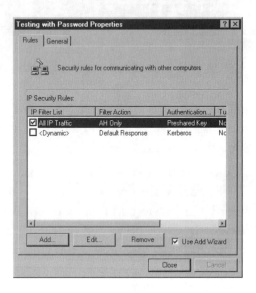

18. If you're sure your computer supports 128-bit encryption, you can skip this next step and go straight to step 19. If your computer doesn't support 128-bit, we'll change the Key Exchange so that the computers will authenticate more quickly. Click the **General** tab, and **Advanced** button, and **Methods** button. Move the two 3DES entries down by selecting each in turn and then clicking on the **Move down** button. It should look like Figure 8.29. Click **OK**, **OK** again, and **Close**.

19. Click **Close**, which takes you back to the Local Security Settings, where you should see your new IPSec policy displayed. Right-click your policy and select **Assign**.

Figure 8.29 Changing the Key Exchange Settings If Your Computer Doesn't Support 128-Bit

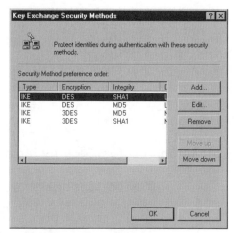

20. Repeat these policy settings exactly (14–19) for the other computer OR export this newly defined policy and import onto the other computer.

21. When both computers have your new policy assigned, make sure you can ping from one to the other. You may have to do this a couple of times whilst the security channel is established before you get a successful response. If it continues to fail, enable auditing and check the Event Log.

22. Load the IP Security Monitor on your Windows 2000 Server. With the **Options** button, change the refresh to be 2 seconds. Edit the file from the shared directory again. You should see details of the policy displayed with the Authenticated Byes counter increasing, but the Confidential Bytes remaining at zero.

23. Make sure the file is closed and your previous capture is closed. Then start capturing again and edit the file under the shared drive again. As soon as the file is displayed, stop and view the capture. If you look through the data captured, you should still be able to see your text displayed. This proves that although your IP Security policy is working (authenticating packets), your data is still unprotected.

24. Back to our IP Security policy. We'll change our filter action through the Manage IP filter lists and filter options. Right-click on **IP Security Policies on Local Machine** and choose **Manage IP filter lists and filter options**. Click the **Manage Filter Actions** and double-click on your **AH Only** Filter Action.

25. You will see it has AH Integrity set (MD5) but both ESP settings are set to **<None>**. Click **Edit** to modify this. On the Modify Security Method page, this time select **Custom** and **Settings** button. We'll leave the top option on but add ESP encryption. To do this, click **Data integrity and encryption (ESP)** and change the **Encryption algorithm** to be **DES** (if you know you can support 3DES, you can select this instead). To make sure we don't reuse the same key, click the **Generate a new key every** option and leave the default at 100000 Kbytes. This dialog box should look like Figure 8.30.

Figure 8.30 Setting Custom Security for AH and ESP Encryption

26. Click **OK**, and **OK** once again. Before we leave this filter action, we'll also modify the name to better reflect our changes. Click the **General** tab and change name from **AH Only** to **AH with ESP Encryption** and click **OK**. Click **Close**.

27. If you check on our policy by editing it, you'll see that the filter action has been automatically updated with the new name and new settings.

28. Repeat this on the other machine (steps 24–27).

29. On both machines, stop and start the policy agent (with **net stop policyagent** and **net start policyagent**).

30. Ping both machines again. If successful your IP Security monitor should show the Confidential bytes now incrementing in addition to the Authenticated Bytes. If you expand the **Security** tab, you should see that it's using ESP for confidentiality (but not authentication) and AH for authentication, as in Figure 8.31.

Figure 8.31 New Policy Settings for AH and ESP Encryption

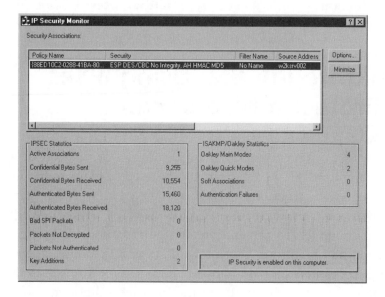

31. Edit the file and capture the traffic. This time you'll see ESP protocol and no readable data (Figure 8.32).

Figure 8.32 Network Monitor Capturing Encrypted Data

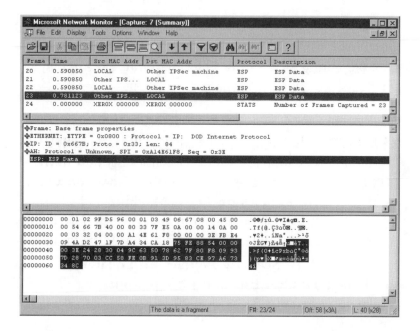

32. Finally, look through your Security Log to verify which security options were in use, and type **netdiag /test:ipsec** to view the full IPSec statistics.

Walkthrough 8.2: Using IPSec to Protect a Web Server

This chapter has concentrated on securing data with IPSec by only allowing certain addresses or ports through, using certificates or passwords between authenticating computers. However, it can also be used to block traffic in much the same way as a firewall can drop packets that don't match a specific pattern.

When you use filters to simply allow or block traffic with IPSec, there is no need for computers to authenticate. It's therefore suitable to use as an additional protection mechanism on your network, even if you don't intend to use IPSec between computers on your network. For example you can even use this for computers that connect directly to the Internet—although you must be careful to specify all the inbound ports you need. This walkthrough only covers Web traffic using http and https. Because there's no authentication required, you only need to configure one computer, which can be part of an NT4 domain or a workgroup.

The steps this walkthrough covers include the following:

- Configuring custom IP Filters for a Web server (allowing http port 80 and SSL port 443)

- Configuring a custom IP Filter Action to block traffic

- Configuring a custom IPSec policy, creating two new rules

- Assigning and testing the IPSec policy

1. Log on (as the local administrator) to a Windows 2000 computer that is running IIS and load the Local Security Settings MMC (**Start | Programs | Administrative Tools | Local Security Policy**). Click **IP Security Policies on Local Machine** and you should see in the Details pane, the three built-in policies which should all be displayed as **No** under the **Policy Assigned** column, as shown in Figure 8.33.

2. Right-click **IP Security Policies on Local Machine**, and select **Manage IP filter lists and filter actions**. This displays the dialog shown in Figure 8.34.

Figure 8.33 The Local Security Settings When First Loaded

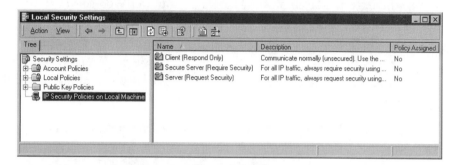

Figure 8.34 The Manage IP Filter Lists and Filter Actions Dialog Box

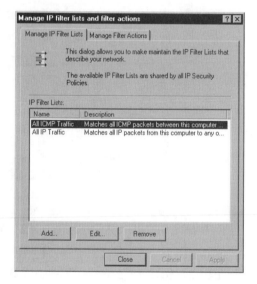

3. We're not going to use these built-in default filters but create two of our own. The first will allow in Web traffic (TCP port 80, and TCP port 443), and the second will block all incoming traffic. Click on the **Add** button, which displays the IP Filter List dialog box. The default name is **New IP Filter List**. Change this to **Allow Port 80 and 443 Inbound**, make sure the **Use Add Wizard** checkbox is set, and click **Add**.

4. This starts the IP Filter Wizard. Click **Next**. On the IP Traffic Source page, set the **Source Address** to **Any IP Address** and click **Next**. On the IP Traffic Destination page, set the **Destination address** to **A specific IP address** and enter the IP address of the adapter that will be used by people connecting to the Web server. For example, if this is a

multihomed server with one adapter connected to the Internet, specify the external IP address. If this is an intranet Web server with only one adapter, simply specify your machine's IP address. Figure 8.35 shows an example where my intranet Web server listens on the address 10.0.0.37. You will notice that this filter uses a classless address, where all bits are checked in the subnet mask, irrespective of what subnet mask the Web server actually uses.

Figure 8.35 Defining the Filter's Destination Address

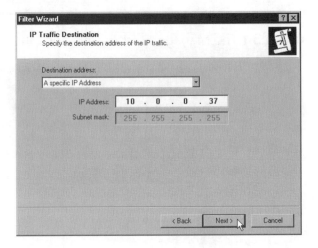

5. With the IP address set, click **Next**. On the IP Protocol Type page, change the **Select a protocol type** to **TCP** and click **Next**.

6. On the IP Protocol Port page, keep the **From any port** but change the lower option from **To any port** to **To this port** and type in **80**, as shown in Figure 8.36.

7. Click **Next** and **Finish**.

8. Repeat steps 3–7, with the only difference being the port number in Figure 8.36 should be 443.

9. You should now be looking at the IP Filter List with two filters added, as shown in Figure 8.37. Click **Close**.

10. Back at the Manage IP filter lists and filter actions dialog box, click the **Add** button again for our second filter. Change the Name from **New IP Filter List** to **All inbound traffic** and click **Add** to start the IP Filter Wizard again.

Figure 8.36 Defining the Filter IP Protocol Ports

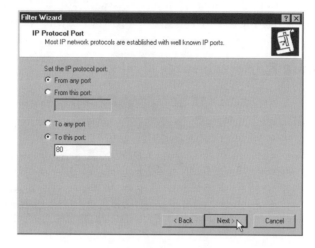

Figure 8.37 IP Filter List with the Two Filters Added

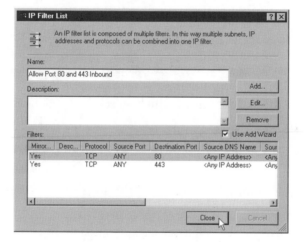

11. Click **Next**. On the IP Traffic Source page, change the **Source address** to be **Any IP address** and click **Next**.

12. On the IP Traffic Destination page, change the **Destination address** to be **A specific IP address**, and as before enter your Web server's IP address and click **Next**.

13. On the **IP Protocol Type** page, keep the **Select a protocol type** as **Any** and click **Next**, and **Finish**. Click **Close** to return to the Mange IP filter lists and filter actions.

14. Click the **Manage Filter Actions** tab. You'll see from Figure 8.38 the built-in default Filter Actions includes a **Permit** filter action, which we will use to allow our inbound Web traffic, but we also need a blocking filter action, which we will have to create.

Figure 8.38 The Manage IP Filter Actions Tab

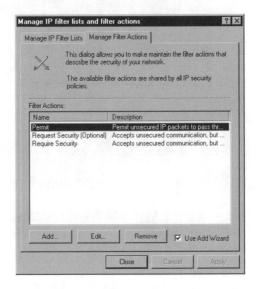

15. Click the **Add** button, which starts the IP Security Filter Action Wizard, and click **Next**.

16. Change the default name of **New Filter Action** to **Block** and click **Next**.

17. On the Filter Action General Options page, select **Block** and click **Next** and **Finish**.

18. Now we've got all the filters and filter actions we need, we can use them in a new IP Sec policy. Click **Close** on the Manage IP filter lists and filter actions dialog box, and back in the MMC, right-click **IP Security Policies on Local Machine | Create IP Security Policy**.

19. This loads the IP Security Policy wizard. Click **Next** and change the name to be **Packet Filter for Web Server** and click **Next**.

20. Uncheck the **Activate the default response rule** and click **Next**.

21. Ensure the **Edit properties** checkbox is set and click **Finish**.

22. This loads up the properties for your policy rules, which are currently blank, as Figure 8.39 shows.

Figure 8.39 Properties for the New IPSec Policy

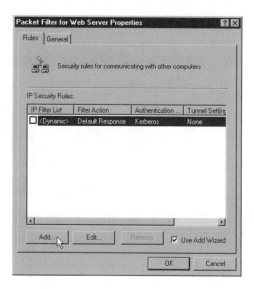

23. Ensure the **Use Add Wizard** checkbox is set (as above) and click the **Add** button, which starts the Create IP Security Rule Wizard. Click **Next**.

24. On the Tunnel Endpoint page, keep the default of **This rule does not specify a tunnel** and click **Next**.

25. On the Network Type page, keep the default of **All networks connections** and click **Next**.

26. On the Authentication Method page, you can keep the default of **Windows 2000 default (Kerberos V5 protocol)**. It doesn't actually matter which authentication option you choose here because with our filters that simply allow or block, authentication will not be used. However, the wizard at this point isn't smart enough to realize that, and you must specify something, so you might as well keep to the default. Click **Next**.

27. If you get a Warning message at this point about Kerberos only being valid on a domain, you can safely ignore it and click **Yes** to continue.

28. You should now be looking at your available IP filter lists, as shown in Figure 8.40 which includes the two custom filters we added. Select the first filter list created, which we called **Allow Port 80 and 443 Inbound**, and click **Next**.

Figure 8.40 Specify the IP Filter Lists to Use

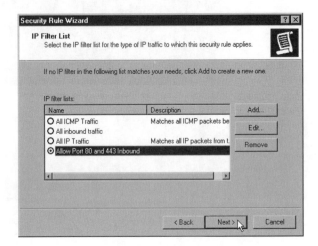

29. On the Filter Action page, select the **Permit** option and click **Next** and **Finish**.

30. You should now be back at the properties for your IPSec policy, only this time it has a new rule listed and enabled, as shown in Figure 8.41.

31. Click **Add** and repeat steps 23–27, only this time on the IP filter lists, select the second filter we created, **All inbound traffic** and then **Block**. Your finished IPSec rules should look similar to Figure 8.42.

32. When you are happy with this, click **Close**, which takes you back into the Local Security Settings MMC. You'll see your new IPSec policy in the right pane. Right-click it and select **Assign**.

33. You can now test that your new IPSec policy successfully allows traffic through port 80 and SSL, and blocks any other traffic. For example, trying to ping the Web server's address should return a "Request timed out." Similarly, a port scan would not show any open ports except the two we allowed on port 80 and 443. To confirm that port 80 is available,

load up IE from another machine and try to connect to the Web server. You don't even need to have an operational Web server to confirm this; a newly installed IIS should return the standard Windows 2000 Under Construction page.

Figure 8.41 Properties for the New IPSec Policy with One Rule Added

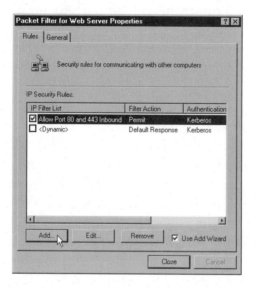

Figure 8.42 Properties for the New IPSec Policy with Both Rules Added

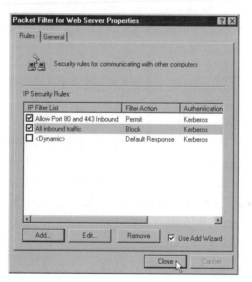

NOTE

We actually defined two filters to achieve this—one for allowing only port 80 and port 443, and another for blocking all inbound traffic. Although there is an overlap in these rules (port 80 and port 443 are also all inbound), it works because IPSec applies the most relevant rules before general rules. This is how port 80, despite also being all inbound, is allowed through.

Summary

This chapter has covered the practical side of implementing IPSec with Windows 2000 when it is being used outside an Active Directory environment. In this environment the default authentication of Kerberos cannot be used, and computers cannot automatically receive a certificate.

Even though you are not running an Active Directory network, there's no reason why you cannot make full use of IPSec to secure data as it travels over the network. It's your choice how securely you choose to enforce this security, and the complexity of when and how the data will be secured. We covered the utilities you will probably require when configuring and testing IPSec and how to use them, and how to configure IPSec policies.

We looked at the built-in IPSec policies and the components that make up these policies so you can modify them, or build your own custom policies. Remember that the most efficient policies to use and troubleshoot will be simple custom ones you build for known computers so that security parameters will be either agreed immediately or rejected immediately rather than having to negotiate down to a common setting.

Building custom policies requires some knowledge of the IPSec algorithms and acronyms, and the workings of IPSec key exchanges. The final section covered key exchange and algorithms to help you better understand the choices available. With a little understanding of how these work, you can see how the built-in policies and suggested default values are often not appropriate, which is why it is always preferable to define your own custom IPSec policies.

Solutions Fast Track

IPSec Planning—Working Out
What You Want to Secure and How

☑ Security requirements when transferring data over a network can be for nonrepudiation, anti-replay, integrity, confidentiality, and authentication.

☑ Work out what data you want to secure and how you want to secure it.

☑ Beware that two IPSec-enabled computers must have security parameters in common. For example a computer that will only use 128-bit encryption will fail to communicate with a computer that can only support 56-bit encryption. However, an IPSec-enabled computer can be configured to communicate with non-IPSec-enabled computers.

☑ IPSec can authenticate computers using Kerberos, Certificates or passwords (preshared keys). Kerberos is the default setting, but this will not work outside Active Directory. Certificates can be used with a third-party Certificate Authority or your own. Passwords are the easiest to configure and troubleshoot but are the least secure.

IP Security Utilities—For Configuring and
Monitoring Secure Communication

☑ There are a number of IPSec utilities you can use to help you configure and monitor IPSec. At a minimum you will probably use IP Security Policy on Local Machine and the IP Security Monitor.

☑ When configuring and testing IPSec, you may also need to stop/restart the IP Security Policy Agent Service and check the Security Log with auditing enabled.

☑ Advanced TCP/IP Options allow you to quickly see whether IPSec is enabled on the computer, and an administrator can change the IPSec policy in use here (but not configure it).

☑ If you are authenticating IPSec-enabled computers with certificates, you will also need the Certificates snap-in and, if you are using your own

CA, a client browser to request certificates and the Certificate Authority snap-in to issue certificates.

☑ The Support Tool, **Netdiag**, provides comprehensive information on IPSec configuration and currently active IPSec data.

☑ The Resource Kit tool, **ipsecpol.exe**, allows IPSec policies to be scripted.

IPSec Built-In Policies—For Minimal Administrator Configuration

☑ Windows 2000 comes with three built-in policies which despite their appearance of offering out-of-the-box security solutions, Microsoft says are examples and not suitable for production networks without modification.

☑ You can use these policies as a first base for IPSec testing, as a reference for possible policy settings, and as a starting point for defining your own policies.

☑ Outside Active Directory, you must change the authentication in these policies from Kerberos to either certificates or passwords (preshared key).

☑ The Client (Respond Only) built-in policy is aimed at workstations that must talk to both IPSec-enabled computers and non-IPSec enabled computers.

☑ The Server (Request Security) is aimed at computers that respond to both IPSec-enabled clients and non IPSec-enabled clients.

☑ The Secure Server (Require Server) is aimed at computers that can only allow secured communication and any traffic that is not secured will be refused.

IPSec Policy Components

☑ IPSec policies consist of rules, filters, and filter actions.

☑ A policy can have more than one rule active at once and each rule contains a list of IP filters and actions that take place when a match is made on the filter rule (for example, a policy can block computers identified by address or subnet, port numbers, or protocols).

☑ Built-in filters include **All ICMP Traffic** and **All Traffic**, but you can add your own for greater flexibility. You can filter on source and destination addresses, subnets, ports, and protocols.

☑ Built-in filter actions include **Permit,** which allows packets through without securing, **Request Security (Optional)** and **Require Security**—and you can add your own.

☑ Negotiating security allows the IPSec-enabled PC to fall back to using unsecured traffic if the responding computer doesn't support IPSec. You can also negotiate different levels of security such as the encryption level (for example, try 3DES first and then DES).

☑ If authenticating computers with preshared keys, you must take additional steps to secure the passwords being used. If authenticating computers with certificates, both computers need a trusted CA in common and a computer certificate issued by that CA.

IP Security Protocols and Algorithms

☑ AH is the abbreviation for Authentication Headers, which ensures the integrity of the whole IP packet (including source/destination address and ports). It cannot encrypt data.

☑ ESP is the abbreviation for Encapsulating Security Payload, which ensures the integrity of the data being transferred by either encrypting it and/or ensuring it wasn't modified in transit. It doesn't protect the IP headers and therefore, without AH, leaves the traffic vulnerable to IP spoofing.

☑ You can use either just AH (Microsoft calls this *Low Security*) or just ESP (Microsoft calls this *High Security*) or a custom combination of the two (for example, AH with ESP encryption).

☑ MD5 and SHA are the two data authentication algorithms you can use, with SHA being the most secure.

☑ DES and 3DES are the two possible data encryption algorithms you can use, but you must have a 128-bit version of Windows 2000 to support 3DES. 3DES is more secure, but requires high processing overheads.

☑ Keys are required to read, modify, or verify data. Both IPSec computers must agree on the key to use using a Diffie-Hellman (DH) algorithm to secure this exchange. For greater security, keys should be dynamically changed after a certain amount of time, or after a certain amount of data has been transferred with them. Both sides must agree on these values at the outset.

☑ Two different types of keys are used with IPSec that correlate to the two exchanges in IPSec of Main Mode and Quick Mode. The Master key is exchanged in Main Mode, and Session keys exchanged in Quick Mode. Typically a single connection between two IPSec-enabled computers would have one Master Key and multiple Session Keys which provides greater efficiency—unless Perfect Forward Secrecy (PFS) is enabled, which offers the highest security at the price of additional processing.

☑ When setting your own custom policies and defining your filter action, always use the **Custom** option if you want a combination of AH and ESP, want to use the higher data authentication algorithm, want to define a key lifetime, or want to negotiate security parameters (for example, try 3DES before DES or SHA before MD5).

Frequently Asked Questions

The following Frequently Asked Questions, answered by the author of this book, are designed to both measure your understanding of the concepts presented in this chapter and to assist you with real-life implementation of these concepts. To have your questions about this chapter answered by the author, browse to **www.syngress.com/solutions** and click on the **"Ask the Author"** form.

Q: We have confidential data on our network, but we use a switched network so that if you were to put a network analyzer on the network you would only see the traffic for that computer. That makes the need for securing data redundant, doesn't it?

A: A false sense of security is one of the most dangerous aspects to guard against when designing your security plans. Although most commonly obtained network analyzers wouldn't be able to see data from other computers on a switched network, this data is far from protected! You can get network sniffers that use Address Resolution Protocol Redirects. These work by redirecting a computer's data sent to the local router to themselves so the packets can be captured and then passed on to the real router afterwards. Because the data arrives at the specified place, nobody is any the wiser that the person using this sniffer has read the data, and possibly modified it in transit. IPSec using Authentication Headers (AH) would protect this data from being modified (but not read) and IPSec using Encapsulating Security Payload (ESP) would protect this data from being read.

Q: We would like to use strong encryption on some of our file servers that host sensitive internal information, so we've got IPSec encrypting all data as it travels to and from the Windows 2000 Professional users that access it. However, we've noticed that it's really slowing down the server with the processor being identified as often running over 90 percent. Are our only choices to lower the security (or stop it altogether) or buy an additional processor on the server?

A: If your processor wasn't bottlenecking until you added IPSec, I suspect it's the overhead of processing the encryption that's tipping it over the edge. You could experiment with slightly lower levels of security or look to buy a new processor, but perhaps a better alternative might be to consider replacing the network card with one that includes a coprocessor that offloads the IPSec processing from the main server's processor. 3Com and Intel offer such network cards that provide considerable network performance for both computers with and without IPSec by handling network processing at the driver level. If you are planning on using IPSec within your organization, these coprocessor adapters are worth adding to your shopping list. However, beware that the IP Security Monitor and **Netdiag** tool, which interrogates the IP Security Policy Agent, cannot provide the IPSec information that is handled at the driver level.

Q: I've got lots of "Event ID 542" messages on my computer, which says something about an invalid encryption algorithm in connection with ISAKMP/Oakley. Does this mean I've got a security problem?

A: There's no security problem in that nobody has breached any security policies you've specified. However, you have security policies which specify 128-bit encryption (3DES), and your version of Windows 2000 does not support this (you can verify this by looking at the **Cipher Strength** under Internet Explorer's **Help | About**). The built-in security policies include the strongest security first and allow computers that cannot support these to negotiate down. This means that usually your computer will be able to successfully negotiate with an IPSec-enabled computer that has 128-bit encryption support (unless they have been modified to only accept the highest security). However, there's little point in your IPSec policies asking for a level of security you can't support, so you could either delete all references to 3DES (which would get rid of this event message in the future) or move it down to the bottom of the list with DES listed first.

Q: I want to secure our Intranet Web server such that a sniffer couldn't see any data that passes between our Windows 2000 Professionals and our IIS5 server. Would the default policies of Client (Respond Only) and Secure Server (Require Security) be sufficient?

A: If you really want to secure *all* data between clients and this server, then no, the default Client (Respond Only) policy is not sufficient. Remember that this policy will never initiate security, which means when it first contacts the Web server it will be in unsecured format. While the Secure Server policy will not allow any unsecured data out, it has no control over accepting unsecured data. If it really was important to encrypt even the initial connection to the Web server, you would have to modify the policy such that all data to this server was secured, and it blocked any data that wasn't secured.

Q: What sort of IPSec policy do I need for VPN clients wanting to use L2TP/IPSec?

A: When you install RRAS on a Windows 2000 server, this automatically adds a policy for L2TP/IPSec, so there's no need to create one yourself. However, you can't see or modify it with the IPSec policy editor (which is annoying!) but you can view it with **Netdiag**, as we discussed in this chapter.

Q: I want to specify an IPSec tunnel so I can secure data sent to our Web server from home. I've specified my tunnel endpoint with the IP address of the Web server and that I only want to tunnel port 80. Does that mean traffic on all other ports won't be using IPSec if I have no other rules or filters?

A: This is a limitation of the IPSec Policy snap-in in that it will quite happily let you specify something it can't support! When using tunneling you can only specify the remote IP address, and all traffic sent to that address will be tunneled, irrespective of what ports or protocols you might also have specified. It's unusual to have to specify IPSec in tunnel mode, and would normally only be used for interoperability with third-party routers that do not support

L2TP/IPSec and/or PPTP. It is not appropriate to secure data between client and Web server—rather it is suited to router to router type situations. In this case of client to Web server you could either use IPSec in transport mode or utilize a VPN server's tunneling. Note that Windows 2000 RRAS does not use IPSec tunneling—rather it uses L2TP and encrypts the data with IPSec in transport mode.

Q: Are there any debugging tools to help determine why our security negotiation is failing?

A: As covered under the IP Security Utilities section in this chapter, the security log is the best place to determine how and where security negotiation is failing. However, for IKE experts, you can enable IKE debugging with a registry key that writes detailed information to a file called **Oakley.log** (and **Oakley.log.sav**) to the **%systemroot%\Debug** directory. To do this you must create a new key called **Oakley** under: **HKLM\System\CurrentControlSet\Services\PolicyAgent**. Under the new key, create the value **EnableLogging** with the data type of **REG_DWORD** and set to **1**. You must then stop and restart the IP Policy Agent Service for this to take effect (no need to reboot).

Remote Access

Solutions in this chapter:

Introduction

Today, the requirement to keep in touch and expand the corporate network for home-workers and those on the road is taken as the norm rather than the exception. The lines for where the corporate network ends has become blurred as more people with modems and Internet connectivity overcome physical distances with the help of remote access solutions that let them conveniently and securely connect to the company network from wherever they are. Remote Access has become an integral part of a company's IT infrastructure, and is a service that is expected to be both proficient and secure, despite restrictions and limitations that come with using technology that must depend on external unsecured and slow networks.

Fortunately, Windows 2000 has grown up from its ancestor operating systems, which assumed that a secure and fast local area network was the order of the day. Instead, Windows 2000 was very much designed with the bigger picture in mind to incorporate distributed networking over slower and unsecured links. This philosophy is very sympathetic to the requirements for a remote access solution such that it can accommodate a wide range of newer connectivity methods and yet provide administrators with a high degree of control and flexibility. These features are there for the taking outside an Active Directory environment, whether you're looking for simple dialup modem access where the need for security is low, to using digital certificates with L2TP/IPSec for access to your entire network, to having a single central configuration point for multiple remote access servers deployed throughout your network.

The three solutions we will look at here—Remote Access Service (RAS), Virtual Private Networks (VPNs), and Internet Authentication Service (IAS), despite having very different images, are actually very closely related in Windows 2000. Not only are they similar to configure, but they can supplement and integrate with each other very well. You may choose to implement one or a mixture, but I would encourage you to consider all three before deciding upon your remote access solutions.

At the heart of all three is the use of Remote Access Policies, which apply equally to Windows 2000 servers outside an Active Directory domain as they do within. True, they are much more complicated than the simple grant or deny access we had with NT4 RAS, but with this added complication comes a wealth of granular control and flexibility to help you fine-tune efficiency and security.

This chapter will cover setting up and configuring RAS, VPNs, and IAS to show you what these services can offer, and how you can make the most of them. Remember, Windows 2000 was designed with scalability in mind, so you can take heart that these solutions can apply to small and simple deployments as well as wider scale solutions that can scale up and out as required. Finally, to ensure remote users will be able to benefit from these solutions with the least amount of maintenance, we'll cover the use of the Connection Manager Administration Kit to deploy remote access configurations to the desktop.

Using and Configuring Remote Access Policies

Remote Access Policies are the hardest part of getting to grips with Windows 2000 remote access services, simply because they are new and using them to grant and control dial-in connections is not as simple as it used to be. Now there are multiple levels of checks and configuration before a remote user will be connected, which offers a much greater granular level of control.

Not only does this allow you to make the remote access server more secure and efficient, but it also allows you to consolidate remote access servers if previously they were unable to support multiple configurations simultaneously. As an example, some departments have one RAS server for dialup access with lower security requirements (such as CHAP authentication and no encryption for legacy clients), and another for VPN access, which requires a higher level of security (for example MS-CHAP v2 only, with encryption). Windows 2000 with remote access policies would allow you to accommodate both sets of security rules, determined by the port (dialup or VPN). Equally, you can now apply different security levels and settings (such as timeout values) to different groups of users, or even set different values depending on the day of the week. We'll cover the configuration choices later.

Previously in NT4 your choices of remote access control was either grant or deny in the user's account properties. On a Windows 2000 server that's offering remote access outside Active Directory, the server is going to be either a standalone server where the user accounts are local to the server, or a member server in an NT4 domain where the user accounts are stored on the NT4 Primary Domain Controller and Backup Domain Controllers. For most people looking for a company remote access solution, it's going to be a member server in an NT4 domain, which is the configuration setup we'll concentrate on most here.

When you read about Windows 2000 remote access administration models, you'll see references to these three different types:

- Access by User
- Access by Policy in a Windows 2000 native-mode domain
- Access by Policy in a Windows 2000 mixed-mode domain

Although it's tempting to believe that remote access policies mean nothing unless you're running Active Directory, this is not the case. If you're not running in an Active Directory domain, the concepts of **Access by Policy in a Windows 2000 mixed-mode domain** are functionally the equivalent of running a Windows 2000 member server within an NT4 domain, and the **Access by Policy in a Windows 2000 native-mode domain** is functionally the equivalent to running a Windows 2000 standalone server. Therefore, for the specific purposes of explaining these outside Active Directory, we'll refer to these different administrative models as:

- Access by User
- Access by Policy on a standalone server in a workgroup
- Access by Policy on a member server in an NT4 domain

Then we'll have a look at the other components of remote access policies—conditions and profiles.

It really is vital to understand remote access policies before you start configuring remote access—they are integral to Windows 2000 remote access, even outside Active Directory. Choose a single policy model you decide best suits your purposes, and then adhere to that choice. If you don't plan your remote access policies in advance, you'll end up with an unsupportable mixture of settings that will be very difficult to maintain and troubleshoot.

Remote Access Administration Models

When users try to connect to the remote access server (whether using RAS modem ports or Internet VPN ports), they need to be authenticated and authorized. Authentication involves the clients proving they are who they say they are—for example matching their usernames with their accounts' passwords. A positive authentication does not guarantee they will be connected however, because they may not be authorized for remote access. This is where the NT4 account would reference the simple **Grant Dial-in** permission option.

Windows 2000 accounts (within Active Directory or on a standalone Windows 2000 server) have an additional option called **Control access through Remote Access Policy** as Figure 9.1 shows. On an Active Directory domain in native mode (where there are no NT4 BDCs and the network has been changed to native mode) this new option will be available. It is equally available to set on a standalone Windows 2000 RAS server. However, you cannot select this option in a mixed-mode Windows 2000 Active Domain, although you can see it. Functionally equivalent to this, you won't see the new option on NT4 domain controllers.

Figure 9.1 New Dial-In Option: Control Access through Remote Access Policy

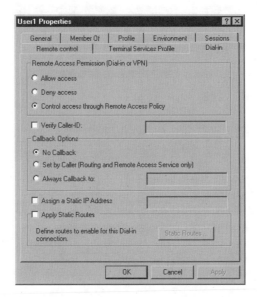

These three options (allow, deny, and control access through Remote Access Policy) on the user account are used in conjunction with two more options on the Windows 2000 server, within the Remote Access Policies. As you can see from Figure 9.2, under the **If a user matches the condition** these are:

- Grant remote access permission
- Deny remote access permission

You might have noticed from the text in Figure 9.2 that Deny doesn't necessarily mean the user will not be authorized; this setting can be overridden by the allow option on a user's account. We'll cover specific examples of how all these work together, but it's important to remember that granting remote access authorization is not simply a yes/no choice.

The dialog box in Figure 9.2 is from the Default Remote Access Policy—the single policy that is displayed when you first install Windows 2000 Routing and

Remote Access and expand the Remote Access Policies. The policy is called **Allow access if dial-in permission is enabled**. For a user to be authorized, they must match at least one remote access policy, which is why a default one is supplied. If you deleted this and didn't have any remote access policies, nobody could be authorized for remote access, irrespective of their account's dial-in permission.

Figure 9.2 Grant or Deny Remote Access Permission Options within the Remote Access Policies

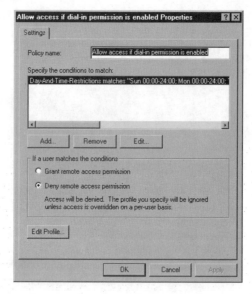

The conditions that make up the default remote access policy are day and time restrictions, which, when you use the **Edit** button to see which days/times are permitted, you'll see are effectively any day and any time.

Although this default setting at first glance might look as though everybody would be authorized for remote access, remember that the default policy setting is **Deny remote access permission**. Therefore, the default setting for a Windows 2000 RRAS server will be to deny everybody remote access authorization unless their account specifically has dial-in granted.

Granting Remote Access Authorization—By User

This is the simplest to explain and understand, and most closely relates to the RAS setting in NT4. You simply set or leave unset the **Grant dial-in permission to user** option within the NT4 user account properties (specified with the **Dialin** button), and keep the default settings in the Windows 2000 remote access policy.

This will allow any user to dial in any time, if their account has the dial-in permission set. If you prefer to refine this, you can modify the Default Remote Access policy—for example, allow remote access only during office hours. However, the final access permission will be down to the setting on the user account, and therefore you must configure each user account individually.

It's an easy remote access administration policy to have because it's simple, but has the drawback of being less easy to configure and maintain because the setting is separate to the Windows 2000 RAS configuration.

Access by Policy on a Standalone Server in a Workgroup

Remember, this is the configuration in which you can select the new option in the account's dial-in options for **Control access through Remote Access Policy**. For all accounts, use this option instead of the individual Allow access or Deny access and then use the Windows 2000 remote access policies to actually determine who will be authorized.

When you do this, the default setting would be denying everybody remote access because the remote access policy we saw is set to **Deny remote access permission** by default. You could change this to **Grant remote access permission**, but that would be no different from selecting the **Deny** on the **Dial-in** tab. Therefore you need to define that certain users (groups) can connect, and others can't. This then becomes a condition of the authorization.

Click on the **Add** button (in Figure 9.2) and you'll see a list of available conditions that can be specified. Choose the **Windows-Group** and the **Add** button, and you'll be able to browse and select specific groups. Once added to the policy you have differentiated those users as deserving different remote access authorization. You may then need to change the option **If a user matches the conditions** from **Deny** to **Grant**, depending on whether you want to explicitly grant access for these groups, or explicitly deny access for these groups.

For example if you wanted all users in your Sales group to be granted access, you could add a new policy with the Windows-Group called something like **Allow Sales Remote Access**, choose the **Windows-Group** condition, and specify the **Sales** group. Then change the policy to be **Grant remote access permission**. Only those users will be granted access. If, however, you wanted to grant remote access to everybody but temporary employees and students, you could add a new policy with the Windows-Group called something like **Deny Temps & Students Remote Access**, choose the **Windows-Group** condition, and specify the groups for the temporary employees and student—and then change the policy to be **Deny remote access permission**.

Access by Policy on a Member Server in an NT4 Domain

In this model, every user account has the **Grant dialin permission to user** set on their account, but who can actually connect is determined by the Remote Access Policy conditions as we saw in the previous model. The difference here is that the default **Deny remote access permission** option can be left, because once the users are positively identified their Grant dialin permission on their account will grant them authorization. The Grant or Deny options in this model have no meaning.

Because you can't use Grant or Deny (as we did in the previous model), you couldn't explicitly deny identified groups because the Deny permission on the policy would be overridden by their account setting. One way around this would be to add a profile setting that couldn't be matched (for example set the **Restrict Dial-In To This Number Only** to an invalid number). We'll cover profile settings later—but it's advisable to explicitly allow remote access (rather than explicitly deny remote access) when Windows 2000 RRAS is running in an NT4 domain.

> **NOTE**
>
> You may have noticed we've said *explicitly* allow and *explicitly* deny— because you can also *implicitly* allow and *implicitly* deny by not including groups in the condition.
>
> For example you can grant only technicians remote access permission by putting everybody's dial-in permission on their accounts to granted, leaving the default remote access policy and adding a new policy above it that denies access to all your groups except the Technicians group.
>
> However, configuring policies with implicit permissions is much less clear and therefore harder to maintain and troubleshoot. For example, any new group you created in your domain would need to be added into the first policy, or they automatically would have remote access permission. My advice would be to only explicitly allow/deny permissions— these policies can get complicated enough without adding implicit permissions!

Remote Access Policy Components

In addition to determining remote access authorization, remote access policy components are conditions and profiles.

We've already looked at two conditions—**Day-And-Time restrictions and the Windows-Groups**. The full list of other conditions can be seen when you choose the **Add** button, and view the list of Attributes. Many of these however, apply only if the remote access policy is configured for a Windows 2000 server running Internet Authentication Service (IAS), which we'll cover later.

Profiles offer a further set of configurations and restrictions on the connection, once it has been authorized. Click on the **Edit Profile** button and you'll see a dialog box like the one shown in Figure 9.3.

Figure 9.3 Editing the Remote Access Policy Profile

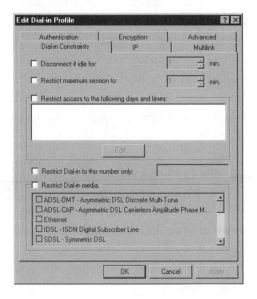

Each option has context-sensitive help for more information, but perhaps the options particularly of note are:

- **Disconnect if idle for** under the **Dial-in Constraints**, to stop users hogging the port if they have forgotten to disconnect.

- **Restrict Dial-in to this number only** under the **Dial-in Constraints**, as mentioned earlier, this can be used negatively by entering a number that isn't matched by your RAS server so it will disconnect the user.

- **IP Packet Filters** under the **IP** tab to restrict the traffic and services once connected.

- **Multilink settings** on the **Multilink tab** but note that Multilink has to be enabled at the server level first (server **Properties | PPP** tab).

- Authentication levels under **Authentication** tab. By default this is set to **MS-CHAPv2** and **MS-CHAP**. Legacy clients may need a lower authentication protocol (for example, non-Windows clients require CHAP). For greater security you can deselect MS-CHAP if you know that all your remote access clients can support MS-CHAPv2. Note that authentication protocols also are set on a server level, under the server **Properties | Security** tab and then **Authentication Methods** button.

- Encryption level under the **Encryption** tab. By default this is set to **Basic** and **Strong**. You must have the 128-bit version of Windows to support Strong. Deselect this if your Windows 2000 server is not running the 128-bit version (**Internet Explorer | Help | About** will display your Cipher value as 56-bit or 128-bit). Conversely, if you wanted to support only 128-bit encryption and you knew all your connecting clients could support this, you could deselect the **Basic** option.

Configuring Windows 2000 Routing and Remote Access (RRAS)

When you first load the Windows 2000 Routing and Remote Access (RRAS) snap-in, you'll be prompted to run the Configure and Enable Routing and Remote Access wizard to help you configure the settings you need. Figure 9.4 shows the options you can select.

If you want to configure a RAS server for modem dialup, you can choose the second option, **Remote access server**. If you want to configure a VPN server because you have a permanent Internet connection, you can choose the third option, **Virtual private network (VPN) server**. Or you can choose **Manually configured server**, or start off with one configuration and modify it (for example choose the Remote access server and add VPN ports so the server supports both simultaneously).

Figure 9.4 Initial Setup Choices from the Routing and Remote Access Server Setup Wizard

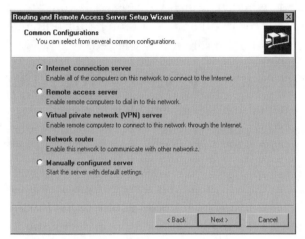

WARNING

After Windows 2000 Service Pack 1 was released, it was noted that there was a bug in configuring the server properly when choosing the VPN option (it wouldn't correctly forward packets). Although this may now be fixed in Service Pack 2 it would be prudent to select the RAS option or manually configure the server.

The wizard will step you through relevant configuration choices; you can change these later, so if in doubt you can select the default and return to these later. Most of these options are server options, so to configure them, right-click your server in the **Routing and Remote Access snap-in** and select **Properties**. The tabs available are:

- General
- Security
- IP
- IPX
- NetBEUI
- PPP
- Event Logging

Configuring General Server Properties

These options decide whether your RRAS server is going to act as a remote access server (RAS and/or VPN) and/or a router. Our only interest here is the Remote access server, so make sure this is selected.

Configuring Security Server Properties

This dialog box gets a bit more complicated. It first of all asks which Authentication and Accounting provider you wish to use—the choices are **Windows Authentication** or **RADIUS Authentication**.

Selecting Windows Authentication will result in users being authorized by this server, using accounts either on this server or within your NT4 domain. Choosing RADIUS Authentication means another server will do this authentication, and your RAS server simply passes on the authentication request and waits for a response to pass back to the client.

Similarly with the Accounting provider you can choose either **Windows Accounting**, **RADIUS Accounting**, or **None**. Accounting information, such as when a user connected and the duration of the call, can be optional (None), or the responsibility of this server or another server. We'll be returning to RADIUS servers later in this section when we look at Internet Authentication Service.

Perhaps the most important server configuration option here, as far as security goes, is rather hidden away under the **Authentication Methods** button. This displays the dialog box as shown in Figure 9.5.

Figure 9.5 RRAS Authentication Methods Settings

These settings configure which authentication protocols will be allowed on this remote access server. You can further refine these choices in the remote access policy profiles—for example configure MS-CHAP v2 and MS-CHAP at the server level and set a VPN policy to accept only MS-CHAP v2. However, you cannot override a setting here—for example, specify only use CHAP in a Dialup remote access policy if it wasn't specified here.

If the remote access policy doesn't restrict which of the authentication protocols can be used, the client will try to authenticate using the strongest authentication protocol it can support. If that gets no response it will negotiate down to trying the next strongest, and so on until an authentication protocol is agreed upon by both sides (and the client attempts to authenticate) or until a common authentication protocol is not found and the client gives up and disconnects. Therefore the settings in this box govern the overall security and flexibility of your remote access server. Set the highest authentication protocols your remote access clients can support, but consider setting less secure authentication protocols to ensure a client will be able to authenticate.

The authentication protocols are listed from strongest security to weakest, with EAP being the strongest (used for example with logon smart cards within an Active Directory Domain) and PAP being the weakest. Select PAP with care—it refers to clear text passwords, which are very vulnerable to exposure.

Configuring & Implementing…

Upgrade to MS-CHAP v2

To ensure remote access clients on a 32-bit Windows platform use MS-CHAP v2 wherever possible because this offers a much more secure authentication protocol, including mutual authentication. MS-CHAP v2 is supported on Windows 2000 by default. However, you may need to check and install upgrades and service packs for other operating systems to ensure they can use it.

For NT4 you must be running a minimum of SP4. For Windows 98 you need a minimum of SP1. For Windows 95 you'll need Windows Dial-up Networking 1.3 Performance & Security Upgrade to provide MS-CHAP v2 for PPTP connections, but MS-CHAP v2 is not supported for PPP connections under Windows 95. 16-bit Windows applications cannot support MS-CHAP v2.

The defaults are for MS-CHAP v2 and MS-CHAP. All Windows clients can support one of these. If you have non-Windows remote access clients you will probably need CHAP, which is supported on a range of platforms and doesn't send the password in clear text. It would be unusual to have a remote access client that couldn't support at least CHAP.

The final option of using Unauthenticated access may be used if you want all remote access users to have the same rights and privileges as your Guest account (rather than setting up individual accounts), or you plan to use Automatic Number Identification/Calling Line Identification (ANI/CLI) as your means of authentication where the authentication is done automatically based on the telephone number of the remote user rather than using a username/password.

Configuring IP Server Properties

As shown in Figure 9.6, this has some vital networking settings for users connecting with TCP/IP (which will often be the majority of your remote clients).

Figure 9.6 RRAS IP Server Settings

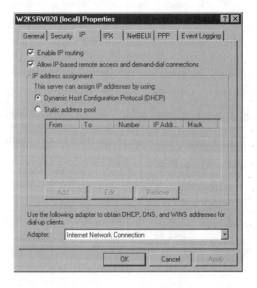

The **Enable IP routing** refers to whether remote access clients should have access beyond the server itself onto the network. Most remote access servers would have this option selected, and it is the equivalent to the **Entire network** option in NT4.

You can also specify whether your server should allocate IP addresses from a predefined pool or get IP addresses from a DHCP server. In most cases, it is preferable to use the central configuration control of DHCP. However, there are a few considerations to bear in mind when using DHCP, including:

- Automatic Private IP Address (APIPA)
- DHCP Address Allocation
- TCP/IP Configuration Options

Automatic Private IP Address

As we discussed in Chapter 6, all Windows 2000 and Windows 98 computers support APIPA by default, which means that if they are configured to use DHCP and a DHCP server cannot be found, they will self-configure with an address from the range 169.254.0.1–169.254.255.254.

It's important to consider the consequences of this when using a Windows 2000 Remote Access Server that is configured to allocate IP addresses for remote clients using DHCP. When the service first starts up, the Routing and Remote Access server will try to contact the DHCP server for a bank of addresses to give out to remote clients. If a DHCP server cannot be found, it will use APIPA and allocate addresses from the 169.254.0.1–169.254.255.254 range (and log this in the Event Log). This means that remote access clients will be able to connect but will be unable to use any network resources—with a rather unhelpful "The network path could not be found" message. However, they will be able to use resources on the RAS server itself.

Ensure good connectivity between your RAS server and the DHCP server (you could put both services on the same server for example with a single scope for remote access clients). If the DHCP server is on a different server, consider disabling APIPA on the Remote Access Server as described in Chapter 6.

DHCP Address Allocation

Windows 2000 is much more DHCP-friendly than NT4 was, and so we see a much more sensible way of allocating IP addresses for remote access clients. We have already said that the DHCP addresses are allocated on the DHCP server by the RAS server when the service first starts, rather than ad-hoc as clients connect.

Where Windows 2000 RAS is different from an NT4 RAS server is that it will ask for just 10 addresses at a time by default. Should these 10 addresses all be allocated to remote access clients all simultaneously connecting, it will then request another bank of 10. NT4 RAS used to ask for the maximum number of DHCP addresses it would ever need right at service startup—which was the number of configured ports plus one. So for example if you configured 100 PPTP ports "just in case" but rarely had more than a third of this number connecting simultaneously, the RAS server will still grab 101 addresses on startup. If you are short of IP addresses, this method of address allocation can easily deplete your scopes, and unnecessarily. Windows 2000 makes much more economical use of these DHCP addresses.

The exception to this way of working is if you have less than the 10 ports configured—for example four COM ports only. Then the DHCP address allocation reverts back to being the number of ports plus one. In our example of four COM ports this would mean the Windows 2000 RAS server asks for just five DHCP addresses.

If you know in advance that 10 is too low a number for the average number of simultaneously connected RAS clients, you can change the default number by editing the registry on the Windows 2000 RAS server. You will need to add a new (REG_DWORD) key called **InitialAddressPoolSize** to the following key: HKEY_LOCAL_MACHINE\SYSTEM\CurrentControlSet\Services\ RemoteAccess\Parameters\IP

Specify the value you want to use—for example, 20 will double the default number reserved by the RAS server. Confirm the new number has taken effect when you next load the RRAS service by checking the number of leased addresses on your DHCP server—all RAS allocated leases will have a modem icon on the DHCP snap-in.

TCP/IP Configuration Options

Most people don't realize that when a remote access client receives an IP address through DHCP, it doesn't receive the standard DHCP options you have configured, for example the domain name, WINS servers, DNS servers, and so on. Any server or scope options will be discarded. All that is passed from the RAS server to the RAS client on connection is the IP address. Not even the subnet mask is supplied. So how does a remote access client function on just an IP address?

First, the subnet address is assumed. For all Windows 2000 clients, the subnet mask will be an all-host address of 255.255.255.255, which safely assumes that all addresses will be remote to the client and therefore forwarded to the RAS server. For down-level clients, the subnet mask assumed will be the default class masks—

so for example an address of 10.10.0.5 will have a subnet mask of 255.0.0.0 on a remote client, even if your DHCP scope has the subnet mask defined as 255.255.0.0.

If you are using nondefault masks (which is common these days) this is something to watch out for when troubleshooting remote access connectivity. Based on the wrongly assumed subnet mask, down-level clients may wrongly try to use their local area network connection rather than their modem when trying to access a remote resource. This can be overcome by manually modifying the routing table on the remote client (for example you could do this within the static routes option on the client's dial-in account properties).

Typical scope options such as the WINS and DNS addresses are taken from the RAS server's settings, so if these are specified incorrectly on the RAS server itself, remote access clients will inherit these incorrect or incomplete settings. One option that cannot be passed in this way is the domain name (for example, company.com). When the RAS server has more than one network card, the particular set of TCP/IP configurations will be taken from the adapter specified on the bottom of the **IP** tab.

Windows 2000 offers a neat way around stripping off these DHCP options by using the new **DHCPInform** message that is used when using DHCP Relay. When you use Windows 2000 DHCP Relay, all the DHCP configuration options will be passed to the client, which is a much better way to keep your TCP/IP configuration central. Note that it doesn't matter if your RAS server is on the same subnet as the DHCP Server—they can even be on the same server and DHCP Relay can still be used to pass the DHCP options to remote access clients.

TIP

Even if you don't want to use any of the new Windows 2000 RAS features such as remote access policies, this ability to pass DHCP options to remote access clients can be reason enough to upgrade your NT4 RAS to Windows 2000.

It's very easy to configure DHCP Relay on the RAS Server. Simply navigate down the IP Routing tree in the left pane until you see the DHCP Relay Agent. If it's not listed, you'll have to add it as an additional Routing Protocol by right-clicking on **IP Routing | General** and selecting **New Routing Protocol**.

Once it's added to your RRAS snap-in, right-click it and choose **Properties**. Specify the IP address of your DHCP server as shown in Figure 9.7.

Figure 9.7 Configuring DHCP Relay on RRAS so Remote Access Clients Receive DHCP TCP/IP Options

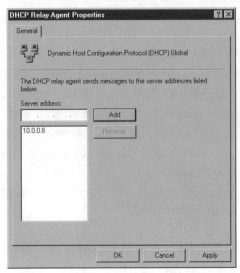

In addition to specifying the WINS server(s), consider deploying LMHOSTS files on remote access clients that have intermittent problems either initially authenticating on the domain, or browsing around the network once connected.

Particularly on limited bandwidth connections, clients can timeout before receiving the IP address to NetBIOS service or name resolution it requires. By having a local LMHOSTS file that contains entries for your domain controllers and key resource servers, you will eliminate the majority of these timeout delays. For example, such an LMHOSTS file might look like the following:

```
10.0.0.10   NT_PDC              #PRE    #DOM:COMPANY
10.0.0.10   "COMPANY \0x1b"     #PRE
10.0.0.11   NT_BDC              #PRE
10.0.0.15   EXCHANGE_SERVER     #PRE
10.0.0.20   DATA_SERVER1        #PRE
10.0.0.21   DATA_SERVER2        #PRE
10.0.0.25   DATA_SERVER6        #PRE
```

Configuring IPX Server Properties

This tab appears only if you have the IPX protocol installed on your RRAS server. As shown in Figure 9.8 it allows you to specify whether to accept IPX connections from RAS clients, and whether they should have access to other network resources. Other options include IPX addressing options.

Figure 9.8 RRAS IPX Server Settings

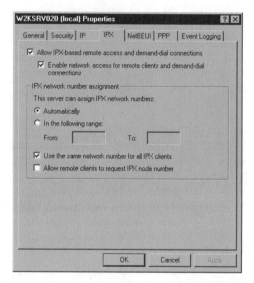

Configuring NetBEUI Server Properties

This tab appears only if you have the NetBEUI protocol installed on your RRAS server. As shown in Figure 9.9 it allows you to specify whether to accept NetBEUI connections from RAS clients, and whether they should have access to other network resources.

> **TIP**
>
> NetBEUI protocol is often suitable for 16-bit clients with low base memory values because NetBEUI is frequently the default protocol on legacy clients, and takes up the least amount of memory. Because it is so lean there is less to configure, and hence less that can be misconfigured.

Figure 9.9 RRAS NetBEUI Server Settings

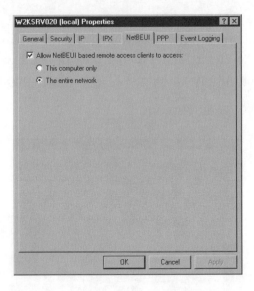

Configuring PPP Server Properties

These options shown in Figure 9.10 include Multilink and Dynamic Bandwidth Control, which, when supported on the remote access client, can make a dramatic improvement to throughput.

Figure 9.10 RRAS PPP Server Properties

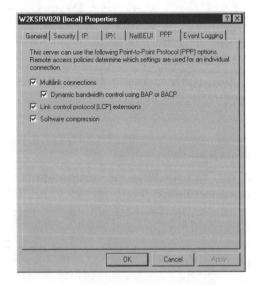

Multilink was available on NT4 RAS and simply refers to using multiple ports to increase the available bandwidth. For example, two 56Kbps modems working together on the client talking to two 56Kbps on the RAS server can offer double the throughput. Note, however, that both sides must have multilink support enabled; usually this works best when the same modem is being used (in theory, different modems with different line speeds can be used). In practice, this setting is used most often with ISDN where you can link two channels together.

Multilink has been improved in Windows 2000 to include **BAP**—Bandwidth Control Protocol. This allows additional links to be added or removed dynamically, according to data requirement. This then frees up unnecessary resources on the RAS server.

Configuring Event Logging Server Properties

This simply allows you to set the level of logging in the Event Log and to set PPP logging, which saves the PPP connection establishment process in a file called **ppp.log** in the **%systemroot%\Tracing** directory.

Configuring Dialup and VPN Connections

This section looks at how to configure your RRAS ports for remote access, whether this is for dialup access (modems attached to your server) or for VPN access (where your server offers a permanent connection to the Internet through one of its network adapters).

VPN connections are suitable for clients that first connect to their local ISP, and with that initial connection established, then dial the RAS server. Because data is being transferred over an unsecure medium (the Internet) it should always be encrypted and the client should use the highest form of authentication protocol it can. Many clients support PPTP, including Windows 2000 and the majority of down-level Microsoft clients (such as NT4, Windows 98, and Windows 95).

Note that a Windows 2000 Server can support both types of connections simultaneously. Even if you want to predominantly offer a VPN remote access solution, you may consider also configuring it for modem access for emergencies (for example if the user's ISP is down), but for greater security, disable the modem ports until required.

When you first load the Routing and Remote Access Service, it will look to see which ports are available on the server, and add these to its list of Ports. These will include any modems installed, any Direct Parallel devices, and VPN ports if you have two network cards installed. The VPN ports will be listed as WAN Miniport PPTP and L2TP.

> **NOTE**
>
> If you initially configured the RRAS server to be a RAS server and not a VPN server, or if you want to configure it manually, it will still list VPN ports if you have more than one network card in your server. However, the number of these ports by default will be 10 (5 PPTP ports and 5 L2TP ports).
>
> If you initially configured the RAS server to be a VPN server rather than a RAS server, the number of VPN ports will total 256 (128 PPTP and 128 L2TP ports), and it will still list your Direct Parallel port and any modems installed.

You can configure which of these ports you want to be used for remote access, and how many should be used, by right-clicking on **Ports | Properties**. Figure 9.11 shows a typical list of RRAS ports where one modem and 10 VPN ports (PPTP and L2TP) automatically have been allocated for RAS. The Direct Parallel port is listed here as an available device, but it's listed as **None**, which means it does not appear as one of the RAS Ports in the details pane.

Figure 9.11 Typical List of RRAS Ports

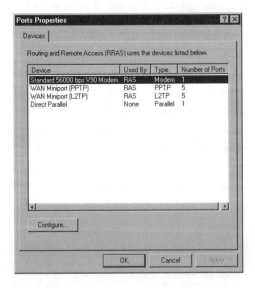

To configure any of these ports, simply select it and then click on the **Configure** button. Figure 9.12 shows the options then available.

Figure 9.12 Configuring Ports for Remote Access Connections

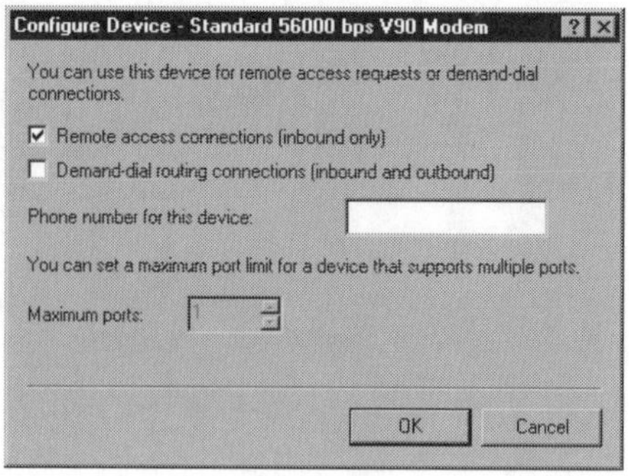

The first option, **Remote access connections (inbound only)**, determines whether the port is available for remote access clients. If you had a modem installed but didn't want to use it for RAS, you would deselect this option. Or for VPN connections, if you didn't want to use L2TP/IPSec connections you could deselect this option so that only PPTP ports were displayed under the RAS port details pane.

Note also the **Maximum ports** option. If you had multiple modems of the same type on your server, you could aggregate them for multilink by selecting a value in the **Maximum ports** field (and also enabling the multilink configuration option as we discussed earlier). For VPN connections this is the option that allows you to increase/decrease the default number of ports allocated, for example increasing 5 to 25. Select a number that matches the number of remote access clients that will be simultaneously connecting and that your server can reasonably service by way of bandwidth and processing. Remember that encrypting data will put a strain on your server's CPU, and L2TP/IPSec will have greater overheads here than PPTP connections.

That's all there is to configuring dialup and PPTP ports on the server. When a remote access client successfully connects, the connection will appear under the **Remote Access Clients** details pane where you can view the username, how long the client has been connected, and the number of ports in use (applicable if using multilink). Double-clicking on the entry will provide more information such as the allocated address and protocol in use. Figure 9.13 shows an example of a connected user called User1, connecting to a PPTP port and using TCP/IP to reach internal network resources once connected.

Figure 9.13 Example of Connected Remote Access Client Details

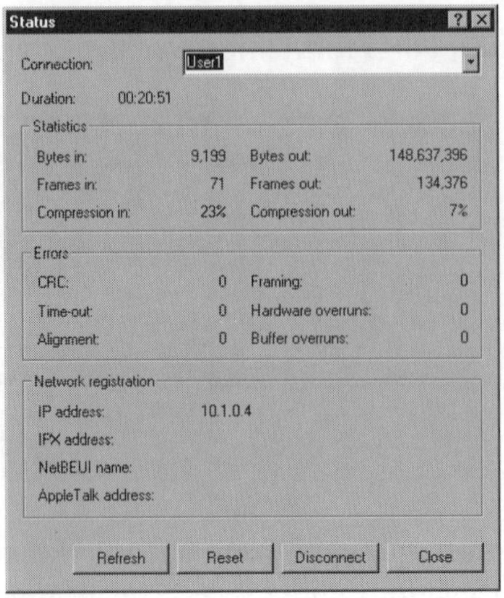

You'll notice from here that you can't tell whether this is a dialup connection or VPN connection. You'll have to look in the Event Log for this, which will tell you the name of the user connected, which port (which will identify a VPN port), and whether the data has been encrypted.

The configuration of L2TP ports can be a little more complicated, so we'll cover this separately.

Configuring L2TP VPN Connections

L2TP ports are new in Windows 2000, and together with IPSec and computer certificates offer a more secure form of VPN connection. Because L2TP ports are used with IPSec, this type of connection offers end-to-end security from remote access client to the final resource if it also is using IPSec. In comparison, PPTP offers only client to RAS server secure communication. Without IPSec, any onwards connection from the RAS server onto the corporate network will not be secured. For many people, this is not an issue if the requirement for internal security is not high—usually the security requirement is on the Internet side.

L2TP ports on Windows 2000 Routing and Remote Access Service work in conjunction with IPSec, which is needed to encrypt the data. Therefore you must be fairly confident of how IPSec functions to use this type of VPN connection; you may need to refer to Chapter 8 for more information on IP Security implementation within Windows 2000. However, when using L2TP/IPSec there's no need to configure specific IPSec policies because a default policy is created for you automatically on both the Windows 2000 server and the Windows 2000 remote access client.

Designing & Planning...

Considerations for L2TP Ports

Despite offering a more secure form of connection for remote access clients, it should be noted that this comes at the expense of additional overheads in terms of configuration and maintenance, and processing. Also, it is not widely supported by all clients. For example, Windows 2000 is the first Windows remote access client that can natively support L2TP/IPSec, so you may have to offer PPTP ports as well on your VPN server to ensure connectivity. However, if you are sure that only L2TP/IPSec clients will be using your VPN server, configuring only L2TP ports for remote access is a good security measure.

The default L2TP/IPSec policy uses certificates rather than a preshared key or Kerberos for authentication. Therefore, both the VPN server and the remote access client must have a computer certificate for authentication that is issued by the same Certificate Authority (CA). The CA used to issue the computer certificates can be a third-party CA such as VeriSign or Microsoft, or you can use your own CA as we covered in Chapter 7 when looking at issuing certificates for web servers. Certainly hosting your own CA provides greater flexibility and control over which certificates are issued, and how.

NOTE

As we discussed in Chapter 8, IPSec requires *computer* certificates and not user certificates, which have been issued by a common Certificate Authority (CA).

The default policy when using L2TP/IPSec is not displayed in the Local IP Security Policies we looked at in Chapter 8 because it is loaded dynamically by the IPSec Policy Agent when L2TP ports are detected (when RRAS is started with L2TP ports or a remote access client attempts a L2TP/IPSec connection). This policy can be displayed with **Netdiag** as discussed in Chapter 8, and also can be seen with the IP Security Monitor when the policy is active.

WARNING

Remember that the successful creation of this L2TP/IPSEc policy depends on the IPSec Policy Agent. For example, if the IPSec Policy Agent is not started when RRAS loads, this policy will not be created. Also if you stop the IPSec Policy Agent after loading RRAS, the L2TP/IPSEc Policy is removed. Therefore, if you must stop and restart the IPSec Policy agent, be sure to also restart the RRAS server afterwards. Because this policy is hidden, this behavior is not at all obvious and should be remembered when troubleshooting L2TP/IPSec connections.

The filters used on the RRAS server with this default policy are in the form of "**Me to Any**," "**Source port: Any**," and "**Destination port: UDP 1701**," where "Me" represents the IP address(es) bound to the RRAS server. There are 16 offers to negotiate security to secure the communication between remote access client and RAS server, which are listed later. All have finite lives for the session keys based on one minute or 250000 bytes.

Remember that the first security options to be met between client and server will be used; so using the default policies on both the server and client may not suit your requirements. You'll get slightly different policy offers, depending on whether your computer supports 128-bit encryption or not—it's intelligent enough to not offer 3DES when it can't support it.

However, it's interesting to note that efficiency rather than security heads the top of the list, which is encrypting and authenticating the payload with MD5. On the first two offers there's no protection for the IP headers (AH) and it lists MD5 before SHA1, even though SHA1 is the stronger authentication protocol. One of the most secure options that protects IP headers and encrypts data is listed third. Note that the last two options won't encrypt the data at all—not the high security configuration you would expect from a virtual *private* connection!

The full list of offers for a 56-bit Windows 2000 computer is displayed next. The equivalent list of offers for a 128-bit Windows 2000 computer is exactly the same from Offer 6 on. Offers 0 to 5 are the same except 3DES is used instead of

DES. Note that this means that if your VPN server supports 128-bit but your L2TP/IPSec client supports only 56-bit, the default settings mean that the server will have to negotiate down from Offer 0 to Offer 6 until a match can be found:

```
Offer #0:
    ESP[ DES MD5 HMAC]
        Rekey: 3600 seconds / 250000 bytes.
                Offer #1:
    ESP[ DES SHA1 HMAC]
        Rekey: 3600 seconds / 250000 bytes.
                Offer #2:
    AH[ SHA1 HMAC] AND ESP[ DES NO HMAC]
         Rekey: 3600 seconds / 250000 bytes.
                Offer #3:
    AH[ MD5 HMAC] AND ESP[ DES NO HMAC]
        Rekey: 3600 seconds / 250000 bytes.
                Offer #4:
    AH[ SHA1 HMAC] AND ESP[ DES SHA1 HMAC]
        Rekey: 3600 seconds / 250000 bytes.
                Offer #5:
    AH[ MD5 HMAC] AND ESP[ DES MD5 HMAC]
        Rekey: 3600 seconds / 250000 bytes.
                Offer #6:
    ESP[ DES MD5 HMAC]
        Rekey: 3600 seconds / 250000 bytes.
                Offer #7:
    ESP[ DES SHA1 HMAC]
        Rekey: 3600 seconds / 250000 bytes.
                Offer #8:
    AH[ SHA1 HMAC] AND ESP[ DES NO HMAC]
        Rekey: 3600 seconds / 250000 bytes.
                Offer #9:
    AH[ MD5 HMAC] AND ESP[ DES NO HMAC]
        Rekey: 3600 seconds / 250000 bytes.
                Offer #10:
```

```
AH[ SHA1 HMAC] AND ESP[ DES SHA1 HMAC]
    Rekey: 3600 seconds / 250000 bytes.
         Offer #11:
AH[ MD5 HMAC] AND ESP[ DES MD5 HMAC]
    Rekey: 3600 seconds / 250000 bytes.
         Offer #12:
ESP[ NO ESP SHA1 HMAC]
    Rekey: 3600 seconds / 250000 bytes.
         Offer #13:
ESP[ NO ESP MD5 HMAC]
    Rekey: 3600 seconds / 250000 bytes.
         Offer #14:
AH[ SHA1 HMAC]
    Rekey: 3600 seconds / 250000 bytes.
         Offer #15:
AH[ MD5 HMAC]
    Rekey: 3600 seconds / 250000 bytes.
```

On a successful L2TP/IPSec connection, you'll be able to see the policy in use with **netdiag /test:ipsec /v**, which will say **IPSec policy service is active, but no policy is assigned**. It will then continue to display the parameters actually in use with the last entry for a 56-bit connection typically being **Integrity: MD5 Confidentiality: DES**, which matches the Security details on the IP Security Monitor (ESP DES/CBC HMAC MD5). Under the Policy Name you'll see **L2TP Rule**.

Modifying the Default L2TP/IPSec Policy

Technically, you cannot modify the default built-in L2TP/IPSec policy, but you can disable it and then define your own using the IP Security snap-in we covered in Chapter 8. For example you could do this if you knew that connecting clients could not support the higher offers. Instead of them having to negotiate down the list until they found the security options they could support, you could define a policy with only these options.

Similarly if you wanted to ensure that all remote access clients used the more secure options of AH with ESP, you could construct an offer list that used only AH and ESP. Or you may want to move some of the less secure offers toward the bottom of the list to ensure that L2TP/IPSec connections were made that fulfill your particular security requirements.

Another reason to disable this default L2TP/IPSec policy is if you wanted to change the authentication from certificates to a preshared key. Microsoft is not at all keen on the use of L2TP/IPSec without certificates, stating that it should be used only for testing. If you decide to use preshared keys with L2TP/IPSec you are unlikely to get any support from Microsoft using this solution. They cite the use of passwords as inherently less secure because:

- Passwords are subject to dictionary attacks, can be guessed, and are passed on by word of mouth or written down.

- Passwords in IPSec policies are stored as clear text in the registry and as such are viewable to any local administrator.

- Support costs to both Microsoft and the implementing company would be jeopardized.

- Using certificates is too easy to not use them.

Designing & Planning…

Special Considerations for Laptops

The point about storing passwords as clear text is more relevant for laptops than desktops and server within your organization. Computers kept solely within the physical confinement of company premises are more likely to have their registry secured from user access. However, laptop computers are often configured more leniently so that users can add and remove hardware and software components independently from the IT department so that they can do this themselves outside the office environment.

If these users had local administrative access to their laptops and were configured to use L2TP/IPSec with a preshared key rather than a certificate, you can appreciate how such configuration would be less secure than using PPTP, because the configuration of the more secure protocol jeopardizes its security.

To disable the default L2TP/IPSec policy, you must add the registry key (REG_DWORD) of **ProhibitIpSec** and set the value to **1** under the following registry key: HKEY_LOCAL_MACHINE\System\CurrentControlSet\Services\Rasman\Parameters.

The computer must be rebooted for this to take effect. Confirm with Netdiag that the default policy is no longer being created when RRAS loads, and then create and assign your own IPSec policy.

Creating Your Own IPSec Policy for L2TP/IPSec Connections

We have already covered the basis of this in Chapter 8, and by looking at the default L2TP/IPSec policy created. However, following these steps will create a basic L2TP/IPSec policy for the RRAS server. You should consult Chapter 8 for more information on the security options involved. Remember, you may also need to repeat these steps for remote access clients—specifically this will be necessary if you want to use preshared key authentication rather than certificates:

1. Load the **Local Security Settings** snap-in and navigate down to the **IP Security Policies on Local Machine**.

2. Right-click **IP Security Policies on Local Machine** and select **Create IP Security Policy**, and then click **Next**.

3. In the IP Security Policy Name dialog box, type in a name for this policy such as **Non-Default L2TP/IPSec Policy**, and then click **Next**.

4. Click to clear the **Activate the default response rule** check box, and then click **Next**.

5. Make sure the **Edit Properties** check box is selected, and then click **Finish**.

6. You'll now be looking at the Properties of your new policy. Click the **Add** button and then click **Next**.

7. In the Tunnel Endpoint dialog box, keep selected **This rule does not specify a tunnel**, and then click **Next**.

8. In the Network Type dialog box, keep selected **All network connections**, and then click **Next**.

9. In the Authentication Method dialog box, select either **Use a certificate from this Certificate Authority (CA)** and use the **Browse** button to locate the computer certificate, or select the **Use this string**

to protect the key exchange (**preshared key**) and type in the password you want to use. Then click **Next**.

10. In the **IP Filter List** dialog box, click the **Add** button, type a name for the IP filter list in the Name box such as **L2TP/IPSec**, click the **Add** button, and then click **Next**.

11. In the **IP Traffic Source** dialog box, under **Source address**, select **A specific IP Address**, which then prompts you to type in a TCP/IP address. Type in the address of your RRAS server that is attached to the Internet. Click **Next**.

12. In the **IP Traffic Destination** dialog box, keep the Destination address as **Any IP Address** (unless you know in advance the specific subnet that will be allocated to connecting remote access clients). Then click **Next**.

13. In the **IP Protocol Type** dialog box, under **Select a protocol Type**, select **UDP** and then click **Next**.

14. In the IP Protocol Port dialog box, under Set the IP protocol port click **From this port**, and underneath, type in **1701**. Underneath that, ensure **To any Port** is selected, and then click **Next**.

15. On the **Completing the IP Filer Wizard** dialog box, click **Finish** and then **Close**.

16. In the **IP Filter List** dialog box, select the IP filter you just created, and then click **Next**.

17. In the **Filter Action** dialog box, if you don't already have a filter action you want to use, click **Add** to do this. Give it an identifying name (e.g., **AH and DES for L2PT/IPsec**) and click **Next**.

18. Make sure **Negotiate security** is selected and click **Next**.

19. Ensure **Do not communicate with computers that do not support IPSec** is selected and click **Next**.

20. Click on **Custom** and the **Settings** button to define which security protocols to use, and their lifetime parameters. When you have defined these, click on **OK** and **Next**.

21. On the **Completing the IP Security filter action Wizard**, click the **Edit properties** and click on **Finish**. There's one more option we need to set to make this secure: uncheck the **Accept unsecured communication but always respond using IPSec** and click on **OK**.

22. Now your new Filter Action is listed, select it and then click **Next** and then **Finish**, and **Close**.

23. You should now be able to see your newly created IPSec policy displayed on the right details pane. Right-click on it and then click **Assign**.

Using and Configuring Internet Authentication Service (IAS)

Windows 2000 offers a RADIUS server called **Internet Authentication Service** (IAS), which integrates and complements the Windows 2000 RRAS service which itself can be configured as a RADIUS client.

Support for RADIUS has been available for a long time in Windows NT4.0, in the form of **Internet Connection Services for Microsoft Remote Access Server** available from the NT4 Option Pack. A later version was called **Internet Connection Services for Microsoft RAS, Commercial Edition**, which can be downloaded from www.microsoft.com/ISN/deployment/icsdefault.asp.

Remote Authentication Dial-In User Service is an industry-standard protocol (defined in RFC 2138 and RFC 2139) to authenticate, authorize, and provide accounting for remote access and router-to-router connections. RADIUS is a client/server protocol and in the context of Windows 2000 the RRAS server acts as the RADIUS client, and the IAS acts as the RADIUS server. Remember the RRAS server properties for Authentication provider and Accounting provider? This could be set to RADIUS Authentication and RADIUS Accounting such that although the RRAS server physically accepts the incoming connections, all client connection requests and information about the connections would be sent to a RADIUS server.

The benefit of this is that multiple RRAS servers can be installed to physically accept the connections, and yet the connections are managed logically by a central RADIUS server. Even when using two IAS servers, the configuration of one can simply be copied over to the other server. So you can see how even without Active Directory, this provides a single repository for configuring, managing, and storing remote access configuration options. For resilience and scalability, an alternative RADIUS server can be used if the first is unavailable (much like a secondary WINS server) or they could be configured to spread the load evenly between them.

Although Windows 2000 RRAS offers new features that make it easier to consolidate RAS servers, there may still be good reasons why you want to use multiple RAS servers—for example to minimize network traffic (put the RAS server on the same subnet as the remote resources that will be used), to utilize multiple modems if your current modem bank is exhausted, or for resilience (for example using two different ISPs to guarantee VPN availability or to safeguard against router failure). Configuring these RAS servers as a RADIUS client would enable you to redirect the authentication onto a central server that was configured with the remote access policies you wanted to use, and perform the account authentication.

You can also use a RADIUS server for accounting information—for example to log who connected when, the duration of the connection, and what services were used. However, the accounting side is less likely to be used in a corporate environment and more likely to be used at an ISP company, or a company offering outsourced services so the appropriate charges could be ascertained.

Unfortunately, some of the features found in the NT4 version of IAS (Commercial Edition) have not been carried over to Windows 2000 IAS. These include being able to offer a Proxy RADIUS service, and the ability to authenticate users in a multivendor environment such as NT domains, NDS, LDAP directories, Microsoft SQL Server databases, ODBC databases, and UNIX password files. This provided great consolidation opportunities because such a wide range of user accounts could be pooled together and configured as one central service. Windows 2000 IAS currently can authenticate only from NT4 domains and Windows 2000 accounts (local SAM and Active Directory). You can extend this, however, by producing custom authentication modules with the IAS Software Development Kit (SDK).

The benefits of using Windows 2000 IAS include support for the new authentication protocols such as EAP, MS-CHAP v2, Dialed Number Identification Service (DNIS) and Automatic Number Identification (ANI), and unauthorized access. And of course the remote access policies can all be defined centrally, which means that even an NT4 RAS server can benefit from remote access policies.

Because IAS is configured with a standard Windows 2000 MMC, you can configure and monitor it from any Windows 2000 server, or from any Windows 2000 Professional desktop or laptop that has the Administrative Tools installed. Additionally Windows 2000 IAS supports RFC-based RADIUS SNMP MIBs so you can include it in your monitoring service.

The adherence to RFC standards means that Windows 2000 RRAS can be used with third-party RADIUS servers (that support RFC 2138 and 2139), and conversely IAS can be used with third-party remote access servers (often referred to as Network Access Servers—NAS) that support RADIUS. This would allow non-Microsoft remote access servers to benefit from the new remote access policies, for example.

RADIUS offers a wide variety of options and features, particularly when used in ISP environments and with third-party implementations. However, this section will concentrate on using and configuring Windows 2000 IAS for central authentication.

Configuring RRAS and IAS

Remember that the RADIUS settings are server-wide, and although you could choose to use the Windows Accounting provider and a RADIUS Authentication provider, you cannot authenticate using *both* Windows and RADIUS on the same RRAS server. When you change the Authentication provider, any remote access policies defined on the RRAS server will no longer be in effect. You will be prompted to restart RRAS and after the restart, the RRAS snap-in will no longer display the Remote Access Policies. However, if you later change back the authentication provider to be Windows again, your remote access policies will still be there.

To change the Authentication provider on the RRAS server, right-click on the server and select **Properties**, and the **Security** tab. Use the pull-down list box under Authentication provider and select **RADIUS Authentication** and then the **Configure** button. Use the **Add** button to define your Primary RADIUS server, and any backup RADIUS servers. Each server's score defines the order in which they should be tried, and the timeout value defines how long the RRAS server should wait before trying the next RADIUS server. The server name should be the IP address or DNS name to be used; use the **Secret** button to type in the password that will be shared between the RRAS server and IAS server. It should look something like Figure 9.14. Once this is set, you'll be prompted to restart the RRAS service.

> **NOTE**
>
> You could use Network Load Balancing with the specified IP address—or use DNS round-robin if using a DNS name—to spread the network load between RADIUS servers.

Figure 9.14 Specifying a New RADIUS Server in RRAS

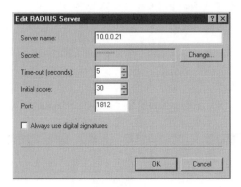

On the Internet Authentication Service server (you'll need to install this as an additional networking service if not already installed) load the **Administrative Tools | Internet Authentication Service** and define any remote access policies you want to use. If you are installing this on the same server as your RRAS server, it will automatically find any remote access policies you previously defined under the RRAS service.

In comparison with the Routing and Remote Access Service snap-in, the IAS MMC one looks rather sparse with just **Clients**, **Remote Access Logging**, and **Remote Access Policies** visible, as shown in Figure 9.15.

Figure 9.15 Internet Authentication Service Snap-In

Remember that clients to this service equate to RAS servers, so we need to add one or more Clients. To do this, follow these steps:

1. Right-click on **Clients | New Client**.

2. Type in a reference for the RAS server, and keep the Protocol as **RADIUS**. Click **Next**.

3. Type in the IP address or DNS name of the RAS server.

4. Change the **Client-Vendor** from RADIUS Standard to **Microsoft**.

5. Type in the same password you entered in the RRAS **Security** tab in the **Shared secret** box, and then repeat it in the **Confirm shared secret** box. This password will never be sent over the network. Click **OK**.

The RAS server details should now appear as an IAS Client, similar to Figure 9.16.

Figure 9.16 Example RRAS Server Configured as an IAS Client

Should you need to change any of these configuration options (for example, the password), simply right-click on the Client entry and select **Properties**. Continue to add more RAS servers as clients as you move them over to using RADIUS authentication.

When using multiple IAS servers, don't forget to add their details onto each RAS server. You will also need to have the same IAS configurations on all IAS servers. The general advice on this is to configure only the Primary IAS server, and then export the settings and import them to the backup IAS servers. To do this, follow these steps:

1. On the Primary IAS server, load a command prompt and type the following: **netsh aaaa show config >IAS.txt**. This stores the IAS configuration settings (including any related registry settings) to a text file called IAS.txt. Obviously you could substitute your own filename and use a relative, absolute, or UNC path.

2. On the first backup IAS server, load a command prompt and copy the **IAS.txt** file. Type the following: **netsh exec IAS.txt**. You should see a message saying **aaaa server configuration successfully set**.

Once a user is authenticating with IAS, you'll still see the remote access client connection details under the RRAS snap-in, and nothing visible will change in the IAS snap-in. However, with the default logging options enabled under the server's Service properties, you'll easily be able to see the authentication parameters used. Usefully these include not only the username but the type of port, the remote access policy being used, and the authentication protocol. For example a successful IAS authentication might look something like the following:

```
User1 was granted access.

Fully-Qualified-User-Name = W2KPRO028\User1

NAS-IP Address = 193.116.96.154

NAS-Identifier = <not present>

Client-Friendly-Name = W2KSRV022 - RAS and VPN

Client-IP-Address = w2ksrv020.company.com

NAS-Port-Type = Virtual

NAS-Port = 7

Policy-Name = PPTP Access For All Salesmen

Authentication-Type = MS-CHAPv2

EAP-Type = <undetermined>
```

NOTE

Being able to determine easily which remote access policy has been used and which authentication protocol has been used, must be a good reason alone for using IAS. It's not easy finding out this crucial information when RRAS is used for authentication!

IAS Configuration with ISPs

Much of the Internet Authentication Service documentation assumes that IAS will be used only by ISPs rather than within a company network. I think there's a good case for using IAS within your company so that you have a central place to configure and store remote access policies. As such, you will be concerned predominantly with RADIUS authentication only.

However, it should be noted how remote access solutions can be distributed between your ISP and your company to achieve cost-cutting benefits. For example your ISP could host the remote access server but require you to run a RADIUS server so that it can authenticate against your internal company accounts rather than duplicating these and risking inconsistencies whenever any account details were changed.

Another example is using compulsory tunneling where your company buys a VPN service from an ISP for home-workers that provides users with an automatic VPN connection whenever they attempt to access your company resources over their dialup adapters. Because the remote access server (NAS) is hosted and maintained by the ISP, configuration costs to the company are reduced, and security is increased because the tunneled connection is automatic rather than relying on the user to specify and use a VPN connection. However, the ISP still needs to authenticate the user with your user accounts, so they could configure their NAS as a RADIUS client to your RADIUS server (IAS).

If your ISP charges for these services on a connection basis, they may also send RADIUS accounting information to your RADIUS server. The accounting information logs who connected and when, the duration of the call, and so on, and logs this to a file. This file can be imported directly into a database so it can be analyzed by third-party data-analysis software.

NOTE

If the NAS will be hosted by the ISP and your company hosts the RADIUS server, you will need to configure your firewall for the appropriate ports. These are UDP port 1812 for authentication and UDP port 1813 for accounting (these may be UDP 1645/1646, respectively, on some older RADIUS implementations—IAS is configured by default for both).

Something to watch out for when your ISP is hosting the remote access server talking to your IAS is the use of ping requests they may periodically send to ensure that your RADIUS server is up and responding. These RADIUS ping requests include fictitious names that will cause them to bounce—a successful bounce means the server is active. However, these can cause problems on the IAS server—for example, unnecessary processing and unnecessary errors in the log files. If you can agree in advance with your ISP what fictitious names will be used, you can configure these to be ignored as far as authentication and logging is concerned by sending an automatic rejection immediately (*Auto Reject*). To do this, you'll need to edit the registry key: HKEY_LOCAL_MACHINE\SYSTEM\CurrentControlSet\Services\IAS\Parameters and add a new **REG_SZ** value called **Ping User-Name** and set the string to be the username that will be used when pinging your IAS sever.

Advanced IAS Configuration Options

If you want remote users to be able to connect without having to supply a user-name and password (for example, be authenticated on their calling number instead), when IAS receives a packet without the User-Name attribute, it assumes the user wants to use guest access. Accordingly, it uses the name of the guest account in its domain as the user identity. In order for this to work, you must have enabled guest access on both the remote access server and IAS, and make sure the guest account is enabled.

Most administrators would baulk at enabling the guest account on a computer that has Internet connectivity, so one way around this is to create a new account that will function as this guest account and then edit the registry on the IAS server to tell it which account has been substituted for the guest account. You'll need to edit the registry key: HKEY_LOCAL_MACHINE\SYSTEM\CurrentControlSet\Services\RemoteAccess\Policy and add a new **REG_SZ** value called **Default User Identity** and set the string to be the substitute guest account name that will be used in place of your guest account.

Configuring & Implementing...

Using Realms

Realms are used by ISPs for routing purposes and act much like domain names in that they identify specific groups. Users from a specific realm can then be treated as a logical group. For example, the ISP can grant or deny certain types of services to users from a specific realm, or differentiate charging costs depending on the realm being used. Another example is providing all your users with a realm that identifies your company, which then results in using your IAS for authentication, or compulsory tunneling.

When the user is connecting with a realm name, and this information is passed to the IAS server, you must define how these realm names equate to your user accounts. You do this with the server's Properties, Realms tab. You'll need to define rules to determine how realm identifiers are replaced (*stripped*) such that they match your Windows accounts.

Similarly, when no domain name is supplied, by default IAS will supply its own domain name. If you want to substitute this for a different domain name, you'll need to edit the registry key HKEY_LOCAL_MACHINE\SYSTEM\ CurrentControlSet\Services\RasMan\PPP\ControlProtocols\BuiltIn and add a new **REG_SZ** value called **DefaultDomain** and set the string to be the substitute default domain name that will be used in place of the IAS server's domain name.

Configuring Remote Clients with the Connection Manager Administration Kit

This handy utility is very badly documented and undersold as an additional tool on a Windows 2000 Server. You no longer have to buy the Internet Explorer Administration Kit in order to be able to distribute fully configured remote access connections for users. These can be fully customized with your own company logos and icons, Help Desk telephone number prominently displayed, automatically downloading up-to-date phone book entries, launching key applications once the remote connection is established, and so on. Or they can use standard defaults, and you just supply the basic connection details required for the client's dialer program.

However, despite reading of all these benefits and features, initially I couldn't find the Connection Manager Administration Kit (CMAK), despite numerous references telling me it should be under my Administrative Tools. It wasn't! Finally, I found the **Connection Manager Components** listed under the Windows components, **Management and Monitoring Tools** when using Add/Remove Programs. This isn't installed automatically so you need to install it.

You may also need **Connection Point Services**, which not only isn't automatically installed, but has to be installed direct from the Windows 2000 Server CD under **\VALUEADD\MSFT\MGMT\PBA**. Then run **pbainst.exe**, which installs the **Phone Book Administrator** (used to create the phone book entries) and **Phone Book Service**, which is an IIS5 extension that works with the FTP service so you can ftp connection entries, and users can download phone book updates if necessary from your Web site.

If you have no need for users to download updated phone book entries, and don't want to run a FTP service (even temporarily), you may have no need of the Phone Book Service. Instead you can supply a static phone book with the appropriate entries with the Connection Manager Administration Kit. However, to do this you'll need to have a phone book file (pbk), which you can easily create with the Phone Book Administrator, or you can use a text editor to supply the required information manually in the specified format. You cannot use your own rasphone.pbk that is created as a result of manually configuring dialup entries in your Network and Dialup Connections—despite the same extension the format is entirely different.

NOTE

IIS5 needs to be running with an FTP service when Connection Point Services is installed in order to create the virtual directories. If necessary, you can manually create this later, but it's easier to let the install program do this for you.

The Connection Manager Administration Kit Wizard steps you through configuring a service profile, the set of files required to configure remote user's connection details bundled into a self-installing executable file that you distribute to users who need remote access. This service profile will work on any 32-bit Windows platform and requires in all, about 1MB free hard disk space. Users must have the Connection Manager v1.2 software installed in order to use your configuration options, which can be included in the service profile. If they already have this installed, the hard disk space required is greatly reduced (requires about 200KB).

The Connection Manager Administration Kit Wizard steps you through the relevant stages of creating a customized connection utility (dialer) for your users. These steps can include adding a Help Desk telephone number, including your own customized bitmaps and icons, specifying programs to run automatically when connected, including a customized Help file, and can even add the PPTP protocol for Windows 9x users (however, this must first be installed manually on NT4 machines). The only stipulation is that users have a modem that is at least 9600 baud, and TCP/IP is installed prior to installation.

The last page of the Wizard will tell you where the self-extracting cabinet file is located so you can distribute it to users—for example on CD or by allowing them to download from your FTP site. When they run it, they'll have a choice of creating a desktop shortcut for their connection, or selecting it from their Network and Dialup Connections (or equivalent). When you distribute this to remote users and partners, there will be far less chance of not connecting to your remote access servers through a misconfigured connection, and it looks very professional because it's all preconfigured and can be branded with your own company image.

However, before using the Connection Manager Administration Kit, you must ensure that your RRAS and IAS work as designed by manually creating connections and testing your server setup. Once these connections are confirmed as working you can use these details to define the connections for your users. This section will step you through the following:

- Manually Defining Connections
- Using the Connection Manager Administration Kit
- How Users Install and Use Connection Manager

Manually Defining Connections

We will assume that you have successfully installed and configured the interfaces that will be used for your connections; in other words your modem(s) on the RAS server and Internet connection, and the modem on your remote access client.

When defining dialup connections for the client side, Windows 2000 makes this incredibly easy with the **Make New Connection** option under the Network and Dial-up Connections. This will load the Network Connection Wizard, which prompts you for the type of connection required as shown in Figure 9.17.

Figure 9.17 The Windows 2000 Network Connection Wizard

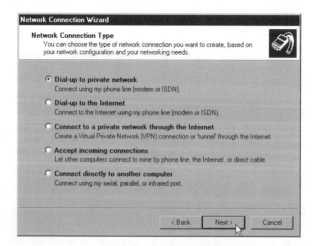

Choose **Dial-up to private network** to specify RAS connections, **Dial-up to the Internet** to specify an ISP connection, and **Connect to a private network through the Internet** to specify a VPN connection (you should have your ISP connection defined first).

For the RAS connection, you simply need to supply the telephone number of your RAS server's modem. The ISP connection will probably load the Internet Connection Wizard—make sure you select the last option: **I want to set up my Internet connection manually, or I want to connection through a local area network (LAN)**. The VPN connection will prompt you to specify the underlying PPP connection—make sure you choose the ISP connection and not the RAS dialup option! Although you can use either an IP address or domain name for the VPN server, for greater security consider using an IP address and not including your VPN server's details on a publicly accessible DNS server.

After you have created the connections, you can right-click on them and select **Properties** to fine-tune their settings—for example, the redial attempt number and timeout value, whether to include the Windows logon domain in the credentials, authentication requirements, which protocols should be used, and so on. Note under the VPN connection you'll have **Automatic** selected under the **Networking** tab, and **Type of VPN server I am calling**. This will mean L2TP/IPSec will be tried first, and then PPTP. If you know users will not use L2TP/IPSec, you can change this to **Point-to-Point Tunneling Protocol (PPTP)** instead to ensure a faster connection.

Once you are happy that all connections are working satisfactorily, you are ready to use the Connection Administration Kit to distribute these settings to users. If you prefer not to use the Connection Manager Administration Kit, you can supply information for users on how to create their own connections manually.

Using the Connection Manager Administration Kit

Using this utility breaks down into two parts—actually running it to create the service profile and the preparation work you need to do before actually running it. Unfortunately, the preparation work is the hardest part. How much preparation work you need to do depends on how much customization you're aiming for. As a bare minimum you'll need to have a phone book that is in a suitable format for Connection Manager Administration Kit, whether that's a static phone book you supply with your service profile or a dynamic one supplied through an FTP site.

Because most companies do not change their RAS server telephone numbers or VPN server names/addresses, I would have thought that hosting an automatic phone book download is overkill, and more suited to an ISP environment. However, the option is there.

This section will guide you through the basics of creating your own service profile for remote access within a company environment. As such we will look at the following:

- Preparation: Creating a static Phone Book
- Preparation: Creating a dynamic Phone Book
- Running the Connection Manager Administration Kit
- Refining Details

> **NOTE**
>
> The Connection Manager Administration Kit and Connection Services offer a very varied and complex number of options. Full details can be found in the online help that accompanies the Connection Manager Administration Kit, the Phone Book Administration, and the Connection Manager Administration Guide.
>
> The Connection Manager Administration Guide can be found online at the following link: www.microsoft.com/windows2000/en/server/help/cmak_ops.htm.

Preparation: Creating a Static Phone Book

The simplest phone book you could create would be one connection—for example, the telephone number of your RAS server, or if you're specifying a VPN connection you'll specify the telephone number of the ISP (the VPN server details will be added with the Connection Manager Administration Kit). When you have multiple RAS servers and multiple ISPs, you will have to decide whether to create one big phone book and let the user choose the appropriate connection, or deploy multiple phone books with only the relevant connections.

The two files you'll need when specifying a static phone book are the **.bpk** file and a **.pbr** file. These files must be in the same directory, share the same base name, and have the same limitation as DOS-based naming formation (no spaces, maximum of 8 letters).

The .pbr file refers to a region file that you have to create manually with a text file. The format of it is simple enough—the first line contains a number that is the number of regions you want to define and will equate to the number of lines minus this line itself. So for example if you had only one region (for example, London) this would be the number 1. The following lines need to be the names of your regions. In my example, my second and last line would be simply London:

```
1

London
```

The format of the phone book is 11 fields, separated by commas and all filled. If a field has no value, it should contain the number zero. The format of this file for each entry is the following:

```
Index,TAPICountryOrRegionID,StateOrPrvinceID,POPName,AreaCode,
PhoneNumber,MinBaud,MaxBaud,Reserved,ServiceType,DUNEntry
```

A single example entry of this for the UK (44), using my first regional number, where my POP name is **Company**, the area code is **0208**, the telephone number is **5441122**, only modem access is allowed, and which has the connection name of **Company RAS Server** is the following:

```
1,44,1,Company,0208,5441122,0,0,0,41,Company RAS Server
```

If you don't fancy creating this file manually, you can use the Phone Book Administrator to do it for you. Once installed, load it and follow these steps to create a single entry in a single phone book we'll call **Company**:

1. Click on **File | New Phone Book** and specify the name you want to use (e.g., **Company**).

2. Make sure your new phone book entry is highlighted, and select **Tools | Regions Editor**.

3. Click on **Add**, and change **New Region** to be the name of the region you want to use (for example, **London**), press **Enter** and click **OK**.

4. Click on **Edit | Add POP** (POP stands for Point of Presence) and you'll see three tabs for **Access Information**, **Settings**, and **Comments**.

5. In the **Access Information** tab, fill in the details as appropriate. You'll notice that the Region list box will contain the region you previously entered. When completed, your dialog box will look similar to Figure 9.18 and you can see how this corresponds to the text file format.

Figure 9.18 Creating the Phone Book Access Information with Phone Book Administration

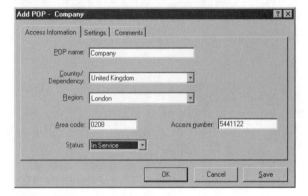

6. Now go into the **Settings** tab and specify the information you want to supply. The default POP settings are probably not appropriate for our needs, so you may want to remove the Sign on and Multicast options (I also removed the ISDN option because my RAS server is modem only). The Dial-Up Networking entry is very important—this is the name users will see to identify their connection, so choose it with care. In my previous example I didn't specify a minimum and maximum analog speed so these fields were filled with zeros. Your tabbed dialog box should look something similar to Figure 9.19.

Figure 9.19 Creating the Phone Book Settings with Phone Book Administration

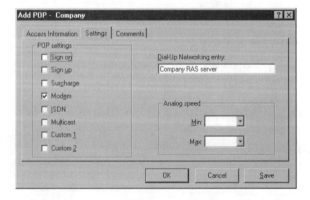

7. Click on **OK**. You should now see some of your phone book entries in the bottom pane, as in Figure 9.20. If you want to go back and edit any details, simply click **Edit | Edit POP**.

Figure 9.20 A Single Entry in a Phone Book

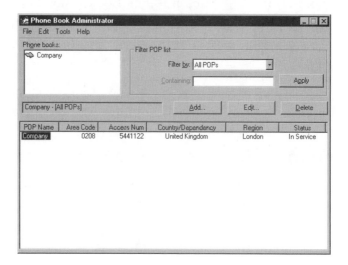

8. Despite defining the phone book entry, we haven't actually created the file yet. To do this, click on **Tools | View Phone Book Files** where you'll see the details again, in the specified field format. Click on **Save As** and save the phone book entry in the default .pbk format.

Preparation: Creating a Dynamic Phone Book

This involves creating a phone book as we did in the previous section with Phone Book Administrator, and then transferring it to an FTP site so users can reference this via your Web service, and download new or changed entries when they dial into your company.

You need to have your FTP virtual directory ready and configured to accept your phone book. The **PBSData** virtual directory is created when Connection Services is installed but you'll need to enable Write access to transfer the phone book, and ensure Anonymous Access is disabled. For security reasons, consider disabling the write permission in between phone book transfers.

Create your phone book just as we did in the previous section, following steps 1 through 7. Instead of saving the phone book as outlined in step 8, click on **Tools | Publish Phone Book** and then follow these steps:

1. Within the Publish Phone Book dialog box, click on the **Options** button and define your IIS server details together with credentials (username/password) to use the FTP site.

2. Click on **OK** and you should now see your server details appear on the bottom right of the Publish Phone Book dialog box.

3. If you're happy with the default directory chosen, which will be used to save current phone book (**\Program files\pba\<POP name>**), click on **Create**.

4. The **Post** button will now become available. Click on this and you'll be prompted to select your dialup connection and connect.

Running the Connection Manager Administration Kit

Once installed, the Connection Manager Administration Kit does indeed appear under the server's Administration Tools and when run, you'll see the first page of the wizard, which looks like Figure 9.21.

Figure 9.21 Running the Connection Manager Administration Kit

To create a basic service profile, which creates a self-extracting file you could distribute to users, follow these steps:

1. On this first page, click **Next**.

2. On the Service Profile Source dialog box, click **Next** to create a new service profile.

3. The Service and File Names dialog box will prompt for the name of a service profile (which will be displayed in the user's connection dialog box) and the name of the self-extracting distribution file. For simplicity it's a good practice to use the same name for both. In my example, I'm calling both **Company**. Type these in and click **OK**.

4. On the Merged Service Profiles dialog box, click **Next**.

5. On the Support Information dialog box, type the text information you want displayed on the user's connection dialog box, for example **Ring (0208) 544 3344 for the Help Desk**. Click **Next**.

6. On the Realm Name dialog box, click **Next**.

7. On the Dial-Up Networking Entries, click **Add** and manually type the name you supplied in the phone book (either the last entry in the text file, or the Dial-Up Networking Entry you specified in Figure 9.19). It should look similar to Figure 9.22.

Figure 9.22 Specifying the Add/Edit Dial-Up Networking Entry

8. Click **OK** and click **Next**.

9. On the VPN Support dialog box you can click **Next** and go to Step 11 if you're specifying a RAS connection. If however, your dial-up networking entry was for an ISP rather than a RAS server because you want to create a VPN entry, click on the **This service profile** and then **Next**.

10. On the VPN connection dialog box, type the IP address or DNS name of your VPN server and keep the other defaults. Click **Next**.

11. On the Connect Actions, unselect all three checkboxes and click **Next**.

12. On the Auto-Applications, click **Next**.

13. On the Logon Bitmap dialog box, click **Next**.

14. On the Phone Book Bitmap dialog box, click **Next**.

15. On the Phone Book dialog box, browse for the static phone book (.pbk) you created—by default this would have saved in your **My Documents** folder. Select it so it's displayed and click **Next**. If at this point you don't have a corresponding region file in the same directory, you'll be warned and not allowed to continue.

16. On the Icons dialog box, click **Next**.

17. On the Status-Area-Icon Menu, click **Next**.

18. On the Help File dialog box, click **Next**.

19. On the Connection Manager Software dialog box, keep the default of selecting the Connection Manager software, and click **Next**.

20. On the License Agreement dialog box, click **Next**.

21. On the Additional Files dialog box, click **Next**.

22. On the Ready to Build the Service Profile, click **Next**.

23. You should now see the command prompt window showing the progress of your cabinet file, and at the end see the final page showing you that the Connection Manager Administration Kit Wizard has completed, and the location and name of your self-extracting file as in Figure 9.23.

Figure 9.23 Completing the Connection Manager Administration Kit Wizard

Refining Details

You can now probably see how you could refine some of the details in the Connection Manager Administration Kit—for example, supplying your own logos, bitmaps, applications that must run when connected, and so on. You can go back and edit an existing service profile to change any of these details. Use the online help for more information—for example how many pixels are allowed for each icon, and so on.

To download a phone book automatically, on step 11 on the Connect Actions dialog box, select the **Run post-connect action (after connecting)**, and on the next dialog box select **Automatically download phone-book updates**. A few pages further you'll see the Phone-Book Updates page, which will ask you to supply the URL of your Connection Point Service server (Web server), as you can see from Figure 9.24.

Figure 9.24 Specifying the Connection Point Service Details

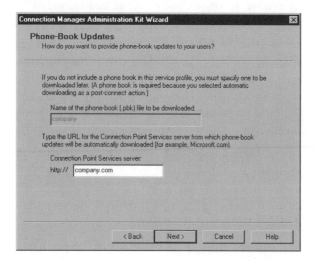

With this setting, the Connection Manager on the user's PC will send a phone book request to this server to see if there are any changes in the phone book, and if so, it will download them. The next time the user starts Connection Manager, the updated entries will be available.

You may also consider editing the Readme file that is provided. The default readme.txt is included with the Connection Manager Administration Kit (in **\Program Files\CMAK\Support** folder), which is then incorporated into the service profile if the Connection Manager software is included. If you edit this before running the Connection Manager Administration Kit your version will end up on users' PCs. This provides an easy way to give users detailed information on how to drive the Connection Manager program for example, or supply alternative methods for contacting your Help Desk—for example, supplying different telephone numbers and e-mail addresses. You could then use the Support Information (defined in step 5, earlier) to reference this file rather than supplying a single telephone message as we did.

Other modifications are possible by editing the Service Provider file (.cms), which is a text file containing the options you have chosen in the Connection Manager Administration Kit. There may be some settings in here that cannot be set through the Connection Manager Administration Kit. You can choose whether to edit them on a per service profile basis, or directly edit the template file so that all new service profiles will have the nondefault values. The template files are created in the **\Program Files\CMAK\Support** folder with the base name of **template**. So if you want to change a setting for all new service profiles, you'll need to edit **template.cms**. Existing service profile files are saved to **\Program Files\CMAK Profiles\<ServiceProfileName>**.

Read through the comprehensive online help topic **Advanced customization: editing service profile files** in the Connection Manager Administration Kit for more information on each available setting. Two settings to note are the following:

- Disabling the **Save password** on the logon details which forces users to securely authenticate on each connection.

- Specifying L2TP/IPSec tunnel connections—PPTP only is the default assumed.

Disabling the Save Password Option

To disable the Save password option, add the **HideRememberPassword** entry under the [Connection Manager] section and set it to be = 1.

Specifying L2TP/IPSec Tunnel Connections

To specify L2TP/IPSec connections, add the entry **VpnStrategy** under the [Connection Manager] section and set it to one of the values in Table 9.1.

Table 9.1 Setting the Tunneling Value, Necessary for L2TP/IPSec Support

VpnStrategy Value	Description
1	PPTP only (the default)
2	Try PPTP and then L2TP/IPSec
3	L2TP/IPSec only
4	Try L2TP/IPSec and the PPTP (Windows 2000 default)

How Users Install and Use Connection Manager

When users run the self-extracting service profile, they'll be asked whether the connection should be available for all users (a computer-wide setting) or for just that user. They'll also be asked whether to add a shortcut for it on the desktop. See Figure 9.25 for this dialog box.

Figure 9.25 Installing the Service Profile

When the program has installed, they'll see the dialog box in Figure 9.26, which displays the name of your Service Profile on the caption bar and your support information.

Before they can connect, they'll need to click the **Properties** button where they'll see different tabbed options, depending on the options you choose with the Connection Manager Administration Kit. The one in Figure 9.28 shows an **Internet Logon** tab and one the one in Figure 9.26 shows an additional **Logon domain** box because the service profile for these includes a VPN connection.

The first time Connection Manager is loaded, users will need to load the phone book—you can't supply this as default. To do this, select the top **Phone Book** button and select the **Access number** as shown in Figure 9.27.

Figure 9.26 Connection Manager When First Loaded

Figure 9.27 Selecting the Phone Book

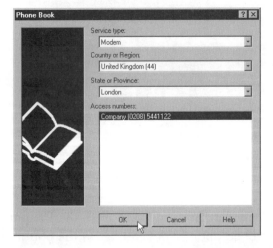

You'll notice on this dialog box that users could choose alternative service types (if you allowed them), and alternative countries/regions and access numbers. When users have selected the details they want to use, the **General** tab should look similar to Figure 9.28.

You'll notice that if you have multiple dialup connections, you could change which one to use with the **Connect using** list box.

Figure 9.28 Connection Manager General Properties

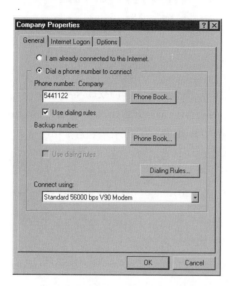

The **Internet Logon** tab allows users to specify their company logon and password, which no doubt will be different from their ISP logon.

The **Options** tab sets the number of redial attempts (defaults to 3) and the idle disconnection time (10 minutes), which can be between never and 24 hours.

Once any options that need to be set are configured, they will remain set the next time Connection Manager is loaded. The user can then simply click on **Connect**.

Walkthrough: Configuring Remote Access Policies

This steps through the creation of two remote access policies for two very different types of users—traveling sales people who must be able to connect over the Internet any time but only with L2TP/IPSec, and home workers who can connect either over the Internet or dialup, but only during office hours. Nobody else should be allowed to connect to this RRAS server that resides in an NT4 domain. It assumes that the RRAS server is already configured and that all the relevant users have been granted dial-in permission on their NT account.

The steps this walkthrough covers include the following:

- Defining a Remote Access Policy for sales people to connect only using L2TP/IPSec, anytime.

- Defining a Remote Access Policy for home workers to connect only during office hours, but using any connection method.

1. If not already loaded, load the Routing and Remote Access MMC (or IAS MMC if using RADIUS authentication) and if necessary expand your local server so you can right-click on Remote Access Policies. Select **New Remote Access Policy** and type in as the Policy friendly name **Sales people with L2TP/IPSec** and then click **Next**.

2. In the Conditions dialog box, click on the **Add** button, click on **Windows-Groups** and then the **Add** button. Initially the Groups dialog box will be blank. Use the **Add** button to select your NT group or groups that include all the sales people this remote access policy should include. Our example includes two groups in the COMPANY domain, called **Sales – East Division** and **Sales – West Division**. When you have added your group or groups, your Conditions dialog box should now look similar to Figure 9.29.

3. We need an additional condition, so right-click on the **Add** button again and this time select the **Tunnel-Type** and **Add**.

4. Scroll down the list of Available types until you find **Layer Two Tunneling Protocol (L2TP)**. Select it, click the **Add** button, and click **OK**.

5. We now have our two conditions of Windows-Groups and Tunnel-Type that we need, as shown in Figure 9.30, so click **Next**.

Figure 9.29 Defining the Sales Groups

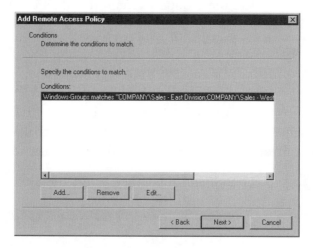

Figure 9.30 Defining the Connection Type

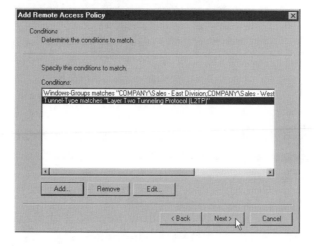

6. In the next dialog box, change the Permissions to **Grant remote access permission**, click on **Next**, and then **Finish**. We don't need to specify anything in the Profile, so click **Finish** again.

7. Back in the MMC, right-click **Remote Access Policies** again for our second policy. Again, select **New Remote Access Policy** and this time call it **Home workers in office hours** and click **Next**.

8. Click the **Add** button to again select **Windows-Groups**, click **Add** and this time select the group or groups that define your home workers, and click **OK**.

9. We need to add the second condition of office hours, so click on the **Add** button in the Conditions dialog box and this time select the **Day-And-Time-Restriction** attribute and click **Add**.

10. Click on the start day and time for your office hours, drag the mouse down to your end of office hours, and then change the setting to **Permitted**. This dialog box should look similar to Figure 9.31.

Figure 9.31 Defining the Office Hours Restriction

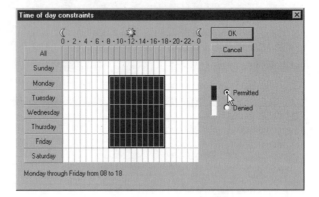

11. Click **OK** to close this dialog box and then **Next**. Again, change the Permissions to **Grant remote access permission**, click on **Next** and **Finish**.

12. Back in the MMC, we have just one more thing to do. Right-click the top remote access policy, **Allow access if dial-in permission is enabled** and select **Delete**. This policy allows anybody, anytime to connect if they have dial-in permission on their NT account. Because this server must allow only specified groups to connect, it's safer to delete this and use only your custom remote access policies. Because our example is based on two different groups of users and there's no cross over between them, the order of these remote access policies doesn't matter. If you had a situation where remote users had more than one remote access policy apply to them, consider the order of the policies and remember that the first matching policy will be used. To change the order, right-click on the remote access policy and use the **Move Up** or **Move Down** options.

13. You can go back into these policies to further refine them, add or edit the groups and conditions, and so on, by right-clicking on them and selecting **Properties**.

Summary

Some of the key benefits of running Active Directory are being able to finely control and maintain central configurations, and being able to encompass newer technologies. And yet with the help of remote access policies and the Connection Manager Administration Kit we've been able to do just that for our remote access solutions by using services, utilities, and configurations that ship with Windows 2000 on a member or even standalone server.

We've covered how remote access policies are the key to remote access solutions in Windows 2000, whether on the remote access server itself, or on another authenticating machine. They control how and when users can connect, whether for dialup, PPTP, or L2TP/IPSec. With L2TP/IPSec connections being a newer and more secure form of remote access, we've looked into how these work rather than just relying on the Microsoft shipping defaults so you are better equipped both to troubleshoot any problems, as well as fine-tune the settings to better suit your requirements.

Finally we looked at deploying the connection information needed on the client side by using the Connection Manager Administration Kit and Connection Point Services—whether you simply want to provide a basic connection with static entries, or a more customized solution that can download new entries to users automatically when they connect.

Solutions Fast Track

Using and Configuring Remote Access Policies

☑ Using Remote Access Policies wisely is the key to centrally controlling remote access authentication and connection configuration.

☑ You can implement different Remote Access Policies administrative models depending on your setup and the requirement for central configuration and control.

☑ Popular remote access policy settings are the conditions of day and time, windows groups, authentication protocols required, encryption levels, and idle disconnection timeouts.

Configuring Windows 2000 Routing and Remote Access (RRAS)

☑ You must choose between authentication and logging on the RRAS server itself, or with a RADIUS server like Windows 2000 IAS. Once you choose to use a RADIUS server as your authentication provider, remote access policies are no longer relevant to RRAS.

☑ Remember to configure the strongest authentication protocols you can, but also remember to include less strong ones (such as CHAP) if required by users for non-Windows clients. Most 32-bit Windows clients can use the stronger authentication protocol MS-CHAP v2 although you may need to update them with Service Packs.

☑ To keep your configuration central, try to use DHCP for IP address allocation for remote access clients. However, this has some considerations including APIPA, and whether DHCP options will be passed to remote access clients.

☑ Each protocol (TCP/IP, IPX, and NetBEUI) can now have its own setting that defines whether remote access clients can use network resources or should be confined to just the RRAS server.

Configuring Dialup and VPN Connections

☑ You can configure Windows 2000 RRAS to offer both dialup and VPN connections simultaneously.

☑ Dialup connections are denoted by Modem ports, and VPN connections by WAN Miniports. You can configure these for remote access, how many should be defined, and whether to use multilink with them.

☑ L2TP/IPSec connections are designed to be used with certificates and with a dynamically and automatically created IPSec policy that offers 16 different security combinations.

☑ If the default policy does not suit your security requirements, you may want to disable this and create your own.

Using and Configuring Internet Authentication Service (IAS)

☑ IAS acts as a RADIUS server for RRAS and other remote access servers, acting as a single and central authentication and logging provider. When configuring RRAS as a RADIUS client, the remote access policies in use will be on the IAS server.

☑ For fault tolerance you can specify one or more backup RADIUS servers, and for load balancing between multiple IAS servers you could use Network Load Balancing or DNS round-robin.

☑ When using multiple IAS servers, configure the Primary with the clients and remote access policies you want to use, then use Netsh to export those settings, and import them onto the other IAS servers.

☑ Outsourcing your remote access servers could be financially advantageous—but the outsourcing company may ask you to run a RADIUS server on your network to authenticate users against your user accounts (your NT4 SAM for example). In this scenario you must configure your firewall to accommodate the RADIUS packets, and consider configuring Auto Reject if they periodically test the online status of your server.

Configuring Remote Clients with the Connection Manager Administration Kit (CMAK)

☑ Always test your connections manually first to ensure they work on all platforms. Certainly the new Network Connection Wizard makes this much easier in Windows 2000 than on previous versions.

☑ Connection Manager Administration Kit (CMAK) is installed under **Windows Components | Management and Monitoring Tools | Connection Manager Components**. You may also need to install Connection Point Services from the Windows 2000 CD to create a phone book, and optionally publish it so that users can download new connection entries automatically.

☑ CMAK is used to gather information about the connection details and any customized information into a self-extracting executable file that produces a Service Profile for the user. When the user installs this, it creates a new network connection (and optionally a shortcut on the desktop), which when loaded displays a connection dialog box from which they easily can connect with the details you provided.

☑ You must decide whether you want to supply a static phone book or a dynamic phone book that is hosted on your IIS server and automatically downloads new entries for connecting users. However, even a static phone book requires a phone book file and corresponding region file for creating the Service Profile. You can use the Phone Book Administrator to create your phone book, or manually create it with a text editor.

☑ Some options can be specified only by editing the Service Provider files with a text editor, such as supporting L2TP/IPSec connections and disabling the Save password option.

Frequently Asked Questions

The following Frequently Asked Questions, answered by the author of this book, are designed to both measure your understanding of the concepts presented in this chapter and to assist you with real-life implementation of these concepts. To have your questions about this chapter answered by the author, browse to **www.syngress.com/solutions** and click on the **"Ask the Author"** form.

Q: How do we configure our NT4 RAS servers to be a RADIUS client so it can use the Windows 2000 remote access policies on IAS?

A: You may first need to update the server with the latest RRAS files, which are available from www.microsoft.com/NTServer/nts/downloads/winfeatures/rras/rrasdown.asp. When this is installed, go to **Control Panel | Network | Services** tab, click **Remote Access Service** and click **Properties**. In the **Remote Access Setup** dialog box, click **Network**. In the **Network Configuration** dialog box, you'll have two Authentication providers listed—Windows NT and RADIUS (if RADIUS isn't listed, you haven't got the latest RRAS files so you'll need to download these and install them first).

Select the RADIUS Authentication provider and then the **Configure** button to add (or edit/remove) your RADIUS server details.

Q: When you have many user accounts, I can see the benefit of controlling remote access permissions centrally in one place, rather than scattered across the user accounts. Verifying that users have this set on their accounts is a burden because you have to go through each account in turn. Other than migrating to native mode Active Directory so we can just use remote access by policy, is there a more sensible and less time-consuming way of verifying the dial-in permission with NT4 user accounts?

A: Fortunately, there is. The **Rasusers** command from the Resource Kit (both NT and 2000) is just what you're looking for! With this, you can display a list of users that have been granted dial-in access per server, or per domain. For example, if your NT4 domain were called COMPANY, the correct syntax would be **Rasusers COMPANY**. If you have multiple domains, create a batch file that will do this for each domain and then collate the responses into one list. This command does take a while to complete however, so use it periodically as an administrative batch command rather than a one-off confirmation on a user's account.

Q: Our firewall has been set up such that it blocks all traffic to our VPN server except PPTP, which explains why it doesn't respond to a ping request. But I'm having problems connecting to it from my client PPTP connection. I can connect to my ISP successfully, but not to the VPN server. Is there any way I can check that the PPTP packets are getting across the firewall?

A: You could use network monitor to see if PPTP packets were coming into the server—but a much simpler solution is to use one of the Windows 2000 Support Tools, **PPTP Ping**. Copy **pptpsrv.exe** onto your VPN server and load it. Then copy **pptpclnt.exe** onto your client and load it, specifying the VPN server's DNS name or IP address (for example, **pptpclnt vpn.company.com**). You won't see anything on the client side other than actually sending out packets, but the server will display the number of packets received and hopefully "GRE protocol test was successful!" Any errors detected should be shown. The most common cause of PPTP connections not getting across firewalls is that although the ports have been configured successfully to allow port 1723, the GRE (Generic Routing Encapsulation) protocol is being blocked. You must allow this protocol (protocol 47) through for the VPN connection to succeed.

Q: On our NT4 RAS server, which provided PPTP access, we used to be able to block all packets except PPTP by selecting the **Enable PPTP Filtering** option with the Advanced button on the TCP/IP properties. Where has this gone in Windows 2000 RRAS?

A: You now have to define this manually; there are many different levels on which you can do this. The equivalent to the NT4 implementation is with TCP/IP filtering under **TCP/IP Advanced Options**. Or you could more precisely define separate input and output filters on the Internet connection from RRAS by going into **IP Routing | General** and editing the properties of your Internet connected adapter. Unlike the TCP/IP properties you can block traffic from certain addresses here, and use source/destination references. And finally you could also specify filters in a remote access policy profile. If you're using only PPTP you'll have to define only TCP port 1723 and protocol 47. If you're now offering L2TP/IPSec as well, you'll have to include UDP 500 and protocol 50.

Q: What's this Remote Access Account Lockout, and how do I know if a user can't connect because their account is locked out rather than other problems like they simply can't remember their password?

A: Remote Access Account lockout is not related to the user account being locked out—it's specifically related to only remote access and defines how many times remote access authentication is allowed to fail against a valid user account before denying any more attempts. It's not set by default, but it's a good idea to set this if you're concerned about dictionary attacks— just don't set it too low or you'll prevent genuinely forgetful users from connecting! You need to set this by editing the registry key: **HKEY_LOCAL_MACHINE\SYSTEM\CurrentControlSet\Services\ RemoteAccess\Parameters\AccountLockout\MaxDenials** and change this from 0 to 1. You'll notice the other key under AccountLockout is the **ResetTime(mins)**, set in hex, which means that 0xb40 equates to 48 hours (which you may want to change). If you cannot wait that long, or want confirmation that a remote account has been locked out, you should see the account details appear under this AccountLockout key in the format **<domain_name:username>**. To manually unlock this account, simply delete their corresponding key.

Q: Can you use scripting commands to configure RRAS and IAS, or do they have to be configured with the GUI snap-ins?

A: They can be completely scripted with the Netsh shell. We used it to copy the IAS configuration from one server to another, but it's a vastly powerful and flexible scripting utility that replaces its NT4 counterpart, Routemon. One of its more useful features is to provide a quick backup of your RRAS configuration by typing **Netsh dump >filename.txt**, which you can later import with **Netsh exe <filename.txt>**, although you might want to check out the Microsoft Support Knowledge Base Q254252 for cleaning up certain entries in the dump file. Another useful job I've just discovered that Netsh can do is change an adapter's status from having a static address to a DHCP assigned address with the command **netsh interface ip set address "Local Area Connection" dhcp**. For a complete listing of syntax and commands, type **Netsh** at the command prompt, and also consult the Microsoft Support Knowledge Base article **How to Use the Netsh.exe Tool and Command-Line Switches [Q242468]**.

Q: I've just copied my IAS server settings to my backup IAS server using Netsh, without any errors displayed. However, they are not appearing in the IAS MMC. What went wrong?

A: The IAS MMC is very unusual in that it doesn't have a refresh option. This means that it cannot refresh its configuration display if it was changed outside the MMC (i.e., with Netsh). You can press F5 all you like (out of habit), but nothing happens! Therefore if you had the IAS MMC loaded and then imported your settings with Netsh, the changes won't be displayed in the MMC until you reload it, even though the settings are in effect.

Q: What's the Advanced tab under the remote access policy profile all about?

A: As you might have guessed from the two default entries displayed showing the Vendor as being RADIUS Standard, these are applicable only for remote access policies on IAS, and if you want to use specific RADIUS attributes that are not covered in the RADIUS RFC 2138. When you click on **Add**, this lists a number of Vendor Specific Attributes (known as VSAs) that you can select to define in your remote access policy. If the VSA you want to use isn't listed, you can define it manually by scrolling down and selecting **Vendor Specific** (which is type 26) and then **Add** to manually define it.

Chapter 10

Internet Connectivity

Solutions in this chapter:

- **Using and Configuring Internet Connection Sharing (ICS)**

- **Using and Configuring RRAS Network Address Translation (NAT)**

- **Using and Configuring Internet Security and Acceleration Server (ISA)**

☑ **Walkthrough: Configuring NAT to Publish a Web Server**

☑ **Summary**

☑ **Solutions Fast Track**

☑ **Frequently Asked Questions**

Introduction

For most of us it is true that Internet connectivity has revolutionized our lives, in both a personal and a business sphere. We have access to more services and more information, which in turn offers a productivity edge and freedom of choice. Previous chapters have already covered remote access solutions for home and mobile workers that extend the company network to the Internet. We've looked at Internet services for external users (consumers and partners) such as FTP and Web sites. But equally the corporate network needs to offer Internet services for internal users—external email, newsgroups, FTP downloads, Web searching and access, and even conferencing and media streaming, to name just a few.

At the network administration level, however, all this comes at the price of financial outlay, functionality, control and configuration, security, and monitoring. Each organization may put these factors at different priorities, but nonetheless they still exist and these services are more difficult to manage than internal services because some of the resources are outside the immediate control of the IT department.

With a view to addressing these issues, many companies are advocating non-routed connections to the Internet—and using network address translation and/or proxying. Translated or proxied connections to the Internet hide the internal network addresses that typically belong to the private address ranges (of 10.0.0.0/8, 172.16.0.0/12, and 192.168.0.0/16). This has two main advantages. First, it means greater security from outside attack because nobody on the Internet will know the internal addresses—only the external (public) address of one perimeter host (the machine running the translating or proxying service). Second, it means that multiple users can use the same public address (*address aggregation*), which saves money, frees up scarce Internet public addresses, and makes controlling and managing Internet traffic easier.

Windows 2000 offers three different Internet connectivity solutions to help address these requirements, which we shall cover in this chapter. Internet Connection Sharing (ICS) is available on Windows 2000 Professional and Windows 2000 Server, out of the box and with very little configuration. It is aimed at the simplest of networks with one Internet address—a small branch network, for example, or a home office network.

RRAS with the Network Address Translation (NAT) routing protocol is available only on Server versions, is available out of the box, and requires a little more configuration. However, it is more flexible than ICS and offers more functionality. This is suitable for multisegmented networks and can efficiently manage multiple Internet addresses.

Finally, Microsoft's Internet Security and Acceleration (ISA) Server (with its predecessor being Microsoft Proxy Server 2) is an additional server product with all the bells and whistles of additional security and control, monitoring, and caching. It is suitable for small networks that require features that the out of the box solutions cannot offer, but it has been specifically designed to scale well across enterprise networks.

All three solutions have their advantages and disadvantages when it comes to assessing those equations of financial outlay, functionality, control and configuration, security, and monitoring. We'll take a look at each solution in turn in the sections that follow.

You also need to take into account how each solution functions with regard to other networking issues, such as the network topology (hosts and routers) and networking services (address allocation, name resolution, and Active Directory). And in the case of ISA Server, we need to include interoperability with its predecessor, Proxy Server 2, for organizations that are already running this and considering upgrading. Although Microsoft is promoting ISA Server as a new product, its technical pedigree undoubtedly lies in Proxy Server 2, and Microsoft is currently offering a supported upgrade path with an attractive upgrade price.

The good news is that all three Internet connectivity solutions will run independently from Active Directory. ICS and NAT were aimed at the SOHO market (Small Office/Home Office), which was never envisaged to run Active Directory. In comparison, ISA Server *was* designed to run within an Active Directory environment so that it could take full advantage of an integrated directory service for better scalability and fault tolerance. To get the most out of ISA Server, you need to run it in Enterprise mode, which interacts with Active Directory. However, you can install ISA in Standalone mode and still take advantage of many options and features, with the choice of upgrading it to Enterprise mode later if you migrate to Active Directory at a later date.

If all these choices seem rather overwhelming and confusing, don't worry; they should become much clearer when we've covered each solution in terms of what is it and how it works. Then you'll be able to put together all the pieces of the jigsaw puzzle and be able to make an informed decision on which (if any) of these Internet connectivity solutions is right for your network.

Using and Configuring Internet Connection Sharing (ICS)

As we've already stated, this is the simplest of the Internet connectivity solutions so that multiple clients can share one Internet address and keep internal addresses hidden. First seen in Windows 98 Second Edition, Internet Connection Sharing was carried over to Windows 2000 Professional and as such offers the cheapest solution because it works on the entry-level operating system, which requires the lowest hardware specification. It also has the lowest administration overheads.

Basic outbound configuration (for example, so that multiple computers can all browse the Web) is as simple as clicking a check box—or two. Typically, ICS will be used with a dialup connection, but there's no reason why you couldn't use ICS with a dedicated, high-speed Internet connection. On the Internet adapter properties, you'll see a **Sharing** tab. You enable ICS by clicking the **Enable Internet Connection Sharing for this connection** option, and if your connection is a dialup, also selecting **Enable on-demand dialing**, as shown in Figure 10.1.

Figure 10.1 Enabling Internet Connection Sharing

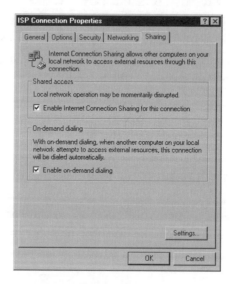

However, once you click **OK** on this dialog box, you'll immediately see an information dialog (see Figure 10.2) telling you that this computer's LAN adapter will be changed to use address 192.168.0.1 and as such it may lose connectivity with other computers.

Figure 10.2 ICS Information Dialog Box

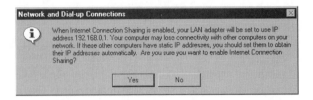

As this dialog box tells you, before other computers can use the Internet shared connection, they may need to change their IP address from static to dynamic (**Obtain an IP address automatically** in the case of Windows 2000). This is because ICS includes a *DHCP Allocator* element that cannot be disabled, but that is designed for minimal configuration.

When ICS is enabled and other computers on the network ask for an IP address, they will receive from this computer an address in the 192.168.0.0/24 range, with their default gateway set to 192.168.0.1 (that is, the same address as the computer running ICS). The DHCP allocation is only for convenient address allocation, however; you could manually set the IP addresses to use the same address details, providing they are within the 192.168.0.0/24 range and the default gateway is set to 192.168.0.1.

By enabling ICS on the computer connected to the Internet, and by enabling automatic addressing on client computers, any address that isn't local to the network will now go over the Internet connection—and so all clients have automatic Internet connectivity with their real address being translated into the single public address.

> **NOTE**
>
> The DHCP allocation is very minimalistic for no administration, which means you cannot exclude or reserve addresses or define other DHCP options, such as the domain name. All you get is the IP address, subnet mask, and default gateway.

The simple workings of this have several implications. The first is that you cannot choose which internal addresses you have—they must use this 192.168.0.0/24 network address range, which is simplest to deploy with automatic addressing. The second is that because of the address range chosen, you can only have a maximum of 254 connecting clients (including the computer connected to the Internet), and by definition it's limited to one segment. You can't run this service in conjunction with a DHCP server, or a router, or a domain controller. If these are present on the network, ICS will close down.

All DNS resolution is handled by the ICS computer's DNS, which is typically the ISP's DNS. There is no provision for a WINS service, but on a single segment, NetBIOS resolution is presumed to suffice. You can augment this with a local LMHOSTS file if you prefer to keep NetBIOS broadcasts off your network.

Other limitations of this type of Internet connectivity include not being able to use some applications. Some applications that are not suitable for address translation will work thanks to the inbuilt NAT editors for FTP, ICMP, and PPTP. Others can be proxied, including H323, DirectPlay, LDAP, and RPC. However, some applications cannot be used with ICS (or NAT), which include IPSec and Kerberos. Outside Active Directory, not being able to use Kerberos should not be a problem, but the limitation of not being able to use IPSec may be a problem. When looking at VPN solutions for a shared Internet connection, you must use PPTP rather than L2TP/IPSec.

Other limitations include a lack of monitoring and logging information (the only information available is limited to the Event Log), and you cannot control access by means of IP address, users, and protocols. Neither can you cache content to reduce bandwidth usage and speed client retrieval times.

ICS Settings

The **Settings** button on the **ICS Sharing** tab is for Applications and Services, which allow you to change the default address translation from dynamic to static.

The **Applications** tab is for configuring outbound applications (from internal client to the Internet), which require a corresponding inbound static port mapping in order to work. This will apply to applications that require a secondary connection, and the ICS configuration needs to know that these inbound connections are linked to the specific outbound applications.

More importantly for most setups, the **Services** tab is for inbound connections (from external client to your network), such as Internet users wanting to connect to any Internet service you want to publish from your internal network, behind your ICS computer. Typically, this would be your Web server, but it could be an FTP server, mail server or telnet server, and so on. You must define a static configuration so that when an inbound connection arrives, the ICS computer knows to which computer it should direct the traffic.

When you first display this dialog box, it shows a list of popular Internet services that you select and for which you fill in the name or address of the internal computer that will be hosting the service. As soon as you select one, it will prompt for the internal computer name or address, as shown in Figure 10.3.

Figure 10.3 Configuring FTP Service with ICS

For services that aren't listed, simply use the **Add** button and define the Service name and port yourself, as well as the name or address of the hosting computer. Figure 10.4 shows a static mapping for a Web service that resides on a computer named W2KSRV01 (this name will be resolved by broadcast).

Figure 10.4 Configuring a Web Service with ICS

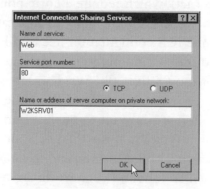

Using and Configuring RRAS Network Address Translation (NAT)

As we've already stated, RRAS NAT as a routing protocol can be used only on a Windows 2000 Server version. Although this makes it more expensive in terms of the underlying operating system and hardware specification, it does offer substantial benefits that limited the ICS solution. Due to its flexibility and added functionality, however, this also comes at the cost of additional administrative overhead. Some limitations that we saw in ICS remain. These include the following:

- NAT cannot be used with IPSec or Kerberos.

- NAT cannot be used in conjunction with routers, domain controllers, or a conflicting DHCP server.

- NAT cannot control access by IP address, or user, or time, or protocols, or content.

- NAT cannot cache content.

- NAT monitoring is limited (can view real-time connections and Event Log entries) with no logging or reporting facilities.

- NAT has no intrusion detection.

The advantages NAT has over ICS include the following:

- NAT can support more than one IP address, which allows for efficient pooling of addresses for automatic load balancing. It also means that inbound services can have a reserved address and that headers need not be translated (more on this later).

- NAT can disable the DHCP Allocator and use a real DHCP server that provides greater control over which addresses are used, which reservations can be used, and other DHCP options that can be configured (such as the domain name and an internal DNS server that must be able to forward requests to the Internet).

- NAT can work with multiple segments by having multiple internal adapters and connecting them all to the Windows 2000 NAT sever.

- NAT clients can use WINS server for NetBIOS name resolution—either from DHCP configuration or by inheriting this from the NAT server when used with the DHCP Allocator.

Installing NAT

NAT is one of the RRAS components on a Windows 2000 Server. It can run in conjunction with other RRAS services, such as the dialup and VPN connections we looked at in Chapter 9. However, it cannot run in conjunction with the DHCP Relay service unless the DHCP Allocator is disabled.

How you install NAT on your RRAS Server depends on whether RRAS is already configured for another component and whether you will be using a demand-dial connection (such as a modem), or a second network adapter that is linked to the Internet.

The easiest setup is if your RRAS server isn't yet configured and you use the Routing and Remote Access Server Setup Wizard we first saw in Chapter 9— only this time select the **Internet connection server** option, followed by the **Set up a router with the Network Address Translation (NAT) routing protocol**. You will then be prompted to select either your Internet connected adapter or, if you will be using a demand-dial connection, the **Create a new demand-dial Internet connection option**, as shown in Figure 10.5. This, in turn, will load the Demand Dial Interface Wizard.

When stepping through the Demand Dial Interface Wizard, make sure you select as your connection type **Connect using a modem, ISDN adapter, or other physical device**. You should then see your dialup adapter listed so that you can select it. Ensure **Route IP packets on this interface** is selected, and then type in the credentials needed to make the connection (for example, telephone number, username, and password).

At the end of the installation, you'll find default ports configured for routing that include your demand-dial interface, a direct parallel port (if it wasn't in use), and five PPTP/L2TP ports. If you want to use only NAT over your demand-dial device, you could disable the other ports by selecting **Ports | Properties**, and for each port other than your demand-dial device, select it and then **Configure** and remove the Demand-dial routing connections (inbound and outbound). Your Ports Properties would then look similar to Figure 10.6.

Figure 10.5 Configuring RRAS NAT for Dialup with the Setup Wizard

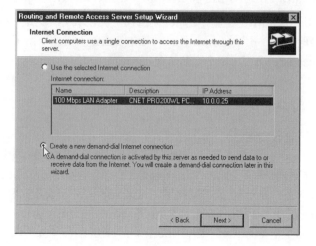

Figure 10.6 Disabling Unneeded Ports for NAT Routing

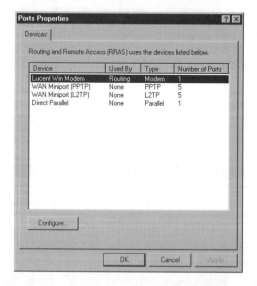

Under the **IP Routing | Network Address Translation (NAT)** you should now be able to see the two (or more) interfaces that include your Internet connection (for example, your modem) and your internal connection(s), similar to Figure 10.7.

Figure 10.7 NAT Configured with a Dialup Connection

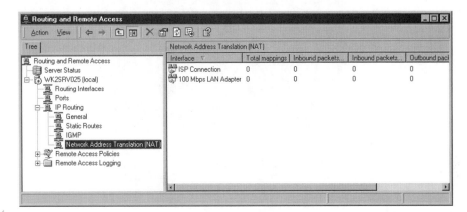

NOTE

If your RRAS server is already configured but you don't want to keep the settings and start anew for NAT, right-click on the server and select **Disable Routing and Remote Access** to delete all your RRAS settings (including any remote access policies). Then you can start again, with the **Configure and Enable Routing and Remote Access Wizard**.

Adding NAT to RRAS

If your RRAS is already configured, you must first ensure that RRAS is configured for routing under the server's properties. If you will be using a demand-dial interface to the Internet (such as a modem) you should select **Router** and **LAN and demand-dial routing**. If you will be using an adapter that has Internet connectivity you can simply select **Router** and leave the default of **Local area network (LAN) routing only**, as in Figure 10.8. Note that you can also use the remote access service at the same time.

If you will be using a demand-dial interface, you first need to ensure that it is configured for routing. Right-click on **Ports | Properties** to see a list of available ports. Your demand-dial device should say **Routing**, not **None** or **RAS**. If necessary, select it and the **Configure** button, then set the **Demand-dial routing connections (inbound and outbound)**, as shown in Figure 10.9.

Figure 10.8 Configuring RRAS for Routing

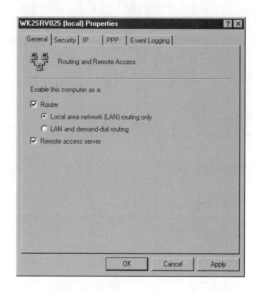

Figure 10.9 Configuring the Demand-Dial Interface for Routing

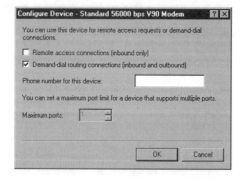

You can now initiate the Demand Dial Interface Wizard by right-clicking **Routing Interfaces | New Demand-dial Interface** as we saw in the earlier section.

With the interfaces configured, you can now select NAT as a new protocol by selecting **IP Routing | General | New Routing Protocol** and selecting **Network Address Translation (NAT)**.

You'll now have to manually add the interfaces you want to use. Right-click on **Network Address Translation (NAT)** and select **New Interface**. You'll see a list of interfaces you can use—you should have at least two available that include either your demand-dial interface or your Internet-connected adapter. Add each in turn, and when you do, you'll be prompted to indicate whether this is for the **Private interface connected to private network** or the **Public interface connected to the Internet**. Figure 10.10 shows an Internet adapter being added and configured as the public interface. When you have finished, you should now have a display similar to the one in Figure 10.7.

Figure 10.10 Adding the Internet Interface to the NAT Routing Protocol

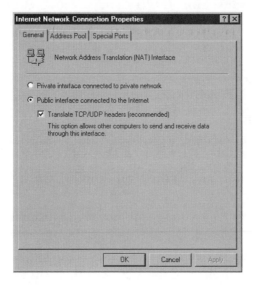

Configuring NAT

There are two elements to configuring NAT. The first is configuring the global NAT properties, and the second is configuring the NAT Internet interface properties.

NAT global properties include the level of information written to the Event Log, how mapping should work, how internal clients receive their IP address, and how DNS names should be resolved for clients. You view and configure these by right-clicking on **Network Address Translation (NAT)** under **IP Routing** and selecting **Properties**. You'll see tabs for the following:

- General

- Translation

- Address Assignment

- Name Resolution

NAT interface properties include the setting for the private or public interface and whether TCP/UDP headers should be translated, the public addresses you want to pool or reserve, and which Internet services you want to publish on your private network behind the NAT server. You view and configure these by right-clicking on the NAT Internet interface after expanding **IP Routing | Network Address Translation (NAT)**, and selecting **Properties**. You'll see tabs for the following:

- General

- Address Pool

- Special Ports

Configuring Global NAT Properties

The **General** tab lets you specify the level of information you want to go in the Event Log.

The **Translation** tab lets you specify how long mappings should remain in memory before being deleted. Usually the defaults of a day for TCP and one minute for UDP would suffice for most setups. The **Applications** button on this tab is the functional equivalent of the **ICS Application** tab we looked at earlier, where you can specify secondary connections.

The **Address Assignment** tab is where we see our first big difference between ICS and NAT. Here, you have a choice of whether you want to use the DHCP Allocator with the check box for **Automatically assign IP addresses by using DHCP**, as shown in Figure 10.11.

If this option is not selected, you can use either static addresses or a full DHCP server. The advantage of using a full DHCP server is that you can offer clients the full DHCP options we looked at in Chapter 6, such as a domain name, an internal DNS server and so on. If you do want to use NAT's automatic addressing, though, you have a choice over the address range used (you can change the default 192.168.0.0/24 to a network address of your choice, such as the commonly used subnetted 10.0.0.0 network), and you can exclude addresses from the range (such as your DNS server, WINS server, etc.).

Figure 10.11 Configuring Address Assignment for NAT

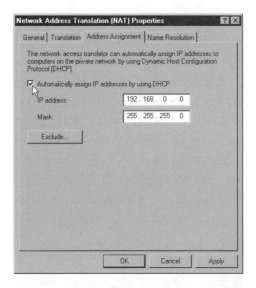

Configuring & Implementing...

Using Multiple Segments with NAT

Note that internal address assignment is global—you cannot set different addresses on the internal NAT interface, which you might want to do if you had multiple segments connecting to your NAT server (with an adapter for each segment). In this scenario, it would be wise to disable the automatic address allocation and use static addressing on connecting clients and, on each client, to set the default gateway to be the same address as the adapter on the NAT server that is on their segment.

However, you could still use the automatic IP addressing with multiple segments, and addresses would be assigned to each client on a first-come, first-served basis, irrespective of which segment they were from. NAT would still work like this, but you would be in the unusual situation of having clients on a different physical segment having the same logical subnet address, which is not ideal from a troubleshooting point

The **Name Resolution** tab applies only to DNS names—not WINS resolution. When WINS names are required to be resolved by internal clients, the NAT server will intercept and proxy these to its configured WINS server and return the response to the client. It's therefore important to ensure that the NAT sever has the correct WINS configuration, particularly if using a multisegmented network where a broadcast might fail.

In comparison, the **Name Resolution** tab is used when connecting internal clients have a DNS name that needs to be resolved. If you have your own internal DNS server for internal names, but that can forward names for which it is not authoritative (Internet names), you can leave unchecked the **Resolve IP address for: Clients using Domain Name System (DNS)**, as shown in Figure 10.12.

If, however, you have no internal DNS server, or if your DNS server cannot resolve Internet names (for example, it is a root server, or it is not connected to the Internet), you must enable this option. The Demand-dial interface option should be selected when your Internet connection is using a demand-dial interface (such as a modem).

Figure 10.12 Configuring NAT to Use DNS Name Resolution

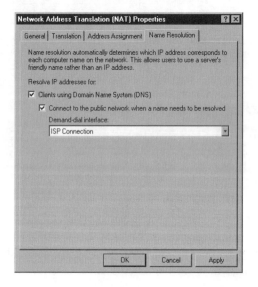

> **NOTE**
>
> Configuring NAT to resolve DNS names means you will not be able to resolve internal host names (if you use them) because all DNS name resolution will go to the Internet DNS server, which, of course, knows nothing about your private network names. One way around this is to use a local HOSTS file on each PC.

Configuring NAT Internet Interface Properties

The General tab lets you toggle between the Private and Public settings for this interface. When set to Private for the internal network connection, no other configuration options are available, and the other tabs are no longer displayed.

The option for **Translate TCP/UDP headers (recommended)** refers to whether the NAT server will automatically translate the source ports in addition to the source address. Usually this is necessary for NAT to work because typically you would have many internal clients sharing the same public IP address. The NAT server chooses a new source port for all outing calls to ensure that its outbound source ports are unique for that computer. It also offers a better level of security for the internal client if its real source port is not in the Internet packet.

Configuring & Implementing…

When Not to Translate Headers

Despite the dialog text implying that NAT will not work without this option set (This option allows computers to send and receive data through this interface), there are genuine reasons why you might want to configure NAT to not translate TCP/UDP headers. It is most likely to be applicable if you had the same number (or less) of internal clients than you had public addresses available, and if you wanted to keep specially configured source ports on the clients' workstations/applications. Although the default source port for a TCP/IP host is to dynamically allocate the next available source port number above 1024, some applications can be configured for a specific source port that is needed, for example, for security reasons on the host or a firewall. If this were the case and the NAT server dynamically translated the source port along with the source address, the connection would fail.

The **Address Pool** tab lets you define the public addresses you want to use, so, for example, if your ISP deal included 12 static public Internet addresses, you could pool them together on a single interface for better throughput on a first-come, first-served basis. But the real advantage of using multiple public addresses is with the **Reservations** button, where you can reserve a specific public address for an internal workstation. This reservation can be used for both outbound and inbound connections, as shown in Figure 10.13.

Figure 10.13 Configuring a NAT IP Address Reservation

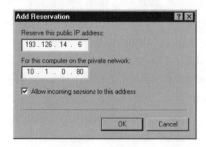

It's most likely to be used when you want to host Internet services on your internal network and want to reserve a specific address for this (for example, your Web site server has its own public address reserved through NAT, which will not be used for other Internet traffic). When you can define a specific IP address mapping (particularly on an exclusive, one-to-one basis), this allows better monitoring and control.

For example, when it is used in conjunction with a firewall, you could tie down only TCP port 80 to be used with a specific public address to help safeguard against attacks on other ports. So, for example, if somebody resolved your Web site address of www.company.com to 193.126.14.6 and ran a port scan detection on this address, he or she wouldn't find any ports available except TCP port 80.

The **Special Ports** tab equates to the Services tab we saw when configuring ICS, where you can define static mappings for internal hosts that you want to publish with Internet services behind the NAT server. You need to define the incoming port (and outgoing port, if applicable) together with the internal address of the workstation. The difference with NAT is that you can specify an address pool (if you've defined an address pool) or the interface.

Monitoring NAT

One of the benefits NAT has over ICS is that you can monitor the service from the RRAS MMC, as well as by checking the System Event Log for any errors or warnings.

The Public (Internet) interface will display statistics for current mappings, and the number of inbound and outbound packets translated and rejected. Figure 10.14

shows the results of just two workstations using outbound connections for Web browsing and email. (I've moved the columns around so that you can more easily see the translated packets rather than the rejected packets which were at 0.)

Figure 10.14 Monitoring NAT Mappings

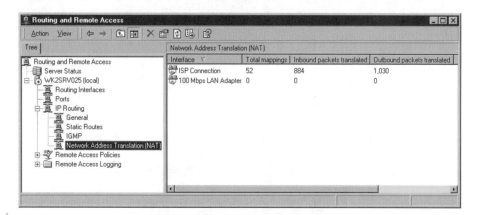

> **NOTE**
>
> You cannot delete a mapping with the Routing and Remote Access MMC, only refresh the mapping information displayed. If you right-click on the Internet interface in the RRAS MMC and select **Delete**, you will delete the interface rather than the mappings it has.

You can get more information on these current NAT mappings—for example, whether UDP or TCP was being used, the private and public addresses being used, and the private and public ports together with the idle time of each mapping's connection. To do this, right-click on the public (Internet) interface, and select **Show Mappings**. You'll see a list of each packet's details, similar to Figure 10.15. You'll notice in this list how the NAT server is performing the DNS lookups for clients because you can see the DNS port 53 displayed.

You can make this display easier to read by right-clicking on the white space in this dialog box and selecting **Columns**. As you can see from Figure 10.16, you can select which columns you want displayed and their order.

More NAT information can be found with the **Show DHCP Allocator Information** and **Show DNS Proxy Information** options, which are available when you right-click on **Network Address Translation (NAT)**. The DHCP

Allocator Information displays statistics about the DHCP packets this server has sent and received, as shown in Figure 10.17.

Figure 10.15 Network Address Translations Session Mapping Table

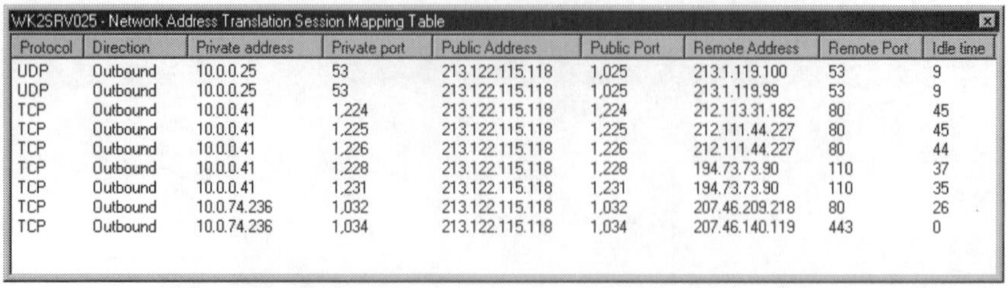

WK2SRV025 - Network Address Translation Session Mapping Table

Protocol	Direction	Private address	Private port	Public Address	Public Port	Remote Address	Remote Port	Idle time
UDP	Outbound	10.0.0.25	53	213.122.115.118	1,025	213.1.119.100	53	9
UDP	Outbound	10.0.0.25	53	213.122.115.118	1,025	213.1.119.99	53	9
TCP	Outbound	10.0.0.41	1,224	213.122.115.118	1,224	212.113.31.182	80	45
TCP	Outbound	10.0.0.41	1,225	213.122.115.118	1,225	212.111.44.227	80	45
TCP	Outbound	10.0.0.41	1,226	213.122.115.118	1,226	212.111.44.227	80	44
TCP	Outbound	10.0.0.41	1,228	213.122.115.118	1,228	194.73.73.90	110	37
TCP	Outbound	10.0.0.41	1,231	213.122.115.118	1,231	194.73.73.90	110	35
TCP	Outbound	10.0.74.236	1,032	213.122.115.118	1,032	207.46.209.218	80	26
TCP	Outbound	10.0.74.236	1,034	213.122.115.118	1,034	207.46.140.119	443	0

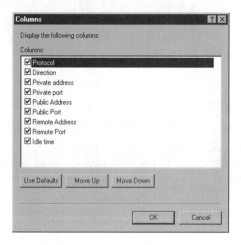

Figure 10.16 Configuring NAT Session Mapping Table Columns

Figure 10.17 NAT DHCP Allocator Information

WK2SRV025 - DHCP Allocator Information

Description	Details
Messages ignored	0
DECLINE messages received	0
DISCOVER messages received	7
INFORM messages received	0
RELEASE messages received	0
REQUEST messages received	26
ACK messages sent	26
BOOTP replies sent	1
NAK messages sent	0
OFFER messages sent	7

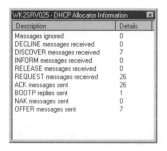

Similarly, the DNS Proxy Information (if using DNS proxying) will show statistical information on this service, similar to Figure 10.18.

You can also track back IP addresses to MAC addresses, as shown in Figure 10.19, by navigating to **IP Routing | General** and right-clicking on the Internet interface and selecting **Show Address Translations**.

Figure 10.18 NAT DNS Proxy Information

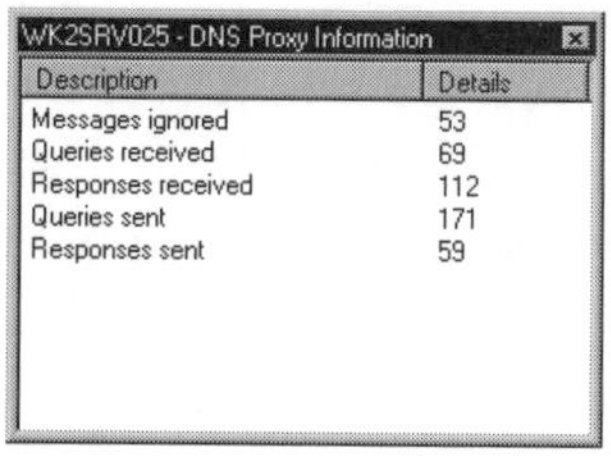

Figure 10.19 NAT DHCP Address Translations

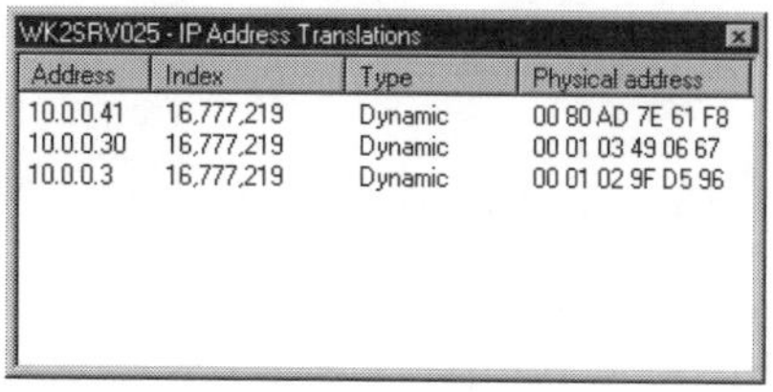

Controlling Connections

You have very little control over ICS and NAT connections. You can't, for example, specify that only some users can have Internet connectivity and others cannot. You cannot define which protocols or sites users are allowed to use. And you cannot monitor historical traffic or break down traffic by user.

Because network address translation works at the network layer, your only control lies at this level—by making your ICS or NAT server unavailable for connectivity (that is, by disabling ICS sharing or stopping the RRAS service). In the case of NAT you can control which PC can use the NAT server by disabling the DHCP Allocator and using restrictive IP address assignment (for example, you could do this through DHCP reservations).

When you're using a demand-dial interface rather than a permanent LAN adapter for your Internet connection, you also have the configuration ability to control when it can be initiated, which can restrict when Internet connectivity is allowed/disallowed. This is possible only when the demand-dial interface is dedicated to NAT, rather than also being used for router-to-router connections.

However, you can control only when the demand-dial interface is *initiated*, not when it can be used. There's a subtle but important difference. If the Internet connection has already been made, the restrictions for the dial-up configuration will not apply. They apply only when the connection is down—for example, after a timeout on either side.

You can also set filters for your Internet connection by using the **Input Filters** and **Output Filters** on the properties of the Internet connection. This approach lets you set restrictions for source and destination address/mask and ports on an exclude or include basis. When defining filters with NAT, though, remember that internal address/mask and ports will be dynamically translated by NAT—so, for example, you couldn't define a filter such that only certain computers could use destination port 80 for Web access because their true source address will be translated into the source address of the NAT server by the time it gets to the Internet connection filter. In most circumstances, NAT filters are useful only for defining the destination port.

Configuring Demand-Dial Restrictions

The two demand-dial restrictive options you can set are **IP Demand-dial Filters** and **Dial-out Hours**, which are both available when you right-click on the demand-dial interface under the **Routing Interfaces**, as shown in Figure 10.20.

Figure 10.20 Configuring the Demand-Dial Interface for Internet Connectivity

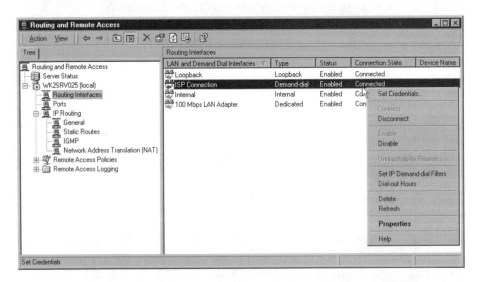

The **Dial-out Hours** allows you to set the time period (according to the NAT server's time) when the dialup connection is allowed to be initiated. This uses a standard block of hours/days with a Permitted/Denied toggle, which allows you to quickly allocate set times for each day, to the nearest hour. For example, Figure 10.21 shows the settings for dial-out being permitted for office working hours, Monday through Friday, 7 A.M. to 8 P.M.

Figure 10.21 Configuring Dial-Out Hours for NAT Internet Connectivity

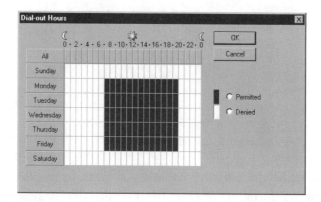

When a user tries to make an Internet connection during a Denied period when the Internet connection is down, the Internet demand-dial interface continues to displays a Connection State of **Unreachable**, and if you right-click this and select **Unreachable Reason** you'll see the message: **The network device cannot connect at this time due to the dial-out hours restriction**. This would prevent a user from coming into the office over the weekend to play Internet games, for example.

The IP demand-dial filters work on the same principle. You can set filters that either allow a dialup connection to be initiated or prevent a dialup connection from being initiated. As before, these settings will have no effect if the Internet connection is already up, and as such they are less useful for NAT but aimed more at demand-dial router-to-router configurations.

Configuring Internet Filters

If you want to restrict what network packets were allowed on the Internet connection (either dialup or permanent LAN connection), navigate to **IP Routing | General**, and right-click on the Internet interface. Under the **General** tab, you'll see buttons for **Input Filters** and **Output Filters**, as shown in Figure 10.22.

Figure 10.22 Configuring Filters for the Internet Connection

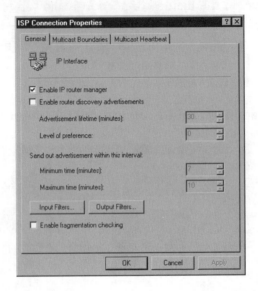

Use these to define the network packets you want to include or exclude. For example, if you wanted to prevent users from connecting to newsgroups for bandwidth and disk storage reasons, you could define an output filter that allowed all packets except those with the destination port of TCP 119 (which is the default port for NNTP). Your output filter would then look similar to Figure 10.23.

Figure 10.23 Configuring the Internet Interface Output Filters to Disallow NNTP Packets

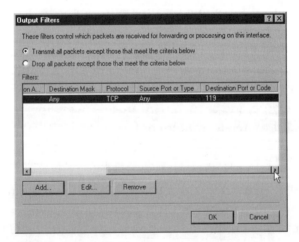

Using and Configuring Internet Security and Acceleration (ISA) Server

Both ICS and NAT allow multiple clients to share an Internet connection for outbound and inbound connections. As we've seen, both solutions have limitations in terms of functionality and control. Some of their biggest drawbacks are lack of control and monitoring for user access and security.

To fill this gap in its Windows 2000 product suite, Microsoft offers its Internet Security and Acceleration (ISA) Server. Many people will know this product in its previous Windows NT 4.0 incarnation as Proxy Server 2, which earned a good reputation for proxying Internet traffic and caching Web content. As the new name suggests, there are two specific components to ISA: The security side refers to firewall features, and the acceleration refers to the extensive caching capabilities.

NOTE

Proxying refers to the ability and authority to carry out a task on behalf of something/somebody else—for example, when you vote by proxy you give somebody else the authority to cast your vote for you. In the context of Internet connectivity it means that a gateway computer that talks to both the internal network and the external network (the Internet) will be used for clients' Internet connectivity. The client never talks directly to the remote resource but sends its traffic to the proxy server so that it can call the resource on the client's behalf.

While this sounds very similar to NAT, the difference with proxying rather than network address translation is that it's done at a higher level—typically at the application level. When a computer is making decisions and performing tasks higher than the network layer (the level at which NAT works) it is able to make more sophisticated choices, which include user and application identity—crucial elements missing from our two previous Internet connectivity solutions. For example, it can distinguish that User1 and not User2 is trying to access an Internet resource and grant or deny that connection based on the user account. Similarly, it can distinguish the difference between User1 connecting to a Web server on the Internet and an FTP server on the Internet—and again grant or deny that connection accordingly.

Many people have said that one of the best things about ISA Server is its flexibility; one example of this flexibility can be seen as soon as you install it. You'll be asked whether you want to install just the firewall features, or just the caching features, or both (both is the default and is referred to as *Integrated mode*). So, for example, if you already have a comprehensive firewall in place, you can install and use just the caching features of ISA Server. Or if you're looking for a dedicated firewall, you can install just that. The two components were designed to complement each other, and with resources permitting, you can safely run both on one server, which helps to reduce hardware and simplifies administrative overhead. Figure 10.24 shows this installation choice.

Figure 10.24 Setup Choices When Installing ISA Server

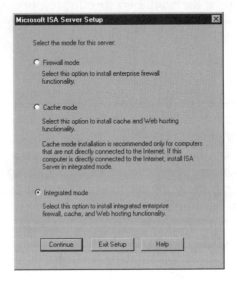

The other important choice we've previously mentioned in the Introduction to this chapter is whether to run in Enterprise or Standalone mode. You can buy ISA Server in Standard Edition or Enterprise Edition. Standard Edition can install only in Standalone mode. Enterprise Edition can install in either mode—it will automatically install in Standalone mode when installed outside Active Directory (for example, in a workgroup or Windows NT 4.0 domain) and will automatically install in Enterprise mode within Active Directory if you have previously run the ISA Server Enterprise Initialization (the Enterprise Initialization modifies the Active Directory schema in much the same way as Exchange 2000 Server requires modifications to the schema before it can be installed).

The two main differences between Standard Edition and Enterprise Edition are price and scalability. ISA Server is priced per processor on both versions, which means that no separate client licenses are required. Standard Edition, though, cannot make use of more than four processors (the maximum that Windows 2000 Server supports—Windows 2000 Advanced Server supports up to eight). In comparison, the Enterprise Edition can use as many processors as the operating system supports. It can also integrate with Active Directory and as such form arrays and make multilevel policies possible.

Designing & Planning...

Arrays in ISA Server

It's important to understand the dependency between ISA Server arrays and Active Directory, particularly when upgrading from Proxy Server.. Although there's an upgrade path for Proxy Server 2 to ISA Server that migrates the majority of configuration settings, remember that you can't use arrays with ISA Server outside Active Directory. Therefore, if using distributed caching on your Proxy Server arrays is an important part of your current Internet connectivity solutions, you may do better to delay upgrading to ISA Server until your network has been migrated to Active Directory. If you specifically wanted the new security features of ISA Server in your Windows NT 4.0 domain, but you wanted to keep your existing Proxy Server arrays, consider keeping your existing Proxy Servers and buying ISA Server as an additional product rather than an upgrade.

You could keep your existing Windows NT 4.0 domain structure and create a new Active Directory domain into which you place your upgraded Proxy Servers (now ISA Servers)—and then form an external trust between the Active Directory domain and your Windows NT 4.0 domain.

Another point worth mentioning about ISA Server arrays is that all members in the array must be in the same domain and the same site. You may want to take this into consideration when designing your Active Directory domain structure if you're interested in using ISA Server arrays. Although Microsoft is trying to encourage larger domains with Active Directory, many people are taking refuge in multiple domains for greater replication control and political/administrative reasons.

Arrays are multiple ISA servers working together, much like a cluster, sharing configuration and resources to provide greater fault tolerance and improved caching performance. Enterprise policies act a little like Active Directory Group Policies—they allow you to configure and enforce policies at an enterprise level to ensure consistency. You can then set further policies at an array level, which can make the enterprise settings more (but not less) restrictive. This is often referred to as using *tiered policies*, which are suitable for hierarchical and distributed administration.

If you currently use chaining (hierarchical caching where users retrieve Web content from the servers physically nearest to them) this is supported on the ISA Server outside Active Directory, and because these servers don't share any configuration, you can even mix Proxy Servers and ISA Servers when chaining. For example, an ISA Server can be downstream or upstream to a Proxy Server.

Another important consideration to bear in mind when considering upgrading from Proxy Server 2 is that IPX clients are no longer supported. Some companies deliberately used IPX as a leaner protocol than TCP/IP on internal networks, as well as profiting from greater security (because an external TCP/IP client by definition would never be able to connect to an internal IPX–only client). Microsoft's Windows 2000 is a TCP/IP oriented platform that generally assumes TCP/IP is running—even outside Active Directory. Before your IPX WinSock clients can use an ISA Server as their Internet connectivity solution, they must have TCP/IP installed and configured.

NOTE

You can currently download a free 90-day evaluation copy of ISA Server (either Standard Edition or Enterprise Edition) from the following Microsoft link: www.microsoft.com/ISASERVER/techinfo/productdoc/default.asp.

There's also an audio-video presentation to talk through the various features and how you might set them. This presentation gives you a good idea of what the product looks like to configure. This can be downloaded from: www.microsoft.com/isaserver/evaluation/demonstration/default.asp

You may also find it useful to read the ISA Server online documentation: www.microsoft.com/technet/isa/isadocs/default.asp

You may notice that these links come from the ISA Server Web site (www.microsoft.com/isaserver), which contains many additional resources that are worth checking on a regular basis.

Another well known external site dedicated to ISA Server information with newsgroups, tutorials, white papers etc is www.isaserver.org.

So, there's a lot to consider if you're thinking of using ISA Server, particularly if you're not currently running an Active Directory network and already have Microsoft Proxy Servers installed. It's not going to be the right solution for everybody, and as an additional product you must purchase for your Windows 2000 server, it's important to qualify and justify its adoption. However, there are exciting new and improved features in this product that you may want to take advantage of when assessing your Internet connectivity solutions—even with the limitations posed when running it outside Active Directory.

The rest of this section will look a little more closely at these features: how they work and what they offer. It is outside the scope of this section to explain in detail exactly how to configure them all. ISA Server is a complex product that comprises many elements and many possible configuration permutations. Not for nothing have complete books been written on the subject. This section aims to provide some basic, background information on the product features in ISA Server that you can use outside Active Directory.

WARNING

If you plan to install and evaluate ISA Server, make sure you do so on a test server where you can start over if necessary. I've never yet been able to successfully uninstall ISA Server (even with the specially designed tool, RMISA, from the **\isa\i386** folder on the ISA Server CD) and have always resorted to reinstalling the operating system. I hope that this will improve with later releases. Note also that you cannot change the server's network identification after installation (server name or domain/workgroup).

Security Features

Microsoft has done a lot of work to make ISA Server a credible enterprise fire-wall—and potential buyers will no doubt feel reassured that ISA Server quickly earned its ICSA Labs Certification (the industry de facto standard for firewall security). The security features include stateful packet, circuit, and application fil-ters that grant or deny traffic based on IP addresses and ports, protocols, and data content. Access control is by policy where you define the elements you want to use in controlling access (for example, by NT4 group, sets of computers, or pro-tocols), and you can even specify allowed days and times.

You can securely publish servers on the internal network, such as your Web server, FTP server, and mail server. You can screen email content by keywords, which, for example, allows you to prevent incoming spam, offensive language, or known virus carriers. Emails that match your criteria can be automatically deleted, held, or forwarded to a different email account. And you can securely set up VPN access for both internal and external clients and for other VPN gateways.

Intrusion detection is included that looks out for a number of well-known attacks including port scanning and those that aim for a Denial of Service. Figure 10.25 shows the relevant dialog box for configuring server Intrusion Detection.

Figure 10.25 Configuring ISA Server's IP Packet Filters for Intrusion Detection

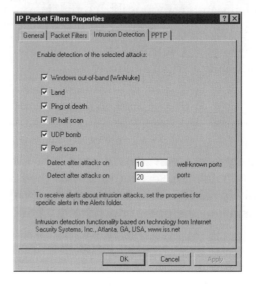

There are also additional alerts that monitor the health and security of the server and that of standard Internet services, such as DNS and SMTP. For example, you'll see alerts for oversized UPD packets, IP spoofing, and IP protocol violation. Each event is highly configurable, as Figure 10.26 shows; it displays the **Event** tab for the DNS intrusion.

When an attack is identified, you can configure an alert to send an email or network message to a designated person, run a program, shut down or start selected services, or simply log an event.

Another security feature is *System Hardening*, which simply uses the same security templates we first saw in Chapter 2—only with the ISA Server MMC front end. As part of the **Configure Firewall Protection**, you'll find the ISA

Server **Security Configuration Wizard**, which prompts for the level of security appropriate for your server, as Figure 10.27 shows.

Figure 10.26 Configuring ISA Intrusion Events

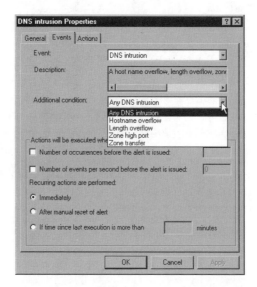

Figure 10.27 The ISA Server Security Configuration Wizard

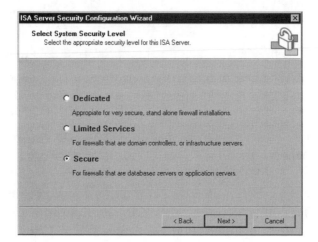

Configuring & Implementing...

ISA System Hardening Templates

We first saw security templates in Chapter 2, and again in Chapter 7 for securing a Web site. Again, the usual advice about applying them should also be remembered with ISA Server: Use cautiously and always test on a nonproduction server first. Make sure you have a backup before applying security templates, either manually or through the ISA Server Wizard. These three choices map to the three built-in security templates we have already seen—ISA Server doesn't include its own templates. The following list explains how the wizard choices map to each template:

- **Dedicated** uses the **Hisecws.inf** template on a standalone or member server, which is suitable only if running the firewall service and no other services.

- **Limited Services** uses the **Securews.inf** template on a standalone or member server, which is suitable for ISA Server running in Integrated mode (both firewall and caching).

- **Secure** uses the **Basicsv.inf** template on a standalone or member server, which is suitable if the server is also running other services such as IIS, mail, or a database.

A new feature in ISA Server is SSL bridging and inspection, which by its very name invariably comes under security features but also benefits performance. This feature allows the ISA Server to act as a HTTP/SSL gateway for external clients. This means that Web computer/user certificate authentication is between client and ISA server, rather than between client and Web server. Or less typically, but perhaps required for secured Web servers, you could convert client HTTP connections to SSL connections on the Web server.

Once the client has been authenticated on the ISA server, the server can open a new HTTP connection (or a new SSL connection) with the Web server. It can also enforce that the connecting client uses SSL and also enforce 128-bit encryption. See Figure 10.28 for the possible configuration options with bridging.

The main benefit of this feature is that you can off-load the additional processing SSL would incur on the Web server. Note that not only must the ISA Server be configured for a SSL listener (as in Figure 10.29) with the appropriate bridging options, but you must also export your Web server's certificate and import it on the ISA server (similarly to how we exported the Administrator recovery certificate in Chapter 3, and imported a Web server certificate in Chapter 7).

Figure 10.28 Configuring ISA for Bridging

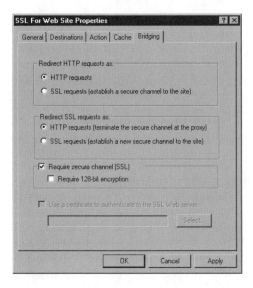

Figure 10.29 Configuring ISA Server for a SSL Listener

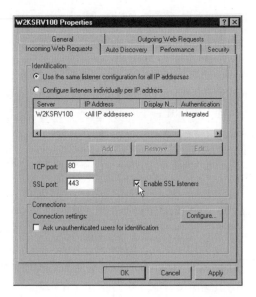

One final change from Proxy Server 2 worth noting under the security features (although rarely mentioned as improved security) is that ISA Server can now function independently from IIS and the Web service. For example, if you previously wanted a proxy server for WinSock clients and wanted to publish your mail server, you couldn't do this on Proxy Server 2 without also running the Web service—which meant that your Internet gateway was as vulnerable as the latest IIS exploit.

Caching Features

We've already covered how distributing caching isn't possible on ISA Server outside Active Directory, so if you're looking for caching abilities you may have already written off ISA Server for your Windows NT 4.0 domain. However, there are new features available for caching that might interest you—even with the limitation that you can't use arrays.

Proxy server caching works on the principle that if one person has asked for Internet content, another user will also ask for it. Rather than let each user ask for the same Web page or FTP file each time, it caches the content so that the next time it is requested the locally stored cached content can be returned to the user—more quickly than if the request had gone over the Internet. This saves on valuable bandwidth, which, in turn, makes other Internet requests quicker. Note that security-specific information (such as passwords, https pages, and cookies) is never cached.

As with Proxy Server 2, you must use an NTFS partition for your caching disk, and by default ISA Server is smart enough to pick out the partition with the most free disk space, rather than default to the current partition. By default it will select a cache size of 100MB if at least 150MB is free (5MB is the minimum allowed). The online Help recommends that you configure the cache at 100MB and then add .5MB for each caching client. Microsoft's Installation and Deployment Guide (isastart.htm from the **\isa** folder on the ISA Server CD) under the Capacity Planning Guidelines recommends 2 to 4 gigabytes for up to 500 users and 10 gigabytes for 500 to 1,000 users. The latest independent tests seem to suggest even higher cache sizes are recommended. The bottom line is this: The greater the cache size (and the faster the disk access time), the more likely you are to see caching benefits.

A hidden but important difference between how caching works on Proxy Server and ISA Server is how the cache is stored. Proxy Server stores cached content in separate files on the chosen NTFS partition, whereas ISA creates and uses a single database file. The database method makes for faster access time, with fewer overheads on the file system driver. It also makes startup and recovery times faster (for example, should the computer crash) because it uses a fixed size rather than dynamically changing.

And last but perhaps most important, the cache is more secure because the database file (**.cdat**) cannot be opened and read with a text editor or Web browser. The only way to access content from the cache is through the ISA service or with the **CacheDir.exe** tool that ships on the ISA CD (in **\Support\tools\Troubleshooting** folder).

The other caching options you can configure include setting a Time To Live value for cached objects, whether to cache dynamic content, how to handle a request if the cached object has expired but cannot be updated, whether unsuccessful Web objects should be cached, and so on. Figure 10.30 shows some of these configuration options.

Figure 10.30 Configuring ISA Server's Caching Properties

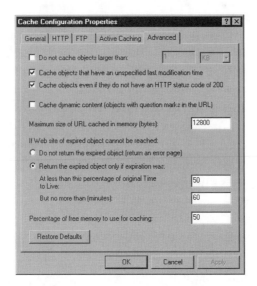

Proxy Server 2 also had *Active Caching* where frequently used Web sites were retrieved and cached during quiet Internet transmission times (note that this is disabled by default). However, new in ISA Server is the ability to schedule active caching and define which sites you want to cache with the same sort of control (and more) that you have with the offline Favorites we first saw in Chapter 3.

For example, you can define how many levels deep the caching should go and whether to also cache linked sites and dynamic content, limit the number of cached objects per site, and define the Time To Live value. Figure 10.31 shows the last page of the Scheduled Content Download Job Wizard where I've defined ISA Server to actively cache the Microsoft ISA Server Web site every day at 10 P.M. Other frequency values you can define are once only and weekly on specified days.

Figure 10.31 Configuring ISA Server's Scheduled Download Job for Active Caching

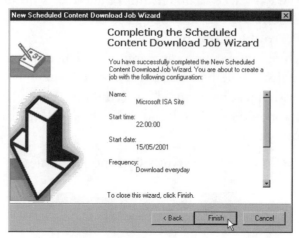

When internal users want Internet content, the caching on the ISA Server is referred to as *forward caching*. In comparison, *reverse caching* is used when external users want internal content—for example, commonly used files or Web pages from Internet servers you're hosting. Typically, reverse caching is employed in an e-business environment where users want a fast response, and you don't want your Internet servers doing unnecessary work. Just as SSL bridging off-loads processing from internal Web servers, so reverse caching can off-load processing from Internet servers—and provide the content users want, faster.

Finally, caching performance in ISA Server has been tuned so that smaller cached objects will be saved to RAM rather than disk—returning these will be faster than returning them from disk. So, the more RAM you add on your ISA Server, the faster the caching responses should appear.

Additional Features

The new configuration interface that uses the Windows 2000 MMC, with taskpads and wizards for common tasks, is aimed at easing the myriad of configuration options that are required. For example, as soon as ISA Server is installed, the Getting Started Wizard loads (see Figure 10.32), which steps you through all the relevant tasks and configurations your installation may need.

Figure 10.32 ISA Server's Getting Started Wizard

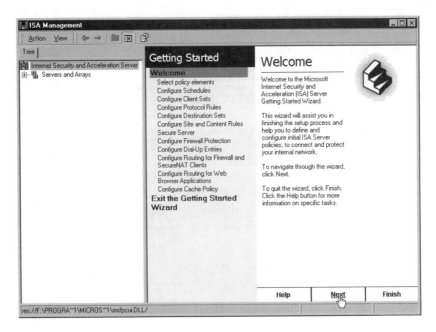

We've already seen a couple of examples of the ISA Server wizards. Figure 10.33 shows the full (unexpanded) configuration options in the ISA Management MMC, and also a typical taskpad with graphical links that invoke configuration wizards.

> **NOTE**
>
> You can toggle on and off the Taskpad view in the ISA Management MMC if you find it more of a hindrance than a help! Simply right-click on an item on the left (scope) window, and select **View | Advanced**.

Other miscellaneous features worth mentioning are the reporting features, bandwidth priorities, and the extensible platform for programmers and third-party solutions.

Figure 10.33 ISA Server's Graphical Front-End Configuration MMC

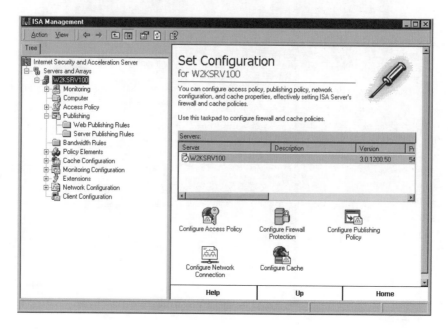

Reporting Features

ISA Server's reporting functionality uses information gathered from log files and can generate reports on an ad hoc or scheduled basis (for example, daily, weekly, monthly), then output them in a report. Five predefined reports are available:

- Summary reports
- Web usage reports
- Application usage reports
- Traffic and utilization reports
- Security reports

For example, from these you will be able to easily determine statistics such as which users, computers, applications, and protocols are used most often, what browsers and operating systems are being used, how effectively caching is being used, average processing time for each request, what security alerts happened, and so on.

Easily viewable bar charts are available within the ISA MMC (under the Reports folder), but you can export the information they contain by saving them in either .htm or .xls format so that you can manipulate the data and produce your own customized reports.

Bandwidth Priorities

New in ISA Server, bandwidth priorities can be set on network connections by utilizing a subsection of Windows 2000 Quality of Service (QoS). After deciding on your server's *effective bandwidth* (the lowest maximum throughput on the server) you need to define bandwidth rules that specify which connections have relative priority over others. These bandwidth rules can be applied to specific users, IP address, protocol, schedule, or content.

Inbound and outbound connections have separate bandwidth priorities. You specify priority bands with different weightings between 1 and 200, with 200 having the highest priority. Then allocate your users/addresses/content one of your priority bands (ISA server uses a default bandwidth priority of 100 for any traffic that doesn't meet the criteria you've specified—you may wish to modify this value).

It's important to realize that bandwidth priorities are not the same as bandwidth restrictions. You cannot, for example, guarantee a proportion of your available bandwidth for a certain type of protocol or for certain users—you can prioritize only that these connections have a higher proportion of the available bandwidth. In fact, the actual bandwidth these connections will have will be dynamically reallocated proportionally as other connections are made and disconnected.

NOTE

Bandwidth priorities are based on a relative weighting rather than absolute bandwidth—you cannot guarantee or limit a set amount of bandwidth.

Extensible Platform

Personally, I think one of ISA Server's best features is that it offers an open and extensible platform. What you see and get when you install ISA Server isn't the end of the story, but the beginning. If there's a feature you want that is missing from the base product or something that needs enhancing, chances are it can be done. It's impossible to produce a product that offers everything to all people, so I think Microsoft has wisely incorporated into this new version the technologies it knows and has experience of with Proxy Server. It has incorporated other companies' technologies to enhance the security side. Then it has actively encouraged developers to take it further, partnering with Independent Software Vendors even before the product shipped so that add-ons would be available.

For example, GFI LANguard integrates its own Internet protection with ISA Server, offering its own virus protection, monitoring Internet usage, and removing potentially dangerous attachments. It does this with an ISAPI extension into ISA Server so that the two products complement each other. Other third-party solutions can similarly improve and extend Internet monitoring and protection, perhaps with their own management and monitoring tools. Extending the base content filters and intrusion detection also seems an obvious market—and one that ISS RealSecure has taken up.

I'm sure as time goes on and ISA Server becomes more prevalent as a viable commercial firewall, you'll have a wider choice of other add-ons. You can keep up to date about ISA Server's third-party add-ons from the following Microsoft site: www.microsoft.com/isaserver/thirdparty/offerings.htm.

At no additional charge, the ISA Software Development Kit (SDK) ships actually on the ISA Server CD (in the **sdk** folder off the root) with numerous samples of administration scripts, Web and application filters, and instructions on how to create an ISA MMC extension. It is also currently available for download (1.1MB) from the Microsoft site: www.microsoft.com/isaserver/partners/default.asp.

ISA Clients

So far we've looked at various features and options on the ISA server, but we haven't explained how internal clients (users and servers) can use these features.

There are actually three different types of ISA clients, and which ones you use will depend on factors such as the level of security and access control required and the client platform. The three different ISA clients are these:

- Web Proxy client
- SecureNAT client
- Firewall client

Web Proxy Client

Those of you familiar with Proxy Server will recognize the first and well-known client that supports standard Web protocols (HTTP, HTTPS, FTP, and Gopher) through a CERN-compatible browser (Internet Explorer and Netscape Navigator and Communicator) that's configured for proxy access.

This type of client can be authorized by username (the default authentication is Windows Integrated, but if Internet Explorer is not your standard browser, you will need to use one of the other Web authentication protocols discussed in Chapter 7). When Internet requests are made through the browser, these clients can use the server's caching facilities.

A change from Proxy Server settings, however, is that ISA listens on port 8080 (by default) instead of port 80—which is a consequence of removing the dependency of IIS from ISA. Port 80 on ISA Server is now used for automatic discovery requests. This default port of 8080 can be changed on the ISA Server's **Properties | Outgoing Web Requests** tab.

As with Proxy Server, you configure the Web browser to manually target the ISA server for proxy access (as in Figure 10.34, under **Tools | Internet Options | Connections | LAN Settings**), or you can use automatic detection (for example, with a script or through DNS/DHCP), which is useful when you have multiple ISA servers.

Figure 10.34 Configuring Internet Explorer for ISA Server Web Proxy Support

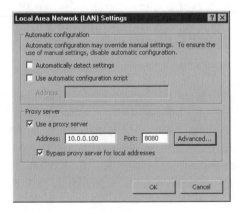

SecureNAT Client

The SecureNAT client works similarly to how our ICS and NAT connections worked on the client side. You configure external traffic to go via the ISA server, and the ISA server translates packets at the network layer.

However, there are a couple of big differences between the simple NAT clients and ISA Server's SecureNAT. First, ISA Server is fully supported in a routed environment with other networking services such as DNS, DHCP, and domain controllers. You may remember that ICS couldn't work with an internal DHCP or DNS servers and domain controllers, and while NAT could accommodate internal DHCP and DNS servers, and even multiple segments, NAT could not work on the same network as routers and domain controllers.

On a single segmented network, SecureNAT clients would define the ISA Server's internal network address as their default gateway—just as we did with ICS and NAT. On a routed environment where the client is on a different subnet to the ISA Server, you must configure the client's default gateways to route external (Internet) traffic via the ISA Server's internal address. As with ICS/NAT, you cannot restrict access by user because this level of Internet connectivity works at the network layer. With ISA Server, though, you can apply access by site, IP address, port, or time of day.

One of the biggest benefits of using SecureNAT is that it will work with any TCP/IP client, regardless of operating system. It requires no additional software to be installed, and as such requires the least amount of configuration on the client side (you simply modify the TCP/IP settings such that Internet access will go via the ISA Server).

Because you cannot use user access security with SecureNAT, it is best employed for computer connectivity, rather than user connectivity. For example, this applies for incoming server requests, such as when unknown users need to access your Web server, mail server, and so on. Your published Internet computers should be configured as SecureNAT clients.

Firewall Clients

Firewall clients are perhaps best known to Proxy Server users as *WinSock Proxy clients*—by their new name. With additional software installed on the client, a Windows client wanting to use an application written to the standard WinSock interface can do this via the proxy server. It's used when standard Web protocols (HTTP/S, FTP, and gopher) aren't being used, such as RealAudio, IRC, and Telnet.

When a WinSock application is being used, the client looks to see if the destination computer is internal or external. When it's internal the traffic is sent directly to the computer. When it's external, it goes via the ISA Server, which can then proxy the connection (providing it is allowed—for example, based on user authentication, protocol, etc.).

The two big differences between the Firewall client on ISA and the WinSock proxy client on Proxy Server are that IPX connections are no longer supported on the client (as previously mentioned), only TCP/IP connections. And there is no 16-bit client version—only 32-bit Windows clients are supported (currently Windows 9*x*, Windows Me, Windows NT 4.0, and Windows 2000).

The other important change between the ISA Firewall client and the Proxy Server WinSock client is how internal addresses are determined. As before, the ISA Server is configured with a Local Address Table (LAT) that is downloaded to connecting clients and that lists all internal addresses. Any destination addresses in the LAT will be treated by the Firewall client as internal and sent directly to that computer rather than via the ISA Server. But new in ISA is the **Local Domain Table** where you can define your internal domains you use (if any). This is an important change in Windows 2000 because previously an external address was defined as one that contained dots (periods) in the name—for example, **company.com** as well as **192.126.12.11**. Now that Windows 2000 is more DNS aware, this simple definition no longer suffices, and so the LAT must be complemented with a Local Domain Table (LDT) where whole domains can be entered with wildcards (for example, *.company.com) or single computers with their Fully Qualified Domain Name (for example, www.company.com).

NOTE

The Firewall client software can be installed directly from the ISA server, or you may prefer to move it to another network software distribution point. The client setup program can be found in **Program Files\Microsoft ISA Server\CLIENTS**, and this directory by default is shared to **Everybody** with **Read** permissions as **MSPCLNT** (showing its ancestor routes when this was referred to as the MicroSoft Proxy CLieNT).

Upgrading Issues

We have already identified a number of upgrade issues to consider if you are already running Microsoft Proxy Server. This section quickly lists the main ones, but if this scenario applies to you, I suggest you read through the "Migrating from Microsoft Proxy Server 2" documentation that comes with ISA (available on the loading screen from the **Read About Migrating to ISA Server** link) and is also currently available to download from the Microsoft site at www.microsoft.com/isaserver/techinfo/deployment/2000/proxymigration.asp. Things to watch out for include the following:

- Arrays are not supported outside Active Directory, so if you're sure you're never going to migrate to Active Directory there is no point in buying the Enterprise Edition (unless you're desperate to use more than four processors). If you are going to migrate to Active Directory in the future, buy the Enterprise Edition and install in Standalone mode. Later when the network is migrated you can run the Enterprise Initialization (link on the loading screen from the ISA Server CD) and then promote the ISA Server to Enterprise mode by joining it to an array.

- IPX is no longer supported for connecting clients.

- The WinSock Proxy Client has been replaced by the Firewall Client, which supports only 32-bit platforms.

- When you upgrade your Proxy Server 2 to ISA Server, you cannot revert back (except with your own backup/restore mechanisms).

- You cannot upgrade if running Proxy Server 1.0, or BackOffice Server 4.0, or SBS 4.0.

- You can install ISA Server only on Windows 2000 Servers (not Professional), and it requires a minimum of SP1 installed.

- For security reasons, plan the upgrade when you can disconnect the Proxy Server from Internet connectivity.

- Although chaining with Proxy Servers is supported, remember that by default the ISA Web proxy service listens on port 8080 rather than port 80, so this may need to be changed so that all chained servers send and listen on the same port.

- While existing cache configuration is migrated, the cache content will be deleted because of different storage mechanisms.

- Although SOCKS is supported on ISA Server as an application filter, any existing SOCKS rules on the Proxy Server will be lost.

- Proxy Server by default allowed Basic authentication as well as NTLM. ISA Server doesn't enable Basic by default (only Windows Integrated, which uses NTLM outside Active Directory) so clients that previously authenticated successfully with Proxy Server may fail to authenticate successfully after upgrading to ISA Server. Check to see if Basic authentication is needed, and if necessary enable it on the ISA Server immediately after the upgrade.

- Web Proxy service permissions are not migrated.
- Active caching is disabled after the migration.

Most other configurations are kept—for example, the Local Address Table, alerts, and log settings. The following configurations are kept but migrated to a different place, according to the new ISA Server architecture:

- Domain filters are migrated into Site and Content rules.
- WinSock permissions are migrated into Protocol rules.
- Publishing properties are migrated to Web Publishing rules.
- Static packet filters are migrated into open or blocked IP packet filters.
- Web Proxy routing rules are migrated into Routing rules.

Walkthrough: Configuring NAT to Publish a Web Server

This walkthrough assumes that you have configured a NAT server with a network adapter for your Internet connection rather than a dialup adapter (such as a modem) because you need a permanent connection to host a Web server. It also assumes that you have been provided with a number of public addresses by your ISP, you have no internal DNS server, and you have correctly configured your Internet adapter (and router).

The steps this walkthrough covers include the following:

- Automatically assigning client addresses in the 10.0.0.0/8 range
- Configuring Internet DNS name resolution
- Defining an address pool
- Reserving an address for an internally published Web server
- Publishing the internal Web server

1. We first need to change the default Address Assignment for clients. To do this, expand **IP Routing** (if not already expanded) in the Routing and Remote Access MMC, and right-click on **Network Address Translation (NAT)** and select **Properties**. Click on the **Address Assignment** tab. Change the IP address box to be **10.0.0.0** with mask **255.0.0.0**. You'll also have to exclude at least one address from this range—the IP address that the NAT server is using on its internal adapter, which should also be in the 10.0.0.0./8 network. To exclude the server's address (and any others on your network that already have statically assigned addresses), click the **Exclude** button.

2. In the Exclude Reserved Addresses dialog box, click the **Add** button and type in the IP address your NAT server is using on its internal adapter (use **ipconfig** in a command prompt if not sure). Click **OK**. If you have any more addresses you need to exclude, repeat this until you have defined all the addresses you need to exclude, and then click **OK**.

3. We could now click **Automatically assign IP addresses by using DHCP**, but we won't just yet until the rest of the NAT properties have been configured. For now, leave this check box as it is. This dialog box should now look like Figure 10.35.

Figure 10.35 Defining NAT's Address Assignment for Clients

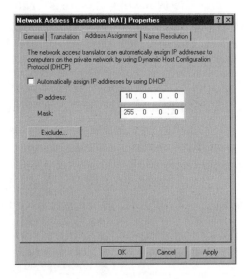

4. There's no internal DNS server, so this NAT server needs to perform the DNS lookups for connecting clients. With the NAT properties dialog box still open, click on the **Name Resolution** tab. Click the **Clients using Domain Name System (DNS)**. There's no need to specify the other two options when you're using a permanently connected adapter for your Internet connection. This dialog box should now look like Figure 10.36.

Figure 10.36 Defining NAT Internet DNS Name Resolution for Clients

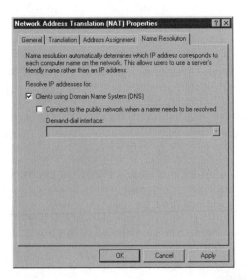

5. Click **OK** to close this dialog box. Now right-click on your external interface under the **Network Address Translation (NAT)**, and select **Properties**. The General tab should have selected **Public interface connected to the Internet** and **Translate TCP/UDP headers (recommended)**; don't change anything here, but click on the **Address Pool** tab.

6. Click on the **Add** button and specify the range of public addresses you want to use on your NAT server. This may be the complete range supplied by your ISP or simply a subset of them so that you can connect other servers directly to the Internet. Specify your start and end address, with the mask. Figure 10.37 shows an example, specifying six addresses starting with 193.112.86.60. When you have finished, click **OK**.

Figure 10.37 Defining NAT's Address Pool

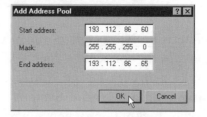

7. You should now see your defined address pool in the **Address Pool** tab. You can always go back and edit these addresses later with the **Edit** button if you want to increase or decrease this range. If you wanted to add another range of addresses that weren't contiguous with your first, simply use the **Add** button again and define your new range.

8. We now need to reserve one of these addresses for an internal server that is going to host a public Web server. Click on the **Reservations** button and you'll see the Reserve Addresses dialog box.

9. Click on the **Add** button and specify the public address you want to be used only for the Web server—for example, the first public address (which in our example was 193.112.86.60). You'll also need to specify the internal address of the server that needs a statically assigned IP address (which needs to be on your list of excluded addresses in step 2 above; if it's not you can add it later). Also click on the **Allow incoming sessions to this address** and click **OK**. When you have

finished, the Reserve Addresses should look something similar to Figure 10.38, where the internal address of the Web server is 10.0.10.80.

Figure 10.38 Reserving a Public Address for Incoming Traffic

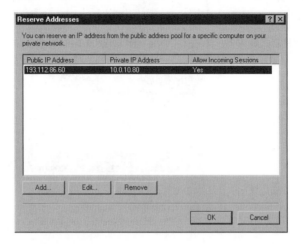

10. Now click on the **Special Ports** tab where we can define that we want to accept port 80 for Web traffic on our reserved address. Make sure **TCP** is selected, and click **Add** to display the Add Special Port dialog box.

11. Because we have only one address pool, we can keep the default of **On this interface**. Specify **80** in both the **Incoming port** and **Outgoing port**. Specify the internal address of your Web server in the **Private address**. Your dialog box should be similar to Figure 10.39.

Figure 10.39 Publishing the Web Server

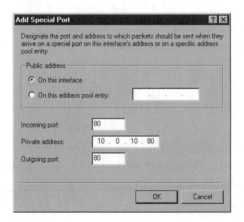

12. Click **OK**, and you should see details of your choices now displayed in the Special Ports dialog box, as shown in Figure 10.40. If you wanted to add other ports for this server (or other internal servers)—for example, adding port 443 for SSL or port 25 for incoming mail etc—you would simply use the **Add** button to build up a list of incoming ports.

Figure 10.40 The Special Ports Details

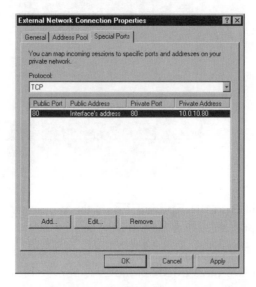

13. Click **OK** and you're ready to go! Right-click on **Network Address Translation (NAT) | Properties** and then click on the **Address Assignment** tab. If you're not sure whether you remembered to exclude the Web server's address from the address range, check now with the **Exclude** button and add it if necessary. Then click the **Automatically assign IP addresses by using DHCP**, and click **OK**.

Summary

We've looked at three different solutions Microsoft provides in Windows 2000 for sharing an Internet connection, with increasing functionality, complexity, and administrative overhead. The two built-in solutions are Internet Connection Sharing (ICS) and the Network Address Translation (NAT) RRAS routing protocol. Internet Security Acceleration (ISA) Server is an additional Windows 2000 product you must purchase on top of Windows 2000 Server, running a minimum of SP1.

Internet Connection Sharing (ICS) is seen as the entry-level solution, first seen in Windows 98 Second Edition and now carried over to Windows 2000 Professional and Windows 2000 Server. Only the Windows 2000 Server version can run the more fully featured and configurable NAT RRAS routing protocol. It addresses many limitations and restrictions that ICS imposed, but still has limitations in terms of running with other networking services, security, monitoring, and control. One of the biggest problems with Network Address Translation (which applies to both ICS and NAT) is that it works at the network layer, and so you cannot control access by user, content, or time.

The most fully featured Internet connection sharing solution Microsoft offers is ISA Server. This is available in two editions: Standalone and Enterprise. You can install both editions as a dedicated firewall or a dedicated Web caching server, or both in Integrated mode.

ISA Server started life as Microsoft's Proxy Server, and there is a supported sales and technical upgrade path for migrating Proxy Sever 2 to ISA Server. There are upgrading issues to consider, however—particularly if you are not currently running an Active Directory network. Written as an extensible product, Microsoft actively encourages enhancements and add-ons—shipping the ISA SDK on the CD, making it available for downloading, and working in conjunction with Independent Software Vendors.

There are many new features in ISA Server that make it a very attractive firewall and caching Internet solution and that address many of the restrictions and limitations seen in ICS and NAT. However, flexibility and a fully featured product set come at the price of greater administrative overhead as well as the financial outlay. Although the ISA Server GUI MMC and taskpads with wizards help in speeding up configuration settings, they are not a substitute for having a sound appreciation and understanding of Internet security and applications. Microsoft claims that its ISA Server is competitively placed in its market with regard to Total Cost of Ownership (TCO) and features when compared with rival caching servers and firewalls. In the same perspective, we must appreciate how ISA Server is not really in the same category as ICS and NAT, despite all three offering Internet sharing solutions on the Windows 2000 platform.

Solutions Fast Track

Using and Configuring
Internet Connection Sharing (ICS)

☑ ICS is the entry-level Windows 2000 shared Internet connectivity solution, supported on Professional as well as the server versions and
requiring the least administrative overhead.

☑ Configuration is simple, but restrictive. For example, internal clients
cannot use a static address, cannot obtain DHCP options, cannot use a
WINS server, and cannot use an internal DNS server.

☑ While both outbound and inbound connections are supported, you can
use only one public address. This means you cannot reserve addresses (for
example, for Internet Web servers) or choose not to translate TCP/UDP
headers (sometimes necessary for security reasons).

☑ Because of the automatic address allocation, you are restricted to a maximum of 254 internal hosts (including the computer hosting ICS).

☑ Not all applications are suitable for address translation—IPSec, for
example, cannot be used with NAT, and if you want to use a VPN
connection you must use PPTP.

☑ There are few monitoring facilities for the Internet connections—scarce
entries in the Event Log are the best you'll get.

Using and Configuring RRAS
Network Address Translation (NAT)

☑ NAT is more sophisticated and involves more configuration than ICS.
NAT can be run only on a Windows 2000 server.

☑ Configuration is more flexible. For example, you can choose the address
range the built-in DHCP Allocator uses or disable it completely. When
you disable it you are able to use a full-blown DHCP server on your
network that delivers all DHCP options such as the domain name,
internal WINS, and DNS servers.

☑ You can use a range of public addresses that can be pooled or reserved. You can also configure that TCP/UDP headers are not translated if this is required.

☑ You are not restricted to the number of internal clients supported, and multiple segments can be used with multiple adapters in the NAT server. However, NAT still cannot be used if it detects routers or domain controllers on the network.

☑ The same application restrictions apply to NAT—you still cannot use IPSec over NAT.

☑ There are much better monitoring facilities for Internet connections— you can see current mappings of internal/external addresses and ports, DHCP and DNS statistics, and a configuration level of Event Log entries. However, there's still no historical logging or reporting.

☑ You can configure static packet filters on the Internet connection and as dialup restrictions. You can also restrict the times and days when the dialup adapter (if being used) can be initialized. However, there is no intrusion detection or alerting, no dynamic packet filtering, no blocking of traffic by site or content or user.

☑ There are no caching abilities with either ICS or NAT.

Using and Configuring Internet Security and Acceleration Server (ISA)

☑ ISA Server is the Windows 2000 replacement for Proxy Server 2, but with its higher level of security and new features, it is being heralded as a new product by Microsoft. However, there are currently attractive upgrade prices for Proxy Server 2 to ISA Server, and there is a supported upgrade path to keep much of your existing configuration.

☑ There are two product versions of ISA Server, Standalone Edition and Enterprise Edition. Both are priced per processor, but the Standalone Edition is considerably cheaper although it supports only up to four processors. You cannot integrate a Standalone ISA Server into Active Directory so that multiple ISA servers can work together and be configured together. Enterprise Edition has no limit on the number of processors supported. It can be installed in Standalone mode or in Enterprise mode if within an Active Directory network. Enterprise mode involves modifying the schema, which then enables multiple ISA Servers to work together for fault tolerance and load balancing and be configured in a tiered fashion for centralized and distributed administration.

☑ You can install ISA Server as a caching server or a firewall server, or both. It is optimized for running both, which reduces hardware costs and offers simplified and centralized management by combining these two Internet services.

☑ Features include safe publishing of Internet servers; screening email content to help prevent spam, viruses, and offensive material; easy setup of VPN connections; intrusion detection and alerting; system hardening with templates; SSL bridging; faster and more secure forward and reverse caching; active and scheduled caching; graphical MMC interface with taskpads and wizards; reporting facilities; bandwidth priorities; and extensible platform.

☑ You have very tight control over access by user, content, site, address, protocols, and schedule.

☑ ISA Clients include the Web Proxy client, the SecureNAT client, and the Firewall client.

☑ Upgrading from Proxy Server 2 has a number of issues that you should consider.

☑ The Microsoft ISA Server Web site currently contains a 90-day evaluation version, online documentation, the SDK, and details of third-party add-ons.

Frequently Asked Questions

The following Frequently Asked Questions, answered by the author of this book, are designed to both measure your understanding of the concepts presented in this chapter and to assist you with real-life implementation of these concepts. To have your questions about this chapter answered by the author, browse to **www.syngress.com/solutions** and click on the **"Ask the Author"** form.

Q: I've got a user who's trying to enable ICS on his laptop so other computers on his home mini network can all use the same dialup connection. He tells me he can't access his dialup connection properties with an error about lack of privileges, and therefore he can't enable ICS. What privileges does he need?

A: You must be a member of the local Administrators group to change the properties of an adapter. Personally, I wouldn't feel very happy about making a user a member of the Administrators group because the adapter properties won't be the only thing he will then be able to access! Because he wants to enable this on a laptop, could this be configured for him by a network administrator when he's next in the office?

Q: I've successfully configured ICS with special ports so that I can play my favorite game with friends over the Internet. However, this works with only one user and I wanted to have multiple workstations on my network all participating. How do I do this?

A: The short answer is that you probably can't. Gaming applications often use multiple incoming ports, and for the ICS computer (or NAT server) to guarantee they are being directed to the correct workstation, you may be able to have only one connection, rather than multiple concurrent connections using the same game. Check with the software vendor if possible, and ask about its NAT abilities and any configuration issues that would allow multiple concurrent access.

Q: I've got a PPTP connection working with ICS, but after the PPTP connection is made, other ICS clients can no longer access the Internet. Is that expected?

A: No, that doesn't sound right to me! I would guess that you've configured the PPTP connection on the ICS computer itself, rather than on one of the clients. When you make a PPTP connection, by default that computer's default gateway changes to be the address of the VPN server. While this is OK for the computer using the PPTP connection itself, it's not OK for connecting ICS clients who can no longer use the underlying Internet connection while it's hijacked by the PPTP connection. Keep only the Internet connection on the ICS computer, and configure and make the PPTP connection from an ICS client.

Q: I'm getting ipnathlp errors 30001 on my NAT server's event log, which identifies IP addresses I've assigned for NAT clients with the DHCP Allocator. What does this mean?

A: In Chapter 6 when we looked at the full DHCP service, we saw how some clients could automatically detect a duplicate IP address and how the DHCP server could check for this itself before offering it to a DHCP client. This is what the NAT DHCP Allocator is automatically doing here—it's sending out a gratuitous ARP with the next available IP address before offering the address to the NAT client and finding that a TCP/IP client on the network already claims to have this address. The NAT server therefore moves on to the next available free address and marks the equivalent of the BAD_ADDRESS with this event log. Try to track down your original IP address owner, or exclude these duplicates from your DHCP scopes.

Q: I'm having problems copying large files over NAT. It looks as if it's worked and I can see the file on the external server, but it's zero bytes and has no contents. Smaller files are OK, so what am I doing wrong?

A: This is a problem when the external adapter has a smaller MTU size than the NAT's client. Usually this would be resolved by the NAT server asking for the larger packets to be defragmented with an ICMP "Destination Unreachable" status; however, this is not forwarded to the client by the NAT server. This is a known issue documented in the Microsoft Knowledge Base article "NAT Does Not Properly Forward ICMP 'Destination Unreadable' Packet" [Q268773], which was addressed in a hotfix post SP1 and is now fixed in SP2.

Q: Why don't my Demand Filters work in NAT? I've configured them such that certain ports are not allowed, but they seem to be ignored.

A: This was a known problem, fixed in SP1.

Q: We have a small branch office that requires low-usage Internet access. They don't need to cache content, and we don't need to restrict access by user, protocol, or time. However, we do want to prevent access to a known number of selected sites. Could we use ICS or RRAS NAT and then use packet filters on the external adapter where we prevent traffic going to and from that IP addresses that these sites use?

A: I appreciate that you don't need all the bells and whistles that ISA Server offers, but you can't guarantee that these sites will not be accessed with your plan. IP addresses can be quite volatile and are not a good way of identifying specific sites. For example, how do you know which addresses those sites use? The address that is displayed when you ping it today might not be the same address displayed tomorrow or the next day. They could be using multiple addresses for DNS round-robin, or they may simply change their Web server addresses. It's not difficult to change a DNS host entry's address—particularly if you manage your own DNS namespace. It is less likely that they would change a Web site name because that is what users remember, not IP addresses. It sounds to me that you need a mechanism to identify domain names, and perhaps content, to safely restrict access to your known sites. Neither ICS nor NAT can do this, and while ISA Server can it sounds as if this may be overkill for the simple Internet control you're after. I would research other companies' products to fit your requirement.

Q: We're really interested in upgrading our Proxy Server to ISA Server while there's a good upgrade offer, and we're looking forward to benefiting from all the new features. We still have a few Windows for Workgroup PCs that access the Internet with the WinSock Proxy client. For political reasons, it will take a while to upgrade these to a 32-bit operating system, and we can't afford for them to lose their Internet connectivity. Does this mean we'll either have to wait before we upgrade to ISA Server, or forgo the upgrade offer and run ISA and Proxy Server side by side?

A: Fortunately, despite the name change between the WinSock proxy client and the ISA Firewall client, they work very similarly. This means that your 16-bit WinSock clients will continue to work with ISA—providing they are running TCP/IP (if they are running only IPX, you must upgrade them to TCP/IP).

Q: Isn't allowing VPN ports on the ISA Server the same as defining the L2TP/IPSec and PPTP ports as input/output filters on the RRAS server?

A: Not quite. When defining these ports on ISA, you're defining dynamic filters. The ports are opened only when a connection is made and closed when that connection is finished. This is in comparison to the packet filtering we looked at on the RRAS server that always leaves the ports open if they have a grant status. This means that dynamic packet filtering used with ISA Server is more secure than the static packet filtering available with RRAS.

Q: Can I configure and manage ISA Server from my workstation?

A: Providing your workstation is running Windows 2000 Professional (with at least SP1) you can install just the Administration tools from the ISA setup program. Choose **Custom**, and you'll see options for ISA Services, Add-in services, and Administration tools. You need only the last option, which then adds the Microsoft ISA Server onto your **Start | Programs** menu, from where you load **ISA Management**. When it is first loaded you must use the **Connect to server** option and specify the ISA server you want to manage. Another alternative, particularly if connecting over the Internet (and RDP is allowed through the firewall), is using Terminal Services for remote administration, as discussed in Chapter 5. As well as the lower bandwidth requirements, you could load this from any Windows platform. Note that you must be a member of the ISA server's local Administrators or Server Operators group.

Q: I'm interested in publishing a VPN server behind the ISA Server. I understand IPSec can't be translated, but is there a good reason why I can't run a PPTP server on my internal network configured as a SecureNAT client?

A: There is a good reason why this won't work—the SecureNAT element works only with TCP and UDP ports. PPTP uses the GRE protocol (number 47) in addition to TCP port 1723, and there's no way to translate this when it comes into the ISA server from an external client. You can create VPN connections from the internal network, and you can run a VPN server on the ISA server itself or on a DMZ, but you cannot publish a VPN server as a SecureNAT client.

The Windows 2000 Microsoft Management Console

Solutions in this Appendix:

- MMC Basics

- Configuring and Creating Your Own MMCs

- Advanced MMC Configuration: Using Taskpads

- Distributing MMCs

- ☑ Summary

Introduction

The Microsoft Management Console (MMC) is used for configuring the majority of the tools and services Microsoft supplies with Windows 2000. A common interface greatly simplifies administration and configuration, which in turn leads to a lower total cost of ownership.

Most administrators find using the built-in MMC tools (for example, those supplied under the Administrative Tools) to be fairly intuitive. No doubt the transition was also helped by familiarity with the IIS4 MMC interface, which has been available for some time. But even administrators without previous knowledge of the MMC can easily find their way around by double-clicking to expand or edit or by right-clicking for a context menu, in much the same way that we use Microsoft Explorer on the various 32-bit platforms that have been around for some time.

In writing most of this book, we assumed that the reader would be familiar with the basics of using and driving the MMC, so we have not provided explicit step-by-step instructions on how to drive the interface that houses the tools we have discussed. For the majority of readers, this material would have been rather tedious, so we made assumptions that it wasn't necessary. However, for readers who are unsure of how the MMC operates, this appendix quickly outlines the basic components and how to drive them. However, it also offers information on how to extend the MMC beyond these basics which is possible when you build your own customized MMCs.

For example, you can make your own life much easier by grouping together common resources and putting them into the same MMC rather than having different MMCs open at the same time. You can hide specific options for a less cluttered interface—an approach that also serves to hide options that shouldn't be accessed when you use delegated administration. Administrators rarely use customized MMCs, perhaps because they're not sure how to do so or because they don't realize it's possible. Thus the aim of this appendix: to explain both the basics and more advanced configurable features of the Windows 2000 ubiquitous MMC.

MMC Basics

When you call up one of the Administrative tools, you're using a preconfigured MMC. In other words, you're actually looking at two different components and how they are configured: the MMC shell itself and the snap-ins it holds. You can keep the MMC tool as it was preconfigured, change it to suit your own requirements, or build your own customized version using some of the elements from the original.

As we mentioned, the MMC is a shell that isn't always immediately obvious. The MMC is actually a program in its own right that can be configured so that it holds the tools you need. Figure A.1 shows what the shell looks like when you load it by itself (for example, by clicking **Start | Run** and typing **mmc.exe**).

Figure A.1 The MMC Shell

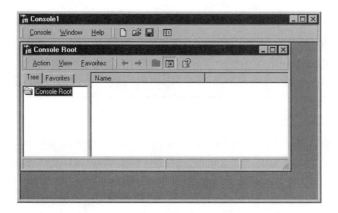

This is loading the MMC in its default, **Author** mode, which we'll discuss when we look at building customized MMCs. Here, we're simply acknowledging how and why all the Administrative tools have a common interface and can be driven in the same way—it's because they all use the same shell.

All the Administrative tools have this vertically split window with the Tree option in the left pane, which could contain options that can be expanded or collapsed by double-clicking on them, in much the same way that you can explore a hierarchical structure of folders in Windows Explorer. This left-hand side of the MMC is called the **Tree** (or **Scope**) **pane**; the right-hand side is called the **Details** (or **Results**) **pane**. It's called the Details pane because it displays the contents, or the details of whatever is selected in the left (tree) side. Just as you select a folder in Explorer and it displays its file contents on the right, so you can select an administrative tool and it displays the components it contains.

The contents of the MMC are *snap-ins*—graphical tools that have been designed to fit (snap) into this shell. So, for example when you load the Routing and Remote Access Administrative tool, you're loading Microsoft's preconfigured MMC with the Routing and Remote Access snap-in. Some snap-ins have *exten-*

sions that extend the configuration scope of the original snap-in. For example, the Internet Information Services snap-in has two extensions, FrontPage Server Extensions and SMTP Protocol. The extensions are dependent on a higher-level snap-in; they cannot be loaded by themselves, but the original snap-in can be loaded without the extension. When you're using the Microsoft built-in Administrative tools, you don't need to worry about the extensions; they are automatically added for you if you have that component installed.

NOTE

The two different terms *tree* or *scope* and *details* or *results* are used interchangeably in Microsoft documentation. The first is considered the *user* terminology and the second the *technical* terminology.

Some tools consist of multiple snap-ins; for example, Computer Management contains multiple snap-ins that locally group together tools you need to manage the computer, grouped under **System Tools**, **Storage**, and **Services and Applications**. But each option itself is a snap-in. For example, System tools consist of the following snap-ins: Event Viewer, System Information, Performance Logs and Alerts, Shared Folders, Device Manager, and Local Users and Groups. Some of these (such as Event Viewer) are listed as separate tools under Administrative tools. For those that are not, you must navigate your way through these built-in MMCs or create your own customized MMC.

When using the Administrative tools, all the MMCs inherit the shell's **Action** and **View** menus in the top menu bar and usually have at least the five buttons you can see in Figure A.1. The menu options for the Action menu change depending on what has been selected, but they are identical to the options available when you right-click that option. Most people find it easier to right-click and choose the option from there rather than select the component, then the Action menu, and then the menu item. You can view or edit an option by either selecting the **Properties** option in this way or by double-clicking it (or, alternatively, using the Properties button on the button bar).

The columns you'll see in the Details pane will differ depending on the snap-in used. They often (but not always) include the Name column from the original MMC, often a corresponding Description, and other status-type information. You can resize the columns by dragging the column headers, sort on them (alphabetically or chronologically) by clicking them, and reorder them by clicking and dragging.

Saving Configuration Changes

It's worth noting that, when you change a configuration option and close the dialog box that holds the configuration option, you have committed your choice without having to use a Save command. There's no Undo option—only a Cancel button within each dialog box. If available, you can also use the **Apply** button, which commits the change while keeping the dialog box open.

Some options take effect only when the service is next started. When that is the case, you will be notified by the configuration utility itself. An example is shown in Figure A.2.

Figure A.2 Prompting to Restart a Service on Configuration Change

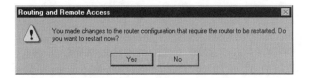

Exporting Information from MMC Snap-Ins

An additional button or option you'll see on most Administrative tool MMCs is **Export List**. In Chapter 6, we mentioned it in conjunction with WINS when suggesting this was a good way of keeping an eye on WINS database entries. However, the option is available on most MMCs and is a really useful addition to the Windows 2000 Administrative tools, but for some reason people rarely use it. The option allows you to export the contents of the details pane to a file in one of the following formats:

- **Text (tab delimited)** With the .txt extension.
- **Text (comma delimited)** With the .csv extension.
- **Unicode text (tab delimited)** With the .txt extension.
- **Unicode text (comma delimited)** With the .csv extension.

This then allows you to import the file into a spreadsheet program such as Excel or a database such as Access or simply into a word processor so that you can include it with your documentation and reports. You'll have saved all column information that is displayed in the Results pane, so, for example, if you used the Export List command with the Services snap-in, you will have a record of not just each service on that computer and its description but also its status and startup type. For example, you could use this Export List with the following:

- Local Users and Groups
- Contents of your DNS/WINS/DHCP databases
- Contents of your IIS services
- Shared folders
- Catalogs
- All the local group policies (for example, the Security options, Administrative Templates, list of scripts, and so on)
- Remote access policies
- RADIUS servers
- Certificates
- Performance logs
- Dfs shares and replicas

Adding Servers

Throughout this book, we have often included instances of adding servers to the same MMC when administering the same service for multiple computers. By default, the Administrative tools MMC will load, focused on the local server. If you were administering multiple servers, it would make sense to add them to the same MMC.

On most MMCs, you can do this simply by right-clicking the root of the MMC console (or using the **Action** menu) and selecting the option that allows you to add another computer. Unfortunately, the exact option name and resulting dialog box differ, depending on the Administrative tool being used. Furthermore, you might or might not be able to browse for the server; it's best if you know the server address or name.

For example, on the WINS MMC Administrative tool, right-click **WINS | Add Server** and you'll see the dialog box in Figure A.3, which allows you to either type in the NetBIOS, host or DNS name, or the IP address. Or you can use the **Browse** button to locate the server.

Figure A.3 Adding Another WINS Server to the WINS MMC Console

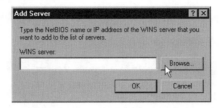

The DHCP Console offers the same **Add Server** option, but the dialog box is extended to include a list of only authorized DHCP servers. However, this list refers only to DHCP servers authorized in Active Directory and doesn't include DHCP servers authorized in an NT4 domain or a workgroup.

Similarly extended, the Routing and Remote Access Console uses **Add Server** (Figure A.4) and lets you specify a computer name, but it has no browse option outside Active Directory. It also lets you automatically add all Routing and Remote Access servers in a named domain. This domain option does work outside Active Directory (in both an NT4 domain and a workgroup).

Figure A.4 Adding Servers to the RRAS MMC Console

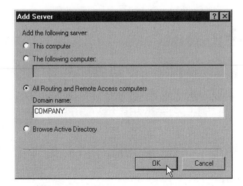

Internet Information Services uses **Connect** and then prompts you with a **Connect To Computer** message (with no browse option).

Some of the Administrator MMC's tools will display only one server at a time. For example, the Event Viewer or Computer Management allows you to change the focus of the MMC from the local computer to another computer, but it won't let you add multiple servers at once without building your own customized MMCs. See Figure A.5 for an example.

Figure A.5 Changing the Focus of the Supplied MMC

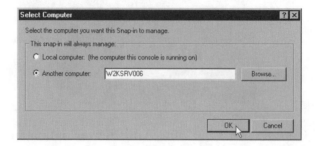

As you can see, there are many combinations available in a tool that's sup-posed to offer a common interface. If in doubt, create your own MMC.

NOTE

You can't add servers to the Internet Authentication Service, which is sur-prising. If you want to create an MMC console that has multiple IAS servers, you have to create your own MMC.

Remote Administration

We discussed the Administration Pack in Chapter 4, when we looked at adminis-tering file and print servers from the comfort of your own desktop rather than on the actual server itself. The Administration Pack (ADMINPAK.msi) can be found in the **\i386** folder of the Windows 2000 server CDs and in the equivalent direc-tory on the Service Pack CD. When installed, the Administration Pack copies over all the administration utilities and puts them all under **Start | Programs | Administrative Tools**. When any of the remote administration tools are loaded, you use the same **Connect to Server** or **Add Server** option that we saw earlier to connect to the relevant server. You will find that some of the Windows 2000 MMCs also work when focused on NT4 computers. These MMCs include the Event Viewer, IIS, Routing and Remote Access, Services, and Shared Folders.

Command Line

Many experienced administrators like to call utilities directly from the command line rather than having to wade through **Start | Programs** and so on—quite simply because it's quicker, if you remember the correct name!

The majority of the Administrative tools are located in the **%systemroot%\ system32** folder, which means that they'll be in the search path and you can run the named utility without having to specify a path. There are a few exceptions to this rule—for example, the Internet Services Manager is located in the **%systemroot%\system32\inetsrv** and the System Information is located in the **\Program Files\Common Files\Microsoft Shared\Msinfo** folder.

TIP

If you prefer to load utilities (including third-party utilities) directly from the command line and they are not included in your search path, this can be a pain. Some of your options include the following:

- You can copy them into a directory included on your search path (such as the %systemroot%\system32 folder).
- You can add their original path to your path statement (under **System | Advanced | Environment Variables**).
- You can call them with a direct path and subsequently use the Run history to repeat the full path or command.
- You can use the Search command to locate the file and launch it from the search results.

Because the utilities are loaded within an MMC and all saved MMCs have an .msc extension, you must specify the utility name with its .msc extension, as we did with the Local Group Policy Editor (**gpedit.msc**), which we covered in Chapter 2. There are a few exceptions to this rule, where the .msc extension isn't needed because the utility also has an .exe extension—for example, Perfmon which loads Performance, and Eventvwr, which loads Event Viewer. However, in the main you need to specify the full .msc extension.

Table A.1 includes most of the Windows 2000 MMC tools we used throughout this book, which you can use outside Active Directory.

Table A.1 Common MMC Utilities

MSC File	MMC Utility
CERTSRV.MSC	Certificate Authority
CIADV.MSC	Indexing Service
COMPMGMT.MSC	Computer Management
DEVMGMT.MSC	Device Manager

Continued

Table A.1 Continued

MSC File	MMC Utility
DRFG.MSC	Disk Defragmenter
DFSGUI.MSC	Distributed File System
DHCPMGMT.MSC	DHCP
DISKMGMT.MSC	Disk Management
DNSMGMT.MSC	DNS
EVENTVWR.MSC	Event Viewer
FSMGMT.MSC	Shared Folders
GPEDIT.MSC	Local Group Policy Editor
IAS.MSC	Internet Authentication Service
IIS.MSC	Internet Information Services
LUSRMGR.MSC	Local User Manager
MSINFO32.MSC	System Information
MSISA.MSC	ISA Management
NTMSMGR.MSC	Removable Storage Manager
PERMON.MSC	Performance
RRASMGMT.MSC	Routing and Remote Access
SECPOL.MSC	Local Security Policy
SERVICES.MSC	Services
TSCC.MSC	Terminal Services Configuration
TSC.MSC	Terminal Services Snap-in
WINSGMGMT.MSC	WINS

NOTE

It would be easy to combine calling up an MMC from the command line with the Windows 2000 **Run As** command, which lets you run an application in a different security context. For example, if you were logged on to your desktop with standard user rights but needed to use an Administrator MMC tool such as Disk Management, you could use **Start | Run** and then type **runas /USER:COMPANY\Administrator "MMC DISKMGMT.MSC"** (where you're using the company domain administrator's account to load the MMC with its associated file). You'll see a command window prompt you for the administrator's password, and then Disk Management should successfully load.

For more information on how to use the Run As command, look up "Starting programs as an administrator" in the online Help.

Configuring and Creating Your Own MMCs

This sounds quite complicated—until you actually do it and realize just how easy it is! You simply load the MMC shell, add the snap-ins you want, and save the MMC. By default, it will then be available under your Administrative tools—and for easy access you could easily copy it to the desktop or load it from the command line.

You might build your own MMC if you wanted to group together related tasks. For example, we saw in Chapter 6 how closely DNS, DHCP, and WINS worked together, and you might therefore want to be able to see their database entries from the same MMC. Alternatively, you might want just a component of an existing Administrative tool—for example, Chapter 4, "File and Print Services," outlined how you could add multiple Shared Folders for different servers. Alternatively, you might want to use the same tool—for example Event Viewer—with multiple servers displayed at the same time in your MMC, which you can't do within the Administrative tool equivalent.

Once you have loaded the MMC console (**Start | Run | MMC.exe**), you choose **Console | Add/Remove Snap-in**. This takes you to the Add/Remove Snap-in dialog box with the **Standalone** and **Extensions** tabs. Because you cannot add an extension before adding a snap-in, select the **Add** button and you'll see a list of available snap-ins for your computer, as shown in Figure A.6. The actual choices depend on the services and components you have installed. For example, Figure A.6 shows the CyberSafe Log Analyst, which ships with the Resource Kit and allows you to analyze the Event Logs (covered in Chapter 4).

Select the snap-in you want and click **Add**, or double-click the snap-in you want (but don't double-click *and* then select **Add**, which gives you two copies of the selected snap-in!). From this dialog box you can select multiple snap-ins. Click **Close** when you have all the snap-ins you want.

Figure A.6 Adding a Standalone Snap-In

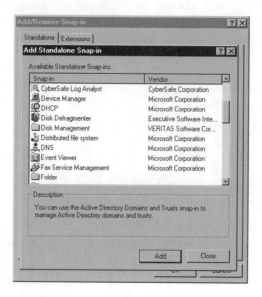

When selecting a snap–in, you'll be asked for its focus. Usually the focus is a local computer or a remote computer, as Figure A.7 demonstrates.

Figure A.7 Configuring a Snap-In Focus for a Remote Computer

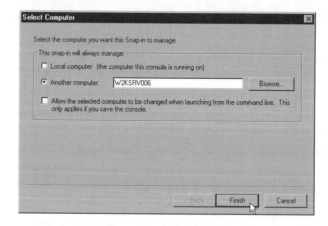

If this dialog box looks familiar, it's because it's nearly the same as the one in Figure A.5, which we saw when we looked at changing the snap–in focus from the local computer to a remote computer. However, this dialog box does have the additional option of allowing the selected computer to be changed when

launching from the command line. This option is used with the
mmc /computer=<computer_name> command.

For example, we could check this option for an MMC that contained the
Event Viewer and Services, which is focused on the W2KSRV006 computer by
default. Let's call the saved MMC **Maintenance.msc** and copy it to a folder
that's on the path (for example, **%Systemroot%\System32**). When we use
Start | Run and specify **maintenance.msc**, the MMC snap-ins will be the
Services and Event Viewer for WIN2KSRV006. However, we could change the
focus and use these snap-ins for any computer (including NT4 computers) by
specifying, for example, **Maintenance.msc /computer=NT4SRV002**, which
would load the MMC with the two snap-ins focused on the NT4SRV002 server.

Using URL Links

The snap-in called **Link to Web Addresses** allows you to group together or to
add a Web URL to your MMC. So, for example, you might have an MMC with
a snap-in for Event Viewer and a number of Web snap-ins that link to troubleshooting event log errors, or you might add RFC references to the RRAS or
ISA snap-in so that you can easily check protocol and port numbers. This is
nothing you couldn't do independently with your browser, but grouping it logically with the relevant administration tool should make your life a bit easier.

Figure A.8 shows an example of a few Web references for Windows 2000
administration and troubleshooting, added into an MMC for easy reference.

Figure A.8 Using Web References in a Customized MMC

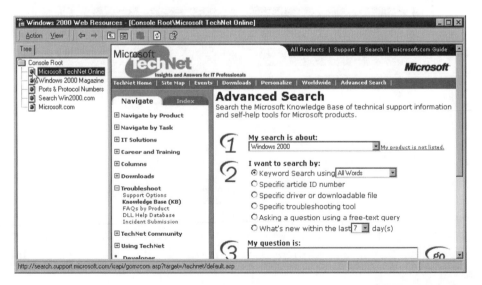

Using Favorites in MMCs

Favorites in MMCs work much the same way as Favorites in Internet Explorer: They provide a shortcut method of getting to the content you most often use. However, instead of saving a URL, which saves you typing the Web address, Favorites in MMCs save the tree path. This saves you having to work your way through the tree levels and options, expanding or collapsing the nodes until you get to the one you want.

Computer Management is a good example of benefitting from Favorites, since it has many options at different levels. If you frequently loaded Computer Management but most of the time used only the **System Tools | Shared Folders | Open Files**, you have to traverse those levels. But if you identified Open Files as a Favorite, you could simply toggle the **Favorites** tab and select the **Open Files** link, which takes you straight to where you want to be.

Another use is when you're combining your own snap-ins into one MMC. For example, Figure A.9 shows a customized MMC, called Server Admin Tools, which includes Computer Management, Local Computer Policy, and Terminal Services Connections. We've already seen in previous chapters how Computer Management and Local Computer Policy have many levels and how Terminal Services Connections contain as many server connections as you define. If all the levels were expanded on this MMC, they would not fit on the page, so instead only the Terminal Services Connections are expanded.

Figure A.9 Multiple Snap-Ins with Multiple Tree Levels and Options

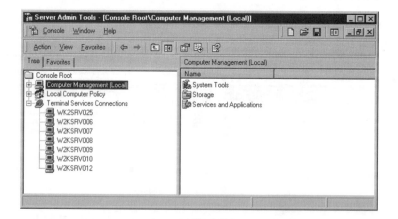

If you had particular options you used on a regular basis, it could make your life much easier if you placed them in your Favorites folder so that you could

navigate to them easily and quickly. Figure A.10 shows a few commonly used options which typically lie several levels deep into the same snap-in. Having them listed as Favorites means that the MMC is responsible for navigating to the correct node in the tree and displaying the correct details.

Figure A.10 Using Favorites for Easy Navigation in MMCs

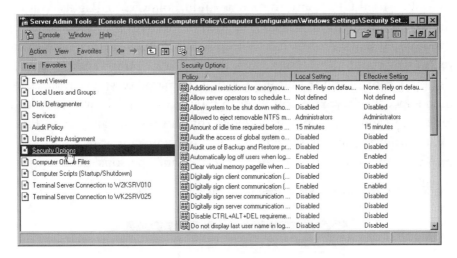

To create an MMC Favorite, simply navigate to the node you want to use in the MMC tree and then select **Add to Favorites**. You can then also select your Favorites from the same menu without having to toggle the **Favorites** tab, as shown in Figure A.11.

Figure A.11 Using the Favorites Drop-Down Menu in MMCs

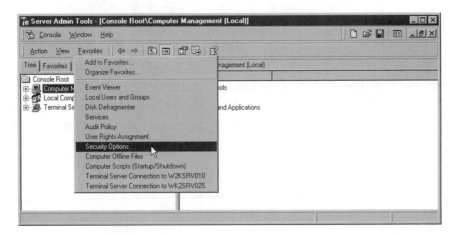

Organizing Favorites

Just as you can organize Favorites in Internet Explorer, so you can organize your MMC Favorites into folders using the **Favorites | Organize Favorites** option we saw previously in Figure A.10. For example, instead of having 11 different Favorites all listed together, you could group at least some into their own folders—often used GPO options such as Audit Policy, User Rights Assignments, and the like could all go into one GPO folder. Alternatively, from a logical point of view, it might make more sense to keep Audit Policy together with Event Viewer, so you could more easily check the auditing options and Security Log.

Use the **Create Folder** button to define the name of your Favorites folder, and then select the **Favorite** you want to move into it, click the **Move to Folder** button, and select your new folder. You can rename and delete Favorites and folders from within the same dialog box, but you cannot reorder them. Figure A.12 shows our same Favorites organized into personal groupings.

Figure A.12 Organizing Favorites in MMCs

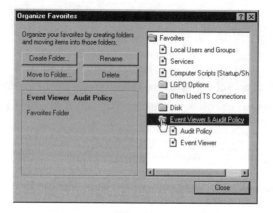

Under the **Favorites** tab, this setup now makes for a less cluttered three Favorites and four Favorites folders. Under the **Favorites** drop-down menu, you'll now have the three Favorites listed, with the folders listed as expanded menus, as shown in Figure A.13. Obviously, the more Favorites you have, the more advantageous it is to organize them. Favorites can also be used when we create taskpads, as we shall see later.

Figure A.13 Using Organized Favorites in MMCs

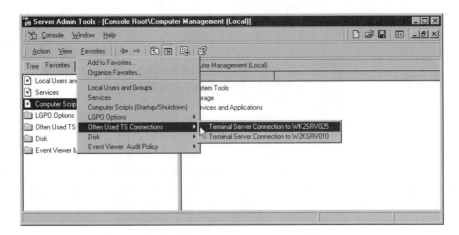

Saving Custom MMCs

To save your MMC with your chosen snap-ins, you simply select **Console | Save As**. By default, you'll be prompted to save the name with an .msc extension and save into Administrative Tools. This means the snap-ins will be readily available when you click **Start | Programs | Administrative Tools**.

However, before you save your MMC, you should select the **Console mode** you want. Set the mode with **Console | Options**, where you can specify one of the modes shown in Figure A.14, which decides the look and scope of the MMC the next time it is loaded.

When you are configuring the MMC for the first time, you need to be in Author mode, which is the default mode when the MMC.exe is loaded and allows you to fully configure it as you want. However, when you want to actually use the MMC or let others use it, you will want them to load it in User mode with varying degrees of control, as shown in the drop-down box in Figure A.14.

If you want a user to have full configuration except for adding or removing your snap-ins or changing console properties, choose **User mode—full access**. Figure A.15 shows an example of a customized MMC called **Networking Services.msc**, which has been previously saved in User mode with full access. You can see that the **Favorites** tab is now missing and the **Console** menu no longer has the **New, Open, Save, Save As**, or **Add/Remove Snap-in**, and **Options**.

Change this setting to **User mode—limited access, multiple windows** and the user will no longer have access to the **Console, Window**, and **Help** menus. However, users will have access to the **Action | New Window from Here** and **Export List** commands, as Figure A.16 shows.

Figure A.14 Setting the MMC Console Mode

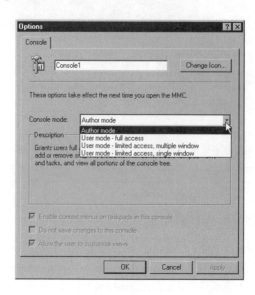

Figure A.15 Example of a Customized MMC Loading in User Mode—Full Access

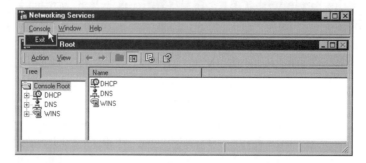

Having multiple windows means just that—you can have multiple windows within the same MMC if you want different snap-ins but not in the same window. To create a new window, you decide your starting point from your existing MMC tree and select the **New Window from Here** command you see in Figure A.16. You can then add new snap-ins to the new window as needed, and you can size or move each window independently—just as you can have multiple documents open in Word.

Figure A.16 Example of a Customized MMC Loading in User Mode—Limited Access, Multiple Windows

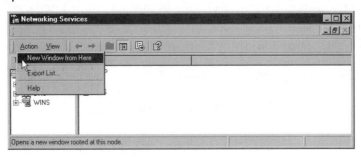

Finally, the most restrictive option is **User Mode—limited access, single window**, which limits the user to just the current window, as you see in Figure A.17.

Figure A.17 Example of a Customized MMC Loading in User Mode—Limited Access, Single Window

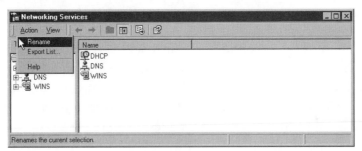

NOTE

You can always open a saved console in author mode by specifying /a after the full msc path so that you can go back in and make author changes. However, a much easier way is to use the Search utility to get to the long path (for example, search for <filename>.msc and the Search results would display C:\Documents and Settings\Administrator\ Start Menu\Programs\Administrative Tools\<filename>.msc), and then right-click the file in the search results and select **Author**.

Changing the Custom MMC View

Another thing you might want to change before saving in User mode is the way that the console itself is configured. You do this by selecting **View | Customize** and you'll see the configuration options shown in Figure A.18.

Figure A.18 Changing the MMC View

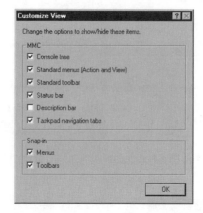

Hopefully, most of these options are fairly self-explanatory, except perhaps the reference to taskpads, which we'll cover later. If in doubt about which element they remove from your customized MMC, try unselecting them and comparing the difference. However, most are useful for users, but you might prefer to remove some or all of these elements for a less cluttered look.

Be careful if you remove the Standard toolbar that allows users to navigate up and down the MMC tree; you can easily create an MMC that allows you go down a level but never back up! However, if you want users to have access to options only through your defined Favorites and hide other options, you need to remove the Standard toolbar and also remove the Console tree so that they have access only to the Favorites. Figure A.19 shows an example of this type of MMC configuration.

By default, users get exactly the same view options that we saw in Figure A.18, unless you unchecked the default option **Allow the user to customize views** when setting the console options, as we saw in Figure A.14. The three options at the bottom of that dialog box become available as soon as you change the Console mode from Author to one of the User modes.

Note that employing the **Do not save changes to the console** option means that users' personal view preferences (included expanded trees) will not be saved and if they can change the view, it will revert back to your saved view when the customized MMC is next loaded.

Figure A.19 Minimal MMC View Options, Using Only Favorites

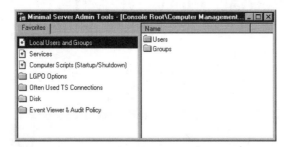

Advanced MMC Configuration: Using Taskpads

Taskpads are ideal for creating a simplified interface in the MMC that groups together common tasks. This interface could be for a limited or restrictive set of administrative tasks that hide other tasks and options that would normally be available in the full MMC, or they offer quick shortcuts for certain commands or Favorites. As such, taskpads are usually touted as suitable for delegated administration, but they're also a great way to customize your own administration tasks. You may remember that the ISA Management MMC used taskpad to good effect, and that they could be toggled on and off. Taskpad views are HTLM pages that can contain a number of items:

- MMC Favorites
- Wizards
- Scripts
- Programs
- URLs

In a way, they are the next step to customization after using Favorites, because taskpads are not limited to snap-in commands and can use HTML graphics. Additionally, you can create multiple taskpad views in a single MMC to logically group or divide the tasks.

You must have at least one snap-in added to the MMC, and then you can use the New Taskpad View Wizard, which is launched from the **New Taskpad View** from the **Action** menu or the context menu.

The New Taskpad View Wizard

After the initial first screen, you'll be asked to select the taskpad display, with the default options displayed in Figure A.20.

Figure A.20 The New Taskpad View Display

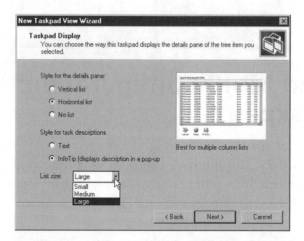

If you're not sure which options to choose here, go for the defaults and experiment with the alternatives later. You're prompted to select the taskpad target, as shown in Figure A.21.

Figure A.21 The New Taskpad Target

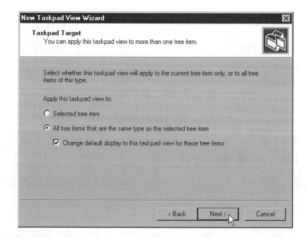

This dialog box is important if you choose a common taskpad command that was available for more than one node (tree item)—say, Open or Properties. Your setting here decides whether you want your taskpad to be available for just the currently selected node or all of them.

You are then prompted for the Name and Description of the taskpad, with the default name taken from the currently selected MMC snap-in. On the last page of the New Taskpad View Wizard, you're prompted to start the New Task Wizard, as shown in Figure A.22.

Figure A.22 The New Task Wizard After the New Taskpad View Wizard Is Completed

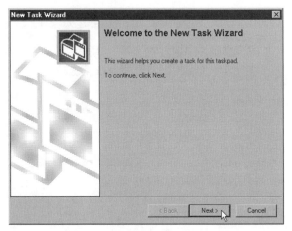

You're prompted to select the command type: menu command, shell command, or navigation command, as shown in Figure A.23.

Figure A.23 Selecting the New Task Command Type

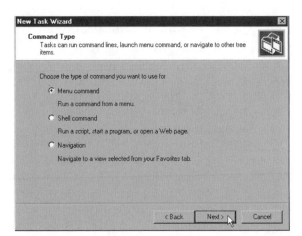

If you select a menu command (the default), your next choice will depend on the snap-in from which you launched the Taskpad view. Our first example uses the Services snap-in because it's quite simple and easily shows how snap-in commands map to the taskpad GUI. I've already loaded the MMC, added the Services snap-in, and created the taskpad from the Services (Local) node. Now we'll add Stop, Start, Pause, Resume, Restart, and Properties as tasks so that they can be easily selected with any highlighted service. Via the New Task Wizard's Shortcut Menu command, we can select any of the commands that would be available for this snap-in, as shown in Figure A.24.

Figure A.24 Selecting the Taskpad's New Task Shortcut Menu Command

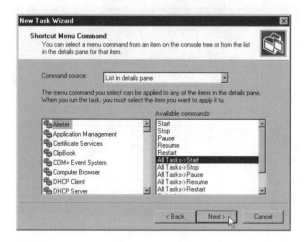

The next page prompts for a suitable Task Name and Description. The following page prompts for a suitable icon (from a limited list) to represent the task, as shown in Figure A.25.

The final page tells you that you've completed the wizard and lists your current tasks. At this point you can run the wizard again to add another task to the same taskpad and select **Finish**, as shown in Figure A.26.

You can carry on adding tasks in this way, until you click **Finish** on this page without the **Run this wizard again** being selected. When I had finished adding the Services commands, they looked like Figure A.27.

Figure A.25 Selecting a Task Icon

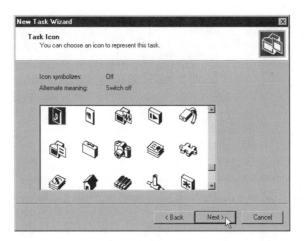

Figure A.26 Completing the New Task Wizard

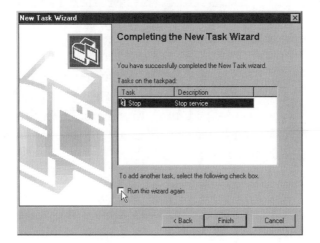

Figure A.27 Example Taskpad Created for Services

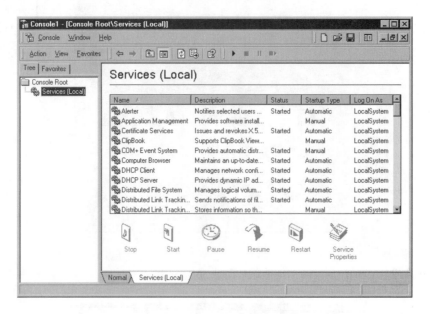

Now you can probably see the resemblance to the taskpads we saw in ISA Management in Chapter 10. This isn't the end product as far as the user is concerned, however. If you want to add or delete your tasks or modify or reorder them, right-click the original snap-in and select **Edit Taskpad View**. (You can also delete the whole of the taskpad from this menu). Then choose the **Tasks** tab. Figure A.28 shows how your currently configured tasks can be changed. The **New** button here calls up the New Task Wizard.

Now when we save the MMC, we have the choice of removing selected items from it. For example, if we removed all the options we previously saw under the Customized View and saved in User mode, the result would look similar to Figure A.29.

TIP

I strongly suggest that you keep two copies of the Taskpad—one for the end product and one in Author mode that includes the Standard menus so you can go back into **View | Customize** to add the Console tree and menus if you want to later modify or add to them.

Figure A.28 Modifying Your Current Taskpad and Tasks

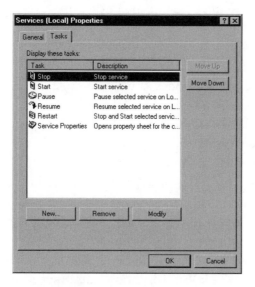

Figure A.29 A Simple Taskpad for Services

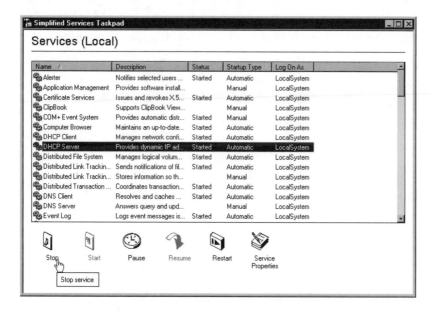

Adding Taskpad Views and Non-Snap-In Commands

Now let's add some tasks to our simple Services taskpad. These tasks include the System Event Log with a URL reference to Microsoft Knowledge Base so we can easily look up event error codes as well as a link to the Add/Remove Programs applet.

First, we need to load a version of the Services taskpad, which includes the View menu so that we can add all the options under **View | Customize**. Then add the Event Log Snap-in, and navigate to the System log and select **Favorites | Add to Favorites**. This series of steps provides the link to the System log in the taskpad.

Click **Services (Local)** in the tree, and select **New Taskpad View**. We need to define a new taskpad in a way that's similar to the way we created the last one, except we need to give it a different name—for example, Maintenance. When going through the New Task Wizard, choose the **Navigation** option as the command type. If you have only one Favorite defined, it will be displayed on the next page for you to select. Finish this task and run the wizard again. This time, select the **Shell** command as your command type. We'll add the Microsoft Knowledge Base of http://search.support.microsoft.com/kb here, as shown in Figure A.30.

Figure A.30 Supplying a Web Reference as a Task

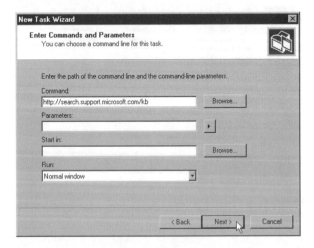

When you've finished that task, add another that specifies the Shell command, and this time supply **appwiz.cpl**, the program that loads Add/Remove

Programs. Because this program resides in the %systemroot%\System32 directory on the path, there's no need to specify the full path or the **Start in** option.

When you've finished the three maintenance tasks, you can then change this taskpad style to have **No list**, because these tasks are not dependent on selecting one of the listed items. You can use the Taskpad bars at the bottom of the window to flip between the original taskpad and this new taskpad. Your customized Services MMC should look similar to Figure A.31.

Figure A.31 Multiple Taskpads in the Same MMC

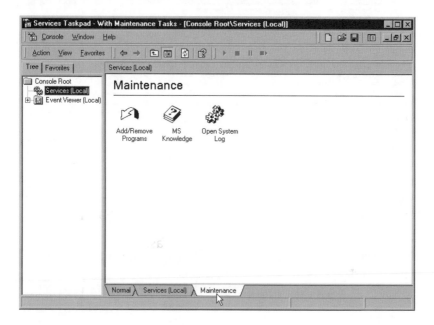

Finally, we'll save this in restricted User mode and remove some of the views. In this case, we'll leave the standard toolbar, which is needed for navigation to and from the System Event Log, and the Taskpad navigation tabs, which are needed to flip between the three taskpad views, as shown in Figures A.32, A.33, and A.34.

Further Customization and Development with MMCs

It is hoped that by now, you have a good idea of what is possible with MMCs and how easy it is to customize their look and behavior. But that's not all! Developers can make full use of the MMC flexibility in any development environment that supports producing COM components (for example, Microsoft

Visual C++ and Microsoft Visual Basic 6.0). You can, for example, include ActiveX controls, DHTML and XML, Extensible Style Language (XSL), and Cascading Style Sheets (CSS), together with even media applications.

Figure A.32 The Normal Taskpad View for the Customized Services MMC

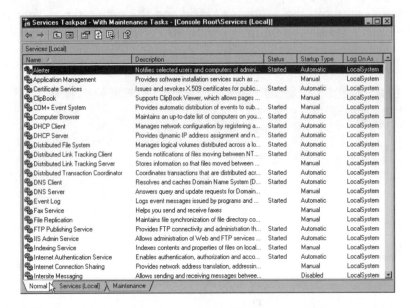

Figure A.33 The Services Taskpad View for the Customized Services MMC

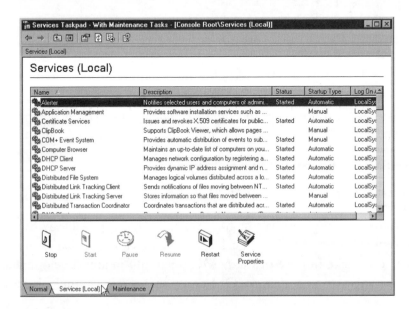

Figure A.34 The Maintenance Taskpad View for the Customized Services MMC

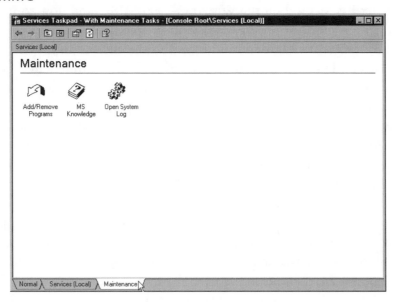

For more information on developing with the MMC, refer to the following MSDN online library on the MMC Overview: http://msdn.microsoft.com/library/default.asp?URL=/library/psdk/mmc/mmcint00_62pj.htm. For information on snap-in development tools, visit http://msdn.microsoft.com/library/default.asp?URL=/library/psdk/mmc/mmcsg002_90j7.htm.

Distributing MMCs

This really is the easy part. Because MMCs (including taskpads) are just .msc files, you can simply copy or e-mail them or make them available on a network. The only caveat to remember is that they won't run on down-level clients such as NT or Windows 9x.

Summary

This appendix has focused on the Windows 2000 MMC and how to use it in its basic form and in more advanced ways. Most people find using this common administrative utility shell quite intuitive, and so throughout this book we have assumed that step-by-step instructions on driving MMC utilities are not necessary. However, some people might appreciate basic instructions on how to use MMCs, if only to confirm that they are using them correctly! If you do not know how to use the MMC shell, it is very difficult to efficiently administer Windows 2000. In addition, although the built-in utilities that use the MMC shell are supposed to all behave the same way because they all use the same shell, we have seen how this is often not the case!

In this appendix that supplements the book's content, we referenced specific examples used throughout the book as well as offering additional examples that are practical for a Windows 2000 administrator. Although you might not need to use some of the more advanced options (such as taskpads), it is helpful to know that these options are there in case a need for them arises.

We covered the basics of the MMC shell and how snap-ins work, how to add multiple snap-ins to the same MMC, how to customize their display, how to use them for remote administration, how you can use Web links and Favorites within the MMC, and finally how taskpads can be used and configured.

Customized MMCs can be very practical, but they also look very sophisticated without the need for any programming, so don't keep them to yourself! The final section looked at just how easy it was to distribute your customized MMCs to other administrators or users.

N

Global Knowledge™

Train with Global Knowledge

The right content, the right method, delivered anywhere in the world, to any number of people from one to a thousand. Blended Learning Solutions™ from Global Knowledge.

Train in these areas:
Network Fundamentals
Internetworking
A+ PC Technician
WAN Networking and Telephony
Management Skills
Web Development
XML and Java Programming
Network Security
UNIX, Linux, Solaris, Perl
Cisco
Enterasys
Entrust
Legato
Lotus
Microsoft
Nortel
Oracle

www.globalknowledge.com